HITLER
The Policies of Seduction

HITLER

The Policies of Seduction

Rainer Zitelmann

Translated by Helmut Bogler

First published in 1998 by
F A Herbig Verlagsbuchhandlung GmbH
München

This edition published in 1999 by
LONDON HOUSE
114 New Cavendish Street
London W1M 7FD

© Text: F A Herbig
© Translation: Helmut Bogler

A catalogue record for this book is available from
The British Library

ISBN 1 902809 03 3

Edited, designed and typeset by Roger Chesneau

Printed and bound in Great Britain by
Creative Print and Design (Wales), Ebbw Vale

The present study was accepted as a dissertation with *summa cum laude* in the winter term 1985/86 by the social and historical sciences faculty of the Darmstadt Technical University. The supervisor of this dissertation was Professor Dr K. O. von Aretin.

Contents

Foreword *by Karl Otmar von Aretin*   9

Translator's Note   12

I. Introduction   13

II. Hitler and the Revolution   33
1. The 'So-Called Revolution' of November 1918   33
2. Hitler's Concept of the State and the 'Obligation to Rebel'   45
3. Hitler's Definition of Revolution   50
4. Hitler's View of Historic Revolutions   54
   a. The French Revolution of 1789   54
   b. The Proclamation of the Third Republic in September 1870   59
   c. The 1848 Revolution in Germany   60
   d. The Jews as Leaders of Revolutions and a 'Negative Example' for Hitler   61
5. Hitler's Revolutionary Claim   62
   a. From 1919 to the Hitler *Putsch* of 1923   62
   b. The Problem of Compatibility between Revolutionary Claim and the Tactics of Legality   63
   Aside: Was Hitler Toying with the Idea of a Violent Revolution in August 1932?   66
   c. Hitler's Portrayal of the NS Revolution: One of the Greatest Upheavals in History – but in a Measured and Disciplined Form   70
   Aside: '... And So We Became Revolutionaries.'   75
   d. The Importance of National Socialism for the History of the World: The Beginning of a Turning-Point in History   80
   e. Continuation or End of the NS Revolution? Hitler's Contradictory Statements and the 'Röhm Revolt'   84

III. Hitler's Social Objectives and His Assessment of the Major Classes of Modern Society ... 93

1. Hitler on the Importance and Origin of the Social Issue ... 93
2. The Importance and Substantiation of the Concept of 'Equal Opportunity' in Hitler's Social Programme ... 99
3. Hitler's Position on the Major Classes and Levels of Modern Middle-Class Society ... 121
   a. The Bourgeoisie ... 122
      – Anti-Social Stance, Ignoring the Worker Question, Rejection of Workers' Justified Claims ... 122
      – Profit Greed, 'Materialism' ... 127
      – Criticism of Bourgeois Nationalism ... 128
      – Middle Class Parties: No *Weltanschauung*, Only Fighting for Seats in Parliament ... 130
      – 'Weakness, Lack of Decisiveness, Lack of Energy, Cowardice' ... 133
      – Inability to Provide Political Leadership ... 141
      – The Bourgeoisie's Political Mission Has Ended ... 143
   b. The Working Class ... 149
      – Definition of the 'Workers' Party' ... 149
      – Hitler's Reasons for Concentrating on the Worker: The Workers as a 'Source of Strength and Energy' ... 152
      – Increasing the Worker's Social Standing; Upgrading Manual Labour ... 162
      – Social Legislation ... 168
   c. The Lower Middle Class ... 170
   d. The Farmers ... 173
4. The Definition of '*Volksgemeinschaft*' in Hitler's *Weltanschauung* ... 177

IV. Hitler's Central Objective: The Revolutionizing of Politics and Economics and the Restructuring of the Economic System ... 198

1. The Underestimation of the Importance of Economic Questions for Hitler's Thinking ... 198
2. Hitler's Position on Political Economy ... 201
3. The 'Secondary Role of Economics' and the 'Primacy of Politics' ... 206
4. Warnings about the Web of Interests between Business and Politics ... 216
5. Market and Plan ... 221
6. Private Ownership and Nationalization ... 240
7. Hitler's Criticism of Capitalism in His Early Speeches ... 263

V. Hitler: An Opponent of Modern Industrial Society? Modernistic and Anti-Modernistic Elements in Hitler's *Weltanschauung*   270

1. Agrarian Utopia as an Ultimate Objective? Criticism of a Misunderstanding in the Interpretation of the Function and Implications of '*Lebensraum* in the East' in Hitler's Concept   270
   a. Substantiation of the *Lebensraum* Concept within the Framework of Hitler's Economic Concepts: Criticism of Economic Expansion and the Autarky Concept   271
      - The Discrepancy between Population Growth and *Lebensraum*   271
      - German Economic Expansion as the Cause of the First World War   272
      - The Theory of 'Shrinking Markets' as an Argument against the Strategy of Economic Expansion   275
      - The Result of Economic Expansion: A Disproportionality concerning Agriculture and Industry, Urbanization and Migration from the Land   280
      - *Lebensraum* and the Autarky Concept   286
   b. Creation of an Agrarian Supplementary Territory by means of Agrarian Settlement   296
   c. *Lebensraum* as a Source of Raw Materials   299
   d. *Lebensraum* as a Market   304
   e. The De-Industrialization of Russia   306
   Aside: Hitler's Criticism of the Export of Capital   308
2. Hitler's Position on Modern Industrial Society   310
   a. Positive Remarks by Hitler about Modern Industrial Society   310
      - The Constant Increase of the Standard of Living as a Premise   310
      - The Highly Industrialized Economy of the USA as an Example   315
      - Hitler on Industrialization and Technical Advancement   318
   b. Hitler on the Destruction of the Environment as a Result of Industrialization   324
3. Hitler's Scientific View of the World and his Criticism of Rosenberg's and Himmler's 'Mysticism'   331

VI. Hitler's Concepts and Objectives in His Domestic Policies   338
1. Hitler's Criticism of Democracy   338
   a. Criticism of the 'Majority Principle'   338
   b. Hitler's Criticism of the Pluralistic System: The Common Good versus 'Special Interests'   343
   c. Democracy as a Form of Rule by Capital   349

		d. Democracy as a Sign of Decadence and Weakness	352
		e. Hitler on Political Freedom	353
	2.	The 'Historic Minority' as a Subject of Revolution	356
		a. The Principles of Élite Recruitment in the Movement Phase and the Theory of the 'Historic Minority'	357
		b. The Problems of Élite Recruitment in the System Phase	364
		Aside: Hitler's Principle: Draw Conclusions about the Race from the 'Ability' and not Vice Versa	375
	3.	The *Führer* State	379
		a. Hitler on the Constitution and the Question of Succession	380
		b. The '*Führer* Principle'	387
		c. Dictatorship as the 'Highest Form of Democracy'	391
		d. Hitler on Federalism and Unitarianism	396

VII. Hitler's Self-Assessment in the Political Spectrum — 404

1. 'Left' or 'Right'? — 404
2. National Socialism as the Synthesis between Nationalism and Socialism — 410
3. Hitler's Assessment of Related and Opposing Political Movements and Systems — 414
   a. Social Democracy — 415
   b. Communism — 419
   c. Hitler's Relationship with Marxism — 422
   d. Hitler's Position towards Stalin — 427
   e. Hitler's Criticism of Italian Fascism and the Reactionary Franco Regime in Spain — 434

VIII. Final Considerations — 439

Notes — 453

Bibliography — 513

List of Abbreviations — 533

Index of Names — 535

Foreword
Karl Otmar von Aretin

A book dealing with Hitler will always generate interest. In this case the interest is doubly justified, because this book is based on the analysis of all of Hitler's written and spoken statements as far as they have come down to us. Until now – astonishing as this may sound – there has been no treatment of all of Hitler's statements. The compilation and publication of his writings ends with the year 1924. As an author of books (*Mein Kampf* and *Hitlers Zweites Buch*), as a commentator and editorial writer in the *Völkische Beobachter* and the *Illustrierte Beobachter* and as a speaker, Hitler left an almost overwhelming wealth of material. Rainer Zitelmann has read all of this, and organized it according to criteria he explains in his introduction. By applying very strict methods of selection, he attempts to eliminate all the statements which reflect current events or situations, in order thereby to penetrate into Hitler's system of thought. The result is well suited to adding important facets to our picture of Hitler.

Hitler appears here as a monomaniacal autodidact who, from his reading of the opinions of his times, put together his own system of thought, the basic theme of which was a primitive Darwinism. The law of the jungle and the eternal free-for-all are the two things which shape the framework of this thinking. War, and in this case racial war and war of extermination of the peoples to be subjugated, are just as much a part of it as his racial ideology, which was based on the insane concept that 'inferior races' such as Jews, gypsies and the mentally handicapped had to be physically destroyed. These two components, with their horrifying consequences, are known. Hans Mommsen, Eberhard Jäckel, Joachim Fest, Martin Broszat and many others have investigated this facet and portrayed it in all its criminal dimensions. They came to the conclusion that war for the conquest of *Lebensraum* and the extermination of 'inferior races' had been Hitler's actual objectives, to which he subjugated all others. This book starts off from this thesis. The conviction of Hitler's criminal nature is, so to speak, its foundation. But it demonstrates that Hitler's Darwinistic *Weltanschauung* did not prevent him from extending it to other fields, to objectives of social, economic and domestic policy, about which, as we formerly believed, he understood little, if anything at all. This verdict will have to be revised.

If we formerly assumed that Hitler had little interest in economic matters, and that the modernization push originating in the NS era was an unintended result (*Dahrendorf*), then our author is able to reconstruct a system from Hitler's statements which certainly also bears modernistic features. Of course, everything had to proceed according to his ideas. Hitler withdrew the basis of existence from whoever refused to knuckle under. The common interest, as Hitler defined it, was the only measuring yardstick to which everything was subjected. He only accepted the capitalist economic system, for example, as long as industry bowed to his will. He threatened it with nationalization several times, and would have been prepared to press the economy into a system of compulsory controls if he had considered this to be more effective for the pursuit of his objectives. Nor was his *Lebensraum* ideology bent on the reagrarianization of Germany within the framework of a blood-and-soil ideology; the *Lebensraum* was – as our author convincingly proves – to create the raw material and market basis for a highly developed industry. The social order of the 'master race' also had some modern features: by virtue of its racial superiority and its technical leadership, it was to rule over subjugated and mentally enslaved peoples.

The picture of Hitler that is developed here from the source material corrects many assumptions previously in circulation about the dictator. Hitler had his own ideas about everything. They were mostly not original in the sense that they stemmed from him; he normally only compiled current opinions. The basic concept of the free-for-all left no room in his thinking for humanity. And while his thinking does shape itself into a logical system, it loses nothing of its horror in the process. We now understand how he was able to discuss matters with experts, and even to impress them with his knowledge and concepts. The image of Hitler as the primitive mass murderer is certainly false. He was a highly intelligent person with the power of rapid comprehension. This also makes it understandable why so many followed him for so long. His thinking was quite impressive in its unity. However, he lacked any moral or ethical foundation. Nothing that would have helped him gain his objectives was inconceivable for him. He did not disclose his actual criminal objectives, or only within his most intimate circle. Therefore, whoever met him met a man who certainly had something to say about specific problems. This book explores the ambivalence in Hitler's person between his fundamentally amoral stance and his outwardly displayed intelligence. He had more far-reaching objectives than the conquest of *Lebensraum* and the destruction of 'inferior races'. The knowledge of these objectives and his opinions about them modify

Foreword

his image without making it less terrible. Basically, Hitler only becomes even more horrible thereby. His whole edifice of ideas, which was frighteningly one-sided, also demonstrates horribly inhumane convictions in his concepts of economic and social politics. What the author has extracted from his statements for the time after final victory is a nightmare. Hitler's admiration of Stalin indicates approximately the direction developments would have taken. Since the individual human being meant nothing to Hitler, and was only noticed insofar as he could be used for the purposes of the regime, this system allowed for any crime whatsoever.

Hitler felt himself to be a revolutionary. In this he envisaged the remodelling of Germany into a state that was solely aligned to the national interest, and in which national interest alone determined the value of the individual. But he also foresaw a social order in which anybody who was prepared to subjugate himself to the maxims of the revolution had free opportunities for advancement. In all of its objectives, Hitler's thinking was stamped by an oppressive inhumanity. That is the conclusion of this study. It is therefore a highly important contribution to the understanding of the personality of the dictator.

TRANSLATOR'S NOTE

About half the book before you consists of original quotations from the writings, but primarily speeches, of Adolf Hitler himself, or from notes of what he said, taken down by various people within his inner circle. Rainer Zitelmann cites these in order to prove his theses about Hitler's *Weltanschauung*, about his ideas, concepts and objectives in various areas of political endeavour.

The problem facing the translator of this book lies in the fact that Hitler spoke – and wrote – a rather strange German as far as grammar and vocabulary are concerned. Being primarily an orator, he never paid much attention to his language, knowing full well that poor grammar and the wrong choice of terms are far less important when speaking than when writing. The decision facing the translator, therefore, is whether to render Hitler's often incorrect German into correct English, and thereby lose the 'flavour' of the original, or to stay as close to the original Hitler as possible, accepting questionable grammar and terminology.

I opted for the second choice, in the belief that the reader would be more interested in reading 'original' Hitler, while being perfectly capable of mentally converting 'Hitlerisms' into correct language, than reading 'pseudo' Hitler after he had been edited according to the Oxford or Webster's dictionaries of the English language.

Helmut Bogler

I
Introduction

'Since we lacked the élite we had envisaged, we had to make do with the human material to hand. The results are what you would expect! Because the mental concept did not agree with the practical possibilities of implementing it, the war policy of a revolutionary state such as the Third Reich necessarily became the policy of reactionary petit bourgeois.'[1]

—Adolf Hitler, 14 February 1945

When the Second World War ended and the facts about the horrors of the extermination camps and about the murder of six million Jews became known to the German people in all their implications, the result was a profound shock which still continues to affect us to this very day.

That the man who had stood at the head of Germany for twelve years now began to be portrayed as a demon is psychologically understandable. The attempt was made to overcome the problem by shifting the sole responsibility on to an insane 'carpet biter', who had succeeded in casting his spell upon the nation with the help of demonic or super-human attributes. Nobody wanted to admit the genuine enthusiasm and jubilation any longer, and the excuse was the claim that the cruel and brutal dictator had excluded any possibility of resistance from the beginning. This, too, was understandable, because the victors were talking about the 'collective guilt' of the whole German nation and the Germans had to oppose this claim if they wished to escape being branded as a nation of criminals without any hope of ever again regaining their lost sovereignty.

None of these reactions, however, was a step towards coming to terms with the past, because the puzzle of how millions of people were able to cheer a man who ordered the murder of six million Jews and unleashed the greatest war in the history of the world still defied solution. Therefore, there was frequent recourse to irrational attempts at interpretation. In a book entitled *Führer und Verführte* (Leader and Misled), published in 1946, for example, the author writes:

> If we therefore make the attempt to comprehend one of the greatest tragedies of mankind in its contexts, conventional, moral or even political frames of reference are no longer applicable, and we must think in larger complexes. We encounter the super-human, the sub-human, even the extra-human, and we must necessarily decide to regard the demon of the German nation, the saviour with the dog whip, as a true genius of spiritual degeneration, as a principle, as a natural phenomenon beyond any possibility of discussion.[2]

While on the one hand Hitler was suspected of possessing, and invested with having, super-human abilities, on the other hand he was not taken seriously. Veit Valentin's oft-quoted statement that the history of Hitler was the history of his underestimation[3] was true not only for the period before 1945, but in the same measure for the period thereafter. This underestimation of Hitler also became apparent when he was portrayed as having acted without any objective or plan, as a power-mad opportunist.[4]

It was Eberhard Jäckel who can be primarily credited with having proved, in his study *Hitlers Weltanschauung* (1969), that Hitler had in fact developed a completely logical *Weltanschauung* which for him was the foundation for his political actions. But even Jäckel still assumed that Hitler had 'only had two real objectives', namely the conquest of *Lebensraum* in the East and 'the removal of the Jews'. For Hitler, according to Jäckel, social, economic and domestic policies had only been the means to an end, namely the achievement of these two central objectives. With this Jäckel remained largely caught up in the 'old' image of Hitler he was criticizing. Hitler had 'indeed been an opportunist in many respects', but this was not supposed to apply to the pursuit of his two basic objectives. Jäckel himself, however, had already admitted that his interpretation of Hitler's *Weltanschauung* 'contributed nothing, or almost nothing, towards solving the question of how and why this man came to power and was able to achieve his objectives to such a horrible degree'.[5]

So this is exactly what remains as the key problem: how was Hitler able to fire millions upon millions of people with enthusiasm, who then followed him almost into defeat, and for the most part voluntarily and not because they were coerced? Indeed, any further illumination of Hitler's objectives of the removal of the Jews and the capture of *Lebensraum* can contribute little to the solution. Hitler, of course, did not come to power because he promised to murder six million Jews and to unleash the greatest war in history. Quite the opposite. Neither anti-Semitism nor the question of *Lebensraum* figured prominently in his speeches in any way during the period (1930–32) in which he achieved his breakthrough as a leader of the masses. But how was he able to achieve such a success? Was it only due to favourable external circumstances, the economic crisis, the humiliation of Germany in the Treaty of Versailles and the collapse of the democratic system of

Weimar? Or was it due to Hitler's talents as a speaker and his demagogic abilities? Both factors certainly contributed, but the main reason was something more: it was – and this is the thesis of this study – Hitler's revolutionary programme which enabled him to become a leader of the masses. This view of Hitler is neither new, nor is it free from controversy. The question whether Hitler was a revolutionary, and National Socialism a revolutionary movement, had already preoccupied Hitler's contemporaries and had always led to controversy. There had never been any question about the Russian October Revolution or the French Revolution of 1789 being genuine revolutions, but from the outset opinions had been divided on whether the National Socialist *Machtergreifung* [seizure of power—H.B.] was also to be defined as a revolution.

There had been no storming of the Bastille or the Winter Palace. Hitler did not come to power as a result of fighting on the barricades, but was legally appointed as Chancellor by Reichs President Hindenburg according to the articles of the constitution of Weimar. Until 1945 the constitution of Weimar was never formally repealed, and most of the members of Hitler's cabinet were certainly anything but revolutionaries.

Nonetheless, the National Socialists regarded their *Machtergreifung* as a revolution. This 'legal revolution', which only began on 30 January 1933 and then systematically abolished the political system of the Weimar democracy by means of a total *Gleichschaltung* [bringing into line—H.B.], is in its way without precedent in history. Until then revolutions were tied to the concept of a violent uprising and the bloody overthrow of the former rulers. The National Socialist *Machtergreifung* did not fit into the tried and trusted concept of what a revolution was or should be.

Defining the NS *Machtergreifung* as a revolution was particularly incompatible with the Marxist understanding of revolution. Despite this, it was the Marxist side which recognized the decisive effect the revolutionary posture of the National Socialists had for their success with the masses. Fascism, Georgi Dimitroff claimed at the Seventh World Congress of the Communist International, was speculating 'on the best emotions of the masses, with their feeling for justice and occasionally even their revolutionary tradition'.[6] Wilhelm Reich, psychoanalyst and Marxist, came to the conclusion

> ... that the revolutionary phraseology of National Socialism had been the decisive factor in winning over the masses. National Socialists had been heard to deny that Hitler represented capital. SA men had been heard to warn Hitler that he should not betray the 'revolution'. SA men had also been heard to say that Hitler was the German Lenin. Those who moved to National Socialism from the Social Democrats and the liberal centre parties were revolutionized masses who had formerly been apolitical or politically confused.[7]

Towards the end of 1935 Paul Sering [pseudonym of Richard Löwenthal—R.Z.] published an article on Fascism in the *Zeitschrift für Sozialismus* in which he drew attention to formal analogies between 'a fascist and a proletarian revolution':

> For both the precondition is the concentration of all hopes on a single pole, around a mass party which has written the abolition of the existing regime on its banners. Faced by either, any attempt at resistance by the purely militarily superior executive organization fails because of the unambiguity of the mass movement. For both, therefore, the formal hallmarks of the revolutionary situation are the same.

While Sering did draw attention to the differences in 'class character', he basically admitted the revolutionary character of National Socialism. Fascism will certainly not abolish capitalism, said Sering, but in a revolutionary way it will implement a new historically necessary stage of capitalism which is characterized by a 'growing need for planning': 'The fascist revolution is therefore a genuine revolution in that – based on economic developments and proceeding in revolutionary forms – it represents an important turning-point in the development of middle-class society.'[8] Despite such insights, both Reich and Sering remained caught up in the view that National Socialism was a form of middle-class capitalist regime.

On the other hand, Friedrich Pollock – a member of the left-wing immigrant group around Herbert Marcuse and Max Horkheimer, who both worked at the Columbia University Institute of Social Research – already came to the conclusion in an essay published in the early 1940s that National Socialism was implementing a 'new order' which formed 'a new economic and social system in opposition to monopoly capitalism'. National Socialism was practising a system of planned economy which was no longer based on the profit principle: 'Profit has lost its primary economic function, namely to direct the flow of capital.' Up to now the National Socialist economic system had demonstrated 'an enormous strength' in all sorts of crisis situations. NS economic policy was 'more efficient ... than any other previous one ... The totalitarian state was able to guarantee this singular right [total employment—R.Z.] to all of its *Volksgenossen* [national comrades, i.e. any who are members of the same national community—H.B.], a right which so far no democratic state had been able to guarantee to its citizens: economic security'. 'Nothing of importance' was being left to the market place; respect for an economic sphere in which the state was not permitted to interfere – a decisive aspect of private capitalism – was being completely ignored: 'The primacy of politics over economics, which has always been so much under discussion in democratic countries, has clearly been established.'[9]

I. Introduction

And just as there were actually some beginnings of a revised evaluation of National Socialism and a recognition of its revolutionary character among left-wing emigrants, so too some conservatives, who had formerly misunderstood National Socialism as being a restorative movement, came to a self-critical realization of their mistaken assessment of the Hitler movement. It is probably Hermann Rauschning, himself a former member of the NSDAP and Chairman of the Senate of Danzig, who recognized the revolutionary character of National Socialism most clearly. Rauschning's book *Die Revolution des Nihilismus* (The Revolution of Nihilism), published in 1938, is ultimately also a criticism and self-criticism of those bourgeois-conservative circles who did not recognize the radical-revolutionary character of National Socialism at all, or not in time. 'Nothing was more shattering for a nationalist in the conservative sense than the slowly dawning realization that this "national awakening", to which he had professed his faith for the sake of such a solution, instead revealed itself as being a cynical, nihilistic revolution in which the legitimate and inalienable values of Nationalism were also being devalued and perverted.' The intention of 'the combination of 1933', i.e. the pact of the bourgeois-conservative forces with Hitler, namely 'to allow this dangerous National Socialism to "use itself up" politically', had failed. The bourgeois-conservative forces, for example Papen, had not recognized the 'revolutionary danger'. 'The conservative national forces believed they had created a political instrument, but in fact they had handed themselves over to a revolutionary force whose doctrine was the movement itself, whose tactics were the destruction and erosion of all values and structures.' National Socialism was, Rauschning went on, not a 'national, but a revolutionary movement. In the failure to recognize this fact lay the fatal mistake of the bourgeois circles. This movement could no longer be derevolutionized but, following its own intrinsic laws, had to continue its development in the sense of an increasingly sharper radicalization.' The misapprehension of the revolutionary character of National Socialism had been favoured by the fact that it had carried out a completely new and previously unknown type of *putsch*. The essence of the new tactic had consisted of first coming to power legally and 'immediately after the seizure of power, to execute the revolutionary act'. Modern revolutions no longer consisted of 'improvised battles on the barricades, but of disciplined actions of destruction'. Their danger lay in precisely this apparently orderly force of upheaval. Initially, however, this had not been recognized. People had still envisaged the German revolution far too much according to the historic pattern. 'But there are no parallels or precedents for the new revolutions of the twentieth century'. The National Socialist revolution, said Rauschning, was 'a new type of revolution, totally different from that of the classic French Revolution'.[10]

Rauschning's realization that Hitler's originality had lain in the concept of a new type of *putsch* was then taken over by historians like Bullock,[11] Görlitz and Quint,[12] Mau,[13] and Faul.[14] Historians like Karl Dietrich Bracher, when speaking about a National Socialist revolution, primarily meant the process of 'bringing into line' which affected all the institutions of German society between January 1933 and August 1934.[15] Other historians, above all George L. Mosse, emphasized a further aspect of the National Socialist revolution. Mosse claimed that National Socialism had primarily been a cultural revolution, but had not aimed at any economic changes.[16] The opinion that the National Socialists were not really interested in the economy[17] is wrong, but Mosse has certainly recognized an important aspect of events when he interprets Hitler's ideology as being a 'proposed solution for the modern alienation of human beings' and states, 'for millions of people the Nazi ideology was an answer to their fears, a release from alienation, and gave them hopes for a better future'.[18]

What Mosse had overlooked, namely the social dimensions of the NS revolution, came into focus when in the mid-1960s authors such as Ralf Dahrendorf and David Schoenbaum came to the conclusion in their research that National Socialism had had the effect of a 'social revolution' whose content had been 'modernization'. The sociological term 'modernization' describes a process of industrialization, urbanization, rationalization, mechanization and secularization during which traditional ties of a regional and religious nature, but also traditional class and status barriers, are dissolved. In principle, this process can take many forms and is not tied to a given social system. In the Western European countries, particularly in Britain and France, it was initiated or advanced by the middle class democratic revolution, and historically was inseparably tied to the Enlightenment, the demand for the implementation of human rights, liberal freedom, political participation and tolerance. This is not, however, the only possible and historically demonstrable form of modernization. As a counter-example we can cite not only developments in Russia, where the Bolshevist Revolution and the Stalinist dictatorship undeniably set off a substantial modernization push and made the leap into a modern, high-tech industrial society possible, but also several 'development dictatorships' in the countries of the so-called 'Third World'. It was therefore only natural to ask whether Fascism and National Socialism could not be interpreted as a specific form of this modernization process.[19] Dahrendorf wrote that National Socialism had 'fulfilled the social revolution for Germany, which had become lost in the convolutions of Imperial Germany and held up by the confusions of the republic of Weimar'. As a totalitarian movement, National Socialism had to destroy the traditional anti-liberal loyalties towards region and religion, family and corporation: 'By this process people are taken out of traditional, individual, often particularly close and intimate relationships and equalized.' This social revolution, however, had taken place involuntarily:

> We can not claim that Hitler set out to unleash and complete this revolution. Quite the opposite: like the whole of the swollen National Socialist ideology, his writings and speeches indicate that the traditions and values of the past were to be resurrected; the Nazis liked to appear Cato-like where in fact they were radical innovators . . . Hitler needed modernity, as little as he liked it.[20]

Schoenbaum argues in a similar vein: National Socialism had not only created a 'new social consciousness' but had also led to a genuine increase in the opportunities for social advancement. 'National Socialism speeded up the already considerable mobility of German industrial society; at least, it created the climate for social advancement and often enough actual examples.' But Schoenbaum, too, came to the conclusion that these outcomes of the National Socialist revolution were the opposite of what Hitler and the Nazis actually intended. National Socialism was therefore a 'double revolution', a

> . . . revolution of objectives and means at the same time. The revolution of objectives was ideological; it declared war on middle class and industrial society. The revolution of means was its reversal. It was middle class and industrial, because in an industrial era even a war against an industrial society must be fought by industrial means, and the middle class is required to fight the middle class.[21]

While we do agree with Dahrendorf's and Schoenbaum's thesis that National Socialism had the effect of a social revolution and of a modernization, this study is intended to demonstrate that both of these authors' second thesis, namely that this process had been involuntary and against Hitler's actual intentions, can no longer be upheld.

Whereas Dahrendorf and Schoenbaum were mainly concerned with the *effects* of the NS revolution, in an essay entitled 'Fascism and Anti-Modernism' published in 1972, Henry Turner dealt primarily with Hitler's *objectives*, and came to the conclusion that the National Socialists had only practised modernization in order to achieve their utopian final objective of a turn away from modern industrial society. In our study we intend to show that the opposite is true: the process of modernization described by Dahrendorf and Schoenbaum, i.e. ongoing industrialization, an increase in the opportunities for social advancement and the removal of traditional class barriers, was not 'unintentional' at all and certainly not against Hitler's will. Quite to the contrary: he intended this. In fact, he wanted to take it even further than it subsequently actually went. Hitler's objective was not, as Turner claims, a return to an agrarian society, but quite the opposite: he admired modern technology and wanted to turn Germany into a highly industrialized country whose industrial potential was even intended to outstrip that of the United States.

Historic research reacted in various ways to Dahrendorf's and Schoenbaum's theories. Authors who were arguing from a Marxist point of view accused Schoenbaum of confusing 'subjective appearance' with 'objective reality'.[22] But even Hans Mommsen, who clearly admits that the period of NS rule had caused a 'substantial push towards modernization',[23] rejects the application of the term 'revolution' to National Socialism and relativates the extent and importance of the actual social changes that occurred during the Third Reich. He claims that 'the socially atomizing effect of the Third Reich was nowhere near massive enough to force back totally the traditional structures of German society and German political tradition'.[24] Despite this restriction, Mommsen admits that 'National Socialism sprang from a modernization crisis which was particularly severe under the conditions existing in Germany'. He adds, however, that 'it remains to be clarified how matters developed on the international level'. Only from there could the question be answered whether it was possible to include Hitler in the group of historic revolutionaries. What was most important to clarify was 'whether this development [modernization—R.Z.] had been initiated by Hitler against his will or with full intent'. Mommsen answers this question in the negative and accuses Joachim Fest, for example, of 'stylizing' Hitler and National Socialism 'to active executors of a process whose beneficiaries they were'. The dilemma of such interpretations primarily affected 'Hitler's role and the relationship between intention and effect'.[25] Even though we cannot agree with Mommsen's thesis, here he does point to a critical factor in many portrayals of the relationship of National Socialism to modernization, namely that the 'international level' – in other words Hitler's objectives and ultimate goals – is omitted. It is precisely the object of this study to investigate this level.

While various authors still deny the application of the term 'revolution' to National Socialism even after Dahrendorf's and Schoenbaum's works, in general their theories did receive widespread notice and agreement by historians. Following Schoenbaum and Dahrendorf, in his Hitler biography Joachim Fest emphasizes the importance of the social impulses which bore up National Socialism. While Fest's statements on whether Hitler's revolution – or, more precisely, the social changes it initiated – had been intentional or unintentional are contradictory,[26] he still comes to the unequivocal conclusion that 'Hitler's place in history lies much closer to that of the great revolutionaries than to that of the retarding, conservative holders of power'. Hitler had not only been a 'figure of German social revolution', but had in general 'drawn the necessary conclusions and reduced the revolution to its modern definition'. Among 'Hitler's most noteworthy achievements, which secures him his place among the great epoch-making revolutionaries, we must include the recognition that revolution in the form of an insurrection was a thing of the past'.[27]

Even though Fest's biography of Hitler was widely acclaimed and quite rightly considered by many experts to be the best biography of Hitler since Bullock,[28] his frequently unorthodox choice of words provoked substantial contradiction. Hermann Graml claims that Fest 'exaggerates' the modernizing effect of National Socialist rule 'in such a manner that it makes the theory lose its tenability'. Above all, Fest ascribes 'far too much in the way of change to a deliberate will to revolutionize. The, let us say, incidental effects of events and developments, which were the results of a policy that was not directed towards change, are underestimated.'[29] Even though we cannot agree with Graml's criticism, he did call attention to a problem in Fest's interpretation. Because Fest does not sufficiently substantiate his otherwise correct theory of the intended revolutionization, and also contradicts himself, he provokes the criticism of those who, like Graml, insist on maintaining that the modernization which came about objectively was at best unintentional. Here again this study is attempting to answer the question which Fest ultimately left unanswered, namely whether Hitler was a supporter or an opponent of modernity. It is still a meritorious contribution of Fest's work to have drawn attention to the 'paradoxical' traits of Hitler's programme, in other words the ambivalence of conservative and revolutionary elements in his *Weltanschauung*, strategy and tactics.[30]

This ambivalent character specific to National Socialism was also the topic Bracher addressed in his 'Tradition and Revolution in National Socialism', published in 1976. Bracher primarily points to one decisive topic, namely the revolutionary content of National Socialism: 'If we continue to adhere to the term for heuristic reasons, then what were the elements in the ideology, programme, objectives of National Socialism – besides the technology of ruling and its implementation as the policy of ruling – that can be described as revolutionary?' Bracher emphasizes quite rightly that 'already for the Hitler of *Mein Kampf* and for his ideology and programme development . . . from the very beginning a very key guideline [had been] that, as opposed to the critics on the left and the competitors on the right, for this movement the non-traditional, non-conservative, non-bourgeois starting-point and content represented an important, possibly its actual, source of power, and finally also the secret of its success with the "masses"'. Bracher's findings are well in line with the fundamental thesis of this study, in which Hitler's conception of himself as a revolutionary will be portrayed, and thereby also a key provided for an explanation of National Socialism's appeal to and effect on the masses. In another article Bracher writes that Hitler

> as an ideologist and as a politician, as the sovereign manipulator of the means and objectives of that movement certainly [had been] a revolutionary . . . If a revolutionary can be described as someone who can combine a radical concept of change with the ability to mobilize the necessary forces, then Hitler may even be called the prototype of a revolutionary.[31]

In recent years other authors have also come around to this point of view and call Hitler a revolutionary. While Eugen Weber, in an article published in 1976 ('Revolution? Counter-Revolution? What Revolution?'), critically examines the instrumentability of the term 'revolution' in historic science in general, he nevertheless basically pleads against its undifferentiated and unreflected use. He primarily criticizes the one-sided occupation of the term 'revolution' by Marxism, which only recognizes the 'left-wing' and 'good' revolution as being such, and disqualifies all other revolutionary movements as being counter-revolutionary. Fascism, in particular National Socialism, had not been a counter-revolution but an alternative form of revolution rivalling Communism.[32]

In view of these differing definitions of revolution, Ernst Nolte brought order into the discussion with an article, published in 1983, in which he differentiated between an 'empirical' and a 'normative' definition of revolution, and the term 'fundamental revolution'. The empirical meaning of 'revolution' as sanctioned by usage, said Nolte, only implied 'a deep-reaching and, in its effect, lasting change, i.e. one that differs from normal changes, not however violence, and it is not restricted to the political sector'. Whether an event was called a revolution or not should not depend on whether the change was judged to be 'good' or 'bad' from the point of view of the observer. Based on this empirical definition of a revolution, the Bolshevist as well as the National Socialist and Fascist seizures of power had to be defined as revolutions. The application of the term 'revolution' to National Socialism only became problematical if one applied a 'normative definition of revolution'. This normative definition, which was primarily orientated towards the contents of the French Revolution of 1789, included certain clear traits which were generally defined as being 'good' – freedom, solidarity, humanity, the advancement of science and technology, democracy, the growth of the material well-being and happiness of mankind, the abolishment of a religious or superstitious view of the world, etc. If the yardstick of this normative definition of a revolution were applied, then one could no longer automatically call the

I. Introduction

National Socialist seizure of power a revolution. The term 'fundamental revolution' had to be differentiated from both the empirical as well as the normative definition of revolution. Nolte applied this term to that process 'which was finally [called] the process of industrialization, de-restriction, modernization, world travel, Europeanization, differentiation, professionalization', which in itself was neither 'good', nor 'clear', nor 'easy', but simply 'fundamentally revolutionary'. If this term were applied to National Socialism, one first had to note that, within the Third Reich, 'capitalism in the Marxist sense of the term' no longer ruled. National Socialism permeated 'a hierarchical and differentiated society with an egalitarian consciousness'. In terms of the fundamental revolution, so went Nolte's thesis, Hitler had been a counter-revolutionary. Nolte's reasoning was that Hitler fought against both capitalism and Bolshevism, but these were 'the two ways in which the fundamental revolution . . . had taken place'. Here one may ask: was not National Socialism – just like today's modernization dictatorships in the so-called 'Third World' – a third possible form of a fundamental revolution which had simply not appeared before in history? However one may choose to answer this question, Nolte immediately relativates that Hitler 'had not already been a counter-revolutionary in the sense of the fundamental revolution because of this. If revolution is simply understood to be the "overthrowing of the existing", then Hitler was not only a revolutionary in his methods, in the end he even almost completely exterminated the former leading class of Prussian *Junker*, and if he had won his war, his victory would have been the greatest revolution in foreign policy that is at all imaginable . . .'[33]

In 1983 Horst Möller came out in favour of defining National Socialism as a revolution with even fewer caveats than Nolte: 'The reflection of the NS seizure of power with the help of sociological-historic models of revolution as understood then, but also as understood today, leads to an unequivocal verdict: the NS seizure of power was a revolution.'[34]

In research we can observe an increasing tendency to agree with the application of the term 'revolution' to National Socialism. The major difficulty, however, is still the problem of the relationship between intention and effect of the revolutionary or modernization process set off by the National Socialists. Where does this difficulty come from?

The thesis proposed by Dahrendorf, Schoenbaum and Turner, that Hitler's objectives had been orientated to the past or had been 'anti-modernistic', is based on a very narrow fund of source material. In part the problem is simply due to the fact that there is still no complete edition of Hitler's speeches, articles and writings. Only for the period 1905–24 do we have the compilation published by E. Jäckel.

It is indeed astonishing that today, several decades after the downfall of the Third Reich, we still do not know what this man said about various subjects. This is a manifestation of the continuing underestimation of Hitler. For a long time Hitler was not taken seriously, and he is still not being taken seriously today, which is demonstrated, for example, by the fact that it is generally held that he knew nothing about economic and social politics and was basically not interested in them. Therefore it was not felt to be necessary to analyze his views on these topics or even first to compile all of Hitler's statements on them. In recent years, however, a change of view is becoming apparent. Not only has a Hitler edition[35] been started, interest in his economic concepts has also begun to develop.[36]

The objective of the research project which resulted in this study was first to compile all of Hitler's statements in his speeches, articles, writings etc. and to analyze them under certain aspects which had previously been grossly neglected in research. The focus was placed on three questions: Did Hitler see himself as a revolutionary, and, if so, how did he define this term? What were his social objectives and how did he view the principal classes of modern middle-class society? What were Hitler's economic policies and how did modernistic and anti-modernistic elements effect his *Weltanschauung*?

It appeared to us that without a clarification of these questions, the problem of the mass effect – the appeal of National Socialism – could not be solved. The question whether Hitler was a revolutionary can only be answered if we first investigate his self-understanding and his social and economic objectives, and thereby answer the question raised by Mommsen about the relationship between 'intention and effect', which is still a key question.

Such a procedure appeared to us to be more sensible than just to hold one of the many definitions of revolution up to Hitler and the National Socialist movement from outside and then to measure how closely they confirmed to this – ultimately arbitrarily defined – abstract term.

The method which we intend to apply is 'phenomenological' in the sense of Nolte's definition. For Nolte phenomenology means ' the understanding of these phenomena as they present themselves on their own behalf'.[37] The phenomenological theory is in essence a method 'which first takes note of an object and then sort of lets it describe itself'.[38] From this we derive the central task of letting National Socialism 'speak for itself' without offering any premature criticism and well removed from such constructions which 'diligently and narrow-mindedly are only avid to collect references'. In view of the hardly manageable plethora of statements, the first question to arise is naturally one of selection. But since, as Nolte points out, 'in the *Führer* movement . . . only the *Führer* can make binding statements', the portrayal of Hitler's

I. Introduction

thoughts must be central, and it must be 'so detailed, must permit the subject to speak for itself so richly, as to exclude any suspicion that only a preconceived schema is to be supported by the selection of individual citations'. What is important, as Nolte underlines, is that it is obviously not permissible to characterize Hitler, 'but then only to cite a dozen statements out of tens of thousands'.[39] By such means any theory at all could be 'proved'. That is the reason why in this study we constantly cite many references – sometimes even very similar ones – from the most varied sources as proofs of the opinions Hitler held on various subjects. While in certain instances this might detract from the readability of the study, even though many parallel citations are only referred to in the notes, we believed it to be important that we support Hitler's previously less well-known opinions on various topics in such detail as to clearly demonstrate to the reader that these are not randomly selected statements which are atypical for Hitler, but rather statements which represent his thinking.

The material for our study is therefore primarily Hitler's speeches, writings and 'conversations'. Besides the known printed sources such as *Mein Kampf*, Hitler's 'Second Book', the 'Complete Recordings 1905–1924' and the 'table talks', our study is based on the still unpublished Hitler speeches and articles of 1925–32, as well as numerous speeches made between 1933 and 1945 which were not taken into account in the Domarus collection on which most investigations are based.

With Hitler's speeches the question keeps surfacing as to when we can 'take him at his word' or when – and to what extent – the immediate reason and purpose of the speech, but particularly the addressee, need to be of primary consideration. We may certainly assume that Hitler's public speeches, articles etc. were written and presented with regard to a specific effect, with the intent to achieve a specific objective. This is particularly true of Hitler's foreign policy speeches between 1933 and 1939, which disclose little of his actual objectives and almost exclusively serve to deceive world public opinion. In contrast to this, however, in his early speeches and articles, as well as in his two books, Hitler speaks about his long-term domestic and foreign policy objectives with an astonishing degree of candour. Ahead of everything else, our investigation confirms what Fest already demonstrated in his Hitler biography,[40] namely that the commonly held opinion that Hitler had 'promised everybody everything' in his speeches was untenable in this form. Nevertheless, it is still quite justified always to keep an eye on the addressee: it goes without saying that Hitler spoke differently at a 1 May rally than he did before a group of industrialists. In this he was a master of demagogy and often succeeded in deceiving both his supporters and opponents about his real views and intentions.

Since Hitler believed that the masses were stupid and incapable of differentiated thinking, his speeches are also composed according to the 'black/white' and 'good/bad' pattern, even if his own thinking about various topics was far more differentiated. This is demonstrated, for instance, by the positive remarks about the Social Democrats and the Communists which he made within his inner circle, as well as by his never publicly expressed criticism of Italian Fascism and the reactionary Franco regime.[41]

In many instances the analysis of the document itself already shows whether Hitler's statements were only tactically motivated or are to be taken seriously. Otherwise we apply a threefold grid in order to separate only tactically intended statements (or such that are obviously only intended as propaganda) from 'programmatic' and seriously meant statements:

(a) A comparison of the internal statements which Hitler made relatively free of tactical and propaganda considerations (e.g. the 'monologues at *Führer* headquarters' or the 'table talks') with his public pronouncements. The internal statements, including his remarks to his immediate associates (e.g. Rosenberg, Speer, H. Frank, Hanfstaengl, Engel, Goebbels, Wiedemann, Schirach, Scheidt and Thöt), which we frequently draw on, can in many instances be used as a sort of 'pattern' against which we can look at the question of the given nature of a public Hitler statement.

(b) A further criterion is the frequency with which specific Hitler statements are repeated, and the consistency and continuity with which he expounded a certain opinion.

(c) A final criterion is the inner conclusiveness of specific statements by Hitler. As a point of departure we are able to take certain fundamental axioms which throughout his life served Hitler as the fixed points from which he derived his opinions on concrete individual problems. If a statement by Hitler can be logically and stringently deduced from the basic principles he developed, then we have a prima facie assumption that we are dealing with a part of his *Weltanschauung* we may take seriously, and not merely with a statement designed for propaganda effect or only meant as a tactical ploy. The most important of these fundamental axioms was Hitler's concept of the 'eternal fight' which for him was founded in social Darwinism. 'I regard fighting as being the fate of all creatures. Nobody can escape fighting if he does not wish to go under', Hitler said in a speech on 23 November 1939.[42] On 30 May 1942 he remarked:

> A highly serious statement by a great military philosopher says that fighting, and therefore warfare, is the father of all things. If you take a look at nature as it actually is, you will find this statement confirmed for all forms of life and all developments, not only on this earth but probably far beyond it. The whole universe appears to

be ruled by only this one thought, that there is an eternal selection process going on in which in the end the stronger keeps his life and his right to live, while the weaker falls. Some say therefore that nature is cruel and without pity, while others will come to realize that nature is only obeying an iron law of logic. Naturally, the one affected will always have to suffer, but with his suffering and his personal view he will not be able to remove this law from this world as it is given to us. The law will remain.[43]

This concept of the 'eternal fight'[44] runs through all of Hitler's speeches, articles, books and conversations like a red thread.

From the end of the nineteenthth century, socio-Darwinistic theories became widely accepted in Germany and were absorbed into various political movements and ideologies. That a 'vulgar-Darwinistically coloured monism' was part of those elements which 'also dominated Hitler during his whole political career'[45] has been generally accepted in research for a long time. But while it has been recognized that Hitler's racial, and above all also his foreign policy ideas, were determined by these concepts,[46] it has not yet been sufficiently taken into account to what extent Hitler's social, economic and domestic policy ideas, as well as his position on the various classes of society, were also predominantly moulded by his socio-Darwinistic view of the world and can actually only be understood in this context. As we will show,[47] Hitler was, for example, a vehement proponent of 'equal opportunity'. One of Hitler's key social-political objectives was that every member of the German nation should have the opportunity to take part in the fight for social advancement – which he defined in terms of social Darwinism – without regard to his former social status, property, education and income. Views such as these when taken by themselves appear to be quite sensible and progressive, but they are derived just as much from Hitler's fundamental socio-Darwinistic concept as are, for example, his conviction of the necessity of conquering new *Lebensraum* or the extermination of 'life unworthy of living'. Occasionally it may appear as if we were able to differentiate between the 'sensible' and the 'criminal' Hitler, but for Hitler himself all of his convictions are derived with the same degree of logic from only a few axioms of his *Weltanschauung*. Therefore there was just as little contradiction between his inhuman demand for the 'removal of the Jews', which in its consequences led to a regime of murder in a form never before experienced in history, and his standing up for the improvement of the chances for social advancement of the worker, which he shared with many humane idealists of his times, as there is between the fact that while he admired the Communists as being 'courageous' and 'brave', he persecuted them brutally, not despite, but because of, this. What at first glance appears to us to be contradictory and incomprehensible turns out to be absolutely logical within the framework of Hitler's total system. To demonstrate this by 'thinking ourselves into' Hitler's thought processes and the inner logic of his *Weltanschauung* is a key objective of this study.

We have identified Hitler's principle of the 'eternal fight' as an important axiom of his *Weltanschauung*, but it is not the only one. A basic thesis of his *Weltanschauung*, which is of central importance for understanding this man, states that one's own race or one's own nation (later on Hitler preferred the term 'nation' to the term 'race') must be at the centre of all considerations and actions. For Hitler this means that the 'individual' and 'humanity' are not relevant points of reference, but only and solely the German *Volksgemeinschaft* [national community—H.B.], or the interests of the German nation as defined by him. He stated in a speech on 1 October 1933 that

> For National Socialism the point of departure for its considerations, its pronouncements and decisions, lies neither in the individual nor in humanity. It deliberately puts *the nation* into the centre of all of its thinking. This nation is for it a manifestation of the blood... It therefore becomes necessary for the individual to finally begin to understand that his own ego is of no importance, measured against the existence of the whole nation, that therefore the position of this individual ego depends completely on the interests of the totality of the nation, that therefore feelings of superiority, self-importance, individual or class conceit are not only ridiculous for the existence of a national community but, above all, that the intellectual and spiritual freedom of a nation are to be rated higher than the intellectual and spiritual freedom of the individual, that the higher vital interests of the community must define the boundaries of the interests of the individual and impose his obligations upon him.[48]

This axiom of Hitler's *Weltanschauung* also runs through all of his pronouncements, and here, too, the conclusions he draws lead to only seemingly paradoxical results: if the nation is everything and the individual nothing, then for Hitler this leads to both the abolition of the certainty of the law for the individual ('right is what is good for the nation') and the right of the state to 'eradicate' genetically defective offspring, as well as to his demand that the enjoyment of private property be subjugated to the common good and his equalizing tendency to abolish the special rights of individual classes, which Dahrendorf has interpreted as the precondition for the development of the modern democratic society of the Federal Republic of Germany.

A further principle was fundamental for Hitler's overall *Weltanschauung*, namely what he called the 'personality principle'. This states that history has only ever been shaped by individual outstanding personalities. The masses on the other hand are stupid and incapable of differentiated thought and judgement. For Hitler they are therefore only 'human material' in the hands of inspired propagandists, who, due to their knowledge of the psychology of the masses, possess the ability to impose their will upon them. There can be no doubt that Hitler regarded himself as being such an inspired personality. He believed that he had not only recognized the great laws governing history, but also understood the problems of the present and the future. 'When I began my political work in 1919,' he professed in a speech on 23 November 1939, 'my strong faith in ultimate success was based on a thorough observation of the events of the times and the study of the causes of those events... Furthermore, I had the clear recognition of the probable course of historic events and the firm will to draw brutal conclusions.'[49] Hitler saw himself to be the executor of a historic necessity and the true interests of the German nation, which he believed he saw more clearly and accurately than the politically immature and stupid masses, and which he could represent better or more consistently than the democratic politicians, who in his eyes were incapable and cowardly.

In this Hitler was certainly prepared to learn; he even possessed a quite extraordinary ability to learn – otherwise he would not have achieved such success – but he always moved within the framework of his basic assumptions, to which he clung 'fanatically' (one of his favourite expressions). On the other hand, this often led to his clinging to an opinion once formed which fitted into his *Weltanschauung*, defining it as an absolute and negating the justifiability of any other diverging opinion. The success which accompanied him both in foreign and domestic politics for almost two decades – his unprecedented rise from being the propaganda speaker of an unimportant Bavarian splinter group that was not taken seriously by anybody to being the lord and master of the European continent – appeared time and again to confirm that he was right, gave him the feeling of a mental superiority over all his critics and reinforced his belief that he himself was 'irreplaceable' and that 'the fate of the Reich' depended solely on him and his inspired abilities.[50]

Tolerance for diverging opinions was not a virtue in his eyes in any case, but rather a sign of cowardice and weakness, as was any show of inconsistency. For Hitler there were no traditional, moral, ethical, social, religious or any other sort of caveats, considerations or restrictions. This radical anti-conservatism which refused to recognize a fact of life if it contradicted his actual or supposed insights – whose absolute correctness he never called into doubt – is what gave his *Weltanschauung* the revolutionary character and singularity that it would otherwise not have had. Taken by themselves, Hitler's insights were neither unusual nor novel. Neither his thesis on the necessity of conquering *Lebensraum* in the East was novel, nor was the concept of the national community, nor were his social and economic policies and objectives. In his Hitler biography Fest has emphasized what Walter Benjamin called the 'social character': 'an almost exemplary amalgamation of all the fears, feelings of protest and hopes of the times; while all of this is grossly exaggerated, distorted and endowed with many an esoteric feature, nonetheless it is never without its connection to the historic background or incongruent to it.'[51] This is what makes the study of the person and *Weltanschauung* of this man so important, even though his thoughts, taken by themselves, can make no claim to originality.

It would certainly also be of interest to trace the origin of Hitler's concepts and the counterparts they have in contemporary opinions, theories and ideologies. However, like Jäckel in his work,[52] as a rule we refrain from doing so. Nonetheless, within the framework of our topic it did appear to be appropriate to intersperse the portrayal of Hitler's thoughts on several key points with references to the differences and similarities between them and the contemporary stream of the 'conservative revolution'.

There are two further points on which we decided to follow Jäckel's procedure. First, the issue is primarily the portrayal of Hitler's *Weltanschauung*, not a description of the social and economic realities of the Third Reich. While at certain points we will draw the connections to certain real developments and manifestations, we will only do this sporadically and not in the sense of a systematic analysis which claims to be complete. This would certainly have gone far beyond the scope of our study. It is accepted fact that Hitler was able to realize some of his ideas, others only partially or not at all. Whether they were implemented or not, however, is not a measure of the seriousness of Hitler's intentions. In his investigation of Hitler's intentions Turner quite rightly emphasized that

> The fact that there were hardly any fundamental economic or social changes in the Third Reich before the war has led most authors to conclude that such upheavals were not seriously intended. There is convincing evidence, however, that the decisive leadership groups within the regime – first and foremost Hitler himself – only regarded the years of peace as a foreword to a far-reaching change of the German social order, which was to be implemented after the military triumph of the National Socialists.[53]

We can agree with this opinion, even though we are not prepared to accept Turner's interpretation as to the contents of these changes of society Hitler intended. As far as this goes, there are far more parallels between the social realities of the Third Reich and our reconstruction of Hitler's objectives than there are between the former and the alleged 'reagrarianization' ideology Turner imputes to Hitler, and for which there was not even the remotest attempt at implementation during the Third Reich. On the other hand, Hitler's revolutionary and 'modernistic' *Weltanschauung* and intentions, as we will present them in this study, equate far more closely to the revolutionary modernization which National Socialism actually did implement. If during the twelve years of his rule Hitler was only able to achieve many of his objectives to a very minor extent, then this has to do not only with the limited period of time to act available to him, but primarily with certain objective difficulties which arose for the implementation of his concepts. In the early years of his regime, for example, Hitler still had to give serious consideration to his conservative allies. While this was particularly true in the period up to Hindenburg's death, in principle this 'hurdle' remained until the end of the Third Reich, because Hitler continued to depend for the most part on the old élite of the military and bureaucratic machine. From 1939 onwards, however, a further difficulty arose, because a state of war was naturally not the right time for a radical socio-revolutionary change, which would necessarily have provoked conflicts with social groups on whose cooperation Hitler particularly depended in times of war. These remarks show why it is not permissible to dismiss certain of Hitler's objectives as not having been serious, or not having been an objective at all, just because during his lifetime they were not achieved, or achieved only to a very minor extent.

There is still a final point where we intend to follow Jäckel's procedure. For the most part we have deliberately refrained from offering our own evaluation of, or moral judgement on, Hitler's concepts. We leave the evaluation of these ideas to the reader, who may and should expect from this study that he will learn Hitler's thoughts in their internal contexts, but not their evaluation from the political or philosophical point of view of the author. This also means that we will refrain from any evaluating comments on the opinions and claims expressed by Hitler. If in every case we were to comment on the tenability or untenability of, for instance, Hitler's portrayals of certain historic events as these appear in his pronouncements, this would not only go beyond the scope of this study but would, above all, constantly interrupt the logical development of Hitler's chains of thought and thereby make them even more difficult to understand. The objective of our study is not only to present Hitler's key theses, but also his reasons and lines of argument which led him to certain conclusions, by 'thinking ourselves into' his *Weltanschauung*. In some instances this may make it appear that we are 'over-rationalizing' Hitler – this at least has been a criticism that has always been raised against any interpretation of Hitler which emphasizes the consistency of his *Weltanschauung*.[54] This impression or objection, however, is far more the outcome of a refusal to recognize the extent to which a *Weltanschauung* ultimately leading to inhuman consequences can still be based on logical reasons, and the long dominating – but still false – image of the totally 'irrational' or even 'insane' German dictator, than that of our method of investigation.

A fundamental consideration must be that for years Hitler has been portrayed as a devil and a 'despicable monster',[55] and by this it has been made virtually impossible for the younger generation to understand the motives of the former large majority which enthusiastically screamed 'Sieg Heil' and placed all of its hopes in Hitler. Under such conditions the younger generation had, and still has, only two equally unproductive and dangerous ways in which to react: on the one hand a simple pitiless moral condemnation of the generation which produced Hitler; on the other hand a preparedness – and this with increasing readiness – to listen to the arguments of those circles who, because some things were actually different from what we have been told, immediately draw the conclusion that perhaps everything was different and that Auschwitz was only a 'gas chamber lie'.

The present study should therefore be taken as a contribution to the 'historization of National Socialism' as demanded by Martin Broszat. 'The normalization of our historic consciousness', Broszat writes, 'cannot exclude the Nazi era in the long run, cannot only take place around it. Even the all-inclusive rejection of the Nazi past is still only another form of suppressing it and placing it under taboo.'[56]

II

Hitler and the Revolution

1. The 'So-Called Revolution' of November 1918

When after four years of war the republic was proclaimed in Germany in November 1918, many Germans, particularly the workers, attached hopes for a better social future to this. But for another segment of the people, the November revolution signified a 'perjured state', a crime: it was tarred with the stigma of the 'stab in the back', and a legend grew up around this term which was to play an important role in the Weimar Republic.

As he reports in *Mein Kampf*, Adolf Hitler learned of the revolution in the hospital at Pasewalk where he had been interned because of blindness caused by exposure to poison gas. He describes his reaction to the news of the proclamation of the republic in impassioned words: 'So it had all been in vain. In vain the sacrifices and hardships, in vain hunger and thirst for sometimes endless months, in vain the hours in which we, although in the claws of mortal fear, still did our duty, and in vain the deaths of two million who died in the process.'[1] Time and again during the years of the battle for power he abused the leaders of the November revolution as 'November criminals', and during the years of the Second World War he constantly repeated that there would never again be a November 1918.

It is quite conceivable that Hitler's extreme reaction, his stereotyped and brutal abuse of the 'November criminals', has obscured the fact that his position on the November revolution was actually ambivalent, and that he assessed it far more positively than many of his contemporaries. In contrast to most of his right-wing and conservative compatriots, he did not mourn the passing of the monarchy and the old authoritarian state. He, as opposed to them, was quite prepared to recognize the justification of a revolution in principle – even at this time and under these circumstances – and for him the term 'revolution' had positive and not negative connotations, so that he was not even prepared to call the 'November deed' a revolution.

In his early speeches, for example in 1921, Hitler spoke of the November revolution as a 'so-called revolution',[2] and in the notes for his speeches he put

Hitler: The Policies of Seduction

the word 'revolution' in quotation marks. Hitler declared repeatedly that no revolution had taken place in Germany at all.[3] 'The revolution of 1918,' he remarked in June 1922, 'was not a revolution, but a revolt by the Jews. Capitalism was to be destroyed, today it marches stronger that ever.'[4] About a year later Hitler again spoke about the 'so-called November revolution, which was not a revolution at all, because basically the system has remained the same... A true revolution would have had to call all those elements to account which plunged us into misfortune.'[5] Hitler explained to his audience that they had 'slept through' a revolution because what they had experienced in November 1918 'was no revolution at all'. It had been, according to Hitler, only 'theatricals', an 'exchange of places' by 'figures'.[6]

In his later speeches Hitler continued to deprecate the November revolution as a 'so-called revolution',[7] a '*putsch* by deserters'[8] or a mere 'revolt'.[9] In the spring of 1932 Hitler spoke to Wagener about the 'pseudo-revolution of 1918'.[10] In a speech in March 1934, in which Hitler demanded the continuation and completion of the National Socialist revolution, he said: 'While the term revolution had been selected for the revolt of 1918, but in the final analysis it had merely been *a change of government*.'[11] At the *Reichsparteitag* [Reichs Party Convention of the NSDAP—H.B.] in 1937 Hitler told the *Deutsche Arbeitsfront* [DAF, or German Labour Front—H.B.] that after the November revolution 'everything continued to exist just as before. I believe that it is we who have achieved the greatest revolution.'[12]

These documentary proofs show that Schoenbaum is mistaken when he claims that Hitler had first spoken about the November revolution as a 'sad revolt' in 1936, whereas 'in his speeches before 1933 he always called it that [a revolution—R.Z.]', and that it was only now that he was 'differentiating it from the genuine revolution under his leadership'.[13] Hitler was – and this has not as yet been recognized in research – never prepared to attribute the character of a genuine revolution to the November revolution.

But what was his position on the results of the revolution? It is known that in later years Hitler was a decisive opponent of the monarchy, and that he assessed the abolition of the monarchy by the Social Democrats to have been a commendable deed. For many conservative and right-wing compatriots of Hitler it was the collapse of the monarchy and the establishment of a republic which made them reject the November revolution so emphatically. It is therefore important to investigate what Hitler said on the subject of 'monarchy or republic' during the early stages of his political activities.

We are able to identify two sets of statements in his early speeches. Hitler frequently said that the question of monarchy or republic – i.e. the question as to which was the better form of government – was secondary because the state was only 'the means to an end'. What was important was the content, not the form.[14] Even during the years of the *Kampfzeit* [time of struggle—H.B.] up to 1933 Hitler sometimes expressed himself in such an ambiguous manner.[15] In addition to such indifferent statements, we also find a series of speeches in which Hitler clearly comes out against a monarchy or in favour of a republic. Already in August 1921 he declared at a meeting of the NSDAP: 'I am not a monarchist, because I do not thirst for the kind of monarchs we have had. We are in favour of a republic, but against a republic of black-marketeers.'[16] In subsequent speeches he repeatedly came out quite clearly against a monarchy and in favour of a republic.[17] Hitler emphasized that he did not fundamentally reject the republic as a form of government, but only its present content.[18] Said Hitler in August 1923:

> We National Socialists would not fight against this republic if it were simultaneously the German Reich. We fight against this republic because this republic proved incapable of again filling the Germans with pride at being a German. We would not fight against the outer form if the content were worthy of the German people.[19]

Turning towards the right-wing and conservative forces, whose primary slogan was the restoration of the monarchy, Hitler declared in September 1923: 'Nobody should delude himself that National Socialism expresses itself in the demand or desire to have the old flags fly again, to have the old authoritarian state resurrected, to have the monarchy restored, in general, to have the former conditions return.'[20] A few days later, in an interview with United Press, Hitler clearly stated: 'I am not a monarchist and I will oppose all monarchist adventurers . . .'[21]

If Hitler did not always state his opposition to a monarchy so clearly, this was probably due less to inner doubts and lack of clarity on this question than to tactical considerations. Hitler felt that it made sense not to commit himself against the monarchy unconditionally, because he hoped the anti-democratic monarchist opposition could contribute to the destruction of the Weimar Republic. In 1929, for example, within the framework of the campaign against the Young Plan, he hoped to gain the support of Bavarian Crown Prince Rupprecht for the plebiscite. After Count Soden, the cabinet chief of the Crown Prince, had harshly declined on the prince's instructions, however, Hitler openly threatened to give up his present – apparently – open-mindedness on the question, and to come out against the monarchy unequivocally in public. In an essay published in the *Illustrierte Beobachter* in early November 1929, Hitler threatened 'to undertake a thorough reform of our position'. He believed it to be right 'then also to have us clearly recognize the republic as the form of government and only declare and continue our most ruthless battle against its present internal enemies and destroyers, the November democracy'.[22]

That Hitler's outwardly displayed alleged neutrality on the question of republic versus monarchy was not based on any internal doubts or actual indifference towards this topic is also confirmed in Wagener's notes. He reports that in Hitler's opinion the nobility had shown itself to have become 'outdated' no later than with the French Revolution. Hitler told Wagener in 1933: 'In Germany the monarchic idea has been laid to rest.' Wagener himself realized 'that he (Hitler) had buried any thought of restoring the monarchy in Germany once and for all, and probably quite some time ago. Only he had never found an appropriate opportunity for apprising me of this.'[23] This point of view, however, did not in any way prevent Hitler from extolling the virtues of a monarchy if he thought this to be advantageous for tactical considerations, as for example to Reichs President Hindenburg, to whom he held out the prospect of restoring the German imperial crown at a later date.[24] From 1933 on, Hitler went over to stating, even clearly in public, that the question of a restoration of the monarchy was 'presently ... unworthy of discussion'.[25]

Hitler did not regard the collapse of the monarchy in connection with the November revolution as a reason to reject this revolution. Looking back to the end of the war and the November revolution in a speech in February 1940, he declared:

> What appeared to be the end for many, in my eyes was actually only the beginning. What had actually been smashed then? Untenable forms were smashed. Forms which could no longer have survived for any length of time anyway. The bourgeois-capitalist world broke down. Its age had simply passed. Such a collapse must come everywhere in some form, and it will not spare anything... Smashed, for example, was the monarchy. The German nation can live without it, it will live better without it... What was smashed then was our bourgeois social order. In the long run the German nation could not have lived with this at all.[26]

As we have seen, Hitler did not develop this point of view only in his later years; it was already well developed at the beginning of his political activities. Later his aversion to a monarchy was to be both reinforced and confirmed, particularly by his visit to Italy in May 1938. Hitler's state secretary Meissner,[27] his adjutant Wiedemann,[28] Reichs Minister Hans Frank,[29] Reichs Press Chief Otto Dietrich,[30] Albert Speer[31] and others all report on Hitler's negative impression of the monarchy in Italy. In his 'table talks' Hitler returned several times to his visit to Italy in 1938 and repeatedly used this as a reason to declare how glad he was that the November revolution had abolished the monarchy in Germany. On 21 September 1941 he said at table: 'That is what I am thankful to Social Democracy for, that it did away with these court interests. I don't know whether the likes of us, as necessary as it had to appear to us to be, would have been able to face up to the House of Hohenzollern in such a way.'[32] In a table talk on 28 December 1941 Hitler mentioned that he had helped Noske and many other leaders of the SPD by having their pensions increased immediately after his return from Italy: 'Thank God, I said to myself, that they got rid of that vermin.'[33] And on 31 January 1942 he emphasized that 'one could really not be thankful enough to Noske, Ebert, Scheidemann, that they cleaned that out here at home'. While their intentions had not been good, 'today the result is to our advantage'.[34]

In his recordings of Hitler's table talks Picker also noted similar statements: 'That our Social Democrats did away with this ferment of German fragmentation,' said Hitler on 5 July 1942, 'he thanked them for by paying them their pensions – among others to Severing'.[35] Hitler's architect Giesler also reports that Hitler had told him in the winter of 1940 that he had increased the pensions of the former Social Democrat ministers immediately after his visit to Italy, 'because in the final analysis they spared me from something terrible. When I think of the *Duce*!'[36] Hitler made a similar statement to Speer: the abolition of the monarchy had been a meritorious deed by Social Democracy, 'a big step forward. Only by this was the way prepared for us.'[37] Hitler's adjutant Wiedemann reports that Hitler had 'repeatedly said that the revolution in "18 had been a precursor for his own intentions, in that it had cleaned out the many dynasties in Germany'.[38] Scheidt, the adjutant to Walther Scherff, Hitler's plenipotentiary for military historiography, writes in his post-war notes: 'Hitler was sometimes wont to say that he actually owed his thanks in many ways to the men of 1918. They had had the courage to take unpopular measures and put an end to many an antiquated practice, so that he had been spared having to handle that himself.'[39] Hitler's Reichs Press Chief Dietrich writes in his memoirs that Hitler had often emphasized that he 'completely recognized as a historic deed' the abolition of the monarchy by the November revolution.[40] After his visit to Italy Hitler told Hans Frank it had been a stroke of luck 'that we lost this monarchy ghost in Germany in November 1918!'[41] As Hitler informed Slovak President Tiso during a conversation in May 1944, he had told Mussolini at the time that if he had not already been a republican he would have become one after his visit to Italy in May 1938.[42]

Hitler particularly despised life at court. Etiquette and 'everything connected with the higher forms of society,' reports Scheidt, 'were anathema to Hitler. Because these manners are based on the differences in rank between human beings which are theirs because of birth or position. Advantages gained by birth in particular were something Hitler simply refused to accept.'[43]

From his total *Weltanschauung* Hitler was a sharp opponent of the monarchy. Part of this was certainly a result of his aversion to having to share absolute power with anybody – even a king – as well as to his fear of events such as later actually transpired in Italy when Mussolini was dismissed by the king. But these were not the only motives on which his rejection of the monarchy were based. As argued by Scheidt, Hitler's refusal to accept differences in rank between people which had only come to them through birth certainly played an important role in his despising this form of government. As we have seen, his rejection was not solely based on the outcome of his visit to Italy in May 1938, where Hitler was basically only looking for further confirmation for his very early commitment against a monarchy.

We can now summarize: at no point of his political activities did Hitler reject the November revolution because it had abolished the monarchy. In this respect he recognized it as the precursor to his own intentions and as a historic step forward.

Many of Hitler's contemporaries, however, were not only mourning the passing of the monarchy, they were longing for the re-establishment of former conditions, the return of the old authoritarian state and, in general, for a return to the forms, values and structures from the past of the old Reich. Hitler was taking advantage of these tendencies for his propaganda when in his speeches he confronted the Germany from before the war, the Germany of 'order, cleanliness, and dependability',[44] with the November republic. On the other hand he also admonished the right-wing parties who were critical of conditions today but 'lauded everything in the past'. He accused them of never being able to differentiate between cause and effect, and in regarding the revolution as being 'the source of all misfortune' instead of 'the result of many mistakes', one of which, according to Hitler, had been 'no breaking down of the class problem'.[45]

In his notes for a speech Hitler wrote on 5 September 1923:

> So if the bourgeois democracy claims
> fault of the revolution, then however
> revolution their own fault . . .
> right wing says revolution is cause
> and is itself to blame for revolution.[46]

Hitler emphasized that the NSDAP 'did not solely consist of stupid reactionaries who only wanted to bring back the old conditions'.[47] He could not see anything positive in the concept of a simple 'reconstruction of the former Reich' as was being pursued by the right-wing parties, because, as he stated in *Mein Kampf*, '. . . we did not want to resurrect the old Reich which had died of its own mistakes, but to build a new state'. He refused 'to identify with those feeble parties whose only political objective is the recreation of former conditions'.[48]

In a speech in July 1925 Hitler explained that the movement had to understand that '*the wheel of history never ran backwards*'. He warned about those elements who believed 'that in a big loop our road would again lead back to former conditions'. This, according to Hitler, was a misconception. If something in the world broke down, then it was for a reason, and therefore it was not permissible to recreate the past with all its mistakes.[49] He repeatedly accused the middle-class parties of having their eye on the past instead of the future and only intending to recreate former conditions.[50] 'Your nationalism,' he said on 6 April 1927, 'is at best a means of bringing the past back to life once again. And our nationalism is the blind faith in the necessity of creating a new condition, since the old one has gone under and is lost.'[51]

He also accused the *Freikorps* [right-wing paramilitary formations—H.B.] and the other paramilitary organizations of intending only to re-establish the old Reich:

> That there is something else besides this, namely that one cannot simply shape the life of a nation by looking backwards and attempting to recreate the past in the future, but that one must sometimes attempt to shift the wheel of history on to a different track and not to turn it backwards in the future, is foreign to them and a far cry from what they intended.[52]

At an NSDAP rally an opposing speaker accused Hitler of only wanting to bring back the condition existing before the war. Hitler replied that he was mistaken: 'For about nine years we National Socialists have now been fighting against the old condition before the war.'[53]

The objective of the middle-class opposition parties, said Hitler in February 1929, had only consisted of a restoration of the past:

> The most daring concept of our large bourgeois parties was the recreation of the former condition, in the field of domestic policy the recreation of the monarchy, the reinstatement of all the individual reigning princes, reinstatement of the German *Kaiser*, but naturally also reinstatement of the German parliament, the *Reichstag* of former times, that shall all remain as it has formerly been ... And it was self-evident that with such backward-looking concepts, such backward objectives, they would never be able to face up to a forward-storming concept [meaning Marxism—R.Z.].[54]

Alluding to reactionary forces such as Papen, Hitler told Wagener in the spring of 1932 that these circles who 'derived their seigniorial rights from former times, now completely overcome, and believed themselves to be solely predestined and qualified for the government – and who, by the way, in their majority only impress us as being particularly stupid, lacking in instinct, and arrogant – simply wanted to recreate the old authoritarian state and thereby also the conditions of the masters and the servants, the upper ten thousand and the lower millions, the propertied and the propertyless, the employers and the employees.[55]

At the Nuremberg *Parteitag* for Employment four and a half years after the seizure of power, Hitler explained that the new Germany was in no way a rebirth of the old: 'It is not a rebirth, but something new, something unique in all of German history.'[56] In his funeral oration for Dr Todt (Reichs Minister for Armament and Munitions) after his fatal accident in 1942, Hitler emphasized with appreciation that Todt had already recognized in 1922 'that the objective of the German uprising could not be the restoration of old smashed forms, but a revolutionization of the German nation and its social order'.[57] Even in his last speech on the radio on 30 January 1945, Hitler, looking back on the year 1918, reproached the former middle-class parties for not having realized

> ... that an old world was fading away and a new world was coming into being, that the issue could not be to support by all means and thereby artificially maintain what had become rotten and decayed, but that it is necessary to replace it by the obviously healthy. A superseded social order had broken down, and any attempt to bolster it had to be in vain.[58]

In summary we can note that Hitler – as opposed to the other right-wing parties – did not mourn the passing of conditions before the war, the old authoritarian state and its social and political structures, but that in his opinion the November revolution had only given the mortal blow to a rotten situation already ripe for collapse. In his domestic policy he opposed the recreation of such conditions, just as in his foreign policy he rejected the re-establishment of Germany's frontiers of 1914. Hitler firmly believed that with such a slogan, which only aimed at the recreation of a former condition, no enthusiasm, no revolutionary drive could be generated, and that it would certainly not be possible to compete seriously with Marxism/Communism and its socialist promises for the future.

So far we have portrayed those motives which certainly *did not* lead Hitler to reject the November revolution, and must now naturally ask ourselves what, then, were the reasons which made him speak about 'the November criminals' and to resolutely condemn the 'deed' of 8 November 1918.

To begin with, Hitler considered the *timing* of the revolution to have been unfavourable. In an article he criticized the fact that a revolution had been 'instigated' in Germany at the very moment 'when only unity could, if at all,

II. Hitler and the Revolution

have saved us'.[59] In a further article at the end of April 1921 Hitler wrote that the attack had been launched 'just at the moment in which the time selected was in itself enough to destroy Germany'.[60] This criticism, namely that the 'timing had been badly selected',[61] can also be found repeatedly in Hitler's speeches.[62] Hitler was of the opinion that 'the point in time in which this revolution broke out was in itself . . . not high treason, but the timing constituted treason'.[63]

The criticism is therefore not directed against the revolution itself, but against the fact that a revolution was conducted in such a difficult military situation. In this, however, Hitler contradicts himself, because he also repeatedly states that a revolution would have been possible and justified if it had increased the power of national resistance instead of leading to Germany's becoming 'unable to resist'. Already on 20 February 1921 Hitler said:

> If the old regime no longer had the power to instil the armies with the spirit that was necessary to hold off disaster in the Fatherland's darkest hour . . . then let this regime fall in ruins. But then this revolution faced a gigantic task from the very outset . . . As an unfettered power it would have had to flow out to the front and untiringly hammer only one thought into the minds of the hundreds of thousands: *You now dare not go back, the old regime is overthrown, no will except that of the people now decides in Germany, but this will shall only be if you preserve liberty for your nation. Whatever you may hope for from this revolution, it can only come about if your nation retains the possibility of free self-determination. We have destroyed the old power out of love of the nation; we intend to defend the new freedom out of an even greater love.*[64]

And on 24 May 1921, at an NSDAP rally, he said:

> What would a German revolution and its men have done? If one had been convinced that the existing form of government had lost its right to exist, then after the establishment of the new form one would have gone to the front, one would have called the troops to the defence of the nation and the people to resistance to the last. One would have concluded an honourable peace and would then have begun to improve everything that needed improvement. That would have been a German revolution . . .[65]

Had the revolution of November 1918 been honestly meant, then one would have had to organize 'the battle against the capitalist West' in order to defend the new social Germany.[66] The republic would have had the duty to again call the German nation to national resistance:[67]

> Had the republic proclaimed on the day of her foundation: 'Germans, unite, onward to resistance! The Fatherland, the republic expects you to fight to your last breath!' millions who today oppose her would be fanatical republicans. Today they are enemies of the republic, not because of the republic, but because this republic was founded on German humiliation.[68]

In his speeches and articles Hitler often compared the November revolution to the proclamation of the Third Republic in France in 1870, which he cited as a model and a positive example of a German revolution that, in his opinion, would have been both possible and legitimate.[69] In his speech to the *Volksgericht* [Peoples Court—H.B.] after the aborted *putsch* of 8/9 November 1923 he explained what the task of the revolution would have been:

> Just as formerly the French Revolution of 1870 was unable to save the French nation, but did save its honour, so it should have saved the honour of the Geman nation even if Germany were to go down. If at the time *Herr* Ebert, *Herr* Scheidemann and *Herr* Barth and all the others had declared, 'German people, under the present regime you will lose the war, this no longer works, we want to be free now [!]', and had they declared at the same time, 'German people, you must now also preserve this freedom for yourself, the whole world is fighting against you, stand and defend yourself [!]' ... then, believe me, most high gentlemen, today the republic would be firmly established and none of us would lift a hand against her.[70]

After a socialist republic had been founded, said Hitler, it should have been obvious that the capitalist environment would now do everything in its power to destroy this socialist state. It would therefore only have been logical now to 'defend the achievements of the revolution in the social field against international capital',[71] but instead the weapons were laid aside. 'If in 1918 a revolution had knocked the state cock-a-hoop in order to erect a strong new Reich in which the people more than before had become the dominating factor ... then to fight against such a state would have been a crime'. This position, said Hitler in a speech in January 1928, was what separated the National Socialists from 'the definition of high treason by the so-called bourgeois world'.[72]

Here indeed lies a decisive difference in the reasons for rejecting the November revolution. While many conservative or monarchist forces rejected the revolution *per se*, Hitler was critical less of the content of the revolution but rather of the fact that it had rendered 'Germany defenceless'. For him the real 'dastardly act' had not been the revolution itself – and certainly not the abolition of the monarchy – but in the capitulation it entailed, leading to the subsequent Treaty of Versailles. If Hitler constantly stressed that the revolution in itself had not been anything reprehensible, he did this in order to differentiate his position from a conservative-authoritarian one which fundamentally negated a right to revolt. In a speech on 21 September 1928 he said:

> What was the November revolution's greatest insanity? One cannot say the revolution in itself, but the way the revolution was conducted, i.e. the rendering defenceless of the German nation. Because foreign policy-wise this delivered the

young socialist state into the hands of the capitalist world and made the consolidation of this creation impossible.[73]

Hitler never tired of repeating this argument in his speeches and articles,[74] namely that the revolution itself had been legitimate and the actual 'crime' had lain in 'rendering Germany defenceless'.

The difference between Hitler's position regarding the November revolution and the conservative-authoritarian view is also underscored by the fact that he reproaches the November revolution with *not having changed enough*, not having been radical enough. The November revolution, said Hitler on 24 May 1921, had changed neither the form of government nor the economic structure, nor the moral values.[75] The November men, he declared on 12 September 1923, 'only wanted to effect a change of people, not of the system'.[76] Years later Hitler told Wagener that while the revolution had put the reins of fate into the hands of the socialists, 'these had been neither prepared for this nor had they known what to do with them. The Jews were then quickly to hand. But the great moment had been missed, and all that could still be accomplished was a bourgeois revolution which found its expression in the constitution of Weimar'.[77] Hitler promised to implement 'what so many may possibly have expected on 9 November 1918'.[78]

When we analyze Hitler's motives for his rejection of the November revolution we are also confronted with the accusation – frequently repeated in his early speeches in particular – that the revolution had been led by Jews,[79] or that it had been carried out by the stock market – that it had been a 'stock market revolution'.[80] It is difficult to decide whether he actually believed this or whether it was simply a propaganda slogan, particularly since we must note that in his propaganda, particularly in the early years, Hitler made the Jews responsible for everything reprehensible, for all evils. In *Mein Kampf* and other places, however, he explains that for reasons of propaganda one should always hold up only a single enemy to the masses, and for Hitler this enemy was Jewry.

What is remarkable – and we may note this as a conclusion – is that Hitler's position on the November revolution differs fundamentally from that of those reactionary circles who deplored the collapse of the monarchy and the authoritarian state, and who were unable to view the revolution as anything except a dastardly 'stab in the back' for the fighting forces.

Insofar as this goes, there are points of similarity between Hitler's view of the November revolution and the interpretation of this event by the movement of the 'conservative revolution' which was popular between 1918 and 1932. Says Mohler:

It is generally accepted that the German 'Right' had uniformly reacted to the experience of this sudden collapse with the claim of a 'stab in the back' of the still

> undefeated German army. Here we may also clearly see how far-reachingly the 'conservative revolution' transcends the existing cliché of 'Right' and 'Left'. Whereas the majority of the 'Right' in the old sense actually does cling to the 'legend of the stab in the back' which robs the defeat of its necessity and portrays it as the 'accidental' work of a group of people insidiously acting in the dark, the conservative-revolutionary forces in Germany for the most part attempt to understand the revolution as having been a necessity and to fathom its meaning.[81]

Hitler's statements on the November revolution in large measure agree with the position of Moeller van den Bruck, one of the principal representatives of the 'conservative revolution' movement during the period between the wars. In Hitler's opinion the revolution had not changed too much, but too little, and it becomes clear from Moeller's statements that for him 'the subsequently so strongly opposed revolution did not appear to be revolutionary enough'.[82] For Hitler the November revolution had only been a change in government, not a 'genuine', but a 'so-called revolution', merely a 'revolt'. Moeller denounces the November revolution as 'false and only half a revolution' and declares also, 'But the revolution was only a revolt'.[83] Other representatives of the 'conservative revolution' put the term 'revolution' in quotation marks when they speak about the events of November 1918,[84] or call it – thus Edgar Jung in his book *Die Herrschaft der Minderwertigen* (The Rule of the Inferior) – the 'so-called revolution'.[85]

As we have shown, Hitler sharply opposed those reactionary forces whose objective was the restoration of an outdated social order he rejected. Moeller criticizes the 'reaction' which 'intends a Wilhelmian restoration' and, in contrast to the reactionary forces who 'have not come to terms with revolutionary changes' and who 'fundamentally regard a monarchy as the best of all constitutionally possible forms of government', emphasizes that 'in the final analysis the downfall of the monarchy can be traced back to its own mistakes'. The reactionary does not concern himself with the reasons for the revolution, 'because he himself is one of them . . . He has still not understood the revolution to this very day.'[86]

Hitler and Moeller also agree in their rejection of a reactionary restoration of the conditions existing prior to the revolution. 'A reactionary is,' says Moeller, 'someone who still regards the life we lived before 1914 as having been lovely and great, yes, grand beyond words'. On this point one should not fall prey to a 'flattering self-delusion' but admit 'that it had been disgusting'.[87]

Hitler probably went even further than the 'conservative revolutionaries' when he defined the November revolution as a historic step forward and the precursor of his own intentions. If he still condemned the leaders of the revolution as 'November criminals', then, as we have demonstrated, he did this not from a fundamentally anti-revolutionary position but because he

II. Hitler and the Revolution

believed that in times of war a revolution was only legitimate if it simultaneously led to a mobilization of forces against the enemy, as had been the case during the 1870 revolution in France. Here we again find parallels to Moeller, who criticizes the revolution for having taken place at the 'most unfavourable moment', but admits that

> The German revolution, like every break with the past, still had great possibilities. When the deceit which the *Entente* was preparing and which Wilson agreed to became apparent, she was given the greatest opportunity for a subjugated state: to incite an enormous wave of emotion in the disappointed people, and by an upsurging movement, to hurl their breach of faith back into the teeth of our enemies.[88]

That the revolution did not take this step is the reason, both for Hitler and for Moeller, why they rejected the 'November deed' – not as with the reactionary forces, however, because of the deed itself, or because of the abolition of the old system that it led to.

2. Hitler's Concept of the State and the 'Obligation to Rebel'

In the previous chapter we saw that apparently far from fundamentally excluding the right to rebel, Hitler admitted it. We now intend to pursue this thought in greater depth. For this we must first familiarize ourselves with Hitler's concept of the state and his criticism of conservative political theories.

Generally known, and quite rightly frequently emphasized by various historians, is Hitler's recurring statement that the state is 'a means to an end', and that this 'end' is the 'survival of the race'[89] or the 'survival of the nation'.[90] The meaning of this choice of phraseology, however, has previously not been seen within the only framework in which it becomes truly comprehensible: Hitler derives the right to rebel from his definition of the state as a 'means to an end'.[91]

In *Mein Kampf* Hitler writes that

> ... a government only has the right to demand respect and protection if it fulfils the requirements of the people, or at least does not cause them any damage. A government as an end in itself cannot be, because in this case any tyranny on earth would be unattackable and sacrosanct. When a nation is being led to destruction with the help of governmental power, *then rebellion by every single member of such a nation is not only a right but an obligation.*

This central passage from Hitler's book opens our eyes to what he really meant when he described the state as 'a means to an end'. A few sentences further on, Hitler emphasizes that it should

> ...never be forgotten that the highest reason for existence of human beings is not the preservation of a state, let alone a government, but the preservation of their race. Once this itself is in danger of being suppressed or even eliminated, however, then the question of legality is relegated to a subordinate role.

And even where the government only uses 'legal' means in its actions, the instinct for self-preservation of the suppressed justifies even an armed uprising against the ruling power. 'It is solely by the admission of this statement that the wars of freedom by the nations of this world against internal, but also external, enslavement could have come about in such overpowering historic examples. Human rights take precedent over states rights.'

Let us summarize at this point: Hitler fundamentally admits a right, even an obligation, to rebel. In order to justify this right, however, he must of necessity turn against the traditional German deification of the state, which does not, like Hitler, view the state only as a mere instrument, a 'means to an end' but rather as an 'end in itself', something holy which derives its justification from itself, from the mere fact of its existence. In the second chapter of the second volume of *Mein Kampf*, entitled *The State*, Hitler goes on to develop this idea in greater depth. He begins with the statement that 'today's bourgeois world is no longer able to envisage anything in common under the term state'. He then goes on to criticize the apologetic sort of approach to political theory which is not searching for the truth but which sees its only objective in 'the preservation at any price of whatever monstrosity of human mechanisms, now called the state, might be the case in point'. Hitler next differentiates between three political theories which he then criticizes. He first addresses the conservative theory of the state, which he characterizes and criticizes as follows:

> The very fact that a state exists is reason enough for its ordained invulnerability. In order to protect this insanity of the human brain an almost dog-like devotion to the so-called *authority of the state* is then required. In the minds of such people a means to an end becomes an ultimate end within the twinkling of an eye. The state is no longer there to serve the people; the people are there to worship an authority of the state which encompasses even the least intelligent form of civil servant.

It was precisely against this concept of the state, which Hitler characterized as being conservative, that he set his definition of the state as being a means to an end. The second theory Hitler criticizes is the one he characterizes as being bourgeois-liberal-democratic. According to this theory, what is primarily expected from the state is 'the favourable shaping of the economic life of the individual'; the appropriateness of a state is primarily assessed according to 'overall considerations of economic profitability'. That Hitler could not agree to such a definition under any circumstances will become clear in Chapter

IV.3. of this study, where we deal with his concept of 'the secondary role of the economy' and the relationship between the state and the economy. Hitler's examination of the third, and in his opinion the numerically weakest group, which believes Germanization – or, in more general terms, the realization of power-political tendencies – to be the purpose of the state, is not relevant here. As opposed to these concepts, Hitler only regards the state as being a means to an end, and he defines this end as 'the preservation of the racial existence of the people'. 'The state is a means to an end. Its purpose lies in the preservation and advancement of a community of physically and spiritually similar beings.' States that do not serve this purpose are, in Hitler's view, 'mistakes, yes monstrosities' and therefore have no right to exist. 'We National Socialists know,' he concludes in his juxtaposition of the existing definitions of the state with National Socialism, 'that with this concept we are revolutionaries in today's world and that we will be branded as such'.[92]

The primary concept from which Hitler started off was not 'the state', but 'the nation'. The concept of a new national policy, said Hitler in a speech in April 1927, 'has less to do with the state. For this concept the focal point is not the *state*, but the *nation*'.[93] Hitler explained his concept of the state particularly clearly in a speech on 9 November 1927, from which we would like to quote at length:

> For some the state is nothing more than a grandiose mechanism which lives in order for it to live, and the authority of the state is what keeps the mechanism alive, and power is what maintains the authority of the state. This comes about reciprocally and has basically no other sense or objective than the existence of this mechanical factor in itself. Then there is another concept which claims that the state is a means to an end, the purpose of this human existence is not the preservation of the state, the existence of the state is rather one of the means which enable the existence of a nation. The content is the essence, it is immortal for ever, and not the form itself.

According to this concept, the state is nothing more than 'the form which must serve the purpose, and when it is no longer capable of preserving and advancing the content, then it must be changed'. Naturally, the content stipulated a specific form, the concept a specific organization: 'But woe to the day the content becomes secondary and the organization, the form, primary'. Hitler sees the cause, necessity and justification of revolutions in the appearance of a contradiction between nation and state, a situation in which the outer form has become independent of its content:

> When in the life of nations the people, the content of the state, are increasingly pushed back over centuries by the purely mechanical existence of the state, then

even the best people there will come into inner conflicts, for no matter how strongly one may proclaim the state to be an end in itself, by this one can not succeed in drawing the individual human being, and particularly great brains, closer to the state, because these are not rooted in the state but in the nation. As soon as state and nation become two concepts which are no longer unified, and the one concept frequently oppresses the other, the oppressed suddenly become accusers and opposition begins to emanate from them; because the source of all life is not the state but the nation in itself.

This 'opposition' which occurs when 'state and nation become two concepts', when the state actually no longer fulfils or is no longer able to fulfil its obligation to preserve and advance the development of the nation, finally leads to the breakdown of the existing state, to revolution: 'When the state removes itself from this duty, accusers will arise from out of the nation and one day the opposition will destroy such a state.' The following sentences clarify the thrust of Hitler's reasoning which, in order to justify the right to revolt had to turn against the German tradition of deification of the state:

> The state is the representation of the life of a nation, and at the moment it loses its mission, it has lost its reason for existence ... It is not there in order to build up this fictitious authority of the state before which the individual citizen has to worshipfully sink into the dust. No, all of this is nothing but a means to uphold the body of the nation.

and:

> When the state is no longer capable of fulfilling this task, then there are only two possibilities left: either the people reform the state and lead it back to its natural purpose, or the state destroys a people.[94]

This concept, which he already developed in *Mein Kampf*, is of such import for Hitler that he again underscores it in his 'Second Book' published in 1928:

> When the leadership of a state appears to be contaminated by the decay of this mentality, then it is the duty of the opposition which alone perceives and represents, and therefore stands for, the true vital forces of a people to pin the battle for the national uprising, and by this for the national honour, to its banners.

Such an opposition had to embrace the concept that besides the 'formal rights of the particular government there were eternal obligations which compelled any member of a nation to do whatever was considered necessary for the existence of the national commonwealth. Even if this were to be a thousandfold opposed to the intentions of bad and incompetent governments.' In Hitler's view, this was the condition existing in Germany. The state had 'become a purely formal mechanism'. It was the duty of the National Socialist movement to 'bring about a basic change for Germany'.[95] In various speeches Hitler repeatedly turned against the 'bourgeois world' which declared the state to be the central point of all events.[96]

Just as Hitler opposed the concept of the state as an end in itself, he also repeatedly attacked the opinion which fundamentally rejected the right to rebel: 'Revolution is also not revolution,' he said on 8 December 1928. 'Nations have often pulled themselves up to a higher morality by means of a revolution'.[97] The only essential question was, what was good for the nation. When a state was rotten and decayed, then the people had to abolish such a state.[98] Hitler believed it was important continually to repeat this idea in his propaganda, because he intended 'a revision . . . of the concept and view of the state'.[99] This new concept of the state led to the proclamation not only of a right, but a duty, to resist. In an open letter to Count Soden, Hitler ridicules the 'wisdom . . . to submit to conditions that are actually destructive'. The 'weakling' will

> . . . always condemn reasons of a destructive nature as such, but never be willing to regard them as the justification, much less the duty, for beginning to resist . . . The question whether a certain condition of decay or suppression now provides a justifiable reason to resist will regularly and constantly be answered in the negative by the weaklings.[100]

Naturally Hitler did not tie this right to resist to any specific legal structure. In early July 1934 Hitler, who also regarded the law only as a mere 'means to an end', and who despised and vilified lawyers more than any other profession,[101] said to Hans Frank, former Bavarian Minister of Justice and later Governor-General of Poland:

> 'Oh yes, if we first had to ask you lawyers whether we were allowed to, then in all of the thousands of years of world history there would never have been a revolution. Revolutions are the big steps forward which suddenly pick everything up, carry it forward and then put it down on the new spot. In a process like that many things just have to splinter and bleed![102] From the point of view of the law, every revolution is illegal. And all you lawyers are really angry about is that you suddenly have to learn a new set of laws because the old one has disappeared.[103]

For Hitler not only the state, but also the law, the economy, the party and the army were mere 'secondary phenomena, means to an end'. And to the degree in which they fulfilled this function, he described them as being 'right and useful'. When they did not fulfil their function, said Hitler in a speech on 30 January 1937, 'they are harmful and must either be reformed or done away with and replaced by something better'.[104] The definition of the relationship between 'the means' and 'the end' is a fundamental requirement for understanding Hitler's *Weltanschauung*. During a talk with Goebbels on 23 February 1937 Hitler said that his great achievement was that 'I have taught the world to again differentiate between the means and the end.' The end was the life of the nation, 'everything else is only a means'.[105] As we have shown, from this Hitler also derived his conviction about the justification and necessity of revolutions, a conviction also shared by other leading National Socialists, as can be seen, for example, from the following statements made by Goebbels in a speech on 15 November 1933:

> Revolutions are necessary in the lives of nations, and they will always come when the natural abilities of a people to develop have become so encrusted and cartilaginous because of the strengthening of their organic life that this leads to a serious threat to the healthy existence of the nation. Crises that can no longer be solved naturally are then either solved by violence or they lead to the downfall of the people they threaten. Therefore revolutions also have their moral justification. They follow a higher moral code than is inherent in legal procedures.[106]

3. Hitler's Definition of Revolution

Earlier we saw that Hitler insisted on calling the November revolution a 'so-called' revolution, and that he refused to recognize it as a 'genuine' revolution. This necessarily leads us to the question of Hitler's definition of revolution.

'What is a revolution? It is the violent change of an existing order by a minority, supported and only made possible by the will of the majority of a nation.'[107] Hitler gave this general definition of the term 'revolution' in a speech on 24 May 1921. The second question he raised and answered was:

> What can be *improved* by a revolution? (1) The form of government, if the existing one justifies this because of deficiencies; (2) the economy of a nation, but only by a slow careful conversion of the existing economic structure such as the MSP [Majority Socialist Party—R.Z.] tried to achieve by a revolution at a time when its theories were still under the scientific criticism of the economists; and (3) in general a revolution is only tolerable if it renews the moral forces of a nation by eliminating the moral and economic corruption that has taken over.[108]

According to this definition, a revolution has three possible dimensions, political-constitutional, economic and spiritual-moral. In Hitler's speeches in 1920 his definition of revolution was still different from the one just presented. While he agreed to the possibility of a political, he rejected an economic and social revolution. In early August 1920 he said that while a political revolution was possible, economic revolution was nonsense, because 'while one can destroy an economy that has existed for ten thousand years, one then has to rebuild it again in the same sense'. A social revolution with the objective of making all people equal was an impossibility.[109] Hitler's scepticism was primarily directed against too abrupt changes in the economic sector. On 27 April 1920, for example, he said that while a political revolution was possible within a matter of a few days, an economic one was not.[110] Changes in the economy, as Hitler underlined on 25 August 1920, could only come about by evolution.[111]

While Hitler was to retain his scepticism towards *too abrupt* changes in the economy throughout his life, one year later he had – as the first quoted passage above demonstrates – already modified the definition of revolution from various speeches in 1920 and recognized the economic and spiritual dimensions of revolution in addition to the political one.

The National Socialists saw their revolution as the attempt to restructure every single sector of human life in the sense of their *Weltanschauung*. It was Goebbels who proclaimed this intent most clearly and emphatically:

> Revolutions, if they are genuine, do not stop at anything. There is no revolution that reforms or overturns only the economic, or the political or the cultural life. Revolutions are breakthroughs of a new *Weltanschauung*. And if a *Weltanschauung* can really claim this designation, then it cannot be satisfied with revolutionarily restructuring only *one* sector of public life, then the breakthrough of this *Weltanschauung* must permeate all of public life; no sector may be left untouched by it.[112]

On 15 November 1933 Goebbels declared:

> The revolution we carried out is a total one. It permeated all sectors of public life and restructured them from the ground up. It completely changed and reformed the relationships of the people to each other, the relationships of the people to the state and to the questions of existence. It was indeed the breakthrough of a young *Weltanschauung*... Revolutions follow their own laws and dynamics. Once they have passed a certain phase of their development they elude the power of control by human beings and only obey the law under which they started. It is in the nature of every genuine revolution that it goes the whole hog and does not admit of any compromise. Either it intends to push through to the ultimate objective – in which case it will have a lasting effect – or it is satisfied with partial successes – then it would be better not to do it at all ... Revolutions never restrict themselves only to the purely political sector. From there they seize all other fields of human life. Economy and culture, science and art are not spared. This is politics in a higher sense then we normally understand it to be.[113]

After the seizure of power Hitler himself also applied the term 'revolution' in this encompassing sense. On 20 February 1938, for example, he declared that the programme of National Socialism meant 'a revolution in most of the sectors of formerly valid social, political and economic tenets and insights. The seizure of power itself was a revolution in the overcoming of existing institutions'.[114] On 12 February 1942 he underlined the necessity of a 'revolutionizing of the German spirit, the German nation and its inner social order',[115] i.e. he admitted both the spiritual as well as the social dimension of the revolution. And about two weeks later, in a table talk, he particularly stressed the social obligations of a revolution.[116] In other words, Hitler used the term 'revolution' in the 'total' sense as defined by Goebbels.[117] For Hitler a genuine revolution was more than just a political upheaval, and it did not exhaust itself only in a radical change of the social and economic structure: it was above all a spiritual re-orientation.[118]

For Hitler the radical re-orientation in *Weltanschauung* was the primary condition for a change in structure. For Hitler it was even the decisive criterion of a revolution that it had to bring about the victory of a *Weltanschauung*, a grandiose new idea, which was to provide the guiding principle for the restructuring of all sectors of life. On 16 December 1925 he criticized the bourgeois right-wing parties for – as opposed to the Communists – not having any *Weltanschauung* at all: assuming the *Deutschnationalen* [German Nationalist Party—H.B.] were to be given full power in Germany, Hitler argued, 'what do you think would change? Do you believe that maybe ten months later any person coming to Germany would know: this is no longer the old Germany, this is a new Reich, a new state, a new nation?' However, if the Communists were to come to power, he continues, after one year one would no longer recognize Germany. This differentiation was not intended as an accusation against the Communists – quite the opposite: the difference between the *Deutschnationalen* and the Communists lay in the fact that the Communists at least had a *Weltanschauung* – even if it was the wrong one, 'but it is a *Weltanschauung*'. The Communists were at least fighting for 'a great idea, even if a thousandfold insane and dangerous one'. This was precisely the difference between a normal party – such as the middle-class parties were, which was already reason enough for Hitler to reject them – and a 'party with a *Weltanschauung* behind it', as were both Communists and National Socialists. A party founded in a *Weltanschauung* claimed exclusivity for its teachings and after having come to power therefore stopped being a party.[119] The victory of a *Weltanschauung* meant, as Hitler emphasized on various occasions, that it put its stamp on the whole of life, that the maxim for all acts was, 'We do not recognize the laws of humanity, but only the law of the preservation of existence, the movement, the idea, or the implementation of this idea.'[120]

Hitler also expounds this concept in *Mein Kampf*. The programme of a *Weltanschauung* meant 'formulating a declaration of war against an existing order, against an existing condition, in brief, basically against an existing view of the world'. Since a *Weltanschauung* was never prepared to share with a second one, it could also not cooperate within an existing condition, 'but [it] feels the obligation to fight against this condition and the whole enemy ideology with all available means, i.e. to prepare their collapse'. The great secret of the French Revolution of 1789, the Russian October Revolution and the victory of Italian Fascism was the 'demonstration of a great new idea', in order to submit the nation to a 'comprehensive restructuring'. 'The conviction of the right to apply even the most brutal of weapons is always tied to the existence of a fanatical belief in the necessity of the victory of a revolutionary new order in the world.'[121]

A movement that was fighting for a new *Weltanschauung*, as Hitler remarked in early April 1927, had the objective of 'completely restructuring all conditions based on new points of view'. A fundamental intent of the proponents of a *Weltanschauung* was to cancel out its party character and, after their victory, to elevate their *Weltanschauung* to become the general frame of reference.[122] After the victory of a traditional parliamentary party basically nothing changed, 'whereas the victory of a new *Weltanschauung* has the effect of an overthrow'.[123]

For Hitler, 'revolution' was therefore a synonym for the victory of a *Weltanschauung*, which by its very nature had to be intolerant and strive for a total restructuring of all sectors of life and all values. On 19 March 1934 he expressed this idea with the following words: 'The victory of a party is a change of government, the victory of a *Weltanschauung* is a revolution, and a revolution which changes the condition of a nation fundamentally and in its essence.' This is the reason why Hitler was not prepared to recognize the 'revolt' of 1918 as a revolution: it was for him merely a change in government. The victory of National Socialism had been the victory of a *Weltanschauung*, therefore this *Weltanschauung* had brought about a 'genuine revolution' which had achieved more in the way of genuine inner restructuring 'than all of the Bolshevist revolutions to date taken together'.[124] The victory of National Socialism, said Hitler on 25 January 1936, had been 'a true revolution of historic dimensions', because it had not simply been a change of government 'but the implementation of a Weltanschauung'.[125]

The focal point of Hitler's considerations had always been the question of power, because the party can obviously only impose its *Weltanschauung* the moment it holds full power in its hands. In fact, this is really the essence of all revolutionary movements – that they constantly make the question of power the starting point and the end point of all their considerations, all their tactical and strategic plans. Even before the seizure of power Hitler admitted quite openly: 'When we finally obtain power, we will keep it, so help us God. We will not let anybody take it away from us.'[126] In his closing speech at the *Reichsparteitag* in 1934 Hitler named as the two essential principles of the national Socialist party: '(1) It wanted to be *truly a* Weltanschauungs *party*, and (2) therefore it wanted *sole power* in Germany without any compromise.'[127] His fundamental principle in the battle for power had been, as he declared in February 1935 when looking back, 'there must be *one will* in Germany, and all others must be overcome'.[128]

The totalitarian character of Hitler's *Weltanschauung* was disclosed in his speech to officers on 26 May 1944 when he emphasized that once he recognized an opinion to be correct, then he had the duty not only to make his fellow-citizens accept it but also to do away with any contrary opinion. Tolerance towards other opinions was merely a sign of uncertainty.[129]

Before we go on to discuss these rather general considerations more precisely and investigate the self-understanding and character of Hitler's revolution, we first want to portray Hitler's assessment of historic revolutions.

4. Hitler's View of Historic Revolutions

The reconstruction of Hitler's view of historic revolutions is often not easy for several reasons. First of all he only expressed himself relatively rarely, and then briefly and 'as an aside' on the great French Revolution, for example; and secondly his verdicts are highly contradictory. This contradictoriness, however, is an expression of the fact that his opinions on the great revolutions, particularly on the French Revolution of 1789 and the Russian October Revolution (which for reasons of systematics we will only deal with further in Chapter VII.3.d.), was characterized by both admiration and rejection.

a. The French Revolution of 1789

According to the testimony of Ernst Hanfstaengl, one of Hitler's closest intimates during his early years, besides Frederick the Great (the particular interest of the 'book devourer') Hitler was devoted to the French Revolution.[130] When Hitler talked about the laws governing the success of a revolution, he frequently referred to the example of the French Revolution. In *Mein Kampf*, for example, he underscored his theory that revolutions are less prepared for by written statements than by the power of great orators with a referral to the French Revolution. One should not believe, said Hitler, 'that the French Revolution would ever have come about through philosophical theories if it had not found an army of malicious agitators led by the greatest demagogues, who incited the passions of the tortured populace until finally that terrible volcanic eruption occurred which paralyzed all of Europe in horror'. Elsewhere in *Mein Kampf* he calls the 'proposal of a great new idea' the secret of the success of the French Revolution.[131]

In a speech to members of the German press in Munich on 10 November 1938 Hitler also cited Napoleon and the French Revolution as proof of the power of propaganda: Napoleon had certainly not won solely as a strategist and inspired leader, but 'this was preceded by the *Marseillaise*, the ideas of the French Revolution', so that Napoleon 'in part reaped what this revolution had previously sown'.[132] Six years later he again explained the same thoughts to officers and generals:

> When formerly the French revolutionary armies deployed in defence of their revolutionary ideals, which despite a Gallic fulsomeness of phrasing did actually enthuse millions, one could observe how traditional, perfectly trained military units simply went to pieces before them, in part because the revolutionary idea had gone on before and begun to render them from inside, in part because it (the revolutionary idea) was superior.[133]

In his diary on 5 March 1945 Goebbels reports that during a conversation on the reformation of the army – which Germany had omitted to carry through but which was planned for the post-war period – Hitler had drawn attention to the fact that the reform of the army in France had not taken place during the Revolution but only in the course of the Napoleonic wars.[134]

We have cited these quite varied references Hitler made to the great French Revolution because they have one thing in common: on the one hand Hitler attempts to derive laws governing revolution in general from certain events of the French Revolution and to apply them to his revolution, and on the other hand he is simultaneously attempting to justify certain of his own views, acts or – as the last quotation demonstrates – omissions by drawing analogies and parallels to the French Revolution. In doing so he puts his own revolution on the same plane as that of the great French Revolution. Basically, however, he remained ambiguous towards it. On 6 July 1920 he said that the French Revolution – in contrast to the November revolution – had been 'national and constructive'.[135] That Hitler rejected the slogans of the French Revolution ('liberty, equality, fraternity'), as we can deduce from a speech on 20 September 1920, actually need not be discussed further.[136] In a speech on 12 January 1921 he again drew on the French Revolution as proof for his own views and spoke in this context about Louis XIV and his 'lush court life' which 'laid the foundation for the subsequent revolution, which in its turn gave a man of the people, the Corsican Napoleon, the opportunity of winning back its former international standing for France'.[137] Such positive statements contrast with other assessments Hitler made. On 18 January 1923, for example, he interprets the French Revolution of 1789 as an attempt 'by the Jew' to incite the 'already partially decayed bourgeois class of the Aryan population against the nobility which he had totally decayed', so that both forces would, finally, completely destroy each other and he could establish his own rule. The Jew did not succeed in this because he lacked sufficient 'brains' to rule the French nation. Therefore, said Hitler, through the revolution incited by the Jew, the bourgeoisie became a power factor in the state.[138]

Besides such obviously abstruse racial-ideological assessments we also find statements by Hitler which are differentiated, as, for example, when on 12 September 1923 he explains that not only the French revolution of 1870, but also that of 1789 – as opposed to the revolt of November 1918 – did result in increasing France's welfare, despite the fact that it had been made by people 'who in the final analysis did not all have their eye on the welfare of France'.[139] In *Mein Kampf* he also contrasts the November revolution with the French Revolution of 1789: while the former had 'not produced a single leader of any stature', the French Revolution had produced a Robespierre, a Danton and a Marat. To surrender to such as these was still quite understandable, but not to a Scheidemann, Erzberger or Ebert.[140]

In an article in the *Illustrierte Beobachter* of 30 July 1929 Hitler takes 14 July, the French national holiday and the day of the storming of the Bastille, as an opportunity to draw a comparison between the great French Revolution and the November revolution. The November revolution, he wrote, had only been 'a more or less wretched pale copy' of the French Revolution. The storming of the Bastille had naturally been quite a different undertaking from the 1918 'revolt by deserters and criminals'. The French Revolution had at least 'produced leaders of stature', even if these had been 'villainous criminals'. One need only compare the 'fanatics of the Convent' (in Hitler's terminology 'fanatic' was anything but derogatory – it was one of his highest accolades) with the 'riff-raff' of the German revolutionary government. 'Above all,' Hitler continued, 'externally the French Revolution was at least a heroic undertaking' as opposed to the German revolution. Out of the French revolution and its 'daring generals' had 'at least emerged a Napoleon . . . An epoch and a historic era which can produce the great Corsican as its ultimate representative is certainly quite something else than a period which finds its most vivid expression in geniuses of the black market.'[141]

Next to such positive statements we also find negative statements on the French Revolution. Hitler's assessment of the emancipation of the Jews which was brought about by the Revolution was, of course, negative.[142] This had resulted in a period of continuous internal unrest without anything of use to the nations having been solved thereby. The French Revolution initiated the 'liberal era', which was 'unable to provide any nation with a really earth-shakingly great idea, but instead gave birth to all the more rigorous tendencies towards dissolution'.[143] As Hitler explains in his 'Second Book', while the bourgeois world had believed it could overthrow the feudal world, 'in reality it only permitted the continuation of its mistakes at the hands of moneybags, shysters and journalists. It never possessed a great idea, but instead immeasurable quantities of conceit and money.'[144]

Six years later, in his culture speech at the *Reichsparteitag* of 1934, Hitler interprets the French Revolution as the beginning of a turning-point in history. It had been the first 'elementary eruption' of an earthquake which had shattered the innermost foundations of a thousand-year-old world of ideas and social order. Hitler assessed this turning-point in history as being neither clearly negative nor exclusively positive. We detect admiration when he speaks about the 'stormy impatience' with which, since this turning-point, man has been attempting to uncover the secrets of the world and his own being:

> Continents have been opened up. Man's advances have progressed upwards, in breadth, and in depth. Into the arctic ice fields as well the zones of tropic deserts and forests, over all the oceans and up to the peaks of the eternal giants of the mountains his drive to explore, his curiosity, and his greed urge him on!

Hitler talks about 'a genius suddenly unleashed as if by magic' which expresses itself in inventions and discoveries and speaks admiringly about the newly upsurging 'major power of physics and technology' as well as chemistry. A world of alleged knowledge and prejudices had broken apart and given way to a new insight, a patriarchal social order had been 'torn asunder', etc. Besides the admiration that echoes in these words, he also sees the 'world ideas of a liberal era' as the precursors of Marxist Socialism and speaks about a magnificent and dreadful play that is being enacted before our eyes. The National Socialist revolution had ended this era of 'chaotic confusion'.[145]

In his culture speech at the *Reichsparteitag* two years later Hitler again turns to the French Revolution and the era it initiated. Hitler's frequently quite colourful and pathetic words reflect his contradictory relationship to this event, which he both admires and rejects. On the one hand he speaks about 'the terrible events of the French Revolution' and on the other of the 'brilliant God of war' who had arisen from its chaos and overthrown a European world already internally undermined by the Revolution's spreading ideas. 'And in ever shorter sequences of time, ever more dynasties fall, ever more states convert their outdated authoritarian forms into what appear to be modern democracies.'[146] In this speech we also find the consideration that the enlightened absolutism of a Frederick the Great and a Joseph II had prevented a similar development in Prussia and Austria. In anticipation of the threatening upheavals, they as monarchs had drawn practical conclusions and in their states thereby 'removed' a large number of the 'inner conditions which apparently justified these' before the approaching revolutionary events, so that 'the infectious power of the French revolutionary idea had already been prevented in Germany right from the outset!'[147] Hitler repeated this consideration again five years later in his monologues at table: 'If Germany was spared the French Revolution, then [this was] only because Frederick the Great and Joseph II were there.'[148]

Hitler, who admired Frederick the Great throughout his life, saw himself as being an enlightened ruler similar to Frederick, who in the twentieth century, however, had been given the task of removing the conditions for the Bolshevist Revolution by overcoming the outdated bourgeois social order step by step. This was to be accomplished by a revolution the idea of which was so powerful and overwhelming that, as he once said to Wagener, 'the French Revolution will appear as child's play in comparison'.[149] In 1932 he threatened 'those who are in power' that if they were to treat the people the way they had been treated before the French Revolution, they could be sure that they would thereby cause a revolution 'which would possibly be even more violent than the French Revolution'.[150]

If we summarize at this point, then the currently held view that the National Socialists had 'seen themselves as being the greatest counter-blow against the French Revolution', while being correct,[151] only describes one side of the relationship to this epoch-making event. Goebbels' frequently quoted statement that with the seizure of power 'the year 1789 had been crossed out in history'[152] should not be interpreted – at least not as far as Hitler is concerned – as if the National Socialist had regarded their revolution as being merely the antithesis to the French Revolution. Hitler certainly defined his revolution as a negation of the 'world concept of a liberal epoch' which had been initiated in 1789, but on the other hand he defined himself as being in the tradition of the age of modernity, technical invention, the destruction of traditional and religious ties and world concepts rung in by the French revolution. As we shall show in Chapter V.3. he did not even roundly reject the ideas of French Enlightenment, but saw them as also being the beginning of a – in his assessment positive – day of reckoning for superstition, irrationalism and religion.

Apart from this quite ambivalent evaluation of the age initiated by the French Revolution, for Hitler the revolution was a positive example to which he referred on various occasions and from which he tried to learn.

II. Hitler and the Revolution

b. The Proclamation of the Third Republic in September 1870

Hitler's assessment of the proclamation of the Third Republic in France in September 1870 was unequivocally positive. As we recall, MacMahon's army surrendered on 1 September 1870 after the battle of Sedan, Napoleon III was captured and three days later, on the initiative of the republicans Favre and Gambetta, came the proclamation of the Third Republic and the formation of a government of national defence. By this deed, wrote Hitler in an article on 20 February 1921, it was intended to restore the honour of the French nation, and this was in fact restored: 'The French were satisfied with overthrowing the imperial regime because it appeared to them to be too weak. In its place they set the revolutionary, nationalistically enthusiastic energy of the republic.'[153] This revolution had, said Hitler in September 1923, clearly increased the welfare of France, because the revolution had been made 'in order to *save* the sinking tricolour'. It was the will to defend the state which had created the French republic in 1870. It was therefore not a symbol of dishonour, but rather a symbol 'at least of the honest intention to preserve the state. French national honour was restored by the republic.'[154] As we have seen in the first chapter, Hitler basically considered a revolution in Germany in November 1918 to have been quite possible and justified – and as a model for such a revolution, which was not tied to the 'rendering defenceless of the nation', he repeatedly cited the proclamation of the republic in France in September 1870.[155]

In a speech on 8 December 1928 Hitler compared the military collapse of France in 1870 to that of Germany in 1918. The slogan in France had been: 'The empire is dead, long live the republic', which was synonymous with 'the weakening resistance is dead, let the powerful resistance begin'. With this France had hardly lost any face in the world.[156] In an article in the *Illustrierte Beobachter* on 6 July 1929 Hitler again compared the proclamation of the 1870 republic in France with the proclamation of the November republic. While in France this change of constitutional form had initially also been carried out by 'the mob in Paris under the leadership of journalists and shysters', and here also it had been the Jews who had ensconced themselves at the head of the nation, 'at least the French republic had been firmly established as a state after only a few months'. While fate had not actually been averted by this, the earnest attempt had at least been made. 'The revolution of the year 1870 forced new weapons into the fist of the French nation, the revolution in 1918 destroyed the weapons of the German nation ... The French republic therefore always had roots in the hearts of many Frenchmen, and not the worst at that. It saved its tricolour from the great war, if not victorious, then at least not dishonoured.'[157]

In his reply to the speech of Social Democrat Wels against the Enabling Law on 23 March 1933, Hitler explicitly refers to the model of the French revolution of 1870. It would have been possible, said Hitler, to have given the German revolution the same drive and the same direction which France had given to its revolt in 1870:

> It would have been within your discretion to turn the German revolt into a truly national one, and if the banner of the new republic had not returned victorious, you would then at least have had the right to declare: We have done our utmost to avert this catastrophe by a final appeal to the strength of the German nation.[158]

c. The 1848 Revolution in Germany

Hitler rarely spoke about the German revolution of 1848, but when he did it was mainly in a positive sense. In an article in the *Illustrierte Beobachter* on 10 November 1928 he accused the 'November men' of having taken the black, red and gold flag of

> ... decent March revolutionaries into their dirty fingers. The patriots of '48 once believed that under this flag they could put an end to the times of wretched German impotency, whereas for the neo-German phoney revolutionaries it serves as the symbol of the dismantling of German honour and German power.[159]

In an article in the *Illustrierte Beobachter* in January 1929 Hitler assesses the March revolutionaries as being 'at least in part upright patriots', who had been prepared if necessary to climb up on the barricades in defence of their greater German ideal. They had been 'pigheaded, yet again valuable people' who were able to perform valuable services and do valuable work once they had overcome the confinements of their party circle. And it did not in any way detract from these people that here, too, the Jews had been the actual puppet masters.[160]

After Hitler had founded the Greater German Reich with the *Anschluss* of Austria in March 1938, in a speech in the *Kaisersaal* in the Frankfurt *Römer* [State rooms of the town hall, formerly state rooms of the German king after his election in the Frankfurt cathedral—H.B.] Hitler even placed himself directly into line with the tradition of the '48 revolution. He was happy to be allowed to enter this city today, as 'the fulfiller of a yearning which once found its most profound expression here . . . The work for which our forefathers fought and bled 90 years ago [i.e. in March 1848—R.Z.] can now be regarded as completed.'[161] Where Hitler spoke of the 'confused revolution' of 1848,[162] as for example in his commemorative speech for Hindenburg on 6 August 1934, there was no general negative assessment intended. As he said in February 1939 at the launching ceremony for the battleship *Bismarck*, it had been a revolutionarily inspired era, 'idealistic in its objectives', but 'confused' in its methods.[163]

In his diary on 6 February 1940 Goebbels reports a conversation with Hitler in which the latter also assesses the 1848 revolution with great goodwill: 'The '48 democrats were Greater German idealists. No comparison to the November democrats. They all hated the dynasties and Austria, because it was destroying the Reich. You have to appreciate this line in order to be able to reach a just conclusion.'[164] We can therefore note that, from the few remarks passed by Hitler on the 1848 revolution, we basically have a clearly positive evaluation of this event.

d. The Jews as Leaders of Revolutions and a 'Negative Example' for Hitler
In the portrayal of Hitler's position on the November revolution, but also during our investigation of his views on the French Revolution of 1789, the 1848 revolution in Germany and the proclamation of the Third Republic in France which he admires as being exemplary, we have seen that he suspects 'the Jews' of pulling the strings behind these events. In Chapter VII.3.d we will show that he originally also saw the Bolshevist Revolution as a shoddy effort by the Jews, although later on he took the view that under Stalin it had lost its original ('Jewish') character.

Despite the fact that they had been instigated 'by the Jew', all of these revolutions were still examples and guidelines for Hitler. Revolutions were always led and organized by 'historic minorities'; this was one of Hitler's fundamental convictions.[165] For him the Jews were such a 'historic minority', i.e. they were the quintessential revolutionaries. This was why he both feared and admired them, a position that, for example, also determined his stance towards Marxism/Communism.[166] During talks with the Hungarian Minister President Sztójay, in which he wanted to convince the latter of the necessity of a 'solution to the Jewish question' in Hungary as well, Hitler even claimed, on 7 June 1944, 'that there would be no revolutions without the Jews', because 'if in times of crisis the Jew is missing, then there is no catalyst available for a revolution'.[167]

On the other hand, Hitler also saw himself as a revolutionary and therefore constantly tried to draw his conclusions from the revolutions he described as being 'Jewish'. Jochen Thies has advanced the theory that Hitler was ascribing his own objective, namely domination of the world, to his enemy, the Jews.[168] For Hitler the Jews were – seen in this light – a negative example, however, not only in their objective and their particular ability to set up world domination, but above all because they were a dedicated historic minority and therefore able to lead and organize revolutions effectively. Hitler admired and feared the Jews for the same reason. That is why he tried on the one hand to learn from them while on the other, because of the particular danger they posed, he was forced to fight them with the most brutal methods to the ultimate consequences.

5. Hitler's Revolutionary Claim

a. From 1919 to the Hitler *Putsch* of 1923

Already at a very early stage of his political activities Hitler emphasized the revolutionary claim of his party and polemized against the proponents of 'law and order'. 'Our party,' said Hitler in a speech in October 1920, 'must have a revolutionary character, because the condition of "law and order" only means continuing to tend the present pigsty'.[169] To be *Deutschvölkisch* [German-national—H.B.] today, he stressed when turning against other national groupings, meant 'not to dream, but to be revolutionary'.[170] 'The salvation of Germany,' he declared in a speech at an NSDAP rally on 29 July 1921, 'can only come from Germans, not from parliament but through revolution.'[171] In his notes for a speech on 26 August 1921 he contrasts 'the revolutionary movements' with 'the parliamentary party' and demands a 'revolutionary programme' which should not tie the forces down but free them.[172]

In the early years of his political activities Hitler strongly opposed participation in elections because he feared that by taking part in the parliamentary system the party would compromise itself and lose its character as a revolutionary movement. In an article published in July 1922 he argued that experience taught that 'if you keep on taking risks you will eventually come to grief'. Not all contemporary politicians had already entered parliament as 'criminals', many of them had originally been idealists, 'just . . . as we are today, but the parliamentary swamp and slime has gradually suffocated their better self and made them into what they are today'.[173]

In July 1921 Hitler demonstratively resigned from the NSDAP. In his statement of resignation he argued, among other things, that the NSDAP had been founded as a revolutionary movement and must therefore reject any parliamentary tactics.[174] 'We do not want to enter the parliaments,' said Hitler in a speech in February 1922. 'Whoever goes into a swamp will perish there.'[175]

In the article on the question of participation in elections already mentioned, Hitler explains that the issue was not to improve or reform the situation and to prevent a 'parliamentary impoverishment'. On the contrary, the only objective had to be the conscious increase and intensification of the damage, until the people finally had their eyes opened and 'the decayed house fell down. We are not improvers, but revolutionary reformers.'[176]

Speaking to the SA in July 1922, Hitler said that the task of the movement was 'one day to revolutionarily restructure Germany from the ground up'.[177] To the frequently levelled accusation by the Left that he was a reactionary, Hitler's reply was that the National Socialists intended a revolution,[178] and elsewhere he spoke of 'the German Germanic revolution'.[179] In a speech on 15 January 1923 Hitler declared that the National Socialists 'were preparing a much greater revolution than the one of 1918'.[180] He defined this 'German revolution' as the 'first step towards creating a state based on a specific *Weltanschauung*'.[181] In the months preceding the 1923 November *putsch*, which Hitler defined as an attempt at a 'national revolution', he expounded the revolutionary claim of the NSDAP: 'What Germany needs is a revolution', not reform', he said in August 1923 in an interview with *The World* (New York).[182] He did not trust Kahr with being able to play the role of a revolutionary. He was not a personality but only an upright civil servant lacking in political instinct: 'Somebody like that cannot achieve anything, only the revolutionary such as Sulla and Ivan the Terrible.' Furthermore, the history of all revolutions taught 'that a man from the old system could never master them, only a revolutionary'.[183]

At an SA rally in mid-October 1923 Hitler announced that a 'revolutionary wave' would wash away everything that had been muzzling Germany for years,[184] and the next day he spoke of a 'Germanic Revolution which will reshape our people body and soul'.[185]

Hitler defined his *putsch* attempt on 8 November 1923 as an attempt at a national revolution. When he 'marched in' at the *Bürgerbräukeller* in Munich he called out, 'I am informing those present that the national revolution has broken out all over Germany.'[186] Until the failure of this *putsch* Hitler had always conceived of the revolution as an act of violence, even when he was also careful not to put himself into opposition to the 'key gentlemen' and the 'actual powers', i.e. 'the representatives of state authority in Bavaria', the *Reichswehr* and the police.[187]

b. The Problem of Compatibility between Revolutionary Claim and the Tactics of Legality

After the failure of the *putsch* Hitler revised his revolutionary strategy and tactics. As he declared when looking back, during his time in prison he had gained the conviction: 'Force will no longer work. The state is already too firmly established, it possesses weapons!'[188] This insight and the modification of tactics resulting therefrom, however, had, according to Hitler, not been understood by many of his adherents.[189] In *Mein Kampf* Hitler explains that the battle would be conducted by 'legal' means for as long as the powers to be overthrown also applied these, 'but we will not baulk at illegal [means] if the oppressor also applies them'. When the state was no longer fulfilling its purpose, then the question of legality only played a subordinate role. Such wording creates doubts whether Hitler had clearly committed himself to the tactics of legality he subsequently pursued while in prison. Another factor militating against this is that in *Mein Kampf* he claims it to be a fundamental mistake by the *Alldeutsche Bewegung* [All-German Movement—H.B.] around Schönerer to have taken part in parliamentarism: 'Going into the parliaments took away its powerful *élan* and burdened it with all the weaknesses inherent in this institution.' Neither did Hitler agree with the argument advanced by the proponents of a participation in parliamentary elections, namely that one should 'erode parliament from the inside' or use it as a forum for the enlightenment of the broad masses of the people. To speak about a 'forum' was only 'casting pearls before the well-known animals'. The result here could be nothing but zero. When the *Alldeutsche* movement had devoted itself to parliament, so went Hitler's argument, it had been given 'parliamentarians' instead of leaders and fighters. Thus it had sunk to the level of an ordinary political party of the day. While these statements seem to indicate that Hitler was still sceptical towards any participation in parliamentary elections, elsewhere in *Mein Kampf* we can read that he was not willing to exclude such a possibility absolutely. The movement, Hitler argued, was anti-parliamentary, and its participation in a parliamentary institution could only have the objective 'of an activity for its destruction, for the removal of an institution in which we must recognize one of the most serious signs of the decay of humanity'.[190]

If Hitler decided to take part in parliamentary elections after his time in prison, this did not in any way signal a change in his attitude towards parliamentary democracy or the relinquishing of his revolutionary claim. As he declared in a speech on 6 March 1929, the National Socialists would 'forge by legal means those legal weapons that were capable of achieving the victory of the movement to the ultimate degree, and we will only see the victory for the movement in our annihilation and extermination of the destroyers of our nation'. As his objective he continued to name a 'non-parliamentary, a German dictatorship of the people', which would 'naturally completely, legally abolish democracy'. What was important was that a different regime be created by legal means. Once this regime had been established, 'then may the Lord our God protect them from this legality'.[191]

Despite his participation in parliamentary elections, Hitler declared that he did not believe in the importance of elections, nor that the fate of the nation was decided solely on election day. 'If we National Socialists yet also walk down this path, then [it is] only because unfortunately today we have no other

II. Hitler and the Revolution

path we can follow without falling prey to the sharpest terror of the state.'[192] Hitler emphasized on various occasions that the National Socialists were not a parliamentary party out of principle but 'under coercion, out of desperation, and the coercion was called: constitution'. While the constitution was forcing the National Socialists to employ these means, it did not force them to pursue a specific objective, it only prescribed a way, a method.[193]

Even though the tactics of legality were successful in the end, they did harbour the danger that Hitler's revolutionary claim would no longer be believed. It was therefore probably more than an attempt at a *post factum* justification of his aborted *putsch* when in his annual commemorative speeches on 8 November he made the *putsch* responsible for his having been able to continue to combine the legality principle with his revolutionary claim. On 8 November 1933, for example, he declared:

> That evening and that day [8/9 November 1923], they made it possible for us to fight legally for ten years. Do not make any mistake about this: if we had not acted then, I would never have been able to found a revolutionary movement, to form and preserve it, and still to remain legal. I would have been told quite rightly: you talk like all the others, and you will act just as little as they do. But this day, this decision made it possible for me to hang on for nine years despite all the opposition.[194]

Two years later Hitler declared in his commemorative speech:

> When this blood had flowed, the first act in the German drama was over. There was nothing left to do. Because now weapon in hand, the legal power stood facing the national freedom movement. And now the insight had to come, that this path could no longer be trodden in Germany. It was over. And now comes the second eternal achievement of the fallen. For nine years I had to fight for power in Germany by legal means. Many others before me had also attempted this. But because they preached legality, they only attracted the weaklings to their movements, only the cowards. The revolutionary people, the forceful, stood outside of their ranks. Had I not attempted this revolution in November 1923 ... then I would not have been able to say for nine years: from now on we will only fight legally. Or else I too would only have attracted the halves.

When opponents within the party stood up to him and criticized the course of legality, Hitler was able to reply: 'Gentlemen! What do you mean, do you want to teach me how to fight? Where were you when we struck our blow? I do not need any instructions from you on revolution or legality. I have done all that. You did not have the courage to. So shut up now!'[195]

That the allusion to the violent revolutionary attempt in November 1923 did in fact play an important role in the conflict with the internal party opponents of the legality course also becomes clear in a letter by Gregor

Strasser written on 7 August 1930, in which he explains his rejection of his brother Otto's criticism. The final break between Hitler and the latter had come about shortly beforehand, and the conflict about the question of a 'legal' revolution had also played a part. Gregor Strasser writes:

> Adolf Hitler and his people never made any bones about the fact that they wanted only one thing, namely control of the state, totally and completely, in order then to implement what they had already outlined and proclaimed in 1919 to be National Socialism. The position was never taken that this seizure of power could only come about in one way, namely by a revolution from the bottom up, although even this attempt was made at the appropriate and given time on 9 November 1923 at the risk of their lives, whereby not one of the people in the 'revolutionary' camp today was involved, nor even a member of the party.[196]

In this line of argument by Gregor Strasser as well as Hitler, the importance of 9 November 1923 for the internal party conflicts becomes clear. Hitler could always point to the fact that he was quite capable of acting as a revolutionary, if necessary even by use of force. But even though Hitler held to the legality course he had proclaimed for eight years, not only many of his adherents, particularly among the SA and the NS left-wingers,[197] but also Hitler himself occasionally developed doubts whether this path would really lead to success.

Aside: Was Hitler Toying with the Idea of a Violent Revolution in August 1932?
In August 1932 an explosive situation developed, the background and contexts of which are still largely obscure. It was after the elections of 31 July 1932, in which the NSDAP had become by far the strongest party, and its members and leaders saw the conversion of their success into the political power so long desired almost within their grasp. On the day after the election Goebbels wrote in his diary:[198]

> Now we have to take over power and exterminate Marxism. One way or the other! Something has to happen. The time of opposition is over. Now deeds! Hitler agrees. Now events have to clarify themselves and then decisions have to be taken. We will not achieve an absolute majority this way. Therefore take a different path. We are facing weighty consequences.

On 2 August he had a meeting with the *Führer*: 'Hitler is pondering. Facing difficult decisions. Legal? With the *Zentrum*? [Catholic Centre Party—H.B.] Makes you puke! The press is guessing at conundrums. All nonsense! We are thinking, but have still not reached any conclusions.' On 6 August Goebbels noted: 'The wave of terror is rising. That is going to lead to murder in revenge and manslaughter. Something has to be done. Something total. Half-solutions are no longer acceptable. New men, new ideas, a new course. And then ruthlessly shake off the reaction. That is the main thing.' Goebbels pins all his hopes on an imminent seizure of power:

> If the *Reichstag* rejects the enabling law [which had therefore already been planned at this time—R.Z.] it will be sent home. Hindenburg wishes to die with a national cabinet. We will never again give up the power; they will have to carry us out feet first. This will become a total solution. While it will cost blood, it also clarifies and cleanses . . . Keep your nerve at the gateway to power. Don't become small. Have courage. The great hour has come.[199]

In the meantime there were rumours afloat in Berlin about a planned National Socialist *putsch*: from the evening of 8 August the policemen on duty in Wilhelmstrasse were carrying carbines.[200] On 9 August Goebbels wrote in his diary about the 'stupidities' of the SA and plans by the Berlin SA chief Count Helldorf which have to be 'acted against', but two days later notes: 'SA is being consolidated around Berlin. Makes the gentlemen nervous. That is the purpose of the exercise. They will most likely give in . . . Consolidating SA. That is quite all right.'[201] Obviously the National Socialists intended to force the 'legal' transfer of power to Hitler by means of the threat of a *putsch* by the SA. Schleicher thereupon had the leader of the Berlin SA brought to him and told him that if this nonsense did not stop, the *Reichswehr* would shoot.[202] Hitler returned to Berlin from the Obersalzberg. He wanted to speak with the Reichs President and demand full power. On the eve of the meeting, as we know from the memoirs of *Freiherr* Ernst von Aretin, a dramatic escalation of the situation developed. Bavarian Minister President Held received a telephone call from Berlin: Hitler had collected 60,000 SA men around Berlin in order to march into the city and force Hindenburg to appoint him as Chancellor. Should Hindenburg refuse, he was to be arrested, and the 'national revolution' proclaimed following the pattern of the Munich *Bürgerbräu* in 1923.[203] A 'march on Berlin' was also being prepared in Brandenburg: in the area of Hohenlychen the SA obtained machine guns and near Neuruppin it attempted to requisition lorries and weapons.[204]

On 13 August the meeting between Hindenburg and Hitler took place. Hitler demanded total power and pointed to Italy as an example: after Mussolini's march on Rome, the king had not merely offered him the position of Vice-Chancellor but conferred full power on him. This he now demanded for himself as well. Hindenburg refused, however, and in a manner Hitler must have regarded as a humiliation. According to Goebbels' 'Kaiserhof' diary, after the failure of the talks with Hindenburg, Hitler addressed the SA. Goebbels noted: 'For them it is the worst. Who knows whether their formations can be maintained.'[205] In the original diary Goebbels wrote on 15 August: 'The events in Berlin have shattered everyone here too. I talked with many pgn [*Parteigenossen*—R.Z.; members of the party—H.B.]. Much despair. The SA raised too high hopes. A mistake.'[206]

It appears to be a fact that during the days around 13 August the SA in Berlin had been mobilized. But had this really only served to exert pressure on Hindenburg? Were there only intentions among the SA men to mount a *putsch*, or were such possibilities also being entertained by Hitler and Goebbels? There are several indications in favour of the suspicion that Hitler himself was considering the possibility of a departure from the course of law at this time. Hermann Rauschning reports a conversation with Hitler in August 1932:

> At the time all of Hitler's thinking turned around the temptation to depart from his self-chosen road of achieving power by legal means and to seize power by means of a bloody revolution. Hitler was constantly being pressured by his most intimate associates to give up his reticence and to begin the revolutionary battle. He himself was torn between his own revolutionary temperament, which was urging him towards impassioned action, and his political deviousness which advised him to follow the sure route of the political combination and to 'take his revenge' only later. There can be no question that in connection with the '32 autumn elections [?—R.Z.] the open outbreak of a National Socialist revolution was impending... This thought kept coming up time and again in conversation: 'the right of way for the brown battalions'. For himself and his entourage Hitler painted pictures of the opportunities that lay in an unexpected occupation of the key points of state and economic power. And he lingered with particular interest on the possibility of bloodily beating down a Marxist opposition in the streets. How far plans for a *coup d'état* had been developed, had been demonstrated by events in the summer. These had not been individual undertakings by local party leaders. They could all be traced back to Hitler himself... Hitler was interested in the battle as an illegal party, it even attracted him, because he hoped for new incentives resulting from illegality.[207]

Rauschning's claim that in August 1932 Hitler had been reckoning with the possibility of 'going illegal' and moving party headquarters abroad,[208] and had therefore asked him about the chances of moving the party headquarters to Danzig, has previously been noted with scepticism, particularly because fundamental doubts have been raised about the value of Rauschning's *Gespräche mit Hitler* [Conversations with Hitler—H.B.] as a source. These doubts are primarily based on the fact that, according to the conclusion of the research done by Fritz Tobias, Rauschning never talked with Hitler in private. It is incontestable, however, according to Tobias, that Hitler, Rauschning and the Danzig *Gauleiter* Forster came together for a meeting at the Obersalzberg on 1 August 1932.[209] This would mean, therefore, that the doubts raised about Rauschning's recordings of conversations would not apply to the talk on 1

August. And, in fact, the statements by Rauschning cited above have meanwhile found confirmation in the memoirs of Otto Wagener.[210]

An interview Hitler gave the *Rheinisch-Westfälische Zeitung* on 16 August 1932, i.e. three days after the abortive talks with Hindenburg, can also be taken as an indication that Hitler was considering giving up the principle of legality at this time, even though the acute explosiveness of the situation had been defused for the time being by having the SA sent on a two-week holiday. In the interview Hitler threatened quite openly:

> There is a right of self-defence, which in the long run we will not let ourselves be talked out of by the maunderings about 'law and order'... The National Socialist movement has fought legally to the utmost extreme, and the butchering will either stop soon or I will see myself forced to order a right of self-defence for my party comrades, which will then really stop the red Cheka methods in a flash.

To the question how he saw the future course of his party, Hitler answered, 'The party is fighting for power. Its course is determined by the method of fighting of its opponents.'[211] What we are supposed to understand this actually to mean becomes clear from Goebbels' diary notes for 28 August 1932: 'We have to achieve power! If the other side violates the constitution, then any obligation towards legality on our part ceases too, then comes tax strike, sabotage, revolt. The question of its downfall will then be settled within a matter of days.'[212]

Even in the table talks Picker recorded, Hitler admits that he had had to master situations 'which had suggested the idea of a *coup d'état* to him'. But he had 'always kept control of himself' not to act in that way, because the danger had been too great, that the use of the power he had held could have caused that power to slip, in other words to create the temptation of a *coup d'état* against him at some point in time. Whether this was really a decisive reason for Hitler to adhere to the principle of legality may be questioned with some justification. What was far more important was a different motive, which Hitler also mentions. He wanted to avoid a possible conflict with the *Reichswehr*, because sooner or later he would

> ... most urgently have to need it ... The stance of the *Wehrmacht* towards his chancellorship had played a particular role in these considerations, because in the case of a non-legal seizure of power the Wehrmacht would have posed a threat as the breeding-ground for *coups d'état* of the nature of the Röhm *putsch*, whereas in the case of a legal take-over of power it was possible to restrict it to its purely military duties for long enough until, with the implementation of conscription, the nation as a whole, and with it the National Socialist spirit, had permeated it, and with constantly growing power, had overgrown all the elements opposed to the National Socialist movement, especially the officer corps.[213]

c. Hitler's Portrayal of the NS Revolution: One of the Greatest Upheavals in History – but in a Measured and Disciplined Form

Considerations for the *Reichswehr* was certainly one, but not the only, motive for Hitler's strategy of 'legal revolution'. His insight into the psychology of the German masses was at least as important. While in view of the political and economic failure of the Weimar Republic large segments of the population desired a fundamental, even revolutionary change in the situation, German traditions of the authoritarian state and obedience to the powers that be were so deeply rooted that most people rejected a violent and bloody revolution.

To Wagener Hitler spoke about a way to socialism 'without overturn, without destruction of most valuable property, without extinction of irreplaceable human lives, and without a relapse into a lower condition of civilization and culture, as well as the standard of living and even life itself'. When Hitler told Wagener that the issue was to convert the German people to socialism 'without the destruction of property and values, without destruction of the culture and the morals and the ethics which set us Europeans apart from the Asiatics or from other races',[214] then this reflects the fear, so typical in German tradition, of too radical, uncontrolled and chaotic revolutionary changes. One of the most important themes of Hitler's speeches after the seizure of power was therefore the reiteration of the disciplined, non-bloody and orderly course of the NS revolution which – even though measured in its form – had been one of the most powerful revolutions in the history of man.

Already on the day of the seizure of power, Hitler said to Hans Frank that there had not been a single incident in the whole Reich: 'That was the most unbloody revolution in history.'[215] In his speech on 23 March 1933, giving his reasons in support of the enabling law, he declared that 'hardly any revolution of such large dimensions had run its course so disciplined and unbloodily as the revolt of the German people in these weeks'.[216] In the appeal on 28 March 1933 to boycott Jewish stores, Hitler spoke of the 'unprecedented discipline and order with which this act of overturning took place', and compared the 'self-discipline of the national uprising' in Germany with the Bolshevist Revolution 'to which more than three million dead fell victim'.[217] In a speech on 22 April 1933, in which Hitler demanded the continuation of the NS revolution, he emphasized that, despite its so deeply permeating effects on all sectors of life, and as opposed to previous revolutions, he had succeeded in keeping the national revolution 'disciplined in the hands of an objective-orientated leadership'. The reason for this was to be found in the fact that previous revolutions had been carried out without objectives by undisciplined hordes of people, only then to turn into their opposites, whereas the German revolution was characterized by a 'singular, wonderfully elastic cooperation between the impulsive popular movement and the considered leadership of the leaders'.[218]

At the *Reichsparteitag* in 1933 Hitler declared that 'one of the greatest upheavals' had been accomplished almost without any spilling of blood: 'Thanks to the brilliant organization of the movement which was the bearer of this revolution, not for a single instant during this historic upheaval did the instrument of leadership get out of hand.' Except for the Fascist revolution in Italy, no other historic action of a similar nature could be compared to the National Socialist uprising with regard to its 'inner discipline and order'.[219] Hitler frequently compared the 'orderly' and 'disciplined' form of the NS revolution with other, 'bloody' revolutions in history. On 14 October 1933, for example, he declared in a radio address that the German revolution had not 'slaughtered hecatombs of human beings' like the French or Russian Revolutions, that it had not, like the uprising of the Communards in Paris, or the Soviet revolutions in Bavaria and Hungary, destroyed cultural monuments and works of art through *Petroleuse*. Quite the opposite: during the German revolution there had not been 'a single display window broken, not a store looted and no house damaged'. Now Hitler was even using the term 'law and order' which he had so sharply rejected during the period of struggle.[220] When, he asked during a speech at the *Sportpalast* on 24 October 1933, had there ever been a revolution conducted so completely free of atrocities as the National Socialist revolution? During the days when 'we were having the revolution' things had been more orderly in Germany than in many countries that had no revolution in progress. Alluding to the French Revolution, he said that, in Germany at least, there had been no guillotine set up and no Vendée created.[221]

Hitler frequently compared this 'measured form' of the NS revolution to the dimensions of the changes effected. On the one hand he spoke of the German uprising as a 'historic revolution' and 'gigantic undertaking', on the other hand he stressed 'that this great upheaval in our nation could take place, first at virtually the speed of lightning and secondly almost without any spilling of blood'. It was the fate of the 'overwhelming majority of all revolutions' to lose their footing in their haste to storm forward to their objectives and 'finally to shatter themselves somewhere against the hard facts of reality'. The reasons why it had been possible in Germany to 'manage' the national uprising 'so exemplarily . . . as this has never previously been the case except during the Fascist revolution in Italy', lay in the fact that it had not been an otherwise disorganized population driven to desperation which had raised the banner of revolt and applied the torch to the existing state, but a brilliantly organized movement that fought with supporters who had been disciplined over many years. It was to the credit of the party and the SA that they carried out the German revolution 'almost without bloodshed and with exemplary adherence to programme'.[222]

In an interview on 17 February 1934 Hitler proudly pointed out that the NS revolution had only caused 27 dead and 150 injured;, no house had been destroyed, no store looted.[223] No revolution in history, he contended on 19 March 1934, had proceeded and been directed with more 'care and judgement' than that of the National Socialists.[224] Two days later he declared that, thanks to the discipline of the National Socialist fighters, 'one of the greatest upheavals in history had been carried out according to plan and in an orderly manner'.[225]

Even after the bloody suppression of the 'Röhm revolt' Hitler declared that it had been his foremost objective to spill as little blood as possible in the course of his revolution.[226] In the opening proclamation at the *Reichsparteitag* in 1934 he asserted that it would remain a rare example for all ages that a gigantic upheaval, which would have been justified in entertaining a thousand desires for revenge, had been ended almost without any bloodshed.[227] On 30 January 1935 Hitler said that 'at no instant during our National Socialist revolution... [had there been] any emptiness anywhere. At no stage of our advance and our struggles was there chaos. The most unbloody revolution in history, and yet one of the most far-reaching!'[228] In his foreign policy speech in the *Reichstag* on 21 May 1935 he declared that in the past two years a revolution had taken place in Germany which was greater than the average human being currently realized. The extent and depth of this revolution had not suffered from the 'consideration' with which it had treated its opponents, because this consideration was not a sign of weakness but a sign of self-confidence and strength.[229] On 1 May 1936 Hitler spoke of an enormous historic upheaval which had been set off by the National Socialist revolution, which, because of its discipline, however, could not be compared to similar events:

> It was not wild hordes who ran through the streets of Germany then and annihilated the works of reconstruction by our nation, destroyed houses and installations, looted the stores – no: but even though outwardly Germany presented a picture of the deepest peace, inwardly the greatest upheaval in German history was taking place, a revolution, legalized by the trust of the people...[230]

A phrase Hitler often repeated was that during the National Socialist revolution not even *one* window pane had been shattered.[231]

On the fourth anniversary of the NS seizure of power Hitler again explained the necessity of a National Socialist revolution: he had often been asked by the bourgeois side why the National Socialists believed in the necessity of a revolution, instead of trying to improve circumstances within the framework of the existing order and with the cooperation of the existing parties. The healing of the need, went Hitler's argument, had not been possible by means of a simple change of government, not by a participation in the circumstances which were causing it, but only through their radical elimination. 'With this, however, under the existing circumstances our struggle had to assume the character of a revolution.' It was not conceivable that such a revolutionary restructuring and renovation could be carried out by the supporters and responsible representatives of the former conditions, nor by means of a participation in the former constitutional life, 'but only by the establishment and the struggle of a new movement with the purpose and objective of carrying out the necessary reformation of political, cultural, and economic life down to their deepest roots, and to do this, if necessary, at the risk of life and blood!' A parliamentary victory by conventional parties hardly changed anything essential in the course and image of the life of nations, whereas 'a true revolution which stems from the profound precepts of a *Weltanschauung* also leads outwardly to impressive and generally visible changes'. But who, Hitler continued, would care to doubt that in the past four years a 'revolution of enormous proportions has swept over Germany?' And it was only due to the singularity of this event that the world, and even some fellow-citizens, had not quite grasped the depth and nature of this upheaval. What was most noteworthy about the course of the National Socialist revolution, was that its legal and disciplined character had made it more difficult for the world and individual fellow-citizens to understand this 'unique historic event'. Because, said Hitler, 'this National Socialist revolution was first of all a revolution of revolutions'. What he meant by this Hitler then proceeded to explain:

> Over the centuries, not only in the minds of the Germans, but even more in the minds of the rest, the opinion has developed and asserted itself that the characteristic attribute of any true revolution must be a bloody destruction of the supporters of the former power, and, in connection with this, a destruction of public and private installations and property. Humanity has grown accustomed to regard revolutions with such attendant circumstances as in some way legal events after all, i.e. to approach the tumultuous destruction of life and property if not with consent, then at least with forgiveness, as being the inevitably necessary attendant circumstance of events which are therefore called revolutions!

And herein lay – if we leave the Fascist uprising in Italy aside – the biggest difference between the National Socialist revolution and other revolutions. In the further course of his argument Hitler repeats the usual phrases about the 'unbloody' revolution during which not a single window pane was shattered and no property was destroyed. It could not be the duty of a revolution to produce chaos, but only to replace something bad with something better. Hitler contrasts this outer form of the NS revolution with the depth of the overturn it achieved. The revolution was so great, that even now the superficially judging environment had not yet recognized its spiritual foundations.[232]

At the *Gauparteitag* [district party congress—H.B.] in Mainfranken on 27 June 1937 Hitler emphasized that in none of the historic cases had such an upheaval been carried out 'more wisely, more intelligently, more carefully, and with more feeling' than in National Socialist Germany. Posterity would one day describe this process as one of the wisest and most brilliant that had ever taken place, 'as one of the greatest of revolutions which in its course did not depart from the path of unconditional legality for a single moment'.[233] In his opening proclamation at the *Reichsparteitag* for Work in 1937, Hitler described the NS revolution as the greatest upheaval in German history. In a time of international unrest Germany could claim to be 'a secure and stable stronghold' because National Socialism had trodden the path to a social revolution without having destroyed the existing order by violence and thereby turning the base of political, economic and cultural life into chaos. 'Having recognized the weaknesses of our bourgeois social order early on, we have endeavoured to build a new social structure by means of a disciplined regeneration.' The NS revolution had indeed also been a revolution, but one without the attending circumstances of 'the blind excess of a mass of slaves gone mad because of their inability to exercise their freedom'. It had not been the mob which had carried out the National Socialist revolution but a community of German people committed to strict obedience.[234]

The disciplined and 'unbloody' course of this 'greatest upheaval in the history of our nation', in other words the 'German revolution' was, said Hitler on 20 February 1938, the expression of the desire to 'emphasize our German Germanic character in the execution of this revolution as well', as opposed, for example, to the French Revolution, 'where for half a decade the guillotine celebrated its bloody orgies, for just as long as German reconstruction has been going on'.[235] In a speech on 23 May 1938 Hitler gave a reason why he forwent revenge and destruction during the course of the revolution, just as he did after the *Anschluss* of Austria (March 1938): 'Who can guarantee that once the excesses have begun, private passions will not also begin to be indulged in, private accounts will not be settled under the guise of a political act?'[236] In view of the events in connection with the suppression of the so-called 'Röhm *putsch*', in the course of which private accounts were indeed settled, this statement by Hitler sounds highly cynical.

How important it was for Hitler to stress the orderly, 'unbloody' and disciplined character of the NS revolution can be deduced from the fact that even in his speech on 30 January 1944, on the eleventh anniversary of his seizure of power, Hitler still points out that a socialist revolution had taken place in Germany without any destruction of property.[237] And as late as December 1944, only months before the final defeat of the Third Reich, in a conversation with the Hungarian 'Leader of the Nation' Szálasi, Hitler emphasized that the economic and social changes in Germany, this 'gigantic revolution', had been carried out 'without the slightest incident'.[238]

The large number of statements cited here, which could be extended by many additional similar statements, show how important emphasizing the specific character of a revolution which was disciplined in its form, but which in content was deep and far-reaching, was for Hitler's self-appreciation and self-portrayal as a revolutionary. It is one of the key paradoxes attached to National Socialism that – in Hitler's self-appreciation and self-portrayal – one of the greatest revolutions in history took the form of a legal, 'unbloody' and disciplined seizure of power and a structural modification of society.

It would certainly be erroneous to assume that Hitler preferred the path of a legal revolution over a bloody revolt for humanitarian reasons – which, according to his own assertions, he rejected as a sign of weakness. The 'legal' and 'unbloody' character of the revolution can only be claimed if this is restricted to 30 January 1933: in the weeks immediately following nothing was still legal – even though the National Socialists did continue to make efforts to keep up this appearance[239] – and in the years up to 1945 more blood was spilt than in virtually any other revolution in history. Nonetheless, this pseudo-legal form was the appropriate form for a revolution in a country with extreme traditions of authoritarianism and obedience, in a country in which terms such as formal order, discipline and quiet stood at the head of the scale of values. With the model of the 'legal, disciplined, non-chaotic' revolution Hitler catered to the actually contradictory needs of broad segments of the population, who on the one hand, and in view of the economic and political collapse of the Weimar Republic, desired a radical change of the social and political conditions, but who on the other hand were too strongly caught up in the German anti-revolutionary and conservative-authoritarian traditions of the state to have understood or accepted any other form of revolution.

Aside: '. . . And So We Became Revolutionaries.'
We have already identified the contradictory needs of the masses for a revolutionary change of society on the one hand and the preservation of the traditional values of authority, obedience and discipline on the other as the conditions for the effectiveness of the concept of the 'legal revolution'. However, we should not exempt Hitler himself from also having this contradictory attitude. Quite the

opposite. Wilhelm Reich pointed to 'the duality of [his] position towards authority' resulting from Hitler's upbringing: 'Rebellion towards authority by simultaneous acceptance and submission.'[240]

As a key to understanding Hitler's development we will quote from his speech of 13 July 1934, in which he justifies the suppression of the so-called 'Röhm revolt':

> We all once suffered from the terrible tragedy that we, as obedient and dutiful soldiers, were suddenly confronted by a revolt by mutineers who succeeded in gaining possession of the state. Every one of us had been brought up to honour the law and respect authority, to obey the orders and decrees emanating from it, in inner devotion to the representatives of the state. Now the revolution by the deserters and mutineers [meaning the November revolution of 1918—R.Z.] forced us to inwardly relinquish these terms. We could not give honour to the new usurpers. Honour and obedience compelled us to renounce obedience to them. The love of nation and Fatherland obliged us to fight against them, the amorality of their laws extinguished in us the feeling for the necessity of obeying them, and so we became revolutionaries.[241]

This extract demonstrates the inner duality to which Hitler and his adherents were subjected: on the one hand being brought up to discipline, obedience and the acceptance of authority, an upbringing that forbids any thought of rebellion or revolution; and on the other the insecurity caused by the collapse of the old Reich, the November revolution and finally the revolt and revolution against the state. On 9 November 1927 Hitler declared: 'On the day on which the old Reich broke apart and the new state formed itself, from former soldiers we became critics, became protest people, against the present state.'[242]

And indeed the year 1918 – i.e. the experience of the November revolution which finally also triggered Hitler's decision to 'become a politician'[243] – appears to mark a turning-point in Hitler's development, particularly in his attitude towards the authority of the state. In a table talk in 1942 he said that until 1918 he had approached any jurist with the idea this was 'the higher life! In fact any state official! My old man was a man of honour.'[244] Now it would be wrong to assume that Hitler's position towards the authority of the state had changed overnight without a break. Hitler himself said in a speech on 24 February 1929:

> There was a time when we ourselves were caught up in all sorts of prejudices. I know for certain that had fate given our movement, assuming it had existed in 1919, the victory, we would only have approached the resolution of certain questions weakly and hesitatingly. One was prejudiced oneself, or maybe less prejudiced than impressed by former times. Over the years one had developed a certain position towards the term 'civil servant', a certain position towards the

term 'minister', a certain position towards the term 'district governor', the term 'president of police', one had developed a certain view of these things, which the state had partly transmitted, because the former state was unquestionably clean, decent and orderly in all these institutions ... And it is good that the present state is slowly doing away with all these considerations of yesterday and that it is showing us its true visage and therefore giving those to come the strength to face it without inhibitions and to do what the hour will one day require. For us today the term 'minister' has changed, the term 'Reichs Chancellor' is a different one, the term 'president of police' is a different one, the term 'judge' is a different one, every term has shifted since then, and in Germany an organization of people is developing which will face all these terms in the future in a new way and without inhibitions.[245]

It took years, however, before Hitler was really able to face up to the representatives of the power of the state without 'inhibitions', and we have some evidence that he probably completely lost these inhibitions, for example when facing generals, only towards the end of his life. For Hitler himself as well as his adherents, this duality was to remain in their stance towards authority, a tendency to rebellion and revolution and simultaneously a counter-tendency, an 'inhibition', an internalization of the values of discipline and obedience. For Hitler himself this contradiction was at the root of his weakness in taking decisions, which many historians have described[246] without being able to explain it convincingly.

An example of this inability to take a decision is Hitler's conduct during his attempted *putsch* on 8/9 November 1923. The events of these two days do not in any way show Hitler as the resolute revolutionary acting with determination that he later painted himself as having been, but far more as a vacillating ditherer unable to take decisions, who was neither able nor willing to bring the revolution he himself had proclaimed to a successful conclusion, who, faced with impending failure, did not even make a serious attempt to save it. Werner Maser writes convincingly of 'Hitler's proven helplessness, insecurity and lack of leadership ability in the decisive situation'.[247] In the final analysis, this lack of decisiveness is explained by the actualization of contradictory tendencies. On the one hand there is the will to proclaim a 'national revolution', but on the other there is the still existing 'inhibition' towards the representatives of the authority of the state. Thirteen years after the *putsch*, Hitler himself stated in one of his annual commemorative speeches: 'And *it was a very hard decision for me to take the Bavarian government into custody and to proclaim a national revolution in Germany. For the first time one had to decide about life and death without oneself having received an order.*'[248] This statement demonstrates Hitler's situation of inner conflict, which ultimately seriously affected his ability to take decisions offensively and with self-confidence. In Chapter

II.5.e we will demonstrate a similar weakness in Hitler's ability to take decisions during the 'Röhm *putsch*'.

Hitler himself was aware of this problem, at least to some extent. In his first speech to the people's court on 26 February 1924, for example, he said:

> I think it is perhaps strange that a man, who for four and a half years, actually almost six years, has learned to respect his superior, not to talk back, to submit blindly, suddenly comes into the greatest conflict that can exist in the life of the state, namely to the so-called constitution.[249]

If on the one hand this internalization of authoritarian modes of thought, the thinking and feeling in categories of command and obey, were a hurdle for Hitler because in certain circumstances they seriously impeded his ability to take decisions, on the other hand this very contradiction was also virtually the precondition for his astonishing success with the masses. Did he not reflect the exact prototype of that fundamental duality which was the determinant for broad sectors of the population? In this light, the concept of the 'legal, disciplined, non-chaotic and orderly revolution' was not only a strategy for gaining power deliberately designed by Hitler, but simultaneously an expression of his own contradictory personality structure – and that of his adherents. An empirical study conducted by Erich Fromm in the 1930s on 'blue and white collar workers on the eve of the Third Reich', which was based on the analysis of over one thousand questionnaires filled in for the most part in 1929–30, came to the conclusion that the character type primarily susceptible to National Socialism was 'rebellious-authoritarian'. With the collapse of the monarchy, so went Fromm's findings, the previously repressed rebellious impulses of those sectors of the population with a fundamentally authoritarian character structure had experienced a strong intensification:

> 'Both the *petite bourgeoisie* as well as, above all, the younger generation, showed rebellious-authoritarian traits and were rebelling against the increasingly more hated authority. The more lenient and weaker authority appeared to be, the more hatred and contempt grew. This emotional need, which was constantly being nourished by helplessness and economic plight, was of itself latent, but could be activated at any time as soon as a political movement presented new symbols of authority signalizing a strength which was foreign to the weak republican, but also to the defeated monarchistic authorities.

During the post-war period such rebellious-authoritarian character types had often joined the Socialist or Communist parties. But 'the National Socialist too opened up escape valves for rebellious feelings', which in part, however, were directed towards other symbols of power than those of the left-wing parties. At the same time National Socialism established new authorities:

the party, the racial community and the *Führer*, whose powers were underlined by their brutality: 'In this way the new ideology satisfied two needs at the same time, the rebellious tendencies and the latent longing for an encompassing subjugation.'[250]

Hitler the person, who was himself the embodiment of this 'rebellious-authoritarian' character type, and his concept of the 'disciplined and legal revolution' equated best, as Martin Broszat aptly phrased it, 'to the simultaneous desire for continuity *and* change, which permeated large sectors of the population'. Characteristic for Hitler and his movement was exactly this 'ambiguous, both revolutionary and restorative relationship to traditional society and values'.[251]

National Socialism shared this dualistic – both 'conservative' *and* revolutionary – stance towards modern society with the contemporary stream of the 'conservative revolution'. However, application of the term 'revolutionary' to this movement is even more doubtful than to National Socialism. Even though the ideologists of this contemporary movement often referred to themselves as being revolutionary, for them this term more nearly meant a spiritual renewal and re-orientation, whereas for Hitler – as with all historic revolutionaries – the question of power always stood at the centre of his considerations. Characteristic for the conservative-revolutionary stream was a frequently 'surprising degree of remoteness from politics', a 'grotesque overestimation of the power of the purely spiritual' and a lack of an 'instinct for power'.[252] Whereas the conservative-revolutionary groupings, circles and writers 'primarily represented a spiritual movement', which was mainly concerned 'with the conquest of new spiritual worlds',[253] Hitler defined a revolution primarily as the gaining of complete political power as the precondition of a change in *Weltanschauung*.

Despite these differences there was a certain affinity between 'conservative revolution' and National Socialism, which was based mainly on the *ambivalence* shared by both. Both stood for the widespread desire in post-war Germany for revolutionary change and the simultaneous preservation of traditional German values and norms. In both the feeling which had befallen many contemporaries was also manifested, that they stood at a 'turning-point in history', in one of those rare globally historic situations, which an author who must be numbered among the members of the 'conservative revolution' had already invoked in 1914 with the words:

> We currently stand at the beginning of one of the greatest periods of mutation in the history of the world, which began in 1912 with the war in the Balkans, and which – drawing most of the nations of the world into its whirlpool – will last for at least a decade, some years before the moment in which . . . Germanness will

explode with elementary force. There will come a gigantic upheaval of everything in existence down to their very foundations in virtually every area.

Germany would, the author prophesied, 'play a similar role in the forthcoming turmoils and wars as France had during the revolutionary period and under the great Napoleon'.[254] Hitler himself was filled with the belief that he and his movement were the active executors of this historic upheaval.

d. The Importance of National Socialism for the History of the World: The Beginning of a Turning-Point in History

Years before his seizure of power Hitler had become convinced of the importance of the impending NS revolution for the history of the world. In a speech on 2 September 1928, which was mainly devoted to the problem of recruiting an élite, he said:

> A look at world history shows manifestations appearing from time to time, which in the course of a relatively short period of time already turn a world around and lead new points of view to victory, even though the carriers of these are initially infinitely small in numbers, whereas the opposition appears to be insurmountable.[255]

Hitler saw the National Socialist party as being such a manifestation, which while, in 1928, still being unimportant and small, would necessarily become successful due to its recognition of the principles of how to recruit an élite, and thereby not just achieve a few social changes but 'turn a world around'.

We know that for Hitler architecture had a special symbolic political importance.[256] In a speech on 9 April 1929 he declared how the future buildings of the Third Reich would symbolize a turning-point in history: just as Fascism today writes on its buildings – 'erected in the first year of Fascism, built in the second year of the Fascist idea, created in the third year of the Fascist state' – so the time would some day come in which one would say: 'erected in the first year of the Third Reich, erected in the second, built in the third'.[257]

In the autumn of 1930 Hitler spoke to Wagener of a 'great turning-point in history' whose content consisted of the 'replacement of the individualistic . . . by the socialistic *Weltanschauung*'. A 'thousands of years old view of life' was being pushed aside by a completely new point of view.[258] Three years later Hitler repeated this thought during a meeting of SA and SS leaders: until now the terms 'individual' and 'humanity' had been the foundations of liberalism and Marxism; the inner dishonesty of these teachings had, however, 'necessarily brought about the turning-point in history through National Socialism, which had overcome the liberalistic formal definition of the state by the living definition of the nation'.[259]

From 1935 to 1938 statements by Hitler began to pile up in which he speaks of the NS seizure of power as a 'historic turning-point'[260] or refers to the NS revolution as a 'turning-point in a . . . millennium of German history'.[261] In a speech on 1 May 1935 he spoke of the gigantic tasks which had to be fulfilled 'such as only very few generations are assigned in history',[262] and in the opening proclamation at the *Reichsparteitag* in the same year he called the NS seizure of power 'one of the greatest upheavals and uprisings . . . which the history of the world knows and will record some day'.[263] In the commemorative speech on 8 November 1935 he declared pathetically that the palls of the sixteen National Socialists who had fallen twelve years ago had 'celebrated a resurrection which is unique in the history of the world':

. . . history will record it as one of the most wonderful and noteworthy manifestations in the history of the world. It will search for comparisons and examples, but it will hardly find an example where, out of such a birth, it was possible to conquer a whole nation and a state in so few years.[264]

On 15 January 1936 Hitler 'prophesied' that 'Future historic writing will, when it attempts to grasp the total content of these three years [1933 to 1935—R.Z.], need more pages than in other ages, maybe ten, maybe twenty, fifty, or even one hundred can claim.'[265] In March 1936 he remarked, 'all of us, and all the nations' had the feeling 'that we are all standing at a turning-point in history',[266] and in a speech given two days later Hitler said that whoever looked at the years 1933 to 1935 impartially would have to admit that in this short period of time 'events of importance for the history of the world had taken place'.[267] Similarly, on 3 July 1936 he declared that while in history decades could not always be counted as all having been equal, the last ten years 'really had been world-shaking'. Only posterity would probably be able fully to appreciate the foundations that had been laid during these ten years.[268] In his speech in the *Reichstag* on 30 January 1937 Hitler spoke about 'the most astonishing epoch in the life of our nation'.[269] At the *Reichsparteitag* in the same year he declared that it was very rare in history that the struggle of one generation had been crowned with such success, 'because much more happened than only the resurrection of our nation: a great historic, unique *forming anew* took place'.[270] During the same party convention he described the conflict with Bolshevism as a gigantic event in the history of the world and said he was sure 'that since the rise of Christianity, the triumphant progress of Mohammedanism, or since the Reformation, a similar event had not taken place on earth'.[271]

On the occasion of the German Architecture and Handicraft Exhibition on 22 January 1938 Hitler again emphasized the function of art in the Third Reich. Since every great age found the 'ultimate expression of its values' in its buildings, and often only after centuries 'was the greatness of an age' understood through its visible documentation in its buildings, therefore one could hope 'that we too may one day count on such a merciful subsequent evaluation'. The exhibit was taking place 'at a turning-point in history'; it documented 'the beginning of a new era'.[272] It was therefore appropriate to take this aspect more strongly into account than before when evaluating art and architecture in the Third Reich. They were possibly not necessarily, as Jochen Thies attempted to prove, an expression of Hitler's striving for world rule, but they certainly intended to document for all time the greatness of the National Socialist revolution and the turning-point in history it initiated.

In his speech to the *Reichstag* on 20 February 1938 Hitler describes 30 January 1933 as 'the day of the turning-point in the history of our nation, then, now and for all time'. January 30, said Hitler, became 'the endpoint of one epoch and the beginning of another. This fact is so uncontested, so self-evident, that we already speak of a German history before the seizure of power and a German history after the seizure of power.'[273] In his proclamation to German youth at the *Reichsparteitag* of the same year Hitler said: 'You have now become the witnesses of a historic event, which often does not repeat itself even in millennia.'[274] In a speech on the sixth *Winterhilfswerk* [annual Winter Help fund-raising campaign—H.B.] about a month later, he declared that the past six years had been among the 'most decisive for German history'.[275] On 10 December 1938 the second German Architecture and Handicraft Exhibition was opened at the House of German Art in Munich. In his opening speech Hitler declared that today one had to build as big as the technical possibilities permitted, in other words to 'build for eternity',[276] because

> We happen to be in a great age of renovation of the German nation! Whoever has not yet tumbled to this will still have to believe it! That is the way it is! For posterity the years 1933, 1934, 1935, 1936, 1937, 1938 will one day mean a bit more than for many a retarded contemporary of today. They will be linked to the age of the greatest resurrection of the German nation, to the founding of a gigantic, great, strong Reich! These years will one day be identical with the rise of a movement to which the German nation owes the fact that out of a hotchpotch of parties, classes and religions, it was merged into a spiritual unit under a united will. Such an age not only has the right, but also the obligation to immortalize itself in such works![277]

In the ensuing years Hitler continued to underline the importance of the turning-point in history initiated by National Socialism. On 30 January 1939 he said that the past six years had been filled 'by the most gigantic event in all of German history',[278] and in his 1 May address to German youth he declared, 'during your youth you have experienced one of the rarest of turning-points in history'.[279]

II. Hitler and the Revolution

In his commemorative speech on 8 November 1940 Hitler said in looking back that from 1925 to 1930 many a citizen had not even been aware 'that one of the greatest revolutions of all times was being prepared... But also many proletarian leaders of Social Democracy or the KPD [German Communist Party—H.B.] did not realize that an upheaval was taking place, moving forward, one of unique dimensions.'[280] In his speech on 30 January 1941 on the anniversary of the seizure of power he declared that no change of government in the history of the German nation had been accompanied by such far-reaching consequences as that of eight years ago.[281] The NS revolution was 'one of the greatest upheavals that had ever taken place on earth'.[282] How deeply Hitler was convinced of the idea that the seizure of power by the National Socialists had initiated a turning-point in history is demonstrated by a remark he made in mid-December 1941: 'At the point of taking over power a decisive consideration for me was: do we want to remain with the present calendar? Or do we have to take the new world order as a sign to begin with a new calendar?'[283] Hitler defined the National Socialist revolution in terms of a fundamental turning-point in world history, which, for example, also manifested itself in the collapse of Christianity:

> Today we are certainly involved in one of the greatest upheavals which human history has experienced. Basically, it is the collapse of Christianity that we are experiencing. This began with the Lutheran revolution. The torch was the theory of freedom of speech and belief; the shock was the uprising against authority.[284]

Hitler also saw the war as a 'historic struggle', as one of 'those elemental conflicts... which – in that they shake the world only once in a thousand years – initiate the millennium of a new age'.[285] In his speech at the tenth anniversary of the seizure of power he explained that everything that had been achieved in the fields of economics, politics and culture since 1933

> ... had, despite all its greatness, to step back before the task we face today. Had National Socialism achieved no more than that which lies behind it, it would already be one of the most gigantic manifestations in the history of the world, but Europe would still be lost despite this.[286]

The statements cited here are not only to be taken as an expression of the self-understanding and self-portrayal of Hitler the revolutionary; they also transmit a picture of the emotional situation which had taken hold of both Hitler and his adherents. They interpreted their actions in terms of the most gigantic revolutionary upheaval in the history of the world, which initiated the beginning of a new age, a turning-point in history. And, for all this, the seizure of power on 30 January 1933 had only been the *starting point* of the revolution, and not in any way its end point.

e. Continuation or End of the NS Revolution? Hitler's Contradictory Statements and the 'Röhm Revolt'

From 1933 to 1934, but also from subsequent years, we have numerous quite contradictory statements by Hitler about the ending, or the continuation, of the National Socialist revolution. When Hitler declares on the one hand that the revolution has already ended, he is very likely to demand shortly thereafter that the revolution now had to be continued and brought to a conclusion. Such contradictory statements can only be understood against the historic background of the so-called 'Röhm *putsch*' and the demand by the SA for the 'second revolution'.

The date 30 June 1934 brought the bloody ending to a conflict between Hitler and Ernst Röhm, leader of the SA, or, more correctly, between the *Reichswehr*, Himmler and Göring on one side and Röhm and the SA on the other. In essence, the issue was Röhm's demand to install the SA as a militia next to the *Reichswehr*, in other words to call into question the *Reichswehr*'s sole responsibility for the defence of the country, or even to replace the *Reichswehr* by the SA.[287] Hitler rejected Röhm's demand because he believed that armaments were primarily a technical problem, for which the military expertise, the technical know-how and the specialized knowledge of the officers corps was of decisive importance. There was also a further aspect, namely the question of the succession to the office of Reichs President. In the spring of 1934 Hindenburg's health continued to decline and there was the danger that, in the event of his death, the question of the restoration of the monarchy would again become acute. Hitler knew that he could only solve the question of the succession to the office of Reichs President according to his own intentions *with* the support of the *Reichswehr*, and was therefore not prepared to risk any sort of conflict with it. Subsequently – primarily in historic literature – this conflict situation was further complicated by the over-interpretation of certain of Röhm's 'socialist' and 'revolutionary' slogans, and by oversimplification, the argument on the question of the arms monopoly and the responsibility for the defence of the country converted into a conflict between the 'revolutionary' Röhm and the 'reactionary' Hitler.

Röhm certainly did give himself a 'revolutionary' flair and also used 'socialist' slogans to underline his claims. It is also true that as a result of the suppression of the '*putsch*', the so-called 'left wing' of the NSDAP, for example the *Nationalsozialistische Betriebszellen-Organisation* [NBO, or National Socialist Factory Cell Organization—H.B.], were eliminated for good. But Hitler simultaneously also directed a blow against the conservative forces around Papen. Edgar Jung, for example, a typical representative of German conservatism, as well as Herbert von Bose were both shot on 30 June,

II. Hitler and the Revolution

even though they certainly had nothing at all to do with the alleged *putsch*. Initially it appeared that the *Reichswehr* had emerged from the conflict as the victor, but, with the elimination of the SA, the inevitable rise of the SS began, which Hitler saw as being the new revolutionary avant-garde. The conflict between Hitler and Röhm was not a conflict between reaction and revolution, but more between the representatives of different models of revolution. The historian H. Mau probably gave the clearest description by saying that the conflict was between 'a revolutionary of the old school' (Röhm) and a representative of 'modern revolution' (Hitler).

Röhm, Mau argues, was a revolutionary in the old style. He had hardly been able to imagine the National Socialist revolution as anything other than the revolutions he knew from the history books: a process which – in a phase of violence to be overcome as quickly as possible, with barricade-storming avant-gardes and the inevitable spilling of blood – overthrows the old order and replaces it with a new one. Hitler on the other hand was

> ... more shifty, more ingenious, more modern than the old-fashioned-straightforward 'pig-headed' Röhm... Virtually on the sly, he had been given the methods of the cold revolution: pseudo-legality, latent terror, splitting the revolution into carefully measured individual actions which could only be recognized later in their overall context, outwitting and deceiving not only your opponents, but also your supporters and allies. And he may also already have had the feeling that modern revolutions no longer storm barricades, but that they can be initiated as a slow process of subversion which lead to more profound changes than previous revolutions ever did, because they not only touch on the institutions, but simultaneously also on the human substance.[288]

It would therefore be too easy to view Röhm as the representative of the NS revolution or its continuation, and Hitler as the one who intended to slow it down, or even to end it. This would only apply if, and only in so far as, we were to turn Röhm's 'traditional' concept of revolution into an absolute and then measure Hitler against it.

The outcome of the conflict between Hitler and Röhm is known. On 30 June 1934 a three-day period of murder began. Besides Röhm and a large part of the leadership of the SA, a number of other 'unwanted' persons who had nothing to do with the affair were murdered. The pretext was that Röhm and the SA had planned a *putsch* with the objective of murdering Hitler. There can be no doubt that his proceeding against Röhm increased Hitler's standing with the public. The apparently quick and determined action strengthened his image as a strong leader who was able to take decisions.[289] Hitler himself constantly emphasized his 'lightning-fast action';[290] in a telegram to the Reichs Chancellor, Hindenburg welcomed his 'determined action'; and in an Order of the Day to the troops, Blomberg underlined Hitler's 'soldierly determination'[291] and during a meeting of the Reichs cabinet on 3 July thanked him for his 'determined and courageous action'.[292] Not only Goebbels admired the 'lightning-fast speed' of the action in a radio address on 10 July,[293] but Hitler himself, in his speech to the *Reichstag* on 13 July 1934, spoke of the necessity of acting 'with the speed of lightning'.[294] On the other hand he also admitted that in recent months he had 'hesitated time and again to take a final decision';[295] and, indeed, the stereotyped appeals to 'lightning-fast action' and 'determined action' were only intended to disguise the fact that Hitler had hesitated for months and had been incapable of reaching a decision in the conflict between Röhm's SA and the *Reichswehr*. Hitler took the position, even though the conflict was already escalating dangerously, that one had 'to let the matter mature'[296] or that he wanted to let 'things boil down'.[297] That he did act in the end had nothing to do with his own 'determination', but with the fact that others, particularly Himmler and Goebbels, then confronted him with a *fait accompli* and by means of forged plans about an alleged *putsch* by the SA forced him to act. In his Hitler biography Gisevius writes:

> ... so that the vacillating *Führer* will not have second thoughts at the last moment as so often in the past, they brutally force him into the adventure ... They [Himmler and Göring—R.Z.] confront Hitler with such a massive forgery that there is no way he can verify it and he has to move forward: they simply let the mutinous SA formations in Berlin and Munich march in to a *putsch* against the sacred person of the *Führer*.[298]

Maser writes: Hitler 'had dithered, waited, had postponed the realization of his objectives to virtually the last possible moment, and up to the moment of the deed itself had still been unclear as to its grievous details, until developments could no longer be stopped'.[299]

The reasons underlying this inability to take decisions resulted – as during his attempted *putsch* on 8/9 November 1923 – from the actualization of the contradictory impulses in Hitler's personality structure, which Reich described with the words: 'rebellion against authority by simultaneous acceptance and submission'.[300] In the 'Röhm affair' Röhm's 'revolutionary' claim corresponded to Hitler's 'rebellious', revolutionary tendencies, whereas, based on his total life and experiences, for him the *Reichswehr* undoubtedly still played the role of a respected and feared authority. Hitler's thought processes were decisively influenced by his time as a soldier and his experiences in the war. He 'accepted the authority of officers in any situation', and for him generals were 'persons commanding special respect'.[301] While Hitler's attitude towards the generals was to change during the course of his later life, particularly after the campaign against France and during the campaign against Russia, Hitler's inhibitions towards the generals were to remain until the final years of the war.[302] Without an understanding of this contradiction in Hitler's thinking and feeling, we are also unable to explain the contradictions in his words and actions in the weeks and months preceding 30 June 1934.

Because of the excesses and acts of violence by the SA, Hitler issued an appeal to the party, the SA and the SS on 10 March 1933:

> Beginning today, the national government holds the executive power in its hand throughout all of Germany. With this, the continuation of the national uprising will be a planned one led from above . . . Annoying of individual persons, obstructing of motor-cars and disrupting of business have to cease forthwith.[303]

On the other hand, on the following day in a letter to Papen, Hitler defends the excesses by the SA against the former's complaint:

> I beg you most insistently, dear Mr Vice-Chancellor, not to bring such complaints to my attention again in the future. They are not justified. The whole German nation should show gratitude towards these men who took this struggle upon themselves, and at the risk of their lives. And I would like to allay all doubts that, should the question ever arise, these men, and with them the German nation, or the government, my place would be at the side of these men.

He had gained the impression 'that there is a planned barrage taking place at the moment with the object of stopping the national uprising, but in any case of intimidating the movement supporting it', and 'I very much have the feeling that our bourgeoisie was regrettably saved too soon. It would have been better to perhaps give it a taste of Bolshevism for six weeks, so that it could have learned to appreciate the difference between the Red Revolution and our uprising.'[304]

Nonetheless, in a speech read on the radio next day, Hitler reinforced his appeal of 10 March. The struggle for power had now found its 'visible symbolic end'; from now on the battle would be 'planned and led from above'. From now on he was therefore ordering 'the most stringent and blindest discipline', so that the German nation, and above all the economy, could be given the feeling of 'unconditional security'. Hitler spoke of the 'victory of the national revolution' and warned against 'petty feelings of revenge' as well as *agents provocateurs* and spies'.[305] In contradiction to the slant of these statements, he declared at a leadership conference of the NSDAP on 22 April 1933 that 'The revolution will only be ended when the *whole German world has been completely restructured inwardly and outwardly.*'[306]

On 14 June 1933 he said, also at a leadership conference of the NSDAP, that the process of the national revolution had 'not yet run out'. Its dynamics still controlled developments in Germany, which were unstoppable in their course to a 'completely new structuring of German life'.[307] Two days later at the conference he stressed that the revolution would 'only be completed when the whole German nation had been newly formed, newly organized and newly built up'.[308] At a leadership conference of the SA in Bad Reichenhall on 2 July 1933 Hitler emphasized the ongoing task of revolutionary re-education and declared that it was the duty of SA and SS *'to continue to carry the great idea of the National Socialist revolution onward until the final victory'*.[309] In contradiction to these statements, at a conference of the Reichs governors on 6 July 1933 he declared there had been more revolutions which had been successful in the initial onslaught than successfully begun revolutions which had been brought to a stop: *'Revolution is not a permanent condition; it should not develop into a permanent condition.* The liberated stream of revolution has to be directed over into the secure bed of evolution.'[310]

At the cultural conference of the *Reichsparteitag* of 1933 Hitler made the following differentiation. At the end of March the revolution had been 'outwardly completed' – completed, however, only insofar as the complete take-over of political power was concerned. 'But only he who remained incapable of inwardly understanding the nature of this gigantic struggle can believe that with this, the battle of the *Weltanschauungen* has reached its end.' *Weltanschauungen*, said Hitler, only regard the achievement of political power 'as the condition for beginning the fulfilment of their true mission'.[311]

In a speech to the *Reichstag* on 30 January 1934 he described the 'continuation of the National Socialist revolution' as the objective of the government,[312] and on 21 March 1934 the *Völkische Beobachter* published an article on a speech Hitler made in Munich to the 'old guard', with the large headline: 'The revolution must go on!'[313]

Even though tactical considerations may have played a role in Hitler's statements, and based on a more detailed analysis they might be interpreted with greater differentiation, the fact remains that in his basic tendencies he was making highly contradictory statements when he first spoke of the NS revolution having ended and then demanded its continuation and completion. That Hitler did not find the decision of how to proceed against Röhm and the SA an easy one, and that in the weeks and months preceding 30 June 1934 he was unsure and vacillated, is also demonstrated by a remark he made in 1942. Hitler spoke of how seldom in history it had been possible to 'lead a revolution over into an evolution. I know *how difficult that was for me personally in many a moment in 1933 to 1934.*'[314] Under this aspect we may also understand why Hitler again – just as with his own *putsch* in 1923 – spoke of 'the most bitter decisions of my life' which he had had to take on 30 June 1934.[315]

It may well be that he regretted this decision in the final years of the war. In a conversation with Hitler, Goebbels expressed the opinion that

> ... in 1934 we regrettably omitted to reform the *Wehrmacht* when we had the opportunity to do so. What Röhm wanted was naturally right in itself, only it could not be carried out in practice by a homosexual and anarchist. Had Röhm been an upright and first-class personality, on 30 June several hundred generals would more likely have been shot than several hundred SA leaders. There is a profound tragedy in this whole development, and today we are being made to feel its effects. At the time, the moment would have been ripe to revolutionize the *Reichswehr*. Under the circumstances, the *Führer* was unable to seize this moment. It is doubtful whether we will ever be able at all to make up for what we missed then.[316]

In his memoirs Speer reports that the Gauleiters had openly expressed regret that the SA had lost to the *Wehrmacht* in 1934. They now saw a missed opportunity in Röhm's earlier efforts to form a people's army. In time, this would have formed an officers corps in the National Socialist spirit, to the lack of which they now attributed the defeats in recent years.[317] Hitler himself may have shared this opinion when he said, for example, 'I have often bitterly regretted not having purged my officers corps the way Stalin did his.'[318]

Further statements by Hitler concerning the causes of his failure[319] make us suspect that with hindsight he regretted his decision of 1934. That barely three years after 30 June 1934 he declares that he had had 'to destroy this man and his adherents to my own deep regret' also speaks for this assumption.[320] On another occasion he said to a circle of higher party leaders that when the time came to write the history of the rise of the National Socialist movement, then Röhm would always have to be remembered as the second man after himself.[321]

When in the concrete situation of 30 June 1934 Hitler decided in favour of the *Reichswehr*, it was only after a long phase of hesitation, of vacillation, and it was only after having finally been confronted with a *fait accompli* by others that he felt compelled to act against Röhm and the SA.

In a speech in the Reichstag on 13 July 1934, in which Hitler justifies his actions on 30 June, he polemizes against those revolutionaries 'who are devoted to revolution for revolution's sake and would like to regard it as a permanent condition'. Revolution was not a permanent condition:

> If the natural development of a nation has been fatally interrupted by force, then this artificially interrupted evolution may again open the way for a natural development by force. However, there is no such condition as permanent revolution, let alone a beneficial development by means of recurring revolts.[322]

In the ensuing months Hitler sometimes emphasized that the battle for power in the state had now ended[323] and that the National Socialist revolution was 'completed as a revolutionary power process' because as a revolution it had

> ... completely fulfilled what could have been hoped for ... Among the Germans revolutions have always been rare. The nervous era of the nineteenth century has found its final ending for us. During the next thousand years no further revolution will take place in Germany![324]

Such remarks were certainly also designed to soothe conservative circles, the *Reichswehr* and those sections of the public to whom Hitler wanted to give the impression that further disruptions of public life were no longer to be feared, and that from now on everything would proceed along calm and orderly paths.

On 9 November 1934, however, addressing his party comrades, Hitler declared that there were still 'many many opponents of our movement in Germany' and every last one of them had to be forced to bow to 'our will'. Therefore 'the party ... [was] not already at the end of its mission, but only at the beginning!'[325] One week prior to this, on 1 November 1934, Hitler had given the Reichs governors a broad hint for their control function as Gauleiters: there were still 'tens of thousands' of political opponents among the civil servants.[326] On 21 May 1935 Hitler emphasized that he 'had once begun the National Socialist revolution by creating the movement, and since then led it as an action', but he knew that 'all of us ... will only live to see the very first beginning of this great movement of upheaval'.[327] During the parade of the 100,000 political leaders at the *Reichsparteitag* of the same year he said:

> Is this struggle now over? The conquest of power is a process that is never, never ended, in other words, if anywhere, then the principle applies here: what you have inherited, always gain it anew in order to possess it! ... So the struggle continues and we come to the period of the second major task, the ongoing education of our nation and the ongoing supervision of our nation.[328]

Even though he had proclaimed several times in 1933 and 1934 that the NS revolution had now finally ended, he declared in his closing speech at the *Reichsparteitag* in 1935: 'But even today we are still involved in the liquidation of a revolution, in other words the National Socialist revolution, in other words the seizure of power, must now slowly reach its completion in the taking over of the leadership.' Since it had not been possible completely to overcome and remove the ferments of the old state immediately, there was a necessity in many sectors to control carefully the 'not yet completely, in a National Socialist sense, secured developments'. It could therefore happen that where the course of government 'was evidently running contrary to National Socialist principles', the party could be forced to intervene by admonishing, and 'if necessary correctively'.[329]

Even in later years Hitler still spoke about the necessity of completing the revolution. In a conversation on 25 November 1940 with the Italian Minister of Justice, Grandi, he said, 'We are faced by social, cultural, economic and finally also legal tasks which are not easy to fulfil. It was the assignment of comrade Frank to carry out a revolution in this sector as well without shaking the state, the society, and the economy.'[330]

In contradiction to his statements that he rejected the idea of a 'permanent revolution', in January 1942 he expounded exactly this concept: 'I assume the National Socialist party will one day erect a firmly established social order, take over positions in the state and care about wealth. Hopefully someone will then come along and start a new club.'[331] This statement is obviously in sharp contrast to his normal pronouncements that there would be no further revolution in Germany in the next thousand years. Hitler naturally knew better when he said on 24 October 1941:

> There is no being, no substance, but also no human institution which does not age one day. But every institution must believe in its immortality if it does not want to give itself up. The hardest steel becomes tired, all the elements decay, and as sure as the earth will one day pass away, so also all institutions must one day fall. All of these phenomena move in waves, not on a straight line, but upwards or downwards.[332]

Hitler found himself caught up in the contradiction that, as the representative of the state, he had to believe in the 'immortality' of the Third Reich, while from a certain position of impartiality he still recognized that this state would one day develop away from its ideals and become socially encrusted.[333] He believed that this process could only be stopped by the continuation of the revolution. In a secret speech as late as May 1944 Hitler said: 'We are not at the end of this revolution, but rather only in the first year of this revolution, so to speak. If I wanted to speak in detail on this, it would take an "eternity". That is impossible.'[334]

Hitler's concept of revolution, which can only be understood against the background of his socio-Darwinistic philosophy of the 'eternal conflict', is quite different from the definition of revolution given by 'conservative-revolutionary' ideologists. Edgar Jung, for example, himself one of the victims of 30 June 1934, rejected the concept of the 'eternal revolution' in his 1927 book *Die Herrschaft der Minderwertigen* (The Rule of the Inferiors),[335] even though an analysis otherwise shows many agreements between Jung's definition of a revolution and Hitler's concept of revolution.[336] The 'predominance of the conservative over the revolutionary idea'[337] we can detect in Jung also applies to Moeller van den Bruck, one of the main representatives of the conservative-revolutionary ideology. Moeller primarily defined himself as being the champion of 'genuine' conservatism, not as a revolutionary. In the final analysis, says Moeller in his principal work *Das Dritte Reich* (The Third Reich), conservatism was superior to the revolutionaries. 'Every revolution will break' against the resistance of the 'conservative powers . . . who have always been and will always be'. Therefore a 'revolution never [has] . . . the tendency to remain revolutionary. A revolution always has the tendency to become conservative.'[338] A statement by Hitler has been handed down which sounds quite similar. On 18 March 1941, in a conversation with Goebbels, he is reported to have said:

> When the able can no longer rise to the top, in the long run there will then be revolution. But the revolution too must be creative and slowly but surely end in the conservative. To reinstate authority has to be the final objective of any revolution. Otherwise it will only become chaos in the end.[339]

That Hitler and Moeller were actually expressing the opposite to each other, however, becomes clear when we look more closely at what each of them meant by the 'conservative' turn of the revolution. Moeller stresses that a revolutionary, once he has to assume the responsibility for the first time, soon finds himself forced 'to in some way adapt his preconceived innovative ideas instead of radically enforcing them, and be it in the form of compromises . . . Therefore he renounces carrying the revolution onward and attempts to reduce it. In the end the revolutionary becomes an opportunist.'[340] For Hitler, as we have seen, the issue was not at all to 'reduce' the revolution, but rather to 'carry it onward', in order to 'radically enforce' the 'preconceived innovative ideas'. To achieve this, however, the revolution had to be led into a new phase which was characterized by the fact 'that the revolution from below, which he had permitted for the time being in his system of a double revolution, was now to be ended, and only the revolution from above continued, the one therefore that *he* would order and initiate'.[341] Rudolf Hess, Hitler's deputy, had expressed this with all the clarity one could wish for in his warning speech on 25 June 1934 during the conflict with Röhm:

> Maybe Adolf Hitler will one day find it necessary to again move developments forward by revolutionary means. But this can always only be a revolution that he directs . . . Adolf Hitler is a revolutionary in the grand style and will inwardly remain a revolutionary in the grand style. He does not need any crutches. Adolf Hitler is the great strategist of revolution. He knows the limits of what is possible with the given means at the given time. He acts after completely dispassionate consideration – often appearing only to serve the needs of the moment and yet looking far ahead in the pursuit of the distant objectives of the revolution. Woe be unto him who, in the delusion that he could do it more quickly, clumsily tramples about between the finely spun threads of his strategic plans. He is an enemy of the revolution.[342]

III

Hitler's Social Objectives and His Assessment of the Major Classes of Modern Society

1. Hitler on the Importance and Origin of the Social Issue

When Hitler was looking back once again to the time of struggle during a table talk in early November 1941, among the things he said was the following important remark:

> The decisive point, I said to myself, is the social issue. To evade this question, that would have been like believing in the seventeenth/eighteenth century that you could get by without abolishing serfdom . . . We had a class society! Only by abolishing it could the forces of the nation be set free![1]

This statement, that the social issue was 'the decisive point', and its resolution the most important condition for setting free 'the forces of the nation', is all the more noteworthy since the opinion has frequently been voiced that Hitler was only marginally interested in social questions and had not attached any importance to them. The question therefore is: can any confirmation be found in the sources showing that Hitler had already attributed considerable importance to social issues in his early years?

In August 1920 Hitler declared that he did not believe that 'ever on earth could a state survive with continuing inner health, if it were not based on inner social justice'. The National Socialists were aware of 'how great the social reforms are which must be carried out, that Germany will not recover based only on small attempts, but that one would have to cut deeply'. Among other things in this context, he mentioned the problems of land reform and social security in old age.[2] Turning against the right-wing middle-class parties, he said in April 1922 that they would have to learn 'that the social concept in a state has to be a foundation', otherwise the state could not stand in the long run.[3]

In *Mein Kampf* Hitler analyzes the reasons for the failure of Schönerer's All-German Movement and draws the conclusions for his own programme. In his criticism of Schönerer the first accusation is an 'unclear concept of the importance of the social problem, especially for a new party that is revolutionary in its essence'. Hitler polemizes against those bourgeois forces who in view of the crying social destitution 'are totally surprised about the lack of "national enthusiasm" of a "young citizen" who has grown up under these very conditions'. The question of the 'nationalization' of a nation was 'firstly also a question of creating healthy social conditions as the foundation for the possibility of educating the individual'. Only then could one expect that a member of this nation would be proud of his fatherland. In order to win over the masses, said Hitler elsewhere in *Mein Kampf*, 'no social sacrifice should be too heavy'. The national education of the masses could only take place via the detour of a 'social uplifting', because this alone would make the creation of those 'general economic conditions' possible, which would permit the individual 'to also participate in the cultural goods of the nation'. A reason to be proud of one's nation was only there when one no longer had to be ashamed of one's class. 'But a nation of which the one half is miserable and careworn, or even depraved, projects such a bad image that nobody should feel any pride in it.'[4]

In his speeches Hitler also frequently emphasized the importance of the social issue. On 15 July 1925, for example, he said, 'If we want to build a true national community, we can only do this on the basis of social justice.'[5] In a speech given in December of the same year, which was published in a special issue of the *Völkische Beobachter* under the title 'The Social Mission of National Socialism', he named the maintenance of the health of the nation as the key reason for the abolition of social injustice. One should not believe, said Hitler turning against the 'bourgeois circles', that a nation could be kept healthy in the long run if it had to work in the mines for twelve or thirteen hours. If one were to maintain such working hours for only a hundred years, the result would be a nation 'that was physically totally broken down'. If one were to continue piece-work and home work at the present rate, then in 150 to 200 years all that would be left would be 'human wrecks'.[6]

This argument, that social need first destroyed the health of the nation, can be found again in various other Hitler speeches.[7] He turned with 'horror' against the idea that social legislation had to be enacted for no other reason than 'that our people will otherwise fall prey to the temptations of Social Democracy, that our people will otherwise turn revolutionary'. National Socialism on the other hand was *not* saying 'we have to give in to the masses to some extent so that they will not revolt', but rather 'we have to have the masses, because these are our people . . . and woe be it if we let these millions perish. We can not practice over-exploitation for ten generations.'[8] Hitler repeated the same thought in a speech in August 1927. Social legislation has always only been determined from one point of view: 'how do we prevent a social revolution, but never from the point of view: how do we prevent the collapse of our people. That is the yardstick with which we intend to measure here.'[9]

Here the connection to Hitler's frequently made statement becomes clear: the state and the economy were only means to an end, which was the preservation of the race or the nation. Since, in his view, unhealthy social conditions were bound to lead to collapse, to the purely physical ruin of the nation, he already attached a great deal of importance to the social issue for this reason alone. It was not pity or sympathy which caused Hitler to emphasize the importance of social issues. He himself admitted in a speech in July 1931:

> ... if someone asks me why are you a socialist, I say because I do not believe that our nation can survive as a nation in the long run, if it is not healthy in all its parts. I cannot imagine any future for our nation if on the one hand I see a well-stuffed bourgeoisie ambling along, while besides it walk the figures of emaciated workers. I ask, what will our future be like, the only thing that interests me is my nation, how will it be in a hundred years, that is all that is important. I am not a socialist out of pity for the individual, only from consideration for my nation. I want the nation that gave us our lives to also have an existence in the future.[10]

Even after the seizure of power Hitler repeatedly stressed the importance of the social issue. On 7 September 1937, for example, he declared in the opening proclamation at the *Reichsparteitag*: 'Among the great problems that continue to fill our times, one of those at the top is the social one.'[11] In his 'monologues' at *Führer* headquarters he remarked on 1 August 1942 that one could only maintain the given social order 'if one kept the people very ignorant'.[12] In his speech on the eleventh anniversary of the seizure of power Hitler looked back at the year 1933 and listed four major tasks which had been set at the time, and as the first he emphasized the 'solution of the social question', because only through this had it been possible to restore the lost internal social peace.[13] All these statements confirm that – as Hitler's state secretary Meissner writes in his memoirs – Hitler paid 'special attention to the social problems and the reconciliation between the working class and the middle class'.[14]

How, and based on what sort of experiences, was Hitler's attention drawn to the social problem, and how did he envisage the resolution of this issue? As far as the first part of the question is concerned, we can only attempt to answer from Hitler's own statements, in which he points to his experiences during his time in Vienna (1908–13) and to his direct personal observations and experiences of social need:

> After the turn of the century, Vienna did belong among the socially most unfavourable cities. Shining wealth and disgusting poverty relieved each other in

> stark alternation . . . The horde of officers, civil servants, artists and scholars was confronted by an even greater horde of workers, the wealth of the aristocracy and business, by bloody poverty. In front of the palaces in Ringstrasse thousands of unemployed loafed about, and underneath this *via triumphalis* of the old Austria, the homeless lived in the twilight and mud of the canals.[15]

We know that Hitler not only observed these social contrasts from the outside but that he was himself directly involved. His description of the 'Vienna Years of Apprenticeship and Suffering' (the title of Chapter 2 in *Mein Kampf*) is in part exaggerated.[16] Nonetheless, with some justification he was able to qualify as a witness to the direct experience and observation of social injustices, which in his rather strange choice of phrase he expresses as follows:

> Hardly in any other German city could the social question be studied better than in Vienna. But one should not deceive oneself. This 'studying' could not be done from the top down. Whoever was not himself in the shackles of this strangling viper, never got to know its poison fangs. In the other instance all that results is superficial blatherings or lying sentimentality.

Hitler describes in detail the 'fate of the worker' and the 'path of suffering of the child of the worker': 'I myself experienced all this in hundreds of examples, in the beginning with disgust, and also with outrage, only then to understand later on the full tragedy of this suffering, its profounder causes. Unhappy victims of adverse circumstances.' Hitler thanked 'providence', which had enabled him to attend school: 'In it I could no longer sabotage what I did not like. It had brought me up quickly and thoroughly.' The harshness of his own struggle for life had saved him from 'capitulating now in pathetic sentimentality before the depraved end products of this development process'.[17]

We cannot simply discount these statements as nothing but clever propaganda designed to achieve a specific effect. Hitler himself was obviously convinced that the direct experience and observation of the social contrasts in Vienna had given him an understanding of the importance of the social issue. In one of his 'table talks' at the end of September 1941 he said:

> Who knows, if my parents had been wealthy enough to let me attend the academy, then I would probably never have come into a situation where I learned to understand social need from the ground up. He who lives outside of social need has to have a door opened for him before he can see it. The years which caused me to experience need in the sharpest form on my own body were one of the greatest blessings for the German nation: otherwise today we would have Bolshevism![18]

In several places in *Mein Kampf* Hitler rejects a position motivated by the sentimentality of 'the gracious condescension of various fashionable females who "feel with the people"'. The issue was not just to doctor the consequences of social injustice, but rather to do away with the causes. The task of any social engagement was the 'removal of such fundamental failures in the organization of our economic and cultural life which must lead to, or can at least provoke, the degeneration of individuals'.[19]

Before we turn to the question of how Hitler envisaged the solution of the social problem, we would like to describe how he viewed the origin of the social issue (discussed in more detail in Chapter III.3.a/b). He saw the beginning of the development of the modern social issue in the 'streaming together of large masses of workers in the cities', initiated by the process of industrialization,[20] 'who were not correctly received' by those who 'had the moral obligation to take care of them'.[21] In *Mein Kampf* Hitler describes this process in detail:

> The gigantic economic development led to a change in the social strata of the nation. While the small artisan slowly begins to die out, thereby making the possibility for the worker to gain an independent existence for himself ever rarer, the latter continues to proletarianize. Thus the industrial 'factory worker' is created, whose prime characteristic can be found in the fact that in later life he is hardly ever able to found an existence for himself. He is without possessions in the true sense of the word, his old age is a torture and can hardly be called living any longer.

Hitler then describes the process of initial accumulation: the splitting off of the direct producer from the means of production, and the development of a class which is forced to sell its labour in order to live. 'Ever new masses of people numbering in the millions moved from the rural villages into the bigger cities in order to earn their daily bread as factory workers in the newly founded industries. The working and living conditions of the new class were far worse than sad.' By the 'senseless transfer of traditional working hours to the new industrial activities', not only was the health of the worker destroyed, but also his belief in a higher form of justice. On top of this came the 'pitiful compensation' which stood in contrast to the 'obviously so much better position of the employer'[22] and, last but not least, the low value society put on manual labour.[23]

In a speech on 26 March 1927 Hitler describes the industrialization process and the development of the worker question: at the end of the nineteenth century more and more factories were built in Germany, one industrial city after the other developed;

> ... everything already closer together, slowly the borders disappeared, electric cables were pulled through so that the whole horizon is one glowing flickering flame and man was proud. Then people said, the chimneys are belching, the steam hammers are pounding, there they are forging the future of our nation. And they had this external grandiose image in front of their eyes, but they did not look inside: there were people standing at all the machines, there were men upon men in the pits, and this fourth class was developing, the industrial proletarian... They began

to regard the industrial worker as necessary, but as a necessary evil. They felt instinctively that there was a danger in this mass. But instead of dispassionately investigating the problem, they tried to shut their eyes and walked on by. And now begins the great historic guilt of the German bourgeoisie. A new class has appeared which the German bourgeoisie did not give a damn about. They let things go as they went. They only rebelled on a few occasions. The time then came, where this new class started to scream for human rights.[24]

While Hitler saw the beginning of the development of the modern social issue in the process of industrialization and the concomitant process of separating the immediate producer from the means of production, this does not mean in any way – and we should note this for future reference – that he rejected industrialization itself. This process of advancement and developing technology was not a misfortune, but a stroke of luck for mankind. Hitler was not criticizing industrialization, but only the blindness of the bourgeoisie towards the newly developing industrial proletariat as being bad for the German nation: 'The German bourgeoisie walks past this class completely indifferently and thoughtlessly, and with this begins the misfortune of the German nation.'[25]

In his speech at the congress of the *Deutsche Arbeitsfront* [DAF, or German Labour Front—H.B.] on 10 May 1933 Hitler identifies a further result of industrialization. With industrialization and the dissolution of the '*petit bourgeois* form of economics' an 'estrangement' between employer and employee had begun, and this process was even speeded up because the share had replaced personal ownership.[26]

How did Hitler envisage the solution to the social issue? We are able to detect several different solution strategies, but the one that was by far the most important for him was the creation of 'equal opportunity'. On 22 February 1942 he said in a table talk:

> For the solution of the social question there are three formulas: the victorious upper class suppresses a lower class that is foreign to it, or the lower class turns on the upper class and exterminates it, or each is given as much room as it needs to develop the abilities it has been given. When a person has the abilities to stand out, I do not look at whether he comes from proletarian circles, and I do not hinder the offspring of my old military dynasties from again proving themselves.[27]

Only a few days later Hitler listed the three major tasks of any revolution:

> Three things are vital in any uprising: to tear down the walls which separate the classes from each other in order to open the way for advancement for everybody; to create a general level of life in such a way that even the poorest has the secure minimum for existence; finally to reach the point where everybody can share in the blessings of culture.[28]

This statement is noteworthy for several considerations. First, it shows that the solution of the social question was for Hitler one of the key tasks of his revolution. Secondly, the last two quotations, as well as that presented at the beginning of this chapter,[29] are noteworthy in that here Hitler is speaking to an inner circle without regard to a specific propaganda effect, without regard to a mass audience. This is of decisive importance for statements on social questions in particular, since in Hitler's public statements a propaganda intent can naturally always play a role. In order therefore to be able to separate social demagogy from seriously meant statements, the statements made in public always require confirmation by others made without propaganda considerations within the inner circle. Thirdly, the last quotation is of interest because here we have an indication of the direction in which Hitler was searching for the solution of the social question, namely by a deliberate increase in social mobility and the creation of 'equal opportunity'.

2. The Importance and Substantiation of the Concept of 'Equal Opportunity' in Hitler's Social Programme

Hitler himself did not use the term 'equal opportunity'.[30] If we use it to describe Hitler's concepts despite this, then it is because this term comes closest to what Hitler actually wanted. His objective was, as Jochmann states in the introduction to Hitler's 'Monologues at *Führer* Headquarters', the creation of a condition in which 'all of the social classes would have opportunities for advancement and possibilities of becoming active',[31] not the equality of all human beings. Hitler rejected such a concept as being absurd. He was far more convinced of a natural inequality existing between the various races or nations,[32] as well as within each nation.[33] In his view, however, the differences between races were far greater than those within the same race.

The theory of human inequality is an argument frequently advanced by conservatives in order to justify existing power structures and social injustice. And this is where the decisive difference between Hitler's line of reasoning and that of conservatism can be found. While Hitler – like the conservatives – does emphasize the importance of an hierarchic order, the hierarchy Hitler means is not the traditional one in existence at the time.[34] As we shall see in the further course of this study, Hitler considered the middle classes to be totally incapable of providing political leadership (all he had for the nobility was contempt), and he wanted to destroy the existing social ranks and political power structures. However, he did not envisage the removal of the former élites as a process of violent destruction which could be carried out in one step, but hoped that, by creating equal opportunities in the sense of his socio-Darwinistic definition of the fight for social advancement, with time the old élites would necessarily be replaced by newly rising forces, particularly from among the working classes. The result of such a process would, of course, not be the equality of all human beings – not even among the 'German national community' – but a new inequality. 'Equal opportunity' in the sense it is used here therefore means the creation of equal starting positions in the battle for social advancement, which will always lead to new inequalities.

In order to prevent any misunderstandings, we must therefore first explore the differences between Hitler's ideas and the concept of equal opportunity as we define it today. When we speak of equal opportunity today, we are referring to *all* human beings, regardless of nationality, colour, sex or religion. With Hitler, however, this demand only applies to the members of the 'German national community', in other words, firstly not to other nationalities, and secondly not to those groups that had been segregated from the racially defined German community, namely Jews, gypsies and those with hereditary diseases. Women are excluded as well, at least as far as holding political office is concerned. *Within* this restricted area of application, 'equal opportunity' has the same meaning we give it today: creation not of the equality of all human beings, but of an equality of starting position, independent of origin, income or the occupations of the parents.

In order to understand why the scope of this demand was restricted to Germans, we must recall that National Socialism – as opposed to most political ideologies – was basically conceived for *Germany only*, and not in any way for transfer to other countries. Wagener emphasizes that Hitler 'only thought in terms of socialism *for* his own nation and *within* his own nation', whereas towards the rest of the world he was a crass egoist and imperialist.[35] Hitler had said to him:

> I have not set myself on the road of politics in order to pave the way for an international socialism . . . I bring the German people a national socialism, the political theory of the national community, the feeling of unity of all who belong to the German nation and who are prepared and willing to feel themselves as being an inseparable but also co-responsible particle of the totality of the nation.[36]

Hitler frequently emphasized that National Socialism was not an article for export. In his closing speech at the *Reichsparteitag* in 1936 he argued that it would be illogical

> . . . to assume that this environment, that somebody who is a fanatical national chauvinist, would want to disclose to, let alone to impose on others, precisely *that*

very idea which alone has created the spiritual and real conditions for his national pride. No: National Socialism is our most valuable German patent.[37]

On 20 May 1942 Hitler rejected

> ... most sharply any attempt ... to export the National Socialist *Weltanschauung*. It is precisely in our interest for the other states to maintain their democratic systems and thereby to march to their inevitable dissolution, and all the more because based on National Socialism, we are slowly but surely becoming the most compact national body anyone can conceive.[38]

The same thing applies to Hitler's concept of 'equal opportunity', which applies to all his political, social and economic ideas: since he believed that he could reduce the social tensions in Germany and create the conditions for the formation of a new, capable élite by the provision of 'equal opportunity', he naturally never considered transferring this concept to other nations or states. Hitler defined himself, always and exclusively, only as being a German politician, so he was bound to welcome unfavourable social conditions and internal conflicts within potential enemy nations.

After these necessary preliminary remarks, we now intend to discuss the importance and substantiation of the concept of 'equal opportunity' in Hitler's social programme. The claim we intend to prove is that from the beginning to the end of Hitler's political activities, over a period of about 25 years, the creation of 'equal opportunity' (in the sense of the definition/modification discussed above) was one of his most important programmatic objectives. Since this has not formerly been taken notice of in historical research, we need to cite and discuss it in detail.

Number 20 of the 25-point programme of the NSDAP that Hitler announced on 24 February 1920 states:

> In order to enable any qualified and diligent German to achieve a higher education and thereby move into leadership positions, the state must ensure a thorough extension of our total public education system ... We demand the education at the expense of the state of particularly well-endowed children of poor parents without regard to their class or occupation.[39]

Hitler repeated this demand in various speeches – on 7 August 1920, for example, when he demanded that

> ... at least anybody who has abilities can also take part in the education system that exists, that at least any child that is intelligent can take part in that which exists, without regard to the social status of the parents, in that, if they are poor, education will be at the expense of the state.[40]

On 12 January 1921 he demanded a reform of the school system according to the motto: 'Let ability win through!',[41] a demand which, as Hitler recorded in his notes for another speech, the November revolution had not fulfilled.[42] On 26 February 1923 Hitler described it as 'the obligation of the state . . . to let able children of any class attend university',[43] and on 5 August of the same year he demanded, 'In this state anybody who is divinely gifted shall be given the possibility of rising upwards from the cradle on. Education must not be the monopoly of one class, it must be provided for the broadest mass of the people.' Simply by 'kicking out the Jews', room for hundreds of thousands of German intelligences could be created.[44]

While the right-wing parties of the Weimar Republic were ridiculing the socialist Reichs President Ebert because he had once been a leather-worker's helper, Hitler was declaring that they were wrong. Even a leather-worker's helper could be a genius and therefore qualified to fill the office of Reichs President.[45]

If we had assumed until now – without knowing Hitler's later internal statements – that he had only expounded such views and demands in his speeches for their propaganda effect, then it becomes clear for the first time in *Mein Kampf* why the demand for 'equal opportunity' was a logical, integral part of Hitler's *Weltanschauung*. In his book Hitler complains that, in general, it was the children of higher class, currently well-situated parents who were thought to be worthy of a higher education. Questions of ability only played a 'subordinate role'. Hitler counters by saying that a farmer's son could 'possess far more talents than the child of parents from many generations of a higher position in life', and it made no difference if the farmer's child lagged behind in general knowledge when compared to the child of the bourgeois, because general knowledge had nothing to do with talent: 'Had the talented farmer's boy also grown up in such an environment from the beginning, then his mental capabilities would be far different.' Today there was really only one field in which the origin of a person was actually less important than his inbred talent, and that was the field of art, and here could be found the best proof that 'genius is not tied to higher strata of society, let alone to wealth'. The greatest artists often came from the poorest families and 'many a little village boy later becomes a versatile painter'. Hitler then bases his further line of argument on this fact: 'It does not speak well for the depth of thinking of the times that such discoveries are not applied to the whole of intellectual life. The belief is that what can not be disputed in art does not apply to the so-called real sciences.' The idea was unbearable 'that every year hundreds of thousands of people completely lacking in ability are being found worthy of a higher education, while other hundreds of thousands with great endowments remain without

III. Hitler's Social Objectives

any higher education'. The loss to the nation was hardly to be estimated. 'If the wealth of important inventions has increased specifically in North America during the past few decades, then also because there far more talents from the lower classes find the possibilities of a higher education than is the case in Europe.' Here the national state would one day have to intervene: 'It has not been given the task' – Hitler has this emphasized in bold type – 'to preserve its decisive influence for an existing social class, but the task of selecting the most able heads from among the sum of the nation and bringing them along to position and authority.' The national state had to regard it 'as its highest duty to open the doors of the state institutions of higher learning to any talent, no matter from what circles it might stem'. Hitler's reasons for the necessity of creating 'equal opportunity' are as follows. The 'intellectual classes' in Germany lacked 'the living connections downwards'. This resulted in their lacking an understanding for the feelings of the masses. 'They have been torn from this context for so long that they can no longer possess the required psychological understanding of the people.' The upper classes had become estranged from the people, but what they lacked most was the necessary 'power of will and determination'. This is the reason why Hitler intended to increase social mobility, in other words the possibilities of social advancement for members of the socially lower classes. In this context he pointed to the Catholic church as 'an exemplary living example'. The celibacy of its priests forced it 'to recruit the replacements for its clergy out of the broad masses of the people instead of from among its own ranks'. Celibacy was therefore the reason for the

> ... unbelievably vigorous power which inhabits this ancient institution. Because this gigantic army of the wielders of spiritual power continuously replenishes itself from the lower classes of the nations, the church not only preserves its instinctive connection to the emotional world of the people but also secures for itself a sum of energy and vigour which in the long run will only ever be available among the broad masses of the people. It is from this that the astonishing youth of this gigantic organism stems, its mental flexibility and steely willpower.

It would be the task of the national state to ensure that 'a continuous renewal of the existing intellectual classes takes place through the supply of new blood from below'.[46]

This line of argument shows that he had not made his demand for 'equal opportunity' primarily for reasons of propaganda. Quite the opposite. It is derived as a logical necessity from certain premises underlying his thinking. First, Hitler considers 'instinct', the power of will and determination, to be more important for political leadership ability than pure intelligence and the level of education. Secondly, he was of the opinion – as we will show in Chapter

III.3.a/b – that these traits (power of will and determination) were almost totally lacking in the upper classes, i.e. in the bourgeoisie, whereas the 'masses', the lower classes of workers and farmers, were for him the embodiment of strength, energy and determination. From these premises Hitler, as we will see in the course of this study, drew a number of conclusions. For example, the bourgeoisie was incapable of political leadership and had to be replaced by a new élite. Of primary importance for the NSDAP, therefore, was the gaining of the working class. It followed that propaganda should not primarily appeal to the intellect but to the emotions. It had to be so radical that it would scare off the 'cowardly' and weak people and draw the courageous, the brave, out of the masses 'like a magnet'.

From the two premises described above, Hitler just as naturally derived his demand for 'equal opportunity', for a deliberate increase in social mobility. The state, so he argues in *Mein Kampf*, had the duty 'to draw out the obviously capable human material and to use it in the service of the general public. Because the state and statesmen are not there to provide a refuge for individual classes, but to fulfil the tasks appropriate to them.' A decisive factor for the 'greatness of a nation' was that it succeeded in training the most able and most talented for the fields best suited for them:

> When two nations compete with each other, which are both equally well endowed, then that one will gain the victory among whose total intellectual leadership the best talents are represented, and that one will be defeated whose leadership is only a huge common manger for certain levels of society or classes, without regard to the innate abilities of its various members.[47]

Because Hitler so strongly emphasized the importance of the élite and of 'great men',[48] he wanted all the more to provide equal education and advancement possibilities for all levels of society, so that at the end of the process of selection the genuinely best and most talented would reach the leadership positions appropriate for them – regardless of their origins, the education and income level of their parents, and so forth.

Hitler also saw the difficulties which would arise when the attempt to realize this demand was made. The objection would be made, he said, that 'you could not really ask the dear little son of a higher state official, for example, to become, let us say, an artisan, because somebody else whose parents were artisans appears to be more capable'.[49] Such a view, however, only resulted from the disdain in which society held physical labour. It was therefore the task of the national state to reduce the social prejudices and to reach the point by means of a re-education process, where physical and intellectual labour were equally respected.[50]

III. Hitler's Social Objectives

Up to now we have seen, therefore, that in *Mein Kampf* Hitler had thought seriously about the problem of increasing social mobility. We have cited and described Hitler's reasons so extensively, primarily in order to make it clear how his demand for 'equal opportunity' logically fits into his *Weltanschauung* or is derived from certain premises in his thinking. We will now investigate the value and continuity of these concepts in Hitler's thinking.

To the *Hamburger Nationalklub von 1919*, Hitler declared on 28 February 1926, 'Because of the restriction in the circulation of blood from below to above, we are lacking willpower, brutal willpower.'[51] In Hitler's terminology this meant that there was too little social mobility, that the workers in particular, or rather their children were being offered too few chances for advancement. In a speech on 26 March 1927 he explained that a nation was only healthily organized when it was assured 'that the most important children necessarily come to the leadership positions. A state is badly organized when it produces classes, when it prevents the pulsating rising upwards of life from below . . .'[52] On 6 April of the same year he declared:

> Every nation in its totality presents itself as a great pyramid, whereby the lowest level, the majority of the people, while being without intelligence, clings all the more energetically to life. As soon as an organization cuts off its upper levels from the broad mass and does not take care that from these broad lower levels life wells up, then it will perish from abstract intellectualism, there will be no more vigour available.

This could be seen in the leadership of the German state, which had lacked the brutal willpower of the lower masses. If the leaders of the state were to have the brutal willpower of the Communists, 'then they would be able to see how Germany would rise upwards!'[53]

In a speech on 9 April 1927 about 'Socialism and Marxism' Hitler explained how he defined socialism. It was the attempt to bridge the gap between 'the highest intelligence' and 'primitive labour' and to ensure that 'the replenishing flow is possible without interruption'. The true socialist could only wish that his nation produced great, important intellects, because their successes benefited every individual. 'He can only wish that the nation be organized in such a way that the capable intellects from below rise upwards as a matter of necessity.'[54] On 17 June of the same year Hitler said that a great inventor could 'stem from the meanest hut', where neither birth nor class counted: 'The great human beings who have brought us our culture did not stem from the classes but from the people.'[55] On 30 November 1928 he lauded the farmer, who by the nature of his trade was constantly forced to 'take an uncountable number of decisions'. When a nation is still healthily organized, so that 'blood [always]

105

flows from down below to up above', it could 'continuously draw new strength from the deepest sources of its strength'.[56] Hitler defined the middle class as a vehicle, a bridge for social advancement. This was one of the main reasons why he criticized the ruination of the middle class: 'If this continues,' he wrote on 29 December 1928 in the *Illustrierte Beobachter*, 'our whole middle class will one day end in ruin. But with this every bridge to a better existence, and particularly to an independent one, will cease, thanks to which a continuous replenishment of our upper levels of life from the lower ones was able to take place before.'[57]

In an article of 1 March 1930, also published in the *Illustrierte Beobachter*, Hitler wrote that the successes of Social Democracy were largely simply due to the fact that

> ... of the activistic forces of our nation with political talents, because of their origin, quite a few were not given a field in which to act within the ranks of the bourgeoisie, nor could ever expect to be given one. It was really so that within the middle class parties there ruled a social class completely shut up within itself, which jealously fended off any penetration by foreign, and especially by talented, elements, and thereby lost all those forces which later were to benefit Social Democracy.

Because the middle class parties 'most sharply rejected any living replenishment of blood from the body of their own nation', it was predictable that they would die out within a foreseeable period of time. Within the NS movement, however, everybody had to 'win for himself' his own position by his own abilities, 'by talent and diligence'.[58]

In his conversations with Wagener Hitler also frequently touched upon the topic of 'equal opportunity'. In a conversation in June 1930, for example, he explained that already in early youth, in kindergarten, in school, in the HJ and BdM [Hitler Youth and its female counterpart, the Union of German Girls—H.B.], all social levels had to come together. There should be no differences of any kind made between rich and poor, high and low, employer and employee. On another occasion Hitler developed this concept in more detail: 'At present we are dragging the greatest dunderheads through the secondary schools and high schools, just because the father has an elevated position or the money to pay for it!' Here one had to be consistent. If the objective was that everybody should receive the education corresponding to his abilities, then the financial means for this would also have to be provided. It should be the responsibility of the occupational organizations, in other words the unions, the farmers' associations, the guilds etc. to intervene with help and support if individual families fell into need because of a large number of children, illness or other reason. This, however, would require the implementation of a different economic order which enabled the occupational organizations to do this. Until this had been realized, the problem would have to be taken care of by the communities or, in the end, by the state. As far as the school fees for the middle school were concerned, one had to take into consideration that a farmer, a worker or a small artisan was not able to support a son or a daughter for longer than eight years of education and to pay school fees on top of that. The farmer, for example, reckoned that from the age of fourteen his children would follow him into the fields or the stables as cheap labour. For the upbringing of a large horde of children a worker's family also had to calculate that the growing children would contribute something to the household from the age of fourteen. It was therefore not enough, according to Wagener's report on Hitler's statements, if such a father did not have to pay school fees for his boy at middle school; he would have to be given additional support on top of that. Since the community had an interest in having the capable youth advance, it was only proper that in this case the community, in other words the state, pay for this support, for example in the form of a contribution for clothing and food to the amount of the wages of an apprentice. In addition Hitler demanded the introduction of free educational material for all. The whole organization of the schools had to be adjusted to securing the education and training of the best of the nation for higher civil service. The omission of this new order was the deepest reason why the Weimar Republic was slowly failing. 'Because', Hitler explained, according to Wagener,

> ... the selection of the best at the moment does *not* extend to the whole nation, but exactly as before primarily to those circles who are already 'on top', who can afford it, and who have the necessary connections. And since these circles are naturally reactionary, leading positions in the state are increasingly being filled by reactionaries, and it is no wonder that reaction is increasingly raising its head.

Hitler continued: the 'present-day descendants of the feudal age', in other words the reactionaries on the one hand and the democrats on the other, would certainly reject his educational policies. The Communists, on the other hand, even though the term 'treason to the fatherland' was foreign to them, were at least honest, as opposed to reactionaries and democrats: 'That is why they will accept our principles of education and schooling. The reactionaries and democrats, however, will not. Because *they* are only interested in the advancement of their own children. But *we* are interested in the élite of the whole nation.'

In another conversation Hitler told Wagener that for pupils who had passed middle school with superior grades in general, or superior grades in certain subjects, the means had to be created for them to take up the appropriate studies, even if the father was a simple workman or farmer. This would require a scholarship, which would not only cover the fees for teaching and the necessary tools for learning, but also housing, clothing and living expenses.[59] As far as the topics of 'equal opportunities' and 'social mobility' are concerned, we can detect, according to what we have learned from Wagener's reports, no differences between what Hitler said in public and what he said in private.

Even after the seizure of power these topics continued to play a major role, both in Hitler's statements in his private circle as well as in his speeches. In an address given on 16 June 1933 at the close of the National Socialist leadership meeting, he demanded that 'a school of practical life be established, which is not only open to certain social classes but to anyone who feels himself called to the political struggle'.[60] In his closing speech at the *Reichsparteitag* in 1933 he declared that the development of a new élite 'from all the classes, occupations and other types of strata' was 'in reality a socialist action', because

> ... by making the effort to find the person born to it for every function in the life of my nation, and transferring the responsibility in this field to him *without regard* to his previous *economically determined* or *social* origin, I am acting in the interest of *all*. And if the term 'socialism' is to have any meaning at all, then it can only have the meaning that with iron justice, in other words with deepest insight, out of the maintenance of the whole we load upon *each one* that which equates to his innate abilities, and thereby to his worth.

During the years of the time of struggle the National Socialist movement had collected the state-building power of the German nation, just like a magnet collects the steel spans, and

> ... from all classes and occupations and levels of life. It has proven itself again that someone might well be able to lead a big business, but often not even a group of eight men. And conversely it has also been demonstrated that the born leaders have sprung from farm kitchens and worker's huts.

Therein lay the NS movement's mission of class reconciliation. A new evaluation of the human being was coming in, not according to the yardsticks of liberalistic thinking but 'according to the measures set by nature'.[61]

To Louis P. Lochner, the representative of Associated Press, Hitler explained on 25 March 1934 that he was in agreement with the Americans when he did not wish to make everybody equal, but paid tribute to the principle of the stepladder – 'Only everybody must be given the possibility to climb the ladder.'[62] These two notions probably reflect Hitler's intention in the shortest and most precise form – on the one hand speaking in favour of a hierarchic

III. Hitler's Social Objectives

order, on the other the recognition of the necessity of giving everybody the same chance to advance. In his closing speech at the 1934 *Reichsparteitag* Hitler described it as a task of the leadership of the state to create the conditions under which 'the most able brains will receive the preference they deserve without regard to origin, title, class or wealth'.[63]

Indeed, as Schoenbaum demonstrates,[64] the National Socialist revolution led to an increase in social mobility and the members of the lower classes were given new opportunities for advancement. What cannot be upheld, however, is his opinion – shared by Dahrendorf and others – that this process had taken place against the intentions of Hitler and the National Socialists. The alleged contradiction between the effect achieved and the intention can certainly not be found in this area. Quite the opposite is true. The process of modernization described by Dahrendorf and Schoenbaum, the increase of social mobility, did not take place against Hitler's intentions, but were very much in line with his social policy programme. In his closing address at the *Reichsparteitag* of 1936 Hitler proudly pointed out that National Socialism had 'opened the way upwards for countless fellow-Germans from the lowest positions'. The German worker could not overlook the fact that 'there is a man at the head of the Reich who was himself a worker barely 25 years ago, that today former land and industrial workers hold countless leadership positions at the lower, and many leadership positions at the higher levels, all the way up to Reichs governors'. With this Hitler is certainly exaggerating the dimensions of the successes achieved to date, just as his claim that he had himself been a worker is, of course, only propaganda. Hitler obviously saw himself forced to admonish the party because it had had to select men for its leadership 'in future more than ever, without any regard to origin, former position in life, birth, or wealth, but filled only with the highest sense of duty and responsibility to the nation'. It should place less value in the 'so-called social deficits', but only in the

> ... personality endowments for leadership of the people and thereby worthiness. In the total build-up of our state the principle must apply that the genius has access to every position regardless of what station in life he comes from ... Particular attention must be paid to ensuring that a bureaucratic ossification does not put the report ahead of the achievement, the recommendation ahead of the value and thereby in the final analysis, birth ahead of worth. We are marching at rapid speed towards troubled times. They will require men of hard determination, not weak *petit bourgeois*. They will not measure people by their superficial social graces, but by the quality and strength of their characters in times of heavy burdens.[65]

In Hitler's speeches we now frequently find a mixture of wishful thinking or propaganda and reality. On 30 January 1937, for example, in his speech on the fourth anniversary of the seizure of power, he said:

> Is there a more splendid and more wonderful socialism, or a more genuine democracy, than that National Socialism which, thanks to its organization, makes it possible that from among millions of German boys the one, if fate wishes to serve itself of him, can make his way to the very head of the nation? And this is not just theory! In the National Socialist Germany of today this is a reality which is a matter of course for us all.

While there were indeed increased chances for advancement during the Third Reich for members of socially underprivileged classes, reality did lag far behind Hitler's objectives and propaganda statements. He could certainly point with justification to the fact that 'many former workers' and farmers' children' held positions of leadership in the NS state 'as ministers, Reichs governors and Gauleiters, some of them are among the highest leaders and representatives of the people'.[66] On the other hand, the universal 'equal opportunity' Hitler was aiming for was still far from being 'a reality which is a matter of course for all of us', as he presumptuously claimed.

Before a meeting of the Kreis leaders at the *Ordensburg*[training institutions for the party leadership—H.B.] Vogelsang on 29 April 1937 Hitler declared that it was the objective of the leadership to gain those people who were capable of leading as leaders in all walks of life by means of a natural selection 'always from among the people'. In his eyes this was the 'most wonderful' and 'most Germanic' form of democracy. 'What can be more wonderful for a nation than to know: out of our ranks the most able can rise to the highest position without regard to origin and birth or anything else. All he needs is the ability. We take pains to search for the most able people. What they had formerly been, what their parents had been, what their dear mothers had been – that makes no difference at all. If they are capable, all roads are open to them.'[67]

The allusion to the increased opportunities for advancement for workers was of course also an effective propaganda tool at the annual rallies on 1 May. At the rally in 1937, for example, Hitler underlined that in Germany 'a world of prejudices' had been cleared away. He himself was already a 'child of the people' and did not stem 'from out of some castle, but came from the place of work' – which, as we know, was mere propaganda, because in his entire life Hitler only worked for a few weeks or months, and could not be defined as a 'worker', neither from his origin nor from his former position in life. On the other hand Hitler was not completely wrong when he continued: 'Next to me stand German people from all walks of life, who today belong to the leadership of the nation: former farm workers as Reichs governors, former metalworkers today are Gauleiters and so forth. However, former bourgeois and former aristocrats also have their position within this movement.' This was true democracy and true socialism. The possibility for anybody to rise even to the

III. Hitler's Social Objectives

highest positions without regard to his class was 'the highest socialism there is, because it is the most reasonable and the wisest'.[68]

In his opening speech at the 1937 *Reichsparteitag* Hitler emphasized that it was of 'the utmost importance' to continue

> ... the careful selection process in the leadership of the nation ... in all areas and not to capitulate in the face of any opposition or inhibitions of a formal nature. The best we have to offer to those to be relieved, to the no longer qualified former pillars of our community structure, is the same equal right as for all.

The fundamental concept of National Socialism's 'social revolution' was, based on insight into the weakness of the bourgeois social order, to

> ... do away with hereditary privileges and to place the leadership of the nation in all sectors of life, but most importantly in the area of politics, into the hands of a new élite, which was selected and found solely according to its inner endowments and worthiness, regardless of origin, birth, social standing or religion.[69]

In his closing address at the *Reichsparteitag* one year later Hitler said that the 'greatest care' of the National Socialist state was to find ways and means 'to ease and pave the way upwards for diligence, energy, vigour, insight, courage and perseverance, insofar as they manifest themselves in the personal'. In the National Socialist state even the 'poorest child' must be able to reach the highest position, provided it has the ability. Then a conflict between the people and the leadership could never develop,

> ... because then every farmer, every worker will always know that the leadership of all is also his leadership, because it is of his own flesh and blood ... In this new Germany from now on every worker's or farmer's child, if it is divinely endowed and blessed, must be able to rise up to the very highest leadership of the whole nation, due to the nature of the support by our organization and thanks to our deliberate leadership selection. Whereas on the other side, even a capital in the millions cannot and must not ever open the way upwards for someone who does not belong to this nation.[70]

These statements at the *Reichsparteitag* in 1937 and in 1938 had more of an admonishing character as compared to Hitler's other boasts cited above. When he said one had to 'continue' this selection process in all areas and must not 'capitulate in the face of opposition and inhibitions', this was an indication that in Hitler's view his concepts had not yet been sufficiently realized, and it was astonishing when he declared in 1938 that 'from now on' every worker's and farmer's child must have the opportunity to rise to the highest positions. Had not Hitler claimed in early 1937, for example, that all this was already a

111

natural reality? He knew, of course, that reality was still lagging far behind the ideal he was proclaiming.

We have already drawn attention in another context to a remark by Hitler in his speech in the *Reichstag* on 30 January 1939. There he declared that the best protection from a possible revolution was the ability of the state to fill all the important positions and to discover the really capable out of the masses of the millions of people. The true revolutionaries of world stature had always been the true leadership personalities whom an 'arrogant, calcified, closed social class' had neglected or not accepted. At another place in his speech Hitler declared that in Germany there were hundreds of thousands of intelligent offspring of workers and farmers who should one day fill the leading positions in the state – together with 'our other educated classes' – but not the members of a foreign people, meaning the Jews.[71]

On 14 November 1940 he pointed to the NS élite schools, the *Adolf-Hitler-Schulen* and the *Nationalpolitische Erziehungsanstalten* [Adolf Hitler schools and national political education institutes—H.B.] as proof that in Germany, despite difficulties, 'the most monstrous of prejudices' had been done away with. Just as the students of these élite schools were selected without regard to their origin, so had all the barriers on the other side of life also been removed – in the administration of the state, where former farm workers had become Reichs governors and former workers Gauleiters or Reichs governors, as well as in the *Wehrmacht*, where thousands who had been enlisted men had been promoted to officers, 'regardless of their origin' and only according to their abilities.[72]

On 10 December 1940 Hitler also declared that for the first time in German history 'basically all social prejudices in recruiting have been abolished' and

> ... all inhibitions of a social nature overcome. And we are now building primarily for the future. You know that we have countless schools, national political education institutes and Adolf Hitler schools. In these schools, there we take in the talented children, the children of our broad masses, workers' sons, farmers' sons, where the parents would never have been able to pay for their children to take part in higher studies, they are slowly coming in here and are being educated here, and later on they will be led into the state, later they will come into the party, they will come into the Ordensburgen, they will occupy the highest positions one day.[73]

In his study on the 'NS élite selection schools', H. Scholtz came to the conclusion that in actual fact the percentage of children from worker's families at these élite schools was 'relatively high in comparison to the mixture predominating at German higher schools'. The statistics on the occupations of the fathers of students at the national political education institutes and the

III. Hitler's Social Objectives

Adolf Hitler schools show that, with 13.1 per cent (NPEI) and 19.5 per cent (AHS), workers' children were relatively strongly represented. At the Adolf Hitler schools the children of workers and employed craftsmen were the third most numerous group after the children of civil servants and white-collar workers, whereas only 2.2 per cent of the students came from the families of university graduates, thereby being by far the smallest group. It had also been decreed that for the Adolf Hitler schools 'pupils from socially less well-off classes . . . were to be given preference'. The conclusion reached by Scholtz, that it 'was unmistakable that Hitler's policy was directed towards increasing social mobility', confirms our investigation of Hitler's *Weltanschauung*. The NPEIs and the Adolf Hitler schools, which for Hitler had the character of being models for the realization of National Socialist principles, were not to be the only attempts to achieve the objective. Included here is the project for the introduction of the *Deutsche Hauptschule* [German secondary school—H.B.] as a compulsory school of selection. This plan was expressly based on point No 20 of the party programme, which demanded that every capable and diligent German be given the opportunity of reaching higher education and thereby entering into positions of leadership. The *Nationalsozialistische Lehrerbund* [NSLB, or National Socialist Teachers' Association—H.B.] in particular, which had been working towards the realization of equality in educational opportunities for a long time, welcomed the introduction of the secondary school as a step in this direction. Expressly referring to Hitler's speech of 10 December 1940, the NSLB demanded the reduction of educational careers determined by class, among other things by the creation of boarding facilities at the secondary schools for the free accommodation of needy children, as well as the abolition of school fees and the granting of economic preferences while attending higher schools. Hitler specifically ordered on 28 April 1941 that outside the *Altreich* [Old Reich, i.e. Germany before 1938—H.B.] the secondary schools were to be created during the war, but this was postponed until after the war in a decree issued on 13 June 1942 by Rust, the Minister of Science and National Education. Nonetheless, 51 such schools were created in Württemberg, 34 in the Palatinate and 51 in the Saarland, in addition to the 1,246 secondary schools created in the territories newly won or occupied since 1938. Besides the National Socialist élite schools, the private boarding schools were also to have their function changed in the National Socialist sense, whereby it was stressed that 'farmers, workers and craftsmen [were to be] given more opportunity than before to have their particularly talented children educated according to their abilities'.[74]

The egalitarian tendencies of National Socialism ran into widespread opposition, particularly from the conservative side. In his study 'Education and

Educational Theories in National Socialist Germany', Lingelbach has pointed out that even educators like Heinrich Weinstock and Theodor Litt, who did not oppose National Socialism out of principle, were critical of its education policy:

> The conservative humanist [Weinstock—R.Z.] was worried about the apparently 'egalitarian' tendencies of the National Socialist mass organizations which were also making the advancement of not 'scientifically' qualified 'élites' institutionally increasingly more possible. The monopoly of the humanistic grammar school was intended to stabilize the traditional hierarchically structured social order even under the political-social conditions of the National Socialist 'national state'.[75]

This position was not untypical for the conservative élites who regarded the social dynamics initiated by National Socialism with scepticism and feared for the loss of their traditional privileges.

In this context, the introduction of the 'non-denominational school', in other words the replacement of the confessional school, ran into considerable opposition from conservative and religious forces. The non-denominational school, a school reform which had been vehemently demanded for a long time by the Liberals and the Social Democrats but whose introduction had been prevented time and again, 'was finally only realized with massive pressure by the totalitarian forces of National Socialism'. Taken as such, the National Socialist school battle appears to confirm totally Ralf Dahrendorf's thesis of revolutionizing and modernizing by dictatorship.[76]

We do not intend to go into this subject more deeply here. A look at the educational policies of the Third Reich does show, however, that efforts were made to implement Hitler's revolutionary ideology in this field as well. But while the demand for the provision of increased opportunities for advancement for workers' children was actually realized in the model schools, the national political education institutions and the Adolf Hitler schools, in the traditional schools the social barriers remained more or less untouched. Overall, the realization of Hitler's ideas remained in its initial stages and only played a minor role for the time being as far as quantity is concerned. Nonetheless, these beginnings should not be underestimated, because the Adolf Hitler schools and the national political educational institutions were models for Hitler. Here the principles of National Socialist educational policy – which were later to be enforced within society in general – were to be rigorously tested for the first time. In his speech on 10 December 1940, which we have already mentioned, Hitler indicated that the ideal he was aiming at had nowhere nearly been reached:

> We envisage a state in the future in which every position shall be filled by the most able son of our nation, completely regardless of where he comes from. A state in

which birth is nothing and achievements and ability are everything. That is our ideal, for which we are now working . . .[77]

This topic plays a key role in his table talks as well, which clearly shows that Hitler was not raising the demand for an improvement in the opportunities for social advancement so frequently in his speeches only for reasons of propaganda but that he attached outstanding importance to the realization of his objectives in this area. At the end of July 1941, for example, Hitler said, 'This is the National Socialist teaching: that you make use of the forces, no matter what social level they come from.'[78] A note by Koeppen dated 18 September 1941 again clearly shows the purely national character of Hitler's concept: 'Within the German nation highest level of national community and possibility of education for everybody, but towards others absolute position of mastery.'[79]

At the end of September 1941 Hitler underlined the importance of the following principles in his monologues at table:

> We have to keep our eye on two things: (1)That all talented youths are educated at public expense; (2) that the gates are open for all talented people . . . And what a role in life does the family background play! It was only under the Social Democratic party that a person who lacked both family and education could become a minister.[80]

At the end of October 1941 Hitler said that it was an important task that for talented workers 'we pave the way and remove the difficulties arising from the fact that we pay too much attention to certificates, to paper'. He himself had been able to gain wonderful experiences in the highest positions within his own movement: 'I have civil servants who are farm workers and who are proving themselves most excellently today.' Hitler was probably thinking of Friedrich Hildebrandt, who had been a farm worker and who was Gauleiter from 1925 to 1945 and Reichs governor from 1933 in Mecklenburg. Above all, said Hitler, everybody had to be given the opportunity to get ahead outside of his profession. 'Ancient China set an example here, as long as the teachings of Confucius were still living: the poorest village boy could become a mandarin.' It was simply not permissible that the whole of subsequent life was dependent on a certificate. He himself, went Hitler's conviction, 'had become a victim of this institution', because – despite his obvious talent – he had been refused admittance to the building academy due to the lack of an *Abitur* [A-level—H.B.] certificate.[81]

Only a few days later in his table talks Hitler came back to this topic: 'It does not depend on a piece of paper, on a certificate, whether somebody gets a position, but solely on how he as a human being is able to handle the tasks he is responsible for.' The measure of selection and promotion, even in the

Wehrmacht, should only be 'ability'.[82] The next day Hitler once again addressed this topic:

> If the broad masses were not involved, then selection would be too one-sided towards the intellectual. The animal power would be missing. The farmer has animal power – he constantly has to take decisions – and so does the worker who, tossed about as a little proletarian, gets to know life from the other side. If brains are added to these people, then you have the epitome of vigour. We must not allow our upper class to close itself off... These people look at everything intellectually, they analyze everything. By this alone, however, one cannot make history. I need the brutal types, who are prepared to draw the consequences from an insight, a healthy natural trait towards the primitive side of brutality, of willpower. The human being's ability to resist belongs to the character side. It becomes marvellous when intellectual superiority is then added on.[83]

On 20 January 1942 Hitler criticized the lack of advancement possibilities for workers in the old army:

> Next to things that were unbelievably good, there were also things unbelievably outdated in the old army, out of this Social Democracy was born, which would never have happened if the army and the navy had not done everything to estrange the worker from the nation, to absorb him. He had no future. An institution that had to have dire consequences! ... On the other hand, any teacher could automatically become an officer. Many did, who were then utter failures. You should not generalize! If somebody proves himself then you know he has the ability to lead.[84]

About a week later Hitler explained that class prejudices could no longer be maintained in a time 'when the proletariat consists of so many highly valuable people as it largely does today!' He wanted to make it possible through the Adolf Hitler schools and the NPEIs that 'even the poorest boy can rise up to any position provided he has within him the abilities to do so'. Furthermore, the party was ensuring that there were possibilities for advancement outside the normal openings in the world of business or in that of the civil service:

> Otherwise there will be revolts. The Jew detects the tensions and is making use of them. A movement must come which pushes back both sides: the feeble-minded conservative and the Jewish-Bolshevist anarchists ... What should be blamed on a child least of all is the occupation of its father: the only thing that decides here is talent and abilities. The child can have the ability the parents did not have ... The strangulation of continuous advancement has to be prevented.[85]

On 30 January 1942 Hitler explained the reasons for his view in a 'philosophical' context:

> We see in every condition and at every point in time on this earth the result of a process of life which is never interrupted. And it is impossible to say at a specific

moment: now this development process stops; it is rather in the nature of the whole development of all things that any sterilization of this process of life must lead to its dying out. On the contrary, it is the essence of nature that the more able will always be lifted upward and set apart, in other words, that inside the nations the path must always be cleared for the able, that it must not be barred by social structures, that inside the nations it must not come to a sterilization of the abilities, but that care must also be taken inside to ensure a continuous flow of fresh blood from below to the top, and that everything which is decayed because it is lethargic should die off, because it must die off, because it is ripe for dying off, and that it should not be held on to.[86]

In a table talk on 12 April 1942 Hitler expressed the hope that he would succeed by a 'restructuring of the German school system' in achieving results in the field of education which would by far exceed those of British colleges. He had had the national political education institutes created for this very reason, and as a principle given them the motto 'To extract and educate the élite of the boys and girls from all levels of German society'.[87] Again in a table talk on 21 May 1942, Hitler reported on the difficulties he had encountered in the realization of many a concept as long as he still had had to take his conservative allies and Reichs President Hindenburg into consideration. How hard it had often been for Hindenburg to free himself from outdated views was demonstrated by his remarks while signing the appointment of Gauleiter Hildebrandt to Reichs governor. At the time Hindenburg had muttered under his breath, Why could the man as a former farm labourer not be content with having made it to the position of a member of the *Reichstag* and now finally hold his peace?![88]

Schoenbaum has pointed out that even in the Army – still, as always, the most conservative branch of the services – a 'silent social revolution' was taking place, that 'the officers corps of the *Wehrmacht*... [was] on the way to becoming the least snobbish in German history'.[89] Hitler himself welcomed and supported this process:

> ... when you look at the promotions of our young officers, here already begins the break-in of our National Socialist national community in its full scope. There are no longer any privileges of the birth certificate, there is no former social standing, there is no definition of wealth, no so-called origin, there is also no former so-called education, there is only a single evaluation: this is the evaluation of the good, brave, loyal man who is capable of becoming the leader of our nation. The downfall of an old world has really been brought about. From this war will come, reinforced by blood, the national community, much stronger yet than we National Socialists, fortified by our faith, were able to transmit to the nation after the Great War.

Germany would emerge from the war 'purified from so many prejudices', and those 'gentlemen' who, as the final remnants of an incorrigible past, were secretly hoping somewhere by their 'blatherings and moanings' to experience a new dawning of their 'class world', would suffer a pitiful shipwreck. 'World history will shunt them aside as if they had never been there.' After the war, Hitler promised, 'the way that his genius, his diligence, his courage, his ability and commitment can at all open for him, will be paved even more for every single member of the nation!'[90]

In 1942, in his annual commemoration address of 8 November, Hitler stressed that National Socialism had 'removed all inhibitions'. Just as anybody could achieve any position in the party if he only had the abilities, and any position in the state was now open to any German, even the poorest, 'so it is also exactly in the *Wehrmacht*, and not only theoretically any longer and as an exception here or there, but in practice today it is so'.[91] These claims by Hitler were certainly exaggerated again, because in the Army certain barriers were only being removed very hesitantly, despite increased chances for advancement. Officer cadets, for example, still had to have the *Abitur*, and this was only changed during the war.[92] What is essential, however, is that the process of equalization which had been initiated was desired and supported by Hitler. He specifically welcomed that 'the *Wehrmacht* is becoming more national socialist month by month . . . how all privileges, class prejudices and so forth are increasingly being removed.'[93] In a conversation with Mussert, leader of the Dutch National Socialists, Hitler said on 10 December 1942 that he had 'decided to tear down all the social barriers in Germany without compunction, in other words, not the destruction of the so-called upper classes, but only the opening of the possibilities for advancement of the really capable'.[94]

On 17 April 1943 Hitler also talked to the Hungarian Regent Horthy about matters of education. He remarked that in Germany he had a leading social class from whom he could not expect that they would let their children become craftsmen and workers. This leading class was naturally attempting to bring its children into positions of leadership. National Socialism, however, was primarily interested in the children of the great masses, for whom only the Catholic church had previously shown interest for the rejuvenation of its priesthood. The talented children could then move into the positions formerly occupied by the Jews. With the latter remark Hitler wanted to persuade Horthy of the necessity and practical possibilities of proceeding against the Hungarian Jews – a major objective of the conversation – and to make clear to him that, in contrast to variously expressed fears, 'everything would continue as before even without the Jews'.[95] On 30 January 1944 Hitler declared that without doubt at the head of all the achievements of the National Socialist revolution stood the careful and insistent restructuring of the former class state into a new socialist organism as a national state. That in this state every

III. Hitler's Social Objectives

young German could become anything without regard to his birth, his origin, his wealth, the position of his parents, his 'so-called education' and so forth, but only according to his own worth, was 'one of the most decisive deeds of the National Socialist revolution'.[96]

In a speech to generals and officers on 26 May 1944 he described the increase in social mobility as being one way to solve the social question, and again pointed to the example of the Catholic church, which continued to recruit its priests from the people. Hitler then continued:

> With this I first solve the social question by bringing a socially infinitely broad element into the leadership. But secondly I also solve it by putting this leadership together out of the best, most vigorous people and thereby withdrawing any possible starting-point for a counter-revolution from the broad masses right from the beginning, but particularly because they see that this state is not a class state.[97]

It was not without importance for the people to be convinced 'that the leadership is absolutely built up from all of the people', that anybody who was capable can become anything, and 'not that he is artificially confronted with difficulties because of his birth, but on the contrary, that he is helped by the authorities to overcome these difficulties'.[98]

To the Hungarian Minister President Sztójay Hitler remarked on 7 June 1944 that it had been a great blessing for Germany that 'we take the replacements for the officers corps and business out of the ranks of the people'. In Germany, said Hitler, 66 to 67 per cent of the officers corps stemmed from the people. He again pointed to the Catholic church as an example, where a boy from the farm could become a cardinal. The principle had to be to preserve the valuable parts of the old class, but to constantly renew these from below.[99]

At the end of June 1944 Hitler pointed out before leaders of the armaments industry that he had ended the class war in Germany. This had only been possible on the condition that the worker could be convinced he was not being discredited socially, that he was not a second-class citizen 'and that his child, just like your own, for example, could become anything if it only had the ability, that is what is decisive'. It is remarkable that Hitler also voiced these concepts in front of business leaders, and not only at 1 May rallies or in so-called 'workers' speeches'. And here, where he could not expect to achieve any sort of euphoria or propaganda effect with such statements, Hitler admitted:

> I never cared about where he [i.e. a talent—R.Z.] comes from, what his name is, or who he is, who his fathers were, his grandfathers, if he has a pedigree or does not have a pedigree, or if you like, whether he has a fortune or not, or so-called upbringing, or eats with a knife or with a fork – it is all the same to me. If he is able to do the one thing, that is what is decisive . . .[100]

on condition, of course, that he was a member of the 'German national community' as defined by Hitler and not, for example, a Jew. But Hitler did not have to add this, because to him it was self-evident.

In this chapter we have listed numerous quotations,[101] first to document the outstanding importance of the concept of 'equal opportunity' for Hitler's social programme and secondly to demonstrate the consistency of his opinions in this field over a period of 25 years. In closing we would like to quote Otto Dietrich, who, because of his job as Hitler's Reichs Press Chief from 1933 to 1945, was very precisely informed about the *Führer*'s views and concepts. He writes in his memoirs:

> The socialist idea Hitler developed originated with the question: by what system can social justice and the harmony of economic interests best be achieved between people who have been given unequal endowments and dispositions by nature? Hitler's answer was: by means of the principle of socialist achievement, in other words, the most just and at the same time most economic solution is brought about by creating an equality of conditions for economic competition. Therefore he supported equal opportunities for everybody, the abolition of all privileges of birth, status and the monopoly of education, therefore he supported the abolition of income without work, the 'breaking of serfdom to interest' and the de-throning of gold as the 'economic factor without effort'.

Elsewhere Dietrich writes:

> Hitler intended to give this condition of a 'classless national and *Führer* state' created through revolution an immortal validity by means of a functional system of permanent leadership selection. To achieve this, the road for those aspiring to leadership from out of the broad masses had to be cleared of all the barriers of birth and property. There was to be only one monopoly in this state: achievement! Continuously and unhindered, the best and eternally youthful forces were to grow up into the leadership and the pulsating life of the nation from out of the people, in order not only to guarantee the stability of the state but also its constant progress and best possible development.[102]

In this statement by Dietrich, the nature of Hitler's concept becomes very clearly visible. Traditional privileges and class barriers are to be abolished in order to open the way for social advancement for the members of socially lower orders – particularly workers. But this, of course, is not in the sense of a concept for the possible development of the individual, but for the optimal advantage of the 'national community'. Hitler was indifferent to the individual as such, who was only important in his function and usefulness for the German national community, and according to Hitler this was best served if traditional class barriers were removed and all members of the national community were offered the possibility of taking part in the battle for social advancement, defined in terms of socio-Darwinism. On the other hand, of course, it is not true when Dietrich writes that the only principle to rule in the state was that of achievement. On the one hand, only the achievements of members of the German national community were recognized at all, from which parts of the population (the 'racially inferior' such as the 'asocial', gypsies, those afflicted with hereditary diseases, Jews) were excluded, even 'eradicated' by definition, and, on the other, political 'fanaticism' could sometimes compensate for lack of education and genuine achievement because the true basis for any advancement was loyalty to the National Socialist system.

3. Hitler's Position on the Major Classes and Levels of Modern Middle-Class Society

The statements by Hitler quoted in the preceding chapters already provide a clue to his position on the middle class, the working class and the other classes or levels of modern society. But it is necessary to deal with this topic in greater detail, particularly since in literature Hitler's view of the middle class has never been treated or investigated. It is known that Hitler was very critical of, or at least highly ambivalent towards, the middle class. As a rule, however, others have been satisfied with quoting three or four statements by Hitler in order to prove this, and then going on to speculate pseudo-psychologically about the '*petit bourgeois*' motives which so infuriated the '*petit bourgeois*' Hitler against the bourgeoisie. Such speculations, however, remain arbitrary and non-provable.

We intend to follow a different path and have therefore compiled several hundred statements by Hitler on the middle class, classified them according to topics, and put them into systematic contexts. The decisive question, of course, is not *whether* Hitler was critical towards, or took a negative view of, the middle class, but *what* the accusations were that Hitler raised against it and how frequently he raised them, the *reasons* he gave for his criticism, the *degree of regularity* with which the specific accusations recur, how public and private statements on this topic relate to each other, how these statements fit into the context of the other elements of this *Weltanschauung*, and what conclusions he drew. Here, too, it is important first to follow Hitler's thought processes and line of reasoning, because he did clearly attempt to explain the reasons for his anti-bourgeois position. Hitler's statements on the middle class rarely have a purely emotional character and they are rarely simply insults or eruptions of hatred (although, of course, there are such statements); Hitler instead voices specific accusations against the middle class, the content of which is reasoned and rationally comprehensible.

We intend to reconstruct Hitler's position towards the working class, the middle class and the farmers in a similar way. We must note in anticipation, however, that Hitler does not give an exact definition of what he means by 'bourgeoisie', for example, or by 'middle class'. For Hitler's purposes, a scientific definition would have been superfluous, because he was primarily interested in defining the role of the individual social groupings within the framework of his revolutionary strategy and tactics. Therefore he apparently orientated himself towards common usage. When he spoke about 'the bourgeoisie' he meant – as can be seen from the context of his statements – both the property-owning as well as the traditionally educated bourgeoisie; in other words, for him these terms include both the entrepreneurs as well as the intellectuals, even though from their socio-economic position the latter would normally more properly belong to the middle class. Hitler apparently defined 'middle class' to mean the 'old middle classes', primarily independent tradesmen such as shop owners and artisans. When Hitler spoke about the 'working class' he normally meant 'manual labourers', in other words primarily the industrial workers.

a. The Bourgeoisie

Anti-Social Stance, Ignoring the Worker Question, Rejection of Workers' Justified Claims

One of Hitler's most frequently raised accusations against the middle class and the bourgeois parties was that they rejected the justified claims of the working class, had no social feelings, were greedy for profits and were completely ignoring the importance of the social issue. When the bourgeoisie was compelled to make social concessions, then it defined these as 'charity' and not as the natural rights of the working class.[103] Social reforms, said Hitler on 30 November 1920, had been given to the people 'as a present, as a favour, instead of as a natural right':[104]

> It is one of the deeper causes of the hatred of millions of national comrades against these 'upper classes' – who in our opinion, however, are mostly the lowest of the low, because we do not intend to define the level of a human being according to his money bags but according to his character – that rights which they as national comrades, and at least in times of war as recognized, because needed fellow citizens, are entitled to *demand*, are being presented to them as 'favours'. It demonstrates the whole moral decay of our society today, that it does not even begin to comprehend how corrupting such a form of 'welfare' must act upon the truly innocently poor.[105]

Hitler accused the bourgeoisie of being 'stupid, conceited, and without conscience', because it had preferred leaving millions of German workers to the mercies of the 'international bank and stock market Jews', rather than to 'climb down from its imaginary throne and to reach out a brotherly hand to the worker of the fist in recognition of justified human social demands'.[106] In a memorandum prepared on 22 October 1922 he wrote, 'For fifty years the German bourgeoisie has not admitted its obligations towards the masses and has left this nation to the leadership of foreign elements.'[107] The right-wing parties, Hitler asserted on 21 November 1922, had sometimes 'not had the slightest appreciation for the worker',[108] they had not been able 'to allow for the social currents of the times'.[109] On 26 February 1923 he declared that it was 'a heavy guilt of the bourgeoisie not to treat the manual workers as equal fellow citizens, in particular to stem itself against any reduction of the excessively long working hours'.[110]

On 24 April 1923 he again sharply attacked the bourgeoisie because it had ignored the justified demands of the workers:

> And then the bourgeoisie, which was also already Jewified, stemmed itself against the rapping of the masses for an improvement of their living conditions . . . Without the boundless stupidity of our bourgeoisie, the Jew would never have become the leader of the German workers. Stupidity was accompanied by pride, in other words, the 'better people' considered it beneath their dignity to climb down to the 'common herd'. The millions of German national comrades would not have become estranged from their nation if the leading classes had taken care of them.[111]

In *Mein Kampf* Hitler also accused the middle class of having 'taken a position uncountable times against even the most generally accepted human demands in a manner that was both most awkward but also immoral', and thereby themselves having become guilty of politicizing the union movement. The bourgeoisie had driven the workers into the arms of Social Democracy by having rejected every socially justified demand. Hitler wrote of the

> . . . insane manner in which the middle class parties oppose any sort of a social demand. The simply narrow-minded rejection of any attempt to improve working conditions, safety devices on machines, the abolition of child labour, as well as the protection of a woman during the months she is carrying a future national comrade under her heart, all contributed to drive the masses into the nets of Social Democracy, which gladly seized upon each case of such a despicable cast of mind. Never can our 'political bourgeoisie' make up for these sins.

The unions had come into being as necessary protective organizations for the workers, in order to help them in their battle for existence, which they had to fight 'thanks to the greed and short-sightedness of many entrepreneurs'. The bourgeoisie, 'blinded by financial interests', had placed the greatest obstacles in the way of this struggle, and 'not only opposed all the attempts to reduce inhumanely long working hours, to end child labour, to secure and protect women, to improve health conditions in the workshop and the homes, but actually sabotaged them'.[112]

In a speech on 15 July 1925 Hitler accused the middle class of not having had a care for the broad masses of the people for sixty years.[113] On 16 December 1925 he said that the workers had been treated 'as being superfluous' and that nobody had had a care for this politically deprived and economically 'extremely badly situated' class; the bourgeoisie had even 'not understood' the worker at all:

> They had not understood, for example, that the transfer of working hours, which might still have been natural out in the country, to the intensity of a modern factory would within only a few years inevitably confront us with a simple question, namely: do you want to forgo a healthy body for your people from now on or not?

and:

> Our bourgeois parties... unfortunately succumbed to the temptation to confront the fight for existence by this fourth estate by political means in order to oppose demands that cannot even really be regarded as social, but are simply purely human problems. Today when we go back and read what outrageous speeches conservative and so-called national liberal party bigwigs once held on the most basic of human issues, when we hear the nonsensical arguments that were voiced against them – always dressed up in the claim that it was all for the protection of the highest national values – then we can understand how Marxism was able to capture and internationalize these broad masses.

The bourgeoisie had 'even opposed social demands that were ridiculously modest as if demented', without, however, having been able to prevent them, and due to this 'failure on the part of the bourgeois parties in the social area' the Marxist labour movement had then come about.[114]

Hitler frequently accused the bourgeoisie of opposing the justified demand for a reduction of working hours:

> The position of the German bourgeoisie was always the same, in that it opposed these attempts at reform and believed it could turn back the hands of time... Only a few years ago the miners had a nine-hour day and wanted to reduce it to an eight-hour day. The whole bourgeois press took the view that this was impossible. When the miners then went on strike, it went completely wild. Now I know very well that at the time hundreds of thousands of those bourgeois joined in the shouting, but only because they did not know what the real issue was. Had they only gone down under the ground once for eight hours, nay only for four hours, they would have said, no, nobody can stand that.[115]

and:

> Do not deceive yourselves that you are being national when on the one hand you do not see this proletariat, and if you happen to meet one you step aside just like our German bourgeoisie did, so that you do not get greasy or dirty, but on the other hand you say, German work has created this, German diligence.

On festive occasions the German bourgeoisie had recalled this, but it had forgotten the people; it had not cared about them. While social legislation had been enacted, it had only been to prevent a revolution, but 'something was lacking, and the masses clearly felt this, namely the inner heart and the inner soul'.[116]

On 21 March 1928 Hitler asked whether the intention was to uphold the 'isolation of the German worker' for ever and ever. If this were to be the case, then the German intelligentsia might as well leave the political stage,

> ... because it then no longer has a mission. This is what we accuse the bourgeoisie of, that it let itself be pushed into this class corner and for decades did not understand the problems of the fourth estate, until this estate fell into the hands of another intelligentsia. Today the German bourgeoisie is moaning: whose fault is it? Your own, you were glad when this broad mass had nothing to do with you. You only wanted their votes in elections.[117]

Hitler accused the bourgeois parties of not recognizing that it was 'insanity' to believe it was enough only to pay the millions of unemployed their unemployment benefits and otherwise not take any note of them. This was 'the political wisdom of the bourgeoisie':

> These people do not see this, as they once did not see that in their industries a fourth estate was developing which represented a political force and must be given its outlet in political life. So they do not see today that a fifth estate is developing which has to be embraced somehow.[118]

On 24 February 1930 Hitler declared that it had been the 'fatal hour' of the bourgeois parties when

> ... they had not been able to tear the fourth estate, which was growing slowly and was initially only an estate, an occupation, out of their factories and place it into the middle of their political world, had not been able to become the leaders of this working class, but instead looked down on them in a partially wretched conceit, pathetic arrogance, and from a superiority which was never there ... That is the terrible fate, from that moment on begins the decay of the world of our bourgeois parties.[119]

In an article in the *Illustrierte Beobachter* Hitler explained his position towards the metal workers' strike in progress at the time. That the political parties of the German middle class for decades 'had regularly opposed almost all of the economic demands of the working class' had in the end cost them all influence on the working class:

> Many a bourgeois who condemns the worker's striving for an improvement in his economic situation with an outrage that is as unwise as it is unjust would possibly suddenly think completely differently if for only three weeks he would have had laid on his shoulders the burden of the work demanded of the others. Even today there are still countless bourgeois elements who most indignantly reject a demand for a wage of ten marks a month, and especially any sharp support of this, as a 'Marxist crime', but display complete incomprehension when faced with a demand to also limit the excessive profits of certain individuals.[120]

After the seizure of power Hitler still spoke on various occasions about the guilt of the German bourgeoisie for having driven the proletariat into the arms of Marxism by its rejection of all social demands by the workers.[121] In his commemorative speech on the fifteenth anniversary of the *putsch*, he declared that the decisive cause of the division of the classes had been 'the social failure of our middle class'. He could very well understand that at the time

> ... a worker could all too easily err in the selection of his place. Because for him there was hardly any place. The bourgeois world had neither sympathy for him, nor any intention of drawing him closer to it ... Socially, too, the division was unbearable. Conceit and class arrogance so completely ruled one side at the time that it is no wonder that class consciousness finally developed in reaction on the other.[122]

This statement shows that Hitler made the middle class – and not the working class – responsible for the division of the classes. Proletarian class consciousness was for him an understandable reaction to the arrogance and the class conceit of the bourgeoisie, which rejected all justified demands of the workers. In an article Hitler had published in the *Illustrierte Beobachter* on 8 March 1930 he had made the bourgeoisie responsible for the development of the class division. Hitler wrote that while it was a part of economic life that a certain division into occupations or classes developed, this separation was 'harmless' as long as it only expressed itself in terms of diverging economic interests. Only when this division led to a 'political rending of the nation', or even to 'a fissure between *Weltanschauungen*', could one speak of a 'serious, possibly deadly evil'. The bourgeoisie 'had been given an economically structured mass and left a politically torn nation behind ... They can neither refute this fact nor resolve it. The word "bourgeoisie" itself has become a class designation. The rising, initially only economically defined new fourth estate slowly became the politically opposite pole.'[123]

Hitler also sharply attacked the bourgeoisie in his table talks and made it responsible for the development of Marxism and the spread of Communism. On 2 August 1941, for example, he said:

> It is no wonder that Communism had its strongest bulwark in Saxony, and that we only won over the Saxon worker very gradually, and also that he is now one of the most loyal: the bourgeoisie there was of an almost imbecile bigotry. In the eyes of Saxon business we were also Communists; whoever supports a social equality for the masses is a Bolshevist! The sins committed against the Saxon home workers are unimaginable. That was a plutocracy such as in England today. In Saxony the *Wehrmacht* had already detected a gradual decay of the human material. I do not blame any one of the little people that he was a Communist, I can only blame that on the intellectual: he knew that for him the poverty was only a means to an end. If you look at this vermin of a bourgeoisie, you still get red in the face today. The masses followed the only way left open to them. The worker took no part in national life. To the uncovering of a Bismarck memorial, for example, or the launching of a ship, a delegation of workers was never invited; all you saw there was top hats and uniforms. For me the top hat is identical to the bourgeoisie.[124]

Profit Greed, 'Materialism'

Hitler, who was himself a convinced believer in the primacy of politics over economics,[125] told the middle class that its whole way of thinking was 'materialistic', in other words only concerned with economic interests. 'It is the undoing of our bourgeoisie', he declared on 6 March 1927, 'that it confuses its profit greed and social arrogance with a national conviction.'[126] On 26 March 1927 he admonished the middle class that it had no grounds to complain about 'how materialistic our times had become'. This 'materialization' was itself the fault of the middle class: 'Up there there is only one God. His name is materialistic life, and he says: business is everything.'[127] In his 'Second Book' Hitler wrote: 'In fact the German bourgeoisie, and with it the so-called national associations, only think in terms of economic politics. Production, export and import, those are the slogans with which they juggle, and from which they expect the salvation of the nation in the future.'[128] To Wagener Hitler remarked that the 'upper 10,000' were

> ... possessed by a fever to own things, a greed, and an economic ego-centralism that overgrew everything else... Their whole thinking and aspiring only culminates in what it says on the bottom line in their accounts and in the outward display of their wealth in material goods. I feel a revulsion, a bothersome contempt when I observe the lives and doings of these people!

In a conversation with Wagener in the spring of 1932 Hitler said that the industrialists, the mine owners and the larger business enterprises 'know nothing except their profit. "Fatherland" is only a word for them.'[129]

When the workers demanded higher wages the middle class or its press often accused them of 'materialism'. Hitler turned this accusation right back on the middle class. When they said that the common people were 'materialistically inclined', then he answered back,

> . . . you are the same first of all. What sort of idealism do you have? How often during our economic conferences do I hear God knows what kinds of big talk? I know very well you are not prepared to make even the smallest sacrifice; every little SA man is prepared to sacrifice his life for his ideal, from up there you do not even recognize any ideal anymore, dear fellow, you wonder when the other one gives you the same answer, I am only living for the wage, in freedom etc. Then you say, what, you materialist. Yes my boy, you are destroying idealism from the top down.[130]

These accusations also recur in Hitler's table talks. On 24 January 1942 he said, for example, that the bourgeoisie only becomes 'heroic when you step on its money bags'; he was therefore hoping that in England ('seen in terms of capital, the richest country on earth') 'an opinion will prevail which says: there is nothing for us to gain in Europe; we still have 16 billion in debts from the old war, to which a further 200 billion have been added'.[131] On 1 April 1942 he criticized that the German ambassadors, for example in Japan, mainly socialized with the great trading houses, because there 'exactly as with our own petty-minded people, everything is judged from the point of view of the dangers or risks threatening their wallets'.[132]

Criticism of Bourgeois Nationalism

Hitler charged that the middle class equated national interests with their own egoistic class and profit interests. When they spoke of 'nationalism' they actually only meant their own economic class interests. The middle class, he argued on 6 March 1927, had given the term '"national" a very special meaning', and this meaning was 'so narrow and trivial that millions of people were not able to understand this term "national"'. The bourgeoisie calls itself national, and the masses now believe that this term is identical to 'anti-social convictions':

> That person is not a nationalist who says: I sing the national anthem, *Deutschland über alles*, and then I go and make my profit, and next day I get up because there is a greasy chap sitting next to me who has not taken off his blue overalls and I cannot sit down next to that. *Deutschland über alles!* My dear friends! The most terrible enemy of our nationalism is profit greed on the one hand and class arrogance on the other.

Nationalism must not be the enemy of 'the human rights of our own nation' [by this Hitler meant social rights—R.Z.] but 'their greatest proponent in all areas'.[133]

On 23 March 1927 Hitler emphasized that being a nationalist did not mean 'fighting for the comfort of one part of the nation and for the maintenance of a condition'. They were not nationals who 'shout hooray and sing the national anthem while drinking wine, while next door stand the unemployed, or undernourished workers come out of the factory'.[134] In a speech on 26 March 1927 Hitler dissociated himself from the middle-class definition of 'nationalism':

> The bourgeois' definition of nationalism puts the proletarian off, they say, these nationalists have not cared about us, only during elections were we good enough, otherwise we were rabble, they did not take notice of us socially, were contemptuous, spit upon us, we were only able to muddle through miserably and in the end could at best have the honour to defend the Fatherland – look here, this nationalism we reject! So do we! That is not nationalism, the German bourgeoisie does not have a clue what the term 'national' means. All it basically understood was a constitutional, and mostly even only a dynastic, and then also an economic definition, but not a national one.[135]

In a speech made on 6 April 1927 on the subject of 'nationalism and patriotism', Hitler said that middle-class politics had made the term 'national' an object of hatred for the lower classes, because

> ... there this term is synonymous with party structures which regularly opposed the new estate [the workers]. Support for even the least of the class interests was identical to the national concept and was declared to be national policy. With this the undoing of the German nation began, in that today there are 15 to 16 million who categorically reject nationalism because it is identical to the interests of certain bourgeois parties, in other words, certain groups instead of the whole German nation.[136]

On 26 June 1927 Hitler defined the line between himself and bourgeois nationalism and emphasized that the National Socialists had

> ... nothing to do with the hooray shouting of a bygone monarchy, nothing to do with the droning out of songs, but our National Socialist movement is nothing but the recognition of the greatness of the nation ... Not when I support a class am I a nationalist, I am only one completely when I support the whole nation. It is not the greatness of a class or an estate, but the greatness of the whole nation which is important for us.[137]

Alluding to the bourgeoisie, Hitler remarked on 6 August 1927:

> The only thing they see in the national community is a re-insurance contract for the profitability of their own company ... How many of them have truly understood the term 'nation' and the term 'national' in its full meaning? How many of the people on the right have already realized that all of the nationalism to date was superficial, that there is no nationalism without a commitment to the nation, that

it is not nationalism when you sing nationalistic songs and stand by while your nation slowly dies, for example because of unhygienic installations. How many have realized that nationalism requires something one can be proud of, and that you can not be proud of a decayed nation. Each time I drive through Thuringia and Saxony and see these deteriorated people, this wretched proletariat, that was ... ... then I am always conscious of the sin that was committed here and I ask myself why nobody ever really gave it any thought.[138]

Hitler criticized the 'bourgeois view of the world' in which nationalism was tied to 'economic concepts', 'dynastic concepts', 'concepts of legitimacy' and 'class concepts'.[139] On 18 October 1928 he declared that a nationalist could only be someone who did not want to belong to a class but who concentrated all his devotion on the 'definition of the nation in itself', on all the people. With this 'the term "national"' is separated from all the superficial hooray shouting, from all specific economic concepts etc.'[140] In the old Germany the term 'national', said Hitler on 6 March 1929, was 'too much attached to a thousand trivial matters which originally had nothing at all to do with this term'. The term had already declined to a 'class term' or an 'economic term'.[141] In his manifesto for the 1929 *Reichsparteitag* Hitler announced that the reason the term 'national' had not become a commonly shared value of the German nation but rather a divisive slogan was certainly not only the fault of Marxism. Just as much to blame were the existing national parties, 'who have not been able to lift this term above the narrow point of view of class and economic interests, and have rather let the nation go under, than to create the social conditions, often even by only very minor concessions, for a generally accepted definition of nationalism'. This 'neglect of social obligations which was excused with economic necessities' later led to the collapse of the Reich, to economic catastrophe.[142] In a speech on 5 November 1930 Hitler argued that when the term 'nationalism' was attached to the belief in the monarchy, to a certain social order or to a specific economic order, then it was made 'unbearable ... for the whole'; this term could never become a practicable foundation for the totality of the nation.[143]

How Hitler himself defined the term 'nationalism' will be treated in Chapter VII.2. In this context it is important that he accused the bourgeoisie of identifying its own egoistic economic interests with the national interest and thereby discrediting the term 'national' in the minds of the broad masses.

Middle Class Parties: No Weltanschauung, Only Fighting for Seats in Parliament
It was of decisive importance for Hitler that politics be aligned to a *Weltanschauung*. As we have already seen in Chapter II.3. ('Hitler's Definition of

Revolution'), he drew the line strictly between parties and movements rooted in a *Weltanschauung*, among which – besides his own National Socialist movement – he actually only included the Communists and the Italian Fascists, and parties completely lacking in any such foundation. The bourgeoisie and the bourgeois parties, as Hitler frequently declared, had no idea, no truly programmatic objectives, no *Weltanschauung*. In his view therefore, they were completely incapable of fighting against Marxism, because, he said on 14 October 1923, 'you can not get rid of Marxism by an administrative ban, for example, you can only get rid of one *Weltanschauung*, and that is what this is, by giving the masses a new *Weltanschauung*. I can only take their God away from the people if I can give them something of full value in exchange.'[144] Hitler therefore believed that Bismarck's laws against socialism had to fail, if for no other reason than because 'an idea that millions greedily suck in cannot be destroyed by force if the sword is not simultaneously the bearer of a new stirring concept'.[145] One could

> ... not take the false idol of Marxism away from the people without giving them a better God. Therefore the laws against socialism of a Bismarck had to fail if success was not achieved in filling the vacuum which had to occur for millions after Marxism had been destroyed. Because, really and truly, only a political child would be able to hope that the workers, once relieved of Marxism, in other words liberated from a proletarian class point of view, would have nothing better to do than to rush to join the ranks of the bourgeois parties, in other words other class or estate organizations.[146]

Hitler also repeated this idea – namely that a *Weltanschauung* can never only be done away with by governmental force but only through another *Weltanschauung* – in several places in *Mein Kampf*,[147] and he accused the bourgeoisie of not representing or having 'any *Weltanschauung* at all'.[148]

In his early speeches Hitler had ridiculed the middle-class parties because they were not fighting for a great idea but only for seats in the cabinet:

> And the parties on the right? Their only aspiration, their highest objective, is the worn-out leather armchair of a minister. For once in their lives to grace one as an 'Excellency', once to be able to sit there free from any attack, not to be subject to any criticism under the umbrella of the Law for the Protection of the Republic – that is the object of all their desires![149]

In a speech on 16 December 1925 Hitler asked:

> What are these bourgeois parties fighting for? They are fighting for new good election weather, for a successful election, in other words for seats in parliament, and so their programme is also nothing more than election slogans... Even leaving aside the divisive term 'bourgeois', what we see before us in the way of middle-class parties is already incapable of opposing the *Weltanschauung* of Marxism because

these parties really are nothing but parties, only fight for party objectives and do not embody a *Weltanschauung*.[150]

On 11 September 1926 Hitler remarked that while Marxism as a *Weltanschauung* was pursuing an objective and was leading people to believe in a paradise in some distant future, the 'bourgeois world in itself had no image of the future to show'. Therefore the bourgeois parties were unable to draw their adherents a picture that was worthy of the ultimate commitment. They were only fighting to win elections'; all they knew was

> ... only one political programme and that said, 'to be allowed to take part', yes, to be able to take part at any price, at the risk of any shamelessness ... today's bourgeois world no longer recognizes a political objective that goes beyond the attempt to take part, in other words to also deceive our people.[151]

The German bourgeoisie, said Hitler on 26 March 1927, did not have a programme, a *Weltanschauung*. It only fought 'in order to be able to take part in the government, in order to get closer to being in clover and sharing in the feast'. The bourgeois parties had nothing to offer besides slogans about 'law and order'.[152] In his 'Second Book' he wrote that the 'bourgeois world' had 'never had an own idea, but rather immeasurable conceit and money. With only this, however, one cannot overcome a world, nor build another one. Therefore the period in history of bourgeois rule will be as short as it is indecently wretched.'[153]

If one looked at the bourgeois party programme of 1918–19, all one could say was, 'how pathetic'. Here a *Weltanschauung* had won, and the opponents presented such a 'minute, little, superficial programme of the day'.[154] Basically, said Hitler on 24 February 1929, the national opposition since 1918 had already 'been nothing but a very naked jealousy about seats in parliament and cabinet positions'. The bourgeois opposition parties in 1918–19 had 'not had any sort of objective for the future'.[155] In an article in the *Illustrierte Beobachter* on 12 October 1929 Hitler criticized 'the inner half-heartedness and worthlessness of a social class', the bourgeoisie, 'whose thinking is only dominated by the point of view of utilitarianism, and who therefore fundamentally deny and reject principles'.[156]

In essence, Hitler was convinced of the superiority of Marxism over the bourgeoisie. On 20 November 1929 he wrote in the *Völkische Beobachter* that if the bourgeois business parties were not able to do Marxism any harm, this was only natural:

> The bourgeoisie in truth has no damned reason for looking down on the proletarian with conceit. Despite all the Marxist brain contamination, he is still not as politically stultified as is the great mass of the German middle class. As a base for

his political activities he has a *Weltanschauung* he believes in, be it ever so insane ... If today one half of their adherents were to leave the Marxist parties for whatever reason, still not even one per cent of them would land in the bourgeois camp! Today it really only attracts the weakest of the weak. I can understand any Social Democrat's or any Communist's inner abhorrence of the bourgeois parties. And if I were not a National Socialist, since I could never be a Marxist, I could not belong to any political party at all![157]

Three days later Hitler published another article in the *Illustrierte Beobachter*, in which he declared that the bourgeois parties, who liked to define themselves in terms of economics, were bound to fall apart the moment 'the next best swindler appears with an even better economic programme. *Weltanschauung* plays no role with these parties.' One of the main evils of which the bourgeois parties were one day going to die was the 'lack of any firm *Weltanschauung*'.[158] And on 4 January 1930 Hitler wrote – again in the *Illustrierte Beobachter* – that the bourgeois parties were 'at best only fighting for their place at the feeding trough. The lack of any concept, any *Weltanschauung* and any ideal makes them incapable from the very beginning of measuring themselves against Marxism.'[159] In a speech commemorating the tenth anniversary of the proclamation on the 25-point programme, Hitler sharply attacked the bourgeois parties: they had 'no ideals, were only fighting for "law and order" and economic recovery' and had no objectives (except the resurrection of the past), and all this was the result of 'a lack of any *Weltanschauung*'.[160]

From his view that the bourgeois parties had no *Weltanschauung*, Hitler derived important considerations for his strategy and tactics. For this reason alone he never really took the middle class seriously as a political opponent, as opposed to Marxism. In the final analysis, even during the Second World War, he saw Bolshevism as being the far more dangerous opponent, because – like National Socialism – it was fighting for a *Weltanschauung*, for a great idea.[161]

Hitler believed that in situations of crisis people looked for firm holds, for a political belief. The problems of daily life the middle-class parties worried about were secondary for Hitler and his propaganda. He emphasized this time and again in his speeches.[162] The commonly expressed opinion that Hitler had told everybody what he wanted to hear and promised everybody everything[163] cannot be upheld. On the contrary, what separated Hitler from the bourgeois parties was precisely that he proclaimed a *Weltanschauung* and never tired of repeating that he 'had no promises' to make.[164]

'Weakness, Lack of Decisiveness, Lack of Energy, Cowardice'
For Hitler two terms belonged indissolubly together – 'bourgoisie' and 'cowardice'. There is hardly a speech, or even a remark, by Hitler about the bourgeoisie

where he does not accuse it of 'cowardice'. Only a systematic analysis of all of Hitler's statements and an insight into his socio-Darwinistic world of thought make it possible to understand the meaning and importance of this accusation of 'cowardice'.

Initially one could assume that this was only another of the usual, emotionally determined insults. Hitler also accused the bourgeoisie of 'stupidity', for example, and of having a 'lack of ability';[165] called the middle class parties 'naïve' and 'without instinct'[166] and 'decayed',[167] and accused them of being 'capable of any nastiness';[168] and called the bourgeoisie 'socially misbegotten'[169] and expressed his 'revulsion'[170] and his 'contempt'[171] of the bourgeoisie.

The accusations of cowardice, lack of energy and lack of decisiveness, as well as of 'weakness', however, occur far more frequently in Hitler's statements over 25 years, and these accusations have a totally different and very important meaning. In order to understand this meaning we have to put ourselves into Hitler's socio-Darwinistically moulded concept of life, in which terms such as 'daring' and 'courage' on the one hand, and 'cowardice' or 'weakness' on the other, play a key role. 'People who prove themselves in battle,' said Hitler on 17 June 1927, 'who make use of the courage and abilities with which nature has endowed them, they should live and the other one should die.'[172] On 5 October 1929 he wrote in the *Illustrierte Beobachter* that life was nothing but a 'game of hazards', and many nations had gone under because of a 'lack of courage' or 'cowardice'.[173] In a speech on 20 May 1937 Hitler declared:

> Because this is very sure, on earth we first have the law of selection, and the one who is stronger and healthier has been granted the right to live by nature. And that is just. Nature does not recognize the weakling, the coward, it does not recognize the beggar and so forth, nature only recognizes him who stands firmly on his ground, who sells his life and sells it dearly, and not him who gives it away. That is the eternal law of life.'[174]

In a secret speech on 23 November 1937 Hitler said that 'daring' and 'courage' were the decisive criteria for recruiting an élite,[175] and on 6 September 1938 he said at the *Reichsparteitag* that 'for the political leader as well, and thereby also for the whole political leadership of a nation, firmness of character, the strong heart, the audacious bravery, the highest joy in responsibility, relentless determination, and the most tenacious persistence are more important than an alleged abstract knowledge!'[176]

In his table talks he said on 4 April 1942 that only 'brave' and only 'very courageous' men could obtain leadership of the state. 'Because among the lower levels of society life itself carries out a hard process of selection, and so these classes display a stone-hard ruthlessness towards a cowardly leadership.' Firmness of character was worth more to him than anything else.[177]

The decisive importance the accusation of 'cowardice' had for Hitler and which he so frequently made against the bourgeoisie becomes clear in this context. 'Cowardice' for him was synonymous with the inability to cope with life, lack of energy and determination led to failure in the socio-Darwinistically defined fight for survival and weakness necessarily had to lead to downfall. For Hitler this applies to whole nations as well as to individuals or social classes. We will see later that for Hitler the accusation of 'cowardice' consistently led to the conclusion that the historic mission of the bourgeoisie had ended, that it was incapable of political leadership and had to pass this on to a new élite. Before we go on to explore this line of reasoning, however, we intend first to show how frequently the accusation of a 'cowardly bourgeoisie' was raised in Hitler's speeches, writings and articles.

Hitler accused the bourgeois parties of the 'cowardly stupidity of sheep'[178] and polemized against the 'whole decayed party clique which calls itself national and is only cowardly'.[179] The slogans of the right-wing parties were 'carefully cowardly', Hitler wrote in a letter of 27 October 1921.[180] On 23 January 1922 he wrote in an article:

> A bunch of cowardly bourgeois shits, shouting hooray with their big mouths, but in reality shaking at the sight of any petty bully, prepared to move over to any new foundation of facts every second day ... That was really some bourgeois society, which fearfully counted votes and clung to mandates while whimpering about the democratic determination of our fate, without realizing that in the hands of cowards even a numerical majority is in practice a minority, because a minority of energy never worries about a majority of numbers, when the minority of numbers is the majority of energy.

Whereas Marxism emanated 'the most brutal confidence in victory', the bourgeoisie was possessed of an 'almost slimy cowardice'. It was therefore the duty of the National Socialists to wage 'first of all a war against the unbelievable cowardice, the weakness which outwardly normally disguised itself by the bashful term of a "nobly bourgeois", well-mannered, highly decent and "scientifically profound" manner of fighting'.[181] The nation, said Hitler on 25 October 1922, was split into two camps, 'the left-wing radicals and the cowardly mass of the bourgeois majority, who can simply never set its cowardice against the brutal force of the Left'.[182] 'Opposed to the bourgeoisie, as a caste by itself, without any connection to the people and in cowardice and dull indifference, stands the deliberate destroyer who drives us to insanity, and who wants the insanity of destruction' – in other words international Marxism.[183] On 24 April 1923 Hitler said that the right-wing parties were 'lacking in energy in the extreme': 'Unspeakably incapable, lacking in energy, and cowardly in addition are all these bourgeois parties at a moment when the nation would not need blatherers but heroes. There is nothing to be expected from that side.'[184]

In *Mein Kampf* Hitler also accused the middle class of cowardice. There was no serious opposition to be expected from that side to a future forceful national domestic and foreign policy: 'Even if in the hour of a coming liberation the German bourgeoisie were to remain in its passive resistance for the well-known bigoted short-sighted reasons, as it once did towards Bismarck, in view of its proverbial cowardice an active resistance is never to be feared.' At various places in his book Hitler makes fun of the bourgeois rallies and meetings:

> Now you have to have seen one of these bourgeois meetings, have experienced the leadership of the meeting in all its wretchedness and fear! Often in the face of such a threat [from the Marxist side to storm the meeting—R.Z.] the meeting was even cancelled. But the fear was always so great that instead of at eight o'clock, it was rarely before a quarter to nine, or even nine o'clock that they got under way. By making ninety-nine compliments the chairman then attempted to make it clear to the 'gentlemen of the opposition who were present' how overjoyed he and everybody else was (a barefaced lie!) about the attendance by men who were not already of their persuasion, because it was only through discussion (which he thereby officially guaranteed right from the beginning) that opinions could be brought closer together, mutual understanding awakened and a bridge built. As an aside, he also assured that it was in no way the intention of the meeting to make people give up their present convictions. Truly not – everyone had to work out his own salvation, but also to let the other one find his salvation, and he would therefore like to request that the speaker be permitted to finish his remarks – which were not going to be very long anyway – and not to offer the world the shameful spectacle of German brotherly hatred at this meeting as well . . . Brrr!

Elsewhere in his book Hitler writes: 'The cowardly bourgeoisie was correctly assessed in this by Marxism, and simply treated *en canaille*. No attention was paid to it at all, knowing that dog-like devotion of the political formations of an old outdated generation would never be capable of resistance.'[185]

In a speech on 'National Socialism and Culture Policy', Hitler accused the bourgeoisie of cowardice in front of 'Jewish art':

> Because what we are experiencing today is the capitulation of the intellectual bourgeoisie before impudent Jewish composers, would-be poets, painters, who present our nation with pathetic filth and who have reached the point where from sheer cowardice nobody dares any longer to say: we do not want that, away with this garbage.[186]

III. Hitler's Social Objectives

In his 'Second Book', in which he explains the reasons for National Socialism's renunciation of South Tirol, he wrote that South Tirol was 'lost through the wretched cowardice of the national bourgeois parties and national formations who capitulated everywhere before the terror of nastiness and malice'. In their 'proverbial incapability and their cowardice which rang to the heavens', the bourgeois parties had 'not only done nothing to allay the hands of the destroyers of the German future, but on the contrary, by the incapability of their leadership in domestic and foreign policy, they have actually aided and abetted these enemies of our nation'. He could 'stand the yapping of these cowardly bourgeois curs as well as that of the national formation intriguers all the more calmly', because he 'knew all too well the average craven cowards within these structures so unspeakably revolting for me'. Elsewhere he wrote that the 'bourgeois stupidity and indecent lack of convictions, greed for money, and cowardice' drove the worker into the hands of Jewish Marxism.[187] On 28 September 1929 Hitler wrote in the *Illustrierte Beobachter* that while Marxism was 'an embodiment of criminality, the bourgeois parties were that of cowardly, indecent baseness. A general calling to account of Marxism is unthinkable without a ruthless destruction of the corpses of the bourgeois parties.'[188] In another article Hitler expressed his hope that 'the conviction of the inability of the current political leadership of our bourgeoisie' be carried into ever larger circles, 'that ever more people recognize how impossible it is to save the nation from its downfall under these pathetic parliamentarian weaklings'. The 'stupid mass of sheep of our pathetic bourgeoisie' was submitting without opposition to the Marxist terror.[189]

When Hitler accuses the bourgeoisie of cowardice towards Marxism, this should not be understood to mean that Hitler was criticizing the middle classes because of their indulgence towards the labour movement or the justified demands of the workers. The opposite is true. As we have seen, one of Hitler's key accusations against the bourgeoisie was that it rejected the justified demands of the worker and took an anti-social position, opposed a reduction of working hours and so forth. Hitler always differentiated between the problems of the working class on the one hand and political Marxism or Communism on the other. He regarded the latter as being 'Jewish agencies' who were only 'instrumentalizing' the justified claims of the working class, in order to gain the workers for themselves, who, as we shall see,[190] embodied strength, courage and energy for Hitler, as opposed to the bourgeoisie. Contrary to the accepted Marxist interpretation, Hitler was not an opponent of Marxism and did not want to destroy it because he was 'inimical to labour' but because he was caught up in the insane idea that Marxism was an instrument of the Jews for the achievement of world domination, and above all because he rejected internationalism, 'pacifism' and the negation of the 'personality principle' by Marxism. Otherwise, however, as we shall see in Chapter VII.3.c, he had quite an ambivalent position towards Marxism, because – quite differently from the bourgeoisie – he admired it in many ways and learned from it.

These differentiations are important because a superficial interpretation could lead to the conclusion that Hitler had accused the bourgeoisie of cowardice towards the working class and intended to motivate it to take a firmer position against it. Such a conclusion can only be reached by someone who unreservedly identifies the interests of the worker with Marxism or Communism, something Hitler – and the issue here is exclusively his own self-understanding and concepts – never did.

There is another thesis expounded by the dogmatic Marxist theory about Fascism which cannot be upheld: that in public, in his speeches, Hitler expressed himself critically about the bourgeoisie and took an anti-bourgeois position, but only for demagogic and propaganda reasons. This opinion is easy to refute, because in his table talks Hitler expressed himself even more frequently, more vehemently and more pronouncedly anti-bourgeois than in his public speeches, which were, admittedly, primarily designed for their propaganda effect. On 5 September 1941, for example, he said: 'In those days I had been so revolted by the cowardice and narrow-mindedness of the bourgeoisie that even today, when the bourgeoisie is pursuing me from reasons of opportunism, I am still fed up. Without my adherents from among the people I would have given up on the German nation.'[191] In another of his table talks he said that during the time of struggle he had conceived 'such a contempt ... for the bourgeoisie'. When a bourgeois occasionally donated 100 or 200 marks he 'thought no end of what a marvellous thing he had done'. It was the little people, however, who had made the real sacrifices: 'All day at work, at night on the road for us, and always risking their neck. In those days politics was made in the street, I looked for people without a collar; a bourgeois with a stand-up collar would have been able to destroy me, everything already won.' Certainly there had also been 'fanatics' among the bourgeoisie, but 'the bourgeois during our time of struggle were all only aesthetics'.[192]

On 27 January 1942 Hitler underlined the importance of 'strength' as opposed to only 'brain' and declared: 'The social class which is only brain finds itself burdened by a sort of bad conscience. When revolutions really come about, it does not dare to step forward, it trusts in the money bags and is cowardly'.[193] After his bad experiences with his bourgeois allies, for example in 1923, he had said to himself: 'Never ... will I ever do something together with bourgeois!'[194] In view of the bourgeois position on the Jewish question, Hitler said in a table talk on 4 April 1942, 'Cowardice, thy name is bourgeoisie.'[195] And on 5 August 1942 he declared: 'When I read the history of the Fascist revolution, it seems to me that I am reading the history of the movement. The same cowardly and lazy bourgeoisie that did not believe in anything, avoided any conflict, always lived in fear of antagonizing the Reds!'[196] Even during the war Hitler often drew analogies with the time of struggle and compared the cowardly bourgeois parties with the enemy countries Britain and the United States, and the German Communists with the Bolshevists:

> Just as the cowardly bourgeois compromise parties were once first manoeuvred into a corner by the Bolshevist world and then swept aside, so today will the bourgeois states disappear, whose bigoted representatives believe they can close a deal with the devil in the hope of being more clever than he is satanic. It is a dreadful repetition of the former domestic German event on the gigantic global political level of today's events.[197]

The statements we have quoted[198] demonstrate the meaning the accusation of cowardice had for Hitler and the consistency with which he tied together the terms 'bourgeoisie' and 'cowardice'. The accusations of 'weakness', 'lack of decisiveness' and 'lack of energy' which Hitler raised almost as frequently were of a similar nature. These accusations can also be traced through all of the 25 years of Hitler's political activities. To cite only a few examples: on 12 April 1922 he said that the actions by the bourgeois right-wing parties were 'extraordinarily petty, narrow-minded, hesitant and timid. They would like to, but they never find the determination for a great deed, because they simply do not comprehend the greatness of the times.'[199] On the bourgeois side, said Hitler in a memorandum prepared on 22 October 1922, not only the recognition of the essential nature of the conflict between two *Weltanschauungen* going on today was lacking, but above all also 'the unbridled determination, therefore the brutal colossus of power on the one side is faced on the other in part by the most pathetic inability'.[200] In a speech on 20 April 1923, in other words during the French occupation of the Ruhr, Hitler elaborates that today the proletariat was

> ... outwardly a pacifist and inwardly a terrorist; the bourgeois, on the other hand, wants to appear as a terrorist to the outside, while inside he is a pacifist. And even less can be expected of someone who is inwardly fundamentally a pacifist than from the contrary. All they do is talk: 'One must', but the determination to act, for the deed, is lacking. Has the bourgeoisie become tighter, more derring-do since 1918? In order to find an answer to this, all one needs to do is to go into the Diet on a half-way empty stomach. Because there sits the élite of the bourgeoisie. Inwardly they have all become democrats. Just as before, they still worship the dead pile of the dead number. They are incapable of recognizing what is necessary and what must be done. Law and order or united front is the ultimate expression

of their political wisdom. With this, however, they are ruining the state. In this law and order they are all cheating each other as best they know how.[201]

For this accusation as well, namely that the bourgeoisie was without energy and strength, weak and lacking in determination, many further instances could be listed.[202]

What had caused this cowardice, weakness, lack of strength and energy according to Hitler's opinion? Hitler believed that as an *ownership class* the bourgeoisie had too much to lose and was therefore cowardly and incapable of exercising political power. In *Mein Kampf* Hitler criticized Schönerer because he had not recognized 'the extreme restrictions on the will to fight of the so-called "bourgeois" circles, already because of their economic position, which makes the individual fear losing far too much and therefore holds him back'.[203] Before the Hamburg National Club of 1919, a decidedly bourgeois audience, Hitler argued that whoever had to preserve material possessions will 'never place his life at risk as easily as he who has no material possessions to preserve ... he who has no possessions dies more readily than he who possesses an estate'.[204] On 21 March 1928 Hitler elaborated: Marxism had

> ... the more determined human material. The vitality, audacity and determination can only be looked for in the German manual labourer, it has been like this at all times. As soon as a person gains possessions, he shifts the focus of his life, concentrates more on the given reality ... A movement which intends to reform Germany can only win over a fraction of the German bourgeoisie.[205]

The consistency – or, if one prefers, the cynicism – with which Hitler thought this concept out to its conclusion is demonstrated in some of the remarks he made at the end of 1943 and the beginning of 1944, when he was even able to discover a positive aspect in the destruction of German cities by the Allies. On 2 September 1943, for example, he said in a conversation with the Romanian state leader Antonescu, 'The belief of the enemy that Germany can be worn down and softened up by the air attacks is a mistake. The opposite is probably more true. This is again a proof that people who no longer own anything fight more fanatically than bourgeois with possessions.'[206]

Let us summarize here: Hitler accuses the bourgeoisie of weakness, lack of willpower and determination, lack of energy and, above all, cowardice. As the reason for these traits, he gives the material possessions of the bourgeoisie, the fact that this class has something to lose. We have already indicated that out of his fundamentally socio-Darwinistic position Hitler necessarily had to come to the conclusion that the bourgeoisie was incapable of political leadership, and that its historic mission had ended. Was Hitler prepared to draw these conclusions?

Inability to Provide Political Leadership

Elsewhere in this study we will portray Hitler's ideas on the recruitment of an élite.[207] Here we must, however, anticipate one aspect of these ideas because this is necessary in our context. Hitler believed the principles of élite recruitment in business and politics to be contradictory, in other words traits which were advantageous for becoming a great business leader were not only useless in politics but even harmful. According to Hitler, the mistake of the capitalist social structure was that the business élite was simultaneously also the political élite.

For the political field, said Hitler on 26 June 1931,

> ... economic achievement does not provide even the smallest measure of degree or value. Here there are completely different virtues. The lowliest soldier at the front who lets himself be shot to death has this virtue to a far greater degree than a great factory owner who will prevent the sacrifice of his own ego and avoid it. For the cowards, the factory owner is the right man, but for the political leadership of the nation the other one is right.[208]

In a speech to the German Labour Front on 10 May 1933, Hitler discussed the principal reasons which had led to the development of the labour movement. As one of these reasons he named the class character of the bourgeois state, in other words the fact that the economic leadership had developed also into the power élite, even though it lacked all the necessary abilities for this:

> This democratization led to the state first falling into the hands of certain social classes who identified themselves with material possessions, with being employers. The broad masses increasingly got the feeling that the state itself was not an objective institution standing above mundane matters, above all that it no longer embodied an objective authority, but that the state itself was the product of the economic desires and the business interests of certain groups within the nation, and that the leadership of the state also justified such a claim. The victory of the political bourgeoisie was after all nothing more than the victory of a social class which had developed out of the laws of business, which for its part did not fulfil even the most minor conditions for a genuine political leadership, and which, above all, made political leadership dependent on the constantly fluctuating conditions of economic life and the effects of this economic life in the areas of the influencing of the masses, the preparing of public opinion and so forth. In other words, the people quite rightly had the feeling that in all sectors of life there was a natural selection going on, always dependent on the suitability for this particular sector of life, except in one sector: in the sector of political leadership. In this sector of political leadership one suddenly turned to that result of a selection which owed its existence to a completely different process.

Slowly the opinion had spread that 'membership in a certain class of life which had developed out of the laws of business also simultaneously held the political capabilities of governing a nation. We have seen the consequences of this error. The class which arrogated this political leadership to itself failed in every critical situation, and in the darkest hour of the nation it broke apart pathetically.'[209]

At the close of the National Socialist leadership conference on 16 June 1933 Hitler expounded the same line of argument. The reason why no political leadership had developed in Germany so far was 'that the previous century increasingly entrusted the political leadership to a social class which developed out of business successes'. Political ability, however, was something quite different from capabilities in the business area. The political leadership had been given to a class 'which because of its purely business determination not only possessed no abilities in the political area and, quite to the contrary, constantly proved that it was particularly incapable in this field'. During this century the state had been almost exclusively governed according to the maxims by which corporations are managed.[210]

One of the deficiencies of the research on Hitler is that, even though he developed them quite clearly in several places, it did not take notice of these lines of reasoning which are crucial to his view of the world, and particularly for his criticism of the bourgeoisie. We therefore intend to cite Hitler relatively extensively on this. In his closing address to the *Reichsparteitag* in 1933 he said:

> The moment when the bourgeoisie as a new class claimed and received the political leadership of the nation, any sensible organic development in the most important area was interrupted. The German bourgeoisie as a social substance was the product of a selection process based less on political than on business functions. With the introduction of money and property as the measure for a certain evaluation within the citizenship, the liberal age had produced a social class which equated to its essential nature.

Not in any way were 'heroic or hero-like attributes' required for membership in this class. 'Yes, quite on the contrary: since business life normally has more unheroic than heroic attributes, the German bourgeoisie was also far less heroic than just "business-like".' Here we find the connection to what we have already explored – heroism; in other words, for Hitler bravery and courage were the key attributes of a political leadership and in his view these were what the bourgeoisie was totally lacking. For him it was therefore a paradox to offer the political leadership of the nation to a class that was particularly distinguished for its cowardice:

> But by virtue of the fact that the German bourgeoisie claimed the political leadership of the nation, a social class *never* born for this task introduced itself to the people as their leaders. Since our new social class had developed from business functions, it could not be assumed that the capability for political leadership was

III. Hitler's Social Objectives

in any way necessarily identical to the social position of the individual German. In other words, just as many people from economically, and therefore socially, inferior levels could be qualified as leaders of the nation, as, vice-versa, numerous members of the highest, particularly business-wise or financially determined social circles had to be rejected.[211]

Here the line of reasoning developed in the preceding chapter on 'equal opportunity' comes full circle. As in many other places, it becomes clear that what Nolte, Jäckel and others have discovered about Hitler's general *Weltanschauung* is also true for his social and economic concepts: an inner logic, a consistency and stringency of the arguments developed cannot be denied, regardless of how one may assess these. Furthermore, we can detect a continuity in Hitler's concepts. The statements quoted above could be extended to include many more, all the way up to a speech Hitler gave in 1944.[212] The final conclusion Hitler drew out of all the premises developed here, in other words out of his conviction of the cowardice of the bourgeoisie, its incapability of political leadership and so forth, is:

The Bourgeoisie's Political Mission Has Ended
In *Mein Kampf* Hitler wrote:

> Our present bourgeoisie has already become worthless for any grand task of mankind, simply because it is without quality, is too bad; and it is too bad, less because of – if you like – *deliberate* badness, than as the result of an unbelievable indolence and everything that results therefrom. Therefore those political clubs which meander about under the common designation of 'bourgeois parties' have for a long time been nothing but interest groups of certain professions and classes, and their most solemn duty is no longer anything but the egoistic pursuit of their interests.

This, and further quotations from *Mein Kampf*, are variously used in the literature as proof of Hitler's anti-middle class position. But they are simply taken as expressions of Hitler's possibly socio-psychologically interpretable, more emotional than rational 'anti-position' against the middle class, without an attempt really to analyze the content of his statements in the context of his overall view of the world. In the statement quoted above, for example, Hitler gives 'its unbelievable indolence', in other words its lethargy, as the *reason* why the bourgeoisie 'has already become worthless for any grand task of mankind'. Here again, however, the line of argument comes full circle. Based on his socio-Darwinistic philosophy, for Hitler the 'indolent', 'weak' or 'cowardly' individuals, nations or social classes no longer have any right to exist – they are 'worthless'. What is interesting is that in *all* of the passages in *Mein Kampf* in which Hitler speaks about the ending of the historic mission of the bourgeoisie,

143

he gives 'weakness and cowardice' as the reasons. Thus also in the following quotation, often cited in the literature, 'One really cannot say what is more pronounced in this bourgeois world, the feeble-mindedness, the weakness and cowardice or the out-and-out shabby cast of mind. This is really a class fate has condemned to go under, but which unfortunately is pulling a whole nation into the abyss with it.' Only a few paragraphs further down Hitler writes: 'Then I realized in the depth of my being that the German bourgeoisie was at the end of its mission and not called upon for any further task.'[213]

While these excerpts from *Mein Kampf* are widely known, it is less well known that in dozens of further speeches and conversations Hitler made similar statements, all the way through to 1945. The view that the middle class was decadent, that its social order was ripe for collapse and that it was at the end of its historic mission, are constants in Hitler's *Weltanschauung*, especially since they follow logically from certain premises of his thinking and were expounded by him independently of specific occasions or considerations of propaganda. In the following we will only cite a few of the statements that point in this direction.

Hitler diagnosed a 'gradual decay of our present bourgeois world'[214] and called this world 'a manifestation of the past'.[215] In his speeches he spoke of the 'decadence' and the 'downfall of the German bourgeoisie';[216] the bourgeois parties for him were 'corpses... who were too bad to live and yet could not die like bad cats'.[217] In his 'Second Book' Hitler prophesied that 'in the history of the world the period of bourgeois government will be as short as it will be indecently pathetic'.[218] In a speech on 10 October 1928 he declared that 'the whole bourgeois-national world is really a failure, is ripe for its downfall',[219] and about two weeks later he said the bourgeois parties were all becoming 'weaker and weaker and will slowly die' – they had to pass away because they had become 'without strength'.[220] On 9 March 1929 Hitler wrote in the *Illustrierte Beobachter*: 'The political collapse of our German middle class is really taking on glorious forms. Never before has a social class gone under in such an almost orgiastic stupidity.'[221] In another article, in which he explained his position on the issue of granting Trotsky political asylum in Germany, he wrote that the German bourgeoisie did not deserve any better, but 'the Jews were to set its house on fire... If Trotsky comes to Germany, for me this would only be the confirmation that fate has ruthlessly and ultimately decided on the destruction and removal of a social class whose rule dragged Germany from its highest peak into deepest misery. The National Socialist movement does not fear impending developments.'[222] The German bourgeoisie, said Hitler on 12 October 1929 in the *Illustrierte Beobachter*, would be removed by political developments; 'And we will also only fully realize in the future that this was the

III. Hitler's Social Objectives

greatest good fortune for our nation!'[223] On 7 December 1929 Hitler said during a rally, 'When the bourgeoisie failed to force the millions of proletarians into the service of the national idea, it had played out its political role, let the fate of Germany slip out of its hand.'[224] On 4 January 1930 he wrote in the *Illustrierte Beobachter* that

> ... the political German bourgeoisie has developed into one of the greatest curses of the German nation. Had the revolution of 1918 only sent the bourgeois parties to the devil instead of the nobility, the German nation could ultimately have honestly thanked Marxism, because for the German nation today the old Roman proverb, in an amended wording, applies more than ever before: Lord protect Germany from its friends of the bourgeois parties, one way or the other it will then be able to deal with its Marxist enemies!'[225]

On 28 June 1930 Hitler wrote in the *Illustrierte Beobachter* that the bourgeois parties and their men 'were capable of any nastiness', that everything 'the bourgeois parties put their hands on' goes under. 'Were Bolshevism not out to destroy the best racial élite, but only to clean out the bourgeois party vermin, one would almost be tempted to bless it'.[226] In similar vein to what he had already written in *Mein Kampf*, on 27 September 1930 he said that 'the German bourgeoisie was at the end of its mission and not called upon for any further task'.[227]

Wagener reports a statement made by Hitler in 1930 in which the latter expressed his understanding that

> ... Bolshevism has simply removed these creatures [the middle-class liberals—R.Z.]. Because they were worthless for mankind only burdens for their nation. The bees also sting the drones to death when there is nothing left for them to contribute to the hive. The Bolshevist procedure is therefore something quite natural.[228]

These and similar statements by Hitler speak against the central thesis which Ernst Nolte develops in his book *Der europäische Bürgerkrieg* (The European Civil War). According to Nolte, the threat felt by the middle class in the face of Communism had been the primary motive for Hitler, from which his actions were easier to understand than before. But while Hitler certainly made tactically clever use of the fears the middle class had of a Communist revolt, he was completely indifferent to the fate of this class he considered to be cowardly, weak and decayed. On 24 October 1933 Hitler expressly declared that if he had turned against Communism, 'then [it was] not because of the 100,000 bourgeois – it can be of complete indifference whether they go under or not...'[229] On 14 September 1936 he repeated this view in his closing speech at the *Reichsparteitag*:

We did not defend Germany against Bolshevism once before because we intended to conserve a bourgeois world or to resurrect it. Had Communism really only intended to do a certain cleaning up by removing individual decayed elements from the camp of the so-called upper ten thousand or out of that of our just as useless *petit bourgeois*, we would easily have been able to let it run on for a while.[230]

In a speech on 30 January 1939 the egalitarian elements in Hitler's thinking become clear – and this egalitarianism (which was only intended to form the basis for the creation of a new élite) was primarily directed against the bourgeoisie, against the former ruling class and its pretensions to special rights and privileges:

But as a social manifestation this new leadership élite must also be relieved from numerous prejudices which I can really only define as a lying and fundamentally nonsensical social morality. There is no position which cannot find its ultimate justification in the advantage that springs from it for the community. What is obviously unimportant for the community, or even damaging for it, cannot be assessed as being moral in the service of a social order. And above all, a national community is only conceivable under the application of laws which are binding for everyone. In other words, it cannot be that we expect or demand that someone obeys principles which in the eyes of others are either nonsensical, damaging or even just unimportant. I have no time for the attempts by dying social classes to separate themselves from real life by means of a hedge of dried-out and unreal class laws and thereby to keep themselves alive artificially. As long as this is only done to secure a quiet burial ground for their own dying out, there is nothing to be said against it. But when they attempt to erect a barrier against ongoing life, the storm of a forward-rushing youth will brush this old undergrowth aside with ease. The German national state of today does not recognize any social prejudices. Therefore it also does not recognize any exempted social morals. It only recognizes the laws of life and the necessities the German people have understood by intellect and insight. National Socialism has recognized them and intends to see that they are respected.[231]

On 24 February 1940 Hitler declared that the bourgeois-capitalist world had already collapsed, its age already long outdated: 'This collapse must take place everywhere in some form or other and it will not fail to materialize anywhere.'[232] The German nation could not, said Hitler, 'live with the middle-class social order at all'.[233] In a conversation with the Hungarian 'Leader of the Nation' Szálasi, Hitler declared on 4 December 1944 that the 'bourgeois European world' would break down ever further and all that was left was the alternative 'that either a sensible social order were created on a national level, or that Bolshevism would take over'.[234]

Even in his final speeches Hitler still expressed his convictions about the necessary collapse of the bourgeois world, of the ending of the historic mission of the bourgeoisie. In his last New Year address on 1 January 1945 he prophesied that

> ... the bourgeois social order is no longer able to resist the storms of today, let alone those of coming times; state after state which does not find the way to a truly social restructuring will descend into chaos. The liberal age has been and gone. To believe one can oppose this storm of the nations by parliamentary-democratic half measures is childish, just as naïve as Metternich's methods were against the mutually reinforcing efforts at national unification of the nineteenth century.[235]

Hitler went on to speak about 'the sunken bourgeois world' and its 'corrupt and socially amoral atmosphere'.[236] In his final radio address he vilified the Jews and their 'best allies', namely those 'insensitive burghers who refuse to recognize that the age of the bourgeois world has just come to an end never to return, that this era of unbridled economic liberalism has outlived itself and can only lead to its own collapse . . .'[237]

The question now arises, however, why, despite his hatred of the middle class, despite his conviction that this outdated class was cowardly, weak and without energy, Hitler entered into temporary alliances with the bourgeois-reactionary forces (as, for example, Hugenberg and Papen). The answer is that Hitler allied himself with these forces not *in spite of* his insight into their lack of capabilities and weakness, but *for that very reason*. It was one of Hitler's fundamental convictions that one should not ally oneself with equal rivals, but with the ones who were weak. However, he was completely aware of the intentions of his bourgeois opponents, or rather allies, and he was only prepared to enter into an alliance in which he – as in the cabinet of 30 January 1933 – had the whip-hand. To conclude from the fact that he allied himself temporarily with middle-class forces that Hitler had any sympathy for these would be just as erroneous as it would be to draw a similar conclusion from Mao Tse-tung's temporary alliance with Chiang Kai-shek and the Kuomintang. Revolutionaries are always on the look-out for allies on their way to power, preferably weaker ones, and they are always aware of the 'second thoughts' and possible intentions of their partners. Hitler had the advantage that he was always underestimated by the bourgeoisie – and, interestingly enough, by the Communists as well – so that today we can agree with Veit Valentin's statement that Hitler's story is the story of his underestimation.

Hitler was aware that his middle-class allies only regarded him as a 'drummer', that they thought they could buy and use him for their own purposes. On 9 November 1927 Hitler said, addressing the 'upper ten thousand':

> And then we can already see you, how you will jubilantly move into this new Germany with your hands raised, as far to the front as possible. Once before we

had the vivid experience of how you go about this, how you let others do the work as good little drummers and, then, how at the last moment you suddenly place yourselves at the head as the great geniuses and then give the Fatherland what is the Fatherland's due and give yourselves what you think is your due. We are not counting on these classes because we know them far too well.[238]

To Wagener Hitler said in February 1931 that he knew very well that the 'businessmen' believed 'they could tacitly lead us astray with their money'. But, Hitler continued,

... the path leading up to the altar of the fatherland is steep, and here and there we have to use steps now and again in order to move ahead. What we are doing at the moment is also nothing more than making use of steps. From there you can also move on in a wrong direction. But we will not do that.[239]

Hitler defined his alliance with the bourgeois forces as being purely a tactical measure, without deceiving himself about the intentions of his allies. In this he differed from his reactionary partners like Papen, who also had – just as he did – the intention of 'using' the other for his own purposes, but who in the final analysis miscalculated the consequences of his intentions and his ability to realize them. In the autumn of 1932, when Hitler rejected Papen's offer of the Vice-Chancellorship and a share in the government, he characterized the intentions of his subsequent bourgeois-reactionary partners thus:

... they say 'the force is there, how about our harnessing the force for ourselves?' They are gradually realizing that we National Socialists are a movement with which they will have to reckon, that I am the born drummer one can make good use of. Why, then, they think, should this brilliant movement with its drummer not finally also find its brilliant commander? This drummer is the one who can drum; they themselves are the only ones who can govern. They all have a 'von' in front of their names, the best and most convincing proof of their ability.[240]

In his closing address at the 'Greater Germany' *Parteitag* on 12 September 1938 Hitler, looking back on the time of struggle before 1933, declared:

Later, after the party had won its place in public life, in other words could no longer be brought away, the fundamental rejection [of the NSDAP by the middle-class parties—R.Z.] was replaced by a tenacious, if tacit hope ... Thus the childish idea came about to one day *spiritually confiscate* this manifestation of the nation which could not be killed, in order then to use it to continue that wise policy which the bourgeoisie had long had to abandon because of its lack of strength. One was therefore longing for the moment when the *drummer* (that was me!) could be replaced by the *real statesmen* (that was the *others*)![241]

b. The Working Class
Definition of the 'Workers' Party'

Why did the NSDAP call itself 'workers' party' when its declared objective was specifically not the pursuit of class interests, but the observation of those 'general interests' which could serve as a platform and common base of understanding for all the social groupings? From its claim, was the NSDAP not far more a 'people's party', and from its social composition not far more a 'middle-class party'? Did not the term 'workers' party' already contain something divisive which could prevent *petit bourgeois* and middle-class groupings from joining the NSDAP? In a speech on 7 August 1920 Hitler explained the twofold programmatic message which was intended to be expressed by the term 'workers' party':

> This is what we thought. If Frederick the Great was able to make the statement 200 years ago, I want to be nothing more than the first official and servant of the state, the first worker, then today we have all the more reason and need to demand that no member of the nation should be ashamed of this name, but is proud to be allowed to call himself a worker. This should be the most important difference that separates us from those who are drones. Whether in the chemical laboratory, whether in the technical construction office or as a civil servant in his office or a worker at a machine, for us the term 'worker' is actually the test, because this term shows who is ready for our movement and who is not. Whoever is ashamed of this term is not ready for our movement, he is still living in a former world. Only he counts for us who is worthy of this term, and worthy to take it upon himself as a title of honour. And it is our objective to win especially those workers for our cause who have been called workers up to now. A national movement that does not have millions supporting it is worthless, is useless. That is the condition, that the national idea does not remain restricted to a few thousand individuals but reaches out and eats its way into the millions and millions who come out of the factories and workshops day after day . . .[242]

The fact that the term 'workers' party' could frighten away, could repel middle-class elements was therefore in Hitler's view not a deficiency but actually a good reason for the term – because the party was already supposed to be a melting-pot of all social classes and levels, a national community in miniature. And there was to be no room in the NSDAP anyway for bourgeois forces who, because of their 'class arrogance', were hesitant to join a 'workers' party'. The second reason Hitler gives for the NSDAP calling itself 'workers' party' is probably even more important. It was the objective of the party to win over those workers who were being called 'workers' – in other words, the manual labourers and industrial workers. Why Hitler was particularly anxious to win over the working class will be explored in detail below.

In a conversation with the poet Hanns Johst many years later and after the seizure of power, Hitler came back to the question why the NSDAP called itself a workers' party. Johst began by saying that Hitler, or rather his party, were considered to be part of the 'bourgeois right wing', which Hitler immediately called 'a mistake', because he could 'never be understood under the aspects of the middle class'. To Johst's question, whether the name 'National Socialist Workers' Party' was a sign that Hitler gave 'the term "worker" precedence over the term "burgher"', Hitler answered: 'I chose the term "worker" because it is much closer to my whole nature and because I wanted to win this term back for the national force... I had to "repatriate" it [the term "worker"—R.Z.] into the power of the German language and the sovereign rights and obligations of the German nation.'[243]

In his closing speech at the 1938 *Reichsparteitag* Hitler said:

> ... whereas the other so-called national formations and associations received most of their supporters from middle-class circles, and even recruited their so-called fighting organizations—as far as one may apply this term—from there, the National Socialist Party was a true people's party even then, in other words the great majority of its supporters consisted of the sons of the masses. The battalions of the SA were recruited from among workers and farmers, small artisans and white-collar workers. They formed the initial cells of the political party and later on filled its local branches. Therefore many of our 'burghers', who had already been worried by the name 'German Workers' Party', were utterly dismayed as soon as they had their first look at the rough fellows who had assembled around the movement as its guard. A national movement consisting of working people! These, however, did not define the term in the exclusive sense as was the case with both the bourgeoisie and the Marxists. From the very first day, for the National Socialist Party the term 'worker' was a term of honour for all those who by honest work—be it in the intellectual or in the purely manual field—were active in the community. And simply because the party was a national party, it therefore necessarily—just like the nation—had to have more manual than intellectual workers in its ranks ... Marxism, on the other hand, from the very first day saw the new movement as a despised rival and believed it could destroy it the more readily by bringing the term 'worker'—which National Socialism had fixated in the sense of a combining of all those who worked—into disrepute with the masses as being in contradiction to the term 'proletariat'. And in fact this was true. Because the proletariat, or more precisely the proletarian parties, had excluded the German brainworker and intellectual from their ranks as far as possible.[244]

Here Hitler is portraying the NSDAP from the time of struggle as a 'national party', in which, however, the 'manual worker' had played a decisive role. While Hitler is exaggerating the importance of the worker element within the NSDAP, in the years from 1930 to 1932 the party had indeed developed into a popular party which was also quite attractive for workers. The results of more recent empirical studies indicate that the workers' share among the voters as well as among the members of the NSDAP was much higher than previously assumed. The workers were indeed – measured against their share of the total population – under-represented among the voters and members of the NSDAP. On the other hand, none of the parties of Weimar – with the exception of the socialist SPD and KPD – could mobilize as many workers as the Hitler movement. Regular shares of between 30 to 40 per cent among the members and voters of the Hitler party force us to revise, or at least modify, the long-held thesis of the middle class. The analyses by Jürgen Falter show that 'between 1930 and 1933 the NSDAP was able to attract members from all the social levels, including the workers, both on the membership and on the voter side, and was therefore socio-structurally a popular party with a pronounced middle-class bulge'.[245]

From its programmatic side as well, the NSDAP can be most readily defined as a 'popular 'party in the modern sense. Modern popular parties attempt to integrate the desires and interests of different social groups into their programmes, or at least to take them into account, or appear to do so, to the extent that they do not only appeal to one exclusive class or estate but are able to recruit their members, supporters and voters from various social classes. This is where modern popular parties differ from the traditional class parties.

On 27 October 1928 Hitler declared that 'The NSDAP intends to gradually reunite the *whole* German nation, *all* the social levels and occupations, and not only to agitate among certain groups as others do.'[246] On 30 November 1928 he said:

> The movement in whose name I speak here is not a movement of a specific class, or a specific estate or occupational group, it is a German popular party in the highest sense of the term. It wants to encompass all the social levels of the nation, all occupations, wants to get close to every German who has the good will to serve his nation, who wants to live with his nation, and who belongs to his nation by blood.

This, of course, was making propaganda more difficult:

> The more one addresses only one social class, the easier it becomes to make promises. One knows from the beginning what each class wants. The civil servants want an improvement of their salaries, the pensioners an improvement of their pensions, the workers an increase in wages, the farmers an increase in food prices, some a closing of the borders, others an opening of the borders. If you are always only addressing yourself to one category, then political propaganda becomes infinitely easy.

But a party which wanted to be a national party could not promise one class something and at the same time promise another class the opposite.[247] The problem of the national, as compared to the class or interest-group, party, lay in that 'in such a party . . . all of the individual interests necessarily cross, and often even cancel each other out'.[248]

Why then did the NSDAP still call itself a 'workers' party'? The primary reason is probably that its main concern was to gain the support of the workers. It was therefore a workers' party from its intentions, even if it was not as far as its actual social composition was concerned. The interesting question which must now be asked is why Hitler attempted to gain the working class for his party and his idea despite all the difficulties involved?

Hitler's Reasons for Concentrating on the Worker: The Workers as a 'Source of Strength and Energy'
In a letter of 3 July 1920 to Konstantin Hierl, Hitler addressed himself to the problem of gaining the worker:

> Your view that our rallies receive too few visitors from the circles of the industrial workers is only partially correct. We do not mistake the difficulties of easily being able to convert workers to our cause, some of whom have already been members of organizations for decades. The condition for this was initially the holding of big mass rallies, in order thereby to gain an effective means of propaganda, particularly for the great mass. Because, as a child of the people, the worker will always only have respect for a movement which presents itself to him awe-inspiringly. Already this confronted us with the necessity – if we wished to guarantee an orderly course of our meetings – of addressing ourselves to a certain lower middle class of which we knew that it thought and felt national, and which only in part was politically homeless due to our present party landscape. With this, our rallies received a very mixed appearance right from the beginning. Next to the civil servant, the tool and die makers, next to the PhDs, the guest-house cooks, and so forth. *But that was supposed to be exactly the objective of our party, not to become a class organization, but a popular party.*[249]

It is unmistakably clear here how, in his usual way, Hitler is trying to make a virtue out of a vice by cleverly presenting an initially unplanned effect as if it had been deliberately intended. While the NSDAP actually was not supposed to be exclusively a workers' party but a popular party, it did want to gain the support of the working class and ran into serious difficulties, because – as Hitler points out – of the traditional ties of the working class to the Marxists parties.

Hitler then goes on to explain how important it was to gain the 'masses' for the party[250] – particularly the manual workers:[251] 'especially the lower levels of the people have remained the purest, and therefore the recovery of the nation can first be expected from them'.[252] 'The strength lies in the workers of the callused fist, these we must gain for ourselves', Hitler declared on 1 March

1922.[253] In a memorandum on the 'Development of the National Socialist Worker's Party', he wrote on 22 October 1922 that especially those segments of the people who were 'internationally' inclined, in other words the workers, were 'the most active and vigorous elements of the nation'.[254] While the middle class was 'lacking in will, courage and energy', the strength 'as always still lay with the broad mass'. There, said Hitler on 24 April 1923, the 'energy' lay dormant. It was not in the political salons that the strength of the nation lay, 'but in the fist, in the brow and in the will of the broad masses'. Liberation would not 'come down from above, but would spring forth from below'.[255]

Here we already have an indication of the reasons why Hitler placed particular value on gaining the working class. In his view, it, as opposed to the middle class, embodied the decisive traits: courage, strength, energy and the determination to fight. He therefore repeatedly declared the gaining of the working class to be the major task of the party: '. . . in future the party will continue to believe', said Hitler on 20 October 1923, 'that with every callused fist of a worker regained for mother Germania, it is doing her a greater service than with the gaining of ten hooray patriots'. A 'Germanic uprising of the people' was only possible 'if the cry for freedom penetrates into the remotest home of a worker and finds an echo there! Germany's salvation is most closely tied to the position taken by its working class.'[256]

In *Mein Kampf* Hitler wrote that a *Weltanschauung* would only stand a chance for victory 'if the broad masses as the supporters of the new teaching declare themselves prepared to take the struggle upon themselves'. He criticized the All-German Movement for not having understood that the 'major emphasis' had to be put on gaining adherents from among 'the broad masses'. In *Mein Kampf* Hitler also gave the reasons for his opinion that priority had to be given to gaining the workers with their vitality and robustness:

> One thing is sure, however: the new class [the factory worker—R.Z.] did not include the worst elements within its ranks, but quite the opposite, in any case the most vital. The over-refinement of the so-called culture had not yet exercised its undermining and destructive effect here. In its broad masses, the new class was not yet infected with the poison of pacifist weakness, but was robust, and if necessary even brutal.

Hitler argued that the working class – as opposed to the intelligentsia – could more readily be organized because it was more disciplined and less vacillating in difficult situations:

> As little worth as an army would have whose soldiers were all generals, and even if only from their education and insight, so little is a political movement as the representation of a *Weltanschauung* worth if all it wants to be is a reservoir of

'clever' people. No, it also requires the most primitive soldier, because otherwise inner discipline cannot be achieved. It lies in the nature of an *organization* that it can only exist when a highest intellectual leadership is served by broad, more emotionally inclined mass. A company of two hundred equally mentally capable people would be far more difficult to discipline in the long run than one with one hundred and ninety less capable and ten highly intelligent ones.

Social Democracy had drawn its greatest advantage from this insight: 'What our bourgeoisie always only regarded with a shaking of the head, the fact that Marxism only attracted the so-called uneducated masses, was in reality the condition for its success.' The platform of a party had to be formulated in such a way that it was capable of gaining those 'who alone guaranteed the *Weltanschauung*-like fight of this idea. This is the German working class'.[257] If in his early speeches Hitler sometimes declared that the Marxist leaders could best use the manual labourer, because while he had 'a big heart, he only had a small brain',[258] then this was less with the intent to insult him. Here too, as so often elsewhere,[259] he was only attempting to learn to understand the reasons for its success and to make use of the insight gained.

We are familiar with Hitler's statements about the principles of propaganda and his theories on mass psychology, which he expounds in *Mein Kampf* in particular. We do not intend to repeat and discuss them in depth here, even though this topic also belongs within our context. When Hitler spoke about the 'mass' or the 'broad mass', he always also and specifically meant the working class. His statements on mass psychology therefore also give us an insight into his image of the worker. Propaganda, said Hitler, should not be directed towards the intelligentsia but 'always only at the masses'. Therefore

> ... its effect must always also be directed more towards the emotions and only very conditionally towards the so-called brain. Every propaganda has to be popular and to adjust its intellectual level to the ability to comprehend of the most limited among those to whom it intends to appeal. Therefore its level of intelligence will necessarily be all the lower, the larger the mass of people is that is to be influenced. And where, as with the propaganda to hold out during a war, the intention is to draw a whole nation into its sphere of influence, the care taken to avoid too high a level of intellectual conditions can not be too great ... The ability of the broad masses to comprehend is only very limited, their understanding small, and on the other hand their forgetfulness high ... The broad mass of a people does not consist of diplomats, or even teachers of constitutional law, yes, not even of generally sensible people able to judge, but of human beings who are just as vacillating as they are prone to doubts and uncertainties ... In its overwhelming majority the people are so femininely endowed and inclined that their thoughts and actions are far less determined by dispassionate considerations than by emotional feelings. These feelings, however, are not complicated, but very simple and uniform. There is not much differentiation involved, but rather a positive or negative, love or hatred,

right or wrong, truth or falsehood, but never half this way and half that way, or some here, some there and so forth.

Hitler built his propaganda on this 'primitiveness of the feelings of the broad masses'. The mass 'in its cumbersomeness always needs a certain amount of time before it is prepared to even take note of something, and it will finally only lend its memory to a thousandfold repetition of the most simple terms'.[260]

According to Hitler's view, therefore, the mass is fundamentally incapable of differentiated thinking, and less directed by rational insights than by emotions. According to Hitler, however, these traits are not to be taken negatively; they are even the necessary conditions for the development of a believing, determined and disciplined fighting unit. According to Hitler's view here – as we have already seen above – 'too much' in the way of brainpower is likely to do more harm than good. Hitler's view of the mass – and also and in particular his view of the working class – was therefore highly ambivalent. On the one hand he despised it, while on the other he appreciated it – in contrast to the middle class – as 'a source of strength and energy', as the bearer of an 'unshakeable faith' which could be converted into determined, courageous and energetic action. And, in Hitler's view, it was these traits, and not education or intellect, which were decisive. It is only against this background that we can understand why he regarded it as the main task of the party to gain the 'lower masses', in particular the industrial workers. 'We need the broad masses in particular', said Hitler on 9 November 1927, 'because this broad mass has at all times always been the bearer of the living energy. It is not as complicated, in truth not as spoiled as our so-called upper classes.'[261] And 'The storm ranks of the future will not only come from the universities, but from the factories and mines, and from the farms.'[262]

On 21 November 1927 Hitler demanded that the party concentrate on gaining the working class:

> We see the future as being secured if we can win over the German worker for it, because he is the source of strength. We believe that Germany can never recover if it does not regain the German worker . . . Our movement turns deliberately to the preservation and care of the German worker. In him it sees the most important element of life . . .'[263]

Time and again their vigour, courage and determination were the reasons Hitler gave for the party having to concentrate first and foremost on gaining the manual workers.[264]

The British historian Peter D. Stachura has proposed the theory that around the middle to the end of 1928 the 'socialist' elements in the NSDAP's propaganda had stepped into the background as well as the party's efforts to gain the working class. The 'reorientation to the right' had been seen as the result of the *Reichstag* elections of 20 May 1928, when the National Socialists had been able to gain only 2.6 per cent of the votes and had been 'bitterly disappointed'.[265] This theory, however, is not very convincing for several reasons. First of all it would appear that Stachura's key premise, that the National Socialists had regarded the result of the election as a defeat, is not true. In his diary on 21 May Goebbels comments quite positively on the results: 'A nice success, but we have deserved it for our work.'[266] Gregor Strasser, the 'Reich Organization Leader' of the party commented on the election results in a newspaper article on 27 May: 'Particularly the joyful insight that the German nation is beginning to take notice of National Socialism's message of salvation. obliges us to keep on spreading this message . . .'[267]

Measured against the outstanding election results the party was able to achieve two years later, 2.6 per cent was certainly not a big success; and the 6.5 per cent which the combined slate of the *Deutsch-Völkische Freiheitspartei* [German National Freedom Party—H.B.] and the NSDAP had achieved on 4 May 1924 may also make this result appear to be a defeat. But the alliance of the German Nationals and the National Socialists was able to achieve its relatively high share in 1924 under the still lingering impressions of the events of the crisis year 1923 and with the positive propaganda effect of Hitler's appearances in court in the case against him just ended. And the sensational result of 1930 was achieved under the impressions already being created by the economic and political crisis which was to ring in the collapse of the Weimar Republic. The results of 1928 were a success for the NSDAP, if for no other reason than that it was the first time it had run alone in *Reichstag* elections and had succeeded in clearly demonstrating its predominance within the 'national' camp. The popular-nationalist block had only gained 0.9 per cent of the votes, and not a single seat; the NSDAP had at least gained twelve.

In a speech at the leadership conference and general convention which took place end of August and the beginning of September 1928 and during which – according to Stachura – the reorientation to the right as a result of the disappointing election results was initiated, Hitler expressly assessed the result as having been a success. To the ringing applause of the members and party leaders attending, he declared:

> For the first time we were completely on our own, burdened with a very evil past, and we can say with pride that we have achieved a resounding success. Not only have we gained twelve seats, we only lost two more by a devilish coincidence, the votes would have been sufficient. We have removed the opposing competition; there is only one national movement still there, without having to borrow from the armed formations. For us it really is a small triumph that the parties which had the

support of the armed formations lost, while we, who did not have this support, have won.[268]

From the point of view of the NSDAP there was therefore no reason to regard the former strategy and tactics as having failed. It appears more likely that Hitler continued to cling to his basic conviction which he had already formed in the early 1920s. The arguments he presented as the reasons for concentrating on gaining the working class remained the same. In a speech on 30 November 1928, for example, he said that when a fellow citizen asked him why he had such a strong belief in the German worker, he would answer,

> ... because the refined tones and genteel behaviour are not able to strike a chord. When a proletarian today brutally gives me a piece of his mind, I have the hope that this brutality can be directed outwards some day. When a bourgeois over-aesthetically murmurs his opinion in my ear, I see that here weakness and cowardice have been added. When a burgher comes wandering by lost in dreams and only goes on talking about culture and civilization and aesthetic global gratification, then I have to say, 'You are lost to the whole German nation, you belong to Berlin West, go there into all that filth and die a miserable death there! Hop your negro dances to the finish.'[269]

In September 1931 Hitler warned Wagener, the chief of the Economic Policy Department of the NSDAP, not to propagate publicly the party's economic plans. He even demanded that they be kept strictly secret. The plans could only be implemented anyway after political power had been won, 'and there too as opponents we will have – besides the Jews – all of private industry, in particular heavy industry, as well as the medium-sized and large property owners, and naturally the banks. And only the devil knows how the army will react. All we can depend on is the middle class, the working class and the farmers'. For the implementation of the plans, however, he also needed the intelligentsia.[270]

Even after the seizure of power Hitler frequently emphasized the particular importance of those classes who, in contrast to the 'superficial intellectuality of our politicizing bourgeoisie', had remained 'intellectually unspoiled, uncomplicated and therefore closer to nature'.[271] Because, in his view, faith was far more lasting and dependable than any 'alleged' rational or scientific insight, Hitler valued the working class as an unshakeable bearer of the faith. The German worker, he said on 16 May 1934, would become the mainstay of the national community primarily because he was 'receptive to this feeling of faith and trust which does not think it necessary to apply the probe of reason to all things, but can blindly commit itself to an idea'.[272]

Such statements are not to be taken as merely currying favour with the working class, even though, of course, they also had propaganda objectives attached to them, but were actually in line with Hitler's thinking. Hitler believed that over-emphasizing the intellect and rational thinking was harmful. As proof let us only cite two remarks from his table talks:

> In certain areas any professorial science becomes a disaster: it leads away from the instinct; the person is talked out of it. A dwarf with nothing but knowledge fears strength. Instead of telling himself that the basis of all knowledge is a healthy body, he rejects strength. Nature adapts to the habits of life, and if the world were to be given into the care of the German professor for a few centuries, then in a million years there would be nothing but imbeciles wandering about here: gigantic heads on a nothing of a body![273]

In another talk he said that 'firmness of character was worth more to him than anything else' and 'a firm character will prevail even with only scant knowledge'.[274]

Hitler's position towards the intellectuals was one of hostility, because in his opinion they were mentally overbred and could not be 'bearers of the faith' for the national community. At the culture meeting of the *Reichsparteitag* in 1938 he declared:

> And I want to differentiate between the people, in other words, the healthy, full-blooded mass of the Germans faithful to their nation and a so-called 'society' which is undependable because it is only conditionally blood-bound and decadent. It is sometimes carelessly called 'the upper class', while in reality it is only the cast-off result of a social misbreed become weak of character due to a cosmopolitan infection of the blood and the mind.[275]

In his speech on 8 November 1938 on the anniversary of the *putsch*, Hitler again contrasted the lower classes with the intellectuals. What he said here makes it particularly clear why Hitler considered the working class to be the most valuable support for the party and concentrated his efforts on gaining the workers:

> And it was readily understandable that this party would primarily gain supporters from among those who were not so much blessed by fortune, particularly from among the broad masses of the people. Naturally, because there more instinct still rules, and out of instinct comes faith, whereas our upper ten thousand are for ever critics out of their intellectuality. They are partially of no use at all as building blocks for a national community, not even today . . . Intellectuality, which runs about in the minds of these tens of thousands of specimens, sometimes looks at the problems a little bit interested, maybe even stimulated, but otherwise always with critical reticence. Maybe it will all turn out differently – who knows? To sacrifice oneself for an ideal, commit oneself to an ideal, that is completely foreign to these people; they do not know that. And they also do not like that at all, and the exceptions only confirm the rule. Therefore they are also completely worthless as

III. Hitler's Social Objectives

building blocks for such a national community. Because they are not bearers of the faith, they are not unshakeable; above all they are not persevering in moments of difficulty and danger.[276]

In the light of what we have discussed so far, it is quite clear that it was also not an attempt to curry favour with his audience when Hitler declared in the same vein in a speech to workers on 14 November 1940:

> You can believe me, my national comrades, I would not have this trust if I only possessed knowledge about the upper ten thousand. I did not enter into political life only with this knowledge. My knowledge is based above all on the German people, on the German worker, on the German farmer, on this mass of millions of good, small, faithful people, who are not as vacillating and as calculating as our so-called upper ten thousand. If all I had known had been these, you can rest assured that I would never have gone into political life. With those you cannot even lure a dog from behind the stove. I entered into political life with my knowledge of the broad masses. I have always placed my trust in this broad mass; with it I built up my party, and I am convinced that with this broad mass I will also survive this struggle.[277]

That Hitler was serious and really did think in this way is not only deducible from the background of his *Weltanschauung* but is also confirmed by the fact that in his conversations with his entourage and in his table talks he frequently expressed himself in a similar vein. After a conversation with Hitler, Goebbels, for example, noted in his diary on 25 July 1940:

> He speaks with contempt about the upper circles. There is not much for us to be got there. We must always remain with the people. He recounts examples from the history of the movement, how he had once spoken in the Berlin National Club and only the cloakroom attendants had understood him.[278]

We have already cited a statement made on 5 September 1941 in another context: in view of the cowardice and bigotry of the bourgeoisie, Hitler would have despaired during the time of struggle if he had not been able to depend on his 'adherents among the people'.[279] On 21 September 1941 Hitler said, 'Whoever wants the deed, needs the faith which can only be found among the masses. The broad mass is not so much burdened by experiences and approaches a new thing with the uninhibitedness of the innocent.'[280] According to a report by Koeppen, he declared on 4 October 1941:

> The broad mass was the most appreciative audience, which really goes along in its primitive emotions while distinguishing itself by a stability which is proof against almost any pressure, whereas the intellectuals vacillate back and forth. He himself had been made to feel this during the time of struggle, in a positive sense by the faithfulness of his adherents, and in a negative sense by the clinging of the broad

masses to the Social Democrats and the Zentrum in elections, even though there had never been a government which imposed on its voters as strongly as this one did.[281]

On 2 November 1941 Hitler again spoke about the worthlessness of the bourgeois forces and claimed that during the time of struggle he had needed people 'who stood up . . . who were prepared to storm a meeting, and on the other hand to govern a Gau'. Only the worker and the farmer had the 'animal power' on which everything depended in the final analysis.[282]

In a table talk on 16/17 January 1941 Hitler recalled:

> In Munich I found a long row of such very loyal people. All of them could only lose, none could win. When I meet somebody from the little people, that touches me so, they clung to me and hastened . . . The upper ten thousand, they only do it out of calculation, they see me as an attraction for their drawing room; others think of protection . . . My love of the people, this has remained to me. I am so personally tied to the people, can think myself into their mentality so well, their worries and joys, because I know all that myself.[283]

On 1 March 1942 Hitler said during one of his monologues, 'If you did not see so much healthy life all round about you would have to become an absolute misanthrope. If I only saw the upper ten thousand, that is what I would be. That I am not is only thanks to my associating with the much healthier broad mass.'[284]

On 8 April 1942, in a table talk, Hitler again looked back to the time of struggle of the NSDAP:

> At the beginning of my political work I set the motto that it was not important to gain the bourgeoisie – which only desired law and order and was cowardly in its political position – but to fire the working class with enthusiasm for his ideas. All of the early years of the time of struggle had therefore been designed to gain the worker for the NSDAP.

In this he had made use of the following means: just like the Marxist parties he had distributed his political posters in screaming red, and had carried out lorry propaganda, wherein the lorries had been covered all over with bright red posters, equipped with red flags and manned by slogan-chanting choruses. He had also taken care that all of the adherents of the movement had come to the rallies without ties and collars and thereby generated trust among the manually working population. Furthermore, he had

> . . . attempted to frighten off bourgeois elements, who without being true fanatics had wanted to join the NSDAP, by means of screaming propaganda, the incorrect dress of the participants at rallies, and such things, and by these means to keep the ranks of the movement free from any cowards right from the beginning.

III. Hitler's Social Objectives

By such and other means he had succeeded in 'attracting so many good elements of the working population to the movement that during one of the last election campaigns before the take-over of power he had been able to have no fewer than 180,000 rallies conducted'.[285]

At lunch on 11 May 1942 Hitler told a story about a 'a bigger than average man from Munich with the strength of a bear'. During the time of struggle he had 'been worth more than one hundred bourgeois'. He had looked like 'a real proletarian', and had been just as well versed in breaking up meetings and capturing the flag of the other side as in protecting the meeting hall during the rallies of his own side. When after the take-over of power this man had once approached him in the garden of the Café Heck in Munich and, dressed in his everyday working clothes, had asked him to sit down with him for a moment, he had been stared at 'almost like a monster' by the 'bourgeois public'.[286]

In his table talks Hitler expressed his respect for the working class. These statements are of particular interest when we contrast them with the contemptuous remarks about the middle class. In one such talk, for example, Hitler said, 'Class prejudices can no longer be upheld at a time when the proletariat consists of such valuable people as is often the case today!'[287] On another occasion he said that England had a wonderful selection of people in its upper classes, whereas the lower classes there were 'dirt'. In Germany it was the other way around, because here 'the section through the lower classes of the population is particularly pleasing'. All one needed do to ascertain this was to go and have a look at the German workers in the Wilhelmshaven shipyard, and then the workers from all the other countries in Europe at the Wilhelmshaven No 4 port entrance.[288]

Hitler was particularly pleased by the new self-confidence displayed by the working class. On 20 May 1942, for example, he said that the training of apprentices had undergone a basic change: 'The same apprentice who had formerly been a "whipping post" and who had involuntarily jumped every time the master craftsman or the journeyman scratched themselves, today after six months' basic training already occupied a job which equated to his abilities and thereby gave him self-confidence.' When he went through the Krupp factory in Essen and saw the workers there, he would think to himself that these workers 'from their inner and outer stance were truly gentlemen to all appearances'. He had been able to make the same observation on the occasion of the launching of the *Tirpitz* at the navy shipyard in Wilhelmshaven: 'How many handsome, stately people with a sovereign noble stance and honest pride on their faces had he been able to see among the workers who had worked in the shipyard on this great project and had now assembled for the baptism.' The miner, however, was and would remain 'the élite among the German working

161

class', because he was shaped internally and externally by a profession which still today was tied to a high risk and was only suited to people who had hardness and determination and were also inwardly prepared to overcome substantial dangers. Therefore everything had to be done 'so that the miner also received the national recognition which was his due', and, as soon as there was peace again, one would have to take special care for the improvement of the standard of living of this particularly state-supporting class of the population.[289] Not only in public but also in his private circle Hitler maintained, as on 25 August 1942, that the only class which had understood him, and in particular his economic policy, had been the workers.[290]

Let us summarize here. Whereas in his speeches as well as in his table talks Hitler regularly spoke negatively about the middle class, his remarks to the working class are always very positive. This applies – to underline the point once again – not only to rallies on 1 May or to so-called 'workers' speeches', where one could assume that Hitler only wanted to flatter his audiences, but to the same degree to his table talks. The reason for his taking this position is easy to explain. For Hitler the workers embodied those attributes which he valued so highly and in which the bourgeois, in his opinion, was so completely lacking – courage, determination, energy and the ability to 'have faith'.[291] Hitler would never have advocated 'equal opportunity' so vehemently if he had not been convinced of the qualities of the 'lower classes', particularly of the working class.

Increasing the Worker's Social Standing; Upgrading Manual Labour
Hitler's verdict was a departure from the evaluation of the worker by society, and he was aware of this. In his view this primarily had to do with the contempt for physical work. One of the major objectives of the social restructuring and re-education advocated by Hitler was the upgrading of manual labour and, in connection with this, the increase of the social prestige of the working class. With this he first wanted to remove existing class prejudices and barriers, but above all – and this has not been taken into account before – to create the conditions for the realization of his concept of 'equal opportunity'. Hitler held the view that the possibilities of realizing greater 'equality of opportunity' was tied to the willingness of parents of middle-class origin to have their possibly more manually gifted children undergo an appropriate training and not to insist on a higher education for them. According to Hitler, this was the only way by which the 'falsely occupied' places in the school system could be made available for the children of workers and farmers. In his opinion, the lack of preparedness of many burghers to have their children undergo training in a craft ultimately had to do with the social contempt for manual labour and the fear of loss of social

III. Hitler's Social Objectives

prestige that went with it. Only if we are aware of these relationships can we understand the underlying reasons why Hitler felt that the improvement of the social prestige of the worker and the recognition of physical work as being of the same worth as brain work were so important.

It is revealing that in *Mein Kampf* Hitler developed his demand for an upgrading of manual labour in exactly this context. Let us recall his line of reasoning once again:

> When two nations compete with each other, which are both equally well endowed, then that one will gain the victory among whose total intellectual leadership the best talents are represented, and that one will be defeated whose leadership is only a huge common manger for certain levels of society or classes, without regard to the innate abilities of its various members. At first glance this appears to be impossible in our world of today. The objection will immediately be raised that you could not really ask the dear little son of a higher state official, for example, to become, let us say, an artisan, because somebody else whose parents were artisans appears to be more capable. This may be appropriate for the currently held opinion of manual work. Therefore the popular state will have to come to a fundamentally different view of the term 'work'. It will have to break away from the nonsense of holding physical labour in contempt, even if this requires centuries of education. As a matter of principle it will assess the individual not according to the nature of his work, but according to the quality of his results. This may appear totally monstrous to an age which values the most witless pen-pusher higher than the most intelligent precision mechanic, simply because the former works with a pen. As already pointed out, however, this mistaken assessment is not due to the nature of things but has been artificially cultivated and was not there in former times. The current unnatural condition is also based on the general symptoms of the sickness of our materialized times.

Hitler differentiated between the material and the spiritual evaluation of work, defining the spiritual value as the recognition which was due to whoever 'used the powers nature gave him, and the national community trained, in the service of his nation'. Then it would no longer be shameful to be a good artisan, but very much so to 'laze the day away and steal the daily bread of the people as an incompetent civil servant'. The nature of the work was not to be evaluated, but the way in which it was done. It is of particular interest that Hitler himself formulated the objection and accepted it as being justified that

> ... in general the spiritual evaluation will be hard to separate from the material, yes, that the declining value of physical work is expressly caused by its low rate of compensation... The inhibitions towards physical work were even more due to the fact that because of the low compensation the cultural level of the manual worker was necessarily reduced and thereby the justification created for a generally lower regard. There is much truth in this. But this is exactly the reason why in

future we will need to be wary of too great a difference between the levels of compensation.

The argument frequently advanced by the conservative middle class, that the commitment to perform would suffer from such a relative levelling of compensation, was also rejected by Hitler. It would be a sad sign of the decay of an age if the only motivation for a higher degree of mental performance lay in a higher wage. The greatest scientific and cultural achievements in the history of man had never

> ... been given to the world out of an urge for money. On the contrary, their birth often entailed a renunciation of the earthly joys of wealth. It may be that today gold has become the sole ruler of life, but one day man will again bow down before higher gods. Today much may only owe its existence to the desire for money and possessions, but there is not much included, the absence of which would make mankind poorer. This too is a task of our movement, that already today it announces a time in which the individual will be given what he needs to live, but which upholds the principle that man does not live exclusively for the sake of material enjoyments. One day this should find its expression in a wisely limited graduation of incomes, which will provide even the lowest honestly working person with an honest, respectable living as a member of the national community and a human being under any circumstances. Let nobody say this is an ideal condition such as the world would not be able to stand in practice and actually will never achieve.[292]

We can see the far-reaching conclusions Hitler draws here. As a short-term objective he advocated an upgrading of the social prestige of the workers through an increased spiritual recognition of manual work; as a long-term objective he envisaged a 'wisely limited graduation of incomes' – a demand, by the way, which in the Third Reich found its expression in the DAF's plans for a restructuring of compensations.[293] Basically, these objectives were stringently derived from Hitler's social objective, the creation of 'equal opportunity'. An increase of social mobility demanded a 'relativation' of traditional social status. According to Hitler, one means to achieve this was the social upgrading and recognition of physical labour. He also advocated this concept in numerous speeches. On 18 September 1928, for example, he said:

> The value of a human being within a national community is determined by whether he can be replaced or not. But when you take the lowliest street cleaner who tends his square metre you cannot say he is worthless. If you were to take him away, you would have to put somebody else in his place. But that he has to be replaced proves that he also represents a certain value. The highest value is to be placed in him who is prepared to put all of his activity into the service of the community, in other words who personally even renounces any extraordinary distinction of his person, and here I ask you to correct the statement you hear a thousandfold from the

mouths of the bourgeoisie: but dear God, if these people were more intelligent, or cleverer, or more diligent, or more committed, then they would not be workers but something else entirely. But why so? It therefore needs a bit of idealism for a person to do his duty even though he knows that fate will not bed him in clover, not him, nor his children. It requires more idealism to do one's duty while knowing all the time that one will never be showered with good fortune.[294]

In his speeches after the seizure of power Hitler gave the workers the feeling that they were appreciated by the National Socialist state. On 1 May 1933, for example, he exclaimed: 'Honour work and respect the worker!' If millions still believed they could draw a conclusion about the worth of the worker from the nature of the work, then this was a bitter error:

> There are many tens of thousands among us who want to make respect for the individual depend on the nature of the work he performs. No! Not what he does, but the way he does it is what must be decisive... Woe unto us if this idealism were to quit our nation and if the value of a human being were only to be assessed according to the material goods of life which rained down on him.[295]

Compulsory labour service was to be deliberately employed as a means of re-education. Labour service had originally been a feature of the Weimar Republic, and, like the Civilian Conservation Corps, its counterpart to the New Deal, was created during the world economic crisis. Its most pressing task – be it ever so modest – was the amelioration of unemployment by means of public work. It was financed by the Unemployment Insurance Office and by the end of 1932 employed up to 250,000 people.[296]

The National Socialists appreciated the economic function of labour service (the creation of jobs), but in Hitler's view its ideological function was more important. In a 'chief's briefing' on 4 April 1933, in which Papen, Reichs Economic Minister Hugenberg and Reichs Labour Minister Seldte, among others, took part in addition to Hitler, Hugenberg warned that labour service could cause 'disruptions for the economy' if, for example, 'people who were in the work process were to be taken out'. The minutes of the meeting then go on to say:

> In reply, the Reichs Chancellor emphasized that labour service should primarily not be seen under economic aspects. He saw it primarily as being an instrument which was outstandingly well suited for the deliberate development of a national community. The controversial term 'work' would regain its honour due to the fact that, without regard to origin and rank, the German people, workers of the hand and workers of the mind, would develop mutual understanding through their common service. Every young German had to undergo the difficulties of this service; they all had to accept the same fate... From this melting pot the German community would emerge.[297]

Compulsory labour service, said Hitler in an interview on 20 February 1933 with Louis P. Lochner of Associated Press, should 'serve as a bridge to overcome class differences by means of a general education to work. As a National Socialist, in compulsory labour service I also see a means to educate people to respect work.'[298] Labour service was to eradicate the 'terrible prejudice' that

> ... manual work was inferior... It remains our unalterable decision, to bring every single German, whoever he may be, whether rich or poor, whether the son of scholars or the son of factory workers, to work with his hands at least once in his life so that he gets to know it, so that some day he may also give orders here all the more readily, because before that he had once had to learn to obey. We are not thinking of only defeating Marxism outwardly. We are determined to remove its conditions... Workers of the mind and of the hand must never stand against each other. Therefore we are rooting out that conceited view which so easily befalls any of us and lets us look down on the comrades who 'only' stand behind a workbench, behind a machine or behind a plough.[299]

The objective of labour service, said Hitler on 23 September 1933, was to educate

> ... even every nice little boy of highborn parents to respect work, to respect physical activity in the service of the national community... We want to educate our nation to give up the insanity of the class arrogance, the class haughtiness, the conceit, that only brain work has a value, so that the people may learn to understand that all work which is necessary ennobles him who performs it, and that there is only one thing which dishonours, namely not to contribute anything to the maintenance of the national community, not to contribute anything to the preservation of the nation.[300]

On 1 May 1934 Hitler described the purpose of the labour service as being to

> ... *force* the Germans from positions of life which do not perform physical work to get to know physical work, and thereby have them gain an *understanding* for those national comrades who work in the fields or somewhere in a factory or behind a workbench. We have to sensibly *kill the conceit* within them, with which unfortunately so many intellectuals believe they must look down on manual work...

The social re-evaluation of manual work was also to lead to a general increase in the social prestige of the worker:

> In the course of the centuries we have learned all too easily to speak about the entrepreneur, about the artist, the builder, to prize the technical and to laud the engineer, to admire the architects, to follow the work of the chemists and physicists

III. Hitler's Social Objectives

with astonishment, but to normally forget the worker. We speak about German science, German craftsmanship, the German industry in general, and *we always only mean one side of it*. And only because of this did it come about that *we not only forgot, but in the end also lost* the most loyal helper.[301]

Hitler emphasized this basic concept of the labour service, namely the re-education of the intellectuals, not only in his annual speeches on 1 May and in his addresses to the *Reichsparteitag*[302] but also in a secret speech to *Kreisleiter* [county leaders—H.B.] at the Ordensburg Vogelsang on 29 April 1937:

> In my view it is necessary, particularly within an organization which is continuing to grow ever more upwards, is becoming bigger, that the individual leaders actually come back to the people from time to time. And we also intend to introduce this, that in our, I would like to say, leadership staff – in itself, basically, and later on for a much longer period of time – the people are again seconded, in some areas already now, in other words they have to go into a factory, they have to go to a farm, the have to go to a shipyard, or some place else, in order to again live completely within the circle of the little people. They must again see and hear all that, experience it, in order then to again know the soul of the people and be able to rule it with sovereignty.[303]

Three months beforehand Hitler had recommended to Goebbels that he form a 'political general staff' of about 30 people who 'could constantly be transferred, above all back into the people, into factories or on the farms, so that they maintain contact to the people'. This recommendation, which Hitler made as a 'means against bureaucratization',[304] Goebbels then passed on during a meeting with his staff on 8 April 1937, in which he explained 'the sense in the delegation of our leading officials':

> Not into an office, but directly to the front, to the worker and the people. Especially the *Landesstellenleiter* [state office leaders—H.B.]. Otherwise this will only become another back area operation. Then also to live for two months on the wages of a worker. Let them get to know that and become familiar with the common people again.[305]

Time and again in his table talks Hitler addressed the problem of the relationship between mental and physical work, wherein he placed special emphasis on the principle that it was not the nature of the work which was important but the way it was executed, and therefore physical work must not be looked down upon as compared to brain work:

> The evaluation of the result of the individual should not be based on whether his work has a special value in itself. Everybody only has one obligation: to do his utmost. If he fulfils this obligation then he is indispensable for the community, regardless of whether he is doing something nobody else is capable of doing, or

something which besides him anybody else could also do, otherwise somebody who achieves something with an effect lasting for years, decades or centuries would need to hold his head so high that he would no longer be able to see the one who sweeps the street.'[306]

In another table talk on 27 January 1942 Hitler said, 'National Socialism says: your occupation has nothing to do with its bourgeois evaluation, that is its consoling aspect.'[307]

Even though on the one hand Hitler was a confirmed believer of the concept of the élite, on the other egalitarian motives play an important role in his thinking. In his speeches he therefore constantly repeated that the evaluation of the individual, in modern terms his social prestige, was to be independent of his income, wealth and occupation.[308]

Until now, however, only one side or function of these pronouncements by Hitler has been recognized, namely the (doubtless intended) integration of the working class by means of increasing its self-confidence and by giving it the social recognition previously denied. In this we should not, however, underrate the aspect already mentioned above: by means of the 're-education' Hitler intended, the traditional social status was to be relativized in order to create the conditions for 'equal opportunity'. Only if the social outlawing of physical work could be overcome in a long process of re-education, and the social prestige of the worker increased, would it also be possible (went the line of reasoning developed by Hitler in *Mein Kampf*) to expect that children of university graduates, for example, would develop a willingness to learn a craft and thereby give talented children of workers the possibility of social advancement. In sociological terms, Hitler saw the relativization of the traditional social status by means of the increase of the social prestige of the worker as the condition for increasing social mobility. As important as this initially more spiritual side of the integration process of the working class Hitler initiated may have been, he was still well aware that all of this would remain without any effect if the *factual* situation of the worker were not improved simultaneously by means of social legislation.

Social Legislation

When Hitler spoke positively about 'Germany before the Great War', he was primarily praising social policy: 'With its social legislation Germany was number one', he said in a speech on 10 December 1919, but added critically that this had been given 'to the people in the form of charity, so that the people might be content'.[309] Germany had been, said Hitler on 25 August 1920, 'the first country which had begun with social care. That was exemplary.'[310] On the other hand, however, he declared that this social legislation had 'never been totally and consequently implemented and developed'.[311] We have already noted an important criticism by Hitler of German social legislation elsewhere: it had remained, said Hitler, 'without effect' because it had been implemented in order to remove its propaganda base for Social Democracy, and to prevent a revolution by the proletariat.[312] Nevertheless, he noted positively, Germany was 'the country which was the first to at least even try to implement a social legislation, to go the route of such a legislation, and has, at least in that which was created, gone on as an example to all of the rest of the world'.[313] While Germany's social legislation had been 'incomplete' and had shown 'mistakes and weaknesses', it had still been better than that of other countries.[314]

On 14 February 1939 Hitler lauded Bismarck, whose 'recognition of the necessity of the state solving the purely social problems by means of a great social legislation' he calls 'admirable'. He had, however, lacked the 'instrument founded in a *Weltanschauung*' in order to be able to bring this battle to a really successful conclusion.[315] It appears obvious that to a certain degree Hitler took Bismarck for his example. The latter's combination of social reforms on the one hand and laws against socialism on the other, said Hitler in a table talk on 2 August 1941, would have 'reached their objective within twenty years had they been pursued with consistency'.[316] In the end Bismarck's attempt failed, not – according to Hitler – because of its insufficiency, but simply due to the fact that within the framework of the capitalist system a consistent social legislation was impossible. In a speech on 8 November 1940 he declared:

> Certainly these problems were solved from the point of view of the times – how else? In other words the state, which was capitalist down to its deepest foundations, could naturally only approach social questions with hesitation and half-solutions which, if they really were to succeed, would have required the state, the national community, to already have had a different visage. That was not the case. But it is all the more noteworthy that at the time one even took up such problems at all, and attempted to solve them within the possibilities of the times.[317]

Hitler repeated the same consideration one week later:

> The attempt had been made to solve these problems with the inadequate means of the times. Also inadequate, because the social order of the state in its deepest foundations was a capitalist one, in other words via the detour of the press and the political parties they financed, business and capital had an enormous influence on public life, so that social legislation always had to get stuck somehow. But the attempt was at least made. The rest of the world did not give these problems any attention.[318]

In Hitler's view there could be no really consistent social policy within the framework of the capitalist system, despite all the welcome attempts. On the other hand, for him social policy was an important lever for making the social integration of the working class possible, which was long overdue and had long been sabotaged by the short-sighted policies of the bourgeoisie. And, indeed, National Socialism then brought noteworthy advances in several areas of social policy, for example the improvement of the protection of young people at work, working pregnant women and mothers of newborn children, and social security.[319] Even the opponents of the regime have admitted these advances to some degree, and also the fact that they made the regime quite popular among the working class. As an example, we can point here to the reform of vacation entitlement, which in comparison to the Weimar era represents a genuine social improvement[320] and which was even recognized as such in the so-called 'Germany reports' by the *Sopade* [Social Democratic Party of Germany (in exile)—H.B.].[321]

In general, the impressions and analyses in these 'Germany reports' unsparingly show the increasing turn of the working class towards National Socialism. In April/May 1934 they say, 'emotionally, the government has its greatest number of adherents among the working class'; shortly thereafter the 'shameful fact' is observed 'that the conduct of the workers permits Fascism to depend on them more and more' (June/July 1934); the workers were 'still strongly obsessed with Hitlerism' (January 1935) and believed, 'despite terror, despite wage decreases, despite enslavement', in the 'great saviour Adolf Hitler' (November 1935); and on many flags one could see that 'the swastika had been sewn over hammer and sickle' (December 1936). The will to resist, wrote a reporter from Berlin in March 1937, was not very widespread, it had to be admitted 'that most of the yielding elements were to be found specifically among the workers. If this were not the case, the regime could no longer exist today.'[322] There was of course also resistance against the NS regime from among the workers, primarily by Social Democrats and Communists. But on balance Hitler's calculation had proved to be correct. In their majority the workers no longer felt themselves as being a foreign body within the state but a respected and courted social force within the 'national community'.

c. The Lower Middle Class

A widespread theory says that Hitler's criticism of the bourgeoisie had been an expression of '*petit bourgeois*' protest and resentment. Accordingly, Hitler had been the prototype of the '*petit bourgeois*' and the NSDAP, in essence a lower middle-class movement. This theory appears to receive confirmation in the fact that a large number of the adherents of the NSDAP actually did stem from the lower middle class, which saw its existence threatened, particularly during the world economic crisis. This led to existential fear among many members of the lower middle class. They saw themselves being crushed between the two major classes, the middle class and the proletariat, and sought an alternative in the NSDAP. And, indeed, in its propaganda and in its polemics against the large department stores, for example, it pandered to these fears and promised the lower middle class a secure future. But how did Hitler assess the *petit bourgeoisie* or lower middle class?

In contradiction to the handy theory just sketched, the lower middle class played only a very subordinate role in Hitler's calculations. We are unable to find any statements by Hitler in his table talks, for example, and have to depend solely on his speeches, on *Mein Kampf* and on the articles in the *Illustrierte Beobachter*. The fact that Hitler only talked about the lower middle class very rarely, in public speeches with clearly demagogic and propaganda intent, could lead us to the conclusion that this class – as opposed to the working class and the bourgeoisie – did not play a key role in his thinking and programmes. Furthermore, the statements we have at our disposal must be regarded with much caution since – as was always the case with his statements on the bourgeoisie and the working class – they cannot be checked against internal statements made within his private circle without any propaganda intent. Much, if not everything, must therefore be regarded as mere demagogy and propaganda, and even in this, as far as Hitler is concerned, the lower middle class only played a secondary role.

We have already cited one remark by Hitler about the lower middle class in another context. In his letter to Konstantin Hierl on 3 July 1920 he attempted to excuse the relative lack of success of the NSDAP among the working class by pointing out that it was first necessary to create an awe-inspiring movement which must necessarily consist of members of the lower middle class, because only such an already numerically strong and powerful movement would impress the worker who was to be won over for the party.[323] Here, however, Hitler – as we have already shown – was making a virtue out of a vice and was only trying to justify to Hierl his relative lack of success with the working class. But, even in this line of argument, the lower middle class was only assigned the role of a social group which might be necessary in the early phase of the movement and whose function was only seen as being purely instrumental under the aspect of the main objective, the gaining of the working class.

On 28 September 1922 Hitler spoke about 'the policy of the destruction of our lower middle class'. Here he criticized the destruction of the lower middle class, for example, through the exploitation by the large department stores. It is quite interesting to hear the arguments with which he explains the importance of the lower middle class:

> But what is the condition of the German worker in this situation? Formerly he had the possibility of advancement. He could become independent and found his own small business, which could become bigger and bigger. No worker can found one of today's public stock companies. He therefore remains a *worker*, and he *must* remain a worker, and a *worker for wages* at that. There is no more advancement for him.

Hitler was therefore primarily interested in the lower middle class because of its function as a vehicle for the social advancement of the worker. For him the destruction of the lower middle class meant a further reduction of social mobility, in other words the chances for advancement for members of the working class. The lower middle class, Hitler continued, should be 'a connecting link between poor and rich'; its 'most valuable task' was 'to bridge the gap between the classes, which must destroy a nation'.[324] Thus the lower middle class was the truly national class because it stood midway between the left and the right side.

In *Mein Kampf* there is only one place where Hitler addresses himself to the '*petit bourgeoisie*' in some detail, and assesses its mentality, which was determined by its middle position between the two major classes of society:

> The environment of my youth consisted of the circles of the lower middle class, in other words out of a world which has very few connections to the purely manual worker. Because, as strange as it may appear to be at first glance, the chasm between this economically anything but well-placed class and the worker of the fist is often deeper than one would think. The reason for this, let us say quasi-hostility lies in the fear a social class, which has just very recently lifted itself above the level of the manual worker, has of sinking back again into the former little respected estate, or at least of still being counted as a part of it . . . And so it comes about that often the one higher up climbs down to his lowest fellow human being with fewer inhibitions than the 'upstart' will ever believe to be possible. Because anybody who by his own vigour manages to struggle upwards from his own station in life to a higher one is necessarily an upstart. And this often very harsh struggle kills all pity. One's own painful struggle for existence kills any feeling for the misery of the ones left behind.[325]

This quotation from *Mein Kampf* is of interest because it shows how Hitler assessed the mentality of the *petit bourgeoisie*. The latter is a class lying between the two major social classes – the middle class and the workers – which often takes sides against the workers out of its economic fear of existence, in other words, its fear of being drawn into the process of proletarianization. The characterization of those 'upstarts' who then separate themselves all the more forcefully from the lower classes, is an accepted part of a socio-psychological line of argument today. While Hitler often spoke most flatteringly about the possible 'bridging function' of the lower middle class in his speeches, he was basically probably more convinced of the opposite. The lower middle class could at best have a bridging function in the objective economic sense, insofar as it could serve as a vehicle for the social advancement of the worker. Politically, or from the view of mass psychology, the value of these social climbers was very doubtful, because they often took a particularly harsh position against the workers out of their fears of social decline. Nevertheless, Hitler did recognize that the fears of existence of the lower middle class could also be made use of politically. He described the tactics of Lueger, for example, who had placed the main emphasis of his political activities on 'gaining social levels whose existence was being threatened, as leading more to an incentive then a "paralyzation" of their will to fight'. Lueger had aligned his party 'primarily towards the lower middle class threatened with destruction' and by this had secured adherents of 'tenacious fighting power'[326] for himself.

This insight may have moved Hitler also to include the fears of the lower middle class in his propaganda. A frequent topic in this was the large department stores which, because many of them were owned by Jews, were a favourite target for the National Socialists and appeared to be well suited for channelling the fears of threatening destruction of the lower middle class – small store owners, for example – in an 'anti-Jewish' direction. If the spread of the Jewish department stores were to continue in this manner, Hitler wrote on 29 December 1928 in the *Illustrierte Beobachter*, then the whole lower middle class would one day end in ruin. 'With this, however, any bridge to a better livelihood, and particularly to an independent one, will end, thanks to which until now a constant replenishment of our upper levels of life from below has been able to take place.'[327] On 29 November 1929 Hitler explained his rejection of the department stores as follows:

> We reject the department store because it demolishes tens of thousands of small stores. These are the bridges over which in the course of the life of the nation with time thousands, yes tens of thousands, of able people from below slowly lift themselves up to higher positions in life. They are the means for the selection of an able class. If you support the department stores, then you destroy this bridge.[328]

While the lower middle class played a certain role in Hitler's thinking as a vehicle for the social advancement of the worker, overall this role was secondary. In his speeches he did chime in – in terms of propaganda, very effectively – with the 'demagogics' against the department stores and deplored the ruin of the lower middle class; he did not, however, pay this class anywhere near the attention he paid to the bourgeoisie and the working class.

d. The Farmers

An 'agrarian ideology' which Hitler is alleged to have advocated is often mentioned as proof that he had anti-modernistic objectives. According to this, while Hitler and the NSDAP did desire a change of society, in the end they wanted to recreate a sort of 'original state' which was characterized by a rejection of industrial society and the idealization of the farmer.[329] We intend to treat the problem of the relationship between the 'modernistic' and 'anti-modernistic' aspects of Hitler's *Weltanschauung* in a later chapter.[330] Here we only want to investigate in general terms what importance the farmer assumed in Hitler's view of society.

In Hitler's early speeches, articles and other notes[331] the farmer or agriculture played virtually no role at all. This is already shown by a cursory glance at the index in the compilation by Jäckel and Kuhn, where for example, the terms 'worker', 'working class' and 'proletariat' give referrals to over 300 pages whereas the term 'farmer' only occurs 27 times in over 1,300 pages, and then exclusively in contexts of very minor importance.

In *Mein Kampf* Hitler developed his objective to gain *Lebensraum* in the East, but, as we will show later, this was only intended for the settlement of farmers *among other things*.[332] In this context, in *Mein Kampf* Hitler also speaks about the importance of the agricultural community:

> The possibility of maintaining a healthy farming community as the foundation of the whole nation can already not be valued too highly. Many of our ills today are only the result of the unhealthy relationship between country and city people. A firm block of small and middle-sized farmers has always been the best protection against social ills such as we possess today. But this is also the only solution which permits a nation to find its daily bread within the circulation of an economy. Industry and commerce step back from their previous unhealthy position and integrate themselves into a national economy based on the satisfaction and balancing out of requirements. Both are then no longer the base for the feeding of the nation, but only a means of support for this. In that they now only have the task of balancing out their own production against the requirements in all areas, they make the whole of the feeding of the nation more or less independent of foreign countries, in other words help to secure the freedom of the state and the independence of the nation, especially in times of difficulties.[333]

This quotation could well be cited as a proof of Hitler's anti-modernistic concepts, and, indeed, such statements are an expression of anti-modernistic tendencies we can sometimes discover in Hitler between 1925 and 1928 but which accompany a far more pronounced modernistic tendency. We must also note here that, in the sentences cited above, Hitler is basically only expressing in a fairly complicated way a simple concept which he also presents elsewhere. While in his view a part of the export of industrial goods had only been necessary to date to finance the import of agricultural products and raw materials, after the conquest of *Lebensraum* in the East an autarkic greater area economy able to supply itself, above all in the sector of food, was to develop, which would make Germany independent in times of crisis and in case of war, and make a part of her exports superfluous in times of peace.

Hitler was worried about the apparently impending ruin of the farmers due to economic developments. On 18 October 1928 he said, 'It must not be permitted to come about that one day nothing is left of our farming community and all that is left is inhabitants of big cities.' This did not mean, however, that he was advocating a 'boundless protective tariff', any more than a 'boundless free trade'.[334]

Hitler not only attributed an importance to the agricultural community under the aspect of securing economic independence, but also valued the traits it had as a result of the way it lived and worked:

> The person who is torn in body and spirit does not develop any strength. This will always only be emanated by him who is externally and internally in complete unity, who is rooted in his native soil; the farmer, for ever the farmer. And also for the reason, because by the nature of his production he is thereby [sic!] forced to take an immense number of decisions. He mows and he does not know whether next day already it will rain and his whole harvest will drown. He sows and does not know whether next day there will not be frost. All of his work is constantly exposed to chance, and yet he still has to come to a decision time and again . . . When a nation is organized in a healthy way so that blood can always flow upward from below, such a nation can always draw strength without interruption from the deepest sources of its strength. Among its leadership it will then always possess men who also have the brutal strength of the person of the native soil, the strength that takes decisions. It is not a coincidence that the greatest nation in the antique world was at heart an agrarian state.[335]

Statements such as this, and similar ones from Hitler's speeches in 1928, could be used as evidence that he had idealized the agricultural community or advocated an 'agrarian ideology'. We should, however, be careful with rash generalizations. It is noteworthy that these sorts of statements all fell into the period of 1925 to 1928, and are in fact almost all concentrated in his speeches of 1928. Neither earlier nor later can statements be found which contain such a degree of idealization of the farmer. We begin to understand this when we consider that 1928 was the year which was characterized on the one hand by an upsurge of the farmers' movement due to the incipient agricultural crisis and leading, for instance, to a mass demonstration on 28 January in which 140,000 people took part,[336] and on the other brought the NSDAP successes in elections conducted in districts with above average numbers of people employed in agriculture.[337] It is therefore quite legitimate for us to assume that statements made by Hitler in his 1928 speeches are not necessarily to be interpreted as expressions of his *Weltanschauung* but are more likely to be propaganda slogans for the purpose of gaining further segments of the agricultural community for National Socialism. Furthermore, Hitler did not only argue ideologically, but partially on grounds of reality and economy. On 3 April 1929, for example, he declared that the result of the ruin of the agricultural community was that 'our domestic market becomes increasingly poorer, that the possibility of placing goods domestically shrinks more and more, and only because the farmer, the great original producer, no longer has any purchasing power'.[338]

From 1933 onwards Hitler's statements about the agricultural community are no longer anything more than hollow phrases without content and are only aimed at a certain audience (farmers). On 3 January 1933 he called the farmers the 'life source of our nation'[339] and on 10 February 1933 the 'supporting pillar of all national-popular life'.[340] Hitler then normally only mentioned the importance of the agricultural community when he spoke to farmers or to their representatives, as, for example, on 5 April 1933,[341] or on 1 October 1933 during a speech to 500,000 farmers on the Bückeberg [the venue for the annual NS rally for the farmers—H.B.]. Here he declared that 'the first and most profound representative of the nation' is the farmer,

> ... that part which nourishes the people out of the fertility of the earth and maintains the nation out of the fertility of his family. Just as liberalism and democratic Marxism negates the farmer, so does the National Socialist revolution deliberately stand by him as the most dependable bearer of the present, the only guarantor of the future.[342]

One of Hitler's closest and oldest intimates, Fritz Wiedemann, who had been his military superior during the First World War and later became his personal adjutant, writes in his memoirs: '... he [Hitler] was not at all interested in agriculture – except in the Reichs Farmers' Day on the Bückeberg'. Minister of Agriculture Darré had also once complained to him that he had now not been permitted to brief Hitler for two years.[343] Wiedemann's opinion that Hitler had not been at all interested in agriculture may be exaggerated. However, he is supported by the fact that in his speeches Hitler only used propaganda phrases when addressing himself to the agricultural community, and only rarely spoke about this class in his table talks, with the exception of the planned settlement of farmers in the *Lebensraum* to be conquered in the East.[344] The only constant in his thinking is the conviction that the farmer was particularly valuable, since his manner of producing and living constantly trained him to 'take decisions', because his occupation was the 'most risky' one there was.[345]

From the few statements in *Mein Kampf* and Hitler's speeches in 1928 we cannot yet deduce that he had fundamentally advocated an 'agrarian utopia'. We will have to investigate later whether the planned settlement of farmers in the East can serve as evidence for such a concept, or be assessed as proof of such an ideology. The discussion so far, however, has shown that Hitler took no interest at all in agriculture or the farmers during the early years (1919 to 1924), nor probably in the years after the seizure of power. The same would appear to apply here as for the lower middle classes: like them, the farmers did not play any outstanding role in Hitler's thinking – in contrast to previous assumptions. The two classes which really did play a big role in Hitler's programmes were the bourgeoisie on the one hand and the working class on the other.

4. The Definition of '*Volksgemeinschaft*' in Hitler's *Weltanschauung*

Having discussed Hitler's view of the individual classes and levels of society, the next question is how he envisaged the relationships between these various social groups. Hitler's objective was the creation of a *Volksgemeinschaft* [a 'national community'—H.B.] in which class war would be abolished. While he rejected class war, he did regard 'economic class interests' as being quite legitimate – as can be seen from the notes to a speech held on 1 March 1922 – as long as they did not call the higher unit of the national community into question.[346] As Hitler emphazised in *Mein Kampf*, the integration of the working class into the national community did not mean a

> ... renunciation of the advocacy of legitimate class interests. Diverging class or occupational interests are not synonymous with class division, but are the natural results of our economic life ... The integration of an estate which has become a class into the national community, or even only into the state, does not take place by way of the descent of higher classes, but by the uplifting of the lower one. The bearer of the process can again never be the higher class, but the lower one fighting for its equality ... The German worker will not be lifted up into the framework of the German national community by detours into feeble scenes of fraternization, but by the conscious uplifting of his social and cultural situation for so long until the most grievous differences can be considered to have been bridged.[347]

When Hitler polemizes against the idea that the integration of the working class into the national community could take place via 'feeble scenes of fraternization', and instead emphasizes the need for a real improvement of the social and cultural conditions of the worker, this is done in clear-cut opposition to the concepts of a 'class reconciliation' ultimately based on a freezing of the existing social *status quo*, or even on the socio-reactionary intention of eliminating any pronounced economic representation by the working class. Hitler, on the other hand, emphasizes that as long as neither through governmental measures nor re-education 'a change in the position of the employer towards the employee occurs, the latter has no other recourse than to defend his interests himself, under appeal to his rights as an equal contracting party within the economic system'. Hitler was of the opinion that 'such a defence was well within the interests of the whole national community, if it were able to prevent social injustices which must lead to serious damage to the whole community of a nation'. He went on to declare that 'the necessity must be regarded as existing for as long as there were people among the entrepreneurs, who on their part did not possess any feelings for social obligations, and not even for the most primitive of human rights'. From this he drew the conclusion that unions, as the organized form of economic representation of the worker, were necessary. Organizing the workers into unions was necessary because

> ... a truly National Socialist education of both the employer and the employee in the sense of a mutual integration into the common framework of the national community does not take place by theoretical teachings, appeals or admonitions but by the daily battle for life. In it, and by it, the movement must educate the individual large economic groups and bring them closer together on the major points of view. Without such preparatory work any hope of the development of a future true national community remains pure illusion.[348]

At the end of 1922 Hitler had advocated the point of view that

> ... in themselves, the unions are not harmful, as long as they are interest groups, like, for example, the British unions. But because the unions are politicizing and therefore de-nationalizing themselves more and more, they have become a danger for the existence of Germanism and share the guilt for our collapse.[349]

He also recognized a strike for the enforcement of legitimate economic demands as being necessary, but no longer within the National Socialist state because there the balancing out of diverging economic interests could take place in other ways.[350] In this Hitler's reasoning is similar to that of today's 'real socialist' states, which emphasize the necessity of independent unions and strikes in capitalism just as vehemently as they do their superfluousness in a socialist state, which represents the interests of the worker as a matter of course.

Here we must again note what we have already discovered elsewhere: Hitler was not opposed to the unions because they represented the legitimate interests of the worker, but because they were controlled by 'Marxism', primarily by the Social Democrats, and were an instrument for class war.[351] The actual reason why Hitler destroyed the unions after his seizure of power was not because he, as a 'lackey of capitalism', wanted to rob the workers of the representation of their interests, but because he feared political opposition to his regime emanating from the unions. The DAF, which was created as a substitute for the unions, was certainly not a union in the traditional sense, but it did perform many similar functions, and by applying massive pressure did in fact succeed in pushing through the interests of the workers and social improvements.

As Mason discovered, the DAF developed into a 'representation of worker interests'; it became 'the proponent of improved living and working conditions for the employer in industry'. This development did not take place against Hitler's intentions, but only became possibly through the commitment of his personal authority. When in the summer of 1934 the activists of the DAF came under massive criticism from, among others, German industry, he 'backed up the DAF' and on 24 October signed a decree on the nature and objectives of the DAF presented to him by Ley [chief of the DAF—H.B.], 'whose "rubber paragraphs" could have legitimized any conceivable social political activity by the DAF'. On 29 August 1936 Hitler signed an appeal by Ley which initiated a competition for the 'National Socialist model enterprise'. In confidence of victory Ley commented, 'The *Führer* has placed an enormous weapon of a social-political nature in our hand – and we know how to apply it!' As a result of the competition between the enterprises for the best social-political achievements, there was a rise in the expenditure recommended by the office for 'the beauty of work' (for company canteens, company doctors, sports facilities, employee housing etc.) from 80 million RM (1936) to over 200 million RM (1938). A Reich Trustee for Labour estimated that the total social reforms of these years – including the payments for holidays – had increased personnel costs for industry by roughly 6.5 per cent. The preponderance of the employer in all company matters had, as Mason has discovered, 'been revised in decisive points'. Whereas Minister of Economics Schacht refused demonstratively to take part in the award ceremonies where the golden flags were presented to the NS model enterprises, Hitler made these awards personally.[352]

When at the end of 1937 the DAF began to try to acquire the responsibility for housing and settlement policy, it ran into bitter opposition from Minister of Labour Seldte. But Hitler backed up the DAF and Gauleiter Bürckel, who was strongly engaged in the social sector,[353] and then finally assigned all housing policy to the responsibility of the DAF in November 1942.[354] These examples from the realities of social policy in the Third Reich cited by Mason – whose overall interpretation, however, does not coincide with our own – show that Hitler did not in any way oppose a pronounced advocacy of workers' interests within the framework of the national community, but that he supported it and tended to take sides with the Labour Front in the conflicts between the DAF and industry.

These clarifications at the beginning of the chapter on the national community are important because we wish to avoid a misunderstanding right from the beginning. If Hitler saw the national community as a means for abolishing the class war, this did not mean that he negated or ignored the continued existence of economic class opposites and the necessity of advocating these interests. He did hold the view, however, that beyond these diverging interests a common platform could be created so that the economically diverging interests need not develop into political fronts. He said on 9 November 1927:

> We cannot remove the economic and occupational differences, but we can change something else, namely the opinion that these differences could ever be abolished by splitting up into classes and one winning out over the other. That is insanity. We oppose this theory with the living theory of the national community, in which head and fist are united, in which the small differences will continue to exist, but in which a common foundation must be the common national interest which grows far beyond the ridiculously petty personal fights, occupational differences, economic battles and so forth. These may still exist in the future. But above and beyond economic battles and occupational differences, beyond all the divergencies of daily life, there is something, namely the community of a nation which numbers over 60 million human beings who have too little ground on which to live, and whom nobody will give life to, unless it will give this life to itself.[355]

Even though Hitler recognized the opposing economic interests of the various social groups, he did believe – at least temporarily – in a relative identity of the interests of all the levels of the people. In a speech on 30 November 1928 he declared that there would 'obviously also be eternal differences in the future within such a national community', but it was

> ... not indifferent ... whether a national community in its entirety was on a declining path and going towards destruction or whether in its entirety it was developing itself upward and possessed the conditions for life ... It is an insanity to promise something to a class today which can only work at the expense of other classes, if one does not have the courage to look the situation of the whole nation in the eye, and this situation is desperate domestically and abroad.[356]

On 12 April 1931 he emphasized that 'it is necessary to only look at the overall interest above the interests of the individuals, that these have to count as the most important, because the interests of the individual can only develop after them'.[357]

After the seizure of power Hitler defined himself as being 'a mediator' between the various class and group interests. Because he knew the various strata of the German people better than many others, he was able to be the 'honest mediator to all sides', because he was dependent neither on the state nor on public office, nor on business or industry, nor on any union. Hitler's statement in front of an audience of workers, that he liked nothing better than 'to be the advocate of those who were not well able to defend themselves',[358] was certainly highly effective propaganda.

Hitler held the opinion that the state should not be the instrument of a class and that it could not be left up to chance whose interests prevailed in the end. In this sense he was a decided opponent of a pluralistic model of society, in which all the groups attempt to assert their individual and special interests.[359] In contrast to this, he underlined the need to 'develop a leadership which stands above the opposing parts and can authoritatively decide about both of them'. On 8 October 1935 he declared,

> We are in the process to also solve the differences on which the class war is based in a factual manner. We are in the fortunate position of being able to implement this factual solution, because we ourselves stand above these differences. I must be permitted to say that I hold myself to be the most independent man in this sense, obligated towards nobody, subjected to nobody, owing gratitude to nobody, but solely responsible to my conscience . . . And under me and next to me all of my co-fighters are just as independent. We are therefore in a position to investigate these problems underlying the class war completely objectively, and to solve them to the best of our knowledge and belief . . .[360]

In order to make good this claim, it was Hitler's primary concern – as we will show in Chapter IV.3 – to establish the 'primacy of politics over economics'. He took special care therefore, that no official of the NSDAP and no official of the state owned shares, sat on a supervisor board etc.[361] In his opinion only the economic independence of the political leadership could guarantee the establishment of the primacy of politics and thereby the possibility to take decisions independently of diverging economic interests.

Another important attribute of the term 'national community' is the claim, or better the intent, to bring about a certain 'equalization'. We have already seen that Hitler was just as much a vehement opponent of the concept of 'general human equality' as he was a proponent of 'equal opportunity'. The basis for Hitler's intended class reconciliation, however, was a sort of partial levelling or equalization in various social sectors.

Hitler regarded such an equalization as being particularly important in times of war. He criticized the German government in the First World War and declared that they should have spread the conviction that

> Everybody will be treated equally, there is now only one commandment and that is called Fatherland, Fatherland, and yet again Fatherland! Whether rich or poor,

whoever offends against it dies! . . . Nobody has the right to believe himself to be superior to any other only because appearances apparently place him in a higher position. The one who has the highest place among the others is not the one who owns the most, but the one who contributes the most to the community . . . The upright man – even if he were to be poor – will, because the maintenance of the body of the nation basically depends upon honesty, have to be counted of more worth than a rich man who possesses fewer virtues which serve the maintenance of the body of the nation.[362]

The wearing of uniforms, which was customary within the National Socialist movement and later on also in the Third Reich, was also an expression of the egalitarian tendency:

Do not believe that we created this uniform as a fad, as part of a game; no, it was a unique necessary insight. We must reach the point where Germans can walk together arm in arm without regard to their station in life. Unfortunately today the crease in the trousers and the blue mechanic's overall sometimes form means of separation. We are building an army of young political fighters and this army wears one dress, and with this we are announcing what else it is that we are, this is just as much all the same of one kind as it was the same of one kind once before, namely in August 1914.[363]

The equalization was to take place even in areas that appeared to be quite secondary. In a conversation on 20 May 1937, for example, Hitler told Abel Bonnard, a member of the *Académie Française*:

Until very recently on board the ships of the large passenger lines there was a shattering contrast between the luxury which was reserved for the passengers and the life led by the crews. On the one hand all the refinements and anything you could desire, and on the other no advantages or comforts, but only difficult living conditions and unhealthy situations. When we demanded that the crews were to be given better quarters we were told that space on the big ships was too expensive for our request to be granted. When we demanded that a special deck was to be reserved for the crews so that they could get fresh air, we were told that this posed technical problems which the engineers had not yet been able to solve. Today the crew on these ships has decent cabins. It has a deck at its disposal so that it can recuperate in decent deckchairs, it has radios for entertainment, it has a dining room where it takes its meals together with a deck officer, and all of these improvements were not so expensive; you just had to have the will.[364]

This is possibly also an example of Hitler's unsystematic and often purely random manner of conducting politics.[365] Apparently Hitler became aware of the shortcomings he mentioned during an inspection of a passenger liner, and thereupon issued the directives to alter them. While it can not be proved in the case at hand, this manner of conducting politics was typical of Hitler. If he happened to come across some shortcoming, this was reason enough for him to

III. Hitler's Social Objectives

become angry, sometimes even enraged, and gave him material for monologues sometimes lasting for hours. As a rule someone – in later years Martin Bormann – then took over the task of issuing a concrete directive to have the shortcoming corrected. It was probably also during an inspection or a trip on a ship that Hitler grew angry about the big differences between the various classes of travel. In one of his subsequent monologues at *Führer* headquarters he said:

> It was frightening to see how still only a few years ago on our large passenger steamers differences were made in the way guests of the 3rd, 2nd and 1st Class were quartered. It boggles the mind that one was not ashamed of displaying the differences in living conditions in such a manner. This is a major field of activity for the DAF. On the trains in the East, all Germans – to segregate themselves from the natives – will ride in the upholstered class, whereby the difference between the 1st and 2nd Classes will perhaps only be that here you have three seats where there are four there. The community kitchen in the *Wehrmacht* is a stroke of luck: already during the World War the food was incomparably better when the officers had to share it too.[366]

On 27/28 September 1941 Hitler said during a table talk:

> Until recently we had four messes in parallel in the Navy. Not too long ago this even cost us a ship. The opinion that one would need to fear a loss of authority if there were no differences made here is unfounded. He who does better and knows more than the others always has the authority he needs, whereas the one who is not superior in ability and knowledge is not helped by the position to which he is elevated by his office. The quarters of the domestic help in Berlin apartments, for example, was a scandal, and those of the crews even on luxury liners was unworthy. I know that this cannot be changed over night everywhere, but the spirit of the times has at least changed.[367]

In his table talks Hitler frequently attacked the double-standards of the 'upper ten thousand' and the nobility, whose 'falseness', as he said on 12 May 1942, made him 'furious':

> A Prussian prince who jilts several dozen women with whom he has had intimate relations and – having grown tired of them – casts them aside like inanimate objects, is regarded as a man of honour by these moral hypocrites, whereas a decent German man who wants to marry the woman who is expecting his child regardless of her social position is inundated in a flood of malicious remarks by them.[368]

In a table talk on 14 May 1942 Hitler said that

> The so-called 'unwritten laws' on officers' marriages 'befitting their station', 'had been emphatically rejected by National Socialism because they were based on a completely mendacious morality. They were the concepts of a bygone world long overcome. According to them, an officer was only permitted to marry girls who

belonged to certain social groups. To marry the honest daughter of an upright master craftsman was considered not to be in keeping with social position and was turned down. Whoever wanted to marry such a girl anyway had to quit active service.[369]

These examples show that within the 'national community' Hitler was advocating an equalization in many areas of life and that for him this equalization was even a condition for the realization of the 'national community'. Schoenbaum has underlined these egalitarian tendencies of National Socialism and drawn attention to the dialectics of freedom versus bondage and equality. By the fact that the worker shared his 'enslavement', in other words, his bondage with his 'former masters', it became, said Schoenbaum, 'paradoxically a sort of equality or even freedom'.[370] Hitler himself declared on 28 July 1942, in a table talk, that the war doubtless required a particularly stringent reduction of freedom:

> What is of decisive importance is that the reduction of personal freedom takes place equally. This applies on the home front, within the *Wehrmacht*, among the troops at the front. The undifferentiated reduction of personal freedom which affects everybody to the same degree will be accepted by the overwhelming understanding majority as being necessary.

The confidence of the people was based 'primarily on the decreed reductions being demanded from all the national comrades in just distribution, and that the leadership also subjects itself to them'.[371]

Hitler could have expected a large measure of agreement from the population when he declared, as he did in a speech on 26 April 1942, that

> In these times nobody can insist on his well-earned rights, but must know that today there are only obligations. I therefore ask the German *Reichstag* for the explicit confirmation that I possess the legal right to admonish anybody to fulfil his obligations, and to have those who in my opinion, as based on conscientious consideration, do not fulfil their obligations, sentenced to common punishment or removed from their office and position, without regard to who they may be, or what acquired rights they might possess . . . I am therefore not interested in whether, in this time of need, a civil servant or an employee can be granted a holiday or not, and I forbid that this holiday, which can not be granted, is saved up for a later time. If there were anybody who had a right to demand a holiday, this would be our soldiers at the front in the first instance, and in the second the men and women who are working for the front.[372]

Such statements by Hitler were also a reaction to the reports by the SD [*Sicherheitsdienst*, or Security Service—H.B.] which spoke of the grumblings among the workers about the unequal distribution of the severities caused by the war. But such announcements by Hitler also provoked great expectations and demands by the workers. The black market was being criticized, for example, in which the workers could hardly take part due to long working hours and a lack of things to trade. The leadership took the SD reports about such criticism extremely seriously. In January 1942 action began to be taken against black marketeering which was approved by Hitler and carried out under Goebbels' direct responsibility. A harsh directive against black marketeering followed in March. The press reported almost daily about sentences of death.[373]

This may serve as an example that it is quite inadmissible rigidly to separate 'objective reality' and 'propaganda' from 'subjective awareness' as done on, for example, the Marxist side, because the propaganda generated an egalitarian awareness and massive demands by the workers. The regime made use of this and showed an 'increasing preparedness to react "revolutionarily", so to speak, to ill feelings'. Goebbels understood the totality of the war to be an active 'revolutionary' measure. He attempted to make use of the class war-like demands and motivations the SD had reported about. As Herbst has stated,

> The socio-revolutionary pathos developed its own dynamics. It animated those who wanted to utilize the emergency situation of the war for a fundamental structural change of the economy and society, and put off those who had trusted in the sacrifices of the war being made up for after peace returned, and that the 'old' order would be restored.[374]

This shows that it was less the sharp separation and far more the dialectic combination of propaganda-awareness-reality which had to lead to the dynamics of revolutionary restructuring of society which were characteristic for the Third Reich.

With the announcement that now everybody, 'whoever he might be or whatever acquired rights he might possess', would equally be admonished to 'the fulfilment of his obligations', Hitler generated the expectation, particularly in female workers, that now the women of the higher-income classes would also be conscripted for work in the same way as themselves. This only took place in part, however, and while the egalitarian claim of National Socialism and the expectations this created did produce revolutionary pressure from below, it was not successfully functionalized for the revolutionary restructuring 'from above' in the manner intended because Hitler did not want to risk a conflict with the economically dominant groups during the war. It would also have required proceeding against important representatives of the regime who, like Göring, openly paraded their luxury and thereby gave the lie to the egalitarian claim of National Socialism.

It has been pointed out repeatedly that one result of the modernization initiated by National Socialism was an advance in women's rights.[375] In view of the basically anti-emancipation position held by Hitler and the National Socialists, this has been made to serve as proof for the theory of the contradiction between intention and effect of the NS revolution. This theory can probably find its strongest justification in this area, but we should also take into account that there were relevant forces within the NS movement which were very positively inclined towards the emancipation process for women. In her study, which for the first time presents us with a differentiated picture of National Socialism's position on the question of women, L. Rupp even speaks of 'Nazi feminists' and casts doubts on the previously held view of a uniform anti-emancipation position of National Socialism 'in total'. 'The misogynist views of the top Nazi leaders, and the views of the Nazi feminists, represent opposite ends of the spectrum of Nazi ideas about women. The great majority of writers on the subject, many of them women, fall somewhere in between.'[376]

Because this would lead 'to the most catastrophic human and political consequences', Goebbels, too, expressly rejected any attempts to force women out of the job market – and not only after labour had become scarce but soon after the seizure of power:

> When 'unmodern', reactionary people declare today that the female does not belong behind a desk, in public office and social welfare installations, because this had not formerly been the case, then this line of reasoning is based on an error. Formerly there simply were no offices and welfare installations in this sense.

By using the same argument, one could just as easily force men out of newly created jobs. But just as the methods of work had changed, so too would the women's share of men's work change.[377] D. Winkler states: 'With this Goebbels was defending the changes in the structure of work and society brought about by industrialization against those anti-modernization tendencies within the party whose ideologists condemned the results of industrialization and desired a return to a pre-industrial society.'[378]

Nonetheless, with good reason the changed condition of women in society can be defined as an area in which the equalizing effects of National Socialism had essentially not been intended. On the other side, there are important social areas in which the equalizing effect of the 'brown revolution' were unquestionably intended by the National Socialists, and even deliberately brought about. In a study on the situation of salaried employees during the Third Reich, Michael Prinz comes to the conclusion that already at the end of the 1930s there had been a clearly noticeable change in the relationship between hourly worker and salaried employee. This was not in any way, as

Prinz emphasizes, the result of a policy of levelling downwards, but the expression of the greater importance the regime attached to the interests of the worker. As opposed to the 1920s, most of the reductions in the differences between salaried and hourly employees instigated by the NS state were due to an uplifting of the workers.

Benefits which had formerly been regarded as typical privileges of the white-collar employee were now also extended to the workers. This applied, for example, to paid public holidays or extended vacations. Without the white-collar employees having to suffer any reductions, they still lost their former privileges and with them the foundation for their pronounced special middle-class class consciousness.

The gradual disappearance of this special consciousness was not only the result of a material and legal equalization process, but also of a changed ideology. 'By satisfying the workers' age-old need for social recognition, and by simultaneously reproaching the bourgeoisie for its historic failures in this area, the NS state achieved a lasting change in the image and self-image of the workers in German society.' Any attempt in public to separate oneself from the workers was criticized or ridiculed as being 'class conceit'.[379]

Egalitarianism, which in Hitler's view was the condition for creating a 'national community', was also to be demonstrated in symbolic actions such as the 'eating of stew', or by charity drives such as Winter Help. Hitler explained the object of the annual collections for Winter Help in several speeches. On 13 September 1933 he said:

> If we understand this concept of national solidarity in the right way, then it can only be a concept of sacrifice, in other words, if one or the other of us says that this is too much of a burden, that you had to give again and again, then one can only reply: 'That is exactly the meaning of a truly national solidarity.' True national solidarity cannot have its meaning in taking. If one part of our nation has fallen into need due to conditions we are all to blame for, and the other, spared by fate, is prepared to take only a part of this need the other is forced to bear upon itself voluntarily, then we say: it is the intention to burden a part of our nation with a certain amount of need so that it helps thereby to make the need of the others more bearable... When all of the people have correctly grasped that these measures must mean a sacrifice for everyone, then from these measures there will not only flow an alleviation of the material need, but something far more powerful will come out of this, the conviction will grow from this that this national community is not an empty term, but that it is truly something living.

The collection drives therefore had not only a material and economic function, but above all also a spiritual one, in that 'in the masses of millions who have not been blessed by fortune' they generated the conviction that 'those who have been more favoured by fortune feel for them and are prepared to voluntarily make a sacrifice'.[380]

As Hitler said in his address on 17 April 1934 to the Gauleiters of Winter Help, it was intended to contribute 'to teaching the people to think socialist'.[381] In his speech to the 1934 Winter Help campaign Hitler polemized against the 'upper ten thousand' particularly strongly:

> Our upper ten thousand apparently do not have even a clue how much sorrow and pain it takes for a mother to first reach the decision and then carry it out, to spare herself and the children further life in this world without hope! ... And here the upper ten thousand in particular, and the masses of a nation who are better off, have a high obligation. And at this point I would therefore like to say quite frankly that the Winter Help drive is counting especially on those who are in a position to make a sacrifice more easily than the broad population. And I expressly say here 'a sacrifice' because I consider it to be hardly honourable when a wealthy man with a high income gives the same amount as somebody who is hardly able to earn his daily bread for himself to a sufficient degree. In contrast to this, I hold that within his means, every individual really does make a sacrifice which he himself will feel to have been a sacrifice. I express the strong hope that what we were able to discover in a number of cities last year will not repeat itself this year, namely that poorer districts mobilized more in sacrifice than the economically better situated. In such cases I am in favour of bringing this shameful fact to the attention of the whole nation in future.[382]

Hitler assessed the integrative function of such actions as the collections for Winter Help and the 'eating of stew' as being very high. In his speech on the Winter Help campaign in 1935 he explained in detail its ideological function in the process of creating and maintaining the 'national community':

> Let us not deceive ourselves. The danger of the sundering of our nation still exists today. Outside of us and all around us the ferments of subversion only lie in wait for the moment when they can one day lead the poison we have eliminated back into our bodies again ... We are all burdened by the past, and many among us Germans also by the present. All the factors of origin and wealth, of knowledge, of culture and so forth, traditions of many kinds, they split the people, they are suited to dissolving the national community time and again. Woe be it if these divisive elements are not opposed by something unifying. Business cannot solve everything; it is in its nature that alongside of success, somehow there always also marches failure. It lies in the nature of this economic battle that already out of the natural and necessary process of selection this path more or less always leads over sacrifices. How easy to just leave these fallen lying! How easy to say: they have fallen, they have stumbled, what do we care? Here the national community must make its appearance, and must help this individual whom economic life has knocked down back up on his feet again immediately, must support them and must integrate them in a new process into the life of the community again.

III. Hitler's Social Objectives

One could of course, Hitler continued, collect the amounts brought in by the drive far more easily by means of a tax, but this would miss the ideological purpose of the drive: 'It is not the state which should force you to do your natural duty, but you should give your feeling for your national community a living expression yourself! You must step up and make a voluntary sacrifice.'[383]

The integration of the national community was to take place on the basis of the National Socialist *Weltanschauung*, the various classes were to come together on the common platform of a obligatory ideology. Hitler emphasized repeatedly that compulsion and force were not sufficient as a foundation for ruling, and that only a '*Weltanschauung*' could serve as a dependable base for society: 'This is simply how it is: in the long run you cannot maintain a regime by police, machine gun and truncheon alone. It also requires something else, some sort of belief in a necessity of the maintenance of the regime for reasons of a *Weltanschauung*.'[384]

In a letter to Colonel von Reichenau dated 2 December 1932 Hitler criticized the appointment of Schleicher as Reichs Chancellor and argued that

> ... neither the police nor the military have ever destroyed a *Weltanschauung*, and even less built a *Weltanschauung* up. Without a *Weltanschauung*, however, no human structure can survive in the long run. *Weltanschauungen* are the only social contracts and foundations on which larger human organizations can be erected.[385]

'The new thought, the new political faith ... the new idea' were, said Hitler in his address on 1 May 1933, to provide the integration base for the national community.[386] On 30 January 1939, in a speech to the *Reichstag*, he declared that the national community 'could not primarily be created through the coercion of force, but through a coercive force of an idea and therefore through the efforts of a continuous education ... National Socialism ... has set up a timeless objective with its national community, which can only be aspired to, achieved and maintained by continuous and constant education.'[387]

In Hitler's view, therefore, the creation and maintenance of a national community was, first, only possible on the basis of a specific *Weltanschauung* and secondly needed a constant education or re-education of the people in order to infuse them with faith in an ideal, a 'great idea'. Without this constant process of education and re-education a national community would be inconceivable. Hitler frequently emphasized the necessity of this 'educational effort' in his speeches and conversations. To Wagener he said:

> The most important thing is the inner conversion of the people, the national comrades, the nation! And that is a political task! Almost all of the people are still caught up in a liberalistic viewpoint. Do you really believe that a dyed-in-the-wool industrialist will suddenly be prepared to admit that his ownership is not a right

but an obligation? That capital shall no longer rule but be ruled? That the life of the individual does not matter but rather that of the total? That the principle of the soldierly sacrifice of life is also to be transferred to the willingness of everybody who otherwise works in industry, or wherever else, to make a sacrifice for the community? This is such a deep-reaching and complete change that the grown-ups are no longer capable of it. Only the youth can be readjusted, newly prepared for and aligned to the socialist sense of the obligation towards the community.[388]

In the address to the leaders of the SS and SA in Bad Reichenhall on 2 July 1933 – which we have already cited in another context[389] – Hitler emphasized that

> ... every spiritual *Weltanschauung*'s revolution *must be followed by the education and shaping of the people* to the ideal which gave this revolution its meaning. Revolutions could only be considered to have been successful when, besides their bearers, they were able to stamp their times with their spirit and insight. The new state would remain a product of the imagination if it did not succeed in creating a new human being. For the last two and a half thousand years virtually all revolutions had failed, with very few exceptions, because their bearers had not recognized that *the essential thing about a revolution is not the take-over of power but the education of the people.*[390]

At a meeting of the SA one week later, on 9 July 1933, he said, 'Our first task consists of the following: We have the power. There is nobody who can oppose us today. Now however we must educate the German human being for this state.'[391]

On 1 May 1934 Hitler again emphasized the long duration of the planned process of re-education: 'True socialism required a complete re-education of the people.' The realization of socialism was therefore an 'enormous task of education', which could only be completed in the coming generations.[392] This work of re-education was far more difficult than the actual seizure of power. In his opening proclamation at the 1934 *Reichsparteitag* he stressed that 'To overturn the power of government in a nation of 68 million individual beings and to take it over is difficult. But to turn these 68 million individual beings of a dead-end world into soul fighters of a new idea is a thousand times more difficult.'[393]

A year later, at the '*Reichsparteitag* of Freedom', Hitler drew attention to the importance of continuing untiringly in 'the education of the German people to a true community': 'We are convinced that this final task is our hardest. It is the one which has to overcome the most prejudices, the one most burdened by the results and bad traditions of a long history and suffers most from the doubts of the faint-hearted.' Only he was a National Socialist

> ... who untiringly feels himself obligated to the idea, who serves it, and seeks support for it ... And therefore, my party comrades, at this Seventh *Parteitag* of

the movement, we want to fight through more sharply than ever before to the recognition that the National Socialist party has an eternal and uninterrupted mission of education of our nation to fulfil, and therein its own proving.'[394]

It was the task of the party, said Hitler in his closing speech at the *Parteitag*, 'by its educational work to provide the National Socialist state *with the National Socialist people to support it*'. In this it must hold the view that '*all Germans are to be educated to become National Socialist in their* Weltanschauung'. The final objective had to be 'in future to provide the national and governmental structures exclusively with National Socialists by the complete encompassing in the party and the circle of its adherents of all Germans by means of the National Socialist enlightenment and teachings'.[395]

A year later, at the 1936 *Reichsparteitag*, in his address to the DAF Hitler again declared 'the education of a new human being who thought socially' to be necessary, which was also a very long process. Again and again the individual had to have 'hammered' into him: 'You are only a servant of your people! Alone you are nothing, only in the community are you everything, only in the ranks are you a power!'[396]

In his closing speech at the *Parteitag* Hitler requested that the party

... continue to represent and emphasize *the socialist character of the present Reich* with the utmost consistency. In these unquiet times the well brought-up burgher is of no use to us who only thinks of his enterprise and who loses sight of the total power of the nation and the reasons underlying it. The goal of National Socialism is not 'Marxist chaos', but it is also not 'bourgeois preservation'. In the past few years we have made infinite progress in the education of our nation to a higher socialist sense of communality. National Socialism, in other words the party, they must continue to march forward here, in order to form a *unique dedicated community* out of a formerly torn and split nation.

The party had, Hitler emphasized, 'to continue more than before with the spiritual education of the national community'.[397]

In Hitler's view, the creation of a national community was not a singular act but a constant task which required, above all, the re-education of people to 'socialist thinking'. Within the process of the creation of a national community, said Hitler on 6 October 1936, the decisive task of the future was 'to educate the German people to become true National Socialists, to a living inner confession and to a genuine conduct in this sense'.[398] On 30 January 1937 he pointed out that a person in the National Socialist state had to be educated, or re-educated, for the whole of his life:

The National Socialist movement has given the state the guidelines for the education of our nation. This education does not begin in a certain year and does not end in another. In the course of human development it has come about that from a certain point in time on, the continuing education of the child must be taken out of the care of the most intimate cell of communal life, the family, and entrusted to the community itself. The National Socialist movement has set this communal education certain tasks, and above all made it independent of a specific age, in other words the teaching of the individual person can never come to an end! It is therefore the task of the national community to take care that this teaching and ongoing education is always in the sense of its interests, in other words the preservation of the nation.[399]

Hitler already intended to re-educate his own generation but believed that this would be a very difficult undertaking because of its many internalized norms, prejudices and behaviour patterns. The 'final implementation of the programme' of the National Socialist movement would take 'until we have brought up a new generation in Germany, which will then have gone through our school'.[400] Hitler emphasized time and again that the task of re-educating the Germans to become a national community was still far from being ended. In his speech on 1 May 1937 he exhorted his audience:

Do not say that this task has been solved and nothing now remains to be done. Life obliges each generation to fight its own fight for this life. And what the centuries have piled up in the way of prejudices and stupidity, that cannot be completely removed in only four years. That does not happen at once![401]

In his address to the DAF at the '*Reichsparteitag* for Work' in 1937 he spoke about the 'many obstacles' which lay in traditions, pet customs, beliefs and opinions 'and above all always again the beloved old habits which number among the most lethargic things that exist on this earth'. It could be far easier to 'overthrow governments' than to overcome such habits, 'because in that which has been overthrown, the old habits then again establish themselves all too easily'. These traditions, habits of thought and customs had to be done away with by constant education and re-education. This 'mission of education' was 'an eternal one, one that remained'. In Hitler's view, an important instrument in this process of re-education were the National Socialist mass organizations, particularly the DAF: 'Formerly we had classes in which people were inoculated with class consciousness. Now in certain organizations we inoculate them with national consciousness.' The DAF had the task of contributing to

... hammering national consciousness into the national comrade ... People tend to cling so strongly precisely to something that is not worth tying yourself to so much. All that has now to be brought out. And this is a wonderful task. And when somebody tells me this has not yet been achieved – we are still only counting the fifth year of our era. Now just leave us 100 or 200 years of time.

III. Hitler's Social Objectives

Man was 'the result of a year-long, century-long, yes, millennia-long process of education'. It was therefore necessary constantly to re-educate oneself, and this re-education was the 'greatest and by far most important task'.[402]

In his speech to the 1937 Winter Help campaign he again emphasized that the drive was to serve the re-education of the national community:

> *Our National Socialist Winter Help is therefore also, purely educationally, possibly the greatest applied social work the world has ever seen* . . . By this form of education this Winter Help should draw the individual person's attention time and again to the fact there are social problems among us.

It was the task of Winter Help to educate people to socialism, because '*Nobody is finally born to be a socialist. You have to be brought up to be one.*' This process of education, however, was never ended but had to be constantly continued and renewed.[403]

The creation of a national community, said Hitler on 1 May 1938, was the 'result of a planned education of our people by the National Socialist movement'.[404] The 'unified body of the people', he remarked at the 1938 *Reichsparteitag*, came about 'through education. Only by it alone can we create the nation that we require and that those will require who intend to write history after we are gone.'[405]

Hitler's statements at the start of the Winter Help campaign in 1940 are of particular interest because the picture of man he develops here contradicts the theories of many 'racial theorists' of the Third Reich:

> National Socialism has always held the opinion that any given position is only the product of upbringing, habit, heredity and can therefore also be redirected again. Because the child which grows up in our nation is not born with any prejudices of status or class origin, it is taught them. Only in the course of his life are these differences artificially forced upon it . . . We bring people up to have a uniform view of life, to a uniform generally accepted concept of duty, and we are convinced that after a certain era of this education *the people will be the products of this education*, in other words they will then represent the new thinking to the same extent that today they still partially embody the old.[406]

This example clearly demonstrates that Hitler is arguing less consistently from the racial-biological point of view than many 'racial theorists' who claimed that they loyally represented the NS *Weltanschauung* in the Third Reich. For National Socialist racial theorists, man was certainly not primarily a 'product of education' but, on the contrary, it was heredity which was decisive. Hitler himself also advocated this racial theory when the topic was the races he denounced as being 'inferior' [Jews, blacks, Slavs etc.—R.Z.] and where he would have flatly rejected the idea that their attributes could be the result of an education or of certain environmental influences. As far as his own 'national comrades' were concerned, the members of the 'German national community' from which these 'racially inferior' groups were to be systematically 'eradicated', he repeatedly emphasized that the differences between them were primarily due to their upbringing, even though he also held the view that this 'Aryan racial core' was composed of various racial elements. On 10 December 1940 he declared that people were 'the product of their education':

> And this unfortunately begins almost with their birth. The little mite in one case is already being swathed differently from the little mite in the other case. And then it goes on like that. And if this goes on for centuries, then suddenly someone comes along and says: Now I want to unwrap you out of your various wrappings so that the core comes out again, because in the core you are all the same anyway.[407]

That people, by which Hitler of course only meant the 'German national comrades', were 'inwardly' all the same and only different because of their upbringing, contradicts the theories of the NS racial theorists, who completely ignored the role environment plays in the development of a person as compared to the factors of heredity.

Hitler advocated the theory of the omnipotence of education in order to justify his demand for a permanent process of re-education, which was far more effective than any measures of force taken by the police. Only in this sense, and not from any humane beliefs, should we understand why he stated in his table talks, for example, that one should 'not put the police on people's necks everywhere', because otherwise the life of the people at home would turn into a 'pure life in prison'. It was the job of the police, said Hitler, 'to observe and radically eradicate the definitely asocial elements', but

> If any sort of harmful consequences were to appear somewhere, we would in fact have to learn not to immediately call for the police, but more to work through education. After all, the NSDAP did not win over the people by threatening them with the police, but by information and education.[408]

It would be a mistake, said Manson, who has also quoted these statements by Hitler, 'to only ascribe such absurd interpretations of his own political achievements to the self-deception of a dictator safe from any contradiction'.[409] It is far more important that Hitler believed in the omnipotence of education and wanted to create the national community not primarily by police power but by the power of a continuous process of re-education and indoctrination.

It was therefore also not an expression of humanitarian feelings when at the end of 1936 Hitler ordered a milder form of application of the 'law governing concealed malice' by the police, or suggested in the summer of 1939 that the

III. Hitler's Social Objectives

shortage of labour could be solved by a drastic reduction of the number of municipal police.[410] It was far more that Hitler was sceptical of the idea of replacing the difficult process of re-education all to quickly with external force, because he regarded measures of external force as being far less effective in the long run than the results to be achieved by a permanent process of indoctrination. This view also found its expression when, immediately before the outbreak of the war, the ministers responsible introduced compulsory coupons for food rationing cards: Hitler 'was furious about the *cards*. He wants them to be withdrawn forthwith and is particularly incensed that everything is again being done with the police truncheon and with threats of punishment, instead of appealing to the sense of honour.'[411]

The process of re-education Hitler demanded was to occupy the people all of their lives. On 26 May 1944, before generals and officers, he drew a picture of the total occupation:

> Because the infant child will already be educated this way in kindergarten. Later on it will then join the *Jungvolk* [literally 'young folk', a preparatory organization for the Hitler Youth for those between the ages of 10 and 14—H.B.]; there its education will continue. From the *Jungvolk* it will move to the Hitler Youth, and there again its education will go on. From the Hitler Youth it will go out into the factories and will again be educated in this way. In every community of apprentices also a uniform education everywhere. At age 18 this youth will later join the party, again the same education. A part will come into the SA – again the same education – or the SS, also the same education. Then it will come into the labour service: continuation of this education. Then it will come into the military and here this education must be continued in the same way, and when the young men leave the military again after two years, they will immediately be led into the political movement again: continuation of this education. Until the man has actually become an old man – a uniform education from infancy on. Believe me, the body of a people that has been trained and shaped in this way can no longer be destroyed, it cannot be made to suffer a year 1918.[412]

Here a key motive for Hitler's attaching such importance to the creation of the national community becomes visible. The shock of the defeat of 1918 had led him to the conviction that only a social national community without regard to origin, occupation, or class could guarantee the stability for a continuing existence in difficult military situations. In the First World War, in Hitler's view, the bourgeoisie had betrayed the national community because it did not subject its egoistic class interests to the communal interest of the nation and opposed all of the justified social demands of the working class. This must not be allowed to happen again, so that a November 1918 would never repeat itself. It was therefore necessary to create an egalitarian national community in which the social demands of the worker were also taken into consideration.

On the other hand, the world war had shown Hitler and his generation an example of the 'national community'. The 'idea of 1914', the communal and egalitarian experience in the trenches, was also to be realized in times of peace, and not only in Hitler's view but also according to the will of a large segment of the German population. This experience provided Hitler with a useful point of departure for the propagating of his 'national community' concept. In August 1920, for example, he declared at a meeting of the Association of German War Participants that 'We need national solidarity and must not count on international solidarity . . . We must learn to understand each other. In the field you were not asked about your convictions either. We must have a national consciousness in us.'[413] In his closing address at the third *Reichsparteitag* in 1927 he again drew an analogy with the experience at the front: 'There was a place in Germany where there was no class division. That was among the companies on the firing line. There there was no such thing as a bourgeois or a proletarian platoon, there there was only the company and that was it.'[414]

On 10 October 1939, during a major speech in the Sports Palace in Berlin, Hitler said: 'We National Socialists once came from the war, the world of our thinking was created by the experiences of war, and in war, if necessary, it will now prove itself!' The time which now 'perhaps faces us', i.e. the war against Britain and France, would 'contribute all the more to strengthening and deepening the National Socialist national community. It will only speed up the process of this social merging into a nation.'[415] In a speech on 30 September 1942, in which Hitler specifically emphasized the egalitarian aspects of National Socialism and stressed that no bourgeois state would survive the war, he again drew attention to the link between the experience of war and the concept of 'national community':

> Because only out of this possibly most heavy battle in our history will come out in the end what we National Socialists, just the way we came out of the First World War, have always envisaged, the great Reich of a national community closely allied in pain and joy. Because this war does also show a great, shining side, namely the great comradeship. What our party has always desired in times of peace, to create the national community out of the experience of the First World War, that is now being consolidated.[416]

On the one hand Hitler took over the community concept of the 'idea of 1914'; on the other he clearly differentiated the former Germany, i.e. the bourgeois class state, from the National Socialist national community:

> And yet another thing differentiates present-day Germany from the former. Then it had a leadership that had no roots in the people; in the final analysis it had merely

III. Hitler's Social Objectives

been a class state. Today we are in the middle of the completion of what grew out of that former war. Because when I returned from the war I brought my experience at the front back home with me. Out of this experience at the front I developed my national community. Today the National Socialist national community is going to the front and you will see from these things how this *Wehrmacht* is becoming more National Socialist month by month, how it increasingly assumes the stamp of the new Germany, how all the privileges, class prejudices and so forth are increasingly being removed, how here the German national community is increasingly imposing itself month by month, and how at the end of this war the German national community will maybe have experienced its strongest test – that is what differentiates the present Germany from the former.[417]

Let us summarize. The national community was intended to overcome class division, primarily by giving outstanding consideration to the social requirements of the worker. By means of a permanent process of re-education, existing traditions, class conceits and prejudices were to be reduced. Tied to that there was a process of equalization in all areas of life. With these concepts Hitler was able to tie in into the very popular 'idea of 1914', in other words, into the community of the trenches, which was now to be transferred to the whole of political and social life. After what has been discussed at the beginning of Chapter III.2 about 'equal opportunity' it should be clear that this concept of the national community also only had an exclusively national validity, was only meant for Germany and not for transfer to other countries. It is also self-evident that Jews, gypsies and other 'racially inferior' people were excluded from the national community to begin with.

IV

Hitler's Central Objective: The Revolutionizing of Politics and Economics and the Restructuring of the Economic System

1. The Underestimation of the Importance of Economic Questions for Hitler's Thinking

For a long time the opinion was widely accepted that Hitler had been ignorant of economic matters and had only attached a very minor importance to economic policy or to questions of the economic system. Following the accepted image of Hitler as the undirected, opportunistic pragmatist, his economic concepts were not taken seriously, and an investigation of these concepts was considered to be either superfluous or impossible. Bullock wrote, for example, that 'In economic matters Hitler thought completely opportunistically. He was basically not interested in the economy at all.'[1]

The verdict that Hitler had thought opportunistically as far as the economy was concerned and had not developed any precise concepts was possibly derived from the observation that in his speeches up to 1933 he only took very imprecise and general positions on economic questions. While the NSDAP had published a very concrete 'emergency programme' in 1932, in which many specific measures of its subsequent economic programme were outlined,[2] the quite decided rejection of this programme by influential business circles moved Hitler to accept the advice Hjalmar Schacht had given him on 29 August 1932 not to present 'too detailed an economic programme' in future.[3] In preparation for the last general elections to be held (5 March 1933), Hitler even emphasized at a meeting of ministers that he recommended

> ... avoiding if possible any detailed information in the election propaganda about an economic programme of the Reichs government. The Reichs government had to unite 18 to 19 million votes behind it. An economic programme that would meet the approval of that great a mass of voters did not exist anywhere in the world.[4]

In the next chapter we will show that one of Hitler's basic convictions was that economics was not suitable as a 'common platform' for the nation because here divergent interests were paramount. Such considerations, but specifically also the fear that a disclosure of his economic concepts would provoke the opposition of big business,[5] caused Hitler in his speeches before 1933 to express himself only very imprecisely and in general terms on economic matters, so that with many of his critics the impression was reinforced that he knew nothing about economics or was in principle indifferent to economic matters. The majority of Hitler's contemporaries, his critics at home and abroad, already believed that Hitler would fail in the economic tasks which were set him. The surprise was therefore all the greater when, against all expectations, his successful mastering of the economic problems turned out to be Hitler's strongest trump card.

In a book published in London in 1939 Claude William Guillebaud drew attention to the contradiction between the more than sceptical prophecies by Hitler's critics and the economic successes of the regime which then actually came about:

> In the autumn of 1936 the success of the first four-year plan was proven beyond any doubt. Unemployment was no longer a serious problem. Full employment had been achieved in the building industry and in the investment goods industries. The national income was rising continually and had reached the volume of the former record year of 1928. Industry and the banks were solvent and savings were increasingly on offer in the capital market. The circle had closed. *The policies which had appeared so daring in 1932–33 had been borne out by events* . . . The doubts abroad, where a successful conclusion to the German experiment had largely been considered an impossibility, had shown themselves to be unfounded. Success was visible to everyone.[6]

After the war the attempt was frequently made to relativize the regime's economic successes. An argument often heard was that the National Socialist government had only reaped the fruits of the economic policies of its predecessor. All the National Socialists had done was to continue the measures of their predecessors – those of the Papen government, for example – on a far wider scale but not to add anything basically new during the early years.[7] Furthermore Hitler had come to power at a most auspicious moment, namely after the high point of the economic crisis had already passed. If these arguments intend to state that there were favourable circumstances which Hitler knew how to make use of, we will not contradict them. If they are intended to imply, however, that under any other government the same economic successes would of course also have been achieved in the same brief span of time, then the greatest scepticism is indicated. But, more importantly, this counted just as little with those millions of unemployed who had experienced the practical failures of the Brüning and Papen governments and who had now again found 'work and bread', as did the frequently cited argument (only partly justified, however) that the mastering of the crisis had been due to a gigantic rearmament programme. Grotkopp has rightly pointed out that the switch to armaments from 1934 on had 'not changed the fundamental character of current economic policy',[8] which, with the help of the Keynesian policy of 'deficit spending', achieved the objective of full employment.[9]

Despite all of the partially even quite justified objections, the fact remains that 'already during the first year of National Socialist rule the number of unemployed went down and the German economy then achieved full employment in barely four years by the end of 1936', and that this secured 'the far-reaching consensus of the German people' for the regime and its policies. 'In the eyes of the population, the NSDAP was the party which had promised "work and bread" and had kept its word, while other affected countries were only slowly recovering from the consequences of the world economic crisis.'[10]

In view of these indisputable achievements of NS economic policy, we ask ourselves how they could have been achieved under the dictatorship of a man who was allegedly totally disinterested in economics and knew nothing about the subject? This image of Hitler obviously requires correction, and the points of departure for such a correction can be found in recent developments. In 1973 the first contribution on 'Hitler's Economic Thought'[11] appeared and subsequently several historians turned their attention to Hitler's economic views.[12] This fact is all the more noteworthy because for decades it had been considered to be impossible or unnecessary to pay any serious attention to the question at all. Numerous books about Hitler's racial and foreign policies appeared, and the opinion slowly became predominant that he had developed very stringent programmatic concepts in these areas. But the investigation of his economic concepts, which had long been completely ignored, has just begun and is still in its infancy. Even though the initial investigations have already produced interesting results, the source material is generally far too limited to be able to make definitive statements about Hitler's economic views.

What is, therefore, primarily of interest is not so much the results to date, but the fact that the possibility and necessity of an investigation of Hitler's economic concepts has been admitted. Peter Krüger, for instance, came to the conclusion that 'until now astonishingly sweeping statements and claims about Hitler's ignorance of and contempt for the economy, and about his inability to think in economic terms, have dominated the field'.[13] For his part, he stresses that Hitler's economic concepts were

IV: Hitler's Central Objective

... consistent in themselves and neither characterized by a lack of understanding nor by contempt of economics. The opposite is more likely true. The economy was the big power in modern life, which could cause the downfall of his political concepts and objectives if one followed economic logic.[14]

We can agree with these findings, which in their tendency have also been confirmed by other historians, but at the same time must note that none of the authors who have previously addressed themselves to Hitler's economic thinking has been able to met the requirements of a reconstruction of his economic concepts.[15]

In the following chapters we therefore intend to reconstruct Hitler's economic thinking, based on the broadest possible source material, and to comment on the research results and controversies to date from the viewpoint of the sources. For reasons of systematics, we will reconstruct – after having discussed Hitler's position towards political economy – his concepts of the 'primacy of politics' and the 'secondary role of the economy', of the relationship between the state and the economy, as well as the relationship in his thinking between the elements of a planned and a free economy and his position on private ownership and the problems of nationalization. In Section 5, which deals with the relationship between modernistic and anti-modernistic elements in his thinking, the economic importance of *Lebensraum* in the East will be discussed, particularly in the context of Hitler's criticism of economic expansion.

2. Hitler's Position on Political Economy

One of the reasons why the importance of economic policy for Hitler's thinking has been underestimated can probably be found in his devastating criticism of the economic sciences. To Wagener, the subsequent chief of the economic policy department of the NSDAP, Hitler said in early summer 1930, that a 'shaking' of the present foundations of political economy could hardly be avoided:

> Science, political economy, and traditional practices . . . are built upon the thousands of years old individualistic views of the past, constructed and cleverly devised by people who think that way, and absorbed into the total feeling, the emotion, yes, even the ethics and the religious beliefs of these people. They will not understand our logic, they will condemn our thoughts, they will denounce our new ethics, and will inundate and pursue us with all the hatred that a *Weltanschauung* doomed to go under is capable of, in order to oppose, to strangle an awakening new *Weltanschauung* which will overthrow all that has gone before.[16]

Hitler was convinced that the official economic sciences were based on hollow dogmas which had proved their ineffectiveness and uselessness long ago — not for the last time during the world economic crisis of 1929–32, to which the accepted theories of political economics had been unable to provide any answers. When Hitler attacked theoretical economics, it was primarily because he believed that its rigid dogmas were not able to do justice to the variables of modern economic life. In his speech to the *Reichstag* on 30 January 1937 he said that he was

> . . . not an economist . . . this means, above all, that in all of my life I have never been a theoretician. But unfortunately I have found that the worst theoreticians always manage to occupy those areas where theory is nothing and practical life everything. It is self-evident that in economics as well, the passage of time has not only led to the development of certain empirical fundamentals, but also to certain practical methods. All methods, however, are a reflection of their times. To make dogmas out of methods means robbing human ability and capacity for work of that elastic possibility which alone enables them to react to changing demands with changing methods and thereby to master them. The attempt to formulate dogma out of economic methods was pursued by many with that thorough industriousness which happens to characterize the German scientist, and then elevated to a science under the name of political economics. And it was only according to the findings of these political economists that Germany was lost beyond any doubt. It is in the very nature of all dogmatists to most sharply reject any new dogma, in other words a new finding which is then rejected as being pure theory. For eighteen years now we can observe the delightful spectacle that our economic dogmatists have been refuted in practice in almost every sector of life, but still reject and condemn the practical surmounters of the economic breakdown as being representatives of a theory which is foreign to them and therefore false.[17]

In essence, Hitler's criticism of political economy is directed against the dogmatization of certain guiding principles and against the inappropriate (in his view) transfer of old methods to new problems and questions. In Hitler's opinion, the new problems of a rapidly changing modern industrial society principally require new and sometimes even unorthodox solutions. He accused political economy of transferring certain solutions which may have been correct and appropriate at an earlier time to qualitatively new problems and situations.

In a speech about National Socialist economic policy to construction workers in Berchtesgaden, Hitler said on 20 May 1937:

> I am not going to tell you that in place of these economic theories of the others I am now going to put a National Socialist economic theory. I would like to avoid the term 'theory' altogether, yes, I would even like to say that what I am going to tell you today is not intended to be a theory at all. Because if I recognize any dogma

at all in the economic sector, then it is only the one dogma that there is no dogma in this sector, no theory at all, but that there is only insight here . . . My achievement, and the achievement of the National Socialist movement itself, only lies in having collected these insights and having put them into a programme, and having enforced this programme in practical reality.[18]

Hitler's criticism of political economy was for him first and foremost a means with which to relativize all the apparently fixed and generally accepted truths and thereby ideologically to create the conditions for the revolutionizing of the economy he intended. Hitler had recognized that he would only be able to restructure the existing economic order if he first exempted himself in principle from any criticism by political economy and generally cast doubt upon its teachings.

One of these teachings – which Hitler rejected – was the necessity of continuing to base the currency on the gold standard. In a speech in the *Reichstag* on 30 January 1939 Hitler ridiculed the teachings of the business sciences:

The effect of the reparations policy has not only cured the German people of many illusions but also freed it from numerous economic ideologies and virtually sanctified financial theories . . . Today we smile about a time when our political economists actually did believe that the value of a currency depended on the amount of gold and foreign currency reserves piled up in the safes of the state banks, and that it was guaranteed by these. We have learned instead that the value of a currency lies in the production capacity of a nation, that increasing production is what holds up a currency, even revalues it under certain circumstances, whereas any declining production results must sooner or later lead to an automatic devaluation of the currency. And at a time when the financial and economic theologians in the other countries prophesied our collapse every three to six months, the National Socialist state stabilized the value of its currency by increasing production most extraordinarily. A natural relationship was created between increasing German production and the currency in circulation.[19]

In a conversation with former American ambassador in Brussels Cudahy on 23 May 1941, the latter expressed his admiration for the clarity and wisdom with which Hitler treated economic problems. If only the American bankers had a part of this insight, said Cudahy, the economic crisis in the United States would not have come about. Hitler, who gladly accepted this praise, answered that he feared 'that in twenty to thirty years he would not be spared being lauded as an exemplary economist by the very same professors of political economy who had fought his economic views until now'.[20]

Hitler held the view that the economic sciences were artificially complicating what were actually fairly simple economic phenomena. He saw himself as the 'great simplifier' who was bringing things back down to a simple denominator again. He said in his table talks that

> All of these things are natural and simple, only you should not let a Jew play around with them. The foundation of Jewish business policy is to make normal business incomprehensible for a normal brain. You start by shuddering before the wisdom of the political economists. If somebody refuses to play along, you say this person is uneducated, he lacks the higher knowledge. In reality these terms have been invented so that you do not understand anything. Today these views have become second nature to millions of people. Only the professors have still not caught on that the currency value depends on the amount of goods backing up the currency. I once had some workers to the hall at the Obersalzberg in order to give them a lecture about money. I received a storm of applause, the people understood that so readily. To give money is only a question of paper manufacturing; but do the workers produce as much more as there is new paper being added? If they stay at work, to begin with, they cannot buy more for all that money than they did before for less. This theory would never have been considered a worthy topic for a dissertation. For that you have to write complicated thoughts about the trade in bottles using terms that are difficult to understand![21]

Hitler's gift of being able to simplify complicated phenomena was also recognized by Schacht: 'Hitler was a genius of resourcefulness. He often found solutions to the most complicated situations that were surprisingly simple, but which others had not seen . . . His solutions were often brutal, but almost always effective.'[22] Hitler himself boasted about his ability to reduce things down to simple denominators. In an interview with French journalist Bertrand de Jouvenel on 21 February 1936, for example, he said:

> I will disclose to you what it was that lifted me up to my position. Our problems appeared to be complicated. The German people did not know how to deal with them. Under these circumstances people preferred to leave them up to the professional politicians. I, however, simplified the problems and brought them down to the easiest formula. The masses recognized this and followed me.[23]

The complicated theories of political economy, which in Hitler's view were not able to offer practical solutions to modern economic problems, were for him only hindrances for positive economic development. On 12 November 1941 he said at the end of a long monologue about economic problems, 'The Continent is reviving. All we have to do for the next ten years is to close down all the university chairs for economics!'[24]

In his table talks Hitler repeatedly expressed his contempt for political economy. On 2 February 1942, for example, he said all the 'nonsense' came from political economy; 'a professor in Munich has announced a completely different "value theory" from that of a professor in Leipzig; but only one of them can be correct!'[25] In a secret speech to officer cadets on 30 May 1942 he spoke against the theory of the necessity of the gold standard:

> In those years when it could not be paid by products and work, in other words by industrial products, America itself exported industrial products and accepted gold for them – an insanity from the point of view of national economics, but political economy was no longer a rational science but only a science of theories.[26]

On 19 May 1944 Hitler recalled during a table talk that in 1929 the NSDAP had issued a publication on questions of economic policy which had been unanimously rejected by the political economists of various universities. He had once made the attempt to talk in depth with a well-known political economist,

> ... with the one among them whom they consider to be a revolutionary, with Zwiedineck.[27] This almost led to a catastrophe. At the time the 'systems state' [i.e. the Weimar Republic—R.Z.] had just taken a loan of 2.7 million in order to build a certain road. I explained to Zwiedineck that I thought this kind of financing was insane. The stretch of road built with it would last maybe five, maybe ten or fifteen years. Interest and amortization of the capital, however, would take eighty years. The burden would therefore be shifted over on to the next generation, and even the one after that. That was unhealthy. We needed radical measures by the government to bring down the interest rates just as radically so that capital became solvent again. Then I told him that I could never ever regard the gold standard, currency and other terms such as these as unchangeable and admirable factors. For me money was only a chit for work performed. It only had value if there was a work result behind it, and only to the amount of this work result. Where it did not represent such a result I could not assign any value to it. Zwiedineck was aghast and very excited. He told me that with such ideas I would knock the system accepted in all of political economy topsy-turvy. The implementation of such plans would inevitably lead to a complete economic collapse. When after the seizure of power I then began to implement my ideas, it was suddenly the political economists who – after a turnabout of 180 degrees – began to scientifically explain the innovations I had brought in to their students and to exploit them.[28]

In actual fact, as we know, political economy underwent a change as the result of the great global economic depression. The policy of public borrowing – previously rejected – became generally accepted and was scientifically developed into a system by the British political economist J. M. Keynes.[29]

If Hitler rejected the official theories of economics, this did not mean that he intended to have them replaced by the teachings of Gottfried Feder, who in the early days of the NSDAP had been regarded as its official economic theoretician.[30] While in the early years of his political activities, as he expressly emphasized in *Mein Kampf*, Hitler had been influenced by Feder's teachings on the 'abolishment of slavery to interest',[31] later on Feder did not play any noteworthy role in the Third Reich, nor in Hitler's economic thinking.

3. The 'Secondary Role of Economics' and the 'Primacy of Politics'

We have seen that Hitler's criticism of political economy cannot be used as proof that he underestimated the importance of the economy. The main reason why various authors were led to the assumption that Hitler had held the economy to be of little account is probably not so much his criticism of political economy but more his thesis of the 'secondary role of economics', which must be regarded as the key element of his economic concepts. That the creation of the 'primacy of politics' was an, if not *the*, essential characteristic of the National Socialist economic order was already recognized by contemporary authors[32] and then confirmed and backed up by subsequent detailed scientific investigations.[33] These analyses, however, are primarily concerned with the actual structure of the National Socialist system of rule, or rather the economic order of the Third Reich, but not with the role the economy played in Hitler's overall view of society.

Despite otherwise varying results, newer research – which for the first time is addressed to Hitler's economic concepts – has also unanimously recognized that Hitler's most important objective was to create the 'primacy of politics', and that his view of the 'secondary role of economics' had to be regarded as the key element in his economic concepts.[34] Hitler's *reasons* for taking this view, however, have not been analyzed, nor have the *conclusions* he drew, which are of decisive importance, especially for his political theory. Turner therefore comes to the incorrect conclusion that Hitler's thesis of the 'primacy of politics' and the 'secondary role of economics' was an expression of a 'deep contempt' with which he viewed economic matters.[35] We will now investigate what Hitler's frequently repeated statement about the 'secondary role of economics' really meant within the context of his economic policy, what the reasons were for the 'primacy of politics' he advocated, and above all what economic, but also political, conclusions he drew from all this.

At a rally of the NSDAP on 26 February 1923 Hitler declared that 'Capital has to become the servant of the state and not its master.'[36] On 24 April 1923 he made a similar statement: 'Capital is not the master of the state but its servant.'[37] In the proclamation of 2 September 1923 which he drew up for the *Vaterländische Kampfbund* (patriotic fighting union), an amalgamation of various nationalist groups and movements, he said: 'In times of need the economy acts exclusively in the service of the Fatherland.'[38] In a speech on 30

September 1923 Hitler for the first time used the expression 'secondary importance' of the economy,[39] and this was later to characterize his position on the relationship between politics and economy. In a fundamental article of April 1924 Hitler explained this concept in detail:

> The belief that by business in itself the nation, the state can be maintained, would be conditional on the concept that the state is first of all an institution which exists for business reasons, therefore to be regarded from this point of view and naturally also governed from it. In other words, a sort of public share company, similar to such a one held together by common, also business reasons, whereby each person owns a certain part, some more, some less, and the majority of the votes decides. Therefore 'business' as the founder of the state! ... Any professor versed in constitutional law, any factory director who has acquired the necessary experience in business, can now govern; a competent and dignified civil servant, however, will in most cases become a sort of Bismarck II, at least in his own opinion. That statesmanship is an art which cannot be learned and therefore has to be innate, which case will occur in the flesh all the more frequently the more politically uneconomically a nation thinks and acts, and the more seldom the more politically economical a people are, is something you will not want to hear, much less accept. In actual fact, business cannot only not 'build up' states, it cannot even maintain them.[40]

In *Mein Kampf* Hitler also discussed the relationship between the state and business in detail. He criticized the belief 'that the state only owes its existence to these [economic—R.Z.] manifestations, that it is first of all a business institution, is to be governed according to business interests, and therefore also depends on business for its continued existence'. Hitler firmly rejected such concepts and instead advocated the thesis that the state had

> ... nothing to do with a specific economic concept or economic development. It is not an amalgamation of contracting business partners within a certain defined living area for the purpose of fulfilling economic tasks, but the organization of a community of physically and spiritually identical beings for the purpose of creating a better possibility for the preservation of their race and the achievement of the objectives of their existence as these have been determined by fate.

A few pages further on Hitler reasons:

> How little state-building and state-maintaining attributes have to do with business can most clearly be seen from the fact that the inner strength of a state only very occasionally coincides with a so-called economic flowering, but rather that in an infinite number of examples this appears to signal the already impending downfall of the state. If the formation of human communities could primarily be ascribed to economic forces or motivations, then the greatest economic development would simultaneously also have to mean the greatest strength of the state, and vice versa.

With this Hitler was not intending to proclaim a reverse natural law according to which only a declining economy could provide the foundation for a strong state and a booming economy was basically irreconcilable with a strong state. What he was saying was that a positive economic development decisively depended on the political framework, and that a one-sided concentration on the purely economic could create a danger for the state, and therefore in the end also for the economy:

> Always when in Germany an upsurge of a power-political nature has taken place, then the economy also has begun to grow; but always when business developed into the sole content of the life of our nation and stifled all virtues beneath it, the state collapsed again and within a time also brought the economy down with it.

One of the decisive 'signs of decline in pre-war Germany' was, for Hitler, the

> ... conditions resulting from the 'economization' of the nation. In exactly the same way in which business rose up to become the master of the state, money became the god whom everybody had to serve and before whom all had to bow down. The celestial gods were increasingly set aside as being obsolete and outdated and instead of to them, the incense was offered to the idol Mammon . . . How far this 'economization' of the German nation had succeeded can probably best be seen by the fact that after the war one of the leading brains of German industry, but above all of trade, was able to express the opinion that business alone would be able to set Germany back up.

Elsewhere in *Mein Kampf* Hitler named as the objective of National Socialism the erection of a state 'which is not a mechanism of business matters and interests foreign to the people but a popular organism'. In the second chapter of the second volume of *Mein Kampf* Hitler – as already pointed out elsewhere – critically discussed various constitutional theories. Here he also rejected the bourgeois-liberal concept 'which primarily expects from the state that it organize the economic life of the individual in a favourable way, which therefore judges from the practical points of view of the overall profitability of business'.[41]

In his speeches during the time of struggle Hitler also repeatedly polemized against the view that 'the so-called economy can be cast as an ultimate sheet anchor'.[42] In his speech to the Hamburg National Club of 1919 at the end of February 1926 he rejected the 'totally incomprehensible belief that business could one day lift Germany up again and rebuild it'. As in *Mein Kampf*, he argued that 'The Reich often stood in a great and powerful blossoming, without a flourishing economy, without flourishing trade and business, it stood there first, and every time the Reich broke apart politically, the economy sank down into its grave with it.' It was 'insanity' to believe

... that one day the Reich could be lifted up by business, an insanity because, based on experience, a flourishing economy does not strengthen the state but rather erodes it internally because if this flourishing economy is not faced by a living political will to maintain, this pure economy will in most cases even become the seductive cause of the destruction of a state.

Hitler obviously regarded phases of economic growth and too one-sided a concentration on business as harbouring the danger of decadence, which must then lead to political, and in its train also to economic, decline. This decline could not then be stopped by continuing to pursue its causes, namely the disregard of the political as well as, in general, the spiritual dimensions and the over-evaluation of business, but only by establishing the 'primacy of politics' over the economy, and in the end thereby also creating the preconditions for a renewed economic blossoming. Hitler accused the politicians of the Weimar Republic of not having recognized these contexts and of propagating exactly the opposite to what alone could save the German nation:

> If we ask ourselves the question: what has been applied and implemented in all these years for German salvation, then we must say – if we are open and honest – to begin with only one thing, the attempt was made to employ business against it. That was the great recipe with which they went into 1920–21 after the initial damage of the war had been overcome. There the belief grew that one day this would not only lead to a flourishing economy but also to a flourishing Reich.[43]

On 26 March 1937 Hitler attacked the bourgeoisie and its belief that business was the cure-all:

> This is now the decadence, the downfall of the German bourgeoisie, that its leading business organism is slackening off. A *Herr* Stinnes was prepared to say that business would rebuild Germany. No, my dear man, you are in the hereafter and can look at Germany from there; business is building up nothing at all. Nations and states have always only been built up by the living force of self-preservation and business was always only a means of feeding them. It was not business that brought Germany down; we fell due to the lack of a unified national organization. Our economy can only be lifted up again by the creation of such a unity within our nation.[44]

On 13 April 1927 Hitler declared that

> ... not only insane political utopia [in other words Marxism] [had] brought this old Reich down, but far more the belief that business itself was not only a factor of state-building, but also of state-maintenance... People were actually convinced that the salvation of the whole nation lay in business alone, and in parallel to this conviction we had a gradual decay of the genuine state-building forces, of our constitutional thinking in total, even defined in the traditional sense.[45]

A key point for Hitler's criticism of the politicians of the Weimar Republic was their belief 'that business is the fate of the nation, that the international interests of business were to be given precedence over the political interests of the various nations, and that these nations had to submit themselves to the international interests of business'.[46] In his 'Second Book' Hitler also expounded the theory of the secondary role of the economy:

> For a nation the danger of engaging in business in the sense of exclusivity lies in the fact that it can all too easily fall into the belief that it can ultimately shape its fate by means of the economy, and that thereby the economy moves from a purely secondary to a primary position, yes, in the end is even regarded as being state-building, and robs the nations and states of those virtues which in the end alone are able to preserve their existence on this earth.[47]

On 9 November 1928 Hitler criticized the 'German entrepreneur' who believed he would be able to

> ... rebuild Germany by business manipulations. We have already seen where this leads to. Here in this hall[48] the attempt was once made to change history, and because this attempt collapsed German business stood up and shouted: German politics will never ever lead Germany back upwards again, business will do that. Where are the voices of those days now? And when the National Socialist movement was founded again for the second time in this hall in 1925, the same business again got up and declared, all you are doing is disturbing the rebuilding of Germany, business will restore Germany and bring her back to greatness. Where are these brilliant political economists? Today we can once again so nicely watch how Germany is being rebuilt by business.[49]

One of the reasons which led Hitler to his belief in the 'secondary role of the economy' becomes apparent in a speech given on 30 November 1928. An overemphasis of the economy was more likely to tear a nation apart than to unify it, because in business there were always necessarily diverging interests of the various classes. Therefore business was completely useless as a common platform and consequently as the basis for the creation of a state:

> At business congresses they say the future of our nation lies on business and in it, and that is ridiculous for many reasons. The most important are: first, business itself is always only a secondary phenomenon and not a primary one. Business does not build states, the political forces build states. Business can never replace the political force, and if a nation does not possess political force its economy will collapse. Business is more burdening than uplifting. Today you see many Germans, especially in middle-class circles, who always say business will forge our nation together. No, business is a factor which is more likely to sunder a nation. A nation has political ideals. But if a nation only lives for business, business must thereby sunder a nation, because in business employers and employees always

oppose each other. Even in a so-called Communist economy... When people only look at business alone, its tendency to sunder becomes apparent.[50]

Hitler developed the same idea on 7 December 1928 at an NSDAP rally:

> The actual development we continue to experience for nine years now, this has as its highest concepts profit, earnings, dividends, wages, working hours, export, import, in brief all of those things that have to split the people and which are completely unable to bring them together. As soon as the republic decided to renounce any continuation of the old traditions of national honour and so forth, at that same moment it had already given itself over to the unscrupulous spirit and sense of business with all of its fatal consequences. Since then we see that top and bottom. Today you can see everywhere: the term 'ideal' has actually become something ridiculous. Millions of people make fun of you if you only just say this word. But the right and proper masters of the republic have completely forgotten that after they have killed the final ideal they will also have removed the last force which could have compelled people to do any sort of duty, perform any sort of service, out of something higher than egoism. With this they themselves have begun to change this republic into a purchase and sales association. They themselves have begun to bring things to the point where in this state only business interests prevail any longer, and that the statement 'business will build up the state and determine its nature' will have become generally valid. This has resulted in the nation thereby being split into two halves, each of which applies this statement to itself, the industrialist, the employer on the one side, the employee, the manual worker on the other...[51]

Hitler is therefore arguing against business interests primarily determining the policies of the state, and pointing to the inevitable consequence that class differences would be increased as soon as the economy were to become not merely the secondary but the primary force. In the ideology which declared business interests to be the primary interests, he saw a cause for class division, and in the final analysis for the dissolution of a social order:

> If today an entrepreneur is only thinking in business terms, then his desire for profit is opposed to the desire of the worker for higher wages. In brief, if everybody only thinks in terms of business, then a nation does not only begin to split into two, it begins to split into innumerable classes.[52]

The old Reich, said Hitler on 6 March 1929, had been completely ruled by the 'concept of profitability'. Up into the highest levels of the state, the terms 'business advantage, profitability, prosperity' had ruled. Since the war, everything was still being regarded only from this point of view:

> Can you still do business under this condition? If so, then this condition is not so bad. Why should a condition in which one can still do business be bad? This concept, which had already ruled all of politics before the war, as long as one can

still profit and do business, as long as one can still achieve something purely business-wise, this concept has become dominant today . . . You can even still do business in total collapse! Why then is collapse something bad if you can still do business . . . Business is everything, the growth of the economy is everything. These, then, are the spirits which govern a nation.[53]

Hitler's concept of the 'secondary role of the economy' is the expression of a criticism of a society and a form of state in which, in the final analysis, business interests dominated. 'The people stand at the head, business is a servant of the people and capital a servant of business, and not the other way around,' he declared on 20 November 1929.[54]

The decisive factors in the political process of decision were therefore not to be business interests: the economy had to subordinate itself to politics. This has obviously nothing to do with a 'contempt' for business. It is merely a definition of the position and function of business within the total framework of a social and political system. Hitler did not underestimate the importance of business; he only wanted to break and turn around a functional connection he believed to be harmful. Politics was no longer to be a function of the economy: the economy was to become a function of politics.

Hitler therefore also criticized the influence the business associations had on politics. On 26 April 1930, for example, he wrote in the *Illustrierte Beobachter*:

The more the economic interest groups eat their way into our political parties, the more impossible any unified operation aimed at great times will become . . . It is particularly bad when on top of everything else associations whose thinking is highly unpolitical gain influence on the political leadership. It is always a capital mistake to want to build a political party out of economic building blocks. I have always most sharply opposed nominating candidates for election out of the representatives of various interest groups.[55]

Such statements show that Hitler's demand for the creation of the 'primacy of politics' was essentially directed against the network of interests between politics and business which is characteristic for the capitalist system as it is expressed in 'lobbyism', as he describes it.

After the seizure of power, Hitler in his famous speech on 21 March 1933, for example, programmatically confessed to the 'primacy of politics' as an objective of his government: 'We intend to reinstate the primacy of politics, which is ordained to organize and lead the battle for life of the nation.'[56] In his speech giving the reasons for his enabling law, he said two days later, 'Here one law will determine all actions: the people do not live for the sake of business, and business does not exist for the sake of capital, but capital serves business and business serves the people!'[57]

IV: Hitler's Central Objective

In Hitler's view the relationship of the state, or politics, to business was to be an unrestricted relationship of rule, in which the rights of the state were in principle not opposed by any rights of business but only by its obligations. The state was therefore always in a position to impose its claims, demands and objectives on the economy and to enforce them. On 30 January 1934 Hitler declared that 'the rule of force of the economically more powerful' was to be replaced by

> ... the higher interests of the community. Because we all know that the gigantic tasks which not only the economic needs of the present show us, but also a critical look into the future can only be completed, if over the egoistic mind of the individual the speaker for the interests of the community holds sway, and his will counts as the final decision.

In this speech, too, he repeated the formula in which his programmatic objective was expressed: 'the people are not there for the economy and the economy for capital, but that capital must serve the economy and the economy the people'.[58]

When Hitler underlined the usefulness of private initiative in business, he never did so without immediately qualifying this by adding that the interests of the community, in other words the political premises to be set by the state, stood ahead of everything else. On 1 May 1934 he declared:

> The authority of the leadership of the nation is the sovereign over all. By the organization and leadership of the national community it creates the preconditions for the effect of the abilities, knowledge and capacity for work of the individual person, but it must also ensure that obligations and rights are not shifted one-sidedly. Therefore it must represent the interests of the community against any national comrade, regardless of who he may be, and insist that they are respected. It cannot admit any privileged groups and classes, but only the given abilities, the given know-how, of the individual person, and from these must determine the mutual obligations which result therefrom and are necessary for the community. Only in such a position of the leadership of the nation, in which it is held above the individual contracting partners of economic life, can the source of confidence lie which is an essential precondition for the economic success of reconstruction.[59]

In Chapter II.5.d we noted that Hitler intended to demonstrate the historic importance of National Socialism and the 'turning point in history' it triggered by means of his monumental building projects. But, in addition, the primacy of politics over economics was also to be expressed in terms of architecture. In his address at the 'culture meeting' of the *Reichsparteitag* of Freedom, Hitler said on 11 September 1935:

> It is impossible to give a nation a strong inner security if the large public buildings do not tower greatly over the works which owe their creation and maintenance

> more or less to the capitalist interests of individuals. It is out of the question to bring the monumental buildings of the state or the movement into a size which equates to that of two or three centuries ago, while on the other hand the expressions of bourgeois creations in the area of private or even purely capitalist building have increased and grown bigger many times over... As long as the vistas which characterize our cities today have department stores, markets, hotels, office buildings in the form of skyscrapers and so forth as their outstanding eye-catchers, there can be no talk of art or even of genuine culture. Here the requirement would be to hold oneself back in modest simplicity. Unfortunately, however, during the bourgeois era the architectural embellishment of public life was held back in favour of the objects of private capitalist business life. The great cultural-historic task of National Socialism will be exactly to depart from this tendency.[60]

This function of monumental buildings has previously not been recognized in the interpretation of Hitler's architectural plans. The secondary role of the economy or private capitalist interests compared to politics, or the ideology of National Socialism, was also to be demonstrated in architecture.

In his 'Memorandum on the Four-Year Plan 1936', written during August 1936, Hitler again underlined the principle that national interests, particularly rearmament and the achievement of Germany's economic independence, were to have priority over capitalist private interests. These national interests were to be implemented with 'determination' and

> ... if necessary with the same degree of ruthlessness... The interests of individual gentlemen will not be permitted to play a role in future. There is only one interest and that is the interest of the nation, and only one opinion, and that is that Germany has to be brought into a condition of self-preservation politically and economically.[61]

In his opening proclamation at the *Reichsparteitag* in 1936 Hitler spoke out against the 'lack of restraint of a free economy' and in favour of a planned economy[62] and declared:

> Neither the economy nor capital are sovereign manifestations and thereby based on their own natural laws, because at the top, and thereby exclusively and solely deciding the laws of life, stand the people. The people are not there for business, business is the servant of the people. And the people and business are not the slaves of capital, capital is only a business tool and therefore also subjected to the greater necessities of the preservation of the nation.

In his culture speech at the same *Parteitag* Hitler declared:

> The lack of restraint of political developments also infects the economy. What was a servant for hundreds of years has now become the master. Under capitalism the tool which was subjugated in order to serve attempts to elevate itself to become the end, and by this new interference in a previously ordered development contributes

IV: Hitler's Central Objective

to the creation of causes of further destruction. With this an apparently impersonal world power interferes into the personal fates of the nations.

Hitler's theory of the 'secondary role of the economy' is irreconcilable with the capitalist economic structure, and Hitler himself emphasized this irreconcilability. Neither in political nor in economic life did the 'uniform line' ever develop 'by itself out of the so-called free play of forces'. With the victory of National Socialism, the

> ... free play of forces has been brought to an end ... Therefore the National Socialist idea and the movement that supports and advances it, which emerged as the victor from the free play of forces, will take over the leadership of the nation, not only politically but also economically and culturally. It will set the tasks and it will determine the tendency of their fulfilment. Nobody disposes of a greater right than it does, nor of a greater inner qualification.

The economy must not be permitted 'to act arbitrarily only according to private interests and personal ideas or for personal advantage'.[63]

These concepts are directly opposed to economic liberalism, according to the theories of which the optimal advantage for the community automatically results from the free play of forces. The common good is a result of the representation in the market place of the egoistic singular interests of private entrepreneurs. Hitler did not share this view and believed that only the clearly dominant role of the state or the political leadership, together with the ruthless enforcement of these defined 'common interests', made an orderly economic life possible.

Based on the logic of a free market and the natural laws of competition, Hitler said, one could in many cases not expect any actions directed toward the common good. One could not, for example,

> ... expect a man who happens to produce nitrogen to say: 'I think it would now be wiser to sell it for 20 per cent less.' No, we cannot ask that. This can only be recognized as being necessary from a higher vantage point, and then you say, 'It must be done.' But we cannot ask it of the man ... Or if, for example, I demand of someone else that he should agree that we in Germany are going to produce our fuel ourselves, but he makes his living in the fuel trade. Well, you cannot expect the man to say, 'I think that is a fabulous idea that you are going to produce your fuel yourself.' Or an international rubber buyer or rubber trader who is now supposed to decide whether we in Germany are to build Buna factories. He will naturally say, 'I think that is crazy, absolutely impossible.'[64]

In all such cases there is obviously a contradiction between the capitalist private and the state-defined general political interests. According to Hitler's view, the state always has the right and the obligation to enforce the general political against the capitalist private interests.

On 30 March 1938 Hitler pointed out that his theory of the 'primacy of politics' had been a basic constant of the National Socialist *Weltanschauung* from the beginning: 'It was clear from the very first that business by itself could not resurrect Germany. The nation first had to come to order politically and thereby organically. Then business was also able to flourish. But politics is the primary thing.'[65]

How deeply Hitler's thinking was determined by the premise of the antagonism between private and public interests is shown, for example, in a statement made during a table talk on 18 October 1941. Koeppen recorded in his notes: 'The *Führer* criticizes the new Japanese government very vehemently. That the business community is very satisfied with the new Minister President was not a good sign.'[66] And in the table talks on 1 November 1941 Hitler called it

> ... one of the most urgent tasks ... to achieve a status in the area of business leadership which is characterized by the following two principles: (1) State interest goes before private interest. (2) If a question arises between state interest and private interest it will be decided in favour of the public and state interest by an authority which is completely independent.[67]

From this Hitler drew the conclusion that political functionaries at all levels should be independent of private business enterprises and must therefore not sit on supervisory boards, own shares etc. Because this view, which is derived from the two basic principles just cited, plays a particularly important role in his economic-political thinking, we will now discuss it in more detail.

4. Warnings about the Web of Interests between Business and Politics

In order to enforce the 'primacy of politics' consistently, Hitler advocated a sharp division between political leadership and private business. He believed that in capitalist states decisions were often not based on political considerations but taken instead in the interests of private business enterprises, because the members of parliament and the leading politicians were closely tied to the business interests of these companies by having seats on their supervisory boards and owning shares. It is surprising that this topic, to which Hitler himself attached very great importance, has not been treated in research until now, even though in 1942–43 Hitler's views led to concrete directives by the party secretariat and the leader of the NSDAP faction.

After a talk with Hitler on 5 April 1940 Goebbels noted in his diary, 'He talks about the level of salary. After the war, every German statesman must be nobly compensated, but will not be allowed to have additional income on the side. Only complete financial independence guarantees highest objectivity towards the problems.'[68] On 14 November of the same year Hitler said in a speech:

> In these [capitalist—R.Z.] countries almost every member of parliament, of the British parliament, is a member of some supervisory board and draws his remuneration. I have forbidden in the German *Reichstag*, already during the time we were still in opposition, that anybody was to be a member of a supervisory board at all. Today this is forbidden by law.[69]

And in actual fact during the time in opposition in the Weimar Republic any *Reichstag* member of the NSDAP had to sign a declaration in which, among other things, he certified that he did not 'hold any position on the supervisory board of a bank or any other business enterprise' and to oblige himself on his word of honour not to 'accept such a position, either directly or indirectly via a third person' after his time as a member of parliament.[70] As we shall see, it was only later that Hitler became aware that his directives regarding the economic independence of party functionaries in the Third Reich had not been put into practice.

On 10 December 1940 Hitler again criticized the interest links between politics and business resulting from supervisory board positions:

> This nonsense we have just abolished here. And all it was was a covering up of profits, nothing more. And above all it was a means of bribery. Because the gentlemen members are supervisors. It was the same here. We have done away with that. No member of parliament may be a director, unless it is completely without compensation. Any compensation is impossible, impossible in any form.[71]

At the end of the preceding chapter we quoted from a table talk in which Hitler declared the priority of public over private interests to be an important principle. In this talk he continued:

> The state can only decide according to the needs of higher public interests, and the state leadership will only have the absolute authority if all those leave it who are committed by belonging to a business enterprise in some form, or are close to it (which is already the case if they hold shares in their estate). Everybody will have to be confronted with the alternative of deciding whether he wants to forgo this and remain in public service or whether he wants to quit this service. The possibility of activities of pure speculation must be completely excluded for men in public leadership positions. They can invest in real property or in state papers, because by this they are tying their wealth to the existence of the state . . . This applies to all men who have seats in the *Reichstag*, are in the service of the Reich or in the *Wehrmacht*, or belong to the leadership of the party. They must be completely separated from these business interests. We have seen where it leads to if in this we

do not act coldly and harshly. Britain would not have stumbled into this war if Baldwin and Chamberlain had not had interests in the armaments industry.[72]

The degree of importance Hitler attached to this topic can be seen from the fact that he kept coming back to it in his table talks. On 24 March 1942 he declared: 'Britain today was so fragile because her total economic system is based upon this capitalist way of thinking.' He, the *Führer*, had therefore

> ... ordered in good time that in Germany no holder of supervisory board positions was permitted to be a member of the *Reichstag*. Because men who hold supervisory board positions or similar positions are completely incapable of thinking objectively about many things, he had further directed that the men of the party were not permitted to be committed privately-capitalistically, nor industrially, nor business-wise. He could also only permit the direct servant of the state, the officer and the civil servant, to invest his savings in negotiable papers with a clear conscience if these were state papers, and any sort of speculation and other dishonest elements were excluded.[73]

One week later Hitler said during a table talk, care had to be taken that

> ... the leading man in the state is independent of any influences by business and could not be forced to any decisions by economic pressure. He therefore had to be supported by a political organization whose strength lay in its deep roots among the people, and which was above any business considerations.[74]

On 10 April 1942 Hitler emphasized in a table talk that he basically had nothing against rich people – a rich man was 'in himself not a socially harmful manifestation' – but one had to limit their political influence.[75]

The key source for this topic is a table talk on 26 July 1942, the great importance of which is underlined by the note preceding it: 'Reichsleiter Bormann has immediately passed the following notes on to Reichs Minister Lammers for further action by the Reichs Chancellory.' Such a note is unique among the table talks or the monologues at *Führer* headquarters. That evening Picker noted:

> After dinner the *Führer* turned to the problem of the business ties of leading men of the party, the state and the *Wehrmacht* and asked *Reichsleiter* Bormann if care had now been taken that no member of the *Reichstag* held any supervisory board positions in private business any longer. *Reichsleiter* Bormann replied that the order had not been executed for the time being but had been postponed until after the end of the war. He suggested that Dr Lammers give a complete picture of the actual status with his next briefing. The *Führer*, who refused to believe that his directive in this matter had not yet been put into effect, then said: No servant of the state was allowed to possess shares. No Gau leader, no member of the *Reichstag*, no party leader and so forth was to be a member of a supervisory board in future regardless of whether this membership was paid or not.[76]

IV: Hitler's Central Objective

Before we continue quoting Hitler's directive and discussing the reasons for it, the underlying factual situation must be explained again. Hitler had already issued several directives which forbade the possession of shares and membership on supervisory boards for political functionaries. Normally Bormann was the central transmission authority. It was his job to convert certain of Hitler's directives into concrete orders. This had obviously not been done in this case, something Hitler initially refused to believe. He must certainly have been very put out about the fact that a matter close to his heart had simply been postponed to a later date (after the end of the war), even though he had assumed that his respective directives had already become political reality. This case could confirm the theory advanced by Hans Mommsen and David Irving that Hitler was not at all the omnipotent ruler he has been regarded as having been for quite some time, but rather a 'weak dictator in many respects'[77] who found little time to devote attention to domestic policies, particularly during the war.[78] We can leave the question open as to whether we may agree with this interpretation in general or whether it is overstated in this form.[79] In the case at hand, Hitler had obviously assumed that his directives had already been implemented, whereas they had actually been ignored. When he learned in answer to his direct question that this was not the case, he ordered Bormann immediately to send the statements quoted below to Reichs Minister Lammers at the Reichs Chancellory. This is what Hitler said in detail:

In the former economic system the great enterprises had not been able to survive without state protégés. Therefore they had taken members of parliament and higher civil servants or men with a title on to their supervisory boards or in other paid positions and regained the amounts paid to these men in the form of profit sharing, director's salaries and such things through large public contracts. In his continuing statements, the *Führer* emphasized that

> ... even a civil servant who leaves public service was not permitted to move into the private business to which he had previously had official contacts. He was only sought after by private business because of his connections, and not because of his professional industrial or business knowledge ... Private industry was after such connections like the devil after the soul of a Jew. If it were therefore permitted that a Gau leader let himself be harnessed for business interests by means of shareholding or a position on a supervisory board, then it could not be prevented that district leaders and mayors were tempted to do the same. With this you had the beginning of corruption. For all of these reasons, care had to be taken that a servant of the state who had invested his fortune in shares would invest it in state obligations in future.

This was the only guarantee that every civil servant

> ... was exclusively linked to the interests of the state in his private interests. In the final analysis the state was not there to lift somebody up into a higher life which

enabled him to develop many connections, and then to stand by while the person in question flew off . . . In order to prevent the servants of the state from one day contemplating their move to private industry, in all larger public contracts with private industry, monopoly contracts had to be fundamentally excluded. For large contracts three to four companies had always to be asked to compete. That was the only way to prevent the civil servants charged with matters of business from building 'golden bridges' for themselves to specific companies. For the same reason care had to be taken that decisions on the awarding of large contracts were taken by a consortium whose members were constantly rotated. Into the armaments office, for instance, one should only call in people from the front who were not committed by any sort of business relationships. And as soon as the attempt was made by means of all sorts of invitations – particularly invitations to go hunting – to get them to commit themselves in certain directions, they should be rotated . . . Germany's strength lay in the fact that the men of the party, the state, and the *Wehrmacht* were not involved in private enterprises. Whoever of these men still had ties of this sort today had therefore to take an unequivocal decision: either he renounced these ties or else he had to give up his public functions.[80]

Hitler's directives were published by the party secretariat in a circular letter on 20 August 1942. The members of the *Reichstag* and other full-time party functionaries were expressly forbidden to be active on 'a management board, a supervisory board, an administrative board or any other organ of any sort of a business enterprise'.[81] This prohibition was reinforced on 26 February 1943 by a circular directive by the leader of the faction of the NSDAP Dr Frick. In this the members of the *Reichstag* were set an ultimative deadline: 'By 31 March 1943 any members of the faction who at present are still on a supervisory board or any other organ of a business enterprise have either to resign from this organ or to inform the faction that they have renounced their seat in the *Reichstag*.' Exceptions from this prohibition were not even possible where 'compliance were to lead to hardships in individual cases'.[82]

This demand for a strict separation of interests between politics and business was, of course, also incompatible with the system of 'self-administration of industry' practised by Albert Speer, the Reichs Minister for Armaments and War Production from 1942 to 1945. It was here that the combination of functions between industry and politics had been realized in its purest form. The opponents of this practice, such as Otto Ohlendorf and Friedrich W. Landfried – who were later to occupy influential positions in the Reichs Ministry of Economics – appealed directly to Hitler in their criticism of this linking of interests. As the result of the meetings involving Ohlendorf, Landfried and Funk in 1942, agreement was reached that the key task of a newly structured and politically upgraded Ministry of Economics was to be the 'opposition against the shifting of [responsibility for] acts of sovereignty to persons and organizations of active business'.[83] In a letter from Ohlendorf to

Himmler dated 16 October 1942 the former refers to a notification by Reichs Minister of Economics Funk according to which the person responsible for such matters, Chief of the Reichs Chancellory Hans H. Lammers, would soon 'notify him clearly in writing of the *Führer*'s opinion according to which the execution of acts of sovereignty by businessmen was to be sharply rejected'.[84]

The fact that Speer's system was still being practised despite this shows how little the picture of the '*Führer* state' drawn by National Socialist propaganda often had in common with reality. Hitler was simply not the omnipotent dictator his opponents in their exaggeration have painted him as being, and he was not the forcefully decisive *Führer* his adherents, and he himself, would have liked him to be. He obviously knew about the corruption of many Gau leaders and other party bigwigs, which he 'forgave them with great tolerance', however, as he did moral transgressions, 'to which he was indifferent anyhow'.[85]

Hitler's demand that business and politics be strictly separated, and his criticism of the 'combination of functions' of leading representatives of capital with holders of public office, was derived directly and stringently from his advocacy of the 'primacy of politics' and his theory of the 'secondary role of economics', because this network of linked interests naturally quite decisively obstructed the ability of the political leadership to assert itself. This caused Hitler much frustration, and he was visibly incensed that his directives on the matter were not being implemented. It also shows that the image of Hitler as the lackey of monopoly capitalism and the willing helper of big business interests is false. He was not interested in the enforcement of the interests of capital, but in the implementation of his *Weltanschauung* and policies against all opposition, even if this came from among the ranks of industrialists, whom – as we shall see in the next chapter – he only regarded as being representatives of the National Socialist state, and whom he threatened, openly or in veiled language, with nationalization if they were not prepared to play this role.

5. Market and Plan

Probably the most important and most controversial question we face in the interpretation of Hitler's economic concepts is the one about the relationship between market economy and planned economy elements in his thinking. Turner has advanced the thesis that Hitler had 'taken the liberal principle of competition as the foundation for his views of domestic business matters'. He points to the connection between Hitler's fundamental socio-Darwinistic convictions and his affirmation of the economic principle of competition. Hitler had regarded free enterprise as being a special case of the fundamental socio-Darwinistic principle, according to which life is a constant battle in which the more competent and the more capable survive.[86]

Barkai disagreed with Turner's interpretation and advocated the theory that the most outstanding characteristic of Hitler's concept was his 'extreme anti-liberalism, the fundamental rejection of the *laissez faire* principle of the unrestricted free market economy initiative of the entrepreneur'. Hitler had not rejected competition as a matter of principle, but he wanted, suggested Barkai, to 'unconditionally subject the individual free play of forces in the economy to the authority of the "national community" and the state'. The attempt to reconcile these two opposites was one of the most outstanding traits of the National Socialist economic concept. While Barkai does succeed with his convincing arguments in casting doubt on Turner's interpretation, he is only partially successful in proving his own. Barkai attempts to explain the weakness of his line of reasoning by claiming that Hitler had hardly expressed his views on these matters in public speeches or articles because he believed it would have been a tactical mistake to attract the hostility of the entrepreneurial class. While this is quite correct, we intend to show that Barkai's theory – that his conviction of the necessity of 'restriction of competition by the state' and 'state control of the economy'[87] stood at the centre of Hitler's thinking – can be proved far more conclusively if we draw on numerous statements by Hitler which Barkai has not taken into consideration or mentioned.

While we agree with Barkai's thesis, this does not mean that Turner's interpretation is completely wrong, because he expressly only refers to Hitler's position on the economy and society *before* 1933. In fact, to a certain extent we can only speculate on Hitler's true position before 1933, because Hitler – as Barkai rightly points out – kept his plans strictly secret, primarily in order not to offend the businessmen. In his talks with Wagener, the chief of the economic policy section of the NSDAP, Hitler underlined the importance of keeping his economic plans secret time and again. In September 1931, for example, he said:

> The conclusion from this is what I have said all along, that this idea is not to become a subject for propaganda, or even for any sort of discussion, except within the innermost study group. It can only be implemented in any case when we hold political power in our hands. And even then we will have as opponents, besides the Jews, all of private industry, particularly heavy industry, as well as the medium and large landholders, and naturally the banks.[88]

In the spring of 1932 Hitler explained to Wagener that, while he was a socialist, at the moment he had to show consideration 'for the men in business for political reasons'. He was against a publication of the party's economic plans because 'there only has to be *one* word in there which is not correct or can be falsely interpreted. All of our enemies will then seize upon that word, and will then not only drag your publication, but our whole party and all of its objectives, down into the dirt.'[89] Time and again Hitler expressly insisted that 'for the time being all of these thoughts and problems are not to be discussed outside of a certain circle'.[90]

In a conversation between Hitler and Wagener which took place in the autumn of 1930 the latter said:

> The economic self-administration structure I have recommended, and the control of the economy by the state which it makes possible, will bring these things [the over-expansion of export and the neglect of domestic food production—R.Z.] back into order automatically. I shall be curious to see when the first big industrialist will come to you and start ranting against this structure and against a planned economy – as they call this – and in the final analysis against me.

Hitler replied:

> That is why it is good that we decide these questions before we get into disputes with these people. And it is also appropriate that we keep our plans secret until we are sitting in the government. Otherwise they too [i.e. big capital—R.Z.] will set the whole horde of uncomprehending industrial workers on us beforehand and we will never gain power.[91]

This conversation between Hitler and Wagener shows that it was precisely those plans aimed at state control of the economy that Hitler wanted to keep secret at all costs before the seizure of power. In a later conversation Hitler accused Wagener of underestimating the political power of the business leaders:

> You are underestimating the political power of these men, Wagener, and of business in general. I have the feeling that we will not be able to conquer the Wilhelmstrasse against them [i.e. the Reichs Chancellory, located in Wilhelmstrasse in Berlin—H.B.]. As much as I therefore consider your plans, which are also my plans, to be correct and necessary, to the same degree it appears to be necessary to hold back these plans completely until we are firmly seated in the Wilhelmstrasse and until we have at least two-thirds of the German people firmly behind us.[92]

This is the reason why it is indeed difficult to determine Hitler's position on free enterprise or planned economy *before* 1933. One of the few sources which provide information about Hitler's economic concepts before 1933 is the notes made by Wagener, who had many talks with Hitler about economic problems.

Wagener's overall impression here was that 'he [Hitler] was obviously of two minds about this . . . He was a socialist and deliberately so. But in his attachment to nature he was constantly able to observe the fight for existence, the struggle to defeat the other one, and to recognize this as a natural law.'[93] With Hitler we therefore concurrently find both elements of a planned economy as well as ones which emphasize the principles of competition and selection. In a conversation with Wagener, for example, Hitler said, 'That is what I keep saying, right from the start there is a lack of leadership in business, a lack of planning! Yes, there is even the lack of any consideration of this, the will to even think about it.'[94] In another conversation he attempted to reconcile the principle of state control with the independence of business:

> If, for example, industrial companies were to decide from a higher insight no longer to compete with each other but to form a community of interests, then each company in itself would remain independent. It would only be integrated into the community production-wise and sales-wise according to a higher plan and according to points of view of common sense and profitability. It will therefore have to relinquish *some part* of its sovereignty in the interest of the whole, and thereby also in its own interest.[95]

As he declared in early 1931, Hitler was looking for a 'synthesis' which would lead to a 'radical removal of all the bad results of industrialization and unrestricted economic liberalism'.[96] On another occasion he told Wagener that

> The liberalism of the industrial nations, the insistence on freedom and self-control over property and jobs on the part of the entrepreneurs has turned into its opposite! Now only the big ones benefit from liberalism any longer, the mass has sunk down to become their servants and to become slaves. Even in the organizations and chambers of the democracies, business sense reigns supreme, the owners of private capital, the big industrial magnates, the trusts, rule the state.[97]

All of these statements are expressions of a critical position towards economic liberalism. Hitler believed that unrestricted economic liberalism had become outdated and had to be replaced by a new economic system. 'We are living in the middle of a turnabout, which is leading from individualism and economic liberalism to socialism,' he said to Wagener in June 1930.[98]

On the other hand, Hitler was a convinced socio-Darwinist and rejected collectivist solutions: 'In all of life anywhere, only a selection process will always be decisive. With animals, with plants, everywhere we look, the stronger, the better, will basically always impose itself.'[99]

Hitler's main intention was obviously to reconcile the advantages of the principles of competition and selection (in the socio-Darwinistic sense) of economic liberalism with the advantages of a state-controlled economy. While the state was to direct the economy according to the principle 'common interest before self-interest' and to set the objectives, within this framework the principle of competition was not to be abolished, because in Hitler's view it was an important mainspring for economic development and technical and industrial progress. What was important, however, was that Hitler did not share the beliefs of the advocates of 'free trade', according to which the common good would come about as a sort of automatic result of the play of the various self-interests. In a speech on 13 November 1930 he said:

> In all of business, in all of life in fact, we will have to do away with the concept that the benefit to the individual is what is most important, and that from the self-interest of the individual the benefit to the whole is built up, therefore that it is the benefit to the individual which only makes up the benefit to the community at all. The opposite is true. The benefit to the community determines the benefit to the individual. The profit of the individual is only weighed out from the profit of the community ... If this principle is not accepted, then an egoism must necessarily develop which will destroy the community. When somebody says that the present age will not stand for such an uneconomic way of thinking, then we have to answer him, a way of thinking is either right or wrong. If it is right, then any age will stand for it, and if it is wrong, then it will be wrong for any age.[100]

In Hitler's view, therefore, the economic egoism of the individual and the principle of competition are important mainsprings of economic life, but they must be held in bounds by the state and not be allowed to unfold without restriction, because the common good does not result from the pursuit of special interests of the individual as the adherents of 'free enterprise' believe. With this the framework has been defined within which Hitler accepted private initiative.

In a speech at the Second Working Congress of the DAF on 16 May 1934, the two sides of Hitler's thinking were clearly expressed. On the one hand, Hitler said, the free play of forces must be granted as broad and free a field as possible; on the other hand it must be emphasized that this play of forces had to remain within the framework of the given human communal necessity, in other words within the framework of the national community. In this speech it again becomes clear that Hitler was transferring his fundamental socio-Darwinistic convictions to the field of economics as well:

> Free life is as natural as the battle out there in nature, which also does not have any compunctions and destroys many living beings, so that only what is healthy survives. If this principle were to be removed by nationalization, then the principles of civil administration would be applied to the structure of our whole economic life and we would experience a pitiful collapse. We cannot achieve any sort of human progress at all in a completely bureaucratic economy.[101]

Hitler was therefore initially also sceptical of a planned economy, even though he did accept the need for state control of business. In a policy speech in the *Reichstag* on 21 May 1935 he declared that the task of making Germany economically independent could 'only be solved by a planned economy', and then added that this was

> ... a dangerous undertaking because any planned economy was followed all too easily by bureaucracy and therefore the stifling of eternally creative private initiative. And in the interest of our nation we cannot wish that, by an economy approaching Communism and the dulling effect on productive energy this entails, the total productive achievement of our existing labour force is reduced, and thereby the standard of living experiences, instead of an increase, all the greater a decrease. This danger is even increased by the fact that any planned economy all too easily abolishes, or at least restricts, the harsh laws of economic selection of the better and destruction of the weaker, in favour of a guarantee of even the most inferior average at the expense of higher ability, greater diligence and value, and therefore at the expense of the common good. If we decided to go this route despite these insights, then we did this under the most harsh constraints of necessity. What has been achieved in the last two and a half years in the areas of a planned provision of jobs, a planned regulation of the markets, a planned structuring of prices and wages, would have been considered to be completely impossible only a few short years ago.[102]

Hitler's reservations against a planned economy are therefore primarily an outcome of his socio-Darwinistic convictions. He feared that the at least partial elimination of free competition could remove a mainspring of business life. On the other hand, from his fundamental principle of the 'primacy of politics' and his concept of 'the secondary role of the economy' he derived the stringent demands of state control of business, because in the final analysis only state control would be able to enforce the state-defined common good against the private interests of the individual.

In view of the successes then achieved by the economic policies of the government, Hitler's reservations against state planning of the economy gradually diminished. In addition, the requirements of rearmament and preparation for war, as well as the attempt to achieve the relative autarky this entailed, required as rational an economic structure as possible. In a speech on the occasion of a harvest festival Hitler looked back on the economic successes achieved since the seizure of power and attributed these to planned economy elements and state measures:

> Certainly, and this is clear, we could not simply let things run on. Such a miracle would not have come about of itself. If Germany intends to live, then it must ... run its whole economy in a manner that is clear and planned ... We cannot manage without a plan. If we were to let things run on according to the principle everyone may do as he likes, then in a very short time this freedom would end up in a terrible famine. No, we have to conduct our business and run our

economy according to plan . . . Therefore the National Socialist government cannot be dependent on any individual interests. It cannot be dependent on the city or the country, not on workers and not on employers. It cannot be dependent on industry, on the crafts, on trade or on finance. It can only accept one obligation . . . The nation alone is our master and we serve this nation to the best of our knowledge and belief.[103]

How important Hitler considered the question of state-controlled planning of the economy to be can be seen from the fact that in August 1936 he personally wrote a 'Memorandum on the Four-Year Plan 1936'. In this memorandum his admiration and fear of the Soviet system of planned economy were expressed: 'The German economy, however, will learn to understand the new economic tasks, or it will prove itself to be incapable of continuing to survive in these modern times in which the Soviet state sets up a gigantic plan.'[104] As we shall see later, Hitler was convinced of the superiority of the Soviet planned economy system over the capitalist economic system. This must be regarded as an essential reason why he so vehemently demanded and enforced the extension of state control of the economy in Germany as well. This motive – namely Hitler's fear, clearly expressed in his memorandum, that if the German economy kept its system of free enterprise 'in these modern times in which the Soviet state sets up a gigantic plan' it could no longer survive – has previously not been acknowledged by research.

At the culture meeting of the 1936 *Reichsparteitag* Hitler declared that 'the free play of forces' had now ended in politics as well as in business.[105] In his opening proclamation he said that it was 'a matter of course that the lack of restraints of a free economy had to be ended in favour of planned direction and planned action'. In this, the National Socialist leadership had always avoided exercising greater influence on business than absolutely necessary. Ahead of all other considerations had always stood the principle that the nation and business were not the slaves of capital, 'but that capital is only a business tool and therefore also subjected to the higher necessity of preserving the nation'. Hitler then went on to set the objective that in four years' time Germany must have become independent of other nations for all those materials

> . . . which can somehow be provided by German ability, by our chemical and machine industries as well as our mines . . . Maybe we will soon again be hearing the criticism from the mouths of the western democracies that we are now also no longer granting business the freedom to do as it likes, but are putting it into the strait-jacket of our state planning. But, my fellow national comrades, you must understand that this is not a matter of democracy or freedom, but of being or not being. The issue is not the freedom or profit of a few industrialists, but the life and the freedom of the German nation.[106]

In his speech on 30 January 1937 on the fourth anniversary of the seizure of power, Hitler sharply attacked the ideology of economic liberalism and expressed his conviction of the necessity of a state-controlled economy:

> There is no economic concept or economic view which can claim to be gospel. What is decisive is the will to always assign business the role of servant of the people and capital the role of servant of business. National Socialism is, as we know, the sharpest opponent of the liberalistic point of view that business existed for capital and the people for business. We were therefore also determined from the very first day to break with the mistaken concept that business could lead an unbound, uncontrollable and unsupervised life within the state. A free economy, in other words one completely left to itself, can no longer exist today. Not only would this be politically intolerable, no, economically too, impossible conditions would result. Just as millions of individual people cannot structure or perform their work according to their own ideas or needs, so also business as a whole can not act according to its own opinions or in the service of egoistic interests. Because today it too is no longer able to bear the consequences of a mistake all by itself. Modern economic development concentrates enormous masses of workers in certain types of jobs and in certain regions. New inventions or the loss of markets can destroy whole industries in one blow. The industrialist may be able to close the gates of his factory, he may even attempt to find a new field of activity for his drive to be active. In most cases he will not go under so readily, and, apart from that, here we are only dealing with a few individuals. But facing these there are hundreds of thousands of workers with their women and their children! Who will take them and who will care for them? The national community! *Jawohl!* It has to. But then it cannot be accepted that the national community is only burdened with the responsibility for the catastrophe of business, without having any influence on, and responsibility for the direction and the control of business by which the catastrophe could be avoided! My fellow members! When in 1932 to 1933 the German economy appeared to be finally heading for complete destruction, the following became even more clear to me than in earlier years: the salvation of our nation is not a problem of finance, but exclusively a problem of the use and employment of our existing working forces on the one hand and the utilization of existing land and natural resources on the other. It is therefore first and foremost a problem of organization. We are therefore also not dealing with phrases such as 'freedom of the economy'; the issue is rather to give the workforce the possibility of a production and a productive activity by all available means. As long as business, in other words the sum total of our enterprises, is able to do this, all the better. But if it is no longer capable, then the national community, in other words in this case the state, is obliged to take care of the employment of the existing workforce for the purpose of a useful production, or to take the appropriate measures for this.

The crucial problem could only be solved by 'a planned direction of our economy' which found its 'most powerful expression' in the setting-up of the Four-Year Plan.[107]

IV: Hitler's Central Objective

Such statements clearly show that Hitler was gradually giving up his initial scepticism towards a state controlled economy and formulating his criticism of the free enterprise system with growing sharpness and increasingly as a matter of principle. In Hitler's view, the free play of forces in the market place in no way automatically resulted in a functioning, orderly and flourishing economy. This economic objective could only be achieved by means of state control of the economy. While Hitler continued to believe that a general nationalization of the means of production was not necessary in order to be able to organize total production rationally, on the other hand he threatened – openly or otherwise – nationalization as a possibility in case the free economy were not able to achieve the objectives the state had set.

On 20 February 1937, for example, at the opening of the International Automobile and Motorcycle Show, he said:

> In one to two years we will be independent of foreign countries in our requirements for fuel and rubber . . . And there must be no doubt, either the so-called free economy is able to solve these problems or it will not be able to continue to exist as a free economy! The National Socialist state will not capitulate under any circumstances before the laziness, nor the lack of intelligence, nor the malice of the individual German.[108]

The sentence that the free economy must either be able to solve the problems, or 'it will not be able to continue to exist as a free economy' was heavily emphasized in the newly published periodical *Der Vierjahresplan* [The Four-Year Plan—H.B.].[109] Hitler, as we shall see in the next chapter, was soon to prove that this threat was meant quite seriously.

On various occasions Hitler emphasized that there was no such thing in business as an untouchable dogma. Free enterprise was not gospel for him either. At the *Reichsparteitag* in 1937 he declared:

> Business is one of the many functions in the life of the nation and can therefore only be organized and directed under considerations of expediency and never treated according to dogma. As a dogma there is neither a socialist economy nor a free economy, there is only a committed economy, in other words an economy which has the overall obligation of providing a nation with the highest and best living conditions. In as far as it fulfils this task without any direction from above, only out of the free play of forces, all the better, and above all very pleasant for the government. In as far as it is no longer able to fulfil its task as a free economy in some specific area, the leadership of the national community has the obligation to give the economy those directions which are necessary in the interest of the preservation of the whole. But when in one or the other area an economy is completely incapable of solving the great tasks it has been set, then the leadership of the national community will have to look for other ways and means with which to satisfy the requirements of the community.

The closing sentences again contain a threat which is only lightly veiled. With his oft-repeated thesis that there were no such thing as dogmas in the field of business, Hitler wanted to make it clear to the business leaders that they had to fulfil the tasks assigned to them by the state, or, should 'the objective set' not be reached 'by these means, the nation itself will take over this work'. Hitler wanted to exploit the advantages of free trade, above all the principle of competition, as the mainspring for the constant growth of the economy but was very sceptical with regard to the possibility of achieving an optimal economic process without state control of business. This scepticism grew, probably based on various negative experiences, and therefore Hitler's announcements or threats that, if private industry were incapable of fulfilling the tasks it had been set, other ways and means would be found to achieve the necessary objectives. In the speech in the *Reichstag* just cited, he also emphasized that Germany could not tolerate 'every individual' being 'allowed to do what he likes'[110] in the field of business.

In Hitler's view the requirements of rearmament in particular prohibited the taking of investment decisions primarily on the basis of personal capitalistic considerations of profitability. Hans Frank (Reichs Law Leader and Governor-General of Poland during the Second World War), for example, reports on a talk between Hitler and Mussolini during the visit to Italy in May 1938. Addressing himself to the problem of iron and steel production Hitler had said:

> But if it should ever again come to war, then Germany's iron and steel production stands prepared for the highest achievements. I am grubbing around in the soil of Germany and where I can find even as little as one thousand tonnes I dig them out. But a procedure such as this can only be done by a state which, like Italy or us, has made itself independent of capitalist methods, for whom the exploitation of national raw materials is only important from the point of view of earnings, in other words so-called profitability. But these raw materials must be gained one way or the other, because what must be important is not whether a capitalist can make money with them but whether the power of the national economy can be increased. This alone is the task, for which – naturally – only the possible degree to which the general welfare can be increased is at all important in the end.[111]

Hitler attributed the success of National Socialist economic policy primarily to state control of the economy:

> But this also required an organization of work which compelled everybody to put the interests of the whole ahead of his own. Here the National Socialist state imposed itself without compunction. Only thereby was it possible for us to install a unified leadership in our economy, which as a result produced those gigantic achievements which benefit the whole nation.[112]

IV: Hitler's Central Objective

Hitler's view that the positive results of NS economic policy are mainly to be attributed to state control of the economy is still shared today by historians. Karl Hardach, for example, writes:

> That the National Socialists were able to implement their extensive rearmament programme without any significant currency devaluation,[113] or any significant reduction of the standard of living of the masses, was only possible because over the years – without following a preconceived plan – they had been able to convert what was left of the German free economy into a planned economy step by step.[114]

The tendency towards bureaucracy which the establishment of the principles of a planned economy entail had also developed in Germany, said Hardach, but

> ... in many respects the system of the 'tied economy' need not shun a comparison with other economic systems of the day. By means of a partial planning and the continued application of the price mechanism as a means of directing the economy, the National Socialists hoped to achieve an harmonious relationship between the adaptability and the stability of the economy. Any running down of their time-consuming search for a new economic order, and the experimentation this required, as having been a senseless and unsystematic attempt to muddle through[115] is a sign of a misapprehension of their intentions and objective possibilities. Rejection of and contempt for the political and social principles of the National Socialists should not make an analysis of their economic system which is free from emotions and prejudices impossible. They considered neither a centralized total planning following the Soviet example nor a free economy of the Western type to be appropriate, but without any dogmatic compunctions instead chose those economic-political instruments they felt would further the ends according to the needs.

We can agree with this opinion, but with one important caveat, namely the wording that the gradual restrictions of the principles of free enterprise had taken place 'without following any preconceived plan' and that the National Socialists had undogmatically helped themselves to the instrument they considered to be useful from case to case could lead to the false conclusion that NS economic policy had been completely pragmatic and free of any ideology. But this is not the case at all. On the contrary, it is characterized by an inner logic by which economic reality was gradually revolutionarily reshaped according to the principles of Hitler's economic concepts. The establishment of a new economic system which, as Hardach himself correctly states, 'was to be an alternative to capitalism and Communism, and meant neither free enterprise nor total planning'[116] was one of the most important objectives of the revolution Hitler intended.

On the other hand we must take into consideration that such an economic system had not been tried in practice before, any more than had Keynes' insights and those of others which revolutionized economic theory. Therefore the practical experiences gained with this economic system in their turn influenced Hitler's economic thinking, and he increasingly came to the conviction that the problems of business could only be solved by centralized planning and state intervention.

In a conversation with the Italian Minister of Justice Grandi on 25 November 1940, Hitler criticized the governments of the democracies: 'They actually do no work but leave everything to civilian initiative and business. With this their problems are not only not solved but simply ignored.'[117] In table talks on 27/28 July 1941 Hitler said that 'A sensible employment of the powers of a nation can only be achieved with a planned economy from above.'[118] About two weeks later he said: 'As far as the planning of the economy is concerned, we *are still very much at the beginning* and I imagine it will be something wonderfully nice to build up an encompassing German and European economic order.'[119] The statement that as far as the planning of the economy was concerned one was still at the very beginning is important because it shows that Hitler was not thinking at all of a reduction of state intervention – not even for the time after the war – but, on the contrary, intended to expand the instruments of state control of the economy even further.

On 5 July 1942 Hitler expressed the opinion in a table talk that if the German economy had been able so far to deal with innumerable problems,

> ... this was also due in the end to the fact that the direction of the economy had gradually become more controlled by the state. Only thus had it been possible to enforce the overall national objective against the interests of individual groups. *Even after the war we would not be able to renounce state control of the economy,* because then every interest group would think exclusively of the fulfilment of its wishes.[120]

Hitler's view of the Soviet economic system apparently also changed from strong scepticism to admiration. As we have shown, we already find the beginnings of a positive view of the planned economy system of the USSR in Hitler's memorandum on the Four-Year Plan 1936. On the other hand, in a conversation with Goebbels on 14 November 1939 for example, he still expresses himself very critically on the Soviet economic system, which he accuses of being over-centralized and bureaucratic and of stifling private initiative and efficiency.[121] Less than three years later, in a table talk on 22 July 1942, Hitler vehemently defends the Soviet economic system and even the so-called 'Stachanow System', which it was 'exceedingly stupid' to ridicule:

> One had to have unqualified respect for Stalin. In his way, the guy was quite a genius! His ideals such as Genghis Khan and so forth he knew very well, and his

economic planning was so all-encompassing that it was only exceeded by our own four-year plan. He had no doubts whatsoever that there had been no unemployed in the USSR, as opposed to capitalist countries such as the USA.[122]

Until now research has not recognized that Hitler's economic convictions, most notably his conviction concerning the superiority of a system of a planned over a free economy, were decisively shaped by his impressions of the superiority of the Soviet economic system. Hitler's admiration for the Soviet system is also confirmed in the notes of Wilhelm Scheidt, who, as adjutant to Hitler's 'representative for military history' Scherff and a member of the *Führer* Headquarters group, had close contact with Hitler and sometimes even took part in the 'briefings'. Scheidt writes that Hitler underwent a 'conversion to Bolshevism'. From Hitler's remarks, he says, the following reactions could be derived: 'Firstly, Hitler was enough of a materialist to be the first to recognize the enormous armament achievements of the USSR in the context of her strong, generous and all-encompassing economic organization.' Hitler's surprise, which also apparently struck Scheidt as well as the other members of the *Führer* Headquarters group in view of their impressions of the effectiveness of the Soviet economic system – a surprise which is perhaps primarily a reflection of the previous underestimation of this system – is expressed in Scheidt's subsequent statements:

> And, indeed, for any eye accustomed to European forms of economy, it was most compelling to see the differences that became apparent when one entered into Soviet territory. Even from an aircraft one observed the sudden change in the cultivation of the land. The many small fields that are characteristic for the European farmer disappeared and gave place to a wide-spaced but still rational division of land. The fertile plains of the Ukraine spread out in gigantic rectangles impossible to overlook, ordered and impeccably cultivated like a carpet of order and diligence, which could hardly be more impressively conceived. It was manifest that here something had been achieved and developed economically, *with which the forms of western economies could not compete in the long run*. This impression is confirmed by the detailed reports of agrarian experts. The same impression is repeated when inspecting even the destroyed industrial plants. Even from their ruins one could see that they had been equipped in the most modern fashion and had disposed a gigantic production capacity.

Scheidt writes that in view of such impressions Hitler had recognized and expressed 'the inner relationship of his system with the so heatedly opposed Bolshevism', whereby he had had to admit that 'this system of the enemy was developed far more completely and straightforwardly. His enemy became his secret example.' The 'experience of Communist Russia', particularly the impression of the superiority of the Soviet economic system, had produced a strong reaction in Hitler and the circle of his faithful: 'The other economic systems appeared not to be competitive in comparison.' About the impression of the rational organization of farming in the USSR and the 'gigantic industrial plants which gave eloquent testimony despite their destruction', Hitler, says Scheidt, had been 'enthusiastic'.[123] As he admitted during a conversation with Mussolini on 22 April 1944, Hitler had become convinced: 'Capitalism too had run its course, the nations were no longer willing to stand for it. The victors to survive would be Fascism, and National Socialism – maybe Bolshevism in the East.'[124]

Hitler's Reichs Press Chief Otto Dietrich writes in his memoirs that Hitler had sensed that

> ... the economic requirements of human large-area development had outgrown the structure of the former self-regulating private capitalistic economic system and that common sense demanded a new, more efficient economic structure, in other words a planned overall management. The economic principle he was envisaging can be expressed as follows: private capital production based on a belief in the common good and under state control![125]

We must note, however, that in this Hitler sometimes played with the idea of calling the principle of private ownership into question and nationalizing important parts of industry – as we will show in the next chapter.

Speer reports that in the light of such tendencies, which were analogous to an actual development in which the influence of the state on business continued to grow, serious 'ill humour' began to spread among industrialists, including the representatives of the armaments industry, directed against the

> ... increasing spread of the power of the party machine on business. And, in fact, a sort of state socialism appeared to be gaining ground in the minds of numerous party functionaries ... Our system of controlling industry the war had caused, and which above all else had also shown itself to be very effective, was well suited to become the pattern for a state-controlled nationalized economic order, so that it was the industrialists themselves who by their improved results were, if you like, delivering tools for their own destruction into the hands of the party leaders.[126]

This background information is required for us to understand the speech which Hitler gave on 26 June 1944 at the Obersalzberg to representatives of the armaments industry.[127] Speer had expressly requested that Hitler allay these fears of the industrialists in a speech, whereupon Hitler asked Speer to give him some cues. Speer reports:

> ... I noted down for him that he should promise the representatives of industrial self-administration that they would receive help in the times of heavy crisis to be expected, furthermore that they would be protected against interference by local

party authorities, and finally an emphatic avowal of the 'invulnerability of the private ownership of the production plants' even when these were temporarily moved underground as plants run by the state, free enterprise after the war, and a fundamental rejection of the nationalization of industry.[128]

None of this was at all in line with Hitler's true convictions. Nevertheless he saw the need to follow Speer's advice and dispel the suspicions of the industrialists.

And indeed, in his speech we find several statements in which he rejects any nationalization of the means of production, declares his respect for private ownership[129] and explains the economic principle of competition in terms of socio-Darwinism.[130] Many of these statements are not to be taken seriously – even if they might have equated to some of his views in former years – because we know from Speer that the purely tactical objective of dispelling the suspicions of the industrialists was the overriding motive. And Hitler did not really succeed in presenting the assurances Speer had asked of him convincingly and credibly. Speer reports on his impression of Hitler's speech: 'In his speech, in which he kept to my cues, Hitler gave the impression of being inhibited. He made frequent slips of the tongue, stopped, broke off in midsentence, lacked fluidity of expression and occasionally confused himself.' Speer also attributes this to Hitler's state of exhaustion. What appears to be more important to us, however, was that Hitler had been compelled to state views which were far removed from his true convictions, and to give a speech which, in contrast to his custom, had partially been written by someone else. And, as Speer noted, Hitler immediately relativized his statements:

> At first Hitler rejected any ideological reservations 'because there can only be one dogma, and this dogma says in short, the right thing is the thing which is expedient'. With this he reinforced his pragmatic way of thinking and *in the true sense took back all of the assurance given to industry.*[131]

In fact Hitler began his speech with the following:

> ... in the liberal state of yesteryear, business, in the final analysis, was the servant of capital, the people, in the opinion of many, a means for business. In the National Socialist state the people are the dominating factor, business a means in the service of the preservation of the people, capital a means of directing business . . . In directing the fight for existence of a nation there can be only one dogma, namely to apply those means which lead to success. Any further dogma would be harmful. I would therefore not shrink back from anything if I knew that one or the other of these methods was failing.[132]

This introduction by Hitler, as Speer rightly notes, was not at all appropriate for reassuring the industrialists. But only if looked at superficially is it an expression of 'a pragmatic way of thinking'. In reality Hitler's statement that there was no dogma in business, had, as we have already shown, more of the function of a warning that for him the system of free enterprise was also not gospel. When he then added that he would 'not shrink back from anything' if one or the other method were to fail, then this too was only a thinly veiled threat which made all of his subsequent avowals in favour of private ownership and against nationalization worthless.

Hitler went even further and told the industrialists that state control of the economy would continue after the end of the war in order to maintain a relative autarky for Germany:

> This, gentlemen, is immediately an area [we should note Hitler's choice of words—R.Z.] where, in future as well, state control will have to intervene. It must intervene here from the vantage of a higher insight. It is an insanity to produce cartridges out of brass in times of peace and to know very well that after three months of war one then has to immediately convert to cartridges out of iron or steel, an insanity! But the brass cartridge is prettier, it is easier to manufacture and furthermore it is well introduced. This is where the task of state control begins, or where it receives its assignment, namely to assure that the higher insight of war is taken into account here.[133]

In the end, the speech Hitler had given on Speer's advice and which Speer had helped to formulate had a completely different result from what Speer had imagined. As Speer summarizes: 'The avowal of a free economy in times of peace, which I had asked of Hitler and been promised, came out far less clearly than I had expected.' Nonetheless, said Speer, some of the statements in the speech had been noteworthy, so he asked Hitler for permission to file it in the archives – which never came about because Bormann prevented it and Hitler remained evasive.[134]

Hitler himself was convinced, as he emphasized in his last radio address on 30 January 1945, 'that the age of unrestricted economic liberalism had outlived itself'.[135] In his final dictations to Martin Bormann about one month later, he said in looking back: 'The crisis of the thirties was only a crisis of growth, albeit of global proportions. Economic liberalism unveiled itself as having become an outdated formula.'[136]

These statements of Hitler's in 1935 to 1945, but particularly from the beginning of the 1940s on, show that he had become a vehement critic of the system of free enterprise and a confirmed adherent of the system of a planned, state-controlled economy. Basically, these convictions were logically derived from his thesis of 'the secondary role of the economy'. If he hesitated from time to time to draw these conclusions, then this must certainly be attributed to his fundamental socio-Darwinistic position, which made him believe in the importance of the principle of competition in business. When his practical experiences, the difficulties with the economy on the one hand and the successes of the experiments with a planned economy on the other, showed him the possibilities of a state-controlled economy, then the step to becoming a convinced adherent of state control was only a short one and basically only consistent. This does not mean that Hitler gave up his convictions of the usefulness of competition in business which he derived from socio-Darwinism. This side of the question was by then, however, no longer essential for his economic thinking, but his conviction was that the system of economic liberalism had outlived itself and that the future belonged to the state-controlled, planned economy.

The example of Hitler's views on the problem of 'market versus plan' is well suited to demonstrate the degree to which the premises of the dictator's *Weltanschauung* were turned into reality. During the early years of National Socialist rule, as Barkai has written in his basic study *The Economic System of National Socialism*, state intervention in the economy was 'incomparable to any other capitalist country, including Fascist Italy, as far as degree and depth is concerned'.[137] In many aspects, the economic policy of the National Socialist was comparable to the recommendations of the 'reformers' among the political scientists, who during the world economic crisis had advocated the thesis that only an active stabilization policy could achieve the objective of reinstating full employment. But while most of the reformers saw their recommendations as being emergency measures of limited duration, and only defined them as being 'initial charges' after which the economy, once started again, could return to free market conditions, these theoretical economic instruments of the reformers in the hands of the National Socialists became 'an ongoing economic and financial control of an economy being directed in the service of the "primacy of politics"'.[138]

Slowly but surely all the sectors of the economy were subjugated to state control. The 'New Plan' set up in 1934 resulted in the complete and direct control of foreign trade. Every single import contract had to be approved by one of 25 'control authorities' organized according to branches of industry. Only on the basis of this approval was the importer allocated the necessary foreign currency by the regional 'foreign currency office'. For all practical purposes the 'New Plan' was nothing but an almost 'total state monopoly of foreign trade'.[139] While private ownership remained largely untouched, the state did create a comprehensive set of instruments for the direct control of investments. The control of raw materials in particular, which had been introduced in March 1933 and formalized by law in July 1934, was used for this purpose. The 28 'allocation offices' also began to use the information they collected for the purpose of deciding on new construction or expansion of industrial plants. This power of confirmation and supervision was transferred to the Reichs Minister of Economics by the Decree to the Law on Compulsory Cartels of July 1933. With this, for all practical purposes, the whole of private investment activity was subjected to state control. Decrees were then issued prohibiting investments for whole industries, for example textiles, paper, cement and glass, but also for segments of heavy industry such as lead and pipes.

Within the framework of National Socialist economic theory, all of this was consistent:

> In the context of a state-directed economic concept, the creation of capital and investments assume a central role. What was at first sensed more intuitively here, namely the importance of investment for the cyclical process of the economy, was soon able to see itself confirmed by modern economic theory, that such an important factor for employment and the balancing of the economy could not be left to the free initiative and the desire to invest of the entrepreneurs.[140]

Wages and prices, which in the capitalist free enterprise system are left to the free play of forces of the market to regulate, were state-controlled in the Third Reich. While there had already been a Reichs Price Commissioner in Germany since 1931, the creation of a new 'Reichs Commissioner for Price Formation' at the end of October 1936 was 'more than just the reactivation of an already familiar institution under a new name. Under the Four-Year Plan it developed into a central control institution for economic policy.' The duties of the Price Commissioner did not consist of merely 'controlling' and correcting market prices, but also of the 'official formation of the price'. The assignment of labour was also state-controlled by means of various instruments and measures. A directive issued in 1936 within the framework of the Four-Year Plan, for example, required every company in the iron and metal industry and the building trade to train a certain number of apprentices as a means of reducing the lack of skilled workers.[141] In summary we can note that the state created a comprehensive planning instrument and by a number of direct and indirect measures controlled the allocation of raw materials, investments, wages, prices and in part also consumption.[142]

It would now be too one-sided, as both Petzina and Barkai have emphasized, to want to explain this policy of state control of the economy only by the necessities of rearmament. The thesis according to which the regime only created these instruments for the pragmatic purpose of an optimal realization of rearmament misapprehends the fact that, completely independently of this, it was a key objective of the National Socialists to establish an anti-liberal economic system and to abolish the economic system based on private capital.¹⁴³ The restructuring of the economic order which had already begun in the early years of the Third Reich was pushed even further during the war. Within the system of the war economy, the state as the sole customer set the priorities, decided what was to be produced in its 'central planning' and allocated the raw materials, labour, energy and transport capacity.

For Hitler none of this was in any way an emergency measure only required because of rearmament and war, but rather a deliberately created instrument for the revolutionizing of the economic order and the establishment of a new economic system that was to be characterized by a synthesis between elements of free enterprise and state control, whereby the preponderance clearly lay on the aspect of state control which was to implement the 'primacy of politics'.

The fact that a planned economy could be installed in Germany so quickly was predicated on a variety of factors. Politically the dictatorship was able to break all opposition, even from the side of industry. Barkai rightly emphasizes that

> It is highly doubtful whether any democratic government of the day could have overcome the opposition by the business interests, which were organized into political pressure groups, in order to implement a uniform unorthodox economic policy, even if it had been able to bring itself to theoretically recognizing these necessities.¹⁴⁴

On the other hand, in German political science there was a long 'étatistic' tradition, which can be traced from Adam Müller and Friedrich List all the way to Werner Sombart.¹⁴⁵ During the world economic crisis, which demonstrated the failure of the capitalist system in view of the problem of full employment, concepts of a planned economy became popular. The Left, particularly the KPD, was critical of, or even opposed, the capitalist system anyway, and propagated the planned economy as an alternative to capitalist 'anarchy of production'. But even political scientists like Werner Sombart admitted in presentations, articles and popular brochures that the future belonged to the planned economy.¹⁴⁶

Hitler was influenced by these concepts, which were widespread within the circles of the 'conservative revolutionaries'. They agreed with the basic premises of his *Weltanschauung*, in which the freedom of the individual (which is cited by the exponents of the free market ideology as the legitimization for their system) had no intrinsic value but where everything had to submit itself to the 'common good', in other words to the interests of the nation as defined by the *Führer*. The practical successes achieved by the application of instruments of the planned economy then confirmed his economic concepts for him. By 1936 the number of unemployed could already be reduced from

Hitler: The Policies of Seduction

5.6 to 1.6 million. At the same time the gross national product rose by more than 40 per cent and national per capita earnings by 46 per cent (compared to 1932).[147] In 1943-44, when Speer was systematically extending the planning system under the war economy, German armaments production achieved a three-fold increase compared to 1941, and this despite the Allied air attacks.[148]

For Hitler the surprisingly effective Soviet war production also appeared to confirm his thesis of the superiority of the planned over the free economy system. And when ideological premises, economic principles derived from these and the practical successes of an economic policy agree to such a degree, it would be mistaken to assume that after the war Hitler would have returned to the 'old' system of free enterprise. The opposite is true. Since the system of a planned economy was in complete agreement with the premises of Hitler's *Weltanschauung*, and had proved itself to be extremely effective in practice, after the war Hitler would (as the industrialists quite rightly feared) not have chosen the path of a gradual reduction of state intervention, but would most probably have continued to extend this system consistently – and his statements indicate this.

6. Private Ownership and Nationalization

The answer to the question of Hitler's position on private ownership and nationalization appears to be fairly simple. It is generally accepted that Hitler recognized private ownership of the means of production and rejected nationalization.[149] To leave it at that, as is generally done, would mean being superficial because this statement is far too undifferentiated and leaves too many questions unanswered.

From the fact that in the Third Reich private ownership was basically left untouched, it has already been generally concluded that Hitler rejected the idea of nationalization as a matter of principle. In the preceding chapter we have already shown, however, that Hitler frequently quite openly used the possibility of nationalization as a threat. In this section we will present several statements by Hitler, particularly from the early 1940s, in which he favours the nationalization of certain sectors of industry. This seems to indicate that during his political rule Hitler underwent a radicalization or modification of various of his economic concepts, similarly to his position on a planned economy. The succinct statement that Hitler was in favour of private ownership leaves the decisive question unanswered: what elements of private ownership remain at all in a planned state controlled economy, in which the owner can no longer freely dispose of his property?

IV: Hitler's Central Objective

In an article on the economic system of National Socialism published in 1941, Friedrich Pollock pointed out the following:

> I agree that the legal institution of private ownership was maintained, and that many attributes characteristic for National Socialism begin to manifest themselves, albeit still vaguely, in non-totalitarian countries. But does this mean that the function of private ownership did not change? Is the 'increase of power of a few groups' really the most important result of the change which took place?[150] I believe it reaches far more deeply and should be described as the destruction of all the essential traits of private ownership, saving one exception. Even the mightiest concerns were denied the right to set up new fields of business in areas where the highest profits were to be expected, or to interrupt a production where it became unprofitable. These rights were transferred in their entirety to the ruling groups. The compromise between the groups in power initially determined the extent and direction of the production process. Faced with such a decision, the title of ownership is powerless, even if it is derived from the possession of the overwhelming majority of the share capital, let alone when it only owns a minority.[151]

It is not the intention of this study to analyze the actual economic structure of the Third Reich. But Pollock's considerations can also be relevant for an analysis of Hitler's position on private ownership. As we know, Hitler's method rarely consisted of simply radically removing an institution or organization but rather of continuing to erode its inner substance until there was virtually nothing left of its original function or original content. For the sake of the analogy only, we should note that the constitution of Weimar was never repealed either, but that its substance and intention were eroded little by little and thereby abolished in practice. These initial considerations should lead us to a very careful analysis of Hitler's position on private ownership and to keep the possibility in mind that his position underwent a change.

In the 25-point programme of the NSDAP, which Hitler had helped to write and which he announced on 24 February 1920, it says under Point 13: 'We demand the nationalization of all the [already] socialized [trusts] companies.' Point 17 of the programme says: 'We demand a land reform in line with our national requirements, the enactment of a law for the expropriation without compensation of land for public purposes. The abolition of interest on land and prevention of any sort of land speculation.' This last point in the programme was amended in the spring of 1928 at Hitler's instigation by a modifying footnote which was to prevent competing parties in rural areas from turning the demand for the expropriation of land without compensation for public purposes against the National Socialists.[152] Point 13 of the programme, which is already worded quite confusingly (nationalization of already socialized companies?!), initially played no role in Hitler's political objectives. While he did demand the 'nationalization of all the banks and the whole sector of finance'[153] on 7 August 1920, for example, in his speeches he generally came out in favour of private ownership and was sceptical of nationalization.

In his notes for a speech on 25 August 1920 he wrote:

Germany as the only state which nationalized.
German model enterprises

I. <u>State administration</u>	<u>Railway</u>
<u>Tax administration</u> etc.	<u>Postal service</u>
Postal service etc.	Telegraph
<u>City administrations</u>	German co-operatives
Vienna – and Berlin – Munich and so forth H Lueger	
<u>Nationalization requires: sense of responsibility</u>	
German <u>civil servants</u>	Only in decades
German <u>state employees</u>	to be <u>formed</u>

<u>without employees with sense of responsibility any total nationalization fraud.</u> (S. Eisner)

In his continuing notes Hitler came out in favour of private enterprise but also demanded the 'nationalization of mineral resources, of artificial fertilizers [and] chemical products', and he also rejected 'socialist experiments' of 'total nationalization'.[154] The sense and context of these notes can be clearly reconstructed from a report on Hitler's speech of 25 August 1920. In his speech Hitler lauded 'the nationalization of the postal and telegraph service' but rejected any 'nationalization without deliberation' because this only meant 'that the citizen has to pay higher taxes'. Germany had 'played the role of pioneer in all areas. That it had worked so well is a credit to the awareness of the civil servants that they had to work for the common interest. It takes years to educate people to the fulfilment of the obligations.'[155]

Hitler approved the nationalizations already carried out, for example the railways and the postal service, but believed that any nationalization first required a sense of responsibility among the civil servants and state employees. This, however, had only been formed in an education process lasting for decades. An immediate 'total nationalization', without having been preceded by such a progress of education, was a 'fraud', which would only lead to the citizens' having to pay higher taxes.

At a rally of the NSDAP on 26 October 1920 Hitler criticized 'plans to communalize and nationalize' in general but also added that 'they do not dare to go after the right places (banks, wholesale trade etc.)'.[156] The demand for the nationalization of banks and the wholesale trade, as we shall see in the next chapter, has to do with Hitler's early economic concepts (strongly influenced by Gottfried Feder), according to which exploitation only takes place in the sphere of distribution but not in the sphere of production.

A campaign by the NSDAP in November 1921 conceived and directed by Hitler against the privatization of the *Reichsbahn* also plays a not inconsiderable role. In a circular letter Hitler wrote to the party on 19 November 1921 he said, 'In view of the threatening squandering of the German Reichs railways for the benefit of private capital, we direct all local groups and sections to oppose this attempt in rallies and evening discussion meetings.'[157] The same day Hitler wrote a detailed article on this topic for one of the NSDAP information publications, in which he said among other things that the 'private capitalization of the German Reichs railways' already under consideration for several months, a 'disposal of most valuable national property', was being rejected by a large sector of the people. 'The work of enlightenment in recent days has caused a certain degree of attention even far into the Right, into the circles of the most imbecilic laziness of thought, as well as into the Left, into the masses of unlimited incitement.' This 'theft of German national property, its squandering for the benefit of private capital', was unfortunately being regarded as being of minor importance by 'numerous so-called national circles, yes, even among national parties', because Stinnes himself was involved in the matter. Hitler argued against the privatization plans:

> And do you really believe that the present deficit of the *Reichsbahn* will be made good by its new owners when ownership is transferred? Is it not completely clear that in future these burdens will again be loaded on to the taxpayer alone, though in a different form, as higher rates etc?

Hitler appealed to the whole party to give this question increased attention:

> The leaders of our local groups have the obligation to untiringly point out this new swindle by the international financial bandits at rallies and evening discussion meetings, and without rest or pause to arouse our nation to resist this squandering of its most valuable national property. Time and again the masses must have drummed into them that in the last three years hardly a day has passed in which the so-called social republic has not squandered German national property, which the so-called reactionary period once created for the German nation in 40 years of hard and thrifty work. The NSDAP opposes any sale, be it in part or total, of the German Reichs railways to private capital. It is convinced that the railways are only the beginning, and that the end will be the complete loss of even the last remnant of the German state economy.[158]

At a rally on 1 July 1923 Hitler was again critical: 'Instead of nationalizing, it [Marxism—R.Z.] is now prepared to deliver already socialized enterprises such as the *Reichsbahn* into the hands of private speculators.'[159] On 6 July 1923 he declared: 'Five years ago people were shouting, we want total nationalization, and what has become of it? Today they are getting ready to convert national companies such as the postal service, the railway, into private enterprises.'[160]

In his early speeches Hitler advocated the nationalization of land[161] but in principle still came out in favour of private ownership. On 28 July 1922, for example, he criticized the 'Marxist theory' which declared that

> ... property as such was theft, in other words, as soon as one moved away from the self-evident formula that only natural resources could and should be common property, but that that which somebody had honestly acquired and worked for was his own, from that moment on even the economic intelligence of a national persuasion could also no longer follow, because it had to say to itself that this theory would mean the complete collapse of any human culture at all.[162]

In the 'Appeal of the National Fighting Union' which Hitler wrote on 2 September 1923 it said: 'Private ownership as the basis for value-producing work will be recognized and protected by the state. Expropriation by means of tax laws is an abuse of governmental power.' It adds, however, that 'capital and business will not be permitted to form a state within the state'.[163]

Hitler's positive position on private ownership led to a conflict within the NSDAP in 1926 when the wing led by the Strasser brothers wanted to support the referendum on the expropriation of the former nobility which the Marxist parties had applied for. At a meeting in Bamberg on 14 February 1926, however, Hitler was able to enforce his rejection of any participation in the referendum. Goebbels, who at the time was still an adherent of the left-wing Strasser faction, soon joined Hitler's position. He described this in his diary on 13 April 1926 with the following words: 'Social question. Totally new insights. He [Hitler—R.Z.] has thought of everything. His ideal: mixture of collectivism and individualism. Land, what is on it and beneath it to the people. Production, because creating, individualistically. Concerns, trusts, end production, traffic etc. nationalized.'[164] Hitler also repeated this concept, said Goebbels, in a conversation on 22 July 1926.[165]

If this note by Goebbels reflects Hitler's view correctly, then it shows that his position on private ownership and nationalization cannot be summarized by a simple, catchy formula. While Hitler favoured private ownership in principle, on the NSDAP platform, on the other hand he had already considered the nationalization of certain monopoly capitalist enterprises. That such thoughts did not surface in his public speeches is hardly strange. As we have already shown, Hitler always demanded of his associates that the economic plans be kept strictly secret because he feared running into the massive resistance of industry if they became known. If his economic views had not gone beyond the unequivocal recognition of private ownership he propagated in public, then this fear would have been unfounded. What we have shown in the last chapter applies here too. Because of the secrecy practised by Hitler, the reconstruction of his economic views before 1933 is extremely difficult. We may, however, safely assume that Hitler continued to reject a 'total nationalization', in other words a conversion of all the means of production into public property.[166]

As becomes clear from Wagener's notes, Hitler's sceptical position on nationalization had to do with his socio-Darwinistic convictions. Wagener reports that in the early summer of 1930 Hitler had said:

> And when I look at the idea of collectivism, then I actually find that it contains and must entail a levelling down, which in a complete nation means nothing else except what is being demonstrated in the insane asylums and prisons. As far as this goes, the whole concept of nationalization in the form in which it has been attempted and demanded so far appears to me to be wrong, and I come to the same conclusion as *Herr* Wagener. We have to bring a process of selection into the matter in some way, if we want to come to a natural, healthy and also satisfying solution of the problem, a process of selection for those who should be entitled – and be at all permitted – to have a claim and the right to property and the ownership of companies.[167]

Against the background of what we have sketched so far we may, after all, believe Otto Strasser – whose report on a dispute with Hitler on 22 May 1930 is unreliable on many points – when he states that Hitler rejected a general expropriation and advocated the view that 'the strong state' would be able 'to let itself be guided exclusively by great issues without regard to interests'. When Strasser had referred to the party programme in which nationalization of the socialized companies (?!) was demanded, Hitler had replied that this *did not* mean 'that these companies had to be nationalized, but only that they could be nationalized, namely if they offended against the interests of the nation. As long as they do not do this, it would simply be a crime to destroy business.' Hitler was therefore rejecting 'total nationalization' but was reserving to himself the possibility of being able to threaten nationalization of companies that did not unresistingly carry out the tasks or achieve the objectives set by the state. In order to abolish the shortcomings resulting from capitalism, one did not need (as Strasser reports Hitler's view) to give the workers any co-ownership or co-determination: 'This is where the strong state must intervene, which ensures that production only occurs in the interest of the nation. If this does not happen in individual cases, then the state takes sharp measures, then it expropriates such a company and continues to run it under the state.'[168]

With this Hitler formulated his concept of the role of private ownership and the position of the entrepreneur in the NS state with precision. After the seizure of power this definition of the role of the entrepreneur was legally fixed in the 'Law for the Structuring of National Labour' (20 January 1934).[169] According to this law, the 'company leader' was the 'trustee of the state' and therefore obligated to the common good of the national community. This interpretation of the role of the owner or manager in the NS state was more important than Hitler's formal guarantee of private ownership. Because, as the reality of the Third Reich – particularly in the war years – showed, this definition of the role of the owner or manager had far-reaching consequences. The *Volksgerichtshof* [People's Court, the highest penal court in the Third Reich—H.B.], for example, handed down extremely harsh sentences against owners or managers who ignored the directives of the state plan.[170]

Even before the seizure of power there had been worries among industrialists that if the National Socialists were to come to power radical economic measures would ensue, leading to a restriction of entrepreneurial freedom. What worried them most was the degree of radicalism in the socio-revolutionary demands raised by the NSDAP. 'In socio-economic matters', Henry Turner shows in his study on the relationship between the industrialists and the National Socialists, 'the NSDAP frequently advocated positions which were practically impossible to separate from those of the extreme Left'.[171] On economic issues – for example on tax laws – the National Socialists in the *Reichstag* often voted with the Communists and the Social Democrats.[172]

For many industrialists this 'tendency to take up a position next to the Left on socio-economic questions'[173] made the NSDAP appear as a danger. The assessment of the National Socialists which predominated in industrialist circles found its expression, for example, in a series of guidelines which Paul Reusch, the founder of the influential *Ruhrlade*, issued in 1929 for the newspapers under the control of his company. In these guidelines the NSDAP appeared together with the Communists, the Social Democrats and the unions as one of the moving forces of Marxism, of its destructive 'class war concept' and of its 'utopian Marxist objectives in the economic sector'.[174] In an analysis which appeared in the periodical of the employers' association on the eve of the *Reichstag* elections of 1930, the NSDAP was criticized for its 'aggressive hostility towards business' and the warning was given that National Socialism belonged to the conspiratorial, demagogic and terrorist elements of contemporary socialism.[175]

Hitler attempted several times to dispel the understandable reservations most of the business community had against the party. On such occasions he was at pains to emphasize his bold and simple recognition of private owner-

IV: Hitler's Central Objective

ship. A well-known example is Hitler's oft-quoted speech to the *Industrieklub* in Düsseldorf on 26 January 1932 to which he had apparently tied the hope that he could persuade the business community to support the NSDAP.[176]

It would, of course, be inadmissible uncritically to call a speech so clearly determined by such objectives a revelation of his 'true opinions', just as it would be nonsensical to take every statement by Hitler in his 1 May speeches as being serious expressions of policy. Particularly in such a speech, in which the objective for which it is held – namely the intention of gaining the support, or at least the goodwill, of industrialist circles – is so clearly predominant, Hitler's statements can only be assessed, with reservations, as being a reflection of his true convictions. This has not, however, prevented many authors from claiming that this speech was *the* programmatic statement by Hitler. The likely reason for this is that such a procedure can so easily support the image of Hitler as a serf of capitalism and a lackey of monopoly capital. However this may be, in his speech Hitler of course stressed his affirmation of private ownership and we intend to follow his line of argument:

> You hold the opinion, gentlemen, that German business must be built up on the concept of private ownership. But you can only uphold such a concept of private ownership if it appears to have at least some sort of a logical foundation. This concept must derive its ethical reason from the insight into a natural necessity. It cannot only be motivated by simply saying: it has always been that way therefore it must continue to be that way. Because during periods of great national upheavals, the shifting of nations and changes in the ways of thinking, institutions, systems and so forth cannot simply be left untouched only because they have previously existed in the same form. It is characteristic for all the really great revolutionary epochs of humanity that they simply walk over such forms only hallowed by age, or only apparently hallowed by age, with an incomparable ease. It is therefore necessary to find reasons for such traditional forms which we intend to maintain upright, so that they may be regarded as being absolutely necessary, logical and right. And there, I must say, private ownership is only morally and ethically justified if I assume that the achievements of human beings differ. Only then can I say, because the achievements of people differ, the results of these achievements also differ. And if the results of the achievements of men are different, it is only expedient to leave the administration of these results to people in about the same ratio. It would be illogical to turn the administration of the results of achievements which are tied to a specific personality over to the next best person only capable of a lower achievement, or to a community which has already proved by the fact that it was unable to produce such an achievement that it cannot be capable of administering the results. With this we must admit that, economically, people are not all equally valuable, equally important, in all areas to begin with. Having admitted this, it is insane to say, in the field of business there are incontestable differences but not in the political area! It is nonsense to build economic life upon the concept of achievement, of the value

of a personality, thereby in practice on the authority of a personality, but to deny this authority of the personality in politics and to set the law of the greater number, democracy, into its place.

An analysis of Hitler's line of reasoning shows that here the issue for him was not the question of private ownership at all. He is only starting off from the views held by the industrialists assembled before him: 'You hold the opinion, gentlemen, that the German economy must be built up on the concept of private ownership.' In his further argument Hitler explains that private ownership cannot be legitimized by pointing out that until now it had been the foundation of business and must therefore continue to be so. Private ownership could only be legitimized by the principle of achievement and the fact of the differences in human achievements. This, by the way, is an important concept for Hitler which, as we shall see later, leads him to the demand for the nationalization of anonymous share companies which in his view are no longer based on the differences between individual human achievements. To raise such demands in front of an audience of industrialists was far from Hitler's intentions. His issue is not even private ownership, but the conclusion that if people are unequal in the field of business, if the personality principle applies here, then this must also be true of the political field. The whole sense of Hitler's statement does not lie in a justification of private ownership but, starting out from their own professed beliefs and interests, in proving the senselessness of democracy to the industrialist. In the course of his speech Hitler paints the spectre of Communism on the wall:

> But if it is claimed on the other hand – and in particular from the side of business – that special abilities were not required in politics and that here there was an absolute equality of achievement, then one day this same theory will be transferred from politics to business. The analogy to political democracy in the field of economy is Communism.[177]

Hitler's reasoning was as follows. If one recognized private ownership – as his industrialist audience did – one also had to draw the conclusion in the political field and make the personality principle (in this context what Hitler actually meant was the *Führer* principle) the foundation of the political system. If one holds fast to democracy, however, then a transfer of the principles in force there to the field of business will soon come about, and this would mean the introduction of Communism. Basically all Hitler's line of argument demonstrates is his ability to put himself into the minds of his audience and, setting out from certain basic convictions of his listeners, to develop a (perhaps only apparently) logical line of reasoning, which ends with the proof of the correctness of his political convictions.

IV: Hitler's Central Objective

Hitler affirmed private ownership not only in front of industrialists but also on other occasions, as, for example, in his speech to the enabling law on 23 March 1933. Here again, however, we must keep in mind that this speech was primarily intended to serve as a camouflage for his real intentions. When he promises in the same breath not to encroach on the independence of the *Länder* [the individual states making up the federal republic of Weimar—H.B.], to respect the rights of the churches, not to aspire to autarky, and only to make use of the enabling law in exceptional cases, then his declarations against 'a business bureaucracy to be organized by the state' and in favour of 'the strongest possible support of private initiative' and the 'recognition of private ownership'[178] are not particularly convincing. In his closing address at the *Reichsparteitag* in 1933 Hitler also justified private ownership by the inequality of human achievements. But in this speech as well, the issue for him was not private ownership but, as in his speech to the Düsseldorf *Industrieklub*, the proof of the illogic of the democratic system.[179]

On the other hand Hitler frequently and emphatically stated that the disposal of his property was in no way the private affair of the industrialist. On 9 October 1934, for example, he declared:

> Therefore wealth in particular does not only have greater possibilities for enjoyment, but above all greater obligations. The view that the utilization of a fortune no matter of what size is solely the private affair of the individual requires to be corrected all the more in the National Socialist state, because without the contribution of the community no individual would have been able to enjoy such an advantage.[180]

On 14 November 1940 he said:

> In Germany, without my having touched private ownership in any way, we have still set limits on ownership, that is to say those limits which lie in the fact that no property can be used to the disadvantage of another. We have not permitted the amassing of capital out of profit on arms, for example; instead we set limits here: 6 per cent, and of these 6 per cent, the first 50 per cent are taxed away, and the remaining 3 per cent, this must be reinvested in some way, or else it too will be taxed away. Anything which exceeds that must be put into a capital deposit and is at the disposal of the Reich, of the state.[181]

On 10 December 1940 Hitler declared that the individual did not have 'the right to dispose completely freely of that which must be invested in the interest of the national community. If he disposes of it personally in a sensible manner all the better. If he does not act sensibly then the National Socialist state intervenes.'[182]

For Hitler the formal maintenance of private ownership was not important. When the state has the unrestricted right to determine the decisions of the owners of the means of production, then the formal legal institution of private ownership no longer means very much. This is what Pollock is saying when he establishes a 'destruction of all of the essential traits of private ownership with the exception of one'. The moment the owners of the means of production can no longer freely decide about the content, timing and size of their investments, essential characteristics of private ownership have been abolished, even if the formal guarantee of private ownership still remains. We know that Hitler preferred a slow erosion of existing rights and institutions in the political or constitutional area as well. In the field of economics the formal legal title of ownership was relatively unimportant for him, as long as the state was able step by step to seize the actual power of disposal over the means of production and land.

In his table talks on 3 September 1942 Hitler said that land was 'national property, and in the end only given to the individual as a loan'.[183] In his speech at the end of June 1944 to leaders of the armaments industry (which we have already referred to in another context), Hitler spoke – in part because Speer had asked him to do so in order to calm down the industrialists – in favour of private ownership of the means of production but also stated as a restriction:

> However – and now we differentiate ourselves from the liberal state – these achievements of highly developed individuals must also lie within the framework of the benefit to all . . . the liberal state holds the view, everything is good which benefits the individual and is useful to the individual, even at the risk of it being harmful to the whole. The National Socialist state on the other hand has the idea, or advocates the recognition, that while the strength lies in the individual, the deed of the individual, the creative action of the individual must still lie in the sense of the benefit of the whole . . . The highest achievements of the individual, but corrected by the interests of a community, which in the final analysis must by its actions and its commitment under harsh conditions, in other words in the war, also cover for and protect the achievements of the individual. It is therefore now only sensible and natural that the achievement of the individual is weighed to that degree to which this achievement benefits the whole. This *modification of the concept of private ownership* is not even the slightest restriction of the individual, individual ability, individual creativity, diligence and so forth, but, on the contrary, it gives the individual the greatest possibilities to develop. It attaches only one condition to this, that the development not be permitted to proceed to the detriment of the community, in other words, in the end, ahead of everything else stands the total interest of the whole.[184]

All of these statements by Hitler have in common that they – as he expresses it – modify the concept of private ownership. What does this 'modification' consist of? Hitler only recognizes private ownership insofar as it is used according to the principle 'common benefit ahead of private benefit', which means, concretely, insofar as it is used within the framework of the objectives set by the state. For Hitler the principle of 'common benefit ahead of private benefit' means that, if it is necessary in the common interest, the state has the right at all times to decide on the way, the extent and the time private ownership is used, and the common interest is, of course, defined by the state.

With this, however, several important characteristics of private ownership have been removed. The moment the legal title of possession and the factual right of disposal separate, in other words when the private person can, for example, no longer freely decide on the nature, size and timing of the investments to be made, essential traits of private ownership have been abolished even though the legal institution formally remains in force. In terms of economic relationships, this may, however, superficially not appear to be the case, because the legal title of ownership, and not the essential determinant of economic form, is viewed as being the key element of the category.

This is one – and possibly the most important – side of Hitler's position on private ownership. In addition to this, however, he lauded certain nationalized sectors of the economy as being exemplary –the railway, for example – and cited them as proof that running a business rationally was possible not only on the basis of private ownership. In a speech at the 100th anniversary of the German railway he declared that

> ... in the railway as it has developed in Germany, we [had to] see the first really large nationalized enterprise, as opposed to the point of view of the pursuit of purely capitalist individual interests. We recognize this first in the organization of railway traffic in itself. In its inner being, the network of the railway was socialistically felt and socialistically conceived. The unique trait of this enterprise is that at the head stands not the question of profit but the satisfaction of traffic requirements.

In other words railway lines are also built in places where they are not profitable but where there is a need for a traffic link. 'It would be an immeasurable step backwards if we were to entertain the thought today of closing down those lines whose profitability is not assured. This would actually mean a return to the worst and most capitalistic point of view.' Hitler was therefore defining the essence of a company run along socialist principles as being that investments were not allowed to be decided on the basis of profit maximization. Hitler's subsequent remarks in this speech carry the heading

> A Warning: ... And secondly we also see the socialist character of the *Reichsbahn* in something else. It is a warning about the exclusive claims of the doctrine of private capitalism. It is the living proof that it is very possible to run a nationalized enterprise without private capital tendencies and without private capital management. Because we should never forget, the German *Reichsbahn* is the biggest

251

company, the largest customer in the whole world. The German *Reichsbahn* can stand any comparison with the railway companies built up purely on private capital ... We see the infinite successes of the capitalistic economic development of the last century, but in the *Reichsbahn* we also have the convincing proof *that it is just as readily possible to build up a company on another basis as a model and example for others.*

The inner organization of the *Reichsbahn* was also proof of its socialist character and convincingly refuted the false opinion that 'management of a large business enterprise was not even conceivable without private capital tendencies'. The *Reichsbahn* was a practical demonstration for the achievability of the concept which put the public good ahead of individual benefit. He knew, Hitler continued, 'that nothing in the world works at one blow, that everything needs its time to develop. But I am convinced that such a development is possible, and that it is our duty to pursue such a development everywhere.'[185]

Hitler's speech is very interesting in several respects. First of all we see that he was not fundamentally opposed to nationalization. Hitler did not at all regard an economic system based on private ownership as the only, or necessarily the best, means of running a business, but even 'warned' against this 'doctrine'. Of course, the 100-year existence of the railway was not the really important event for him; he only used this as an excuse to present his criticism of the capitalist system of economy. The timing of the speech is also interesting, namely the turn of the year 1935–36. In the last chapter, in which we discussed Hitler's position on market versus plan, we came to the conclusion that he had apparently partially modified, or developed, his economic concepts some time around 1935. He expressed his criticism of the system of free enterprise more aggressively, more fundamentally and more clearly than in the preceding years, and increasingly became an adherent of a state-controlled, planned economy. In parallel to this, his position on private ownership and nationalization also apparently underwent a change. The bold and simple declarations that he stood on the grounds of private ownership, so frequently made in previous years, become more rare, while his referrals to the limits to the right of free disposal of property, his threats of a possible nationalization and his considerations within his inner circle with regard to the nationalization of whole branches of industry become more frequent.

Let us recall Hitler's threats that we cited in the preceding chapter:

The Ministry of Economics only has to set the national economic tasks, and private industry has to fulfil them. But if private industry does not believe it is capable of doing so, then the National Socialist state will find its own way of solving this problem ... German industry, however, will learn to understand these new economic tasks, or it will have proved itself to be incapable of continuing to exist in these modern times, in which the Soviet state sets up a gigantic plan. *But then it will not be Germany which will go under, it will at most be a few industrialists.*[186]

Thus was Hitler's quite open threat in his memorandum on the Four-Year Plan of 1936.

On 17 December 1936 Hitler gave a speech to industrialists which showed, according to Louis P. Lochner (former member and later chief of the Berlin office of Associated Press of America), how he 'really saw the world of business and how he intended to deal with it once he was no longer burdened by tactical inhibitions'. The speech equated to an ultimate demand to exploit even the most meagre raw materials for the benefit of the home country, leaving all considerations of profitability aside. He would give industry a final chance to make those natural domestic sources of material which had formerly not been considered worth exploiting flow on its own initiative – or else! 'The word "impossible" does not exist here!' he screamed at the meeting in a cracking voice. 'I will no longer stand for the practice of capitalism to acquire titles to natural resources, which are then left lying unused because their exploitation appears not to be profitable. If necessary I will have such resources confiscated by the state in order to bring them to the utilization they merit.' The manner in which Hitler spoke that day reminded one, said Lochner, of 'an ill-tempered road construction foreman who is giving the workers in his column hell because they had not met their target'.[187]

If Hitler spoke to industrialists in such a harsh tone, within his inner circle his position towards businessmen was expressed without any reticence. Goebbels, for example, noted in his diary on 16 March 1937:

> Lunch with the *Führer*. Large group at table. The so-called industrial leaders are under heavy attack. They do not have a clue about real political economy. They are stupid, egoistic, unnational and narrow-mindedly conceited. They would like to sabotage the 4-year plan, out of cowardice and mental laziness. But now they have to.[188]

The following day Goebbels noted in his diary: '*Führer* heavily attacks the industrial barons who still practise a silent reserve against the 4-year plan',[189] and on 8 September 1937 he summarized Hitler's statements at the party congress as being 'strongly against high-handedness of business. Woe to private industry if it does not fall in line. 4-year plan will be executed.'[190]

In May 1937 Hitler declared:

> I tell German industry for example, 'You have to produce such and such now.' I then return to this in the Four-Year Plan. If German industry were to answer me,

'We are not able to', then I would say to it, 'Fine, then I will take that over myself, but it must be done.' But if industry tells me, 'We will do that', then I am very glad that I do not need to take that on.[191]

These threats are only understandable in the context of the conflict between the owners of the iron and steel industry and the National Socialist state, or rather the authors of the Four-Year Plan, which was escalating at the time. According to the maxims of the Four-Year Plan the two major problems at the time were an extension of smelting capacity and the increase of iron ore production. The extension of the iron and steel industry, however, met with the severe opposition of the owners. Their serious reservations were primarily based on the fear that further exploitation of the iron-poor German mineral deposits would be uneconomic and, in the export of iron and steel products, would negatively affect the competitive position of German industry compared to foreign industry. There was also the fear that too great an extension of smelting capacity would lead to sales problems as soon as the armaments boom was over.[192] After a meeting with the most important representatives of the German iron and steel industry on 17 March 1937 it appeared as if the owners were prepared to follow Hitler's, or rather Göring's, directives. In fact, however, despite their agreement, during the ensuing months nothing happened on the industrial side which could have indicated that the extension of the ore base was being enforced. On 16 June 1937, in a joint meeting of the Four-Year Plan, the Ministry of Economics and the iron industry, Göring accused the industry of still resisting the exploitation of German ore. At the same time he announced the setting up of a new plant but left the question open whether the state or private industry would become its owner. Similarly to Hitler, he also threatened the industrialists: 'It has long been necessary to also exploit German ore ... where this is not being done we will take the ore away from you and do it ourselves.'[193]

That such statements by Hitler and Göring were not empty threats became clear to the industrialists no later than on 23 July 1937, when Göring announced the formation of the 'AG for Ore Mining and Iron Smelting Hermann Göring' to the industry. Göring's *coup* caused considerable bewilderment among the industrialists. While parts of the industry still continued their attempts to steer a course which was independent of Göring's demands, under the impression of a *fait accompli*, and out of fear of more far-reaching measures, other industrialists were now willing to co-operate. 'Despite these events,' Petzina summarizes, 'the dispute remains remarkable enough because it demonstrates that the interests of private industry did not automatically agree with the interests of the regime, and that in case of a conflict the regime did not have any compunctions about realizing its objectives even against the opposition of parts of heavy industry.'[194]

IV: Hitler's Central Objective

The development which had begun with Hitler's and Göring's repeated threats finally led to the creation of the Reichswerke Hermann Göring, which by 1940 employed 600,000 people. The plant in Salzgitter finally became the largest in Europe. With this, the National Socialist state had shown that its oft-proclaimed 'primacy of politics' was deadly serious, and that it would not hesitate to become active itself and to build up state-controlled enterprises in areas where private industry resisted the execution of state directives. The procedure adopted in the case of ore mining and smelting assumed the importance of a precedent for the actions of the National Socialist state. In future, Hitler was able to calculate, out of fear of similar measures private industrialists would be more willing to follow the directives of state planning without damaging objections.

Under such conditions a 'total nationalization' – which Hitler continued to regard with scepticism – was of course no longer necessary. On the other hand, in his speech of 20 May 1937, which we have already cited, he remarked that there were

> ... areas where I can say they are ripe for nationalization. These are the areas where I do not need any competition, where there is none anyway, where the age of inventions is past anyhow, and where in the course of many decades I have slowly been given a diligent civil service, above all where there is no competition, for example in transport and so forth.[195]

Hitler was therefore quite prepared for nationalization in certain sectors of the economy, but only under certain conditions and premises. Hitler's reservations against 'total nationalization' – and this also becomes clear in the speech cited – resulted from his socio-Darwinistic convictions, which he also transferred to the field of economics. The fear that a general nationalization would remove the mainspring of competition, and thereby one of the primary causes of economic development, still made him oppose a comprehensive nationalization of all of the means of production.[196]

Hitler remained true to his tactic of initially attempting to 'win over' private industry for the realization of his projects, and, if it could not be 'convinced', to take the matter (as he often expressed it) into his own hands, in other words to realize the project by creating state companies. A further example after the Hermann-Göring-Werke is the foundation of the *Volkswagenwerk* by the DAF. This was also preceded by a violent struggle with industry. Hitler believed that the automobile was the means of transport of the future, but only on the condition that a cheap 'Volkswagen' that the masses could afford could be successfully produced. He therefore immediately became enthusiastic about designer Ferdinand Porsche's idea to design such a car, but set him the condition that the sale price (which Porsche had already calculated very modestly at 1,550 RM) had to be substantially reduced even further. 'It must be possible,' he told Porsche, 'to give the German people a motor car whose price is not higher than formerly that of a middle-range motorcycle.'[197] While this project was technically and economically feasible, it was rejected by private industry. The German automobile industry tried to sabotage the project from the very beginning because it feared that it would be cultivating its own competition and thereby endangering the sales of the more expensive models. During the period from 1934 to 1938 Porsche – whom Hitler had commissioned – 'fought a battle against the whole of the German automobile industry, a secret, subterranean battle'.[198]

In several speeches, particularly at the annually recurring automobile shows, Hitler therefore criticized German industry, which did not realize that if the automobile was really to become the means of transport of the future it would have to become a consumer article the masses could afford and not remain a luxury article for the few. When Hitler finally saw that he was not going to succeed in 'convincing' the private industrialists, he installed a 'plenipotentiary' for automotive transport within the framework of the Four-Year Plan and founded the *Volkswagenwerk*, which under the authority of the DAF then proceeded with the project. At the international automotive and motorcycle show Hitler declared on 17 February 1939 that he had come to the realization

> ...that in the end industry could not come to such a structuring of their production on their own initiative. I therefore decided to install a plenipotentiary for this task in the person of Colonel von Schell, who within the Four-Year Plan will now issue the directives which are binding for all offices.[199]

In his biography of Porsche, Quint writes:

> The fact that the Volkswagen became a KdF car [KdF = *Kraft durch Freude*, or 'Strength Through Joy, an NS mass organization under Robert Ley which organized leisure activities for the masses—H.B.], that finally the DAF alone took over the construction and the financing of the plant, and with this the responsibility for the car, that party comrade Ley, who knew devilishly little about automobiles, became the patron of this car, and his loyal assistant Dr Lafferentz played an important role in the planning from then on, that the state took over the Volkswagen concept so radically, all this was only the result of three and a half years of intensive attempts to set the Volkswagen on its wheels with the help of the German automotive industry, which had, via its national organization, initially welcomed and supported it pro forma – the initiative came from Hitler, the *Führer* of the state, and one hardly dared say 'no' openly – but had in actual fact tried to prevent it with all of its might.[200]

IV: Hitler's Central Objective

These conflicts with private industry, which we have highlighted with the examples of the disputes with the iron and automotive industries, led to an increasing radicalization of Hitler's position. On the occasion of a conversation on 14 February 1942 with Goebbels about the problem of increasing production, Hitler said:

> ... here we have to proceed rigorously, that the whole production process has to be re-examined, and that the industrialists who do not want to submit to the directives we issue, will have to lose their plants without any regard to whether they will then be ruined economically.[201]

While Hitler remained opposed to 'total nationalization' – for the reasons already discussed – he now no longer excluded the nationalization of important branches of industry, for example the 'anonymous public share companies' of the power industry and other key industries. On 24 March 1942 he declared in a table talk:

> Private ownership as the property of the individual was to be unconditionally protected! It was something quite natural and healthy when somebody took a part of the results of his work and used it to create family property. If this family property consisted of a factory, then as long as the family has a healthy progeny, this factory will certainly be better managed, and therefore also more successfully managed for the national community, by a member of the family than, for instance, by a civil servant. Insofar he could readily emphatically advocate the security of private industry. But he opposed anonymous private ownership in the form of shares just as emphatically. Without having to do anything himself, the shareholder receives higher dividends when the workers of the share company are diligent than when they are lazy, or a brilliant engineer stands at the head of the company, or even when a crook handles the business of the share company. If the shareholder were then so clever in his anonymity to hold shares in several share companies, he would pocket the profits from pure speculation without having to fear losses which he could not compensate for on the other side. He had always rejected and fought against such easy speculation income. If there was anybody who had a right to such profits then it was the whole nation, the workers, the engineers, who worked for the increased profits of such a share company and were otherwise not being paid according to their contributions. *The anonymous share company therefore belongs in the hands of the state*, and, for those who were looking for an economic investment for their savings, the state could issue state obligations which were uniformly valued and which carried a certain interest rate.[202]

The conclusions Hitler draws here are basically logical consequences of his speech to the *Düsseldorf Industrieklub* in 1932, although he would naturally have felt it to be inappropriate to draw these conclusions in front of an audience of industrialists and he might himself not have been ready at the time to think the consequences of his premises through to their final conclusion. Let us recall. Then Hitler had emphatically rejected the argument that it had always existed as being a legitimization of private ownership. The only legitimization he accepted was achievement, or rather the differences in achievements. The statements made in his table talks almost exactly ten years later are only logical conclusions from this line of reasoning. The cutter of coupons, the pensioner, i.e. the shareholder, could not derive his dividend from a personal contribution he had made to the company in which he held shares. This was different in a family company, in which – at least superficially – the profits of the owner appeared as a reward for his achievement and his willingness to take a risk. The whole trend of modern capitalism, however, was moving towards the large public share companies and away from the small family company. There was increasing separation between the owners of the means of production and those who used them or actually managed them. Marxist-Leninist economic theory calls this phenomenon 'parasitical capitalism'. N. Bucharin, for example, writes:

> This class of the bourgeoisie is extremely parasitic; it develops psychic traits which actually relate it to the decaying nobility at the end of the '*ancien régime*' and the leaders of the financial aristocracy of the same period. The most characteristic trait of this class, which sharply separates it from both the proletariat and the middle class of a different type, is – as we have already seen – its alienation from business life. It does not participate directly in production, nor in trade, its representatives often do not even clip the coupons personally.[203]

It is also exactly this class, as opposed to the 'bourgeoisie' of a different type, that Hitler was referring to when he criticized the anonymous share companies and spoke out against 'easy income from speculation' which to a large extent eliminated any economic risk.

What is important, however, is not Hitler's criticism but the consequences he drew from it. Theoretically, two consequences would be possible. The one would be going back to the private family company, the breaking up of the big monopolies and returning to free competition. But this was only a spurious alternative, because it would only recreate the condition which with inner necessity by a process of concentration and centralization of capital would lead back again to the big monopolies and anonymous share companies. Marxist economic theory therefore calls this alternative reactionary-*petit bourgeois* criticism of modern monopoly capitalism, whereas the 'socialist alternative' is naturally to nationalize these large enterprises, to convert them into the property of the state.

It is exactly *this* conclusion Hitler drew when he said that the 'anonymous share companies belong in the hands of the state'. But he went much further

IV: Hitler's Central Objective

and demanded the nationalization of the power industry. In the monologue just cited he went on to say:

> The monopoly on power belongs to the state which could issue state obligations and thereby interest people in its monopoly companies and therefore above all in the state itself . . . What was true for the power industry also applied to the management of the other essential raw materials: oil, coal, iron, as well as water power. As far as this was concerned, capitalist companies had to be abolished.

Let us summarize so far. Hitler was in favour of nationalizing the following enterprises:
- the big share companies,
- the power industry,
- all other branches of industry which produced 'essential raw materials', for example the iron industry.

He then went on to declare that 'already in his youth . . . he had occupied himself with the problem of capitalist monopoly companies', to criticize the 'unclean. . . business methods of anonymous shareholders', and sharply turned against the linking of political and economic interests.[204]

The following day (25 March 1942) Hitler again addressed himself to this topic. He emphasized that

> . . . the Reich also has to keep its hand on monopolies, and thereby on monopoly profits [he meant the monopoly profits in the occupied Eastern territories—R.Z.]. For some incomprehensible reason, consideration had already been given to leaving the tobacco monopoly in the occupied Eastern territories to Herr Reemtsma [Philipp Reemtsma, a tobacco industrialist in Hamburg—R.Z.]; the *Führer* had forbidden that out of hand and emphasized that, from the outset, the tobacco monopoly could only be given to the Reich itself. In the Reich itself, as he, the *Führer*, had long demanded, a monopoly tobacco industry had to come soon! For the same reason, over there [i.e. in the occupied Eastern territories—R.Z.] the greater part of the cultivated land had to remain state property as before, so that the profits from agricultural production in this gigantic state domain would be to the exclusive benefit of the state and could be used to cover the war debts. Quite apart from that, the required surplus of agricultural products was only produced by large estates anyway.[205]

These statements about the economic organization planned for the occupied territories in the East are particularly important for the following reason. As we shall show in the next chapter, the *Lebensraum* to be conquered in the East was for Hitler primarily also a source of raw material and a market and was not at all only intended for the settlement of farmers as research has assumed to date. This insight could, however, lead to the misconception that Hitler had waged the war against Russia for the purpose of imperialistic expansion in the service of monopoly capitalism. The opposite is true, because Hitler was, as the statements just cited above prove, in favour of the organization of the economy in the East being state-controlled from the beginning.

When on the one hand Hitler demanded the nationalization of large segments of German industry, on the other he still had reservations because of the over-centralization which would result. As we will show in Chapter VI.3.d, he was critical of any over-centralization. With this, however, he fell into the contradiction that both state control of the economy and the totalitarian political system he advocated had inherent centralistic tendencies.

With Hitler this contradiction expressed itself in a certain inconsistency when on 26 July 1942 he said in a table talk that the restructuring of the power industry should take place 'neither in the form of socialism nor with a centralistic tendency'. He went on:

> In the NS state the state administration intervenes quite naturally in the interests of every individual if this becomes necessary for the whole. Therefore the NS state could grant private initiative a much greater freedom, because the state reserved itself the right to intervene at any time. But the state should not take private industry into its own hands, because this would lead to a terrible over-administration and the paralysis of the areas controlled. On the contrary, the NS state should foster private initiative as far as possible. Therefore he, the boss, was thinking of the following set of rules. In future basically every farmer who had the right conditions should provide himself with a wind motor. If his farmhouse lay on the banks of a stream, then the farmhouse should be readily connectable to the stream in order to generate the required electricity itself. The monopolies of certain companies, who today normally inhibited the private initiative of the individual national comrades in the area of power generation, had to fall as a matter of principle. Furthermore, it was readily possible for the communities to generate their own electricity, be it with coal, be it with water power they have at their disposal. The government should be glad when an individual village or the individual city took care of their power generation themselves. The Gau self-administration authorities should also take care of electricity generation for their own areas if they had the possibilities of doing so . . . It was therefore not at all desirable for all of the small and medium-sized power plants to be run by the Reich instead of by the communities and the Gau administrations. In addition it should also still be possible in the future that the owner of a mill, for instance, generate electricity for himself and his community. The state itself should only take over the administration of those great waterworks or power plants that were necessary to maintain the composite power system.

Hitler declared further that he had the strongest reservations against the centralization Speer intended. In the field of politics and the economy 'any centralization is bound to stifle initiative out there in the country'. The main thing was

... that the power industry was taken out of the speculation by private industry. But otherwise an individual mill owner or an individual factory should still be allowed to generate their own electricity, and the mill or the factory also be permitted to give the superfluous electricity they did not need themselves to other consumers.[206]

These statements by Hitler, which are based on previous recommendations made by the NS economic theorist and power expert *Dr Ing.* Lawaczeck,[207] are, in part, obviously contradictions of his concept announced only a few months before aimed at the total nationalization of the power industry.[208]

We can therefore note that Hitler had two alternative concepts which could certainly be linked in theory but which were an expression of the fact that until the final years of his life he was caught up in a fundamental contradiction. On the one hand he was a vehement proponent of the concept of the 'primacy of politics' or, as he expressed it, of the 'secondary role of the economy'. *One means by which the 'primacy of politics' could be enforced was the nationalization of large sectors of the economy.* On the other hand Hitler always retained his scepticism towards total nationalization. This scepticism was derived from another axiom of his *Weltanschauung*. As a socio-Darwinist he valued the principle of competition as a mainspring of economic progress and growth and feared that a 'total nationalization' could lead to over-centralization and a stifling of private and local initiative. This is also a reason for his oft-emphasized recognition of private ownership – particularly noticeable in his speeches before 1935. The principle of private ownership, however, underwent substantial modifications with Hitler because he rejected the unrestricted right of decision with regard to the nature, amount and timing of investments by the owners of the means of production. Moreover, just as we are able to ascertain for the years after 1935, in particular after 1941–42, that Hitler expressed his criticisms of the system of free trade ever more fundamentally and with increasing sharpness and became a convinced adherent of the control of the economy by the state, we are now also able – and this is the result of this chapter – to establish a tendency towards a greater receptiveness for concepts of nationalization.

The war was, of course, not the right time for the implementation of radical concepts of nationalization such as were projected by Hitler in his table talks in March 1942. He and other leading National Socialists were well aware of this, and they already had difficulty dispelling the fears of nationalization held by industrialists. A memo by Himmler of 21 October 1942, for example, states that 'during the war'(!) a 'fundamental change of our completely capitalistic economy is not possible'. Anybody who was to 'fight' against this would provoke a 'witch-hunt' against himself.[209] Situations of war are the worst possible times to provoke conflicts of domestic policy, particularly with those groups on whom the effectiveness of the war economy happens to depend. Nonetheless, it was Himmler's SS which by its enforced development of the SS plants which were amalgamated in the gigantic Deutsche Wirtschaftsbetriebe GmbH concern was attempting to create the conditions for a radical restructuring of the economic system and the reduction of private capitalism.

In a report prepared by an SS *Hauptsturmführer* [an SS rank equivalent to Captain in the Army—H.B.] in July 1944, the question 'why does the SS engage in business activities?' was answered as follows:

> This question was raised specifically by circles who think purely in terms of capitalism and who do not like to see companies developing which are public, or at least of a public character. The age of the liberal system of business demanded the primacy of business, in other words business comes first, and then the state. As opposed to this, National Socialism takes the position: the state directs the economy, the state is not there for business, business is there for the state.[210]

The degree to which Hitler's programmatic statements had become the guiding principle of practical politics at lower levels as well becomes clear here. According to Enno Georg, the creation of as encompassing an SS concern as possible extended the hope of being able, after the war, to direct the economy of the Reich even more strongly than before, towards an even more strictly organized 'state command economy':

> There can hardly be any doubt, that with a longer continuation of the National Socialist regime, the process of expansion of the SS business enterprises would also have continued. The files contain a large number of projects which were to be undertaken after the war. But the longer such a development went on, the more the structure of private business – whose forms and legal rules the SS knew how to exploit opportunistically – would have been eroded. With the increasing accumulation of SS businesses, the path to a functional and structural change of important sectors of the German economy was already being trodden.[211]

Actual development was therefore moving – under the motto 'The state commands the economy' – towards a reduction of private capitalism, and Hitler welcomed this trend.

Our investigation has shown that the sweeping theory that Hitler had been a confirmed believer in private ownership and an opponent of nationalization can no longer be sustained because it hides the contradictions – and also the development – of his economic concepts. Hitler thought about economic questions in a far more discriminating manner, and less sweepingly, than has previously been assumed. He was searching for a system which could combine the advantages of private initiative and business competition with the advan-

IV: Hitler's Central Objective

tages of state direction, including the possibility of a nationalization of certain sectors of the economy.

7. Hitler's Criticism of Capitalism in His Early Speeches

In the preceding chapters it has become clear that Hitler was a critic of the capitalist system, even though he did value certain of its advantages, primarily the principle of competition. Our investigation has shown that this criticism was rationally founded, in that the term 'rationality' does not necessarily have to include a positive evaluation because it can also serve inhumane objectives such as it ultimately did within the system of the Third Reich. Hitler's criticism first resulted from the contradiction between the interests of private profit and the interests of the state, which for him were identical with the needs of the 'national community'. His demand for the 'primacy of politics' was directed against the dominance of private capitalist profit interests and in the final analysis implied both the demand to exchange the free enterprise economy for a planned economy and the possibility of nationalizing certain sectors of the economy if the contradiction between private interests and the interests of the 'national community' could not be reconciled any other way. Secondly, Hitler criticized the phenomenon which in Marxist political economy is known as 'the anarchy of production'; in other words, from the contradiction between the rationality of the individual company and the lack of planning of the total economy he derived the demand for an active business planning by the state.

We have again summarized these two key elements of Hitler's criticism in order to demonstrate how widely his 'criticism of capitalism' formulated in his early speeches differs from his later convictions. While we must describe Hitler's later criticism of capitalism – whether we agree with it or not – as being quite rationally founded, this can hardly be said to the same degree of his earlier economic views. Yet these too do not lack a foundation 'in theory' because they were decisively influenced by the theory of 'slavery to interest' as formulated by the engineer Gottfried Feder. Even though this theory raised an anti-capitalistic claim, it still stood diametrically opposed – as we will show later – to Marxist economic theory, something that can no longer be said in this form for Hitler's later economic views.

In his policy speech on 13 August 1920 on the question 'Why are we anti-Semites?', Hitler explained his views, which we first intend to cite in detail. He declared that the National Socialists were being accused of only fighting against stock market and loan capital and not against industrial capital. Industrial capital, however, was something one could not fight against:

What is industrial capital? It is a factor which is gradually changing in size, only a relative term. Once it had meant the needle, the thread, the workshop and maybe the few pennies in cash the master tailor in Nuremberg possessed in the thirteenth century. It was the sum he needed for his work, in other words the tool, the shop and a certain sum that would make it possible for him to live at all for a certain time. Gradually the little workshop developed into a big factory, and for all practical purposes we still see the same thing; because the formerly small weaving frame later became the loom, and then the mechanical loom, but the latter is just as much a tool as the most primitively constructed first loom, and the workshop, formerly a little enclosure, a room, became the big factory. But workshop and tool, machine and factory in themselves are not a value which produces value by itself, but only a means to an end, only become value-producing when you work with them. The thing which produces value is work, and the little penny the little craftsman may have possessed at the time in order to survive dismal times, to be able to buy cloth, has increased tenfold, a hundredfold, and today again stands before us – only now we call it capital for the continuation of the company in bad times, that is working capital. And here I would like to underline something! A tool, a shop, a machine or a factory and working capital, that is industrial capital, that is something you can not oppose at all. You may be able to ensure that it is not misused, but you cannot fight against it. This is the first big swindle being practised on our nation, and it is being practised in order to draw its attention away from the real battle, to tear it away from the capital that should and must be fought, from loan and stock market capital.[212]

Let us pause to reconstruct Hitler's concept of capital. He defines capital as a 'tool, shop, machine or factory and working capital'. From the point of view of 'middle class' political economy, this is not necessarily wrong because it also defines capital as 'a producing means of production'. Seen from a Marxist point of view, however, Hitler is confusing the nature of capital with its manifestations.

This confusion of the nature with the form of capitalist production conditions becomes even more apparent in Hitler's differentiation between 'stock market and loan capital' and 'industrial and working capital':

Stock market and loan capital [said Hitler] comes about in a fundamentally different way. Whereas the small craftsman is dependent upon the strokes of fate which can hit him during the day, on the overall situation, during the Middle Ages maybe on the size of his town and its prosperity, on the safety in this town, today too this capital, in other words the industrial capital, is tied to the state, to the nation, dependent on the will of the people to work, dependent also on the possibilities to acquire raw materials and to offer work, to find customers which really buy the work, and we know very well that a collapse of the state can sometimes make the greatest values worthless, devaluate them, as opposed to the other capital, the stock market and loan capital, which earns regular interest without any regard to whether the owner on whose property these 10,000 marks

IV: Hitler's Central Objective

lie goes under himself or not. The debts remain lying on the property... Here we already see the first possibility, namely that this form of money growth, which is independent of all of the events and happenstances of normal life, must necessarily gradually grow to become gigantic sums, because they are never hindered and always continue to go on uniformly, until in the end they have only one drawback, namely the difficulty of being able to continue to place them. In order to place these moneys one has to go over to destroying whole states, annihilating whole cultures, abolishing national industries, not in order to nationalize, but in order to throw all this into the maw of this international capital, because this capital is *international*, as the only one on this earth which is at all international, it is international because its holders, the Jews, are international because of their being spread all over the world. And here everyone should actually already throw up their hands in despair and say to themselves, if this capital is international because its holders, the Jews, are spread internationally all over the world, then it must be insanity to think that one will be able to fight this capital of the same members of this race internationally ... Therefore this capital grew and today rules practically the whole world, immeasurable as to the amounts, inconceivable in its gigantic relationships, uncannily growing and – the worst part – completely corrupting all honest work, because that is the horrible part, that the normal human being who today has to bear the burden of the interest on this capital has to stand by and see how despite diligence, industry, thrift, despite real work, hardly anything is left to him with which only to feed himself, and even less to clothe himself, at the same time as this international capital devours billions in interest alone which he has to help pay, at the same time in which a racial class is spreading itself out in the state which does not do any other work than to collect interest for itself and to cut coupons. This is the degradation of all honest work, because every honestly working human being has to ask himself today: does it make sense if I work at all? I will never get anywhere anyway, and there there are people who can live without doing any work – in practice – and who practically even rule us, and that is the objective. One of the basic foundations of our strength is to be destroyed, namely moral definition of work, and that was also the brilliant idea of Karl Marx, that he falsified the moral concept of work, that for the destruction of the national economy, and for the protection of the international stock market and loan capital, he organized the whole mass of the people who were suffering under this capital.[213]

Let us summarize. Hitler differentiates between (national) working or industrial capital and (international) stock market and loan capital. While industrial capital is dependent on work, the acquisition of raw materials, the possibilities of the market etc., stock market and loan capital is 'a form of increase of money which is independent of all of the events and incidents of normal life'. The holders of this capital, however, are the Jews, who, as the only 'international' race, are the only class of holder possible for this capital. The brilliant fraud committed by Marxism lay in attacking national working or industrial capital and thereby sparing international stock market and loan capital.

Here again we see that Hitler's so-called criticism of capital is exactly the opposite of the Marxist theory. When Hitler claims that interest payments on stock market and loan capital are independent of defects in the national production process, and that this was the true source of exploitation whereas the profit of the entrepreneur was the reward for the 'mental work' he had performed,[214] he is accurately describing the 'outer appearance' which conditions of production assume on the surface of middle-class society, but without plumbing their true nature.

In the final analysis it appears – according to Marxist theory – on the surface of middle-class society as if exploitation had its origins in the sphere of circulation and not in production. With this, however, it would be possible – from a Marxist point of view – to explain the economic reason for Hitler's hatred of the Jews: since for historic reasons that are well known the Jews were strongly represented in trade, in the banks, etc., Hitler identified them as the actual exploiters. Since he had localized the sphere of circulation as being the place exploitation occurs, his theory, as mistaken as it is, is logical in itself. It is just as logical that he has to define Marxism as an instrument of Jewry, with which it detracts from the battle against interest-earning stock market and loan capital as the source of all exploitation, a theory which is confirmed to him by the fact that not only many 'stock market and bank capitalists' but also numerous leaders of the Marxist labour movement were Jews.

On 31 August 1920 Hitler declared: 'Karl Marx, the founder of the Red International, was a deliberate falsifier of the social concept... He fights against industrial capital but leaves the *loan capital* of the Jews untouched, because he is a Jew. German industrial capital today amounts to 15 billion, loan capital to 300 billion.' The report on this speech in the *Völkische Beobachter*, however, emphasizes that Hitler is criticizing interest-bearing capital as a matter of principle, and not simply because it is 'Jewish': 'We are fighting,' said Hitler, 'against any *big capital*, regardless of whether it is German or Jewish, if it is not based on productive work but on the principle of interest, an income without work or pains.'[215]

We find this differentiation between industrial and loan capital in many early speeches by Hitler. At an NSDAP rally on 10 September 1922, for example, he said: 'This capital, the industrial capital, works creatively. Loan capital, however, works destructively. By sacrificial work industrial capital creates, the untouchable loan capital only satisfies the ego of its owner without work, it earns interest, it increases at the expense of others.'[216] The main differences he saw between industrial and stock market capital are illustrated by his notes for a speech on 22 November 1922:

IV: Hitler's Central Objective

```
              What has one fought.
    Industrial capital – Stock market capital
              Difference Interest
   I. Personal                I. Impersonal
   II. National               II. International
```

What was fought against?

```
                    Tools + workshop + working capital –
I. Industrial capital
                                   I. diligence
                   dependent on    II. talent
                                   III. the state
                   therefore national

                   Interest concept
II. Loan capital
                                   diligence
                   independent of  talent
                                   the state²¹⁷
```

In the preceding chapter we have shown that Hitler saw private property as being legitimized by the principle of achievement. Thus far he recognized the concept of private ownership as an expression of the 'principle of personality' which he valued highly. Here certain connecting lines to Hitler's criticism of stock market and loan capital become clear. What is essential for him is that the latter, as opposed to industrial capital, is not dependent on 'diligence and talent' but is completely independent of these. Industrial capital is 'personal', stock market capital 'impersonal'.

While in his later speeches and other statements Hitler criticized capitalism far more fundamentally, and while the ideological constructions just cited hardly play a role any longer, there are still lines of continuity to his early convictions to be found in certain areas. When Hitler advocates the nationalization of 'anonymous' share companies, and in this context deliberately points out that the shareholder is drawing 'profits from pure speculation without loss' and risk and that 'he had always rejected and fought against such effortless income from speculation'[218] it becomes clear that he is still drawing on Feder's ideology as the reason for his plans. By then, however, such referrals were only of minor importance.

At the beginning of his political career Hitler – as he deliberately emphasized in *Mein Kampf* – had been deeply impressed by Feder's theories. At what point Hitler began to draw away from these concepts can no longer be decided with any accuracy. In *Mein Kampf* there is a passage which indicates that he had recognized the problematical aspects of Feder's theories early on, at least in part:

> Any, and even the best, idea becomes dangerous when it begins to believe that it is an end in itself, whereas in reality it is only a means to such an end – but for me and all true National Socialists there is only one doctrine, the nation and the Fatherland... Every thought and every idea, all teachings and all knowledge, must serve this purpose. Everything has to be examined from this point of view and either used or rejected according to its appropriateness. In this way no theory can ossify into a deadly doctrine, because all things are only there to serve life.[219]

With these statements referring to Feder's theory Hitler intended to indicate that for him the teachings of the party's official economic theorist were not a dogma because he obviously already had inklings of the problems involved in implementing them in practice.[220]

As we know, in the late 1920s and early 1930s Hitler then gradually withdrew from Feder, whose 'career' came to an end once and for all in August 1934 when he was replaced as state secretary in the Reichs Ministry of Economics. From then on Feder was only a professor at the Technical University of Berlin with a chair for housing and settlement, regional planning and urban development. Feder's career reflects the change in Hitler's economic concepts. At the beginning of his political activities, he himself apparently knew little about economics. While he claimed in autobiographical notes written on 29 November 1921 that from his 20th to his 24th year he had undertaken 'a thorough study of the teachings of political economy',[221] in view of the economic naïvety of the speech cited above we may question this just as much as his statement that he had studied Marx's *Das Kapital*.[222] Nonetheless, Hitler was obviously able to make up for at least some of these deficits during the course of his life. As Wagener confirms, he at least attributed great importance to economic policy. Wagener writes that Hitler was 'not a man who granted the economy any sort of primacy, no matter in which area'. On the other hand, however, he emphasizes that Hitler had shared his own view of the importance of economic and social policy without any reservations:

> I had no doubts that for the 'National Socialist Workers' Party' the setting of unconditionally clear objectives and the affirmation of unequivocal guidelines in the area of economic and social policy were a *conditio sine qua non*. And whenever I talked with him about such matters, I always found complete agreement and support in Hitler.[223]

Werner Ziegler, Director-General of the German National Theatre, who was acquainted with Hitler, writes in his memoirs that, based on his own experience, 'Hitler's thoughts on all economic questions, on political economy, on finance, on global economy, and on the various branches of industry all the way down to the most complicated question of iron and power supply, were of a most profound nature' and that his statements to businessmen (which Ziegler witnessed) 'displayed an astonishing command of the topic'.[224] This assessment by Ziegler, whose competence to judge such a matter may well be questioned, might be over-stated, but to a certain degree does apply to the 'later Hitler', whereas the 'early Hitler' was obviously interested in economic questions but still so naïve that he initially made Gottfried Feder's theories the foundation for his so-called 'criticism of capitalism'.

V

Hitler: An Opponent of Modern Industrial Society? Modernistic and Anti-Modernistic Elements in Hitler's *Weltanschauung*

In the introductory chapter we presented the thesis maintained by Schoenbaum, Dahrendorf, Turner and many other historians that Hitler's concepts had been 'anti-modernistic', or that he had rejected modern industrial society and only made temporary use of it for the purpose of waging war. Since Dahrendorf and Schoenbaum it has been widely accepted that National Socialism had *objectively* caused a great modernization thrust, but simultaneously it is generally claimed that this came about against Hitler's intentions. Turner writes, for example:

> In order to cure the problems of the highly industrialized Germany of the twentieth century, they [Hitler, Himmler, Rosenberg and Darré, whom Turner jointly classifies as belonging to an anti-modernistic direction in the NSDAP—R.Z.] prescribed the resurrection of the cult honouring blood and soil. They intended liberating a large part of the Geman people from the industrial world and making their return to the simple life in the country possible.[1]

Turner goes on to claim that 'during the years in which he was attempting to gain power in one of the most advanced industrial nations of the world', Hitler 'had regarded the economy from an agrarian point of view'.[2] In the next section we intend to show that the thesis that Hitler had been an opponent of modern industrial society, and that he had pursued the anti-modernistic utopia of a 'reagrarianization' of German society, is based on a number of misunderstandings and can no longer be sustained after a closer examination of Hitler's statements.

1. Agrarian Utopia as an Ultimate Objective? Criticism of a Misunderstanding in the Interpretation of the Function and Implications of '*Lebensraum* in the East' in Hitler's Concept

In this context, one of the important questions is about the function in Hitler's concept of the *Lebensraum* to be conquered in the East, and how this was to be structured. Because Turner bases his thesis of the anti-modernistic nature of Hitler's objectives primarily on the argument that the *Lebensraum* Hitler wanted to conquer in Russia was to serve exclusively for the settlement of farmers and therefore for a reagrarianization. 'As settlers in the East, these colonists would again lead the simple, pure life of the common people of their ancestors and, as in times gone by, form a class of courageous freemen and an inexhaustible reservoir of warriors for future conflicts.'[3] But in any case, says Turner,

> ... for him the gaining of *Lebensraum* fulfilled a one-sided purpose of agrarian policy ... Indications that in this context Hitler was also thinking about wider economic concepts and, for example, giving consideration to the possibility of gaining power and raw materials, can at best be found in reports by contemporaries, but not in his own writings.[4]

As our investigation will show, this is wrong. The settlement of farmers was merely *one* element, but, beyond that, *Lebensraum* had a decisive function for Hitler as a source of raw materials and a market.

We must now first step back a little, because the function of *Lebensraum* in Hitler's concept can only be understood in the context of his criticism of economic expansion and his ideas on autarky. Without this comprehensive context, the question of *why* Hitler wanted to conquer *Lebensraum* in the East, what *function* this was to fulfil and how he *envisaged that it would be structured* cannot be answered.

a. Substantiation of the *Lebensraum* Concept within the Framework of Hitler's Economic Concepts: Criticism of Economic Expansion and the Autarky Concept

The Discrepancy between Population Growth and Lebensraum

One of the theories that is fundamental to Hitler's *Weltanschauung*, is that of the contradictory inter-relationship between *Lebensraum* (the base for food production) and population. One of the basic requirements of human existence is a certain *Lebensraum*, in other words, a certain territory which provides the base of subsistence in a comprehensive sense (i.e. agricultural land, raw materials, sources of power etc.). While this territory forms the base, it also limits the economic possibilities. In the given *Lebensraum*, a certain number of people can live, but this number is naturally not static and constantly increases under normal conditions. Above a certain stage of development the limited territory, in other words the available *Lebensraum*, comes into contradiction with the rising number of people. The base of subsistence is no longer assured.

In such a case there are several possibilities of reacting to the incongruity, in other words the disparity, which has come about between population growth and

Lebensraum. One possibility is migration, a phenomenon which assumed a certain importance in Europe around the turn of the century. Another possibility is birth control and a third solution is the increase of exports, so that food and raw materials can be imported in exchange for the industrial goods exported. A fourth possibility, finally, is the extension of the *Lebensraum* – which can only be achieved by force. It is well-known that this theory we have briefly sketched here was held by Hitler, can be found in many speeches and articles and is expounded in detail in *Mein Kampf* and in Hitler's 'Second Book'.[5]

What is essential in this context is, first of all, that Hitler defined economic expansion, i.e. the export of goods and capital, as a reaction to a disparity between population and base of subsistence which had already occurred. This is not to say that Hitler regarded *all* exports as being explainable by this disparity, but only the highly intensive and extensive increase of industrial production as the result and expression of a disproportionality which had occurred in the development of the relationship between farming and industry, and which made the subsistence of a nation out of the resources at its disposal no longer possible. And Hitler rejected this specific reaction to the incongruity between population and base of subsistence. Since this criticism assumes vast importance in his speeches and articles, and since without understanding it we can not understand Hitler's concept of autarky, nor his concept of *Lebensraum*, we will now discuss it in detail. In doing this we must first differentiate between the following three lines of reasoning:

1. The strategy of 'economically-peacefully conquering the world' was an illusion, because, as the Great War had shown, a policy of economic expansion also led to war in the end.
2. The possibilities of an economic policy greatly orientated towards export gradually declined as a result of the shrinking of the world market caused by the industrialization of former agrarian countries.
3. Such an economic policy increased the disproportionality in the development of farming and industry and ultimately led to the destruction of the agricultural class.

The conclusion from Hitler's reasoning is that only the conquest of new *Lebensraum* can remove the disparity between population and land and provide the foundations for an autarkic economy.

Let us now turn to the first line of reasoning with which Hitler criticized a policy of economic expansion.

German Economic Expansion as the Cause of the First World War
One of Hitler's basic convictions, and something research has not taken into account to date, was that wars, at least in modern times, are mostly due to

economic reasons. Behind the diplomatic causes of a military conflict Hitler always assumed deeper economic reasons, which he considered to be the real motives behind the wars.[6] In a table talk on 10 October 1941 he said: 'Originally war was nothing more than a battle for the feeding place. Today the issue is natural resources. According to the will of creation they belong to the one who fights for them.'[7]

Based on this view, Hitler believed that the Great War could ultimately be traced back to economic causes, and here mainly to the reaction by the British – in his view, quite natural – to the threat to their economic interests posed by Germany. Hitler for the first time expounded this thesis of German economic expansion being the cause of the Great War in a speech on 17 April 1920:

> The German offered the Englishman strong competition. The German engineer and so forth soon pushed the British one aside. We began to export goods . . . It would only have taken a few more years and Germany would have become the foremost trading nation in the world. Britain recognized this and adjusted her policy accordingly. First the attempt was made to bring Germany down by economic means like duties, labels on German goods ('Made in Germany') and so forth. This did not succeed, however. Since that time hatred of us grew into the immeasurable and Britain was already considering destroying us by a war. The British policy of encirclement![8]

In a speech on 26 May 1920 Hitler explained as the cause of the World War that 'England . . . began to fear German competition on the world market . . . England did not have any means of bringing Germany down peacefully, and so she took up the means of violence.'[9]

On 17 June 1920 Hitler reasoned:

> Germany's rise, its freeing itself from British capital, the competition on the world market, its rising exports, its flourishing colonies which made the mother country independent of the raw materials from British colonies, the transatlantic shipping lines, its important merchant fleet, and finally its dangerous Navy, coaling stations and the Army were *the envy and the fear of Britain and the reason for the war.*[10]

He repeated this thesis in many speeches and also in *Mein Kampf.* There he argued that German economic expansion had necessarily had to lead to 'Britain becoming our enemy one day . . . It was more than senseless, but quite in line with our own naïvety, to get excited about the fact that England reserved herself the right to one day oppose our peaceful activities with the brutality of the violent egoist.'[11]

How important this argument was for Hitler can be seen in the frequency with which he repeated it in speeches, articles, writings and conversations.[12] It not only appeared in his early speeches, but also after the seizure of power. In a table talk on 23 July 1941, for example, Hitler argued exactly as he did twenty years earlier in his speeches.[13] This assessment of the causes of the Great War therefore appear to be a fundamental constant in Hitler's thinking.

Hitler's view that the German strategy of economic expansion had been a primary reason for the Great War equated to the theory of British envy of German trade as the cause of the war, which was widely held in Germany at the time. In a book by Johannes Haller published in 1922, the author said that the thesis of British envy of German trade as the reason for the world war 'had been repeated during the war . . . until it became wearying, and after the defeat its advocates never tired of constantly preaching it anew'.[14] Reputable persons and scientists expounded this theory in innumerable appeals, speeches, books and articles.[15] In one of the most widely read books of the times, Hermann Stegemann's *Geschichte des Krieges* (History of the War, published in 1917), which according to the Hitler intimate Ernst Hanfstaengl was one of the former's favourite books,[16] the Anglo-German conflict is also primarily explained in terms of trade policies and identified as having been a primary cause of the war.[17] This widely held theory of the times – which modern historic science rejects, at least as far as its being the sole explanation for the First World War is concerned – was formerly drawn upon by the various political tendencies in order to support their theories. Even within the framework of the Leninist theory of imperialism, the claim that Germany's extraordinary economic development, and the competition this led to with other imperialistic powers, especially Britain, was bound to lead to war gained importance.

Hitler's thesis was therefore not original and could count on wide acceptance. But the conclusions he drew from it, and the way he linked it to his economic and foreign policy concepts, were no longer so readily generally acceptable. For Hitler the issue was not to accuse the British morally because of their envy of German trade. Such a naïve way of looking at things would hardly have been in agreement with his socio-Darwinistically and power-politically coloured view of the world. For him the fact that Britain had to react to German trade competition by declaring war was only natural, and completely justified and understandable from the point of view of British interests. Hitler's conclusion was that, therefore, if a peaceful strategy, in other words 'the peaceful economic conquest of the world', also ultimately had to lead to war, then it was basically an illusion. The disparity between population and *Lebensraum* could therefore not, according to Hitler's logic, be reconciled 'peacefully', because even the peaceful strategies, i.e. policies of economic expansion, ultimately had to lead to armed conflict and exactly with the country which was his ideal as an ally. For Hitler the attempt to solve the disparity between population and *Lebensraum* by means of a policy orientated towards export was, in the final analysis, a 'detour' which was already extremely problematical and impractical for other reasons, to be discussed below. One of the principal reasons for Hitler's scepticism of the feasibility of this way was the theory of 'the shrinking markets'.

The Theory of 'Shrinking Markets' as an Argument against the Strategy of Economic Expansion
This theory can be found for the first time in a speech Hitler gave on 6 August 1927. Here he again developed his theory of the disparity between population and the base of subsistence and discussed the various possibilities of bringing the two factors into agreement again:

> Then there is also another possibility, namely the export of goods. But this possibility is a deceiving one. Not only Germany is heading towards this industrialization and is forced into this industrialization, but also England, France and Italy. And recently America has also entered into this line of competitors, and the most difficult thing is not the increase of production, the most difficult thing is the increase of sales. That is the problem in this world today, in this world which is industrializing everywhere, which is fighting for these markets.

Germany's economic problems had to become bigger, said Hitler,

> ... because firstly world competition is growing from year to year, and secondly because the other nations to whom we have delivered our products so far are also industrializing, and because the lack of raw materials is bringing us into an ever more unfavourable position from the start, compared to the other states and peoples of the world.[18]

About two weeks later Hitler repeated this thought in his closing address at the third *Reichsparteitag*:

> We National Socialists must immediately raise the objection here that it is not industrial production which will be hardest in future for the European nations; far more difficult will the increasing of sales be in the coming decades. And one day we will arrive at a dead end, because even the states who at present are not yet completely ripe for industrial production are slowly giving themselves over to industrialization. These states will still not be able to satisfy their requirements locally out of their own national power. With this alone one day an increase in the difficulty of selling industrial products will come about, and this will become all the greater insofar as it no longer concerns only one country, but in Europe quite a number of countries. It is natural that increasing competition will force these countries to gradually employ ever sharper weapons. One day the sharpness of this initially economic battle will be replaced by the sharpness of the sword.[19]

This thesis of the trend towards shrinking markets also did not originate in Hitler's own thinking but had been widely held in Germany for a long time. It was drawn upon by economic theorists of different schools and by the adherents of opposing political persuasions for the support of their theories. At the turn of the century the well-known political economist Werner Sombart had been the first to formulate the 'law of the falling export rate'.[20] In a presentation given in 1928, the key theses of which were repeated in a popular brochure in 1932 entitled 'The Future of Capitalism',[21] Sombart had expressed the opinion that 'the continuing industrialization of the agrarian nations' would cause industrial export to slow down, because 'the newly capitalist nations would no longer satisfy their needs for industrial products from the old capitalist nations to the same degree as before'.[22]

Ferdinand Fried (pseudonym of Friedrich Zimmermann), one of the main proponents of the autarky concept, had already begun to advocate the thesis of 'shrinking markets' in 1929 in the well-known conservative-revolutionary periodical *Die Tat*. According to Otto Strasser, his book 'The End of Capitalism', in which these articles had been compiled, had had a greater influence on the economic concepts of the NSDAP than any other. Hitler himself had also read it.[23] Fried claimed that it was 'naïve optimism' to believe one could 'continue the increase of import and export indefinitely'. The exchange of goods had already

> ... shrunk to a minimum, because the debtor countries no longer hungered for finished products, nor the creditor countries for raw materials. The one side no longer needed finished products because by now it has been equipped to produce its own goods, the other no longer needed raw materials because nobody was willing to buy the finished products these raw materials had been made into.[24]

Marxist theorists such as Rosa Luxemburg and Nikolai Bucharin also argued that because of the shrinking of free markets – caused among other things by the industrialization of former agrarian countries – the problems of exports would increase and the inevitable outcome would be imperialistic wars for the safeguarding of these markets.[25]

These theories did not lack a foundation in reality. After the war, not only had protectionism increased, but industrialization abroad had led to heavy competition in markets which had been served by European exports before the war. Furthermore, since the world economic crisis, internationally falling prices had led to the reduction of their foreign trade quotas in most countries, in other words, to a reduction of the share of foreign trade in national income. 'This development', Eckart Teichert states in his study 'Autarky and Large Area Economy in Germany 1930–1939', 'confirmed, and not only in Germany, the pessimistic assessment of the beneficial function of the global division of labour'. In 1925, in Britain, the Balfour Committee had argued against a further industrialization of the colonial countries under direct referral to Sombart's 'law of the shrinking export rate'. Even Keynes used this 'line of argument so fervently taken up'[26] in Germany for his prognosis about the development of the terms of trade in the industrial countries.

What is important for our discussion is that the theory of the 'shrinking markets' played a key role in Hitler's economic thinking and was emphatically advocated by him in his 'Second Book' as well as in numerous speeches and articles between 1927 and 1937. If we do not understand the importance this thesis had for Hitler's economic thinking, we can understand neither his autarky concept nor his *Lebensraum* concept in their contexts. We therefore intend to cite extensively, beginning with Hitler's 'Second Book':

> The market of today's world is not an unlimited one. The number of industrially active countries has constantly increased. Almost all of the European nations suffer from the insufficient and unsatisfactory ratio of their territory to their population, and are therefore dependent on world exports. In recent times they have had the American union added on, in the east Japan. With this, a fight for the limited markets begins automatically, which will become all the sharper the more numerous the industrially active nations become, and on the other hand the more limited the markets become. Because while, on the one hand, the number of nations fighting for the world market increases, the market itself gradually shrinks, in part due to self-industrialization under their own power, in part by a system of branch companies which are increasingly being set up in such countries out of purely capitalistic interests . . . The more purely capitalistic interests begin to determine today's economy, especially the more general financial and stock market considerations gain a decisive influence, the more this system of the foundation of branches will expand, but with this also the industrialization of former markets . . . artificially carried out and, in particular, restricting the possibilities of export of the European mother countries . . . The greater the difficulties of export become, the harsher the fight for the ones remaining will be waged. And if the initial weapons in this battle lie in price structures and the quality of the goods with which one tries to compete each other into ruin, the final weapon here too ultimately lies in the sword. The so-called economically peaceful conquest of the world could only occur if the earth were to consist of only agrarian nations and were to have only one industrially active economic nation. But since all the great nations today are industrial nations, the so-called economically peaceful conquest of the world is nothing but the fight with means that will only be peaceful as long as the stronger nations still believe they can win with them, in other words, actually, that they can kill the others by a peaceful economy . . . But should a really powerful nation believe that it cannot defeat another one by economically peaceful means, or should an economically weaker nation not want to let itself be killed by an economically stronger one through gradually having the possibilities of feeding itself cut off, then . . . in both cases the fog of economically peaceful phrases will suddenly be torn asunder and war, in other words the continuation of politics by other means, will step into its place.[27]

Let us again trace the logic of this line of reasoning. The European countries, the USA and Japan were fighting for a limited market. And this market was even further reduced by the capital export of the industrially developed countries setting off the industrialization of the formerly underdeveloped nations. With this, however, they were not only curtailing their markets in the long run, but also unwillingly raising new competitors for themselves. The sharpening battle for markets would initially be fought with economic means, but ultimately would inevitably lead to war.

In a speech on 18 October 1928 Hitler said, 'What do we mean by global economy? It [the nation—R.Z.] must produce and try to sell that. One should not forget that it is not simply the increase in production that does it, one forgets that there are quite a number of other nations who are in the same situation.'[28] Hitler again pointed out that 'this sales possibility becomes ever more restricted by the industrialization of the world to begin with, and because the number of nations which are based on this means of subsistence is constantly increasing'.[29] On 30 November 1928 he called it

> ... nonsense when our industry says today that the problem of German business is the problem of increasing production. No. The problem of business is the increase of sales. It is a total misapprehension of economy itself, of the big economic-political points of view, when it says increase of production. It is easy to increase production. Our automobile factories, for instance, can increase it immediately. But not sales. It is because our domestic sales are too low, and because therefore production costs are too high, that we can not enter into competition abroad. The problem of the economic expansion of a nation is the question of securing the markets, and these are limited on this earth. A large part of the markets is already occupied by other countries. By colonial policy, Britain has secured almost one quarter of all of the markets in the world. The raw materials are also secured. Germany is coming in too late. There is a violent battle going on for the existing markets, in which the issue is life or death ... German politicians forget that in the end this battle will be decided by the greater strength. If the British, for example, realize that they cannot remove us economically, they will reach for the sword.[30]

In numerous further speeches and articles Hitler continued to develop his theory of the 'shrinking markets',[31] including his well-known speech at the *Düsseldorf Industrieklub* on 26 January 1932.[32]

How important an argument for his *Lebensraum* concept the thesis of 'shrinking markets' had become for Hitler can also be seen from the fact that only a few days after the seizure of power he again repeated it in his programmatic address to the commanders of the Army and the Navy. What has been often cited is the well-known statement by Hitler as noted by Lieutenant General Liebmann: 'How should political power, once it has been gained, be used? Not decided yet. Perhaps for gaining new export possibilities, perhaps – and probably better – conquest of new *Lebensraum* in the East and its ruthless Germanization.' This statement has rightly been cited as proof of the continuity of his objective of conquest of *Lebensraum* in the East. What is less well known, however, is how Hitler explained the necessity of *Lebensraum* in the sentences immediately preceding: 'Future increase of export senseless. World receptivity is limited and production is over-extended everywhere. Only possibility to put army of unemployed back in partially lies in settlement. Needs time, however, and radical change not to be expected, because *Lebensraum* for German nation too small.'[33]

In his speech in the *Reichstag* on 21 May 1935, in which Hitler, among other things, gave his reasons for his autarky concepts and the need for state control of the economy, he repeated his thesis that the international market was 'too small' and was 'furthermore practically being continually restricted even more by numerous measures and a certain automatic development'.[34]

One of the most important documents which, while not uncontroversial with regard to its value as a source, has repeatedly been cited as proof of Hitler's readiness for war is the so-called 'Hossbach notes' reflecting Hitler's important speech to military and political leaders on 5 November 1937. Here, too, where as reasons for the necessity of war Hitler again discusses all other possible strategies, he comes back to the thesis of the 'shrinking markets': 'Participation in the world economy: this has limitations which we will not be able to overcome... In particular it must be taken into basic consideration that since the World War an industrialization of former food exporting countries had taken place.' The line of reasoning here again leads to the result that 'the only solution – for us perhaps only appearing as a dream – lies in the gaining of a larger *Lebensraum*, a desire that through all the ages has been the cause for the formation of nations and the migrations of peoples'.[35]

Let us summarize what we have discussed so far. The second major argument which Hitler sets against the strategy of 'the economically peaceful conquest of the world' was a purely economic one. The looming industrialization of previously underdeveloped agrarian countries caused by the capital export of the industrialized countries was leading to an ever-increasing reduction of the markets, i.e. the possibilities of selling. In the long term, therefore, the disparity between *Lebensraum* and population could not be solved by a one-sided, export-orientated economic strategy but only by the conquest of new *Lebensraum*.

In addition to the reasons discussed so far, Hitler fields a further argument against the strategy of economic expansion.

The Result of Economic Expansion: A Disproportionality concerning Agriculture and Industry, Urbanization and Migration from the Land

Hitler defines the cause and essence of the strategy of economic expansion as follows. In view of the incongruity which had come about between the base of subsistence and the population, a large proportion of food – but also raw materials – had to be imported, which was only possible by means of a substantial increase in the export of industrial finished goods. This, however, would lead to a disproportionality between farming and industry. Migration from the land and an exaggerated increase of the population in the large cities would be the results. Alleviation could again only be brought about by the conquest of new Lebensraum, which secured the base of subsistence out of own resources. Therefore this Lebensraum should *also* serve for the settlement of farmers.

This line of reasoning by Hitler has led to many misunderstandings because it was taken as proof of his alleged objective of 'reagrarianization' and therefore misinterpreted as an expression of a fundamental anti-modernistic position. In *Mein Kampf* Hitler laments the fact that

> ... the renunciation of the gaining of new land and its replacement by the insanity of a global economic conquest ... in the end had to lead to an industrialization which was as unrestricted as it was harmful. The first result of most weighty importance was the weakening of the farming class this led to. In the same measure in which this decreased, the mass of the proletariat in the big cities grew ever bigger, until finally the balance had been completely lost.[36]

On 18 October 1928 Hitler argued that the economy was only healthy 'if it represents the balancing out between the production of the products of the soil and the production of the products of industry'. If this balance were disturbed within a national economy because it had gone over to exporting industrial products in order to import the missing food, the result was a migration of the people into the cities and a desertion of the country:

> This desertion of the land can be carried to such a point that a nation is not even remotely able to support itself from its soil. This is the principle upon which Britain rests. She has neglected her own soil, reduced farming, created gigantic parks and so forth. The British people have lost their own farming and rest completely and totally on their world economy.

The worst thing about industrialization was

> ... that the people forget how to think healthily. The masses slowly begin to determine politics. They say: We want cheap bread, open all the borders in order to satisfy that. The people adjust themselves to industry. With this a part

of agriculture is destroyed according to plan. A part of agriculture now goes over to industry. With this the harmful influence of industry is again increased. Everything migrates into industry and finally there is no longer any possibility to sell.[37]

Hitler feared that this development tended to lead to the complete destruction of the farmers.[38] The ruining of agriculture and the simultaneously ever-increasing economic dependence on foreign countries (as markets and for the importation of agricultural products) would lead to the point where Germany would collapse with the first catastrophe, 'that with the slightest threat to her international business relations she is exposed to death by starvation'.[39]

Because of the shift in the balance between city and country, said Hitler on 30 November 1928, the people in the cities ultimately lost 'their way of thinking rooted in the soil; they no longer have a feeling for their [own] agriculture. These people have only one wish, to obtain cheap food.' And since cheaper food could be supplied from abroad, the big city demanded the opening of the borders, with the result that domestic agriculture collapsed even further. This in turn led to further migration from the land, a further growth of the big cities, to a strengthening of the demand to open the borders and so on, the result finally being the destruction of agriculture. Britain had at least been careful enough to secure her world markets by means of colonial policies, but if Germany were to follow the same route without this precondition it would one day lead to collapse.[40] Besides this economic problem resulting from the disturbance of the balance between agriculture and industry, the destruction of the farming class had further undesirable effects because the farmer – based on the nature of his business – had been brought up to accept risks and be decisive. The destruction of the farming class would lead to people no longer being prepared to stake something, to accept risks, and consequently they would waste their lives away.[41]

Let us summarize Hitler's line of argument up to this point. Over-industrialization led to the neglect of agriculture and the balance between the two sectors of the economy was increasingly disturbed and finally resulted in the destruction of the farmers. Hitler's conclusion was that one should turn away from a policy of economic expansion and conquer new *Lebensraum* in order also to restore the disturbed balance between agriculture and industry. Was this demand the expression of an 'anti-modernistic' persuasion or did it imply a concept of 'reagrarianization'? Did Hitler's argument pretend to claim that one should turn the whole process of industrialization around and again become a purely agrarian state? Obviously not. Hitler was only establishing the disproportionality between agriculture and industry, and in the conquest of *Lebensraum* he saw a way of re-establishing the disturbed balance. In the final analysis, for Hitler the *Lebensraum* to be conquered in Russia was no more than what the colonies were for Britain, France and other industrial countries, i.e. an agrarian attachment, a source of raw materials and a market. None of this, of course, had anything to do with a basic rejection of industry and 'anti-modernism'.

But perhaps there is another aspect of Hitler's line of reasoning which could be cited as proof of his anti-modernism, namely his criticism of big cities. In the source material we investigated we found thirteen statements by Hitler which document a negative position on big cities. Of these statements, however, eight were made in 1927–28, three in the period between 1929 and 1931 and only two in later years. Even though we are, of course, not attempting to make any statistical claims, this information is still important because, as we have already seen in the chapter on Hitler's position on the farmers,[42] between 1925 and 1928 there were apparently some anti-modernistic elements to be found in Hitler's speeches and writings. These can probably be explained in terms of his attempts to exploit the agricultural crisis for propaganda, or rather to convert it into National Socialist election victories, because we do not find such statements either before or afterwards. As with most of the other statements indicating an idealization of the farmer, the statements cited above, in which Hitler expresses his criticism of migration from the land and urbanization as the result of economic expansion, were made in 1928,[43] with only one exception.

A remark which could serve as proof of 'anti-modernistic' elements in Hitler's *Weltanschauung* is contained in a speech of 13 April 1927. Here Hitler laments the 'destruction of the good in our people' which was taking place in the big cities by the 'bastardization and the decay which remains as a result of bastardization'. This 'decay', said Hitler, was leading to

> ... an unproductivity of our big cities ... It is no wonder that among the great men of a city like Vienna there are no Viennese, because nothing great can grow out of this kettle of bastards any longer. Everything which is great has come to Vienna from the healthy agricultural provinces. And it will be the same here. Nothing great can come out of the melting pots of our big cities any longer.[44]

On 23 January 1928 Hitler lamented the 'gradual pollution of the body of our nation by the poisoning of the blood in the big cities',[45] and in his 'Second Book' he wrote:

> A specific danger of the so-called economically peaceful politics of a nation, however, lies in the fact that it first makes an increase in population possible, which then finally is no longer in a sound ratio to the subsistence provided by its own soil. This overfilling of an insufficiently large territory with people often also leads to

serious social damage, in that the people are only concentrated in centres of work which are then less like centres of culture and more like abscesses on the body of the nation, in which all evil vices, bad habits, and illnesses appear to be united. They are then above all breeding grounds for the mingling of blood and bastardization, including mostly the dilution of the race, and thereby those festering centres in which the international Jewish maggot of the people thrives and takes care of the continuing ultimate decay.

Elsewhere in the book he also bemoans the 'niggerization and jewrization of our people in the big cities'.[46]

Hitler's ambivalent position on big cities becomes clear from a speech he made on 18 September 1928:

> In the last century, because of the impossibility of feeding our fresh supply [Hitler meant 'progeny' (*Nachwuchs*) but, apparently thinking in terms of 'human material', chose the term 'supply' (*Nachschub*)—H.B.] from our own soil, we concentrated this fresh supply in our big cities. They have become the nucleus of the industrial development of the megapolis, of technical progress, of constructive genius, of ability in business, but also of all social illnesses and the rootlessness of these people.[47]

Hitler was therefore not rejecting big cities simply because of industrial development. He even valued them as the 'nucleus' of technical progress, constructive genius and ability in business. His criticism of the big cities was not derived from any rejection of industry, but from his racial ideology. Because most of Jewry was concentrated in large cities such as Vienna and Berlin, he saw these as the breeding ground of 'racial intermingling'. His experiences in Vienna in particular led to a criticism of big cities that was motivated by racial ideology. The logical conclusion is, however, that once Hitler's racial programme, the 'removal of the Jews',[48] had been completed, his key reason for his criticism of big cities would also have been removed. Only one point of criticism would then be left, which Hitler stated, for instance, in a speech on 30 November 1928: The big city 'alienates' its inhabitants from 'the soil'

> ... because millions of people live in the big city, who may well eat three times a day, but without rendering account to themselves where the food comes from. They work in a factory, in the office, in the plant, and are convinced that they are thereby earning their bread. But they forget that this bread has to be brought in from somewhere, that the increase of purely industrial work does not already mean an increase of the daily bread. Because the daily bread of a nation is initially conditioned upon the extent of its own available *Lebensraum*.[49]

Hitler therefore believed that the shift in the balance between agriculture and industry caused by the strategy of economic expansion, the occurrence of a disproportionality between both sectors of the economy, was no longer recognized in all its consequences by the inhabitants of the big cities because, based on their own experiences, they no longer gave account to themselves of the relationship between the two fundamental factors, '*Lebensraum*' and 'population'. This view in itself cannot be taken as proof of an anti-modernistic element in Hitler's thinking, any more than the other quotes presented so far. There is only one statement, made in a speech on 8 December 1928 (which we have already cited in another context), which shows that in 1928 Hitler had apparently partially advocated an anti-modernistic agrarian ideology: 'Completely different ideas from former times now dominate our nation, and in Germany the territorial policy of the German nation is gradually being transformed into economic policy. The soldier no longer stands in the foreground, but the businessman, no longer the farmer, but the entrepreneur . . . the city has replaced the village.'[50] A further statement which can be advanced as proof of Hitler's anti-modernistic criticism of the big city and his agrarian ideology stems from 1929: 'Perhaps it is the farmer who has the most instinct, who is familiar with the concept of risk, who must dare to sow regardless of whether the heavens give their blessing . . . In the asphalt spirit of our big cities the people today have gradually lost their instinct.'[51]

On 3 July 1931 Hitler again criticized the strategy of economic expansion and spoke of the risks attached to the unpredictability of sales. As the second 'negative aspect' of economic expansion he mentioned 'the amassing of great masses of people in our big and global cities'. This was leading to a negation of the concept of property, because 'one can hardly define the ownership of property as the base of an economic structure, when from the beginning it is impossible for uncounted numbers of people to ever achieve ownership of property'. A further result of the amassing of great numbers of people in the big cities was the social effect of life in the big city which led to illnesses, polluted the people and eroded them. The 'greatest danger', however, was the alienation of the city-dweller from the soil, but above all the development of the idea that 'the farmer is a burden upon the nation, that the agriculturalist in some way is a blemish on the nation, that tilling the soil is a necessary evil'. This point of view then led to the city-dweller calling for cheap food imports, for the opening of the borders, with the result that agriculture continued to be destroyed and the farmer ruined.[52]

Hitler also made statements to Wagener[53] which were critical of the big cities. He apparently always retained a certain scepticism towards a one-sided development of the city,[54] but this does not mean that he wanted to break up the existing cities and resettle their inhabitants in the country. Quite the opposite. As the megalomania of his urban building projects proves, he had no intentions at all in this direction. On 4 October 1941 Koeppen noted a statement by Hitler in which he emphasized that he rejected the resettlement of city-dwellers in the country: 'This would be a waste of effort and money out the window.'[55]

Hitler had no intention of settling farmers only in the *Lebensraum* to be conquered in the East; he also wished to found 'a number of bigger cities'.[56] Within Germany, however, he was 'against the creation of further cities of the dimensions of Berlin. It is more than enough for the Reich that it has a five-million city (Berlin), two two-million cities (Vienna and Hamburg) and many cities with one million inhabitants. To further increase the size of our big cities in order to orientate the whole cultural life of larger areas of the German Reich towards them is nonsense.'[57]

Let us summarize. One of the lines of reasoning – even if not the most important – against the strategy of economic expansion which, in the end, also led Hitler to the demand for new *Lebensraum* is as follows. This strategy leads to an ever-increasing disproportionality between agriculture and industry, which in the end must lead to the destruction of domestic agriculture. This is accompanied by migration from the land and a disproportionate growth of a few industrial centres. To conclude from this argument that Hitler had intended to break up the big cities and resettle their inhabitants in the country (in the *Lebensraum* to be conquered in the East) is not permissible. As we have shown, Hitler did not fundamentally reject big cities at all, but only certain of the manifestations of life in big cities which he defined negatively.[58]

If the line of reasoning we have portrayed is in itself already not proof enough of a fundamental anti-modernistic position allegedly held by Hitler, the untenability of such a claim is additionally underlined by the fact that this line of reasoning represents only *one* of Hitler's arguments, and the one he presented with the least degree of frequency! Far more important for his criticism of economic expansion are the two theories discussed initially, which he presented much more frequently as an argument against this strategy, namely (1) As the Great War had shown, the 'economically peaceful conquest of the world was impossible, because competition in trade also had to finally lead to war – especially with Britain. (2) This strategy was very limited, primarily because – due to the industrialization of the formerly underdeveloped countries – there was a trend towards shrinking markets. But if Hitler rejected an economic policy that was orientated one-sidedly towards export, then the consequence can only be that he was envisaging an autarkic economic area in which the disturbed balance between industry and agriculture could be restored and self-sufficiency in terms of raw materials become possible.

Lebensraum *and the Autarky Concept*

Hitler was aware that, in view of the limited resources in raw material, the creation of autarky for Germany was basically not possible. In the final analysis, such an concept could only be realized within a pan-European economic structure, including the *Lebensraum* to be conquered in Russia. This conquest of *Lebensraum* would then solve the incongruity between population and base of subsistence which could not be solved by economic expansion.

If we follow this logic while taking Hitler's foreign policy programme into account, however, we come to a contradiction. Hitler wanted to realize autarky on the basis of the *Lebensraum* to be conquered in the East. But since, based on the experiences of the Great War, he wanted to avoid a war on two fronts, he desired an alliance with Britain. This alliance was to be built upon the following premise. In view of the upward development of the USA and the Soviet Union, Britain could no longer uphold its traditional concept of a 'balance of power' on the Continent, or only at the cost of its position as a world power. Hitler was prepared to guarantee British colonies overseas, but in exchange demanded a free hand for his expansion to the East.[59]

Hitler was also sceptical of a policy of economic expansion because he feared provoking Britain – as before the Great War – and thereby endangering the realization of his concept of an alliance. In *Mein Kampf* he had expressly stated: 'No sacrifice should then have been too great in order to gain England's sympathy. Colonies and sea power should have been renounced, and British industry spared the competition.' This also implies a 'renunciation of world trade'.[60]

For Hitler, on the other hand, the strategy of economic expansion was a necessary outcome of the already existing incongruity between *Lebensraum* and population. In order to bring both factors back into line again, and to realize an autarkic large-area economy, the conquest of new *Lebensraum* was first necessary. But before this *Lebensraum* had been conquered, autarky could not be realized, from which it follows that trade had to continue, and therefore competition, primarily with Britain, which destroyed the conditions for a treaty with her, and finally therefore also the possibility of conquering new *Lebensraum*. We are dealing here with a *circulus vitiosus* of which Hitler was certainly well aware. His solution: by first employing emergency measures, for example the production of synthetic raw materials and the substitution of such raw materials that would otherwise have to be imported, to achieve a limited 'temporary' autarky and thereby create the conditions for both an alliance with Britain and for war. After the conquest of *Lebensraum* in the East, a true autarky which could be maintained in the long-term could be created out of the 'temporary' autarky with the aid of the raw material and agricultural areas now available. The 'temporary' autarky was therefore only an emergency solution.

Until now Hitler's autarky concepts have mostly been traced back to the necessities of waging war. And this does indeed play a role, because, based on the experience of the blockade at the end of the Great War, he wanted to prevent a recurrence of such a situation. On the other hand, autarky was also necessary in order to be able to realize the idea of an alliance with Britain. But we must always differentiate between two autarky concepts, the 'temporary autarky' as it was to be achieved by means of the Four-Year Plan, i.e. by the substitution of synthetically produced raw materials for natural raw materials (rubber, fuel etc.), and the actual autarky, which was only conceivable within the framework of a pan-European economic area including the *Lebensraum* to be conquered in the East.[61]

Only if we keep this context in mind can we adequately interpret Hitler's *Lebensraum* concept and his statements on the problems of autarky. In *Mein Kampf* and in his 'Second Book' he emphasized the link between *Lebensraum* and autarky. The *Lebensraum* to be conquered will facilitate a 'national economy of requirement and exchange', in which the imbalance of the development of agriculture, trade and industry would be abolished:

> By their [industry and trade—R.Z.] now only still having the task of providing the exchange between domestic production and requirements in all sectors, they make the total nourishment of the nation more or less independent of foreign countries, and therefore contribute to securing the freedom of the state and the independence of the nation, particularly in times of trouble.[62]

In this quote, as well as in Hitler's 'Second Book',[63] we detect that he had apparently taken the experience of the blockade at the end of the Great War into consideration. Since for him, based on his socio-Darwinistic *Weltanschauung*, war was an eternal fundamental condition of human existence,[64] the state had to be able at any time to wage a war. This meant first of all that it had to be resistant to blockade, in other words autarkic as far as possible. We have seen, however, that Hitler was advocating an autarkic economy for reasons that were quite independent of such considerations, but which could only be achieved on the basis of the *Lebensraum* to be conquered.

On 10 October 1928 he declared:

> An economy can basically only feed a nation healthily if it remains within the inner circle of the nation. How often have we National Socialists not advocated the position from this point as well. A national community is only healthy when the original production of the soil can feed the industrial forces, when one part is the customer of the other part. Then the nation is independent from without, and the

body is healthily organized within. As soon as a nation is too small, however, to make this internal circulation possible, and is forced to enter the outer circulation with its economy, at that same instant this nation joins the battle for power.[65]

While on the one hand autarky therefore facilitates the waging of war, on the other hand – and this is what Hitler wants to express here – in a situation in which a nation *cannot be* autarkic, competition in trade unavoidably leads to war, because the limitations of *Lebensraum* require the pursuit of a policy of economic expansion. On 18 October 1928 he said that an economy was only healthy 'when it provided the exchange between the goods of the production of the soil and the goods of industrial production', in other words 'when the total economy remains within an internal circulation'.[66] We should again note that Hitler is speaking about an *exchange* between both sectors of the economy. This cannot have anything at all to do with the alleged objective of 'reagrarianization'.

In view of various statements by Hitler in which he advocates autarky[67] before 1933, it becomes questionable whether, as Otto Strasser reports, he actually did say during the debate on 22 May 1930 that he too was 'envisaging such an autarky as a goal in the future, but that this would only become possible at the earliest in one hundred years, because we simply could not survive without the exchange of goods with the world economy'.[68] According to this, Hitler is alleged to have called the objective of autarky advocated by Strasser the 'most vile dilettantism'. Strasser reports Hitler as saying:

> Do you believe we can ever withdraw from the world economy? We depend on the importation of all important raw materials. We are no less dependent on the export of our own industrial goods. During the past few months I have just had this necessity of the global economic network described to me from East Asia and everywhere, and we cannot stop this development, nor do we want to.[69]

While we do not want to accuse Strasser of having invented this statement by Hitler – which is quite possible – he is certainly reporting specific objections Hitler had in highly exaggerated terms. In essence the debate probably went as follows. While Otto Strasser was pushing for as rapid a realization of the autarky concept as possible, Hitler declared that this could not be achieved at short notice because of the existing world economic links. That he is supposed to have said that autarky could only be realized in one hundred years at the earliest is not credible. Hitler knew that with Germany's *existing* raw material base, and with the existing 'limited *Lebensraum*', autarky could hardly be achieved. But after the conquest of *Lebensraum* in the East he considered the achievement of autarky, even if not absolute autarky, to be quite possible within the framework of a pan-European economic order. And there can be no doubt that Hitler intended to conquer the *Lebensraum* in Russia during his lifetime, and not one hundred years hence.

When in his speech on 23 March 1933 on the enabling law, for example, Hitler declared that 'the geographic situation of our German poor in raw materials does not completely permit an autarky for our Reich', and that 'there is nothing further from the mind of the Reichs government than opposition to export',[70] he is both telling the truth and lying at the same time. He was certainly aware that Germany in its existing borders would hardly be able to achieve autarky in view of the lack of raw materials. What he was keeping hidden, of course, was the fact that he intended to conquer new *Lebensraum* in the East, in order thereby to create the conditions for a constant supply of raw material to Germany without the necessity of a greater participation in world trade.

Until this *Lebensraum* had been conquered, however, Hitler had to achieve a temporary autarky. He was naturally falsifying the facts when – as in his speech in the *Reichstag* on 21 May 1935 – he claimed he was basically 'convinced that the strict realization of economic autarky of all the states ... would be unwise and in its results harmful to the nations' but that the conduct of the other nations were forcing him 'to either gain the missing raw materials himself by means of complicated procedures, or, if this was not possible, to substitute them'.[71] The attempts begun in 1935–36 to realize a relative autarky through the production of synthetic raw materials or by substituting them were only determined by the objective of having a blockade-proof economy in case of war. They had nothing to do yet with the economic-political objective of National Socialism, with true autarky, which only appeared to be achievable on the basis of new *Lebensraum*.

In his memorandum of August 1936 on the Four-Year Plan, from which we have already quoted repeatedly in other contexts, Hitler assigned the German economy the task of being 'capable of war in four years'. This meant, in concrete terms, that Germany had to be completely independent from abroad in the supply of fuel, rubber and iron ore. In his memorandum Hitler emphasized that this road [the substitution and production of synthetic raw materials for the achievement of a relative autarky—R.Z.] only had to be followed temporarily and as an emergency measure. It was of course correct, he argued, that agricultural production could no longer be increased by any substantial degree, and that it was impossible at the moment to produce certain raw materials artificially that were missing in Germany, or to replace them by other means. It was therefore completely needless to keep repeating these facts, 'in other words to ascertain that we lack food and raw materials, but what is important instead is to take those measures which can bring about a *final* solution for the *future*, and for the interim a *temporary* relief'. By 'final solution' Hitler meant the 'extension of the *Lebensraum* or the base of raw materials and food for our nation. It is the task of the political leadership to solve this question one day.'[72]

At the so-called 'Hossbach Conference', Hitler's famous address to military leaders on 5 November 1937 which serves as proof of his determination to wage war, he also discussed the question whether autarky could be achieved under the existing conditions of a limited *Lebensraum*. Hitler's answer was that in the sector of raw materials only a limited, but not a total, autarky was achievable. Autarky could be achieved as far as coal was concerned, but in the area of ore the situation was much more difficult: 'Requirement of iron – self-supply possible, and light metal, other raw materials – copper, tin, however, not'. As far as fibrous material was concerned, self-sufficiency was possible as long as the reserves in wood lasted, but this was not a 'long-term solution'. In the area of food the question of autarky had to be answered with a straight 'no' because 'a further increase of production by burdening the soil which was already showing signs of exhaustion due to the use of synthetic fertilizers' was hardly possible any longer. Hitler's conclusion at the 'Hossbach Conference' was that autarky was not achievable under the existing conditions and that relief was only possible by the conquest of new *Lebensraum*.[73] Here again the degree to which Hitler reasoned economically, and how closely linked the topics of 'autarky', 'war', and '*Lebensraum*' were in his thought processes, can clearly be seen.

Although Hitler emphasized in several speeches that even under existing conditions it was necessary to gain as much independence as possible from abroad, and also drew attention to the successes achieved in this area,[74] he was still clearly aware that 'today's circumstances did not make it possible' for Germany 'to withdraw from the world economy. They force us, already out of need, to take part in it under any condition.' While Germany had attempted with its Four-Year Plan to relieve 'foreign markets from German competition' – a statement that was not only meant tactically, but was again a reminder of his thesis that in order to realize the alliance with Britain, Germany had to give up the greater part of its world trade! – 'what cannot find an economically satisfactory solution in this territory which we have at our disposal today will have to be solved by taking part in world trade'.[75]

After beginning the war against Russia, Hitler repeatedly underscored the link between his *Lebensraum* and his autarky concepts. On 17/18 September 1941, for example, he explained: 'The battle for world hegemony will be decided for Europe by possession of the Russian space, it will make Europe into the most blockade-proof place on earth.'[76] Here the long-term perspectives of Hitler's foreign, or rather war, policy become apparent. Once the *Lebensraum* in Russia has been conquered, Europe could achieve complete autarky and no longer be strangled by any sort of blockade. With this, however, the starting conditions for the later conflict – here Hitler was primarily thinking of the conflict with the USA, which in his view was unavoidable[77] – would have become extremely favourable.

On 25 September 1941 Hitler stated in his monologues that life had to be based on 'sales possibilities which lay within one's own sphere of power. Today I can say: Europe is autarkic, insofar as we can still prevent that a giant state continues to exist which uses European civilization in order to mobilize Asia against us [meaning the Soviet Union—R.Z.].' As a reason for his autarky concept he again cited proof against blockade, but also added further quite unrelated arguments:

> A European policy is also right, I believe, when it holds itself away from the desire to export to all the world. The white man's world has destroyed its own trade all over the world. On the other continents the European economy no longer has sales territories. With our production costs we can no longer compete there. We are so much at a disadvantage everywhere that we can not get in anywhere. And the whole world is scrambling after the few export articles that are still required abroad. In order to participate in this I have to pay such high export duties that the requirement of our own nation has an enormous power, a colossal work result, taken away from it. Only with the few new inventions can we engage in trade for a while ... Germany is the only country today which has no unemployed because we did not adjust ourselves to foreign markets! The country we are now opening for ourselves [i.e. Russia—R.Z.] is only a source of raw material and a market for us, not a field for industrial production.[78]

We will return to Hitler's last remark in Chapter V.1.e when we show why he rejected the export of capital in principle, and therefore also the export of capital to the *Lebensraum* conquered in the East. What appears to be the essential point in his statement here, however, is that he explains his autarky concept completely independently of any ideas about a future war and primarily bases it on the theory of 'shrinking markets'.

The link between *Lebensraum* and the autarky concept becomes particularly clear in a statement by Hitler made on 13 October 1941: 'There is no country which will be autarkic to a greater degree than Europe.' His reason: the immeasurable raw materials of the Ukraine. Hitler's example for the intended autarkic large economic territory was without doubt the USA. 'If I were in America, I would not be afraid; all one needs to do is to build up a gigantic domestic economy. With those nine and a half million square kilometres of land, the problem would be completely solved in five years.'[79]

The autarky concept should not be interpreted as only being an interim solution. It was not primarily a means of war, but the main objective of the war, and thereby again the condition for further wars. Insofar as Hitler's autarky concept reflected his long-term foreign policy plans, the 'temporary' autarky of the Four-Year Plan was, on the one hand, to enable a blockade-proof economy in order to be able to survive the coming war, and, on the other, to be an economic tool with which to make Britain more inclined to accept an alliance with Germany. The 'final' solution, the conquest of *Lebensraum* in the East, was to provide a truly autarkic pan-European large economic area, and thereby create the conditions for further wars, above all for the later war with the USA. Hitler warned against repeating the mistake after the Great War and not maintaining autarky after the war:

> I do not want to repeat one mistake. We build ourselves up what we had already had in the World War, an autarkic economy. Then it failed because we could not exploit it people-wise. The work which is squandered in the production of unproductive goods had to find its compensation. Instead of the domestic market, however, it was the foreign market we hurled ourselves into out of profit greed, after the war, in order to pay our debts. That we were given loans for this purpose only thrust us in deeper. At the end of the war we had already arrived at synthetic rubber. Instead of continuing to produce it, we went back to natural rubber after the war. We imported petrol even though the Bergius process[80] was already there. That is the most important thing after the war, to immediately build up the autarkic economy.[81]

The base for this autarky, said Hitler, was the *Lebensraum* in the East with its plentiful raw materials.[82]

On 26/27 October 1941 Hitler said that national and political independence was

> ... just as much dependent on autarky as on armed might. What is decisive: not to fall back into the mistake of throwing ourselves into world trade. We do not need more than three to four million tonnes of merchant shipping. To get coffee and tea from the African continent is enough, we have everything else in Europe.[83]

In a conversation with Finnish Foreign Minister Witting on 27 November 1941 Hitler sketched the global political perspectives after the end of the war: The USA and Britain would without doubt drift into 'a terrible social crisis at great speed', whereas Europe had already overcome the heavy social crises:

> So we must recognize that in the end Europe is completely dependent upon itself. The most important task was now to exploit *for* Europe the richest and most fertile part of Europe [meaning European Russia, especially the Ukraine—R.Z.], which until now had been organized *against* Europe ... Europe had to mobilize its own resources, and this would be done. Europe could become autarkic and would make itself autarkic ... It was a gigantic task to develop Europe into an autarkic structure, a task which was solvable, and with only relatively small adjustments...

All the wealth of the huge European Russia had not been made available to Europe, not even to the Russian people, but had only been used to build up a gigantic armament against Europe.[84]

Here again the actual function of *Lebensraum* in the East in Hitler's economic concept becomes clear. It was not to be a means of reagrarianization, but of creating the possibility of realizing the autarky concept within a pan-European framework.

Hitler also explained these contexts during a table talk on 27 July 1942. By the conquest of the territories in the East, almost all of the necessary raw materials would fall into Germany's hands:

> In the restructuring of the Reich there is one thing we should always keep in mind: it was essential that the state be large enough to be autarkic. This could again be seen in this war by the difficulties Italy was having because it lacked coal, and Britain, whose existence was being endangered by the sinking of ships.[85]

The size of the *Lebensraum* was therefore of primary importance to Hitler, to enable the achievement of independence in the supply of raw materials and thereby of autarky. On 9 August 1942 Hitler again explained how rich in raw materials the *Lebensraum* conquered in the East actually was: 'We will be, including cotton, the most autarkic state there is.'[86]

In his speech to the leaders of the armaments industry at the end of June 1944, which we have already cited in another context, Hitler sketches the perspectives of a victorious war:

> But the victorious war will give us above all the foundations – and it will give them to us because I am not considering any poor sort of compromise – it will give us the foundations in order then to actually secure the conditions for its future activities for the German economy. Because by now everybody must have seen, despite all the inventions, how sensitively dependent we Germans in our former *Lebensraum* structure and *Lebensraum* size are on imports which are done by countries who perhaps want to or do not want to. If a country does not want to supply us with tungsten, then it does not supply us. The simple pressure by another country is enough to cause us great worry. If somebody else does not want to give us any nickel, the mere pressure by one country is enough and we have great worries about nickel. If another country bars our supply of chromium, then we have great worries about chromium, about molybdenum and so forth. Gentlemen, it is just as important to bring these absolutely indispensable materials into – I do not want to say – the possession of the Reich, but within the sphere of power of the German nation, within the power sphere, as it is necessary to secure the necessary grain areas, beet areas, potato areas and so forth. This is also a part of it. Because this is also a part of securing the continuity of its work in the future for the economy. The state, which shapes and leads policy here, has the obligation to secure those things for the economy power-wise, which it needs to be able to work constantly and with continuity in the longer term.[87]

In his last dictations to Bormann the objective Hitler envisaged again becomes clear. A large economic area such as the USA would permit the achievement of autarky:

> The United States disposes in practice of the conditions for an autarkic economy such as we envisage for ourselves. They dispose of unlimited space in which their energies can extend themselves without restrictions. On our part, we hope for Germany that we may one day succeed in securing her economic independence within a *Lebensraum* which is appropriate to her population. A great nation needs sufficient *Lebensraum*.'[88]

The continuity of Hitler's concepts, from *Mein Kampf* all the way to the final weeks of his life, has now been demonstrated. The function of the *Lebensraum* to be conquered in the East – and this is the conclusion from this chapter – can only be understood in the contexts of Hitler's criticism of economic expansion and his autarky concept. In this we should not overlook the fact that his demand for autarky was linked both to the discussion going on at the time and to actual economic developments. Without understanding these links, the effectiveness of Hitler's *Weltanschauung* cannot be understood. Teichert has demonstrated how centrally important the demand for autarky was in Germany in those days. In this, the experience of the blockade during the First World War was certainly *one* argument for the proponents of such a concept, but not the only argument, or even the main one. We must keep in mind that one result of the First World War, which was dramatically reinforced by the world economic crisis, was a 'loosening of international economic ties'[89] with a trend towards economic nationalism and a regionalization of trade policy.

We have already pointed out in the context of the portrayal of Hitler's theory of 'shrinking markets' that at the time there was widespread pessimism in Germany as far as exports were concerned, which then automatically led to the demand for autarky. Teichert therefore also finds:

> 'Autarky' and 'large-area economy' were popular slogans which were being promulgated by a flood of books, brochures and articles which was simply immense. All of these publications signalized pessimistic expectations within the machine of the state and the business bureaucracy, in scientific political economy, journalism and among the general public as far as the future importance of foreign trade and the world economic order were concerned.[90]

Ferdinand Fried, a vehement proponent of the autarky concept, was able to state in his book *Autarky*, published in 1932, that 'Hardly a term tossed into the current public debate has incited the emotions so much as "autarky", and there is no term about which so heated and bitter a controversy is going on today as "autarky".⁹¹ There was, as Goerdeler wrote, 'an almost demonic movement towards autarky'.⁹²

The demand for autarky was closely tied to a fundamental criticism of the capitalist system and the objective to supplement or replace it with state control of the economy or a planned economy. Fried himself makes this connection right at the beginning of his book:

> Autarky is to free trade as a planned economy is to a free economy. Neither are logical, contradictory opposites; one is only the historic replacement, the *organic* development of the other. It follows that planned economy is one form of 'organisation' of the free economy, autarky one form of organization of free trade, of the free exchange of goods in the world.

In all this the conservative-revolutionary proponents of the autarky concept did not, of course, demand the conquest of new *Lebensraum* for the realization of the concept as did Hitler. Fried, for example, interpreted the demand for autarky as being an expression of a 'recollection of one's own soil' which 'was opposed to the old imperialistic nationalism. The nation which is being born today out of the German revolution is intensively directed inward, wants to be sufficient unto itself.' But this also meant that autarky was only conceivable within the overall framework of an anti-modernistic turnabout, which, for example, included reagrarianization and the reduction of consumption. Fried therefore demanded the 'return to the country of the human masses stranded in the big cities', a 'strengthening of agriculture and a gradual reduction of the influence of the city, better: the big city'. A nation which was fighting for its freedom and independence should 'also be able to do without coffee, oranges or chocolate'.⁹³ Sombart as well, who like Hitler derived his demand for autarky from the trend of 'shrinking markets', also pleaded for a reagrarianization: 'The way that leads to this objective of a greater national independence is clearly marked: it is reagrarianization, which also appears to be destined to play a decisive role in the inner structure of our economy.' For him this actually meant that the current (1932) quota of rural population, which had sunk to 30 per cent, was to be brought back up to the position in 1882 (42.5 per cent), and this equated approximately to the number of unemployed in the coming years.⁹⁴

Such concepts were naturally unacceptable to Hitler. They were far to 'defensive' for his 'warlike' and 'offensive' way of thinking. If one intended to create autarky *without* accepting a reduction in industrial production, if one wanted to re-establish the disturbed proportionality between agriculture and industry and still continue an enforced industrial development, the only way remaining was to conquer new *Lebensraum*, which could then provide the raw materials and food base for the realization of autarky. Of course, most of Hitler's contemporaries drew back from this consequence – even the proponents of autarky. Here we clearly see the degree to which Hitler's *Weltanschauung* was a product of his times, i.e. a reflection of current popular theses, and to what extent it was an original product of the man himself. Quite unoriginal and very much 'in line with current thinking' was Hitler's pessimism about exports and the demand for autarky he derived from this. But the radical consistency with which he demanded the militant conquest of new *Lebensraum* for the realization of this concept, the ruthless thinking-to-the-final-conclusion of premises others dared not think through to the end, were characteristic for Hitler. We must note, however, that even the demand for new *Lebensraum* for the safeguarding of a blockade-proof economy was not a completely new idea. This concept had already been projected in the plans of the Army Supreme Command (Ludendorff) at the end of the First World War. Hitler took over these concepts as well as some of the theories of the political scientists and combined them into a new system within the framework of his *Weltanschauung*. The difference from the autarky concepts of 'conservative-revolutionary' contemporaries such as Fried lay in the fact that Hitler *did not* advocate a concept of reagrarianization in the sense of a reduction of the industrial sector. On the contrary, the newly conquered *Lebensraum* would not only serve to abolish the disproportionality between agriculture and industry, it was primarily to be a source of raw materials and a market, and thereby a means for the increase of industrial production.

b. Creation of an Agrarian Supplementary Territory by means of Agrarian Settlement

In the following sections of Chapter V.1. we intend systematically to portray the various economic functions Hitler allocated to the *Lebensraum* in the East. Let us begin with the best-known function by far, the settlement of farmers.

In his 'Second Book' Hitler wrote:

> An additional 500,000km² of land in Europe can provide new homesteads for millions of German farmers, but also provide the strength of the German nation with millions of soldiers for the decisive case. The only region in Europe which could be considered for such a land policy was then Russia. The thinly populated western regions bordering on Germany, which had already once before received German colonists as the bearers of culture, also came under consideration for the new European land policy of the German nation.[95]

If Hitler wanted to settle 'millions of German farmers' in the *Lebensraum* to be conquered in the East, then it was because in his view the fertile Ukraine was well suited as an agrarian supplementary territory to Germany. In Germany proper, as Hitler had repeatedly stressed, an increase of agricultural production was no longer possible. Because of synthetic fertilization of the soil and intensive cultivation, the limits of an increase of agricultural production had long been reached or already exceeded. Therefore Germany was to remain a highly industrialized central area, which would then, however, require supplementary *Lebensraum* in the East. It is self-explanatory why Hitler held back such plans in his public speeches after the seizure of power, and generally from 1930–31 on, and he did not again mention the topic of 'the conquest of *Lebensraum* in the East' in his *public* statements after 1933. His internal statements show, however, that he continued to hold fast to this objective.

When after the attack on the Soviet Union the realization of his plans had apparently moved within immediate reach, Hitler returned to his concept. And here an overall concept becomes apparent which aimed at a ruthless enslavement of the indigenous population and the settlement of 'soldier-farmers'. On 27 July 1941 Hitler declared in his table talks:

> Nothing would be more mistaken than to want to attempt to educate the mass [of the indigenous population—R.Z.]. Our only interest is that the people, let us say, learn to keep the traffic signs apart, they are presently illiterate and they should remain so. But they must live well, that is in our own interest. The southern Ukraine, especially the Crimea, we will settle exclusively with Germans. I have no problem with shifting the population there to some other place. The German settler will be a soldier-farmer, and for this I will take the *Kapitulanten* [the old word for a soldier who enlisted for longer than the statutory term of the draft—H.B.], may they be related as they please . . . In future we will have a standing army of at least 1.5 to 2 million. With the discharge of the twelve-year-termers we will have 30,000 to 40,000 *Kapitulanten* available each year. If they are the sons of farmers, the Reich will provide them with a completely equipped farm.

These soldier-farmers were to be armed, 'so that in case of danger they will be immediately available as an armed force'.[96]

Hitler rejected any attempt to educate the Russians:

> The German has made himself hated throughout the whole world, because wherever he appears he immediately begins to play the teacher. The other nations did not gain the slightest advantage from this, because the values they were offered were not values for them. The sense of duty the way we define it does not exist in Russia. Why should we want to educate the Russian to this? The 'Reichs farmer' will live in outstandingly beautiful settlements. The German offices and authorities will have wonderful apartments, the governors palaces. Around the offices all that is necessary for the maintenance of life will be built up. And around the city there is a ring of 30 to 40km of lovely villages, interconnected by the best roads. What comes next is the other world in which we will let the Russians live as they

like, only we control them. In case of a revolution we then only need to drop a few bombs on their cities and the matter is settled.

Since Hitler intended to evacuate the Russians, and did not include them in his development plans because they were racially 'inferior', the question arises where the people for the realization of his settlement plans were to come from. On the one hand, as we have seen, these were to be the *Kapitulanten*, on the other hand those 'Nordic' people who up to now had emigrated to America: 'We must not permit any Germanic person to go to America from Europe any longer. The Norwegians, Swedes, Danes, Dutchmen must all be channelled into the Eastern territories, these will become segments of the German Reich.'[97] And so the connection to Hitler's racial concepts becomes clear.

We could belittle such plans as the fantasies of a megalomaniac, but we should not forget that at the time, Hitler was closer to the possibility of their implementation than at any time before or after, and that in the end he was only prevented from converting them into reality by the united efforts of the whole world. On 19/20 August 1941 Hitler said in his monologues that the Ukraine and the Volga basin would one day in the future be the 'granary of Europe. We will harvest a multiple of what is now growing on this soil.'[98] Germany would, said Hitler on 17/18 September 1941, 'be a grain exporting country for all those in Europe who depend on grain. In the Crimea we have tropical fruit, rubber plants (with 40,000 hectares we will become independent), cotton. The Pripet Marshes will provide us with reed.'[99]

Hitler expected that 'a stream of people' would set off for the East, 'because for the farmer that countryside is beautiful which produces a lot'. In twenty years' time the migration from Europe would go east instead of to America as before. 'In the Black Sea we obtain an inland sea with an infinite wealth of fish. Through the soya beans in the Crimea we uplift animal husbandry. We will harvest a multiple of what the Ukrainian farmer is able to take from the soil today.'[100] As Koeppen noted, Hitler declared on 4 October 1941 that 'in 50 years there should be five million German farmsteads settled there [in the East—R.Z.]'. This was already necessary for military reasons, because that was the only way to control such a large continent.[101] All one needed to do was to increase the production of food in the Ukraine by 50 per cent, said Hitler on 12 November 1941, then it would still lie 30 per cent below the German average: 'With this we create a complete supply of bread for 25 to 30 million people additionally. The same applies to the Baltic states. Agriculture-wise they are surplus areas, but also Byelorussia. It would be ridiculous if we were not able to get this continent into shape!'[102] Time and again in his table talks Hitler projected his idea of the 'soldier-farmer' in the East[103] and talked of his conviction that the quality of the soil available there would motivate the farmers to settle in the East.[104] From the East, Hitler declared, 'we will take out ten to twelve million tonnes of grain each year'. In one hundred years, so went his vision of the future, 'millions of German farmers will live there!'[105]

This concept, which Hitler developed in his table talks, merged logically with his economic theories. Based on the incongruity between *Lebensraum* and population, in time an imbalance between agriculture and industry had developed which had required increased foreign trade activities. A large proportion of exports had been required to obtain the necessary food and raw materials in exchange. The new *Lebensraum* in the East removed this disparity between population and base of subsistence. As a supplementary agrarian territory it served to restore the proportionality of both sectors of the economy.

The conclusion from this chapter is that the plans to settle farmers in the East played a major role for Hitler but they cannot be cited as proof of a concept of 'reagrarianization' of German society. Above all, the function as the 'granary for Europe' was only one function of the Eastern *Lebensraum*. Besides that, it was also to serve as a source of raw materials and a market.

c. *Lebensraum* as a Source of Raw Materials

Let us recall. Turner claims that for Hitler the gaining of *Lebensraum* had had a

> ... one-sided purpose of agrarian policy ... Indications that in this context Hitler was also thinking about wider economic concepts and, for example, giving consideration to the possibility of gaining power and raw materials can at best be found in reports by contemporaries, but not in his own writings.[106]

This claim is all the more astonishing as there is much proof that Hitler also regarded the new *Lebensraum* as a source of raw materials. In his 'Second Book' he wrote that in Germany before the war 'the supply of raw materials to many an industry ... [ran into] serious difficulties' and could only be obtained from abroad, in other words by importation – a means which, as we know, Hitler rejected. Hitler regarded the acquisition of new territory as the best way of solving this problem. The size of the *Lebensraum* of the USA, above all the Americans' wealth of raw materials, was the reason for its economic superiority. The future of Germany in its present borders, however, must 'appear to be very dark and sad, particularly in view of the limitations of our own raw materials and the threatening dependence on other countries this leads to'. Hitler also saw the importance of Russia in terms of energy production, because he emphasized in his 'Second Book' that Russia was 'the owner of oil wells which today have the same importance as did iron and coal mines in the last century'.[107]

These statements show that the factor of raw materials played an important role in Hitler's thinking very early on. In a speech on 10 October 1928 he again addressed himself to the 'importance of the land problem' and discussed the reasons for the economic superiority of the USA and the Americans' higher standard of living. The reason was not to be found in the economic structure of the USA, but simply in the fact that America possessed 'sufficient wheat land, sufficient natural resources, gigantic forests, gigantic ore deposits, gigantic coal fields, gigantic oil well areas... in brief, America is the land of enormous natural resources'.[108] The *Lebensraum* in the East was to create a cohesive continental empire, whose wealth not only in arable land but also in raw materials and sources of energy would be comparable to that of the United States. When Hitler turned to the problem of the disparity between population and *Lebensraum*, he certainly did not only lament the lack of arable land, but also 'the lack of raw materials', which now had to be imported from abroad.[109]

Hitler repeatedly argued, in turning against the Marxists, that a different economic order could also not remove these deficits which resulted from insufficient territory: 'Man does not live by ideas, but by grain and corn, by coal, iron, ore, all of those things that lie in the land. And if this land is missing, all theories become useless. It is not a problem of the economy itself, but of the land.'[110] From such statements we see that *when Hitler spoke about the disparity between the base of subsistence and population, he did not in any way restrict this to the lack of arable land but just as much to the lack of necessary raw materials. For Hitler 'land' stood for both factors.*

At the end of June and in early July 1931 Hitler addressed the raw material problem in two speeches. He did not primarily explain the economic expansion he was criticizing in terms of the lack of food – he only mentioned this factor in second place – but in terms of the need to import the missing raw materials in exchange for industrial goods:

> That we were able to achieve the standard of living of the prewar period at all had to do with our having artificially extended the borders of our confined *Lebensraum*, in that we became accustomed to an economic order, or an economic system, which gave us the possibility of producing more of certain goods in Germany than we needed ourselves, and with the surplus of these goods, to bring in all that was lacking, what was not there but still needed then and now, that means to begin with, innumerable raw materials which we do not possess at all and which we need if we want to maintain our standard of living, which we would also like to measure against the standard of living of the nations around us. Innumerable raw materials our *Lebensraum* does not have; we must therefore acquire them...[111]

We know that Hitler rejected importation as the way of acquiring raw materials. A lasting solution could therefore only be provided by the acquisition of new *Lebensraum*, in order to gain these raw materials from his own land. On 3 July 1931 Hitler declared that the present *Lebensraum* was 'too poor in natural resources which today's industry requires as raw materials, in other words, the limited *Lebensraum* will force us again and again to search for relief'.[112] In 1931 Hitler also explained his concept of the conquest of *Lebensraum* in the East to Wagener in terms of the missing raw material base in Germany: 'And in addition Europe needs the grain, the meat, the wood, the coal, the iron, and the oil from Russia in order to be able to survive in the decisive battle against America.'[113]

Ernst Hanfstaengl, one of Hitler's closest intimates in the early years before the seizure of power and later his foreign press chief, reports on a meeting between Hitler and a Japanese professor which took place at the turn of the year 1931–32. In this conversation Hitler emphasized that both Japan and Germany needed 'raw materials which secured our independence from world markets and therefore our future as nations'.[114] In his foreign policy speech in the *Reichstag* on 17 May 1933 Hitler analyzed Europe's economic situation as follows: 'The present economic situation of Europe is characterized by overpopulation in western Europe and the poverty of the land in certain raw materials in this region, which are indispensable for securing the standard of living these regions with their ancient culture are accustomed to.'[115] In his speech in the *Reichstag* on 28 April 1939, in which he replied to a message from President Roosevelt, he again drew a comparison between Germany's limited and America's wide *Lebensraum*:

> You have a country with enormous wealth, all the natural resources, fertile enough to feed more than half a billion people and to supply them with everything they need ... The fertility of our country cannot be compared to the fertility of yours. Innumerable natural resources which nature has put at your disposal in unlimited amounts we lack.[116]

What Hitler did not add, of course, was that he was not prepared to accept this disparity between Germany and the USA, but that by the conquest of new *Lebensraum* in Russia he intended to create a continental empire in Europe which would be comparably rich in raw materials and would be in a position to confront the United States.

When, after the attack on Russia, the possibility of achieving this plan appeared to have become imminent, he not only spoke about the need to settle farmers in the East but just as much about the enormous economic perspectives which the possession of Russian raw material and energy resources would open up. On 19/20 August 1941 Hitler said during a table talk, '... we will also supply Europe with iron. If one day Sweden does not want to, fine, we will take it from the East'.[117] On 17 September 1941, as Koeppen noted, he spoke about

> ... the importance of the conquered ore region of Kriwoi-Rog. Even if the complete repair of the gigantic facilities may take as long as one year, exploitation of the ore deposits must be given priority and all efforts made. Production of about 1 million tonnes of iron and ore per month practically solves all the calamities in the area of supply, because some sort of relationship to the availability of iron in sufficient quantities exists to everything.[118]

About a week later he said, 'The land we are now opening up for ourselves is only a source of raw materials and a market, not a field for industrial production.'[119] With this Hitler obviously meant that the *Lebensraum* in the East was not to become a site for industrial plants producing finished goods.[120] What is important is that he specifically described the conquered territories as 'sources of raw materials'. A few weeks later, in a table talk on 13 October 1941, he again said that the conquered *Lebensraum* would make autarky possible for Europe:

> Where can we find an area with iron as rich as that of the Ukraine? Where nickel, coal, manganese, and molybdenum? These are the sources of manganese from which America still bought. In addition the possibility to plant oil and rubber plants! With 40,000 hectares under cultivation our total rubber requirement is satisfied.[121]

A few days later, on 18 October 1941, Hitler declared that the Russian lakes would provide Germany with 'inexhaustible reed plantations. Right on their shores, the factories for the refinement of the cellulose must be built.'[122] On 26/27 October 1941 he called the Ukraine a 'European India' and declared: 'Nobody is ever going to drive us out of the East! We had a monopoly in potash. We are now adding a monopoly in bread, coal, iron, wood.'[123]

On 26 October 1941 Koeppen noted the following: 'The *Führer* then said that this war would make Europe largely independent of the colonies. If earlier wars had already made us independent of sugar cane, Chile-saltpetre, indigo, quinine, this war would bring self-supply in india rubber, rubber, and cotton.'[124] And on 4 February 1942 Hitler declared that 'it is only common sense that tells us to go east ... In the East there is iron, coal, grain, wood ...'[125]

On 30 May 1942 Hitler gave a talk to future military leaders on the topic 'Was the Second World War Unavoidable?' In it he repeated his theory of the necessary balance between *Lebensraum* and population and emphasized, in this context, that he saw *Lebensraum* primarily as a source of raw materials:

> If one does not want to extend the *Lebensraum*, then one day a disparity must occur between population, which constantly grows, and *Lebensraum*, which stays the same. This is nature's intention: by this she forces man to fight, just like every other creature in the world. It is the battle for food, the battle for the foundations of life, for raw materials which the earth offers, the natural resources which lie within her, and the fruits she offers those who cultivate her.[126]

V: Hitler: An Opponent of Modern Industrial Society?

In these few sentences Hitler's socio-Darwinistic *Weltanschauung*, his theory of the link between population and *Lebensraum*, are clearly expressed, as well as the fact – and this is important in our context – that he regarded *Lebensraum* primarily in terms of raw materials and natural resources.

In a table talk on 9 August 1942 Hitler again mentioned the raw materials or mineral resources which made the East appear so valuable to him: 'Wood we have enough of, iron unlimited, the largest manganese deposits in the world, oil, everything is swimming in it!'[127] On 28 August 1942 he mentioned that he had now read a description 'according to which the Caucasus is certainly the richest area in mineral resources, it consists of primary rock, gneiss and granite. I did not know that there were nickel deposits there as well.'[128] How greatly impressed Hitler was by Russian raw material resources is also expressed in a lengthy conversation he had on 10 December 1942 with Mussert, the leader of the Dutch National Socialists: 'Gigantic raw materials were available in the East, regardless of whether one was thinking of agriculture or of ore. Russia was without doubt the richest country in the world. One need only think of the ore deposits in Kertch, of the oil reserves, the rare metals and so forth. In addition Russia had the most valuable raw material of all: human beings.'[129]

The purpose of the conquest of new *Lebensraum* in the East was sometimes even expressed quite openly in National Socialist propaganda. At an NSDAP rally on 17 November 1942 Goebbels, for example, explained the reasons for the war as follows:

> When we therefore advanced, and still continue to advance to the East, then not only for purely theoretical reasons, not only in order to save Europe [this was normally a favourite topic for NS propaganda—R.Z.]. If the issue were only Europe, we would love to hand Europe the responsibility for her own salvation. But rather, on top of all else, to extend our own *Lebensraum* . . . Now *we* want to possess the wheatfields on the Don and Kuban and with this have *our hand on the breadbasket of Europe*! We now want to possess the *oil wells* and the *iron and coal and manganese* deposits. *We* want to acquire a colonial possession on our own European territory and *that* is our limited objective . . .[130]

All of these statements show that while the Ukraine was certainly *also* to become the 'granary of Europe' for Hitler, and while the *Lebensraum* to be conquered *also* had the function of a supplementary agrarian territory as we have shown in the preceding chapter, that was not all there was to it. At least as important to him were the mineral resources and the raw materials, the iron ore, nickel, manganese, molybdenum, coal and, above all, the oil wells in Russia. The reason he needed these raw materials was, of course, for the supply of German industry, which was therefore to experience an enormous upswing.

This has nothing to do with a concept of de-industrialization or a 'reagrarianization utopia'. Perhaps Hitler's view that there should be no industrial production of finished goods in the East has contributed to this misunderstanding, a view which can only be understood within the context of his fundamental rejection of the export of capital. Before we turn to this topic, we will first discuss another function of the conquered Eastern territories. Hitler not only saw them as a supplementary agrarian territory, as sources of raw material and energy, but also as markets – an aspect which has been just as much overlooked as the one just discussed.

d. *Lebensraum* as a Market

Compared to its function as a supplementary agrarian territory and a source of raw materials, *Lebensraum* as a market was only of secondary importance for Hitler – at least, he only began to develop this perspective after the attack on the Soviet Union had been launched, when he announced his visions of the future shaping of the now conquered *Lebensraum* in his monologues at *Führer* headquarters.

His ideas on this topic show that he regarded the population of the Soviet Union as 'natives', a term he even used at one time or another. On 17/18 September 1941, for example, he said: 'We will send the Ukrainians headscarves, glass necklaces and whatever else pleases colonial peoples.'[131] The next day he declared:

> The sales possibilities for consumer and finished goods on the Russian market will give Saxon industry an unexpected upswing [Saxony was known for its many small manufacturers of trumpery—H.B.]. If one were then to put the indispensable alcohol and tobacco under a state monopoly, one would have the population in the occupied territories completely under control.[132]

This statement shows that, as a result of the conquest of *Lebensraum* in the East, Hitler was not in any way envisaging a reversal of the process of industrialization; on the contrary, he even expected an 'unexpected upswing' for Saxon industry. On 25 September 1941 he also specifically described the East as being a future 'sales territory' for German industry[133] – a sales territory, as he elaborated on 13 October 1941, not only for Germany, but for all of 'the nations we take into our economic order'. These were

> ... to share in the natural resources of the developed Eastern territories and should find the markets for their industrial production there. All we need to do is to open this perspective to them, and they will integrate themselves into our order. Once this territory is organized for Europe it will mean the end of all unemployment.[134]

V: Hitler: An Opponent of Modern Industrial Society?

On 14 February 1942, in a conversation with the Croatian ambassador Budak, Hitler said that the inhabitants of the Soviet Union lacked

> ... even the basics that were necessary to live. The people there do not even have the most simple pots and pans, the most simple tools, and during my drives through the country I have not seen one woman who had worn even the most modest jewellery. And all this in a country whose land was richer than any other in Europe. If we were once to regulate these territories, then the people there would acquire more than they had ever dreamt of, and in their masses would represent an enormous purchasing power for European products. It was ridiculous: there the Europeans ran all the way to Eastern Asia, to China or God knows where in order to find markets for their products and all the while there was now a market with almost unlimited possibilities opened right on Europe's borders.[135]

On 6 August 1942 Hitler again developed his inhumane concept of the total subjugation of the 'ridiculous hundred million Slavs', who had to be 'absorbed or driven out':

> At harvest time there will be a market held in all the larger hamlets where we will bring our trumpery. In the same market grain and fruit will be sold. When somebody has sold something he can immediately buy. Our products will achieve an equivalent which is notably higher that our manufacturing costs. The difference must be to the benefit of the Reich, so as to pay off the costs of the war in this way. The agricultural machine industry, other specialized industries, the transport industry, the consumer goods industry, receive a gigantic upswing. The cheapest and most garish calico is wonderful here.[136]

These and other statements show the degree to which Hitler, who was influenced to an astonishing degree by the stories of Karl May[137] [one of the most widely read German authors of adventure stories about his hero among the Indians, the Arabs, etc., abounding with the most primitive clichés about the 'natives'— H.B.], regarded the colonization of the East as a counterpart to the colonization of America, with the 'soldier-farmer' as the cowboy and the 'natives' as the Indian to whom one could sell cheap jewellery, trumpery, alcohol and tobacco. On 8 August 1942, during a table talk, Hitler's thoughts in this direction became perfectly clear:

> With the partisans there is a battle here as there was in the Indian wars in North America. The stronger race will win, and that is us... In the autumn, at all the train stations, we will have to set up a market on one side, like a German country fair, and next door to it to install a delivery station for grain. There must be everything there in the way of trumpery that you normally find with us out in the country. Saxony will experience an upswing in its industry like never before. We will have an export industry. There its creativity can engage itself yet once again.[138]

We do not need to discuss the inhumanity of Hitler's colonization plans – he himself variously describes himself as an opponent of humanity because it contradicted his socio-Darwinist concepts – but one aspect of Hitler's view is of interest in our context. When he spoke about an upswing of various special industries and the transport and consumer goods industries, when he repeatedly dreamt about the upswing German industry would experience with the conquest of *Lebensraum* in the East – on the one hand because of the infinitely broad raw material base, on the other as a market – none of this had anything to do with an 'agrarian utopia' or the desire to turn away from industrial society.

On the other hand, our results could lead to the conclusion that the theory of economic imperialism can contribute far more to the explanation of the National Socialist will to expand than so-called 'middle-class' historians have been willing to admit to date. The realization that for Hitler the conquest of *Lebensraum* in the East was not a means of 'reagrarianization', and that he specifically regarded Russia as a source of raw materials and a market, will certainly be drawn upon by Marxist historians as support for the thesis of a 'Fascist imperialism'. What speaks against such an interpretation is, as we have shown above, the argument that Hitler roundly rejected the exploitation of these sources of raw materials in the service of private capital profit interests and advocated instead that the economy in the East should be organized by the state from the very beginning. How far this would still permit an argument in the direction of 'state monopoly capitalism', cannot be discussed here. What should at least be noted is that Hitler, as his refusal to industrialize Russia demonstrates, clearly rejected the practice of capital export which was characteristic for the phase of monopoly capitalism.

e. The De-Industrialization of Russia

When Erich Koch, the Reichs Commissioner responsible for the Ukraine, was a luncheon guest of Hitler on 18 September 1941, Koeppen noted:

> The tendency of the *Führer*, who regards the destruction of the big Russian cities as the condition for the duration of our power in Russia, was further reinforced by the Reichs Commissioner, who wants to break up Ukrainian industry as far as possible in order to bring the proletariat back to the country.[139]

As already noted, Hitler also declared in his table talks that the conquered Eastern territories were 'for us only sources of raw material and markets, not a field for industrial production',[140] and this is also confirmed by Speer: 'According to his [Hitler's] will the occupied Eastern territories were later even to be de-industrialized, because industry promoted Communism, as he believed, and bred an undesired intelligentsia.'[141]

Here we already see a motive why Hitler rejected an industrialization of Russia. Industry and big cities, in Hitler's view, would reinforce and mobilize the possibilities of resistance and the will to resist of the enslaved 'natives'. Therefore industry, both heavy as well as consumer goods, was to continue to have its focus in Germany. There, as we have seen, however, it was to experience an upswing like never before. Again, therefore, Hitler's rejection of an industrialization of Russia has nothing to do with a fundamental anti-modernism, with a rejection of modern industrial society, but is derived from his concept of subjugation and enslavement, which would nip any possibility of resistance in the bud. And since a proletariat was more readily capable of solidarity and politics than the rural population, and the cities were always more likely to be the cells of revolutionary uprisings than the villages – at least, according to Hitler's way of thinking – he wanted to concentrate industry in the West as far as possible. 'As far as possible' means that Hitler was naturally not so naïve as to assume that the raw materials could be exploited without any plant at all. This is demonstrated, for example, by his remark on 18 October 1941, which we have already cited in another context, that 'The Russian lakes in particular would provide us with inexhaustible reed plantations. Right on their shores, the factories for the refinement of the cellulose must be built.'[142] The creation of an infrastructure was also a self-evident condition for the industrial exploitation of the Eastern territories:

> The region must lose the character of an Asian steppe, must be Europeanized! For this we are now building the great traffic lines in the southern tip of the Crimea to the Caucasus. Along these traffic lines the German cities will be strung like pearls on a string, and around these lies the German settlement.[143]

On 26 February 1942 he said he would build a 1,500km long autobahn in the occupied Eastern territories: 'This I will settle, like a string of pearls, every fifty to one hundred kilometres, in addition a few larger cities.'[144]

Hitler was therefore even in favour of building cities, and was planning the creation of a comprehensive infrastructure in the East – but only for the Germans and other settlers from Scandinavia, the Western countries and America. The 'natives' were to be 'sifted' according to racial criteria, i.e. 'the destructive Jew will be sent out completely', and those segments of the population of the Ukraine Hitler considered valuable were to be Germanized. 'There is only one task: to bring about a Germanization by taking in Germans and to regard the original inhabitants as Indians.'[145] The de-industrialization of Russian industry and the destruction of Russian cities was accompanied on the other side by the concept of the building of new German cities and the creation of an encompassing infrastructure. The concentration of industrial plant, however, was to take place in the centre of Europe, in the German Reich.[146]

In order to be able to understand Hitler's rejection of an industrialization of Russia, we must discuss his basic position on the export of capital, because his plans for the reduction of industry in occupied Russia are directly derived from his criticism of this. During our portrayal of Hitler's criticism of economic expansion we kept this aspect out of the discussion to a large degree because the topic there was primarily the export of goods. Here we now intend to briefly describe why Hitler opposed the export of capital.

Aside: Hitler's Criticism of the Export of Capital

We have seen in the context of Hitler's criticism of economic expansion that he believed that the export of capital from the industrialized countries to the underdeveloped countries would increase the rate of their industrialization even further, leading to an increasing limitation of the world market. Such a 'system of branch companies', Hitler continued in his 'Second Book', was being

> ... created more and more in those countries out of purely capitalistic interests ... But what must be considered here: the German nation, for example, has a vital interest in building ships to China in German shipyards, because thereby a certain number of people of our nationality are given the possibility of obtaining an amount of food which they would not possess out of our own no longer sufficient land. But the German nation has no interest in, let us say, a German finance group or a German company setting up a so-called branch shipyard in Shanghai, which then builds ships for China using Chinese labour and foreign steel, even if the company itself thereby makes a certain profit in the form of interest or dividends. Quite the opposite, because the result of this will only be that the German finance group will receive so and so many millions, but the German national economy will lose a multiple of this amount because of the orders lost.

Hitler also believed that the 'purely capitalistic interests' were dominating the economy more and more, and that the system of branch companies would therefore continue to spread.[147]

In his line of argument Hitler is therefore differentiating between the general interests of the German nation and the special interests of certain capitalist enterprises. And where the export of capital lies solely in the interest of a profit maximization for capitalist enterprises, and not in the interest of the German nation, Hitler rejects it. The conclusion from this is that in a National Socialist state, in which capitalist interests are no longer decisive but where the 'primacy of politics' has been established, capital export must be reduced more and more. In a speech on 26 June 1931 Hitler again used the example of a factory in Shanghai and complained that the

V: Hitler: An Opponent of Modern Industrial Society?

formation of such branch companies 'can possess a capitalistic interest, but must be harmful to the German nation'.[148]

In a meeting of the Economic Committee of the Reichs government on 24 April 1933, where the German positions for the world economic conference in London were to be decided, Hitler lamented the fact that

> ... during the last twenty years we have given up principles which formerly led to the building up of our economy. One of these, for example, is the bringing of manufacturing to the site where the raw materials are to be found. If this export of the means of production is continued without limits, then the conditions for life of European industry will simply cease.[149]

Hitler therefore recommended that one of the objectives for Germany's negotiations at the world economic conference should be an agreement between the industrialized nations for the 'limitation of the export of the means of production', i.e. the limitation of the export of capital.[150]

Hitler's rejection of any industrialization of the *Lebensraum* to be conquered was therefore the outcome of a general scepticism about the consequences of capital export to the underdeveloped countries. The reasons that led Hitler to take this position became particularly clear in a table talk on 25 September 1941:

> The British have industrialized India to their own detriment. The result: unemployment is rising in England, the British worker is becoming impoverished. The millions of unemployed in America! One would need to begin a whole new economic policy there, give up the gold standard, and instead set up a production domestically.

From this line of reasoning Hitler drew the conclusion already mentioned, that for Germany the *Lebensraum* in the East was 'not a field for industrial production'.[151]

The same argument can be found in another table talk on 31 January 1942. Hitler again cites the example India and Britain, and we should note that Hitler frequently described Russia as being Germany's India, i.e. it was to have the same economic function that India had for Britain, although he did not to want to repeat one important mistake. Hitler agreed that Britain should regard India as a market, for calico for instance, just as Russia was to be a market for Germany, but added:

> In this the calico was initially delivered from Britain. Only later did they build factories over there. They took the capitalistic point of view. The discontinuation of the shipping and the cheap labour would bring, so they believed, an increase in profit which they should not miss. For this Britain today has an army of unemployed numbering two and a half million![152]

309

As can be seen from the last two quotations, Hitler believed that industrial production should be 'located . . . inside', instead of furthering the industrialization of the colony or the pseudo-colony (which was what the *Lebensraum* in the East meant to Hitler). The reason was that while it might offer advantages for a capitalist enterprise to set up branch companies on the spot because there was cheap labour there and shipping costs could be saved, this would, as the example of Britain had demonstrated, lead to unemployment in the home country.

It now becomes clear that Hitler's rejection of an industrialization of Russia was not derived from a rejection of industrial society, but out of his fundamental scepticism towards the export of capital, which in the end would lead to unemployment at home. The sites of industrial production were to be concentrated in Germany, and were to undergo an enormous upswing, both because of the almost unlimited raw materials and energy reserves in the *Lebensraum* conquered in the East, and because of the new sales possibilities there.

We have now discussed the various economic functions of *Lebensraum* in the East. It should be noted here that *Lebensraum* also had functions for Hitler outside the sphere of economics. He also advocated the theory that as large a *Lebensraum* as possible would be of decisive military-geographic importance in the future.[153] Our reason for discussing the functions of *Lebensraum* in such detail is that the settlement of farmers and the de-industrialization Hitler intended are cited as *the* proof for the 'agrarian utopia' Hitler allegedly advocated, and for his opposition to modern industrial society.

2. Hitler's Position on Modern Industrial Society

Independently of the question of the economic functions of *Lebensraum* in the East, in this chapter we intend to discuss Hitler's position on industrial society and attempt to determine whether we can discover a fundamental rejection by him of modern industrial society, permitting us to claim that Hitler was pursuing 'anti-modernistic' objectives.

a. Positive Remarks by Hitler about Modern Industrial Society
The Constant Increase of the Standard of Living as a Premise
Hitler's position on modern industrial society, on technology and on mass production cannot be adequately interpreted without first knowing his criticism of 'an undemanding nature' and his thesis of the constant increase of the standard of living caused by the dynamics of constantly rising needs.

On 6 March 1927 Hitler again spoke about the contradiction between population and the base of subsistence, and in this context attempted to refute the view that an adjustment of both factors could be achieved by means of 'domestic colonization', by the extension and intensification of agriculture. Hitler argued that whatever a nation might gain through domestic colonization would be 'more than made up for by the nation increasing its own demands unendingly over the years, the individual not being so undemanding, the individual having greater needs, so that what comes out of the soil in addition is vanquished by the increased needs'. This development was not only to be noted in Germany, but all over the world.[154]

About three weeks later Hitler repeated this line of argument in more detail in a speech. Here, too, he opposed the view that the contradiction between population and base of subsistence could be solved by means of, for example, artificial fertilizer. While production had in fact been greatly increased by this, it had still not been sufficient to feed the increased population:

> Why? Because in the course and changes of time not only did the number of people increase, but also the needs of the individual human being grew, in other words what has been cultivated out of the soil in the way of an increase at best serves to satisfy the needs of the individual which are constantly growing. The needs of the ancestors, let us say in this city one hundred years ago, were only a fraction of those it has today. We do not become aware of this, but that is still the way it is. Man constantly makes greater demands, and the non-fulfilment of the greater demands is felt more painfully today than eighty years ago, when they were perhaps not there yet. But it is a specific undoing which drives man forward. He sees the peaks of his society and constantly wanders after them like an army. In front are the scouts, then the advance guard and behind it the army, behind that the train comes, and so too the people, they have their points before them. Perhaps 300 years ago these points did not yet have all that in the way of natural products and the goods of life, which the people of today have on average. Today man does not look back, but ahead, towards the points of today.[155]

Hitler apparently believed in a natural law according to which man's needs and demands are constantly rising. He had already developed this thesis in *Mein Kampf*[156] and also advanced it in his 'Second Book'. There, however, he added a further argument:

> Here a standard of living is created as an example, primarily by the knowledge of the conditions and life in the American Union. Just as the needs of life in the countryside increase by the gradual knowledge and influence of life in the big cities, so do the needs of life of whole nations increase under the influence of life in better situated wealthier nations. Often a nation feels a standard of living to be insufficient which only thirty years ago would have appeared as a maximum, simply because it has learned about the standard of living of another nation . . . The more space is bridged by modern technology and especially by traffic, and the nations move closer together, the more intensive their mutual relations become, the more

311

will their living conditions rub off on each other and attempt to balance each other out. The opinion that a nation with a certain cultural potential and also an actual cultural importance can be kept below an otherwise generally accepted standard of living in the long run by an appeal to insights or an ideal is wrong. The broad masses, in particular, will seldom develop an understanding for this.[157]

Let us summarize Hitler's line of argument. Man's tendency towards a constant increase of his needs, which has always existed, was being substantially heightened today because, due to the development of the international communications network, the example of others, particularly that of the USA, was increasing the demands of other industrial nations and reinforcing the clamour of the masses for a constant increase of the standard of living. Hitler himself was, as we shall see, an admirer of the technical and industrial capabilities of the United States and the high standard of living these permitted.

As he underlined on 26 June 1931, Hitler started off from the fact that 'our nation has achieved a certain standard of living and regards any slip downwards from this standard of living as an intolerable hardship'. He added that the justice of such a view of the nation could not be denied.[158] At the Congress of the General Council of the Economy on 20 September 1933 he declared that the issue was

> ... above all to fight against the ideology of the lack of needs and the systematic reduction of needs, in other words against the cult of primitiveness emanating from Communism. This Bolshevist ideal of the gradual regression of the demands of civilization must inevitably lead to the destruction of the economy and all of life ... The issue is not that everybody practises restriction but that everybody tries to move forward and to improve themselves. The German economy can only survive based on a certain defined level of needs and a very specific cultural demand by the German nation.[159]

Hitler also rejected this 'theory of primitiveness' in his speech on 15 February 1936 at the International Automobile and Motor Cycle Show in Berlin. While all new inventions initially benefited only a limited group of people and were therefore seen as 'luxury articles', after a certain time the former luxury articles became the most natural thing in the world for the masses. 'It is just as little unsocial to buy an automobile as it was formerly unsocial to replace the traditional oiled skin in one's window with a piece of modern glass. In practical application as well, the development of such an invention inevitably begins with a few, in order then to draw ever larger circles, and gradually to embrace everybody.' This also applied to the automobile, which in future would have to develop from a luxury article into a mass product. For Hitler the automobile industry was 'promising and full of opportunity to an unheard of degree', which he again proved using the United States as an example, where there were already 23 million motor cars in circulation and a further three to four million being produced annually, whereas in Germany the actual number was just under 450,000 and the number produced in 1932 only 46,000. In this context he criticized the German industrialists who had not recognized that

> ... the motor car must become an instrument of the general public, or else the development possibilities slumbering in it will not arrive. The motor car is either an expensive luxury object for a selected few, and therefore not of any real importance to the economy in the long run, or it should really give the economy an enormous upward drive, which it is capable of doing from its very nature, but then it must develop from a luxury object of a selected few into a consumer object for everybody.

This could only happen if the 'purchase, running, and maintenance cost of this car were brought into a tolerable relationship to the income of the broad masses of our nation, as we can see this having already been solved in America as such a brilliant example'.[160]

Here Hitler's thesis of the necessity for a constant increase in the standard of living is demonstrated by a practical example. This, however, applied not only to the consumer goods industry but also, for example, to the possibilities of tourism. In his table talks he said on 27/28 September 1941:

> In future every worker will have his vacation, a few days that belong to him alone, and once or twice in his lifetime he will also be able to take his ocean cruise. It is wrong to say: 'No, for God's sake, the people will lose their undemanding nature!' An undemanding nature is the enemy of all progress. In this we resemble the Americans in that we are demanding, whereas a Spaniard, for example, prefers to make do with a few olives a day just so that he does not have to do any work at all.[161]

On 2 February 1942 Hitler spoke with admiration about the modern methods of production of the Americans and railed against the opinion that

> ... such an increase in production methods had to lead to the workers' becoming breadless. Yes, but this consequence only happens if I do not create relief by increasing the standard of living in another area! Man was primarily a farmer, he made his things himself. He did not produce more than he needed himself. In the measure to which he succeeded in improving his methods, he was able to spare individual people and shift them over to the crafts. Seen from the larger view, the German nation has only twenty-seven per cent of its population working the soil, everything else something else. And in the crafts it then went the same way. By the application of genius to the methods of production people were spared everywhere. And now the foolish thinking began. The standard of living should not be raised further! Whereas progress lies in life being made more pleasant for the

people! As long as the food supply is secured! Then I cannot spare too many people! I simply build double the length of the stretch of autobahn, if I now need only half as many for a result which only a few years ago required double the number of workers.[162]

On 5 July 1942 in table talks Hitler came to speak about

... the extraordinary lack of demand of the people in southern Italy ... In such a lack of demand there lies a great danger. Because since the majority of mankind tends towards idleness, it loses the desire to do anything far too easily when it sees that one can also live without all that.[163]

In a speech at the end of June 1944 Hitler said that the demands of the people were the

... nourishment of industry. This is the condition for the life of the economy. Take a nation that has no demands, then you can pack up three-quarters of the economy. If you succeed in constantly awakening new needs, and on the other side making it clear to the individual that he will only achieve the satisfaction of these needs by work, time and again by work, then we will gradually increase the standard of living of our nation, and many elements that formerly had a class-rending or destructive effect, acted in a society-destroying way, will then become class-uniting in the course of time.[164]

Such statements by Hitler, his whole theory of the constantly rising needs and the demand for the constant increase of the standard of living he derives from this support the thesis that 'Hitler's genuine achievement in economic policy' had been 'the recognition of the legitimating function of a consumption-orientated policy of full employment'.[165] One of the deficits of many of the portrayals of the reality of the Third Reich is that the orientation towards consumption, which the regime deliberately fostered, has largely escaped notice. It is an achievement of the study by Hans Dieter Schäfer (*The Split Consciousness*) to have moved these formerly unnoticed aspects of the reality of National Socialism into our field of vision: 'With private home, car/trailer, radio/television, camera, kitchen machines, detergents, hygiene/cosmetics etc., values were propagated during the rearmament boom, which our consciousness almost completely associates with the twenties or the Adenauer period.'[166] The key importance the regime assigned to the satisfaction of private consumer needs can be proved by the fact that – as opposed to the situation in Great Britain – even under the burden of 'total war' civilian production was not substantially reduced: in 1944 it was still at 93 per cent of the level of 1938.[167] Speer's assignment in 1941 to increase armaments capacity was subsequently restricted by an order from Hitler 'to again increase the manufacture of products for the general supply of the population'.[168]

V: Hitler: An Opponent of Modern Industrial Society?

Let us summarize. Hitler's theory that the constant increase in the standard of living was a necessary law of modern industrial society disproves the view that he had only made use of industrial society under duress because he needed it for the war and that his ultimate objective had been the realization of an anti-modernistic agrarian utopia.[169] Such an intention would have been irreconcilable with Hitler's concepts – in Hitler's own words, the expression of 'a cult of primitiveness', an ideology of 'lack of demands' or the expression of the 'Bolshevist ideal of the gradual regression of the demands of civilization'. It should be noted here that Hitler regarded the constant rise of the standard of living as 'an objective' law and also, as his statements clearly show, that he welcomed it – not because he saw the increase of material well-being as the possibility of increasing individual happiness but because he regarded the constant increase of needs as a sort of 'barb' which preserved people from passivity and thereby finally followed the law of the 'eternal battle' which he defined in socio-Darwinistic terms. Hitler's objective – and this will be stressed again at the end of this chapter – was not, as Turner claims, the return to a 'mystically and eclectically prepared past' and a 'flight from the modern world'.[170] Quite the opposite. His example was the highly technical industrial society of the United States, of which he was contemptuous because it lacked culture, and whose capitalist economic system he criticized but whose industrial power he nonetheless admired.

The Highly Industrialized Economy of the USA as an Example

In his 'Second Book' Hitler writes that 'the size and wealth' of the American domestic market permit 'production figures, and thereby production plants, which make the product so cheap that despite the enormous wages it no longer appears possible [for the European powers—R.Z.] to underbid them':

> [The] size of its own domestic market, the wealth of the same in purchasing power, but again also in raw materials [guarantee] the American automobile industry its sales figures . . . which already permit methods of manufacture which would be impossible in Europe because of the lack of these domestic sales possibilities. The result is the enormous export capabilities of the American automobile industry. And what we are dealing with here is the general motorization of the world, an issue, therefore, with an importance for the future that is immeasurable. Because the replacement of human and animal power by the motor is still at the beginning of its development, the end cannot even be imagined today.

We have already seen that Hitler was of course not prepared to accept this superiority of the USA fatalistically. The conquest of *Lebensraum* in the East was intended to create just as large a domestic market and just as broad a base of raw materials for Germany as the USA already possessed, which would then result in Germany also being able to create modern production facilities and to achieve huge production figures (for example, in the automobile industry). As well as the size of the *Lebensraum* and the wealth of raw materials, Hitler also advanced a third argument for the superiority of the USA – a 'racial' one. The contradiction between population and base of subsistence in the European countries had resulted in emigration to the USA, which had thereby received the racially valuable 'Nordic forces of Europe'. Emigration, according to Hitler's firm belief, 'necessarily [draws] the more resistant, daring and determined people out of the body of our nation' and thereby worsens the racial mix in Germany, or the European countries, to the same degree that it provides the USA with top people. 'The American Union is not by coincidence the country in which at present by far the most, sometimes unbelievable, inventions are being made. America as a young, racially selected nation stands before ancient Europe which has lost infinitely much of its best blood through wars and emigration.' And of course Hitler did not intend to accept this fact either. His solution was, on the one hand, that new *Lebensraum* had to be conquered in order to solve the disparity between population and base of subsistence, and thereby to remove the need for emigration to the USA or to direct emigration to the East; and on the other hand the European countries had to follow 'a deliberate national racial policy because only this could save them from losing the initiative to America'.[171]

Furthermore, in the high degree of social mobility of American society, and in the fact that there the members of the lower classes were given far better chances for advancement, Hitler saw one of the major reasons why 'during the past decades the wealth of important inventions increased so extraordinarily, especially in North America'.[172] Hitler concluded that here as well Germany had to follow the example of the United States and improve the chances for social advancement. He was therefore orientating himself towards the industrially highly developed United States with its 'unbelievably daring inventions' and attempting not only to analyze but finally also to remove the reasons for this superiority, so that Germany or Europe could break American superiority in this field.

Major Engel, Army adjutant to Hitler from 1938 to 1943, noted in his diary on 5 September 1938:

> During a walk F. [the *Führer*—R.Z.] talked at length about the traffic problems in the world and claimed that the development of cars and the increase of production would lead in less than ten years to the roads no longer being sufficient to handle the traffic. He had attached very specific concepts to the creation of the VW plant. It was not only to be a good source of foreign currency for the Reich, but above all to replace the worker's bicycle. He would not rest until, in the course of the years,

production had reached such a level that, in a time he would like to live to see, at least every skilled worker would have his Volkswagen. The time would come when via the motorcycle – which, by the way, he did not like at all – the small car would even replace the bicycle. These would only still be ridden by boys and little girls. The extension of the autobahn was going far too slowly for his liking, but it could simply not be done faster because the steel and armaments industry had to be kept in mind as well. One country besides himself had so far recognized the traffic problem and that was the United States. There they had already begun some years ago to build large bypasses around the cities. Above all they had built multi-lane roads, while in Germany, because of the antiquated means of transport, as the horse was called, whole companies of district administrators were fighting like crazy to hold on to the summer lanes. He would sort out this ridiculous view and he had already given orders to the Go leaders. In 50 years the horse would only still be an object for parade in the Army, or be gazed at with the same amazement by the youth in zoos and circuses, as the camel and the elephant are today.[173]

These statements show not only Hitler's enthusiasm for the automobile but also his orientation towards the USA, which, he asserts, is the only country to have recognized the substantial traffic problems which would result from its inevitable development.

On 2 February 1942 Hitler demanded in his table talks that an increase of production had to be achieved in the area of coal and ore because the whole of industry was based on coal and iron. To achieve this increase, however, more modern and more rational methods were required:

On this alone are the great successes of America based. They produce the same amount as we do with a third of our human effort! We have always said: German craftsman's work. They wanted to make people believe that this was something unachievable. That is all bluff. A big modern press will stamp that out for me with an accuracy that is not possible at all with our handiwork. They also run their automobile factories with a minimum of people. The first German factory of that kind would have been the Volkswagen plant. We are still a long way away from where the Americans are! ... The whole thing is work by automats, therefore they can also hire any idiot. Training, that is unnecessary there![174]

Hitler's admiration for the modern American methods of mass production was quite distinct from the anti-modernistic criticism of such advanced manufacturing methods, which was also popular within the circles of the 'conservative revolution'. Whereas Fried, for example, complained that in American goods 'no human work is in there any longer' (?!), compared 'America's incapability of quality' – for which he mentioned the American automobile industry so much admired by Hitler as an example – with German quality work and drew the conclusion that 'American principles cannot be transferred to German business, principles of mass, of rational logic, not of tradition, feeling, quality',[175] Hitler's statement that 'we are still a long way away from where the Americans are' clearly demonstrates that the highly industrialized American society was the benchmark for his efforts and objectives.

We must emphasize that this does not mean that Hitler admired American society or 'culture'. On the contrary, it was the technical and industrial development which fascinated him. He therefore also criticized the nature of German polemics against the United States when in the National Socialist press, for example, the Americans' technical standards and degree of industrialization were portrayed negatively. On 27 March 1942 he dictated a direct order to the correspondents on how the polemics against the USA were to be conducted and which arguments should not be used:

> It has recently been observed repeatedly that unsuitable arguments have been used in the polemics against the USA. What we cite against this nation is primarily its total lack of culture. The disgusting adulation of film stars, for example, demonstrates a general lack of truly great ideals. The extreme degree of sensationalism, which does not even shrink back from the most revolting displays such as female boxing, wrestling in filth and mud, the public showing of freaks, the parading of the relatives of particularly vile criminals and such things is telling proof of the lack of culture in this country. In view of this fact, we deny Mr Roosevelt the right to sit in judgement over Germany. This is the line of argument that should dominate our accounting with this hypocrite. It is completely wrong, however, to ridicule the attempts at the development of civilization in the United States. What is decisive in contrast is that progress has not found its most noble field of cultivation and achieved its greatest successes in the USA but here with us in the Reich.[176] Germany has the best roads in the world, the fastest cars are built here. This has been clearly demonstrated by the results of the great international races. German scientists and inventors have created new elements which are being ridiculed in the USA of all places.[177]

This decree from Hitler to the correspondents shows once again that he was an adherent of industrial progress, that he envied the Americans and that he was attempting to keep pace with their development and outdo them. This is exactly the opposite of dreaming about pre-industrial conditions and the perfect world of an agrarian utopia.

Hitler on Industrialization and Technical Advancement
In a speech on 6 March 1927 Hitler described the process of industrialization and its social consequences:

> You have to imagine that there was a day when there were no factory workers in our nation. Only gradually was small craftsmanship driven out. In place of the little sewing needle and the little tools grew the factories. Now this was not in itself a

misfortune for mankind, but a stroke of luck. Today you will not find a poor little hut in which there is no window pane. Three hundred years ago window panes were a rarity. Why? Machines make it possible that today this can be manufactured so cheaply that everybody can have this today. When you go outside today you see bottles stuck into the gardens. They are used to border flower beds with and so forth. Such a bottle was a rare piece a 100 years ago, which equated to the work of many days. Today they are used to decorate the gardens. There was a time, barely 80 years ago, when only 70 per cent of the people had boots, and these only wore boots on Sundays. And there were only a few per cent who had more than one pair of boots. The ratio between the wages of labour and the output of labour is continually becoming smaller.[178]

In further discussion Hitler turns to the social consequences of this process of industrialization, to the development of the proletariat, the indifference of the middle class to it, the development of class conflict etc. These were the negative results of industrialization. We have already portrayed Hitler's criticism in detail in Chapter III.3.a/b. What is important in this context is that Hitler regards the process of modernization or industrialization *itself* very positively. It is not a misfortune but a 'stroke of luck' for mankind, because it permits the increase of the standard of living. The 'misfortune' only begins the moment the bourgeoisie starts to ruthlessly exploit the proletariat, to resist the justified demands of the workers, such as a reduction of overlong working hours etc.

On 26 June 1927 Hitler again came back to his favourite topic, the inevitable motorization of the world: 'We are living in an age of the motorization of the world . . . The motorization of the world is making enormous progress. It creeps into cities and villages. More and more it is beginning to replace the power of man and the animal with the power of the motor-driven machine.' This 'whole upheaval, whose extent we are no longer even able to imagine' was the work of the Aryan, who was the only one who was a creator of culture.[179]

In literature the picture still prevails that Hitler had been the representative of a reactionary or anti-modernistic faction within the NSDAP, whereas Otto Strasser had led the progressive and socialist wing. This erroneous opinion will have to be corrected once we have understood the following controversy of the definition of progress as Strasser himself reports it. In his report about the dispute with Hitler on 22 May 1930 Strasser writes that he had told Hitler that 'I had to deny the so-called progress of mankind to begin with, because I was unable to regard the invention of the toilet as a work of culture.' To this Hitler had replied: 'You certainly cannot deny that mankind has developed enormously, starting from the Stone Age to today's marvels of technology.' Strasser objected that he did not believe in the progress of man and was of the opinion that 'man has been and will remain unchanged for millennia, even if his outer appearance changed'. Turning polemically to Hitler he asked him whether he actually believed that 'Goethe had been "retarded" because he did not drive a car, or Napoleon, because he had not yet listened to the radio. What we call progress I regard – following my law of the triune bipolarity – as being various stages of an ageing process, whereby it was only a relative term whether this was called progress'. Hitler had replied to this that 'all of this was deskbound theories because practical life actually did prove day by day the gigantic progress of mankind, which always only received its impulses from great individuals'.[180]

This dispute points up a substantial difference between Hitler's *Weltanschauung* and the historic view of the 'left wing' National Socialists, who were strongly influenced by conservative-revolutionary ideologists like Moeller van den Bruck and Spengler. Unlike Hitler, Strasser recognized no progress in history but appealed to the so-called 'law of the triune bipolarity'. According to this, history was a series of alternating swings of the pendulum between 'liberalism' and 'conservatism' which repeated itself every 150 years as a natural law. This 'theory', which Strasser defined as an 'extension of Spengler's teachings',[181] was just as irreconcilable with Hitler's belief in progress and optimism for the future as was Spengler's prophecy of the 'Decline of the Occident', against which Hitler held forth on various occasions.[182] Hitler's appeal to progress, which he saw primarily in the development of technology, shows that he stood in the tradition of those concepts of the nineteenth century which had been rejected so determinedly by the conservative-revolutionary theorists and their adherents among the National Socialists.[183]

Hitler once said to Wagener, 'Remember Faust! A Faustian will, a Faustian definition of nature and its forces, the possibilities of technology and human genius – these must be the true characteristics of an awakening new age.'[184] In an interview with Associated Press correspondent Louis P. Lochner Hitler again turned to the topic of the value of great technical inventions and declared that the purpose and objective of any progress had to be to make a nation, all of humanity, happier.[185] Such an appeal to 'progress' has nothing in common with a point of view that is culturally pessimistic and critical of civilization.

We have mentioned Hitler's belief in the future of the car and the automobile industry several times, and he gave his opinions about this subject very often.[186] On 19 October 1941, in table talks, he spoke about the necessity of a unified standardization in the technical area:

> Why do we need a hundred different shapes of wash basins in the German Reich? Why the differences in the measurements of doors and windows? Every time you move into a new apartment you have to buy a new set of curtains! For my car I find spare parts everywhere, but not for my apartment. The reason is the possibility of

earning money with something new, which is offered by patterns of usage, patterns of taste and patent law. In one, two years this nonsense must stop! ... The desire to provide our millions with a higher level of living forces us to standardize and to use standardized building blocks wherever individual design is not necessary.[187]

Hitler was generally in favour of technical innovations. One had to pay attention that 'the penchant for inertia of conservative life did not gain power over the striving for the development of new technical possibilities,' he said on 28/29 January 1942. 'Need forces us to always keep to the forefront as far as technical progress is concerned; it alone secures the lead!'[188] On 9 February 1942 Hitler admitted: 'I am, and I say this quite openly, a fool for technology. He is always in the front who comes along with amazing technical innovations.'[189] With Hitler we can almost speak of a 'technology freak'. He wanted to 'technologize' all the areas of life where this was at all possible. On 28 February 1942, for example, he spoke about his intention 'as soon as there is peace, to build one million homes every year for five years ... And there we must make sure that the achievements of technology are finally also applied where they are still completely lacking to date: the housewife has to be given relief!' Hitler then painted the picture of a modern, fully mechanized home:

> Not only that the apartment blocks have the kindergarten in the immediate vicinity, the housewife should no longer be required to bring the youngsters there herself, she presses a button and the nurse appears to fetch the children. The housewife should furthermore no longer be required to carry refuse and garbage from the kitchen down the stairs, or to bring up the heating material: all this must be taken care of by appliances in the apartment itself. The alarm which wakes her up in the morning should also simultaneously boil the water that is required for breakfast, and whatever else there is in the way of such means of making life easier. I have a man who is only waiting for me to tell him to modernize housekeeping technologically. Robert Ley is waiting to employ his means in this direction![190]

In a table talk on 11 May 1942 Hitler addressed the subject of the building of the underground in Munich and declared, in this context, that 'it always depends on exploiting all the technical possibilities in order to shape or to preserve the appearance of a city'.[191]

As far as waging war was concerned, Hitler did not share the view that the fighting spirit of the troops was all that mattered and that technology was secondary by comparison:

> In war he always proved himself to be the best – that means the most successful soldier –who disposed of and had mastered the newest technical means, not only of attack, but also of transport and supply. An 'either/or', either soldier or technician, was about the most impossible thing there was in war. Therefore also

only that strategy was really good which developed technology and its application to the peak.[192]

In a table talk on 28 July 1942 he said that it had been a mistake during the First World War to have refused freeing the labour force required to build tanks as late as 1917, just as it had been too late to have discharged roughly 80,000 workers for the building of submarines only in 1918. With this the military leadership had committed a 'cardinal mistake, because it had renounced an improvement in the technology of war in favour of the manpower volume of the *Wehrmacht*'. But what is decisive for victory in any war is that one always 'possesses the technically superior weapons'.[193]

Despite these insights into the importance of technology for modern warfare, Hitler sometimes did not recognize the usefulness of technical innovations. The best known example is his mistaken decision concerning the Me 262, Germany's first jet fighter, whose production he initially forbade, probably because his negative experiences with the He 177 heavy bomber had made him sceptical of all new prototypes.[194] Such mistaken decisions on Hitler's part are certainly not an expression of an anti-modernistic rejection of technology. On the other hand, there were many cases in which he recognized the importance of a technical innovation, or of its effect on military tactics, sooner than the majority of the military professionals. He took the decision to set up integrated independently operating panzer divisions and armies against the opinion of the overwhelming majority of the professionals. During the first two years of the war the new army formations, which in 1938 only the German Army possessed, proved themselves to be weapons which decided campaigns, and they were later copied by all of the other armies. Haffner has called their creation 'Hitler's personal achievement and his greatest contribution in the military field'.[195]

On the other hand, Hitler appears not to have recognized the importance of scientific research for the development of the technology of war to the necessary degree, as Ludwig has pointed out in his study 'Technology and Engineers in the Third Reich'.[196] Hitler attached more importance to suggestions for the improvement of weapons technology which came directly from the troops.[197] Most probably this position resulted from the initially prevalent '*Blitzkrieg* strategy' and the subsequent insight that Germany had to avoid a lengthy war of material and attrition. From this perspective, the decision in favour of technical improvements and innovations applicable in the short term, and against systematic basic research which could only have been made practicably applicable in the long term, becomes understandable.

When, on the occasion of the transfer of Todt's offices to Speer, Hitler insistently advised the young architect to cling to proven methods, and above

V: Hitler: An Opponent of Modern Industrial Society?

all to draw primarily on 'technicians' in the armaments industry, we may take this as an attempt to create a 'primacy of technology'. At the end of July 1942 Hitler even agreed with a decree according to which the supervisory boards of armaments companies were only permitted to contain a maximum of 20 to 30 per cent members from banks or the legal profession, whereas the majority had to consist of experts from the industry.[198] While such decrees, and the statements cited above, demonstrate that Hitler was aware of the importance of technology and technicians for modern warfare, we must also note that, quite independently of military considerations, he was generally fascinated by the promise technology held for the future. He clung to his autobahn project even though the military experts were unanimously sceptical of its military value.[199] When he declared on 18 July 1942 in his table talks how much 'the autobahns had become dear to his heart',[200] he was not referring, as Ludwig has rightly pointed out, 'to the attack possibilities of an aggressive war policy, but to a belated manifestation of the technical design interests of his own youth'.[201] His enthusiasm for the possibilities of technology surfaced during his election campaign trips in 1932. Hitler was the first speaker at elections who travelled by aeroplane, a fact that was extensively exploited by NS propaganda. Even in his evening table talks during the war he categorically maintained that, as compared to the ship, the future certainly belonged to the aircraft,[202] and on 13 June 1943 he prophesied during one of his evening monologues at *Führer* headquarters that 'Today technology is still facing an enormous development.'[203]

Such statements in particular demonstrate the fundamental difference between Hitler's modernistic *Weltanschauung* and the anti-modernism of many representatives of that prevailing trend of the times called 'conservative revolution'. Quite in opposition to Hitler, many supporters of this school of thought believed that in the twentieth century the classic age of epoch-making inventions had passed and that mankind could now basically only continue to exploit the technical solutions already known.[204] The global economic crisis appeared to be a manifestation of the fact that the development of industrial technology was, in principle, over, and over-production and mass unemployment were seen as being clear indicators of this by the representatives of this school of thought.[205]

While Hitler also succeeded in exploiting this trend for his purposes, and in 'instrumentalizing' such anti-modernistic motives for his battle against 'the system', he did so without really identifying himself with their teachings. This led to massive disappointment among the members of this school of thought. Werner Sombart may serve as an example: in 1934 he noted sceptically that, among the National Socialists, 'quite a lot have still not recognized the demonic

323

power of technology and believe in it and its marvels and therefore in eternal progress'.²⁰⁶ And Hitler was in fact not alone in his enthusiasm for technology. Leading National Socialists like Fritz Todt, Robert Ley, Joseph Goebbels and Albert Speer vehemently opposed any tendencies which were anti-modernistic and hostile towards technology and shared with Hitler the belief in the possibilities of technical progress.²⁰⁷ In view of this dominating positive assessment of modern technology in the Third Reich, it is small wonder that Sombart's criticism was immediately rejected in a review in the *Völkische Beobachter*: 'National Socialism's opinion on technology does not agree in the slightest with that of Sombart ... For us modern technology is the offspring of the Nordic spirit. It expresses the power of our humanity.'²⁰⁸ Nonnenbruch, the economics editor of the *Völkische Beobachter*, was able to state in 1939 that 'The opposition against technology has broken down so thoroughly that there is nothing left for those who still continue to engage in it but to break down themselves.'²⁰⁹

But it was not only their position on technology which separated the National Socialists from the representatives of anti-modernistic schools of thought which could often be linked to the 'conservative revolution'. We have shown that Hitler himself had a positive view of historic 'progress', and that he not only shared the belief in progress but vehemently defended it against internal party criticism. Here lies a fundamental difference from the 'conservative revolution', which Armin Mohler has defined as a 'negation of the concept of progress'.²¹⁰

The fact that the National Socialists were able to also tie those anti-modernistic schools of thought into their coalition of the dissatisfied, who based their rejection of capitalism on a backward-looking criticism of civilization, led to the latter misunderstanding National Socialism as the realization of their own objectives.²¹¹ It would mean a prolongation of this misunderstanding if we were to amalgamate Hitler's objectives with the anti-modernistic utopia of these forces. There was only one point on which Hitler saw the justification of these criticisms of civilization, namely in the criticism of the destruction of nature.

b. Hitler on the Destruction of the Environment as a Result of Industrialization
If we systematize Hitler's criticism of the consequences of industrial development, we can distinguish two principal arguments: (1) The social consequences of industrialization (the development of an industrial proletariat which was not integrated into society). For this Hitler did not blame industrialization *itself*, but the bourgeoisie with its greed for profit.²¹² (2) The negative ecological consequences of industrialization, i.e. the destruction of the environment.

V: Hitler: An Opponent of Modern Industrial Society?

Since we have already exhaustively treated the first point, we will now discuss the second point, which played a role in Hitler's table talks. In his public speeches, questions of the protection of the environment played hardly any role at all. Hitler only occasionally expressed his scepticism of fertilization of the soil and its consequences, and listed the fact that a further intensification of cultivation was no longer possible as an additional reason for the gaining of new *Lebensraum*. In a speech on 14 November 1940 he declared:

> What we cultivate out of our soil is the most immense, but we do not know, however, how long the soil is going to stand this. We stimulate it with every conceivable kind of artificial substance. We do not even know whether that is healthy for our own lives, but we stimulate it with artificial fertilizer and so forth, and try to take out as much as possible.[213]

In a table talk on 5 July 1941 Hitler spoke about the limitations of natural resources. He believed that

> ... oil could still be found in thousands of places; with coal we know what happens when the coal reserves are taken out: caverns are created; with oil we do not know whether the caverns do not refill themselves from reservoirs invisible to us. Man was perhaps the most dangerous microbe one could imagine: he takes out everything from the earth without asking whether these are perhaps substances of vital importance for life in another region, which is possible looking at the earth through a microscope to find the reason for the destruction which is becoming noticeable on the surface of the earth.[214]

On 2 August 1941 Hitler spoke in favour of exploiting water as a source of energy:

> With us, because of the power of private capital interests, the exploitation of water power is still in its infancy. Major water power must mainly hold to the major customers, the chemical industry for example. Otherwise we will have to even pay premiums for every horsepower gained in the style of our former use of mill power: the water flows, all you have to do is build a step and you have what you need; whereas coal will come to an end one day, water is always there renewed. All of that can be much better exploited than at present. You can build step behind step and make use of the slightest incline, thereby get a regular flow of water and can build it bomb-proof. The new Fischer process[215] is one of the most brilliant inventions ever made ... If all of our cities were to use the Munich sludge process for the production of gas (Munich covers 12 per cent of its normal requirement that way), that would make an immense difference. In the Welser Heath the gas comes up from the ground: the city of Wels is heated with it; it would not surprise me if they were to find oil there one day. But the future is clear: water, wind, the tides; for heating we will probably use hydrogen gas.[216]

That Hitler was concerned with the problem of energy is also confirmed by his architect Hermann Giesler. In connection with the city planning project for Munich, Giesler and the engineer Adolf Gerke gave extensive consideration to the possibilities of alternative energy, above all to thermal power stations.[217] According to Giesler, Hitler was very interested in this, and during a conversation in late summer 1940 he said:

> The energy problem already concerned me during the time of struggle. I talked about it repeatedly with engineer Feder and Keppler. Now, of course, it concerns me to a greater degree, because energy not only determines the standard of living of a nation, it determines its existence! It is a European problem and in the end it can only be solved within a pan-European framework. Coal is the European raw material with the greatest importance for the economy, other countries and regions are blessed with oil. Since we have to husband our coal despite our large reserves, I have primarily ordered the exploitation of water power – in Norway as well. I have asked *Dr* Todt to seriously consider the possibility of exploiting the tides on the Atlantic coasts. But the transport of electric power has its spatial limitations.[218]

Hitler was aware, at least to some extent, of the problems under discussion today: the limits of chemical pollution of the soil, the scarcity of resources and the generation of alternative energy. Sometimes he even recognized ecological contexts, as a remark made on 28 September 1941 shows:

> We have to be careful not to go too far in the organization, because then an unforeseen catastrophe could easily turn the whole system off. It would not be right in view of the high quality of the soil in the Ukraine to say: here we only permit the cultivation of grain. No, there should also be livestock farming there! Nature herself attempts to make the regions of the earth as autarkic as possible, and man must pay attention that he preserves this mixed system. So we will leave the swamps, not only because we need them as terrain for manoeuvres but also because of the weather, to counter the danger of becoming a steppe. They act like a sponge; it could otherwise be that one day the whole harvest is destroyed by heat waves.[219]

In a table talk on 7 July 1942 Hitler declared that it was 'proof of the cultural decline of a nation when its people cut down the forests without taking care for the appropriate reforestation, thereby robbing the wise water economy of nature of its most important precondition'.[220]

Even though Hitler was a 'technology freak' as he himself said, and prophesied a great future for the aeroplane and the automobile, he also saw the negative side of future developments. On 28 July 1942, for example, he remarked that

> ... it was good that he would only live to see the beginnings of aviation. Because when all the possibilities had been completely exploited, the air would be full of

aeroplanes. And the people who would have to stand for all that engine noise and all that back and forth in the air would not know how beautiful the world had once been when aviation was still in its infancy. One had to keep in mind that every horsefly, every little mosquito in its flight made a noise that was audible for the human ear. And how much less conceivable was therefore an engine for an aeroplane that did not make a racket. He believed it was preposterous to remove the noise of the screw or rather the propeller. And then what about four 4,000-horsepower engines in our big aircraft, which at full power each equated to the electricity output of the power plant of a city with 40,000 inhabitants?[221]

In order to solve the problem of noise pollution by automobile traffic Hitler, as Picker reports, proposed pedestrian zones in the city centres and street tunnels for motor traffic in the city.[222] To his architect Giesler, who had been entrusted with the city planning for Munich, Hitler is alleged to have spoken at length about the traffic problems and their solutions. Giesler's report must be viewed with a certain degree of scepticism, however, because his book was obviously written with the intention of making Hitler appear in a favourable light. But since other associates of Hitler also report that he had taken the problems to be expected as a consequence of the coming motorization very seriously and searched for solutions to them,[223] Hitler's statements on this topic as reported by Giesler may be regarded as being genuine, at least in essence. Giesler reports Hitler as having said:

> As far as the car can be avoided in the inner city – exceptions will be permitted – in its stead as a means of mass transportation the underground offers itself, as well as the tram with a completely new carriage profile moved under the street area. With this the streets in the inner city will have been relieved, the streets will again equate to human dimensions like they did for hundreds of years. How can we meet the pressure of traffic which the rising level of motorization will inevitably bring with it? ... Until now there are three autobahns leading to Munich, in the end phase of the restructuring there will be six autobahn approaches or streets with a cross-section profile of an autobahn ... As soon as they stab through the autobahn ring they will become city speedways, but in addition they will receive the sideward access lanes to the secondary streets and the local city traffic. But in parallel to these three autobahn-city speedways – and this is important – we have the rights of way of the underground. In other words, below the car, underneath the means of private vehicle traffic lies the mass transport, the rail, the underground. If we then plan a parking deck between the two traffic levels, as you have done for the new east–west axis, then we not only gain the parking space, we also have a perfectly smooth transition from the private vehicle traffic of the car to the mass transport of the underground suited for the city, and a further connection to the under-pavement tram. The car, coming in from outside, from the autobahn, the autobahn ring, but also from the cross and inner city ring roads, can park, and, based on the configuration of the underground stations, the longest way from the parked car to the station is 200 to 250 metres. I think that this is quite reasonable. We therefore

create a further level for 'standing traffic', a buffer, and a transition between private traffic and mass transport.[224]

We cannot discuss Hitler's plans for urban development in detail here. What is interesting in our context, however, is Hitler's statement, as reported by Giesler, that with this concept

> ... the pollution, the alienation of streets and squares that were built to the specifications of the automobile, is removed. The inner city remains homey, noise and exhaust fumes are reduced, and the accident rate will also go down. Because of exhaust fumes and noise pollution, an overpass for automobile traffic in the city is just as senseless as putting rail traffic on stilts. All of this is at the expense of humanitarian conditions and the urbanity of the city organism. Streets and squares in the inner city must belong to the pedestrian ahead of anything else! ... The solution of the traffic problems of the future has priority, not only for Munich! We can already predict today that private traffic, the car, will make demands on the street area to a degree that we cannot even imagine yet. Such a development is already looming. Despite a possible redirection by the autobahn ring, the street area will be overstrained, a second level for mass transport by rail has to be built. By this automobile traffic will be brought down to a reasonable level, otherwise the inner city will suffocate from the cars and their exhaust fumes![225]

Even though Hitler was an outspoken proponent of modern industrial society and technology, he criticized the negative effects of industrialization and the far-reaching interventions by man into nature. Chemical cultivation of the soil and its consequences for health and the ecology; scarcity of resources and dangerous interventions by man into nature; water, wind and the tides as future sources of energy in view of the limited reserves of other energy sources; cultivation of the soil according to the laws of nature; warnings about the ecological consequences (changes in the climate) of the draining of swamps or the clearing of forests; noise pollution as a result of the increase of air traffic; noise and fume pollution as well as overcrowding of the cities as a result of increasing automobile traffic – for Hitler, however, none of these was a reason to reject modern industrial society in general, and, in his optimistic view of the future, he believed he could find solutions to the problems that would arise.

One may call Hitler's criticism of the consequences of industrialization and modernization 'anti-modernism', but then it was a highly modern anti-modernism. The same applies in many ways to his criticism of big cities. We have already mentioned this subject elsewhere and seen that Hitler was not against cities in principle, not even big cities, but was sceptical of an increased growth of the big cities and the creation of new big cities. Giesler claims that Hitler

V: Hitler: An Opponent of Modern Industrial Society?

regarded industrial conurbation as an expression of a 'disruption of the necessary balance'.[226] That Hitler expressed himself in this manner is doubtful, but we should not see his criticism of the big cities within the context of an alleged 'agrarian utopia' but more in the context of his scepticism with regard to the consequences of the industrialization process for the human environment.

Even though ecological topics certainly did not play a central role in Hitler's ideology, leading conservationists such as Walther Schoenichen hoped that National Socialism would bring about a profound change in the treatment of nature, a turn away from merely thinking in terms of resources, and the salvation of endangered natural monuments.[227] One was therefore able to read in the periodical *Naturschutz* in 1934: 'The friends and proponents of conservation . . . expect [from National Socialism—R.Z.] the fulfilment of many a demand and desire so important for our nation, for which in former times any sympathy could simply not be expected.'[228]

In 1935 a Reichs Conservation Law was actually passed by which, for example, all Reichs, state and local authorities were required to 'involve the responsible conservation authorities in any decision process concerning measures or planning which could lead to substantial changes in the landscape so early on, that the requirements of conservation may be taken into account'.[229] A Reichs office for conservation was also set up[230] and, by a ministerial decree, the 'fostering of the concept of conservation specifically made mandatory' in the schools.[231] But, on the other hand, the fostering of technical and industrial development had the opposite effect.[232] Therefore many conservationists only expected a fundamental change after the conquest of new *Lebensraum*, which would make it possible, for example, to extend the existing national park of Bialowies (Poland) from 46 to 2,600 square kilometres, or even, according to the intentions of Reichs Minister Seyss-Inquart, 'to set up a conservation area in the grand style from the Grossglockner to the Grossvenediger [mountains in Austria—H.B.]'.[233] The war, however, after the victorious conclusion of which one hoped 'to secure larger areas for conservation without regard to existing property rights or economically more attractive competing forms of exploitation',[234] first led to the greatest destruction of the environment that was conceivable at the time.

On the other hand it should not be overlooked that in the building of the autobahns, for example, quite intensive efforts were made to take ecological aspects into consideration. *Dr* Todt, who was responsible for road construction, demanded a harmony between technology and nature in the completed project, and thereby, said Ludwig, observed both modern ecological principles of engineering and contemporary 'organological' ones, together with the

329

'nationalist ideology they were rooted in'.[235] Hitler was acting in accordance with such considerations when in March 1935 he ordered a stop and immediate review of work already in progress near Bayreuth. Todt was deeply affected and submitted without any objections because 'by building works, or rather the projected line, the danger of a disruption of the landscape threatened'.[236] At the end of 1935 Todt wrote in a personal letter to the owner of a civil engineering company:

> The German landscape is something unique, we have no right to disrupt, let alone destroy it . . . If it were not already reverence for the beauty of our homeland, then it would at least be the knowledge of the indispensable and irreplaceable recuperative value of our countryside, which we would have to observe in any constructional interference with nature . . . When we build in this our native landscape, then we have to be clearly aware that, and how, we intend to preserve its beauty, and how we can restore it in a new form in those places where it has already suffered.[237]

In 1934 Todt, reacting to an expert opinion by the conservationist Seifert, had already ensured that every construction management group of the autobahn organization had a scientifically schooled 'landscape advocate' assigned to it, who on the basis of his botanical and biological knowledge and experience was charged with ensuring that the new traffic lanes were to grow back into the landscape 'organically' after the necessary earthworks had been completed. The 'harmony between nature and technology', said Ludwig, 'was actually given priority in road construction'.[238] Sieferle concludes:

> Today it is seen as being an almost involuntary irony that in road construction, of all places, the requirements of conservation and protection of the landscape were fostered so intensively . . . For the purely technocratic road builders, however, these were all superfluous ideological additions, which contradicted the singular purpose of traffic. In the post-war era they were therefore largely removed again. Technology should look rational, simple, geometrical, like technology in effect, because only then was it considered to be honest.[239]

Let us summarize the results of this chapter. We do not wish to dispute that in Hitler's *Weltanschauung* and in the reality of the Third Reich certain 'anti-modernistic' elements can be detected in the sense of scepticism towards specific consequences of technical and industrial progress, which also led to some initial stages of practical attempts to correct the effects of industrialization on the environment. This does not, however, affect the fact that, in principle, Hitler was a vehement proponent of 'technicalization' and industrialization, and an adherent of the concept of a constantly growing economy and a constantly increasing level of consumption.

3. Hitler's Scientific View of the World and his Criticism of Rosenberg's and Himmler's 'Mysticism'

The process of 'modernization' also includes a secularization and rationalization of thinking which was initiated by the Enlightenment and accompanied by faith in the power of human reasoning, the rejection of mysticism and irrationality and an increasingly more scientific view of the world. How does Hitler's *Weltanschauung* compare with this, and in this sense, must it perhaps not be seen as an expression of 'anti-modernism' after all?

One of the assumptions made and not questioned is that National Socialism was not only a protest against liberalism but also against the rationalism of the nineteenth century, that it must be interpreted as a counter-movement to the Enlightenment, as an expression of an accentuation of the (perhaps previously ignored) 'mystic' and irrational side of human life. This may be true to some extent if we apply it to Himmler's and Rosenberg's ideology, but for Hitler the thesis has no validity in this form. To be sure, Hitler was very aware of human irrationality and was prepared to exploit it unscrupulously in the service of his ideas. This was the purpose of the mass parades, the consecrations of flags, drums, symbols etc. which Hitler knew how to stage and use.[240] But we also know that Hitler used these means very consciously, very deliberately, and therefore 'rationally'. When in *Mein Kampf*, for example, he explained in terms of mass psychology the reasons why he held his rallies in the evening and not during the day, this may be taken as an example of a very carefully considered and therefore rational use of human irrationality.

Hitler was basically convinced that his *Weltanschauung* was a rational, scientifically based theory. When we now discuss his speech at the culture conference of the *Reichsparteitag* of 1938 in detail, we will demonstrate how questionable – with reference to Hitler – is the interpretation of National Socialism as an expression of the accentuation of the 'mystical' and 'irrational' side of human life against the rationalism of the Enlightenment and the nineteenth century. In his speech Hitler again began with architecture, which had the task of expressing 'the universal will of an age. The religious, inwardly directed mystical world of the Christian Middle Ages found forms of expression that were only possible, yes useful, for that world. A Gothic stadium is just as unthinkable as a Roman railway station or a Byzantine shopping mall.' National Socialism on the other hand was a

> ... cool set of teachings of reality of the most sharply scientific insights and their mental formation. By our having unlocked and continuing to unlock the heart of our nation for these teachings, we do not wish to fill it with a mysticism which lies outside the reasons and objectives of our teachings. In its organization, National

Socialism is probably first and foremost a popular movement, but under no circumstances is it a cult ... Because National Socialism is not a cultic movement but a national-political doctrine which has developed solely out of racial discoveries. In its intention there is no mystic cult, but instead the care and leadership of the nation as defined by blood. Therefore we have no cult rooms, but only meeting halls for the people, no cult areas, but only assembly and parade areas. We have no sacred groves, but sports arenas and playgrounds. And the hallmark of our meeting halls is not the mystic darkness of a cult room, but the brightness and the light of an auditorium or hall which is as beautiful as it is useful. Therefore no cultic ceremonies take place in them, but only rallies by the people of the kind we have learned to hold during the course of a long struggle, are therefore familiar with, and want to preserve for ourselves in this way. Therefore the movement must not tolerate mystically inclined occult investigators of the hereafter sneaking in. They are not National Socialists, but something else entirely, and in any case something that has nothing to do with us. At the head of our programme does not stand some mysterious presentiment, but clear understanding and therefore open confession ... There was an age in which semi-darkness was the precondition for the effectiveness of certain teachings, and today there is an age in which light is the basic foundation for our successful actions. But woe be it when because of the insidious insertion of unclear mystical elements the movement or the state itself gives unclear assignments. There is already a danger in giving some sort of order for a so-called 'cult place', because this already creates the necessity of inventing so-called cult games and cult rites for later on, which have nothing to do with National Socialism. Our cult is solely care for the natural and therefore that which is divinely willed.[241]

These statements are directed against Himmler and Rosenberg, even though Hitler does not mention their names.[242] It is therefore all the more questionable when Turner writes in his article 'Fascism and Anti-Modernism' about a mainstream of the NS utopia which was represented by 'Hitler, Himmler, Rosenberg and Darré' and which allegedly had discovered 'its guiding principles in the early Middle Ages, but also in pre-Christian, even prehistoric times' and which intended to solve the problems of the highly industrialized twentieth-century Germany by 'a resurrection of the cultic adulation of blood and soil'.[243] This may apply to Himmler and Rosenberg, but Hitler clearly separated himself from such attempts. In his table talks on 23 September 1941 he emphasized that 'National Socialism must never attempt to ludicrously imitate a religion in a cultic way, what applies to it always is to only scientifically develop a theory which is nothing more than the "cult of reason".'[244] National Socialism as a scientific theory, as the 'cult of reason' — such wordings should be grounds enough to re-examine the theory that National Socialism had in principle defined itself as a counter-movement against the Enlightenment and the rationalism of the eighteenth and nineteenth centuries.

V: Hitler: An Opponent of Modern Industrial Society?

One of the main topics of Hitler's monologues was the relationship between science and religion, and he maintained that, with the advance of science, the church would go under: 'Science will be the victor,' he said on 14 October 1941 and again warned: 'A movement such as ours should never let itself be drawn into this metaphysical field of totally uncontrolled thought processes. It has to stay in the field of an exact science. The party should not be a substitute for the church. Its job is of a scientific-methodical nature.'[245] On 24 October 1941 Hitler again spoke on his favourite subject, namely the superiority of science over religion. What is of particular interest is his remark: 'When we read polemical treatises from the French seventeenth or eighteenth century, or the conversations between Fredercik II and Voltaire, then we have to be ashamed of the low level of our meagre contemporary insight!'[246] That with his criticism of religion, his 'cult of reason' and his belief in the superiority of science Hitler deliberately places himself in a line with the tradition of the French Enlightenment once again speaks against the thesis that National Socialism had to be regarded as a protest against the Enlightenment and rationalism.

The degree to which Hitler's thinking was determined by science can also be seen from his repeatedly expressed idea to combat the church in Germany by building large astronomical observatories:

> These clerics! All I need is to see such a black inferiority come walking by! The brain was given to man to think with; and when he then wants to think, such a black grubby little bug goes and burns him at the stake! I can see the building before me, classical, as beautiful as anything: the astronomical observatory on the Pöstlinghill in Linz. The temple of idolatry already there I will remove, and put this up there instead. In future every Sunday tens of thousands of people will go through and all will be entranced by the vastness of the universe. As an inscription I can imagine only this: 'The Skies Praise the Honour of the Eternal!' With this we will educate the people to a religion, but an anti-cleric one, we educate them to be humble.

The Russians, said Hitler, were purely negative in their rejection of the church. His museum should be positive as well: 'I will put the statues and busts of those great men in there who opened up knowledge and removed superstition, and who attempted to see a new view of the world.' The best thing to open people's eyes with was 'the picture':

> A single small telescope in a village and a world has been broken through! We have to break away from the concept with which the cleric operates, that knowledge changes with time while belief stays the same: Oh, how has knowledge changed, but the belief of the church has stayed the same![247]

On 5 June 1942 Hitler demanded that everything had to be done in future to prevent a mental retardation of large segments of the German population, regardless of whether this expressed itself as religious insanity or as some other form of mental derangement. He had therefore ordered that, as far as at all possible, astronomical observatories were to be built in all the larger cities, because experience taught that observatories were the best means of extending people's view of the world and thereby prevent 'mental retardation'.[248]

Hitler's scientifically determined view of the world was expressed in such statements, and his whole criticism of religion – his 'biologism' must also be included here! – puts him into the context of the rationalism of the nineteenth century. This is why he so frequently and so vehemently opposed tendencies in his party which saw National Socialism as a new religion or a new 'myth'. During a table talk on 11 April 1942, for example, he emphasized yet again that Rosenberg's book *The Myth of the 20th Century* 'could not be regarded as an official work of the party'. He had

> ... expressly refused at the time to give this book the character of a party dogma, because its title was already false. Because you could not say that you wanted to set *The Myth of the 20th Century*, in other words something mythical, against the spirit of the nineteenth century, but as a National Socialist you had to say, that you were setting the faith and knowledge of the twentieth century against the myth of the nineteenth century.[249]

Speer reports that Hitler had also spoken out against Himmler's SS myth:

> What nonsense! Now we are finally at the point of entering into an age that has left all mysticism behind it, and now he is starting off at the beginning again. We might just as well have stayed with the church. It, at least, has tradition. To think that I might one day be elevated to become an 'SS saint'! Just imagine that! I would turn over in my grave!

Hitler and Goebbels, Speer reports, ridiculed Himmler's weird ideas and pseudo-religious views.[250] In his diary Goebbels reported a conversation with Hitler on 19 August 1935 in which Hitler said, 'Rosenberg, Himmler and Darré have to stop their cultic nonsense.'[251]

Hitler, on the other hand, repeatedly made the claim that his *Weltanschauung* was based on strictly scientific discoveries. In a speech on 26 May 1944 he gave a definition of his understanding of the term:

> *Weltanschauung* is nothing more than a way of looking at all the problems of existence according to scientific discoveries such as those we are offered today. This means I assess the problems of life in such a way as scientific discoveries permit today. Whether this is then an eternal truth, we can leave that aside for the moment, but there was a time when man was so well developed in his ability to

V: Hitler: An Opponent of Modern Industrial Society?

observe that he first recognized that the lights in the firmament had been moving lights, and he was now convinced that everything stood still, his Earth stood still, which in antiquity had already been recognized by the Greeks as being a sphere, and that these lights were moving, which meant that the Earth is the centre of the world. This Ptolemaic system was a *Weltanschauung*. It was wrong, but for mankind it was an infinite advance compared to the primitive, stupid way of looking at things of, let us say, a tribe of negroes. One day, or in the course of the centuries, a new, better scientific discovery comes along and this whole Ptolemaic system of an Aristotle is overthrown in the end, and in its place steps the discovery of a Copernicus, a new view of the world opens up . . . In other words scientific knowledge changes. The only thing that is important is to take the newest scientific knowledge to heart and to look at the problems of life based on this . . . In other words, a view of everything that transpires around us from the vantage of the newest scientific discoveries![252]

We might now interject that Hitler's racial ideology had nothing to do with science. This is certainly true, but what is important in this context is that from the very beginning Hitler attempted to explain even his hatred of the Jews 'rationally' and 'scientifically'. In his very first discussion of the 'Jewish question', namely in a letter written on 16 September 1919, Hitler complains that up till then anti-Semitism had 'only had the character of a mere emotion'. This was wrong, however, because 'anti-Semitism as a political movement must not, and cannot, be determined by moments of emotion, but by the discovery of facts'.[253] In his study on 'Hitler's *Weltanschauung*' Jäckel has convincingly demonstrated that, even on the basis of his racial theory, his hatred of the Jews and his concept of the necessity of conquering new *Lebensraum*, Hitler had still developed a stringent, logical and conclusive *Weltanschauung*. Even where for us the irrationality of National Socialism becomes most obvious, namely in its racial ideology, Hitler was convinced that he stood on the foundations of proven biological and historical discoveries.

As far as his demand for new *Lebensraum* in the East is concerned, a second constant in his *Weltanschauung*, we have shown that he was well able to derive and explain it logically in terms of certain economic premises. One may reject the premises and judge his conclusions to be immoral and criminal, but the logic of his reasoning remains conclusive. Konrad Heiden had already ascribed 'a strange ability to reason logically' to Hitler:

He is able to develop something from a given premise with a compelling conclusiveness, and where the premises are correct he comes to astonishing conclusions. But, to begin with, his premises are only correct within a certain sphere, namely within that of the politically reacting person. Furthermore, he lacks an eye for measuring terms and judgements against each other; he is able to derive lines of development, but not to identify contradictions.[254]

In his thinking, Hitler was far more rational than has previously been assumed, and, as paradoxical as this may sound, he was also firmly convinced of his rationality where he was irrational. As an adherent of a 'cult of reason' and a decidedly 'scientific theory' – at least as far as its claim was concerned – as well as in his opposition not only to religion but to any form of 'superstition', 'mysticism' and irrationality, Hitler was an offspring of the nineteenth century, even though he refused to admit this. From Hitler's point of view National Socialism was not primarily a counter-movement against rationalism and secularization but rather its most perfect form of expression. What made Hitler different is that for himself he believed in the power of reason, in logical rational deduction, but not for the masses, who – as he had already written in *Mein Kampf* – were guided less by reason than by emotion. But the cold exploitation of this fact, the propaganda and strategy of political rallies, which deliberately took the irrationality of man into account, show that here Hitler himself was again rational. If we attach rationalism and secularization to the term 'modernism', in his thinking Hitler was then certainly modern, notably in his own self-definition.

The conclusion from the fifth section of our study is clear: Hitler's objectives did not have an 'anti-modernistic' character as research has previously claimed. This assumption was based on a number of misunderstandings, mainly on the misinterpretation of the functions of the *Lebensraum* to be conquered in the East. Hitler, however, intended neither 'reagrarianization' nor opting out of modern industrial society. He defined himself as a deliberate executor of that process of modernization which is characterized by industrialization, technicalization and rationalization. We have already shown, in Chapter III.2, that Hitler also deliberately intended the social implications of this process, i.e. primarily an increase in social mobility.

With the refutation of the theory that Hitler had been an opponent of modernity, however, the question of whether one may describe him as a revolutionary has been clearly answered, because, as we have already shown in the introductory chapter, the main objection to defining Hitler as a revolutionary was that the process of modernization he initiated had been unintentional. The alleged contradiction between the intention and the effect of Hitler's revolution does not exist. The basis for this contradiction was not an antagonism between Hitler's objectives and means, his intentions and effects but simply a misinterpretation of his objectives by historic research.

Even though we have shown in the last chapter that Hitler was a vehement advocate of modern industrial society, this does not mean that he was in favour of the political form of a modern pluralistic democracy. The opposite is true, of course, and in the following section we intend to show why, and with what arguments, Hitler rejected democracy. But this rejection of democracy is not a contradiction to the modernity of his *Weltanschauung*. Democracy is one, but by no means the only, possible political form in which the process of modernization can take place.

VI

Hitler's Concepts and Objectives in His Domestic Policies

1. Hitler's Criticism of Democracy

It is well known that Hitler was an opponent of democracy and was aiming at replacing this form of political and social organization with a different one. What is less well known, however, are the arguments with which he criticized the democratic system and, above all, how the different lines of argument are weighted. In the following pages we intend to portray Hitler's more important and most frequently made accusations against democracy. In doing this we have to differentiate between the following lines of argument:
– Criticism of the 'majority principle'
– Criticism of the policy of 'special interests' (criticism of pluralism)
– Democracy as a form of rule by capital
– Democracy as a sign of decadence and weakness

a. Criticism of the 'Majority Principle'
One of the arguments most frequently advanced against the democratic form of government by Hitler was directed against a key point within this system, namely against the principle of decision by the majority, as this manifests itself primarily in elections. Hitler's position towards the masses was ambivalent. On the one hand he recognized the importance of the masses in a modern society, and knew above all that a revolutionary movement had to be a mass movement, while on the other hand he held the masses to be stupid and incapable of judging.

The true meaning of democracy, said Hitler on 28 July 1922, was the 'herd-wise outvoting of intelligence and true energy by the number of the dead mass'.[1] Because Marxism negated 'the value of personality' and the concept of authority, the

> ... freedom of action and creative possibilities of personality were cut off, the genius of leadership was fettered so as to paralyze any free development, and in place of all this comes the democratic principle of a determination by the majority, which always only means the victory of the more common, the worse, the weaker,

and above all the more cowardly, the less responsible. *Personality is destroyed by the mass.*[2]

Hitler's criticism of the majority principle is again tied into his socio-Darwinistic philosophy, because he always regarded the mass as being 'without a sense of responsibility' and 'cowardly', whereas bravery and heroism were only embodied in the 'historic minority' and the individual. 'Any true strength is a characteristic of only a few people, otherwise we would not have the term "hero"', Hitler declared on 30 October 1923. He continued:

> The mass consists of the average, of democrats. But one hundred blind do not make up one seeing, a thousand cowards not one hero, a hundred thousand parliamentarians not one statesman. Cowards vote for cowards as their leaders so that they are not called upon to show heroism, and the stupid the most stupid, so that everybody can still have the feeling that he is still a little bit better than the leader. *A nation that is subjected to the decisions of the majority is in danger of going under.*[3]

In the portrayal of Hitler's position on the middle class we have already seen the importance the accusation of 'cowardice' had within his socio-Darwinistic *Weltanschauung*. It is only from here that we can understand Hitler's 'adulation for heroism' which Vappu Tallgren has quite rightly called an essential element of his *Weltanschauung*.[4] And since the mass simply does not consist of 'heroic appearances', it searches, so went Hitler's argument, for cowardly parliamentarians to represent it, who in their turn again shun responsibility. In his testimony before the court after his *putsch* of November 1923 Hitler said that the decisions of the majority 'would always be negative. They are the inferior, the worse. The decision of the majority is always a weakness. The only one who will win in the end is the one who knows how to pull the majority along on strings.'[5]

We can only speculate about what sort of experiences caused Hitler to become such a sharp opponent of parliamentary democracy. In *Mein Kampf* he writes that he had always hated (the Austrian) parliament,

> ... but not as an institution in itself. On the contrary, as a freedom-loving person I was unable to imagine any other form of government, because given my position towards the House of Habsburg, the mere thought of some dictatorship would have appeared as a crime against freedom and against any sort of reason.

He had also felt a sort of admiration for British parliament.[6] Whether this is true or not is difficult to say. Hitler also claimed initially to have rejected anti-Semitism and to have been positive towards Social Democracy,[7] and it may well be that this is only a clever rhetorical tactic to 'convert' the reader by telling the story of one's own alleged 'conversion'. Hitler wrote that he had been hostile towards the Austrian parliament from the beginning and seen it as being unworthy of its great example, i.e. the British parliament, because, based on universal suffrage, an 'outvoting' of the Germans within the Habsburg state had come about. After he had frequently attended sessions of parliament, however, and gained the impression of a chaotic mess, he came to a fundamental rejection of parliamentary democracy:

> What made me stop and think right from the beginning and most importantly was the obvious lack of any responsibility of an individual person... Is not any concept of responsibility tied to a person? But can one make the leading person of a government responsible in practice for actions whose coming into being and implementation are exclusively attributable to the will and desire of a plurality of people?

Any brilliant deed in this world was the 'visible protest of genius against the inertia of the mass'. Did one really believe, Hitler queried, 'that progress in this world . . . stemmed from the brains of a majority and not from the minds of individuals?' But because the democratic-parliamentarian principle of majority decision rejected the authority of the individual and 'in its place put the number of the crowd, it sins against the aristocratic basic principle of nature, whereby her definition of aristocracy in no way has to be embodied in today's decadence of our upper ten thousand'. The parliamentary system inevitably led to an

> . . . unbelievable flooding of total political life with the most inferior appearances of our times. Just as the true leader will withdraw from a political activity which mainly cannot consist of creative achievement and work, but rather of bargaining and dealing for the favour of a majority, so will exactly this activity suit the small mind and therefore attract it.

The great minds, the brilliant individual personalities, would just as much reject 'becoming the lackeys of stupid incapables and windbags as vice versa, the representatives of the majority, that is stupidity, hate nothing more fervently than superior brains'. If, in spite of all this, in an exceptional case a real personality could be found who was prepared to govern within the framework of this system, then if he succeeded at all in reaching a position of power he would immediately be pushed out of it again by the united front of the majority and irresponsibility. Hitler then goes on to say that the political understanding of the masses was not sufficiently well developed to reach certain general valid political conclusions and to select the people capable of dealing with them. So-called 'public opinion' was determined by the press, and so the 'political opinion of the masses was only the final result of a sometimes quite unbelievably persevering and thorough manipulation of soul and mind'.

The parliamentarians finally elected did not, in their majority, possess the specialized knowledge or the competence to decide the topics under discussion in parliament:

> The tipping of the scales will always come about by a majority of the ignorant and incapable, because the composition of this institution remains the same, whereas the problems to be dealt with extend to almost every field of public life, and would therefore require the constant change of the deputies who are to judge and decide them. It is impossible to have the same people decide about problems of transportation, who decide, let us say, about high foreign policy. They would all have to be universal geniuses such as hardly really appear once in hundreds of years. Unfortunately, however, here we are not dealing with real 'brains' at all, but with puffed-up dilettantes who are as retarded as they are conceited, with an intellectual demi-monde of the most disgusting sort.[8]

The arguments with which Hitler attacked democracy in his speeches are always the same, and culminate in the accusation that the mass was incompetent to take political decisions and could be manipulated by the press,[9] that it was not creative and only the individual (e.g. the inventor) could be,[10] but above all that a majority never embodied determination, daring, insight and farsightedness[11] but always only cowardice, inability, stupidity, lack of knowledge, mediocrity, weakness and half-heartedness.[12] The most frequently raised accusations are those of stupidity, cowardice and weakness.

In his propaganda Hitler frequently cited the army, or various other sectors of life, as examples of the senselessness of the majority principle. For example, in a speech on 6 August 1927 he said:

> Or if I were to say, the army will now be led according to democratic principles, that means in future each company will vote whether it wants to attack or does not want to attack, and the majority will vote how to attack, where to attack and what to attack with and so forth, then the man would certainly say to me, that means the destruction of the army. Or if I were to tell him that the railway will now be organized so that all the railway men can vote on which trains are to run and when the trains are not to run, and the pointsetters vote on whether they want to set the points or not, then he would say, that means collapse. *Jawohl*, you know that it is impossible to build up the whole state on this foundation, but that does not alter the fact that you place the decision in the hands of the majority, that means the individual achievement you otherwise value so highly, you throw to the will of stupidity, to the majority.[13]

Hitler attempted to make democracy appear absurd or ridiculous by advancing the argument that, under certain circumstances, the fate of the whole nation could depend on only one vote, and that the vote of 'the cowgirl Zenzi'. Here is an example of Hitler's rhetoric:

> That means it can come about, for example, that there is a vote on whether Germany should pursue this road in its foreign policy, or another road, and there is a vote on this and in the end it all depends on one man and that is, let us say, Hieronimus Oberhuber who is now going to decide German foreign policy one way or the other. The man casts his vote. But now you have to imagine how he got elected! He himself was only elected by a majority of one vote, and this vote was a cowgirl. This Miss Zenzi was to go and vote. Actually she would not have gone. But with the help of spiritual encouragement and advice she found herself moved to do so. She was told that the cross belonged on number seven. This piece of paper is what Oberhuber owes his being elected to. Just imagine, the German nation owes its foreign policy achievement to this fair damsel. There are enough damsels of this sort running about. You can even find them in the best families.[14]

Hitler argued that it was quite conceivable that

> ... even very wise men were not able to reach a completely clear understanding of particularly difficult issues. But it would be a capitulation by the leadership if it were then to turn such problems over to public treatment and opinion. Because it would then be expecting more wisdom from the mass than the leadership itself possessed.[15]

One of the consequences of Hitler's line of reasoning was, of course, that the 'plebiscites' conducted in the Third Reich were not intended to serve the purpose of decision-making or a discovery of the truth, because they would then have been an expression of the despised majority principle. Although Hitler and other NS leaders took the results of these votes quite seriously, it was, as Hitler himself emphasized in numerous speeches,[16] primarily for their propaganda effect of demonstrating the unity of the German national community to the world. In a speech to the district leaders at the Ordensburg Vogelsang on 29 April 1937 he declared that the people should not be burdened with something which was already causing the better brains serious headaches:

> I only want to give you one example. It is not possible that, for example, a party leader racks his brains to reach, let us say, a decision and discusses it with his associate, but about which not even the best brains can reach complete agreement, but this party leader then goes and puts the decision he could not agree with his best associates up to the people. This means in other words, that he assumes the people are more intelligent than he and all of his selected associates.[17]

As an example Hitler named the difficult situation before the decision to send the army into the demilitarized Rhineland. In such a situation it would be preposterous to burden 'a little human worm who does his job out there day after day, who from his whole education, his whole insight, his knowledge, is not even in a position to judge the consequences of these problems to the slightest degree' with such a decision. One could now raise the objection, Hitler went on, that he himself had conducted a plebiscite:

> But first I acted. I acted first and then, however, I only wanted to show the world that the German nation stands behind me, that is what it was about. Had I been convinced that perhaps the German nation was not prepared to go along here completely, I would have acted anyway, but then I would not have held a plebiscite. Then I would have said: I will simply take this on my own responsibility. But it is quite clear, somebody has to take the decision, somebody has to find the strength to decide.[18]

We have now heard the arguments with which Hitler criticized the fundamental democratic principle of majority decision. But Hitler also knew that the democratic system does not solely consist of voting, but is organized into parties and lobbies which have the task of formulating political demands and articulating interests where the individual is incapable of doing this.

b. Hitler's Criticism of the Pluralistic System: The Common Good versus 'Special Interests'

It is one of the basic tenets of any pluralistic social theory that within industrial society there is a warp of contradictory interests. This heterogeneity is accepted and a homogeneous society not aspired to. The common good, so goes the argument of the proponents of a theory of pluralism, cannot be determined *a priori* but develops from the conflicts and compromises between the social groups *a posteriori*, the realization of the common good therefore being the result of political competition.[19]

Hitler criticized the democratic system because he rejected the thesis that the common good developed automatically from the conflict between the various interests. According to his view, the common interests had to be advocated and imposed by the state against the particular interests of individual groups. But this was only possible for the strong state organized according to the *Führer* principle, at whose head there were men who had the insight into what was right and necessary for the common good.

In his speeches he compared class and party politics, which only ever advocated the specific interests of a class or party and were therefore 'harmful to the nation', to 'national politics', which advocated the 'interests of the whole nation'.[20] All parties had to be opposed, said Hitler on 18 October 1928, 'who primarily want to advocate professional interests'. One reason Hitler criticized this sort of policy was his belief that, in a pluralistic democracy, the short-term interests dominated the long-term ones, and that the various party and interest groups were incapable or recognizing these long-term tasks of the future or of taking them on. The parties all acted according to the motto,

> We don't care what happens after we're gone! So let us see if we can grab as much as we can get out immediately. This is a criminal principle. It gradually leads a nation to destruction. It is important that we say, what you are doing is a vice. You are not thinking about the future today. But one day a future will come which will curse you.[21]

He accused the political parties of not pursuing any long-term perspectives for the future, and of even attempting to justify their petty politics of the day with Bismarck's statement that politics was the art of the possible. But Bismarck had had, wrote Hitler in his 'Second Book', 'an exactly defined and clearly marked political objective in mind'. It was impertinence to insinuate that

> ... he had only achieved his life's work by the accumulation of the political possibilities that happened to be there and not by mastering each situation with a view to the political objective he was envisaging ... His successors have neither a political objective nor even a political idea, and instead bumble along from today to tomorrow, and from tomorrow to the day after, only to then attempt to portray their politically senseless and aimless stammering as being the art of the possible by appealing to the very man whom in part they themselves, and in part their spiritual ancestors, had caused the most serious worries and most bitter battles.[22]

Here a fundamental contradiction between the democratic theory of a pluralistic society and Hitler's definition of politics becomes evident.[23] According to a pluralistic definition of politics, the political decisions have to orientate themselves on the *status quo* and only to aspire to marginal changes, thereby bringing about a step-by-step solution of the problem. In doing this, it is not adequate means which are being sought to achieve fixed objectives, but, *vice versa*, the objectives are adjusted to the available means. The most important impulses for political decisions are not derived from overriding objectives but from existing shortcomings.[24] And it is against this political practice of 'muddling through' that Hitler's arguments are directed.

In another context we have already quoted a passage in which Hitler emphatically objected to the influence of economic interests on politics.[25] Here, too, he is in contrast to the pluralistic concept of democracy, because this regards the influence of economic interest groups as being legitimate and necessary. Hitler fundamentally opposed the view that 'the fate of the community is derived from the fate of the individual', as the traditional class parties maintained. It was rather the other way around, in that the fate of the community, in other words the common good, had priority. 'A correction of the fate of the individual, or the various groups of the nation, cannot be made unless the fate of the totality of Germany, defined as a state and a nation, is not improved.'[26]

We have already been made aware of this view of Hitler's in the context of his criticism of the economic system of free enterprise. The common interest took priority over the individual interests and depended mainly on the overall situation, and not *vice versa*. The pluralistic theory of society, however, assumed that the common interest could not be determined *a priori* but could only be derived as the end result of the advocacy of various individual interests (by parties and lobbies). Hitler, on the other hand, frequently affirmed in his speeches that the National Socialist movement 'did not represent any interests of any sort, except those of the German nation in its totality',[27] in other words that it rejected any politics in pursuit of special interests. He accused the other parties of 'never [having been] the representatives of the people, but always representatives of special interests', in actual truth, however, 'primarily only having thought of themselves'.[28]

To Wagener Hitler lamented that 'there were so few people who had an eye for the whole. They are all always interest cliques; they all interpret things according to *their* advantage and *their* chances to profit.'[29] On another occasion Hitler told Wagener that 'in the coming socialism' the issue would only be 'the total, the community, the nation'. The individual would only play a subordinate role and would be prepared to sacrifice himself 'if the community requires it, if the common good demands it'.[30]

Hitler defined socialism as the unconditional and ruthless imposition of the common interest upon the individual and group interests. Socialism meant, he said in a speech on 5 November 1930, that

> ...now the right thing is what serves the whole and not the individual... The whole is the primary, the essential, only through it does he receive his share of life, and when his share contradicts the laws of the whole, then human common sense must point out that the interest of the whole must take precedence over his interests.

For Hitler socialism meant the 'subordination of the individual' and his interests under the benefits of the whole. The economist who stepped up to him and claimed that it was the other way around, that the benefit of the whole resulted from the advocacy of the interests of the individual, 'had got things upside down'.[31] Hitler was therefore opposing parliamentary or pluralistic democracy with the principle of socialism as he defined it. In a speech on 8 November 1930 he remarked that

> ...socialism means in the ultimate and deepest sense advocacy of the interests of a whole against the interests of the individual, in other words I do not regard it as being necessary that the interests of the individual are pushed to the fore, but quite the opposite, that the interests of the whole stand in front. When the interests of the whole stand in the foreground, then the interests of the individual will also be

guaranteed, because, when egoism reigns, it is not the individual who breaks down first, but the collapse of the whole is the destruction of the individual.[32]

After the seizure of power Hitler described as a key task the building up of an authority which must be

... independent of the momentary streams of the spirit of the age, above all independent of the streams which are made to appear by economically limited and restricted egoism. A leadership of the state must develop, which appears as a genuine authority, and an authority which does not depend on any social class.[33]

In Hitler's view, only such an authority would be able effectively to represent the common interests against the egoistic claims of the individual. His opinion, already mentioned in Chapter IV.4, that political functionaries should be independent of business – that is, they should not hold positions on supervisory boards etc. – was derived from these premises, as was his advocacy of a state-controlled economy. Hitler believed, as he outlined in a speech in the *Reichstag* on 30 January 1934 that

... the gigantic task which is set us not only by the present economic need, but also by a critical look into the future, can only be solved when, above the egoistic sense of the individual, the advocate of the interests of all has the say and his will is recognized as the ultimate decision.[34]

Hitler readily saw that there are a plethora of diverging interests in a modern industrial society. Under the conditions of a capitalist economy and a political democracy – under which, in Hitler's view, the state did not have the independence and authority to impose the general against the individual interests – he also recognized, as we have seen, the justification for having unions, for example, as a necessary corrective to the egoistic pursuit of economic interests by capital. In the National Socialist state there was also the necessity, said Hitler in his closing address at the *Reichsparteitag* of 1934, that 'a compensation be found between the understandable and natural interests of its individual walks of life'. This compensation, however, should not be 'the result of the horse-trading of parliamentary black marketeers' but 'it should be the result of a just weighing of what can be given to the individual within the framework of the community as determined by a sovereign regime which is only responsible to this common interest'.[35]

On 12 March 1936 Hitler declared:

I too, of course, have seen, and see, the various interests which exist within a nation. I too see the city dweller, the craftsman, the farmer, the white-collar employee, the entrepreneur, and I understand that they all believe that they have to pursue their special interests in a special way. But I also know that if these pursuits of special interests degenerate into a lack of restraint, none of them will be able to realize their interests in the end, but all of them together only destroy their interests. As opposed to this I have taken the position that a regime must be independent of such interests. It must keep its eyes fixed on the interests of the whole ahead of and against the interests of the individual.[36]

The National Socialist leadership of the state, said Hitler at the *Reichsparteitag* in 1936, was a 'sovereign one, and one standing so high above any economic ties that in its eye the designations "employee" and "employer" are unimportant terms. There is no employer and there is no employee before the highest interests of the nation, but only those entrusted with tasks by the whole nation.'[37] In other words, everybody had to submit unconditionally to the authority of the National Socialist state and to perform his task solely within the framework of the objectives set by it. Hitler designated himself as being 'the man who will take care with ruthless determination of the higher, common interests of the nation founded in reason and reality, against the egoism of the individual'.[38] With this definition of the relationship between individual and general interests, Hitler projected his alternative to a pluralistic democracy. The common interests were bindingly defined by the National Socialist state and its *Führer*. He recognized the 'common good' and was able with all his authority to impose it against all the interest groups.

In his speech to the district leaders at the *Ordensburg Vogelsang* on 29 April 1937 Hitler discussed the view that the definition of the state and the democratic system contradicted each other. He believed that democracy was undergoing a world-wide crisis:

> Because what we understand by the term 'state' today, what shows itself as being reality under the term 'state' is the natural contradiction to the term democracy. This state developed, and all the states developed, by overcoming the pure interests of pigheadedness and also the egoism of the individual. Democracy sets out to place the individual into the centre of the whole event. It is impossible now to avoid the crisis in the long term which must result from such a duality . . . This struggle, which I call the crisis of democracy, is unavoidable, and it will come over all of the states of the world, inevitably come, whereby decades are of no importance . . . What is sure is that in the long term the state cannot exist under the leadership of a parliamentary democracy. That is sure. And it is sure that out of the contradiction that exists between this parliamentary democracy and the state, a crisis must develop, a tension and therefore one day also an easing of tension.[39]

Hitler was therefore basing his reasoning on an antagonistic contradiction between the terms 'state' and 'democracy'. It lay in the essence of the term 'state' that individual interests were lifted up into a higher unit; it lay in the essence of the term 'democracy' to place exactly those individual interests into the centre. From this contradiction Hitler declared the necessity of replacing democracy by an authoritarian form of society. This authoritarian state legitimized its demand upon the individual by the claim that it was enforcing the higher and general interests of the nation:

> We will never tolerate in the national state that anything sets itself over the authority of this national state. Be that whatever it may be, not even any church. Here too the unchangeable principle applies, the authority of the state stands over everything else, that means this living national community. Everything has to subject itself to this authority. If somebody attempts to take up a position against this authority, then he will be bent under this authority, one way or the other! There is only one authority possible, and this can only be that of the state, on the condition that this state in its turn only recognizes as its highest objective the preservation, protection and maintenance of a certain nation.[40]

This last remark was important for Hitler's *Weltanschauung*, because in contrast to an étatistic tradition he only permitted the claim of the state to authority when it served the 'interests of the nation'. Where it did not fulfil this purpose, the nation – as we have discussed in Chapter II.2. – had the right, and even the obligation, to rebel against the state.

Hitler described the state he projected as an alternative to the democratic system as a 'national state': 'The former class or caste state has developed into the German national state. A state which was once defined and ruled by interests of individual groups has now become a Reich which belongs solely to the German nation.'[41] The National Socialist world of ideas, said Hitler in a speech on 31 Januray 1941, represented

> ... the overcoming of individualism ... not in the sense that it curtails individual freedom or paralyzes the initiative of the individual but only in the sense that the total interest of all stands above individual freedom and any initiative of the individual, that this common interest is what regulates, what determines, if necessary what inhibits, if necessary also what commands.[42]

Let us summarize. Hitler rejected not only the principle of majority decision but also pluralistic democracy, in which lobbies and parties advocate their sundry interests. The arguments with which he criticized pluralism were neither clearly 'right wing' nor 'left wing', simply because criticism of pluralism by the Right and by the Left had many points in common. Whereas the conservative criticism of pluralism focused on the term 'common good', which is defined by the state, Marxist criticism was based on the claim that the alleged pluralism of the democratic system was only a camouflage for the actual dominance of the interests of capital. And it was exactly this opinion Hitler shared when he criticized democracy as a form of rule by capital.

c. Democracy as a Form of Rule by Capital
In a speech on 9 June 1927 Hitler said that the present system was not realizing rule by the people:

> In reality it is not the people who are ruling today, but capital. Do not claim, my dear comrades from the Left, that you are ruling! How many Germans actually have any concept of political life? They all only know what it says in the papers and what they read. But the newspapers are not made by the people, but by the 'hacks' who are being kept by capital.[43]

On 18 September 1928 Hitler declared that the Socialists had not achieved their objective because 'the capitalist idea today dominates the world more than ever before . . . Nobody believes that big capital has been smashed. Today it rules . . . more impudently than ever before.'[44]

In a democratic state, said Hitler in his 'Second Book', the political processes of decision take place under pressure from that

> . . . public opinion whose producers were the political parties and the press, who in their turn where given their final instructions by puppet masters who were hardly discernible. With this the interests of the nation were pushed more and more into the background as compared to the interests of certain and special groups.[45]

In the portrayal of Hitler's position on the middle class we have already seen that he believed that the democratization of the state had led to 'the state first falling into the hands of certain classes of society who identified with property for its own sake, with entrepreneurship for its own sake'. The state was then no longer an objective institution but an 'expression of the economic will and the business interests of certain groups within the nation'.[46]

It was dishonest, said Hitler on 12 September 1938, when the democracies described themselves as governments by the people and called the authoritarian states dictatorships, because 'what is called democracy in the other countries is in most cases nothing more than a captivation of public opinion achieved by means of clever press and money manipulation and a deceitful exploitation of the results achieved thereby'.[47] In Germany before the Great War, he said on 14 November 1940, capital had had 'an enormous influence on public life via the press and the former parties subsidized by capital', which had caused all social legislation to fail.[48]

Hitler developed his criticism of democracy in detail in a speech on 10 December 1940:

> You know that this democracy distinguishes itself by the following: they say that this is government by the people. Now then, the people need some sort of means by which they can express their thoughts or their desires. If we then take a closer

look at this problem we now discover that the people there have no convictions, but get their convictions served to them, of course, as everywhere else by the way. And the important thing is now: who decides these convictions of a people? Who enlightens a people? Who educates a people? In these countries it is actually capital which rules, that means a crowd of a few hundred people in the end, who possess enormous fortunes and who are completely independent and free because of the strange way public life is organized there. Because they say 'we have freedom here' and by this they mainly mean 'free enterprise'. And free enterprise they define as the freedom not only to acquire capital, but above all to use capital freely again, to be free of any state, that means national control, in the acquisition of capital, but also to be free of any state and national control in the use of capital. That is the definition of their freedom in reality. And this capital then first creates a press for itself. They talk about the freedom of the press. In reality each of these newspapers has a master. And this master is its financial backer in every case, in other words the owner. And this master now directs the appearance of this newspaper, not the editor. If he wants to write something other today than what pleases the master, then he gets kicked out next day. This press now, which is the absolutely servile unprincipled villain of its owners, this press now shapes public opinion. And the public opinion mobilized by this press is then divided into parties. These parties are as little distinguished from each other, as they were formerly distinguished from each other here with us.[49]

The opposition too, Hitler went on, was only a pretence. In the capitalist countries there were crass class differences and social tensions:

In these countries of so-called democracy it is not the people at all who are placed in the centre of their considerations. What is important is only the existence of these few makers of democracy, that means the existence of those few hundred gigantic capitalists, who own all their values, all of their shares, and who thereby completely direct these nations in the final analysis. The masses do not interest them in the slightest. Exactly like formerly our bourgeois parties, they only interest them at election time, then they need their votes ... No, believe me, in these states, and this is demonstrated by their whole economic structure, under the mantle of democracy there rules the egoism of a relatively very small group. And this group is not corrected and controlled by anybody.[50]

In Hitler's polemics the audience (he gave his speech to armaments workers) and the purpose (the propagandistic mobilization for the war against the Western powers) played a role, of course. However, these factors should not be overestimated, because the view he expressed here fits in completely with his statements in his table talks, for example, where we have already seen that he believed that, in the capitalist system, the ministers and leading politicians were bribed by capital with positions on supervisory boards and the ownership of shares.[51]

In view of the persistence with which Hitler expounded the theory that, by means of manipulation of the press, democracy was only a camouflaged form

VI: Concepts and Objectives in Domestic Policies

of government by capital, and in view of the inherent logic of these arguments, there is no reason to doubt that the statements cited above did reflect his true opinion. What is more, Hitler expressed these opinions not only in front of workers, but also, for example, in his address on 30 January 1941, the eighth anniversary of the seizure of power. In his polemics against the capitalist enemy states he declared:

> Here, too, they make do with phrases, they talk of freedom, they talk of democracy, they talk about the achievements of the liberal system, and all they mean by it is the stabilization of a regime by a social class which is enabled, thanks to its capital, to lay its hands on the press, to organize and to direct it and thereby to shape public opinion.[52]

In the light of what we have discussed in this work so far about Hitler's views on social and economic policy and his self-understanding as a revolutionary, such statements are hardly surprising. They actually fit in completely with the picture of Hitler developed so far. While we must keep in mind that, in his speeches denouncing democracy as a form of rule by capital, his first concern was the propagandistic unmasking of the claim to democracy by the enemy states, there can be no doubt that Hitler himself shared the conviction that democracy was finally nothing more than a form of capitalist rule and manipulation.

The only possible doubt whether all this was nothing more than calculated propaganda could at best be founded in the one-sided picture of Hitler – primarily influenced by a dogmatic-Marxist school of history – having been a lackey of monopoly capital, a pawn in the hands of Flick and Thyssen. Such a position can be understood as being a defence, because a conservative school of history is only pointing to certain similarities between Communism and National Socialism in an attempt to discredit the former. This, however, is certainly not our intention. Nor is the issue to certify a conformity between the two 'totalitarian' ideologies and regimes simply because both agree in their rejection of a pluralistic and parliamentarian democracy. What is interesting, however, is that Hitler's criticism of democracy not only agrees in content with certain conservative positions (for example the contrasting of 'special interest policy' and 'common good'), but also with Marxist positions (for example the polemics against democracy as a camouflaged form of rule by capital). In this Lothar Kettenacker is correct when he states that 'National Socialism was capable of anything, but certainly in any case of a policy which in practice could be more anti-middle class and anti-capitalist than later generations, who are imbued with just this awareness, would consider to be theoretically permissible'.[53]

At the end of this chapter we will discuss Hitler's view that democracy only ruled in historic 'periods of decay' and was an expression of 'decadence'. What reasons does Hitler present for this view, particularly within the context of his socio-Darwinistic basic philosophy? Moreover, how does Hitler develop his argument against the claim raised by the proponents of the democratic system that it is the emphasis on freedom and tolerance which distinguishes this form of government from the others?

d. Democracy as a Sign of Decadence and Weakness

In *Mein Kampf* Hitler calls parliamentarism 'one of the most serious signs of decay of mankind'.[54] It had been forgotten, said Hitler in a speech on 30 November 1928, 'that the world has only had the period of democracy for a very short time, that this is a sign of decay, that the Roman state and England had not been democratic republics in the sense of today, but that they had been aristocratic republics'.[55]

He repeated this view in several speeches and articles. On 2 March 1929, in the *Illustrierte Beobachter*, he wrote that 'in the history of the world this parliamentary-democratic system has only ruled in very minute periods of time and regularly only in periods of the decay of nations and states'.[56] Democracy, he said on 26 June 1931, was never creative.[57] He called the 'replacement of the value of personality by the levelling term of the number in a democracy' a manifestation that only appears 'in times of the decay of the nation'.[58] No state, he declared in a speech at the *Reichsparteitag* in 1936, had been created by today's democracy, 'but all the great nations experienced their destruction through this form of democracy'.[59]

How did Hitler reach the conclusion that democracy was a sign of decay, of decadence? We have already seen in the discussion of his criticism of the majority principle that he associated parliamentary democracy with such terms as 'weakness' and 'cowardice'. In his socio-Darwinistic view of history, however, 'weakness' and 'cowardice' stand for 'unfit for survival' and 'decay'. Anything weak and cowardly has no right to live and must go under, be this individuals, classes of society, systems of government or nations. This was one of Hitler's most fundamental convictions. But how did he come to associate democracy with these terms? As paradoxical as this may sound, one of the key reasons was that in a democracy he had the freedom to fight against democracy, to ridicule it, and finally to defeat it with its own weapons.

His repeatedly stated objective was to defeat 'democracy with the weapons of democracy'.[60] 'We defeated our opponents on their own democratic base,' he announced on 15 January 1936 on the anniversary of the victory by the NSDAP in the state elections in Lippe-Detmold in 1933.[61] The National Socialist revolution, he said on 30 January 1941, 'defeated democracy by democracy during democracy!'[62] Hitler considered a repetition of this event within the National Socialist regime to be impossible because

> All of the boneheads who are counting on a return to the past would have to decide to go the same route I did. That means a nameless one would have to come along and begin the same struggle that I began, but with the difference [that] I defeated democracy through its own insanity! No democracy can remove us, however. We have removed the preconditions for a return to such a game for the coming centuries.[63]

Hitler was only able to interpret it as being weakness when a state permitted a movement to be founded, developed, organized and put in uniform whose declared objective was the destruction of this very state. The 'cowardice' of the Weimar Republic before the National Socialists, that is, the negligence of the police and the authorities and the tolerance of the state, was not admired by Hitler as a sign of liberalism and freedom but despised as stupidity, cowardice and weakness – and therefore as a sign of the necessary downfall of democracy. What was true for domestic policy was also true for Hitler in foreign policy. Just as he was convinced of the cowardice and weakness of the middle class and its political parties, so did British appeasement policy confirm his conviction that democracy was weak and outdated.

e. Hitler on Political Freedom

In a speech on 29 April 1937 in which Hitler developed his thesis of the contradiction between the definition of the state and democracy, as well as his view of the world-wide crisis of this form of government, he came to speak about the problem of the relationship between freedom and force:

> What we see around us is also only conceivable by the concentration of the labour of millions of individual people. And they are all thereby somehow naturally bound and improved in their unrestricted personal freedom. This may be painful for the individual. I believe that somewhere and somehow there is a small amount of an anarchic drive to rebel naturally hidden in everybody. But that is simply of no use at all. If we believe in a mission of mankind, then we have to believe that man must define and reaffirm this mission through his achievements. But when we decide to trust in human achievement, then we must accept that all these achievements can only be achievements by the community. And if we trust in achievements by the community, then we must recognize that any community somehow requires the concentration of all the forces, that it is not conceivable to say: now go and do everything you want to do, but that it is necessary to give the order: *now go and do what one will wants.*

Hitler was therefore legitimizing the restriction of human freedom by the necessity of producing communal achievements which required a uniform co-ordination. The alternative to this was chaos and anarchy:

> Because if you were to let the total mass of a nation run free according to the point of view of democratic freedom of action, and there is only the harsh either/or, then, my party comrades, we can imagine what kind of a spectacle such a nation would present when seen from above. An anthill, I believe, would still be a marvel of organization and discipline, because there too there are rules which have to be obeyed. But if we were to let the people run free, if today we were to establish the principle that each one do what he considers to be proper, right, orderly, correct and so forth, then mankind would not advance by the road of the enjoyment of freedom, but it would, on the contrary, destroy, and thereby lose within a short time, everything that millennia of a disciplined concentration of man have achieved.

The 'concentration of all human activity' was nothing more than a commandment of common sense:

> And therefore the precondition for such a concentration, namely the creation of an authority, is simply a commandment of common sense, or common sense itself. Compared to this, I would like to state, democracy in the final analysis is the dissolution of concentration and therefore the opposite of common sense; it is insanity.[64]

In a speech to farmers on the occasion of the harvest thanksgiving festival in 1937 Hitler declared that there was 'no freedom of the individual, just as there is no freedom of the class', because nature constantly forced people to perform work they did not like, to achievements which were not always pleasant.[65] Such restrictions of freedom were, according to Hitler's view, also those restrictions, for example, that were imposed by the obligations of the labour service. The children of the higher-placed families in particular had to be forced to perform physical labour in order thereby to lose their class conceit. 'Insofar as the interest of the national community permits freedom for the individual, it is given to him. Where his freedom interferes with the interests of the national community, the freedom of the individual ceases. Then the freedom of the nation takes the place of the freedom of the individual.'[66]

In his table talks Hitler based the restriction of human freedom on the argument that the

> ... greatest measure of cultural achievement ... can only be reached by a strict concentration into a state organization ... Without organization, that means without force, and thereby without renunciation by the individual, it will not work. Life itself is nothing but an ongoing renunciation of personal freedom. The higher a person rises, the more easy it must become for him to give things up! Because, based on his extended vantage point, he must be all the more aware of the necessity of giving things up.[67]

In another table talk, Hitler explained that 'it is not individual freedom which is a sign of a higher level of culture, but the restriction of individual freedom by an organization which includes as many individuals of the same race as possible'. The more the reins of a strict state organization were loosened and individual freedom given room, the more one directed the fate of a nation on to the path of cultural regression. A community could, simply, only be created and maintained by force. For this reason it was wrong, for example, to criticize the methods of Charlemagne, or today of Stalin in the Soviet Union.[68] What was important, Hitler said in a table talk on 28 July 1942, was that the restrictions on freedom were the same for everyone.[69]

While some of these statements about freedom and force were couched in such general terms that even a democrat could agree with them, the anti-democratic and totalitarian character of Hitler's ideas is proved by his rejection of the concept of tolerance. The democratic system was, seen from its claim, based on the principles of freedom of opinion and plurality of political persuasions. Hitler strictly rejected these principles:

> ... when I have recognized an opinion as being correct, then I not only have the obligation in a state to impart this opinion to my fellow citizens but beyond that also the obligation to remove contradicting opinions. This may be regarded as being intolerant. But, my officers, all of life is an eternal intolerance. This nature also teaches us. Nature is intolerant of anything that is not right and therefore weak ... Nature already removes the weakest and the weak among the most primitive forms of life ... It is insanity to imagine today that political concepts should be tolerant. Tolerance is only understandable as a sign of inner insecurity. But the moment I am inwardly completely sure about a problem, I not only have the right to impart this problem or this opinion, but the duty to remove the others ... There is no tolerance in nature. Nature is, if I take 'tolerance' as a human term, the most intolerant thing there is. It destroys everything that is not quite fit to live, that does not want to defend itself, or is not able to defend itself, this it removes, and we are only a speck of dust in this nature, man is nothing more than a little bacteria or a little germ on such a planet. If he attempts to evade these laws, he does not change the laws but ends his own existence.[70]

These statements clarify once again why Hitler rejected democracy in particular. Democracy as a tolerant form of government, which not only tolerates but even demands a plurality of *Weltanschauungen* and political persuasions, was for Hitler weak and therefore doomed to go under. Tolerance of one's political opponent was for him primarily a sign of weakness and insecurity. But the revolutionary character of his *Weltanschauung* is proved by the fact that he put the question of power into the centre of his considerations and was convinced of the necessity of bringing the political opponent down with all available force and authority.

Let us summarize. Hitler did not define the freedom of the individual as a value in itself but believed instead that the precondition for human progress was the restriction of personal freedom. The freedom and tolerance granted in the democratic state was not a positive value for him, not a strength of this system, but a clear sign of weakness and decadence. His conviction of the necessity of revolutionary substitution of democracy by an authoritarian form of government was derived from his socio-Darwinistic *Weltanschauung*. Democracy had proved its weakness, especially by its tolerance, by the freedom it granted to its political opponents. Since nature did not accept the weak and the cowardly, but only the strong, the uncompromising, the replacement of democracy by another form of government was inevitable. How did Hitler envisage this other form of government? What were the principles upon which it should be based? And, if he did not accept the decision of the majority, the 'principle of majority' he ridiculed, on what foundation should the system he aspired to be based?

2. The 'Historic Minority' as a Subject of Revolution

We have seen that Hitler rejected the 'majority principle' as the basis for the formulation of political demands and objectives in the democratic state. He also wanted to get rid of the former élites in the long term, even though he initially still had to make use of them. But what was to take the place of the élites and the 'majority principle' he criticized? What were the principles according to which the new élite was to be recruited? Even though this question – which is so important for understanding Hitler's politics – played an outstanding role in his speeches and writings, until now any closer examination of his concepts in this area has been lacking. These, however, are of central importance for our topic, because every revolutionary is immediately faced with the question of the subject of the revolution, in other words the question of organizing a revolutionary élite which acts as the bearer of the revolutionary restructuring of the state. Furthermore, it is also a fundamental question for any political system how the political power élite is developed.

Hitler opposed the 'majority principle' he rejected with the theory of the historic role of the 'minority', which was to be the bearer of the revolutionary process and occupy the decisive positions of power in the new state. It was not the majority which made history, he maintained, but above all active, conscious minorities. However, since Hitler declared that all the traditional features of the former élites were secondary, or without importance or harmful (education, property, social prestige, occupation, income etc.), and even intended to do away with all that, the question arises by which methods, according to which principles and criteria he intended to recruit his new revolutionary élite, in other words what he called the 'historic minority'.

Hitler's concepts require a clear differentiation between two phases, namely the 'movement phase', i.e. the time of struggle before the seizure of power, and the 'system phase' after the gaining of political power.

a. The Principles of Élite Recruitment in the Movement Phase and the Theory of the 'Historic Minority'

It was one of Hitler's most frequently repeated basic convictions that history is never made by majority decisions but always by the efforts of deliberate, organized minorities. 'Great historic events,' said Hitler on 30 January 1922, 'are always and exclusively only forced upon the lethargic mass of the whole by minorities with strong faith.'[71] In a speech on 25 October 1925 Hitler said:

> Only a minority in which activity and daredevilry dominate is capable of a revolution. All revolutions have been the result of a minority prepared to fight, so also the one on 8 to 11 November [1918]. Only because the USPD made itself independent as an active fighting minority could the revolution be carried out. This was the lever where the National Socialists have to hook on.[72]

Hitler was therefore deliberately orientating himself with Marxism, and regarded a radical, relatively small party such as the USPD (the left-wing splinter group of the SPD) as an example of the 'historic minority' he wanted to collect within the NSDAP.

But how did Hitler intend to ensure that a 'historic minority' actually did come together in his party? Hitler's answer to this was that because to declare one's belief in National Socialism led to ostracism, and because activities on behalf of the ideals of the movement could involve serious physical dangers (for the SA), the ones to join his movement would automatically only be the truly brave and daring idealists, while the opportunists and the cowards would avoid it. This conviction, which was fundamental to Hitler's theory of recruitment of an élite, first appeared in a speech made on 28 July 1922 when he addressed the SA men:

> ... whoever is today a leader of the German nation on our side, so help me God, has nothing to gain, but only perhaps everything to lose... Whoever fights for you today, he cannot at present gain great honour, even less gain great wealth, more likely he will land in jail. Whoever is your leader today already has to be an idealist because he leads those against whom apparently everything conspires. In this lies an immeasurable source of strength.[73]

In *Mein Kampf* Hitler emphasized that anybody who joined the movement had to know in advance that 'the new movement offered honour and fame before posterity, but could offer nothing in the present'. The more a movement has to offer in the way of easily 'gainable' positions and jobs, the greater will be the attraction of inferior people, until finally these political part-timers will swamp a successful party in such numbers that the upright fighter of former times will no longer recognize the old movement and the newly joined will reject him as a noisome 'undesirable'. With this, however, the 'mission' of such a movement is done with.[74]

Hitler therefore also regarded participating in elections and sending deputies into the parliaments as being a great danger for the revolutionary character of the party.[75] If the party were only to appear determined and radical, then only a few

> ... comrades in arms [would join] from a society ... which was not only physically, but all too often also mentally, outdated ... Opposed to us stands the infinite army of the not necessarily wilfully bad, but of the mentally lazy, indifferent, or even the ones interested in the maintenance of present conditions. But in exactly this apparent hopelessness of our gigantic struggle lies the grandeur of our task and also the possibility of success. The battle cry which either scares away the petty spirits right from the start or quickly makes them lose heart becomes the signal for the joining together of the true fighting spirits. And one must be clear about this: *When in a nation a certain sum of the highest energy and determination appears to be united towards one objective, and thereby removed for ever from the lethargy of the broad masses, this small percentage has risen up to become the masters of the total number. World history is made by minorities when this minority of numbers embodies the majority of will and determination. What many may regard as a burden today is actually the precondition for our victory. In the magnitude and difficulty of our task lies the probability that only the best fighters will unite to fight for it. In this élite lies the guarantee of success.*

If we accept this idea, then it was important to keep the number of the members of the party as small as possible so that it would not become 'diluted' by 'unheroic' and 'cowardly' people and thereby lose its revolutionary character. Hitler therefore made a clear distinction between 'adherents' and 'members' of the party:

> When a movement nurses the intent to tear a world down and erect a new one in its place, then there must be complete clarity within the ranks of its own leadership about the following principle: *Any movement will first have to sort the human material it has gained into one of two groups, into adherents and members. It is the task of propaganda to gain adherents, it is the task of the organization to gain members. An adherent of a movement is he who declares himself to be in agreement with its objectives, a member is someone who fights for them ... Adherence is rooted in insight, membership in the courage to personally advocate and spread that insight. Insight in its passive form suits the majority of mankind which is lethargic and cowardly. Membership requires activistic convictions and therefore suits only a minority of mankind ... Resounding success of a revolution in* Weltanschauung *will always only be gained when the new* Weltanschauung *is taught to all the people if at all possible, and if necessary, subsequently forced upon*

them, whereas the organization, the idea, the movement should only encompass the number that is absolutely necessary to occupy the nerve centres of the state in question... Organizations, in other words numbers of members that grow above a certain size, gradually lose their fighting power and are no longer able to support the propaganda of an idea with determination and aggressively, or rather to utilize it. The greater and inwardly revolutionary an idea now is, the more activistic will its membership become, because there is a danger to its supporters tied to the revolutionary power of the idea which appears to be suited to keeping the petty, cowardly petit bourgeois away from it.

Therefore the propaganda of a party had to be as radical and inciting as possible, because this scared the 'weaklings and hesitant natures away' and prevented them from 'penetrating into the first nucleus of our organization'. The radicalism of the propaganda guaranteed that only really radical people joined the organization.[76]

In his speeches Hitler normally cited the Soviet Communist party, or the Italian Fascist party, as proof of the efficiency of a small, radical party based on a *Weltanschauung*. In a speech on 12 June 1925, for example, he said:

The Communist party in Russia only has 470,000 members; they control 138 million. 580,000 Fascists rule the Italian state. That is a troop which can not be torn asunder. That is where the strength and the power lies. If we had 600,000 men who would all submit themselves to this objective we would be a power.

Hitler was convinced that the time of illegality and persecution (the NSDAP had been banned after the abortive *putsch* attempt in November 1923) was a touchstone which would show who really belonged to the historic minority and who did not:

Times of persecution are almost necessary for the movement, they are perhaps a critical test of nature. The one who is healthy shall be dedicated to life. The illnesses of the movement are the moments of persecution, they are only great periods of purification. Whoever flees in such periods should not be held back.[77]

According to Hitler, the party goes through different stages of its development: (1) The movement is hushed up. (2) The movement is ridiculed. (3) Then persecution sets in. (4) The phase of success. During the second phase – and this was good – some of the 'vacillating adherents' deserted the party. During the period of persecution, however,

... the flight from its ranks begins. But if only the nucleus of a movement loyally and unshakeably holds fast to the flag, then this danger must be overcome. If the adherents are convinced of the rightness of the idea and the honesty of the determination, then the nucleus will never go under during the persecution but emerge from it with renewed strength. When a movement has overcome the curse of ridicule, then it is good to carry out a purification from time to time, and this is normally taken care of by the enemy. Whoever does not stand fast under the barrage of persecution also belongs out of the movement.[78]

In Hitler's view, therefore, the dangers of persecution, ostracism, or even physical dangers were not something negative but led to only idealists and fanatics (for Hitler a positive term) joining the party or remaining loyal to it. This was an important difference compared to the middle-class parties:

Subject one of these bourgeois parties to such persecutions as we are subjected to, and then you will see if anything still remains of them! In this lies the sign that our movement cannot be suppressed despite all the persecutions. We have not become fewer, we have gained disciples. Whoever joins our movement is constantly walking between the fulfilment of his duty and the gates of the prisons.[79]

These views are again only understandable within the context of Hitler's fundamental socio-Darwinistic convictions. The movement was to unite the active 'historic minority', the brave, courageous men determined to fight. The radicalism of the propaganda on the one hand, which scared away the middle-class 'cowardly' people from joining the party, and ostracism and persecution on the other, which purged the party from the 'cowardly' elements, guaranteed that the 'historic minority' joined together in the movement. This élite was not distinguished by education, occupation, class, or wealth – these were more likely hindrances because they gave a man too much to lose[80] – but by daring, courage, unshakeable faith and fanaticism. However, since these attributes could always only be found among a minority of the nation, too strong a growth of the party finally led to its weakening. Here again Hitler was learning from Marxism, and he analyzed the reasons for Social Democracy's change from a revolutionary to a reform party:

Over the years the Marxist movement, organized into the Social Democratic party, became ever bigger and more encompassing in volume. But this increase actually meant an inner weakening, because the ultimate goals of the Marxist *Weltanschauung* are so radical that they can only be fought through by an absolutely fanatical unit of shock troops. After Social Democracy had exceeded a certain measure of adherents, it had to fall to the danger of a so-called 'bourgeoisization', had to gradually become ever tamer, and it could not be avoided that one day this army of the old prewar Social Democracy numbering in the millions would more or less come to terms with the existing state and would basically end as a reform party, which would advocate certain economic interests of the mass of the employees and gradually leave the ground of radicalism already from its basic tendencies. That is why in the fifth month of the war a split occurred, which some of the leaders had organized within an extraordinarily sound framework, and which from the very first day displayed such radical tendencies that the group which was prepared to commit itself to these tendencies could only be very small, whereby the former Independent Party took a position against the war loans in the most brutal manner and accused Germany of being guilty of the war. Because of the most extreme exaggeration of these radical objectives the size of the new movement was limited, but with this the probability was also given that its adherents would only consist of the most radical elements prepared for the extreme. And later on this calculation worked out completely.

The USPD had had 'the best human material within its ranks, all of them infatuated, brutal, ruthless brains, who because of the extraordinarily far-reaching fanatical objectives of the movement could themselves only consist of the most fanatical and most determined people. Later on these brains then made the revolution possible.'[81]

The important characteristic of such an élite, the decisive criterion for whether this was 'the best human material' (as Hitler expressed himself) or not, was the willingness to embrace sacrifice and heroism, not social status. Hitler tried to explain this to his middle-class audience during a speech at the Hamburg National Club of 1919:

> By and large a nation will always consist of three parts, the big, broad, lethargic mass, the middle class which is gravitated to wherever the power resides at the moment and where success is, and probably to where the lack of courage makes it appear to be advantageous. Opposed to this broad mass on the other side stands a small part of heroism, of heroism in all sectors of life, of spiritual heroism, of actual heroism, which is ordained for leadership. Do not think that this part stands exclusively on intelligence, it goes down all the way to the farmers, down into every factory. That is an élite, which is better and better. They are prepared to put back their own ego, their own interests compared to the interests of all, to stand for their nation, be it a very humble person, a better sort of street cleaner, or a professor, or an entrepreneur,[82] or anybody else, that makes no difference ... And this most important part can be found throughout the whole nation, in every class. It is the better blood.[83]

Hitler developed these principles for the recruitment of an élite in many more long speeches, from which we can only quote in part here.[84]

For the time before the seizure of power, we only want to point to two further fundamental speeches on the topic of the recruitment of an élite. On 2 September 1928 Hitler gave his most important speech under the heading 'On the internal energy of the National Socialist party'. Here he developed the theory of the alleged natural law and necessity of victory for a party if it understood the laws of the creation of an élite and acted according to them.

Throughout world history, Hitler began his presentation, there have been individual manifestations from time to time, which already within a relatively short span of time 'turn a world around and lead new opinions to victory', even though the bearers of these ideas 'are infinitely small in number, whereas the opposition is apparently insurmountable'. Such a rise of an idea – as Marxism is – could only be understood if one had understood the principle of selection in the political field. It was

> ... the task of an age to sort out the people, to find out those whose specific value was a particularly high one, because out of some organization or other, or total number, that fraction is pulled out which has a particularly high personal value... But if I succeed in pulling out and collecting the most highly valuable achievements from this chaos by means of a specific process, then the preponderance of this whole lies in this part which unites a specific value within itself to the highest degree. When an idea succeeds in securing the highest specific individual values for itself, then it embodies the historic minority which makes history.

Hitler then went on to ask, But how can an idea now secure these 'highest individual values' for itself?

> The answer to this was given to us by historic experience. Every *Weltanschauung* which appears to be correct, at least according to examination from without, but which stands itself absolutely contrary to an existing condition which has become ossified within itself, will then one day possess the majority of the energy if it wages its battle ruthlessly and is ruthlessly supported by the other side. It does not require much courage to do one's duty silently within an existing organization, but more courage to fight against an existing condition. As soon as a person aggressively goes against an existing condition, he will have to find more courage than the one who defends it. Motion requires more courage that merely standing still. The attack attracts those people to it who possess more courage. Thereby a condition which contains a danger becomes a magnet for people who like to court danger. A programme with radical ideas will attract radical people. An organization such as *Rotfront* [a radical left-wing counterpart to Hitler's SA—H.B.], which has the most brutal sense of aggression from the start, will also only gain people who are analogously inclined. Movements with a radical persuasion attract people of radical persuasion by the nature of their tendency, those with cowardly tendencies people with a cowardly nature. When I now equip a movement with radical tendencies, what is added is the reaction of the existing condition. The opposition by the mass begins to further sift even this small number. What then remains is a minority of determined hard people. This process alone is what makes it historically explainable why certain upheavals took place which started off with only a very few people and gave the world a new appearance. Added to this we now also have the active opposition of the existing state. All the parties, public opinion, take sides against us. In this lies the unequivocal, I would like to say almost mathematical reason for the coming success of our movement. As long as we are the radical movement, public opinion shuns us, the existing factors of the state oppose us, so long will we collect valuable human material within us, even then when, as they say, all human reason is against it. The future of our movement lies in this, that by this

process we slowly, indestructibly collect the historic minority, which in Germany will perhaps number between 600,000 and 800,000 people.[85]

On 24 February 1929 Hitler repeated this line of reasoning. For him those people were valuable who swam 'against the current', but not those who swam with it – because one did not need any strength for that:

> Whoever runs with the public mass, whoever stays in it, does not need any daring, he does not need any courage. Whoever accepts the events of the day, who submits to them, does not need any heroism, he does not need a sense of sacrifice. He can always make money out of it. Only the one who dares to declare war on the spirit of the age, he needs courage and he needs heroism. Only whoever dares to set himself against a fact which has become second nature and to proclaim another idea, another opinion, he must then also make sacrifices. And only the one who needs courage and has to make sacrifices will be capable of courage and sacrifice. The wonderful thing about it is that there is after all an inner link between the programme and the people.[86]

If we follow this line of reasoning, we discover that it does not lack a certain inner logic. Of course, it also applies to the same degree to any radical movement, and to the KPD to an even higher degree than to the NSDAP, because during the days of the Weimar Republic it was far more heavily persecuted by the state. Hitler recognized this and, as we have seen, was of the opinion that in parties such as the USPD, or in organizations such as the *Rotfront*, the 'best human material' was also being collected. This did not apply to the bourgeois parties, however, who were only defending the *status quo* and therefore only attracted the cowardly people. This explains why Hitler only took Marxism seriously as an opponent and not the parties of the middle class.

There is a second conclusion to be drawn from Hitler's theory. If an emphatically radical movement attracts all those people who have nothing to lose, then this will include many dead-beats who have failed in normal everyday life and who, while perhaps being useful for certain purposes – as SA fighters, for example – will hardly be the élite with which one can build up the new state.

Wagener reports that Hitler was well aware of this problem. Towards the end of 1930 and the beginning of 1931 Hitler told him he had to take

> ... everybody who puts himself at my disposal. If I find many among them who have failed, what of it? They are certainly more prepared and determined than others to build a new future for themselves, to fill their impoverished lives with a new meaning. Yes, they are even often the better fighters, the more ruthless advocates of our concepts, the more fanatical flag bearers of our faith. Who would you rather see in the political organization than such fighters?

Wagener reports that these statements led to a controversy between himself and Gregor Strasser, during which the latter said that only those people advanced to become leaders of the party and its formations 'who are nothing and have nothing'. Wagener objected with indignation: 'And these nonentities are then supposed to be political leaders!', whereupon Hitler interrupted the dispute:

> You see. That is why I am in favour of the *Führer* principle. You are both right. We are dependent on those who offer themselves. And unfortunately these are not always the best. Therefore we must not permit them to speak freely and say whatever they want. All they may advocate is what they are told to from higher up. Only one person can lead. They are only strong enough to obey.[87]

Therefore the '*Führer* principle' was also a conclusion from Hitler's recognition of the fact that while the 'human material' gained according to his principles might consist of brave and daring it did not necessarily always need to consist of intelligent people.

Even after the seizure of power Hitler still quite frequently spoke about the problem of recruiting an élite. In Chapter III.3.a we discussed one of the trains of thought that were of central importance for his theory, namely that in business and politics the principles of recruiting an élite contradicted each other, and it was therefore completely wrong to elevate the business élite, in other words the bourgeoisie, to become also the political élite. Hitler's statements on the recruitment of an élite made after the seizure of power can be divided into several main groups of statements. On the one hand he naturally looked back to the time of struggle – in commemorative speeches and addresses at the *Reichsparteitage*, for example – and again repeated the principles of recruitment of an élite[88] we have already discussed. On the other hand, he also addressed himself to the principles and problems of recruiting an élite in the system phase, which were of a totally different nature than in the movement phase.

b. The Problems of Élite Recruitment in the System Phase

Let us again trace the logic of Hitler's line of argument. Commitment to a radical political movement requires courage, because its members or adherents are exposed to ostracism, and under certain circumstances even to political oppression, persecution and physical dangers. But this is exactly the reason why the real élite, that is, the 'historic minority', the most determined, courageous and consistent men gather together in this movement or party. But what happens if the movement is successful or has even already acquired the political power? Then a commitment to such a movement no longer requires any courage; on the

VI: Concepts and Objectives in Domestic Policies

contrary, the commitment *against* this movement would require courage, whereas the opportunists are the ones who would join the party. Obviously, therefore, Hitler's statements on the principles of recruiting an élite only apply to the movement phase, i.e. the 'time of struggle', and not to the period after political power has been gained. Was Hitler aware of this problem, and, if so, how did he react to it?

In the preceding chapter we quoted from a speech by Hitler made on 8 July 1925 in which he differentiated between the various phases in the development of a movement. The first three phases were: the movement is hushed up; the movement is ridiculed; persecution of the movement. But Hitler also mentioned a fourth danger:

> When a young movement holds out the promise of success, when you can already see victory beckoning in the distance, then *the great migration* begins. Then people come from all sides who push their way into the movement and who will soon be marching not only in the ranks but even at the head. These are the ones who did not want to make sacrifices, not to suffer deprivations, but who now hurry so that at the finish line of the movement they will have gained a seat in parliament, or some other sort of advantageous place in the expected kingdom of heaven to be reached down here on earth.

The best example for such a fatal development was Social Democracy: 'With time, others push their way in and give the concept a new shape.'[89] In *Mein Kampf* Hitler also discussed this problem in detail. The 'greatest danger' for a movement was an abnormally rapid growth in membership due to rapid successes:

> Because as much as a movement, as long as it has to fight bitterly, is avoided by all cowardly and egoistically minded people, so quickly are these wont to become members when developments have made the great success of the party become probable or it has already occurred. To this can be traced why many victorious movements suddenly fall back out of an unexplainable inner weakness shortly before their success, or, better before the final accomplishment of their intentions, give up the battle and finally die. As a result of their initial victory so many bad, unworthy but especially cowardly elements come into their organization, that these inferior people finally gain preponderance over the ones with fighting power and then force the movement into the service of their own interests, pull it down to the level of their own meagre heroism and do nothing to complete the victory of the original idea. The fanatical objective has then become blurred, the fighting power paralyzed, or, as the bourgeois world is wont to say quite rightly in such a case, 'the wine has now also been mixed with water'.[90]

Hitler was addressing the fundamental problems of any revolutionary movement, namely 'degeneration' and 'opportunism'. The example he primarily had in mind was apparently Social Democracy, which, by becoming

365

parliamentary and the too large growth of its membership, had lost the character of a revolutionary party and degenerated into a mere reform party. How then, Hitler asked, could the revolutionary character of a party be maintained even after success had been achieved and the power in the state already gained? His answer was in *Mein Kampf*:

> For a movement it is therefore very necessary, out of the sheer instinct for survival, that as soon as success has placed itself at its side, it immediately stops all induction of new members, and from then on only increases the size of its organization with the utmost caution and after thorough examination. Only by this will it be able to maintain the nucleus of the movement genuinely fresh and healthy. It must then assure that only this nucleus alone then continues to lead the movement, that means to decide the propaganda which is intended to lead to its general acceptance, and as the holder of power, to undertake the actions that are necessary for the practical achievement of its ideas.[91]

When a movement is successful and 'victory appears to be ready to attach itself to its flag', Hitler warned in a speech on 18 September 1928, then suddenly 'inferior elements' rush in in great numbers:

> Then, namely, when the battle is done and the entry into the conquered city takes place, then these vacillating cowardly egoists begin to rush in in hordes in order to march in at the head of the fighters into the conquered castle, not as attackers but as a rabble which has only changed sides with a certain alacrity and far out in front so that they achieve a success first! These are actually scoundrels. The rogues can be found in any movement as soon as it achieves victory. Woe unto such a movement if it does not protect itself against such elements and attempt to remove them. One day it will possess these elements.[92]

As we know, the success about which Hitler was warning here was first achieved by the NSDAP in the elections on 14 September 1930, when, compared to the elections of two years before, it was able to increase its votes from 810,000 to 6.4 million and the number of its seats from 12 to 107. And, in actual fact, the development Hitler had feared had to a certain degree already begun. As Joachim Fest writes in his Hitler biography about the situation after the September elections in 1930, 'the opportunists, the anxious', began to adjust to the new power structure:

> ... it now became 'in', in many cases, to belong to the NSDAP. Already in the spring Prince August Wilhelm ('Auwi'), one of the sons of the *Kaiser*, had joined and remarked that where a Hitler led, anybody could submit himself; now came Hjalmar Schacht, who had helped formulate the Youngs Plan and had defended it against the criticism of the National Socialists, and many others followed. Already in the two and a half months to the end of the year, the membership of the NSDAP rose by almost exactly 100,000 to 389,000.[93]

A similar development, though of far greater proportions, took place after the seizure of power in 1933. The NSDAP, which in 1933 had been able to depend on about 849,000 members,[94] took in 1,644,881 new party members between the 'upheaval' and the first ban on new memberships, an increase of 193 per cent. Almost two-thirds of the 2,493,890 party members in the early summer of 1933 consisted of what the 'old fighters' called the 'March casualties', in other words primarily of those opportunists which Hitler had said in *Mein Kampf* would join the party in the phase of its success.

In a speech in the *Reichstag* on 30 January 1934 Hitler again addressed himself to these 'elements'. More dangerous than the other enemies of National Socialism, among whom he deigned to mention specifically Communists, bourgeois intellectuals, reactionaries and national ideologists, were

> ... those political migratory birds who always appear at exactly the place where in summer time the harvest is in progress. Subjects of weak character, but who as true fanatics of opportunism, hurl themselves upon any successful movement and attempt by overly loud shouting and a conduct of one hundred and ten per cent, to prevent from the beginning, or to answer, any question about their former origin. They are dangerous because under the mask of the new regime they are only attempting to satisfy their own personal interests, and thereby become a real burden for a movement for which millions of upright people made the greatest sacrifices for many years without, perhaps, ever even having believed in their imagination that they would ever be compensated for what they had taken upon themselves for their nation in the way of suffering and deprivation. To cleanse the state and the party of these noxious parasites will be an important task, especially for the future.[95]

In his closing address at the *Reichsparteitag* in 1934 Hitler also turned to the problem of recruiting an élite in the system phase. It was important, Hitler declared, to restrict the increase in party members to those who offered the guarantee that they actually did belong to

> ... that minority which up to now has always made history due to its value. When formerly the natural battle, the given requirements and the sacrifices demanded automatically carried out a healthy selection and prevented chaff from being added to the wheat, then we must now ourselves ensure this prevention for the future by means of conscientious methods of the most stringent tests. Once it was dangerous to become a National Socialist, and therefore we received the best fighters. Today it is useful to 'latch on' to us, and we therefore have to be careful of the inflow of those who only want to do cheap business under the symbol of our struggle and our sacrifices. Once our opponents ensured, by means of waves of prohibition and persecution, that from time to time the movement was again cleansed of this light stuff which had begun to find its way in. Today we ourselves must conduct the inspection and reject what has proved itself to be bad and therefore inwardly does not belong to us. The great virtues of sacrifice, loyalty and obedience, in which we

were formerly tested from time to time by the persecution by our enemies, we must now subject to our own test. And whoever does not pass this test must leave us.[96]

Baldur von Schirach, Reichs Youth Leader and later Hitler's Deputy in Vienna, reported that Hitler had often told him while the movement was still small: 'I shudder to think of the day on which the big herd will flow in to us.'[97]

In *Mein Kampf* Hitler had already advised a stop on new member admissions in order to deal with this danger of the 'opportunists', to prevent the inflow of opportunistic elements into the party after it came to power. In 1933 such a stop was actually decreed, but only after over 1.6 million new members had been admitted. And since the NSDAP ran into financial problems and needed many new party comrades able to pay, the stop could not be maintained and was rescinded for a time, first in 1937 and then again in 1939, which once more led to such a massive inflow of new members that the élite principle could factually no longer be upheld.[98]

In view of these difficulties Hitler returned time and again in his speeches to the key problem of the principles according to which the recruitment of the élite was to take place in the system phase. On 29 April 1937 he again described the method of recruitment of an élite in the movement phase, in which 'this selection [had been] very easy to make'. For the future, Hitler went on,

> ... we must now still try to somehow, I would like to say mentally, continue this process which was formerly favoured, of course, by the struggle for power of the movement. And to continue it in a similar manner. In the future we cannot, naturally, give ourselves an artificial opposition so that we can see who is now brave or who now goes forward ... But with this we now lack the possibility of finding out in the normal way by battle who is now especially born to it. We must now employ something else, and the natural selection process with us in the future already begins in youth, in other words we have two assessments of the boy,

namely the scholastic assessment by the teacher, but in addition above all the assessment by the *Jungvolk* [the preparatory stage for the Hitler Youth, similar to Cub Scouts in relationship to Boy Scouts—H.B.] and Hitler Youth, where the leadership abilities of the individual were tested. The potential leaders trained in the Hitler Youth, said Hitler, are then 'subjected to harsh tests, and there the very first test is of their manhood, their personal manhood – because I protest against the view that umbrella weaklings can ever become political leaders'. What was important above all, was that heroism be made the basis of the selection process, so that it would be certain that

> ... the political leadership generally consists of courageous, also personally brave men ... And here we now also have the test possibility for the future. They will tell me: 'Now wait a minute, there can still be a political leader in the future some

VI: Concepts and Objectives in Domestic Policies

time, and he does not have the courage to jump out with a parachute or to do something like that.' Then I have to say: 'No, no, no, no! No, no! I have nothing against this man, he can become the leader of some association of pastry-cooks, or something like that, I have nothing against that. But he will only become a political leader if he is brave.' During the time of struggle I was able to test that in other ways. Then I could say: Go into the rally! There are ten thousand Communists outside, they shout, throw rocks at him, there he can then jump with his parachute straight into the rally. Now I cannot do that unfortunately, now the guy has to somehow show in another way that he is a man, that he is hard, that he is determined, that he has courage, that is necessary. Only by this means of a systematic selection, an unconditional appeal to manhood, will we get a political leadership in the future as well, which is really hard and which will then – and of this you may be sure – be respected by the nation.[99]

As a substitute for the missing possibilities to prove oneself in the political struggle, Hitler wanted to introduce artificial 'tests of courage', which were to show who was really brave and heroic and therefore qualified and ordained for political leadership. In a secret speech to political leadership trainees on 23 November 1937 he called it

> ... the primary task of these NSDAP order schools, to later introduce the tests of courage as a matter of routine, in other words to break away from the opinion that only the soldier had to be brave. Whoever is a political leader, is always a soldier. And whoever is not brave cannot be that. He has to be prepared to commit himself at any time. In former times, right from the start courage had to be the precondition to find the way into the party. And it was. Today we have to erect artificial hurdles, artificial ditches, which he now has to get over. Because if he is not brave then he is worthless for us. But if they now tell me, yes, but there are now others who come along, the 'only-geniuses' ... Geniuses alone are totally worthless in political life if they do not possess character. In the political leader, character is worth more than so-called brilliance. Courage is more important than wisdom or insight. The important thing is that we build up an organization of men who are dogged, tough, but who also – where necessary – ruthlessly pursue the interests of the nation.[100]

Let us now sort these statements into the overall system of Hitler's *Weltanschauung*. The point of departure is the socio-Darwinistic concept according to which, in nature, the brave and courageous wins and the weak and cowardly is destroyed. From this Hitler derived a basic emphasis on heroic values, a hero-worship that was of decisive importance for his *Weltanschauung*. From this, the view that only courageous men were called upon to be political leaders follows automatically. And since courage could no longer be proved by entry into the party alone as during the movement phase, and instead opportunists were often more likely to come into the party, artificial 'tests of courage' had to be introduced in the élite schools – Adolf Hitler schools, National

Political Education Institutions and the *Ordensburgen* of the NSDAP – in order to separate the cowards from the courageous. But, above all – and this is a further logical conclusion – the opportunities for advancement for the worker had to be improved because he, as opposed to the bourgeois, distinguished himself by determination, courage, the willingness to take decisions and energy.[101]

As logical as this concept may have been, Hitler was aware that it alone was not sufficient to solve the problem. The 'power chaos' so typical for the Third Reich, in other words the battle of competition resulting from the overlapping competences and responsibilities of various institutions, has often been interpreted as one of Hitler's deliberately employed methods of making the 'selection of the stronger', in the sense of his socio-Darwinistic philosophy, possible in the system phase.[102] The importance of these 'polycratic' elements within the NS system is being discussed just as controversially[103] as the reasons for this phenomenon are being interpreted.

William Carr has summarized the various possibilities of explanation offered by the research on Hitler.[104] Hitler's Bohemian lifestyle and his inability to take decisions are cited as a possible explanation.[105] It has also been claimed that Hitler deliberately created confusion and insecurity in order to maintain his power according to the principle *divide et impera*. But above all, says Carr, following the interpretation other researchers have advanced before him, 'it fitted into his socio-Darwinistic concepts. In his conviction, one could certainly depend on nature revealing which party in a political battle for power would prove itself to be the weaker, and one only had to wait patiently until the battle was over.'[106] This theory is plausible insofar as it offers an answer to the problem of recruiting an élite in the system phase which is a logical outcome of Hitler's socio-Darwinistic premises. On the other hand we must note that there is hardly any proof to be found in the sources that Hitler had deliberately planned in this way. We can cite only a remark made by Speer, according to which Hitler, when asked about his practice of entrusting several different people or organizations with the same task, had said, 'Then the stronger will prevail.'[107]

Neither the 'tests of courage' at the élite schools nor the organization of a planned 'anarchy' could, of course, be taken as convincing answers to the problem of recruiting an élite in the system phase – and specifically not, because the organization of the élite, i.e. the party, continued to grow, despite Hitler's maxims as developed in *Mein Kampf.*

Hitler stated in a monologue on 19 November 1941 that the party 'should not take in any ballast, no fellow-travellers, and the ones already taken in it will have to reject again'. But he did not conduct any purges similar to those practised in the Soviet Communist Party.[108] In view of the growth of the party, he most probably intended to build up an alternative élite organization in the SS, which would equate more closely to the principles developed in *Mein Kampf*. On 3/4 January 1942 he said:

> The SS should not grow too big, because then we can keep it at a level that is unreachable.[109] Like a magnet, the formation must attract everyone who belongs to it, it must develop solely from within itself. It must be made known that all of these formations carry their blood debt with them so that the boys who only want to brag stay away . . .[110]

As in the domestic struggle, the war – by means of the élite organization of the SS – was also to show who was truly courageous and brave, and to collect these elements into an élite.

In view of the 'over-inflation' of the party, Hitler hardly saw any further possibility of again restructuring it into a revolutionary élite. The SS was intended to take its place, as a statement made by Hitler in a table talk on 27 July 1942 shows:

> According to the will of the *Führer*, the RFSS [*Reichsführer SS*, i.e. Himmler] should in future collect the *best of the party*, and therefore of the nation, in the SS. The SS should apply far harsher and stricter criteria of selection than the party does. The SS should also make far higher demands on the character and stance of individuals in everyday life than the party does. The SS should train its individual members far more comprehensively and effectively than the party is able to do this. Because the SS is again only a fraction of the whole, and in order to maintain the élite it should remain numerically small.

Hitler naturally differentiates between the party and the armed SS:

> It is not possible to make the same assessment of the man from the armed SS as of the man from the party SS. Today the man of the armed SS is measured primarily as a soldier, and this will probably remain the same in the future and necessarily so. If a man of the armed SS is a particularly good soldier, then he will normally not be blamed if he is not so outstandingly well versed in the area of *Weltanschauung* . . . while on the other side in the party SS only an evaluation according to stance, character and achievement for the nation takes place. In the party SS the RFSS is to collect and lead the best of the party and the best of the nation. In the armed SS, in addition, he should collect and educate in the concept of the Greater German Reich a military force whose men are completely firm in *Weltanschauung* and were being made so.[111]

Only in this sense, namely the loss by the party of its revolutionary qualities as an élite and its tremendous growth, and as an answer to Hitler's problem of recruiting an élite in the system phase, can the rise of the SS in the Third Reich and the creation of the SS state be explained. These contexts have not yet been sufficiently taken into account within a comprehensive overview. This does not mean, however, that Hitler had already given the party up completely. On 31 July 1942, for example, he remarked that 'the movement must later on appear like this, that for one organized party comrade there should be nine others who were not registered in the card file. In future the party should only collect the politically active minority.'[112]

Because nobody has as yet fully appreciated the inner logic of Hitler's concepts of recruiting an élite in the movement phase, it has also not been recognized that many subsequent developments can only be understood from the fact that Hitler was no longer able to transfer these principles to the system phase and was still constantly searching for a way out of his dilemma. Hitler repeatedly lamented that 'such a selection of leadership as the party experienced it in the time of struggle . . . [was] no longer possible today'.[113] His reservations towards an over-centralization of the Reich and its bureaucratizing, which have also previously not been investigated, can also, as we shall see, only be understood within the context of his search for a solution to this problem.[114]

Hitler's loyalty to the old élite formed during the time of struggle – variously reported and sometimes even appearing to be irrational – can also only be understood in this context. Fritz Wiedemann, Hitler's military superior in the First World War and later his personal adjutant, writes in his memoirs: 'One of Hitler's outstanding traits, which was irreconcilable with a true leader, was his inability to separate himself from elements who had perhaps once been useful to him during the time of struggle but who he should definitely have got rid of when he became chancellor of the Reich.'[115] This reaction by Hitler was certainly not based on sentimental motives, as has sometimes been assumed.[116] His 'unquestioning loyalty unto death' to his 'old fighters' came from his conviction that the élite gained in the movement phase, in other words, those members who had come to him at a time when it was still a 'sacrifice' to commit oneself to the party had most surely proved their courage, bravery and leadership abilities. In view of the lack of any convincing principles for the recruitment of an élite in the system phase, Hitler was obliged to cling even harder to the members – in his view proven members – who had already come to him before the seizure of power.

Hitler had pointed out in *Mein Kampf* that 'from the root stem of the old movement', i.e. the members who joined the party during the movement phase,

> . . . all important positions in the conquered territory [were] to be filled [and the] whole leadership formed. And that until the former principles and teachings of the party have become the foundation and content of the new state. Only then can the reins gradually be given into the hands of the constitution of this state which has

been born out of this spirit. This will normally again only take place in a mutual struggle, because it is less a question of human insight than of the play and effect of forces which, while they can be recognized in advance, cannot be directed for ever.[117]

When Hitler recalled the time of struggle, what he emphasized above all was the value of the people who had come to the party in those days. In a speech on 24 February 1941, for example, he said:

The times of the hard former battles necessarily entailed a selection of the leadership . . . These hard times created an élite of first class men, who also often caused worries – that is clear. Men who are worth something are gruff and often also prickly, and in normal times one sometimes has to worry that these spines stand out next to each other – and not against each other. But at the moment when dangers arise, that is a guard of determined people. This selection, which for the soldier is brought about by war, which makes the true leaders appear, this selection only comes about through battle in political life as well. That was a result of this slow development, this constant battle against opposition, that we gradually received a leadership with which you can dare anything today.[118]

On 3/4 January 1942 Hitler recalled: 'Our old National Socialists, that was really something wonderful, in those days all you could do in the party was lose everything, not gain anything.'[119] On 16/17 January 1942 he declared: '. . . I always judge people according to how they behaved during the time of struggle.'[120]

The reason why Hitler was tied to his old party leaders in such a way can now be understood. He also knew, however, that while many of his old party comrades were 'brave' and 'courageous', they did not possess the necessary professional knowledge to be able to administer the state or manage a business. In many sectors he therefore leaned on the old civil service structure which, while it had been 'brought into line' was, of course, not yet National Socialist. As Mommsen has pointed out, with the exception of the replacements of the top positions of the administration, the military and the associations which had been brought into line, the regime avoided any systematic interference in the position of the traditional élite. A decisive change was only brought about by 20 July 1944:[121] the assassination attempt on that date revived the latent resentments against the members of the traditional élite, not only in the National Socialist leadership but also among the mass of the adherents of the NSDAP.[122]

Hitler gradually recognized that he had failed because of the lack of a concept for the recruitment of an élite in the system phase. To achieve power at all, and to secure the administration of the state, he had been forced to form an alliance with those forces for whom he basically felt the deepest contempt. In his

Bormann dictations, Hitler declared on 14 February 1945 that the war had come

> ... much too soon ... with regard to our moral preparedness. I was not given time to educate the people to my policies. I would have needed twenty years in order to let a new National Socialist élite mature, an élite of young people who had grown up under our teachings from infancy ... For lack of the élite, as we envisaged it, we had to make do with the human material available. The result is what you would expect! Because the spiritual concept was not in agreement with the practical possibilities of its implementation, the war policy of a revolutionary state such as the Third Reich necessarily became the policy of reactionary *petit bourgeois*. With few exceptions, our generals and diplomats are men of yesterday, who are waging the war and conducting the politics of a bygone age.

As an example, Hitler cited the policy towards France which had been 'complete nonsense':

> It would have been our task to free the French workers, to help them to win the revolution. The issue was to ruthlessly sweep aside an ossified bourgeoisie – those heartless and unpatriotic scoundrels. But what sort of friends did our great diplomats in the Wilhelmstrasse [seat of the German Ministry of Foreign Affairs—H.B.] uncover in France? Small-minded accountants who decided to appreciate us in the belief we were occupying the country in order to protect their strongboxes, and who were determined to betray us as soon as this appeared to be possible without punishment! Our position in the French colonies was no less idiotic. Here too, our great geniuses from the Wilhelmstrasse were in their element! Real classic diplomats, military people of the old school, and East Elbian *Krautjunkers* – such were our helpers for a revolution of European dimensions! They sank their teeth into the concepts of the last century on how to wage war. And we should never at any price have played France's game against the peoples who wore the French yoke. On the contrary, we should have helped them to free themselves from this imposition of France's will, if necessary we should even have incited them to do so. In 1940 there was nothing to prevent us from doing this in the Middle East, nor in North Africa. Instead, our diplomats resorted to strengthening France's position in Syria, Tunisia, Algeria and Morocco. Our cavalier politicians preferred maintaining social relations with elegant Frenchmen instead of returning the friendship of the insurgents; they preferred to breakfast with stick-swinging colonial officers who were only thinking of deceit and betrayal, than with Arabs – who would have remained our loyal allies.[123]

In this and other statements, Hitler's intention to find the reasons – and also the guilty – for the defeat of the Third Reich becomes clear. Faced with defeat, he discovered the truly guilty in his domestic and foreign policy allies. It was the bourgeois élite – and here he identified the underlying cause for the failure of his policy – upon which he had been forced to lean because he had not succeeded in creating a National Socialist élite. He was therefore unable, for example, to form an alliance with the Arab freedom movements, he could not revolutionize social conditions in France and so forth. On 25 February 1945 he said:

> The ideal formula for me would have been to first secure the preservation of the German nation, to bring up a National Socialist youth, and then to leave the waging of the inevitable war to future generations, insofar as the power then embodied in the German nation would not have frightened her enemies off. Then Germany would have been morally and materially prepared, equipped with a corps of civil servants, diplomats, a general staff of men who had imbibed the spirit of National Socialism with their mother's milk and had been shaped according to these principles. The work I set myself, to conquer a place in the sun for the German nation, is too much for one man, too gigantically encompassing for one generation![124]

Let us summarize. Hitler had developed a logical concept of how to recruit an élite in the movement phase, which was not transferable to the system phase. While he attempted to modify and adapt this concept to the changed conditions after the seizure of power, he did not succeed in creating a National Socialist élite which could have replaced the traditional élite. Therefore he had to lean extensively on the bourgeois forces who followed him out of opportunism but not from a true National Socialist spirit.

There is perhaps one final question that will occur to the reader. We have described Hitler's concepts of the recruitment of an élite in the system and in the movement phase, without the 'racial' argument having surfaced even once. This, however, contradicts the accepted view of Hitler's racial ideology. When we think of the recruitment of an élite, we probably often associate this with the blond, tall, blue-eyed SS man. Had Hitler been a racial ideologue to the degree previously assumed, then for the development of his new élite he would primarily have had to apply racial criteria. That this took place in part within the SS and agreed with the concepts of Himmler and other NS ideologues is beyond doubt. But what was Hitler's position on this problem?

Aside: Hitler's Principle: Draw Conclusions about the Race from the 'Ability' and not Vice Versa
In order to be able to understand the inner logic of Hitler's reasoning here, we must first familiarize ourselves with certain basic premises from which he started. According to Hitler's view there were not only racial differences between the nations, but also within the community of Germans. While all of its branches belonged – compared to the Jews, for example, or the Slavs – to a higher, i.e. more valuable, race, the German nation was still not a uniform race, but was composed of different racial elements.[125] According to Hitler's under-

standing, there were racial elements, for example, which were more musically, others which were more technically-scientifically, again others which were more politically gifted or capable, and so forth. While this is a rather strange, basically no longer biological definition of race, we must accept it as it is if we want to understand the inner logic of Hitler's reasoning at all.

Hitler started with the question of how, within a nation, one could recognize which people could be allocated to which racial groups. Theoretically there were two possible ways of doing this. Either we took a person's external attributes (e.g. the shape of the skull, size, the colour of eyes and hair) and then allocated him to a certain racial group according to these criteria, or we took the empirically visible specific abilities of a person and recognized, by these, to which racial group he belonged. Hitler rejected the idea of selecting the political élite (or any other élite) according to external 'racial' attributes. What was conclusive was the specific ability of the person. If by his commitment to the radical revolutionary party a person showed himself to be brave and courageous, for example, then this proved that he should be allocated to that racial element within the German nation which was politically endowed and therefore chosen for political rule.

If we penetrate more deeply into this line of reasoning, we cannot help noticing that Hitler was leading his racial ideology *ad absurdum* by his own arguments, because if in the end his theory came down to meaning that one selected certain people for certain sectors by checking on their ability in these sectors, then it made little sense to add that these people therefore possessed the racial element of, let us say, 'political' or 'artistic' ability. The racial argument was obviously only an 'add-on' and not necessary anywhere for the logic of the line of reasoning. Therefore it did not lead to any practical consequences, in the sense, for example, that the political élite was being selected according to externally recognizable criteria (which, by the way, Hitler and the party élite would not have fulfilled). The racial argument only had a consequence – but a fatal one for the person concerned – insofar as those people who had been excluded from the German national community to begin with – such as Jews, gypsies and the mentally handicapped – were not examined for their abilities but, with only a few exceptions, exterminated as being racially inferior.

Hitler gave the most extensive presentation of his views on this matter in his speech at the *Reichsparteitag* in 1933. He started off from the thesis that the German nation was composed of various racial elements, and that National Socialism appealed to the potential élite, in other words the 'heroic' race.[126] But, as he developed his reasoning further on another occasion, 'you cannot only conclude from the race about the abilities, but also from the abilities about the race. This means, therefore: it is not necessary to first discover the musically gifted people as a race in order then to entrust them with the care for music; music will discover the race by finding the ability.' In other words, the question which people within the German national community were to be allocated to the racial element which stood out because of its musical abilities answered itself through the ability of these people, through their musical talent. The other method Hitler rejected was first to investigate the external racial elements which were constitutional for a musically talented person and then to collect such people and 'entrust them with the care for music'. Hitler only used this absurd example (the absurdity of which, as Hitler was well aware, basically only resulted from the absurdity of constructing a 'musically' or 'technically' gifted *race*) in order to demonstrate that the political élite could not be selected according to external racial attributes (as one might perhaps have suspected), but exclusively on the basis of its talent and ability, which, as we have discussed in detail, manifests itself in this area in the aggressive commitment to the radical revolutionary party. Hitler explained that the question by which method he could select the heroic people, in other words the future political élite who existed in all social classes, had been of decisive importance to him:

> There was only one possibility here: one could not conclude about the abilities from the race, but from the abilities one had to draw the conclusion about the racial suitability. And the ability could be determined by the nature of the reaction of individual people to a newly proclaimed idea. This is the infallible method to search for those people one wants to find. Because we all only listen to the note to which our innermost being is attuned.[127]

Hitler regarded it as his achievement that he had forged the German nation into a unit, into the 'national community', over and beyond all religious, social and other barriers. He had no intention of destroying this unity by propounding different racial elements and thereby introducing a new set of criteria of differentiation leading to disunity. In June 1930 he said to Wagener:

> If we examine the question of the advantages and disadvantages of keeping the races and tribes in our German fatherland apart from the vantage point of this insight, then all we see is disadvantages! The staging of the racial problem would only split the German people further apart, incite them against each other, atomize them, and thereby make them without importance foreign policy-wise. I have therefore already forbidden it several times, and at the next meeting of the Gau leaders I will again forbid most sharply that racial theory and racial problems are even talked or written about. We must do exactly the opposite! National community, national community, has to be our battle cry! Everything that unites the classes and binds them together must be brought forth, cared for and fostered, and everything that

separates them, that reawakens the old prejudices, again must be avoided, fought against, removed... We alone can and must decide about the racial question, you and I, and Rosenberg and one or two others. Because for us this is a key and a pointer. But for the general public it is poison! And what is more, all it will do is awaken feelings of superiority and inferiority complexes. And those are the surest means of destroying a national community.[128]

Therefore Hitler rejected developing an élite according to external racial criteria. In a monologue on 27 January 1942 he said:

Racial war need not break out if people are selected not according to their appearance but according to their achievements. Looks and ability are often quite far apart. You can make the selection according to the appearance, and you can make it – as the party has done – according to the test of life.[129]

In a speech on 26 May 1944 Hitler again said that the recruitment of the élite must not in any way depend on external attributes, but must be carried out solely on the basis of ability because the able person thereby proved that he belonged to a special race:

We have now united these racial nuclei within our nation. What is important now is that – as rich as the spectrum of the abilities of the German people now is – I bring out first and foremost the racial nuclei of the various abilities which were originally the bearers of these abilities; that means, therefore, I have to ensure that in the case of an artistic talent, that racial nucleus gradually comes into effect throughout the whole German nation which is artistically talented. Now, gentlemen, this does not come about by a selection in which I say, 'Who looks artistic?', but here the miracle appears, that the note finds its representative in the end. That means in other words: when I strike a certain note, then in the piano, for example, that string will respond which is attuned to this note, and when I need a certification of a certain ability and switch on free development here, then those elements will respond who in the final analysis are really ordained by nature, that means based on their racial endowment.[130]

We can therefore see that, with his whole line of reasoning about the recruitment of an élite, Hitler is leading racial ideology *ad absurdum* – insofar as it attempts to claim validity within the German national community. The racial argument is not necessary at any point for the logic of the argument: the whole concept could be presented without the racial element and the practical consequences would remain the same.

Nonetheless, during the Third Reich, and particularly among the SS, there was a widespread primitive racial ideology in evidence whose proponents did not 'conclude about the race from the abilities', as Hitler demanded, but, *vice versa*, 'from the race about the abilities'. Himmler expressly avowed the principle of 'selecting the person on outward appearance',[131] whereby size, the shape of the face and the colour of hair and eyes, as well as build, were the decisive criteria according to which an applicant for the SS was allocated into one of five categories.[132] Hitler himself, who was undeniably a fanatic racist as far as the Jews and the others who had been 'excluded' from the national community (gypsies, the handicapped etc.) as well as other nations were concerned, still opposed the propagation of racial topics *within* the German national community. 'The *Führer* sharply deplores work of all racial committees,' Goebbels noted in his diary on 26 June 1936.[133] Goebbels himself, whose appearance would also hardly have fulfilled the criteria of the SS, vehemently turned against the 'nonsense of race materialism, which does not look to position and persuasion but to peroxide blond'.[134] On 7 September 1937 he became excited about an essay by a lord mayor: 'Now external physical attributes are supposed to be decisive for promotion. Nonsense of the first magnitude'.[135] On 28 October 1937 he noted: 'Discussed racial policy with Dr Gross. I confront him with our false principles of selection. According to these, most of the leaders of today would have been rejected.'[136] We may conclude from this aside that on racial-political questions as well there could be no talk of a uniform ideology of 'the' National Socialists.

3. The *Führer* State

We have now discussed Hitler's criticism of the 'majority principle' and his theory of the 'historic minority'. Based on what we have learned, the most we can say at this point is that Hitler considered it to be a key task to replace the existing élite by a new élite he called the 'historic minority', which was to be created by a special process. We also know that Hitler constantly emphasized the so-called '*Führer* principle' as an alternative to the democratic system. Did Hitler put his concepts of constitutional and domestic policy into more concrete terms than these? There are still some open questions: What did Hitler mean by the '*Führer* principle', and how did he define it? Did he intend to set up a new constitution, and, if so, what was it to contain? How did Hitler intend to handle the question of his succession? What was his position on the question of federalism versus unitarianism? Did Hitler define his rule as a dictatorship? We intend to answer these, and further questions, in this chapter. We will show that a renewed investigation was important in this case as well, because until now we have known too little about Hitler's political self-understanding, the contents of his concepts, and above all the reasons for them within the context of his *Weltanschauung*.

Jäckel writes that Hitler had not only been disinterested in economic and social questions, but also in domestic and constitutional questions. Jäckel's reasons are (1) that Hitler's definition of 'the state as a means to an end' shows his pragmatic-opportunistic view of such questions; and (2) the fact that the constitution of Weimar had never been repealed and replaced by a new one, and that Hitler had not even legally settled the question of succession ('the heart of any constitution'), proved his indifference towards such questions.[137] We have already dealt with the first argument in Chapter II.2 and shown that Hitler's choice of words was not intended to express any sort of disdain for questions of domestic policy but to be a criticism of conservative constitutional theories and the German tradition of idolizing the state, and above all to serve as his justification for the obligation and the right to revolution. We now intend to discuss Jäckel's second argument, i.e. the constitutional question.

a. Hitler on the Constitution and the Question of Succession

Hitler writes in *Mein Kampf* that it was

> ... the greatest mistake to believe that only because one possessed the power one could suddenly carry out a certain reorganization simply out of nothing without already having a certain basic stock of people who had already been prepared for this, particularly as to their convictions. Here too the principle applies that more important than the outer form, which can very quickly be created mechanically, is always the spirit which fills such a form. It is quite readily possible, for example, to dictatorially graft the *Führer* principle on to a state organism by means of an order. But this will only come alive if it was able to develop itself gradually from the smallest beginnings, and to receive over many years by the constant selection which the harsh reality of life carries out without interruption the leadership material necessary for the execution of this principle. One should therefore not envisage suddenly pulling the draft of a new constitution out of a briefcase and then being able to 'introduce' it by means of an order from above. One can try something like that, but the result will most certainly not be viable, in most cases already a stillbirth. This reminds me of the origin of the constitution of Weimar and of the attempt with a new constitution to also donate to the German nation a new flag which had no inner relationship to the experience of our nation during the past half a century. The National Socialist state must also guard itself against such experiments.[138]

Let us retrace Hitler's line of reasoning. The outer form of a constitution does not in any way guarantee the inner functionality and viability. If once in power, one attempts to artificially 'graft' on a constitution without having first re-educated the people, or the new élite so that they inwardly affirm the state, then this state will not be viable, 'in most cases already a stillbirth'. As proof of this he cites the Weimar Republic, in which a democratic constitution existed but which lacked the essential precondition, namely the support of strong and committed groups of people. What is therefore of primary impor-

VI: Concepts and Objectives in Domestic Policies

tance for Hitler is the development of the 'historic minority', i.e. the élite which actively carries and supports the new state and gains the support of the masses for it through propaganda or 're-education'.

Hitler's statements to a circle of party comrades, about which Albert Krebs, head of the Hamburg district of the NSDAP from 1926 on, reports, point in the same direction:[139]

> Initially [Krebs reports in his memoirs], in reply to a question I had raised, Hitler sketched in broad outline the picture of a National Socialist reform of the constitution and legislation. With heavy, and not totally unjustified attacks against jurists and bureaucrats, he expressed the opinion that a legislator should always only create a framework, but not a work of statutes and clauses fixed down to the last and most minute detail. Life should not be smothered by letters, organic development not made impossible. Hitler expressly cited Britain as an example, whose true nature, however, he obviously did not correctly recognize or portray, either from a lack of knowledge or from a deliberate doctrinaire misinterpretation.[140]

Important here is Hitler's statement that 'organic development should not be made impossible'. Hitler rejected 'too timely' a constitutional legislation, not out of disinterest in questions of domestic policy but because such a procedure would have contradicted his concept of the permanent revolution. To cement an existing condition by means of a constitution worked out in detail would mean arbitrarily to interrupt the process at a certain stage.

After the seizure of power Hitler did variously announce a reform of the constitution,[141] but these announcements were probably primarily tactics. Otto Meissner, who had already been a State Secretary under Ebert and Hindenburg and was later also to be one under Hitler, reports that according to the impressions he 'gained of him from [Hitler's] meetings with Hindenburg and other confidential discussions in the inner circle in those days [shortly after the seizure of power—R.Z.]' he had believed it was probable that Hitler,

> ... after his originally revolutionary start, after the failure of his Munich *putsch* and his experiences with the rivals in his party, had come to the conclusion that for reasons of both domestic and foreign policy it was advisable to give up the revolutionary methods of his fight for power as soon as possible and to go the way of evolution, which alone could secure the stability and duration of his government and its recognition abroad. After he had come to power legally, he had the serious intention to have the *Reichstag*, as a constitutional convention, decide on a reform of the Reich and the constitution in order to remove the excesses and exaggerations of parliamentarianism and to govern with a corrected constitution under the control of a parliament while permitting a factual opposition. During the early period of his office he repeatedly made statements to this effect in personal conversations and emphasized that he did not reject democracy itself but that he

wanted to replace the present party democracy by a direct democracy of the citizens of the state structured from the bottom to the top. The community and district leaders should be elected, the Gau leaders and ministers appointed by the *Führer* and confirmed by the voters in a plebiscite, the laws enacted by a senate in which all of the occupational classes should be represented. When and why he gave up the idea of such a constitutional reform, whether the capitulation without resistance of the existing parties and consideration for the radical elements of his movement as embodied in Goebbels, Hess and Himmler, or whether his own urge for total power led to this change of mind will probably never be decided.[142]

In actual fact Hitler had not undergone any 'change of mind' but only deceived his conservative allies, men such as Hindenburg and Papen, about his true views and intentions during the extremely critical phase immediately after the seizure of power. Hitler's alleged plans that Meissner reports on, which were only directed against the 'exaggerations of parliamentarianism' and the 'existing party democracy', and which promised a rapid reform of the constitution and the ending of the revolution, are far too obviously tailored to Hindenburg's world of thought and political convictions to be taken seriously.

Hitler most certainly feared that too detailed a set of constitutional regulations could restrict his autocratic rule, but more important was the fact that he wanted to keep the condition of revolution open for as long as possible. A constitution would have artificially broken the revolutionary process off at a certain point by cementing the result of a certain stage of its development. Hitler also had to be suspicious of formal constitutional constructions, because the period 1930–33 had demonstrated that the constitution could be suspended through its own means if there were no longer any powerful forces available to defend it. If we tie all of these arguments together, it becomes clear why Hitler was highly suspicious of the usefulness of formal constitutions. In case of doubt they could not help him, but they could very easily harm him.

As far as the question of succession that Jäckel mentions is concerned, this is something Hitler frequently addressed himself to. His plan was to form a senate consisting of the oldest and most reliable party members, which would then elect his successor. Already at the end of 1930 he had Professor Troost build a senate chamber in the 'brown house' in Munich, the seat of the Reichs leadership of the NSDAP. Wagener reports that towards the end of 1931 Hitler had said that one must always be prepared for the possibility that something could happen to him at any time. He had therefore decided he would now finally have to go about constituting the party senate:

> You know that this party senate is charged, and responsible for it to the party, with ensuring that the national and socialist principles of the party will always be respected, and in particular that no side offends against them . . . Should I depart

this life ahead of time, without such a party senate a power struggle for the leadership would then break out, which I always conjure up in my mind when I feel how different the views and thoughts of my various associates are. The struggle would not only be about the leadership, but also about the objectives and the programme.[143]

In a speech to the Reichs and Gau leaders on 6 August 1933 Hitler also announced the formation of a senate, which was to consist of 'the oldest, most proven and most loyal party comrades'.[144] On 13 December 1934 a Law on the Succession to the *Führer* and Reichs Chancellor was passed: 'Until the creation of a new constitution for the German Reich, in case of his death or some other form of termination of the offices of Reichs President and Reichs Chancellor united in his person, the *Führer* appoints his successor.'[145] Based on this law, Hitler appointed Göring as his successor in a document issued on 19 December 1934. On 1 September 1939 Hitler said in the *Reichstag*:

Should something happen to me in this struggle, then my first successor is party comrade Göring. Should something happen to party comrade Göring, then his successor is party comrade Hess. You would then be sworn to the same blind loyalty and obedience to him as you are to me! In case something were also to happen to party comrade Hess, I will now convene the senate by law, which shall then elect the most worthy, that means the most courageous, from among its ranks![146]

Hitler returned to this topic repeatedly. Goebbels reported about the ideas Hitler developed during a conversation on 3 November 1939:

The future senate should include about 60 people. Not only office holders, but also men of merit. Not all of the Gau, and certainly not all of the Reichs leaders. A committee of proven National Socialists. Frick's suggestion with 300 names is roundly rejected. The *Führer* said he [Frick] would be lucky if he were to be included himself.[147]

On 5 February 1941 Hitler again discussed constitutional and succession problems with Goebbels:

The most important content of the future constitution is the procedure of the election of the *Führer*. He will be elected by the top leaders of the movement, the *Wehrmacht* is unpolitical and has nothing to do with this. It will only be sworn to the new *Führer* immediately after the election. Monarchy always contains the danger that a complete fool reaches the top. This is prevented here. The leader of the state needs a certain maturity, which only comes with a certain age, even in a genius. Therefore the intended have to be given every possibility to become active. They should be enabled to familiarize themselves with the whole state. There are large and small *Gaue*. Later the Gau leaders will also be rotated and then have possibilities for advancement. As in the party, the central power in the state has to be made as strong as possible. It should not administer, however, but lead. It has the money, the power, and the legal right to take great initiatives. The party must also dominate within the state. Without the party, the state can not lead. S[ee] Italy, where the state commands the party. And with what degree of success we now see.[148]

Hitler's table talks also show that the assertion that he had not been interested in constitutional questions, and had not had any concept of how to regulate the succession, is wrong. During such a talk on 31 March 1942, for example, he addressed these questions in detail. The importance of these statements is underscored by the fact that during the evening meal Bormann passed Picker a card with the directive: 'Do not simply dictate the memo on this conversation, whose importance you probably do not even recognize, but sit down at your desk after the meal and write out your memorandum in more detail.' Hitler addressed the question of how one could succeed 'in bringing the best to the leadership of the state'. This was a big problem for which there was no solution in sight that did not contain its own source of error. The republic, in which the whole nation elected the head of state, had the disadvantage that it was possible with the help of money and advertising 'to bring the greatest of fools to the top'. If the head of state was elected for life, then there was the danger that he would engage in 'egoistic power politics', whereas if there were a change in the head of state every five or ten years, then the stability of the leadership of the state was not secured and the execution of long-term plans cast in doubt. Hitler also rejected other possible constructions, including a hereditary monarchy, which he rejected as a matter of principle. By a balancing of the pros and cons of the various constitutional forms, said Hitler, he had come to the following conclusions:

1. The chances of not getting a total idiot as the head of state were greater in free elections than otherwise . . .
2. In selecting the head of state, a personality had to be looked for who, as far as anyone could judge, guaranteed a certain stability of leadership for a longer term. This was a condition not only for the successful administration of the state, but even more for the execution of any greater state planning.
3. It had to be ensured that the leading man in the state was independent of business influences and could not be forced to any decision by economic pressures. He therefore had to be supported by a political organization which had its firm roots in the people and was above business considerations.[149]

For Hitler the most important criteria for the selection of a leader were therefore the stability of the leadership of the state and the independence of the head of state from business interests. These priorities must be seen within the context of Hitler's criticism of democracy. According to his view, in the democratic system the heads of government were only working with an eye to the next election and had no interest in long-term concepts for the future. In addition, in a democracy the politicians were bribed by capital and therefore incapable of taking independent political decisions.

In his further statements Hitler specifies his constitutional concepts as follows:

1. The German Reich had to be a republic. The leader had to be elected. He was to be given absolute authority.
2. As a collective there had to be a parliament which had to support the leader and, if necessary, intervene in the leadership of the state.
3. The election of the leader was not to be conducted by this parliament, but by the senate. The senate was to be given limited authority. Membership in it was not to be permanent, but had to be tied to certain of the highest positions, whose holders also had to be rotated. Based on their upbringing and development, the members of the senate had to be imbued with the concept that no weakling, but only the very best, was to be elected as leader.
4. The election of the leader was not to take place before the eyes of the public but behind closed doors . . .
5. Within three hours after completion of the election the men of the party, the military and the state were to be sworn to the new leader.
6. The most precise and sharpest separation between legislative and executive had to be the top commandment for the new leader. Just as within the movement, the SA and SS were only the sword for the execution of the political directives of the party, so must the executive refrain from engaging in politics and only execute – if necessary with the sword – the political directives it received from legislative authorities.[150]

Hitler's concept of the constitution was therefore as follows. There was to be a republic, at whose head stood a leader elected by the senate. Membership in the senate was to be tied to the highest positions and changed. Besides the senate there was to be a parliament which had to support the leader, but which could intervene in the leadership of the state if necessary. The legislative and the executive had to be strictly separate.

Hitler repeated this idea in a table talk on 24 June 1942:

Next to the structured leadership of the state on the one hand, on the other must stand the absolutely secured instrument of public power, the executive, as a strong bond of the Reich. The executive, at its head the *Wehrmacht*, then the police, the labour service and youth education and so forth, can only lie in one hand. When this is secured, then nothing can happen to the Reich. The most dangerous thing is when the executive is, or wants to be, the leadership of the state as well. Rivalries between various sectors of the *Wehrmacht*, various territories and so forth will then begin, which have formerly already caused a large number of otherwise effective states to go under.

To the question of the election of the head of state Hitler, in continuing his line of thought, said:

> If something were to happen to me some day, then the new head of state should not be elected by the whole nation, just as the Pope is not elected by the mass of the faithful, or the Doge of Venice by the whole population of Venice. If the mass of the people were to be involved in such an election, then the election would become a matter of propaganda. And propaganda for or against individual candidates tears the nation asunder. If a small group [he was thinking of a senate] were to conduct the election, and the opinions were hit upon each other, that is of no importance whatsoever. One has only to be smart enough not to let the differences of opinion become known outside. After the election is over, the one who has received the most votes, just as in the election of the Doge, or the election of the Pope, is then the head of state regardless of the differences of opinion during the preparation of the election. And because within three hours of the completion of the election the *Wehrmacht*, party, and civil service are sworn to the new head of state, the order of public life is guaranteed absolutely.

Such a system did not, of course, guarantee that in every case an outstanding leadership personality will necessarily come to be the head of the Reich. But it would always be a man who is so far above the average that he does not pose any danger for the Reich as long as the total machine is in order.[151]

These plans, the senate as well as Hitler's other constitutional concepts, were not realized during his lifetime. We have already mentioned the reasons at the beginning of this chapter. For Hitler, far more important than any formal constitution was the development of an élite which could carry the new state, replace the old élite and oversee the re-education of the people. He also wanted to postpone the creation of a fixed form for as long as possible and instead have this develop organically in the course of the revolutionary process. In addition to these motives, there may also have been a further element. During his lifetime Hitler did not want to have his power curtailed under any circumstances by any sort of institutional restrictions. He moreover did not consider any of his associates capable of really becoming his successor. In less than two months after he had publicly appointed Göring as his successor, he said in a speech before the commanders-in-chief of the *Wehrmacht*: 'Neither a military nor a civilian personality could replace me . . . I am convinced of the power of my brain and of my determination . . . The fate of the Reich depends on me alone.'[152]

In a conversation with Mussolini on 19 July 1943 Hitler declared that he believed no greater man would come after him who was better able to handle matters, and that therefore a decision in this war had to be reached in his lifetime.[153] In his last dictations to Bormann, Hitler said on 25 February 1945 that other statesmen could depend on their successors 'who begin at the same

VI: Concepts and Objectives in Domestic Policies

place where their predecessor stopped; replacement men who continue the same furrow with the same plough'. But he asked himself 'unendingly where among my immediate associates was the capable one to be found to carry the torch onward which will one day slip from my hands'.[154]

Scheidt reports that after Hess's flight Hitler had addressed the question of the succession:[155]

> During this period Hitler no longer wanted to have a man of his generation appointed as his successor, but a younger one. He was considering Reichs Youth Leader Baldur von Schirach.[156] He was to be systematically groomed for the role ... The development of the war had assumed a far more serious character since the winter of 1941/42. This then made Schirach also appear to be unsuitable to Hitler. He needed a man who would not shrink from anything and who would be his equal in the lack of scruples. He therefore hit upon State Secretary Heydrich, whom he called 'the man with nerves of iron' ... But Hitler had never publicly excluded Göring from the succession, not even when it had already become completely clear that the failure of this paladin was the greatest cause for the loss of the war, excepting the failure of Hitler himself.[157]

If Hitler did not consider any of his associates capable of succeeding him, this should not only be taken as an expression of his overestimation of himself. Hitler was probably well aware that he was the only figure of integration within the whole National Socialist system of rule who was accepted by the German people and without whom the existence of the system was inconceivable. Kershaw has convincingly demonstrated that the high esteem in which Hitler was held stood in inverse ratio to the reputation of the party and the other NS leaders.[158] Hitler, and only Hitler, was the integrating bond of the Third Reich, and no second could stand beside him. That was what made the settlement of the succession so extremely difficult. But that Hitler had shown no interest in this problem, or that he had not developed any principles for solving it, is wrong, as the statements from the table talks cited above prove. We now intend to continue and investigate how Hitler envisaged the structure of his *Führer* state, and must therefore of course first answer the questions of the content of and reason for the so often cited '*Führer* principle'.

b. The '*Führer* Principle'

We have already discussed the most important preconditions for understanding the '*Führer* principle' Hitler propagated, namely his criticism of the majority principle and his theory of the 'historic minority'. In a speech on 27 April 1923 Hitler declared:

> What our nation needs is leaders, not of the parliamentary kind, but prepared to enforce what they believe to be right before God, the world and their conscience,

even against majorities. If we succeed in bringing such leaders out from among the mass of our people, then a nation will again crystallize around them.'[159]

The people, so Hitler believed, 'are not longing for majority decisions, but for leaders. The German Reich was not the work of a majority decision, but of one man – Bismarck.'[160] Hitler was therefore of the opinion that a leader had to enforce his decisions against the will of the majority if necessary (today we would say he has to be able to take unpopular decisions), but he also believed that the masses longed for a leader they could obey.

As Albrecht Tyrell has convincingly demonstrated, during the early years of his political activities Hitler did not yet see himself as being this leader, but as the forerunner of someone else. His self-understanding only changed after the aborted *putsch* of November 1923. During his imprisonment in Landsberg, says Tyrell, Hitler had to admit to himself that all of the 'leadership personalities' in whom he had trusted with 'an almost blind faith' had failed.[161] His understanding of himself underwent a change, and he now began to see himself as the coming *Führer* of Germany. During his Landsberg imprisonment he then wrote *Mein Kampf* and developed the '*Führer* principle' as an alternative to the democratic parliamentary system.

What was important for the *Führer*, according to Hitler, was that he had a solidly based *Weltanschauung* from whose principles he would no longer deviate. A key term Hitler associated with the '*Führer* principle' was 'responsibility'. He described a system in which the leader was elected 'in a free election' but then had the obligation to 'fully accept all responsibility for his deeds and omissions' as being a 'truly Germanic democracy': 'In it there is no voting by a majority on specific questions, but only the decision of one individual who then has to back his decision with his fortune and his life.' Elsewhere in *Mein Kampf* Hitler developed the principle according to which the party and the future state were to be developed. The party, or the state, was built from the top down; the *Führer* appointed his sub-leaders personally. The basic idea of the '*Führer* principle', which Hitler later never tired of repeating, was: '*Authority of every leader downwards, and responsibility upwards.*'[162]

Hitler *did not* maintain that the *Führer* was infallible, or that a subordinate could not be capable of judging a specific matter more correctly. In a speech on 12 June 1925, for example, he said:

> Beyond any doubt, in certain cases there will be a brain in a subordinate position which actually thinks more correctly than the leading organizers. It is in the nature of an organization that the power of the organization is all the greater, the more the individual will is forced back. An example from the Army: Let us assume, out there lies the front. A big general attack is scheduled for 21 March at 9 a.m. Among the

dozen corps commanders there can doubtless be one who says to himself: 'For this or that reason the 27th would be the right day, and not the 21st.' From a factual point of view he can be right (can be a 'Napoleon'). The man has the right to express his opinion. But even though he may be right a thousand times over, he still does not have the right to say: 'Out of my most holy conviction I consider it better to attack on the 27th!' A leader can be mistaken, without any doubt. But even the worst directive is more likely to lead to the objective than freedom of action will!

He, too, could be mistaken occasionally, Hitler admitted in the same speech. This was, after all, in the nature of man.[163] Krebs and Schirach claim, on the other hand, that in June 1930, or in January and May 1931, Hitler had proclaimed his infallibility as '*Führer*-Pope'.[164] But these alleged statements by Hitler should not be cited as uncritically as this has frequently been done in literature, not only because they are not confirmed anywhere in the 'safe' sources but also because in his speeches Hitler expressly admitted that he too 'could be in error and make mistakes'.[165] The issue was not the question of fallibility or infallibility, said Hitler on 16 September 1935, but just as an army commander could not permit the commander of a unit, or in the end even the individual soldier, to use his own ideas and opinions as the yardstick when casting doubt on the correctness of an order he has been given, in the political setting of objectives and leadership also no 'wild lone wolf could excuse his conduct with a claim to the correctness of his opinion or to the error of the view, directive or order issued by the party'.[166]

Hitler believed that, all things being equal, to act at all, i.e. to obey an order, was still better than, by giving up the *Führer* principle, to leave it to the individual to act according to his own judgement but thereby to destroy any possible co-ordination, and as a result to prevent any action, be it right or wrong. Therefore the individual had to submit to the order from above. This authoritarian concept was contradicted, however, by Hitler's opinion that sometimes disobedience could also become necessary. In certain situations, he said in a speech on 14 October 1923, there was 'an even greater obligation, namely the obligation of the German man, not to do the duty, his "duty"! History shows us men who, when the issue was the salvation of the Fatherland, had the courage to disobey.'[167]

For Hitler the term 'duty' was tied to certain conditions without which it was not valid. In Germany, said Hitler on 28 February 1926,

> . . . there [reigned] a very incorrect definition of the term 'duty'. Here with us in Germany, the term 'duty' was deliberately turned into a doctrine, into an end in itself, even though it is only a means to an end . . . Let it be said in contradiction: if there is anything that could be an end in itself, then it is obedience unto death. All of this is only sensible if such obedience takes place in order to preserve

something else in the life of the nation . . . Duty was completely natural as long as one knew that this large administrative apparatus, even if it was bad, was prone to inadequacies, was administered bureaucratically, served one purpose: the welfare of a nation, that all of this decreed joy of battle had only to serve this purpose. On the day that a wicked hand dared to destroy this precious thing, duty logically had to cease, or it became the strongest weapon of the destroyers of the Reich.

Hitler then went on to speak out against 'the lack of the courage of one's convictions'. This courage consisted of 'taking a decision, not when there is no order given, but when it is against the will of general opinion'.[168] In *Mein Kampf* Hitler had objected to 'the paralysis of our definitions of duty and obedience'. In the fatal hours of the nation, obedience and duty were 'a doctrinaire formalism, yes, pure insanity'. In such hours, personal responsibility manifested itself against a whole nation.[169] These statements are not without importance, because in the times of catastrophe during the Second World War they turned against Hitler himself. With reference to the paragraph from *Mein Kampf* cited above, responsible officers turned against the senseless resistance and destruction in a war already lost long beforehand.[170]

When on the one hand Hitler demanded 'unconditional obedience', on the other he also turned against the 'authoritarian state'[171] and proclaimed the necessity of independent and responsible action. In a monologue, for example, he declared:

> The *Wehrmacht* has the highest decorations for someone who acted against an order and by his insight and determination saved a situation. In an administration, any departure from a regulation costs you your head. The term 'exception' is foreign to it. Therefore it lacks the courage to accept great responsibility.[172]

Such statements reflect Hitler's contradictory relationship with authority, which prohibits any attempt to summarize his position by means of a simple formula. While it is certainly correct to interpret Hitler and the Third Reich as the embodiment of authoritarianism, the opposite is also true. Just as Hitler was against the German tradition of idolizing the state, in which the state was now only 'an end in itself' instead of 'a means to an end',[173] he also attacked a blind obedience which no longer enquired after the sense and purpose of obedience and admired 'the courage of one's convictions', i.e. responsible action – without, or even against, an order from above – in situations of danger for the Fatherland. Only if we understand this contradiction and Hitler's ambivalent position towards authority on which it is based can we adequately interpret him.

Such ambivalence is normally important for an understanding of Hitler's political concepts. Any emphasis on only one side of his thinking would be an impermissible handicap which would obstruct the view of the man's

Weltanschauung, policies and personality. There is another ambivalence in his relationship to democracy and dictatorship, government by the people or the individual. We have already seen that Hitler rejected the 'majority principle' and opposed it with the principle of the 'historic minority' and the solely responsible *Führer*, but he also believed that 'true democracy', or government by the people in its highest and most perfect form, could only be realized in the *Führer* state. This ambivalence of authoritarian-democratic and 'democratic'-populist elements in Hitler's thinking is important for an understanding of the attractiveness of his ideas and his system. A one-sided interpretation clearly aimed at the elements of oppression and dictatorship, which was particularly popular in post-war Germany because it was also meant to serve as an exoneration from any responsibility for the crimes of the regime, obstructs any possibility of understanding the reasons for Hitler's success and the attraction of National Socialism.

c. Dictatorship as the 'Highest Form of Democracy'

In his early speeches Hitler frequently demanded: 'We need a dictator who is a genius if we want to rise again.'[174] This wording of the 'dictatorship of genius'[175] is an expression of Hitler's hero-worship and is linked to certain traditions of the cult of genius in the Germany of the nineteenth century. On 4 May 1923 Hitler, who, as already mentioned, did not see himself as the coming *Führer* at the time, declared:

> What can save Germany is the dictatorship of the national will and national determination. There the question arises: is the required personality there? It is not our task to search for the person. He is either given by heaven, or is not given. Our task is to forge the sword the person would need, if he were there. It is our task to give the dictator, if he comes, a nation which is ready for him![176]

'We want,' said Hitler on 5 September 1923, 'to become the supporters of the dictatorship of national common sense, national energy, national brutality and determination.'[177]

While Hitler frequently used the term 'dictatorship' in his early speeches,[178] after his release from the Landsberg prison he used it only seldom. This is probably first due to the fact that he was pursuing the concept of the 'legal revolution' and had formally to acknowledge the constitution of Weimar, but it was also due to a change in his self-understanding. Had he formerly demanded the dictatorship for someone else because he had not yet seen himself as the coming leader of Germany; this was far less presumptuous than if he now propagated his own dictatorship which, according to his changed self-understanding, he would have had to do to be consistent.

The 'dictatorship' could only become legitimate, as Hitler critically objected to Papen's plans and intentions on 16 August 1932, as the 'bearer of the national will':

> A dictatorship is also only conceivable if it is the bearer of the national will, or has the most assured prospects of becoming recognized as such a bearer of the national will within a short and foreseeable time. But I do not know of any dictatorship in world history which was finally able to transform itself into a new and accepted form of state, that had not grown out of a popular movement.[179]

In Hitler's view, a dictatorship merely as a rule by force did not promise any possibility of stability.

After the seizure of power Hitler frequently rejected the accusation that he was a dictator. This was probably first an attempt at self-justification, because the term 'dictatorship' had negative connotations. But it must also be taken into consideration that Hitler hardly saw himself as being a dictator in the conventional sense, even though, no later than August 1934, he united such far-reaching powers in his person as only a dictator can possess.

Hitler objected on several occasions to the accusation from abroad that he was a dictator, and pointed to the high level of confidence of the German nation in his leadership, which was supposedly expressed in the plebiscites.[180] According to statements by Wiedemann, Hitler actually did assess popular opinion

> ... primarily according to the election results. He did not take into account, or did not want to take into account, that the vote was less a reflection of actual popular opinion than of the cleverness of his Gau leaders who were responsible for this opinion and therefore for the number of affirmative votes.[181]

Goebbels' diaries also show that the NS leadership took the results of the plebiscites quite seriously as being 'barometers of opinion'. The result of the vote on 19 August 1934, which Hitler had conducted after the death of Hindenburg and the unification in his person of the offices of Reichs Chancellor and Reichs President, was commented upon by Goebbels with disappointment. Even though, with a participation of 95.7 per cent, the plebiscite had brought 89.9 per cent affirmative votes, the result apparently did not meet the high expectations of the NS leadership. The result in Berlin, at least, was interpreted by Goebbels as a failure:

> Election over ... foreign press so-so. The serious ones good. But our failure still remains the main topic ... Berlin result very bad. In part our own fault ... Lunch with the *Führer*. Many people there. Discussion about reasons for failure. Each one looks for them where they do not affect him ... More speeches and contact to the people ... More firmness against enemies of the state.[182]

VI: Concepts and Objectives in Domestic Policies

Goebbels' comments on the 98.8 per cent result of the plebiscite which Hitler held on 29 March 1936 after the occupation of the demilitarized Rhineland read quite differently:

> Lunch [with] *Führer*. We are all tense... The first results. Hardly believable. Time and again. I go to the Ministry. The trend continues. I still wait with publication ... Triumph upon triumph. And now the messages of victory pour in. Unendingly ... The nation has risen. The *Führer* has united the nation. We could not have hoped for this in our wildest dreams. We are all dazed. The *Führer* is very calm and silent. He only lays his hands on my shoulders. His eyes are quite wet ... He is unspeakably happy.[183]

The reports on the mood of the people prepared by the SD [Security Service—H.B.] and other authorities indicate that the results of the plebiscites did actually reflect popular opinion. It would certainly be too easy if one were to assess them as being primarily the result of the falsification of election returns and manipulations.

In Hitler's view, dictatorship and democracy only appeared to be contradictions because dictatorship, or the authoritarian state, was best able to realize 'true government by the people'. While Hitler rejected parliamentary democracy, he simultaneously claimed for himself that he had not simply abolished democracy but had lifted it to a higher plane. This element, which is important for Hitler's political self-understanding, and which had already played a certain role in his speeches and conversations during the time of struggle, can be shown in the following. 'Now what does "government by the people" mean in the highest sense of the word?', he asked in a speech on 9 June 1927. 'Government by the people', in Hitler's definition, was

> ... the system which brings the greatest benefit to the whole. I cannot set up a principle [meaning the 'majority principle—R.Z.] which is against logic. Government by the people is a government under which the people do not suffer any harm. A condition which brings the others happiness for ever. Government by the people lies in a system which permits that a nation is led and directed by its most capable brains. Government by the people is a government of responsibility. Government by the people is service for the people. You will surely all understand that a people is of course not served by a regime which consists of aristocrats, but by a man of the people, a capable brain, who reaches the top.[184]

While today in actual fact it was not the people but capital that ruled, National Socialism was striving for a true government by the people. This, said Hitler on 18 September 1928, would not be realized through the majority principle, not by 'a system which in reality means government by stupidity... No, government by the people means to bring the best brains of the people to power.'[185]

On 6 March 1929 Hitler declared that democracy could not be opposed by the aristocracy of birth,

> ... but only by the aristocracy of reason, genius, determination! If today a Communist turns to me and says you are against democracy, against the rule of the people – no, I am not against the rule of the people, I am only against the rule of the élite of the stupidity of a nation, that is all. Because I object that the representation of a nation should only be found in its stupidity, and profess my belief that the only true representation of a nation lies in genius, in its daring, in the superior reason. Put the best of the nation at its head and subject the people to their rule! As long as one gives oneself over to the mob, it is not the people who rule but the froth, not that rules which sinks to the bottom because of its value, but that which because of its lack of value swims on top and noisomely forms bubbles there. This is the only declaration against democracy which has any justification.[186]

In several conversations Wagener had with Hitler in 1930 and early 1931 the latter explained this theory of the contradictory identity of democracy and the *Führer* principle. 'The term democracy', said Hitler in a conversation with Gregor Strasser and Wagener in the summer of 1930,

> ... has been usurped by the parliamentarians, and they claim for themselves that parliamentarianism is identified with democracy. But in pure parliamentarianism I can neither see the right form, nor in parliamentarians the right men, to truly represent and govern a nation. The true self-administration of a nation, which for me is the deepest sense of democracy, can certainly not be achieved by way of pure parliamentarianism, but only by way of an organization of self-administration, in which the best and most capable must rise to the top.[187]

In his opening proclamation at the *Reichsparteitag* in 1933 Hitler said:

> In that we negate the parliamentary-democratic principle, we advocate in the sharpest way the right of the people to decide their own lives. But in the parliamentary system we do not see any true expression of the will of the people, which can logically only be a will to preserve the nation; in it we see instead a distortion of this, or even its about-turn. The will of a nation to preserve its existence manifests itself most clearly and usefully in its best brains![188]

In his speech in the *Reichstag* on 30 January 1934, the first anniversary of the seizure of power, he said:

> The will to preserve this [national] substance has to find that appropriate expression which becomes visible and vital as the will of the people, and also becomes effective in reality. The term 'democracy' is thereby subjected to a detailed examination and clarification. Because the new government is only a better expression of the will of the people against the outdated parliamentary democracy. But then the new state can only have but one task, the appropriate fulfilment of the conditions necessary for the continued existence of the nation. By relieving them

of all purely formal republican legitimistic or democratic concepts, its government will become just as much a leadership by the people as the leadership of the people grown out of the inner national conditions is the government of the state.

The National Socialists, he declared elsewhere during the same speech, were 'truly the better democrats'.[189]

The thesis of the identity of democracy and dictatorship by the people is, as we know, also one of the fundamental theorems of Leninism and Stalinism. Lenin, Stalin and Mao Tse-tung all claimed that the dictatorship of the proletariat (which was realized by the rule of the proletarian party) was in reality a higher form of democracy than bourgeois parliamentarianism.[190] These claims, just as the statements Hitler made, should not be interpreted exclusively as an attempt to shroud the reality of a dictatorship in democratic phrases. Modern totalitarian dictatorship actually is a qualitatively new form, which cannot be reduced to the principle of the rule of an individual by force but is characterized by a synthesis of dictatorial and plebiscitary elements. A dictatorship of modernization, such as not only Stalinism but also National Socialism and Maoism represent, always also leads to certain forms of equalization and participation. Hitler was therefore able to stress the 'democratic' character of his system by, for example, pointing to the increased opportunities for advancement for workers and farmers, i.e. to more 'equal opportunity'.[191] Both National Socialism as well as Marxism/Leninism are based, at least implicitly, on a differentiation between the *volonté général* and the *volonté de tous*. Rousseau's theory of the social contract admits the possibility that the general will, which orientates itself towards the preservation of the community and therefore has a normative character, and the will of the majority, which is determined by elections, do not coincide. Similarly, Leninism differentiates between the objective and the subjective interests of the proletariat, and the party becomes the authority which, based on its knowledge of the conformity to the natural laws of history, represents the objective interests of the proletariat, even where the latter has not yet even become aware of them. Hitler believed that the 'majority principle', in other words the *volonté de tous*, did not in any way express the true general will, i.e. the *volonté général*, which can only be adequately interpreted by the party and its *Führer*. The theory of totalitarianism is correct when it identifies such similarities between National Socialism and Communism. One should, however, record such similarities soberly and without the intent to defame communist or socialist systems and movements.

At the close of this section we intend to discuss a further question related to constitutional policy, namely Hitler's position on federalism and unitarianism. Since the relationship between the independence of the individual states to the authority of the central government of the Reich has always been a key constitutional problem in Germany, we shall now investigate whether Hitler took a position on this, and if so, what it was.

d. Hitler on Federalism and Unitarianism

In the tenth chapter of *Mein Kampf* (Volume II), Hitler addressed himself in detail to National Socialism's position on federalism and unitarianism. In a historic look back he expressed his admiration of Bismarck, who had carried out the process of the centralization of the Reich with extraordinary care and thereby shown 'the greatest considerations for habits and traditions'. It would, however, be completely wrong to attribute these considerations

> ... to his conviction that the Reich now possessed sufficient sovereign rights for all time. Bismarck did not hold this conviction in any way. On the contrary, he only wanted to leave to the future what would have been difficult to carry out and to bear at the moment. He was hoping for the gradually balancing effect of time and the pressure of developments themselves, to which he attributed more power in the long run than to any attempt to break down the momentary resistance of the individual states immediately. With this he demonstrated and most excellently proved the greatness of his ability as a statesman. Because, in reality, the sovereignty of the Reich has constantly increased at the expense of the sovereignty of the individual states. Time has fulfilled what Bismarck expected of it.

Hitler started off from a historic trend towards centralization caused by the development of transport and mass communication:

> All the states in the world are surely moving towards a certain unification in their internal organization. Germany too will not be an exception to this. Today it is already nonsense to speak about a 'state sovereignty' of the individual states, which in reality does not exist already because of the ludicrous size of these formations. Both in the area of transport as well as administration, the importance of the individual states is constantly being reduced. Modern traffic, modern technology, constantly cause distances and space to shrink. What was formerly a country is only a province today, and countries of the present were formerly regarded as continents. The difficulty, solely in terms of technology, of administering a country like Germany is no greater than the difficulty of administering a province like Brandenburg was one hundred and twenty years ago. Overcoming the distance from Munich to Berlin is easier today than that from Munich to Starnberg was one hundred years ago. And the whole territory of the Reich of today, in relationship to contemporary transportation technology, is smaller that any given medium-sized German state at the time of the Napoleonic Wars. Whoever closes his eyes to the consequences of the facts as they are will be left behind by the times. People who do this have existed throughout the ages, and there will also always be some in the future. But they can hardly slow down the wheel of history and never bring it to a stop. We National Socialists cannot afford to blindly pass by the conse-

quences of these truths. Here too we should not let ourselves be deceived by the phrases of our so-called national bourgeois parties.

However, Hitler continued, the obligation for the National Socialists could arise 'to most sharply oppose such a development in the state of today', not for reasons of principle, however, but for reasons of tactics, because centralization led to a domestic strengthening of the power of the system of government which they had set out to do away with. In Hitler's view, the National Socialists should attempt to exploit the opposition of individual states for their battle against the system. In this he drew a clear line between himself and the Bavarian particularists. Hitler was not interested in the independence of Bavaria as an objective in itself, but in the revolutionary exploitation of the conflict between Bavaria and the Reich:

> While, therefore, the Bavarian People's Party is attempting to obtain 'special rights' for the Bavarian state from a faint-hearted, particularistic point of view, we have to use this special position in the services of a higher national interest which is directed against the present November democracy.

Here, too, we see how Hitler orientates himself with the tactics of the Marxists, who he had accused only a few pages before of having functionalized the anti-Prussian mood by cleverly pretending, as had the leader of the Bavarian Soviet Republic Kurt Eisner, to be the champions of Bavarian interests to which they were actually completely indifferent.[192]

In various articles in the *Illustrierte Beobachter* Hitler also explained his tactics – already tested practically in the autumn of 1923 in Bavaria – of exploiting the problem of the independence of the states as a lever for revolutionarily intensifying the contradictions of the existing system. On 10 November 1928 he wrote that the issue was not 'to give Bavaria extra favours' but to turn the individual states into 'furnaces of national emotions of freedom and uprising'.[193] Because Hitler knew that the fight for Bavarian independence could be applied as a lever in the fight against the state, after the seizure of power he had to proceed as quickly as possible to the destruction of the independence of the states, particularly Bavaria. He rightly feared that his opponents could now attempt to use this lever. And, indeed, in 1933 Hitler's opponents attempted to link the fight for Bavarian independence to the fight against the new rulers.[194] As we know, Hitler abolished the independence of the states in a revolutionary process. But this process for the abolition of state independence should not only be seen as the result of power-political necessities. As we have seen, in *Mein Kampf* Hitler had already identified a historic trend towards centralization, whose executor he regarded himself as being.

In a speech at the *Reichsparteitag* in 1933 Hitler identified a continuity between the historic abolition of small statehood in Germany and the abolition of the independence of the states in the course of the NS revolution:

> What would Germany be if not already generations before us the scandalous nonsense of German small statehood had not stopped, which benefited the German people nowhere, but only their enemies everywhere? ... *The National Socialist movement is therefore not the conservator of the states of the past, but their liquidator in favour of the Reich of the future.* Because as a party it is neither north German nor south German, neither Bavarian nor Prussian, but only German, in it every rivalry of all the German states and tribes dissolves as being without substance.[195]

On 20 February 1938 Hitler said:

> The National Socialist revolution would have remained half-hearted if it had not imposed the interests of the nation as a whole upon the former states, and above all upon their so-called own sovereign roots ... The future of the German Reich was only secure from the moment the Reich became the sovereign and exclusive representative of the German nation. The iron principle that a nation has the right to a Reich made it possible to *release Germany from the paralysis of numerous individual state ties* and subsequently led to a development of power which today gives the individual national comrade within the individual states a far greater benefit than would ever have been possible in the past. It is only now that we have succeeded in all sectors of our national existence in setting those truly great tasks, and above all in securing those material means which are the conditions for the realization of great creative plans ... *great traffic routes, gigantic industrial buildings*, unique city plans and buildings, enormous bridges are today experiencing their planning, are ready for their building, or are already partially completed![196]

Dahrendorf called the 'restriction and ultimate abolition' of the rights of the states an attack on 'one of the characteristic traditions – and faults – of German social structure' and interpreted it as a part of the social revolution triggered by National Socialism.[197] The overcoming of narrow regional ties and traditions is in fact one of the essential attributes of the process of modernization. But this too – as the statements by Hitler cited above demonstrate – did not take place as unconsciously as the proponents of the theory of the contradiction between intent and effect of the NS revolution assume. When Hitler declared that the NS revolution had freed 'Germany from the paralysis of numerous ties of the individual states' and thereby created the conditions for the 'realization of great creative plans ... gigantic industrial buildings and great traffic routes', this showed that for him the abolition of the states was not merely a necessary evil in the course of the process of gaining political power. Hitler saw himself as the executor of the process of modernization, in the course of which the forces for the development of a modern industrial society were freed by the removal of regional ties and fragmentation.

On the other hand, in *Mein Kampf* and in his early articles Hitler had warned about the harmful effects of an unreflected over-centralization of the Reich. We see from his table talks that Hitler, even though he welcomed the historical trend towards centralization, also saw the danger of a bureaucratization through over-centralization. Faced with the fact that the jurists in the central authorities in Berlin often insisted on regulating even the most minute details – the type of street lamps, for example – Hitler said on 1/2 November 1941 that one should not be surprised that

> ... the country is becoming filled with hatred of Berlin! Ministries should lead, but not burden themselves with the implementation. The administrative apparatus has developed into a purely mechanical mechanism. We will overcome this when we decide in favour of as far a decentralization as possible. The extension of the frontiers of the Reich already force us to this. One should not believe that a decree which makes sense in the *Altreich* [the old Reich, i.e. Germany with her 1938 borders—H.B.] or parts of it has the same meaning in Kirkenes and the Crimea. It is not right to want to administer this gigantic Reich from Berlin in the way we were used to.

In the same talk Hitler declared: 'Just like the authorities in the old police state, our administration today still regards the citizen as the underling who, being politically under age, requires constant spoon-feeding.'[198]

Hitler's advocacy of decentralization does not contradict the fact that he basically welcomed the process of centralization but is rather a criticism of bureaucracy as the context of the statements cited above show. Within the framework of the centralization he welcomed, Hitler was in favour of the development of independent authorities on the lower level and against interference and restriction by a centre intent on regulating everything. He therefore did not regard France as the ideal model of the modern state, because French centralization had led to a bureaucratization of all sectors of life. The French, said Hitler on 16 November 1941, were the worst possible example: 'The ideal state of the jurists and lawyers! A structure which mobilizes the living forces where they exist will be able to manage crises in which a jurist state fails. A great reform of the administration will have to take place there!'[199]

In a table talk on 3 May 1942 Hitler attacked the 'Berlin ministerial bureaucracy'. They were 'confusing the tasks of the central authority, which should only set the direction and intervene where damages occurred, with a unitarianism which was suffocating life out there completely'. This was all the more dangerous because during the last twenty years the ministerial bureaucracy had almost completely regenerated itself out of its own ranks. It was therefore necessary to develop as many good administrators as possible throughout the country and then infiltrate the ministerial bureaucracy with them. But such people, who would also be of use in practice, could only be developed if they were given the opportunity to demonstrate their abilities in their own administrative organizations. Hitler believed that 'the more decentralized the Reich is administered, the easier it would be to find good people for the central authorities who actually do know where they should issue directives to the administrations out there, and when they have to intervene'.[200]

Hitler's advocacy of a greater independence and more initiative must also be seen within the context of the problem of recruiting an élite in the system phase. Only when the Gau leaders, for example, were given independence and not interfered with in everything could really capable men prove themselves. Hitler declared on 24 June 1942 that, in the organization of the Reich today, he was utilizing the experiences he had gained in the organization of the party in the time of struggle:

> If he had then made the Gau leaders into a sort of Gau kings who had only received the very key directives from above, he was now giving the Reichs deputies far-reaching freedom of decision – even if he ran into objections by the Reichs Ministry of the Interior. Only if the Gau leaders and the Reichs deputies were given sufficient room to act on their own could talents be identified. Otherwise the only thing to develop would be a stupid bureaucracy. Only if the corps of regional leaders was given responsibility, could responsible people be recruited, and thereby a sufficient reserve of capable brains for overall leadership tasks.

In relation to the great freedom he had granted the Gau leaders and Reichs deputies, he had automatically demanded unconditional discipline towards the orders of the top leadership. But in this he had 'assumed, as a matter of course, that with its directives the top leadership would not attempt to interfere in the so-called detail work, because the local conditions for this were different everywhere'. In this context, said Hitler, he wished specifically to emphasize that, in the organization of a Reich, nothing was more harmful than too strong a regimentation of self-administration. As Bismarck had said in 1871, at the time France had also broken down due to a lack of self-administration because 'its small departments had been without their own leadership possibilities and therefore without initiative, [and] they had doggedly waited for directives from Paris'.[201]

During a table talk on 22 July 1942 Hitler complained that in the *Altreich* things had developed over time in such a way 'that too much was being looked at from the vantage of the provincial backwater and therefore was being regimented and proscribed down to the smallest degree'. The mistake of 'constant regimentation' had to be avoided at all costs in the occupied territories in the East. He wished, therefore, that Berlin should only issue 'the large directives' for the occupied Eastern territories. The decisions on daily affairs had to be taken on the spot by the responsible regional commissioners.[202]

We have already quoted Hitler's statements on the partial decentralization of the power industry in another context. This project was also based, as the same table talk (26 July 1942) clarifies, on Hitler's scepticism towards over-centralization and over-regimentation. If a field of activity were regimented in detail by civil servants in Berlin, said Hitler, then it would be impossible to develop useful brains who thought and worked independently in the *Gauen*:

> Only out in the *Gauen* do the fresh talents constantly grow, who had to be treated with care, that means left to work as independently as possible, so that they matured for subsequent assignments in the Reich. If a field of activity was solely regimented by Berlin, then no talents would surface any longer in the administration concerned, then everything would fall into a dogged ministerial bureaucracy and the Reich would become dependent on the people who might be developed by the ministries.[203]

Hitler's rejection of the too stringent regimentation and spoon-feeding of the lower levels of administration by the centres often also expressed itself in his own conduct, which was then interpreted as an 'inability to take decisions'. Wagener writes that

> Hitler actually never gave orders. He did not, in fact, want to take decisions. He avoided, yes he even omitted, to say: I want to have this in such and such a way. Instead he explained his more or less philosophical line of thought couched in general terms to his associate or within a certain circle, and declared that this should be taken in such and such a way, looked at from such and such a point of view, decided on such and such a principle, and this and that taken into consideration. Then it became the task of the individual to issue his directives and work in his area in such a way that the general direction outlined by Hitler, the great objective that was gradually crystallizing in these conversations, was aspired to and achieved over time.[204]

It was therefore Hitler's way normally to only give general directions but not to decide the detail of a matter himself. He only set the principles which were to be taken into consideration for the decision which was to be taken independently at a lower level. This conduct by Hitler has been interpreted as an expression and manifestation of a lack of decision which was deeply rooted in Hitler's personality.[205]

We have already shown in Chapter II that some of the frequently cited examples of Hitler's indecisiveness – his conduct on 8/9 November 1923, for example, or during the weeks and months preceding 30 June 1934 – are not to be taken as expressions of any 'reluctance to take decisions' which is not otherwise explained, but as the result of an actualization of his ambivalent relationship to authority. Other examples which are cited as manifestations of Hitler's inability to take decisions – for example, his habit, as reported by Heinz Linge, of giving long and voluble 'presentations', in order not only to convince everybody but also to familiarize them with all of his various reasons, instead of simply giving a precise order – should be regarded less as a reluctance on Hitler's part to take decisions but as a manifestation of his scepticism towards over-regimentation and interference with lower-level authorities. Maser also admits that with Hitler one could normally not count on concrete and detailed orders, but he was quite readily prepared to give unequivocal and precise orders when he was familiar with the details of the matter at hand from his own experience.[206] Hitler's conduct was an outcome of his belief that the details of a matter should normally not be decided by the central authority but independently 'on the spot'. We have seen that Hitler, even though he basically welcomed the historic trend towards centralization, still often warned of the consequences of an over-centralization which expressed itself in interference and regimentation at the lower level. This prevented the development of truly independent brains at the lower levels.

We see that there are three elements which come together at this point. First is the attempt to find an answer to the problem of the recruitment of an élite in the system phase. From this the criticism of over-centralization is derived, because such a development prevents the training of really capable elements on the lower level. From this in turn we can derive Hitler's habit of refusing to decide the details himself and only issuing the general guidelines under which the decision was to be taken, which has frequently been described as a 'reluctance to take a decision'.

Let us summarize the results of this chapter. Hitler addressed himself in detail to the question of federalism or unitarianism which is so important for any constitution. In view of the development of modern technology, particularly transport, he believed that a trend towards centralization was unavoidable. While the abolition of the independence of the states was initially a power-political necessity because he feared his opponents could copy the concept he advocated, i.e. the tactical exploitation of the contradictions between the Reich and individual states (particularly Bavaria) for the destabilization of the system, Hitler also saw himself as the executor of a historic trend towards centralization. On the other hand, he warned of the consequences of over-centralization which would lead to over-regimentation by the authorities in Berlin, and therefore to the stifling of responsibility and initiative on the lower levels.

At the end of this chapter we are able to state that Jäckel's claim that the fact no new constitution had been introduced in the Third Reich was an indication that Hitler had been disinterested in questions of domestic and constitutional policy can no longer be upheld. Hitler, who rejected 'too timely' an enactment of a constitution because he feared artificially and arbitrarily cutting off an organic development within the process of the revolution at a certain stage of development, still addressed himself in detail to many questions of domestic and constitutional policy, including the question of succession.

Chapter VI has shown that, in the field of domestic policy, Hitler did indeed have conclusive concepts and objectives as well. A democrat will certainly reject these most emphatically. But this does not alter the fact that they are conclusive. Hitler's criticism of the 'majority principle' and pluralistic democracy, his thesis of democracy as a form of rule by capital, his advocacy of a strict separation of politics and business and the creation of the primacy of politics, his contrasting of 'the common good' to 'the politics of interests', his theory of the 'historic minority' and his concepts of the *Führer* state all fit together logically and are in close context to his social and economic views as well as his socio-Darwinistic philosophy. Our investigation has shown that 'thinking your way in' into the world of Hitler's concepts permits us to understand many contexts and modes of conduct (for example, his 'reluctance to take decisions') which would otherwise appear to be inexplicable.

VII

Hitler's Self-Assessment in the Political Spectrum

1. 'Left' or 'Right'?

The views, positions, concepts, ideas and theories held by Hitler, which we have learned about in the preceding five chapters, are often surprising, because we would more likely expect them from a left-wing revolutionary but not from a reactionary from the far right such as Hitler. This raises the question: was Hitler really 'right wing'? Sebastian Haffner has pointed out that the only opposition which could really have become dangerous for Hitler came from the right: 'From its vantage, Hitler was on the left. This makes us stop and think. Hitler can certainly not be so readily sorted into the extreme right of the political spectrum as many people are in the habit of doing.'[1]

The only effective opposition to Hitler, in actual fact, represented by conservative and in part also monarchistic forces such as Beck, Halder, Oster, Witzleben, Goerdeler, Popitz, Yorck and Hassell, stood to his right. Dahrendorf has pointed out the dilemma of German resistance to Hitler which, while certainly having been highly moral, still did not mark a step forward on the road of German society to a constitution of liberty:

> What is even worse is that it was Hitler who effected that transformation of German society which alone made the constitution of liberty possible, while the resistance to his regime appeared in the name of a society which could serve as a base for nothing but an authoritarian regime.

July 20, 1944, and the persecutions set off by the failure, meant, said Dahrendorf, 'the end of a political élite'.[2]

As Hans Mommsen has shown, the German opposition to Hitler, which recruited almost exclusively from the upper class and here primarily from the nobility, regarded National Socialism and Bolshevism as being identical. Trott said, for example: 'What presents itself to us as a dirty brown muck at home faces us with Asian hardness and brutality in Moscow'.[3] Hassell feared that 'socialism in the Hitlerian form' inevitably had the objective of destroying the upper classes through an 'internal Bolshevization'.[4] And in a memorandum prepared by Lieutenant-Commander Liedig at the end of 1939, which illuminates the opinions of the group around Oster in Intelligence and is also typical of the political concepts of Beck and Halder, it says: 'A revolutionary dynamics of destruction of all the historic links and all the cultural tie-ins which once made up the dignity and fame of Europe is the only, and the total, secret of his [Hitler's] statesmanship.'[5]

From the very beginning of his political activities Hitler had to contend with the accusation from the right that he was a 'Bolshevist' or Communist, just as he had to contend with the accusation from the left that he was a 'reactionary' or a lackey of monopoly capitalism. In a programmatic speech which Hitler gave on 13 August 1920 he took exception to the accusation that he was a Communist. On the one hand, he complained, they say: 'If you advocate what is in your programme, you are a Communist'; on the other hand, he was being denounced as an 'arch reactionary' and a 'militarily completely contaminated retrograde'.[6] On 17 February 1922 Hitler declared:

> Whether we stood up a thousand times against the regime of Wilhelm II, for the Marxists we are still reactionary monarchists thanks to a mendacious press; whether we fight against Bolshevism, and we are the only ones who *really* fight, for the 'nationalists' we remain Bolshevists ... In this way, from right to left there is nothing but a great lie.[7]

In an interview with the *Rheinisch-Westfälische Zeitung* on 16 August 1932 Hitler said:

> Certain right-wing circles call us Bolshevists, and the Bolshevists in their turn claim we are reactionaries, barons, big capitalists, serfs of entrepreneurs and God knows what else... The internal Marxist enemies of Germany know after their years-long deception of the German people that the National Socialist movement will really honestly take care of the German working person. The bourgeois reactionaries know that we will replace their policy of weakness by a policy of national strength. Both suspect that the time of class and special interest battles is approaching its end, and that on the ideological platform of National Socialism the German nation will be given back its unity.[8]

In another context we have already cited a statement of Hitler's in the 'monologues': 'In the eyes of Saxon industry we too were Communists. Whoever advocates social equality for the masses is a Bolshevist!'[9]

It is of course erroneous to call Hitler a Marxist or a Communist, even if this is still being done by conservative forces today – no longer with the object of defaming National Socialism, however, but with the intention of discrediting left-wing socialism or social democracy. F. J. Strauss said in an interview on 29

September 1979 that 'Hitler and Goebbels were both Marxists at the bottom of their hearts'.[10] This classification is just as far from Hitler's political self-understanding as is the thesis of Hitler being the reactionary agent of monopoly capitalism, which Soviet-Marxist history keeps repeating as a stereotype.

Nevertheless, until today Hitler has been regarded as belonging to the right almost as a matter of course. This classification, however, at least contradicts Hitler's own concept of himself as well as his self-portrayal. Hitler never described himself as being a right-wing politician, but always criticized both left-wing and right-wing political movements and parties to the same degree. The following passages from the report on a speech on 26 October 1920, for example, are typical:

> Now Hitler turned to the right and left. The national right lacked a social concept, the social left a national one. He admonished the right-wing parties: if you want to be national, then climb down to your people and away with all this class conceit! To the left he called: you who have declared your solidarity with the whole world, first show your solidarity with your own national comrades, become Germans first! Is this the way the heroes look, who intend to destroy the world, but crawl before the foreign nations in fear that something might be taken amiss out there? You who are truly revolutionaries; come over to us and fight with us for our whole nation! Your place is not over there as drovers for international capital, but with us, with your nation![11]

On 19 November 1920 Hitler said that his party 'was not fighting against the right or left but was taking what was valuable from both sides'.[12]

In his notes for a speech on 20 July 1921 he wrote:

> right — left
> war profiteers — state destroyers
>
> both do not care what country they live in.[13]

In a letter written on 6 September 1921 to the leader of the Hannover district group of the NSDAP, Hitler declared that the party was not being built up by mergers with other national-popular groupings but by gaining the forces of the extreme left and extreme right: 'But there is no value in joining up with such weak formations. *What we need is to attract powerful masses, preferably from the extreme left and extreme right wing.*'[14] Hitler regarded only the truly extreme forces, the idealists of the extreme right and extreme left, as being suitable for the new movement. 'In the ranks of us National Socialists,' he said on 28 September 1922, 'the disinherited from the right and left must come together.'[15] And on 26 February 1923 he declared: 'Our movement must comprise both extremes, left and right. Here Spartacus man, there officer. Both groups are idealists.'[16]

> Our task will be to give our nation a national feeling again, and to unite this with social happiness because with us, only he will be *national* who is aware of his highest *social* obligations, while we will only be able to call him *social* who is *national* in the truest sense of the word. For this reason, the two extremes are flowing together in our movement, the Communists from the left and the students, the officers from the right. Both were the most active elements, and it was the greatest of crimes that both once stood opposed to each other in street battles. Because of many years of incitement the Communists, as the idealists of Socialism, regarded the reactionary officer as their deadly enemy. On the other hand, in the meantime, the officers marched against the Spartacists because they had to regard the proletarian who had been seduced by the Jew as the deadly enemy of their fatherland. Within our party in its storm department [i.e. the SA—H.B.] we have already succeeded in uniting these two classes.[17]

Hitler's objective was the development of a movement which would abolish the contradictions between left and right and unite the most active, most spirited elements from the extreme right and the extreme left within itself. At a rally on 24 April 1923 Hitler defined his position in the political spectrum: 'So today our movement is the sharpest extreme against two extremes.'[18] In *Mein Kampf* he wrote that the new movement must appeal to the 'dissatisfied', above all to those 'tired of voting' and the

> ... many inclining to the fanatical extreme of the left side. And the young movement should turn to these first of all. It should not become an organization of the contented, satisfied, but it should unite the tortured and restless, the unhappy and dissatisfied, and it should above all not swim on the surface of the national community but root in its depths.

A young movement did not take 'the material of its adherents from the camp of the indifferent . . . but from mostly very extreme *Weltanschauungen*'.[19]

Hitler's intention primarily to unite extreme forces from left and right in his movement of the 'extreme against both extremes' can only be understood in connection with his theory on the formation of an élite in the movement phase. The people who followed radical slogans and joined extreme parties, regardless of whether on the right or on the left, thereby showed that they were not the opportunists or career-minded who wanted to adjust themselves to the system but brave and courageous fighting spirits who were also prepared to make sacrifices for their political convictions. And with this they proved that they belonged to the 'historic minority'.

Hitler did not define himself as belonging either to the left or to the right: 'The political work of our two groups, left or right, is of no importance to the

German nation in its totality, as long as this work only encompasses group work, and as long as it does not become a work to overcome these groups.'[20] His objective was therefore to overcome the traditional left/right contrast, so that in his speeches he normally attacked both the bourgeois right as well as the Marxist left to the same degree.[21] At the end of April 1929 he declared: 'And the sense which comes from such an idea [National Socialism] is, it must free itself in a cry for national freedom which flows over both right and left.'[22] In a speech commemorating the tenth anniversary of the announcement of the 25-point programme of the NSDAP, Hitler looked back:

> You could see how they cautiously felt their way towards each other, the fighters from the barricades right and left, how they gradually came to like and know each other: he is a fine fellow too, he also has ideals, a man who is prepared to die for an ideal is always good, you can come to an agreement with someone like that. The National Socialists came about. Their name already unites two extreme terms, the national and the socialist joined together in one word. What tore our nation apart most strongly suddenly became the cement which joined it most strongly and united it inseparably.[23]

In February 1931 Hitler told Wagener that he feared that a civil war would break out between the left and the right:

> This means two dangers are looming for Germany. First that of a reactionary dictatorship of the right, and second that of an uprising on the left under Communist leadership. Both mean civil war ... At the moment of a *putsch* by the right, the workers would react by a general strike, the Social Democrats and the Communists with insurgence and opposition. With time, however, the police and the *Reichswehr* can gain the upper hand. But it would be a terrible spilling of blood, which would not even end with a stable order. In this battle we ourselves would be torn apart into socialists and nationalists. Because true National Socialism is firstly still not clear to most of them, and furthermore it could neither decide to march with the reactionaries against the German workers nor with the Communists against the nationally minded German middle class. We would therefore also go under in this maelstrom.[24]

When on 24 February 1941 Hitler looked back to the announcement of the party programme in a commemorative speech, he again emphasized the character of the NSDAP which from the beginning 'had neither subscribed to the right or the left side'.[25] When he was recalling the time of struggle in his monologues on 30 November 1941, he said: 'My party at the time consisted of ninety per cent of people from the left. I could only use people who had fought.'[26] In a speech on 30 January 1942, on the anniversary of the seizure of power, Hitler declared that he had had 'to turn against both sides', against the left and the right.[27]

VII: Self-Assessment in the Political Spectrum

Hitler did not regard himself as being either on the left or on the right, but wanted to overcome both extremes – not in the 'middle', however, but by a new extreme in which both were abolished. On 26 May 1944 he said:

> In those days the definitions of both terms were diametrically opposed to each other. Then one was on the right side of the barricade and the other on the left, and I went right in between these two fighters, in other words climbed up on the barricade itself, and therefore was naturally shot at by both. I attempted to define a new term under the motto that in the end, nationalism and socialism are the same under one condition, namely that the nation moves into the centre of all desire... In those days I had heavy battles both from the left as well as from the right.[28]

We know, however, that Hitler did not proceed against the left in the same way as he did against the right. Some dedicated monarchists were also delivered into the concentration camps in certain cases, and some conservative middle-class forces, such as Papen's associates Bose and Jung, were also shot just like the SA leaders on 30 June 1934. In the balance, however, it is incontestable that the Communists and the Social Democrats had to bear the greater sacrifices. While they were being tortured and murdered in the concentration camps, the right-wing middle class and the capitalist forces were still making good money in the Third Reich. This has nothing to do with Hitler's preference for the right, however – quite the opposite. He regarded the right-wing and middle-class forces as being cowardly, weak, without energy and incapable of any resistance,[29] whereas he assumed the left to have the brave, courageous, determined and therefore dangerous forces. And, as we shall see, for him these were more appealing then the middle-class conservative elements he despised and basically no longer took seriously as opponents. This ideologically mistaken assessment was to avenge itself, however, because it was not the Communists who became a danger for him. He had convinced many of them, who had become fervent adherents of National Socialism. Others offered resistance which was certainly admirable but still impotent. The actual dangers came from other forces, from conservative middle-class men such as Goerdeler, from Hassell and Popitz, who can only be described as extreme reactionaries, and from monarchists like Oster and Canaris.[30] At least from 1938 onwards, these forces carried on a systematic conspiracy and opposition which was not at all doomed to failure from the beginning.

It was only towards the end of his life, when he appreciated the total and irreversible failure of the Third Reich, that Hitler recognized that it had been a mistake to proceed one-sidedly against the forces on the left and to spare those on the right. At a conference of the Gau leaders on 24 February 1945 he said, as his adjutant von Below reports, 'We liquidated the left-wing class fighters, but unfortunately we forgot in the meantime to also launch the blow against the right. That is our great sin of omission.'[31] In view of his failure, Hitler searched for an explanation for his defeat and recognized that his alliance with the middle-class and right-wing forces – without which he would, however, never have come to power – was irreconcilable in the long run with the radical revolutionary policies he had conceived. And he had not 'forgotten' to launch 'the blow against the right', but, based on his ideological premises, had simply not believed it to be necessary – at least until 20 July 1944 – to proceed against his opponents on the right whom he despised as being weak, lacking in energy and cowardly. In view of the war plans Hitler was pursuing, proceeding against the right, which played an important role in business, the military and the civil service, would moreover hardly have been possible, particularly since he would thereby have provoked a dangerous 'war on two fronts' in domestic politics.

Let us summarize. Hitler defined himself as being neither left nor right, and was striving for a synthesis, an overcoming of both extremes.[32] In order to come closer to Hitler's political self-definition, it appears to us important to try to trace Hitler's attempted synthesis of nationalism and socialism, because that, and nothing else, was what National Socialism wanted to be.

2. National Socialism as the Synthesis between Nationalism and Socialism

The nineteenth century had produced two great ideas: nationalism and socialism. Based on the Marxist tradition of socialism, a melding of the two ideas was impossible, because as Marx wrote in his *Communist Manifesto*, 'The workers have no fatherland.'[33] Nonetheless, around the turn of the century there were already attempts being made – or at least consideration was being given – to unite both ideas in a synthesis. The liberal Friedrich Naumann was pursuing the thought of a 'national-social' movement which was to gain the worker for the national power state. With regard to National Socialism, its claim to being a synthesis of nationalism and socialism was often not taken seriously or rejected.[34]

For Hitler the contradictory terms 'nationalism' and 'socialism' were identical on a higher plane:

> Any truly national idea is social in the final analysis, that means whoever is prepared to commit himself to his nation so completely that he truly does not have any higher ideal than only the well-being of this, his nation, whoever has understood our great song *Deutschland, Deutschland über alles* in such a way that there

is nothing in the world for him which stands higher than this Germany, people and land, land and people, is a socialist.[35]

The national concept, said Hitler in a speech on 29 January 1923 'is identical for us Germans with the socialist one. The more fanatically national we are, the more we must take the welfare of the national community to heart, that means the more fanatically socialist we become.'[36] The higher term for Hitler is 'nation'. *For Hitler, socialism was the ruthless pursuit of the interests of the nation domestically according to the principle 'common good ahead of egoism', 'nationalism' was the ruthless pursuit of the interests of the nation abroad.*[37]

As we have seen in the portrayal of Hitler's position on the middle class, he sharply rejected bourgeois nationalism because it identified egoistic class and profit interests with the interests of the nation. This made the bourgeois definition of nationalism incompatible with socialism:

> But what is the meaning of this term? What does nationalism mean? . . . If I wish to be national, this means that I want to serve this people, and if I want to serve a people, this can only mean that I want to contribute to this nation surviving, that it can preserve its existence, that it earns its daily bread, and that it can continue to develop, physically and spiritually. But if I want to be national in this sense, then I must understand that the future of our German nation will only develop favourably if we lead a people which is healthy into this future.

Just as Hitler accused the parties of the right of having falsified the actual sense of the term 'nationalism' and to have turned it into its opposite, he also accused Marxism of having falsified the meaning of socialism. The purpose of socialism was

> . . . to improve the fate of the masses, to lift them, to give them bread, and culturally raise them. The purpose of socialism should also be that within it a people become healthy, that the people rise upwards in this socialism. And if I recognize that socialism should not be a phrase of a party, but a teaching for the uplifting of the poorest, the most lowly of a nation, the improvement of their situation in life, then I must understand that I will only achieve that if the whole national community is prepared to do this, if a whole nation places itself at the service of this movement.

The 'changing around of these two terms "socialism" and "nationalism"' meant

> . . . in reality a coming together of both. Because what then occurs, socialism becomes nationalism, nationalism socialism. They are both one, socialism and nationalism. They are the greatest fighters for their own people, are the greatest fighters in the fight for existence here on earth, and with this they are no longer battle cries against each other, but a battle cry which shapes its life according to this

motto: We do not recognize pride of estate, just as little as pride of class. We know only one pride, namely to be the servants of a people.[38]

For Hitler 'National Socialism' also meant that 'Socialism can only exist within the framework of my nation' because 'there can only be approximately equals within a national body in larger racial communities, but not outside of them'.[39] Hitler's socialism therefore had an exclusively national claim to validity, just as we emphasized at the beginning of Chapter III.2

Hitler's claim to be forming a synthesis between nationalism and socialism was primarily based on a *social* reason. Hitler believed that neither of the two embattled classes – bourgeoisie and proletariat – was strong enough to defeat the other, i.e. that there was a certain state of balance between the two classes. This fact would finally lead to the downfall of the whole nation. But if neither class were strong enough to overcome the other, then a class war on this basis was no longer sensible: the contradiction had to be resolved on a higher level, a new idea, a new force had to appear, which could form the common platform for both embattled parties.

Here we see an interesting point of contact between that Marxist interpretation of Fascism which stands in the tradition of the so-called 'Bonapartism Theory' and Hitler's self-understanding. The Bonapartism Theory as advocated from August Thalheimer[40] all the way to Eberhard Jäckel[41] assumes that the autocratic ruler 'comes to power in stand-off situations' in which 'one part of ... society ... [is] no longer strong enough, the other not yet strong enough, to rule the state'.[42] Fascism in the form of 'Bonapartism' develops, according to Thalheimer, when 'all the classes lie on the ground exhausted and without strength',[43] i.e. in a situation in which none of the classes can defeat the others any longer.

As he declared on 8 November 1930, Hitler assumed that

> ... both parties have already lost the strength to overcome each other ... neither of both camps who today are fighting each other is still capable of completely overcoming the other spiritually ... If in Germany neither is capable any longer of spiritually overcoming the other, there are only two possibilities left.

Either Germany will go under, said Hitler, or the nation had to be led back together again on 'a third platform': 'The two existing concepts have become paralyzed. There is only one possibility, to create a third concept and on this third platform to newly reunite the German nation.' When the concepts of nationalism and socialism under which the bourgeoisie and the proletariat march into class war were really irreconcilable, said Hitler, then the unity of the German nation would come to an end. But since socialism only meant 'the representation of the interests of a whole over the interests of individuals', while nationalism only meant 'commitment to one's nation',[44] both terms were ultimately identical.

In a speech on 13 November 1930 Hitler asked whether the two *Weltanschauungen* still had 'the strength to overcome the opponent'. Today one could see, went Hitler's answer, 'that at the end of this internal war between nationalism, bourgeoisie and Marxism, both directions lack the convincing strength to overcome the other part'. Even twelve years after the November revolution one had to note that 'in reality the two camps were facing each other with stacked arms'. Both worlds – bourgeoisie and proletariat – 'stand facing each other exhausted, hardened and closed off within themselves'. Therefore only a 'third idea' could form a new platform which would enable the continued existence of the German nation. Hitler saw this new platform in the synthesis of the national and the socialist idea:

> If we burden the term 'socialism' with all of the dogma which social democracy and the Communist party have put into the term, and if we burden the term 'nationalism' with all of the dogma which the bourgeois parties have put into it, then the terms actually are absolutely divisive. But that is not necessary and does not lie in the terms themselves. I do not have to link the term 'socialism' to any ideas the Social Democratic Party has put into it, and I do not need to identify the term 'nationalism' with opinions of the present bourgeois parties. On the contrary, these terms should be cleansed of foreign additives.

Then we would have the following: socialism meant nothing more than that 'the benefit of the whole takes precedent over the benefit of the individual'. In the whole of business life the concept had to be done away with, that the benefit of the individual was essential and that the benefit of the whole developed from the benefit of the individual. The opposite was true. Therefore the term 'socialism' had proved itself to be identical to the term 'nationalism'. Nationalism only meant 'commitment of the individual to the benefit of the whole ... Sacrifice of your life for your nation. Is there a greater sacrifice of my own interests, than to give my life for my nation?'[45]

Let us trace Hitler's line of reasoning once again. The two embattled classes, the bourgeoisie and the proletariat, no longer had the strength to overcome each other, to win out. Neither of the two extremes could reunite the German nation on its platform by abolishing the other extreme. Therefore a new platform had to be found, a 'third idea', based upon which the continued existence of the German nation would alone become possible if it were not to be consumed in a class war which no side could win in the end. This 'new idea', however, must unite within itself the former *Weltanschauungen* of both embattled classes, nationalism and socialism – unite them and abolish them. By negating the two terms in their present (Marxist and bourgeois) form, they were simultaneously lifted up and abolished within a higher form, namely National Socialism. It started off with the identity of the two contradictory terms. Just as socialism primarily meant subordination of the economic interests of the individual to the interests of the whole, so, in the end, nationalism was nothing more than a willingness to subordinate the ego to the community of the nation.[46]

In his speech on 24 February 1941 at the commemoration ceremony for the proclamation of the party programme, Hitler again declared that his idea of melding socialism and nationalism had ultimately sprung from the insight that no class could defeat the others. The bourgeois ideal, said Hitler, was

> . . . limited socially, the Marxist unlimited internationally. But basically both movements had already become sterile. At the time I first appeared here, no sensible person could still expect that a clear victory could be achieved here. And that was what was important. If the nation were not to finally split apart, then one side had to emerge from this battle, if it was inevitable, as the one hundred per cent victor. But that was already impossible then, because the movements had already begun to dissolve within themselves and to split up.[47]

Here, as in other quotations, the parallels between Hitler's own view and the Marxist analysis of Fascism orientated towards the Bonapartism Theory become clear. Seen socially, National Socialism for Hitler was the attempt to overcome a stand-off in the fight between the two big classes, the middle class and the working class. In terms of social policies, Hitler regarded his concept of National Socialism as the 'third way' between the two extremes of capitalism and Bolshevism.[48] And, as Klaus Hildebrand emphasizes, this claim was certainly one of the important reasons for Hitler's success.[49]

3. Hitler's Assessment of Related and Opposing Political Movements and Systems

We have seen that it makes little sense to sort Hitler into the traditional left/right spectrum. While his theory – as we have portrayed it here so far – contains more 'left-wing' than 'right-wing' elements, the racist component of his *Weltanschauung* already prohibits our classifying him as belonging to the political left. In order completely to appreciate Hitler's political self-understanding, i.e. his self-evaluation within the political spectrum, it is necessary to portray his position with regard to opposing and related political movements and systems. Of particular interest in this context is Hitler's position in relation to the left (Social Democracy, Communism or Stalinism) on the one hand and to Italian Fascism as well as the reactionary Franco regime in Spain on the other. While it is customary to assume that Social Democrats and Communists, whom he persecuted with the greatest harshness, were politically the furthest removed from him, and Italian Fascism and Franco's Spain were politically more closely related to National Socialism, we intend to show that, while not exactly the opposite was true, this view will still have to be modified quite substantially.

a. Social Democracy

There are many statements by Hitler in which he expressed admiration for the Social Democratic party. 'The Social Democratic Party,' he said on 27 April 1923, was 'the best organized movement not only in Germany but in the whole world.' It was also 'the most disciplined party in Europe.'[50]

In *Mein Kampf* Hitler claimed that he had originally been quite positive towards Social Democracy. While this claim cannot be clearly proven, there are indeed reports that in 1918, before the overthrow of the (German) Soviets, Hitler had unsuccessfully tried to join both the USPD, i.e. the radical split-off from the SPD, and the Communists.[51] Among other things this would explain numerous statements by Hitler in which he assesses the USPD surprisingly positively and even over-evaluates it.

In his book Hitler explained his original sympathy for the Social Democrats as follows:

> That it [i.e. Social Democracy—R.Z.] fought for universal suffrage and the secret ballot made me inwardly happy. My reason told me already then, that this was bound to lead to a weakening of the Habsburg regime I hated so much . . . Therefore this activity of Social Democracy was not displeasing to me. That it also was attempting to uplift the living conditions of the worker, as my naïve spirit was still dumb enough to believe, also appeared to me to speak more in its favour than against it.

What he did not like from the very beginning, said Hitler, was the hostile position of Social Democracy towards the battle to preserve Germanism in Austria and the 'pitiful wooing for the favour of the Slavic "comrades"'. Hitler then described how, as a worker in the construction industry, he gained the first negative experiences with Social Democracy, or rather the unions, which were cause enough to have a closer look at them. He then analyzed the reasons for the success of Social Democracy – the methods of propaganda, for example – and attempted to learn from them. His negative position towards Social Democracy or Marxism only developed fully, however, after he had begun to recognize the influence of the Jews in this movement:

> *Only the knowledge of Jewism alone offers the key to understanding the inner, and therefore the true intentions of Social Democracy.* Whoever knows this race, from

415

his eyes sink the veils of erroneous concepts about the objective and the purpose of this party, and out of the mist and fog of social phrases, the grinning countenance of Marxism rises upward.

In *Mein Kampf* Hitler also dealt with Social Democracy in another context. In his view the SPD had declined from a revolutionary party – because of its too large membership – to a mere reform party. While he agreed that the Social Democratic leaders still had the objective of revolution,

> ... what was left in the end was only the intention and a body that was no longer fit for its execution. *One can no longer carry out a revolution with a party of ten million members.* In such a movement one no longer has an extreme of activity, but a broad mass of the middle, therefore inertia.

While Social Democracy had therefore 'continually lost the character of a brutal revolutionary party', its radical active part had split off: 'Independent party and Spartacus union were the storm battalions of revolutionary Marxism.'[52] In another context we have already quoted from Hitler's speech at the Hamburg National Club, where he developed the same line of reasoning, out of which he then finally derived the need for the creation of a small, tightly organized and extremely radical core party.[53]

Hitler tried to learn from Social Democracy's success as well as from its degeneration to a mere reform party, but he always remained an admirer of the old Social Democratic Party. In a speech on 12 June 1925 he said:

> The SPD did not come about overnight. Whoever wants to study it must study the course of its development, how it grew out of small workers' associations, how it developed extraordinarily logically and appropriately! Now it has 15,000 employees. The instinct for self-preservation of this bureaucracy alone is a guarantee of its continued existence.[54]

Hitler did not, of course, normally express his admiration for Social Democracy in his public statements. His private statements, however, show that he was far more positive towards Social Democracy than towards the middle-class parties. In a conversation with Wagener in June 1930 he said:

> Now I come to the Social Democrats. There we find the great mass of the good, industrious, diligent German people from all the tribes and levels ... The racially most impeccable and best German people live together in Social Democracy. But unfortunately under the wrong leaders. But that is not their fault!

It was the task of the National Socialists to liberate these 'people led astray' from their false leaders and to gain them for the cause. Let us compare this assessment of the SPD with Hitler's evaluation of the DVP, the business party, the house owners etc.:

> ... a milling about of ants, which from early morning to late in the evening are diligently and busily running back and forth on the paths of business, occasionally addressing each other, then busily rushing off again, some lugging heavy burdens, at least a briefcase which, besides bread and butter and toilet paper, contains completely irrelevant documents, which for the person concerned, however, momentarily appear as valuable mortgage bonds for the satisfaction of his ridiculous greed for profit which is totally without importance for the course of world history. This is a racial mixture of the common sort. It is harmless, unimportant, politically without strength. It only vegetates.

Hitler's verdict on the Democratic Party was even more negative: he simply called it 'a stinking sore within the nation'. His assessment of Social Democracy was very positive by comparison.[55]

In his table talks Hitler also repeatedly commented positively on Social Democracy, normally in the context of his praise for having abolished the monarchy in the November revolution.[56] In such talk on 18 September 1941 he said, as Koeppen noted, that

> ... the greatest corruption had been among the parties of the centre, whose politicians had all been bribable and purchasable subjects without exception. One could not say this about the leading Social Democrats [Braun, Severing, Löbe] in any way. Therefore hardly any of them had gone into the concentration camps. It had also not been necessary for Braun to flee abroad. The *Führer* is convinced that today these former Social Democrats are all long convinced supporters of the Third Reich. To the vote on the Saar, and now again at the outbreak of the war, Severing had voluntarily offered to issue a proclamation to the former Social Democratic workers. The *Führer* rejected this for reasons of principle.[57]

In his table talks on 28/29 December 1941 Hitler again praised Social Democracy for 'having got rid of this vermin' (i.e. the monarchy) and declared that he had helped everyone who was not 'a base enemy' ('then off into the KZ with him') by, for example, increasing the pensions of Noske and other people after he had returned from Italy: 'But I could never permit these men to issue political statements for me, which Severing, for example, repeatedly offered to do. It would have looked as if I had bought that! I know that one of them said, "More than we ever imagined has been achieved!"'[58]

In a table talk on 1 February 1942 Hitler declared:

I make a difference between the figures of 1918. Some of them slid into it like Pontius into the Credo: they never wanted to make a revolution. These include Noske, Ebert too, Scheidemann, Severing, in Bavaria Auer. But I could not make allowances for that in the battle against these people or accept any excuses. Only after victory was I able to say: I understand your reasons. But the people from the Zentrum were base, like Spiecker for example. They worked with lies and deceit.

> Brüning too was a subject without character, Treviranus a scoundrel. Such a little Marxist proletarian grew up in a world he did not even understand; but these swine: Hilferding, Kautsky!

'Former Social Democracy', Hitler went on in the course of the conversation, 'was only lacking a leader. It did the worst possible thing of all, without wanting to, it even ran on ahead of the development that could no longer be stopped.'[59] Hitler was therefore prepared not only to recognize the positive achievements of Social Democracy, but also to differentiate between its various representatives. He stressed, however – and this is important – that during the time of struggle he could not take such differentiation into consideration.

Another positive evaluation of Social Democracy, this time primarily of Scheidemann, can be found in a table talk on 27 January 1942. Here Hitler spoke about the signing of the Treaty of Versailles, lauded Scheidemann and criticized the Zentrum politicians Wirth and Erzberger: 'There were Social Democrats who were prepared to go to extremes. It was Wirth and Erzberger who did it!'[60] The background to this remark was that on 20 June 1919 Social Democratic Minister President Scheidemann had resigned with his cabinet, formed on 13 February 1919, because he rejected the Versailles peace conditions. Wirth, on the other hand, was one of the most outspoken advocates within the Zentrum party of a policy of reconciliation and compensation. Erzberger (assassinated in 1921) signed the armistice and in Scheidemann's cabinet argued in favour of accepting the peace treaty. On 24 August 1942 Hitler returned to this topic: 'That it turned out differently then [(i.e. at the time of the signing of the Versailles treaty—R.Z.] we only actually have to primarily thank the Zentrum for. The Social Democrats did not want that, therefore also Scheidemann's premature statement.'[61]

These statements by Hitler show that even though in his propaganda he defamed all the parties of the Weimar coalition as 'November criminals' without making any distinctions, in actual fact the guilty ones for him were only the leaders of the Zentrum, while he regarded the abolition of the monarchy as a positive achievement to be counted in favour of Social Democracy. For Hitler the 'crime' of the men of November was not the revolution and not the abolition of the monarchy but the 'rendering defenceless of Germany', i.e. the signing of the Treaty of Versailles. And since the Social Democratic Minister President refused to sign the treaty, for Hitler there was basically no blemish remaining on Social Democracy as opposed to the middle class politicians of the Zentrum.

Hitler's sympathy for Social Democracy becomes understandable within the context of his views as we have portrayed them in this study. Its advocacy of equal opportunity and the social needs of the working class were just as little reason for him to reject it as were its economic views. What made him an opponent of Social Democracy were the elements of Marxism which he constantly criticized most sharply in his speeches – advocacy of parliamentary democracy, in other words of the 'majority principle' Hitler was so contemptuous of, internationalism and pacifism. Before we turn to the investigation of Hitler's basic position on Marxism, we will first discuss his position on Communism, because for him Social Democracy and Communism were merely the moderate and the radical versions of Marxism.

b. Communism

Hitler's position on Communism was characterized by a strange ambivalence. He admired and feared Communism for the identical reason. If we understand the motives for his admiration, i. e. trace these reasons out of Hitler's own mental premises, then we will also understand the other side of his position, his fear of Communism.

Hitler admired Communism because it, as opposed to the middle class forces, 'fanatically' advocated a *Weltanschauung*. He admired it because it brought along all those traits and abilities which he regarded as the essential attributes of the 'historic minority' capable of enforcing its will on the majority. As adherents of a radical ideology, the Communists had proved that they did not belong among the opportunists but among the brave and courageous who were prepared to make sacrifices for their ideals. Exactly those attributes of the Communist movement which were considered to be particularly reprehensible from the point of view of bourgeois liberalism provoked Hitler's greatest admiration – the sharp opposition to bourgeois society, the totalitarian character of the ideology, the unrestricted will for power and the clearly stated objective not only to fight all political opponents 'fanatically' but, ultimately, to remove them completely.

We must note here that it is an essential weakness in Ernst Nolte's interpretation not to have discriminated between the quite different motives underlying middle class and National Socialist anti-Communism. Since the anti-Communist position of large sectors of the middle class stemmed from Communism's anti-liberal position and its fighting opposition to the bourgeois system, it cannot be true that Hitler, as Nolte writes, 'shared all of the anti-Communist emotions of the post-war period'.[62] Certainly, anti-Communist motives played a not unimportant role with both the middle class and the National Socialists, even though it did not have the central importance in Hitler's ideology that Nolte claims.[63] However, we should not overlook the substantial differences in the reasons and content of middle class anti-Communism compared to Hitler's anti-Communism, particularly since Hitler often admired exactly those things which motivated middle class anti-Communism to a large degree.

Hitler variously cited the Communist Party of the Soviet Union as proof of the efficiency of a small radical élite party orientated to a *Weltanschauung*, which was succeeding with only 470,000 members in ruling over 138 million people. 'That is a troop that cannot be torn apart. That is where the power and the strength lies. If we had 600,000 men who were all committed to this one objective, then we would be in power,' Hitler declared in a speech on 12 June 1925.[64] Hitler specifically admired the intolerant character of Communism, which was aiming at the ruthless implementation of a radical *Weltanschauung* and acting on the premise that 'We recognize no laws of humanity, but only the law of the preservation of the existence of the movement, the idea or the execution of the idea.'[65]

If we follow Otto Wagener, who reports on Hitler's view of the various political movements and parties in the Weimar Republic, then he differentiated three groups within the Communist party – the 'idealists', the 'despairing' and the 'racially decayed'. The first two groups 'could again become valuable', because they 'were actually good, character-wise, but had either fallen prey to their ideology or their fate', whereas the third group was 'not useful . . . for the battle of development'.[66] In another conversation with Hitler, which Wagener has not dated, the former said that while the Communists were betrayers of the Fatherland, they were at least honest as compared to the reactionary and the democratic parties, which is why they would also support the education and school principles (aiming at 'equal opportunity') of National Socialism.[67]

After the seizure of power Hitler openly solicited members from the Communist party. In a speech on 8 October 1935 he declared that if the Communist 'comes back to his senses and returns to his nation, then he is highly welcome to us'.[68] The leader of the DAF, Robert Ley, reports:

> One of the strongest among many impressions was that moment when, at the last *Parteitag* in Nuremberg [in 1935—R.Z.], the *Führer* went among the workers who had marched up outside his quarters and welcomed them. How old? What occupation? Where did you formerly stand politically? One of them answered: '*I was a Communist.*' The *Führer* takes the head of the young man between his hands, looks at the young man for a long time and says: '*So will you all come! You must all come this way!*'[69]

In a table talk on 2 August 1941 Hitler remarked that he did not blame

> . . . any one of the little people that he had been a Communist; I can only blame an intellectual for that. He knew that need for him had only been a means to an end.[70]
> . . . Thälmann, that is the archetype of such a little man who could not act otherwise.

The bad thing about him is that he was not as clever as, for example, Torgler.⁷¹ He was the mentally retarded one, that was why I could let Torgler go, while I had to hold him fast, not out of revenge, but only because he is a danger. As soon as the big danger in Russia has been removed he can go where he likes... The pact with Russia could never have determined me to assume a different position towards the internal danger. But I prefer our Communists a thousand times to Starhemberg, for example. They were robust types, who if they had spent a longer time in Russia would have come back completely cured.⁷²

It is noteworthy that Hitler compared the reactionary 'Austrofascist' Prince von Starhemberg – who took part in the fight for freedom in Upper Silesia and 1923 in the Hitler *putsch* but later came into conflict with the NSDAP, and who had been the national leader of the Austrian 'Home Defence' since 1930 and was later Vice-Chancellor under Schuschnigg – with leader of the KPD Thälmann. During the time of struggle Hitler had sharply criticized the Austrian home defence formations because they allied themselves with the middle-class parties.⁷³ Hitler's remark that he 'preferred the Communists a thousand times over' to men such as Starhemberg was merely consistent within his *Weltanschauung*. He naturally felt himself to be closer to the brave and courageous Communists, who were fighting for the ideal of a *Weltanschauung* like he was, than to the bourgeois reactionary forces. In another table talk on 2 November 1941, during which he talked about the 'time of struggle' and his 'contempt' for the bourgeoisie which he had developed at this time, he said, 'The Communists and us, those were the only ones who also had women who did not flinch when the shooting started. Those are decent people with whom alone you can maintain a state.'⁷⁴

In order to express his sympathy for the Communists, Hitler claimed untruthfully in a table talk on 28/29 December 1941 that Thälmann was 'being treated very decently in the KZ, he has his own little house in there'. Torgler, Hitler went on,

> ... was released; he is working in Germany on a work about socialism in the nineteenth century. I am convinced that he set fire to the *Reichstag*, but I cannot prove it. Personally I have nothing to blame him for, he has also completely turned away from it all. If only I had perhaps met that man once ten years before! He was actually a wise man.⁷⁵

Hitler was convinced that he had won over not only the majority of the Social Democrats but also most of the Communists. During a meeting with the Bulgarian regency council on 17 March 1944 he declared, 'In Germany the National Socialist party had completely absorbed the Communists, with the exception of the criminal elements who had been brutally suppressed.'⁷⁶ And we know in fact that during the time of struggle there had been much fluctuation between the SA and the *Rotfront*. That many Communists became convinced adherents of National Socialism after the seizure of power is small wonder. The KPD always claimed that Hitler would never conquer unemployment, above all that he was a vassal of France, an anti-national traitor to the ideal of bringing Austria into the nation etc. and that he would never revise the Treaty of Versailles. But since the opposite of all this then came about, and in addition the National Socialists also pursued a partially progressive social policy which even fulfilled certain demands that had stood no chance of realization in the Weimar Republic, it is only logical that many Communists turned to National Socialism, which was fulfilling so much of what the KPD had demanded and was in agreement with it with regard to its anti-bourgeois direction of attack.

How can we then explain that, in view of his sympathy for the Social Democrats and the Communists, Hitler still proceeded against them far more sharply and brutally than against the bourgegois reactionaries he so cordially hated? As with the Jews, in Hitler's assessment of his Marxist opponents admiration was mixed with fear. He admired the Jews for their 'racial purity' and feared them for the same reason. He admired the Communists for being idealists, for being men who were prepared to make sacrifices for their *Weltanschauung*. But with this they represented a dangerous élite, quite different from the 'cowardly and opportunistic' bourgeois. And Hitler's measures depended on the degree of danger, actual or assumed. For him all Marxists were highly dangerous to begin with, because he had himself taken over their methods of propaganda and learned much from them. We will therefore now discuss Hitler's fundamental position on Marxism, before we turn to his position towards Stalin.

c. Hitler's Relationship with Marxism

If we ask ourselves what it was beyond mere cheap polemics and propaganda that Hitler criticized in Marxism[77] we must primarily look at three points: 'But the teachings of Marxism', said Hitler on 2 April 1927, 'put pacifism in the place of fighting, in place of race the International, in place of the person democracy.' With this, however, Marxism was a declaration of war against 'the three fundamental pillars on which man rests'.[78]

We know that the principle of the 'eternal battle' was the key point in Hitler's *Weltanschauung*. Since for Hitler only battle guaranteed a constant development upward, both in nature and in society, he rejected humanism and pacifism, which he identified as essential elements of Marxism.

The second accusation Hitler made against Marxism, namely that it put the International in place of race, does in fact point to a fundamental difference between Marxism and Hitlerism. Whereas Marxism propagated the solidarity of the proletarians of all nations in the fight against capital with the objective of world revolution, Hitler was convinced of the inequality of the various races and the superiority of the Aryan and defined his socialism as a 'National Socialism', i.e. as socialism that was not intended to make all of humanity happy but had only been created for the German nation.

The third accusation also identifies an important, though more theoretical than practical, difference between Marxism and Hitlerism. Hitler accused Marxism of paying homage to the 'majority principle' and denying the 'personality principle'. Even though Hitler's criticism of democracy (rule of capital) agreed on many points with Marxist criticism, in the final analysis they were based on contradictory premises. While Marxism – at least in theory – demands the spread of democracy, for example through the Soviet democracy, Hitler fundamentally criticized the democratic principle of the majority decision. The points Hitler criticized in Marxism are not necessarily specifics of the teachings of Karl Marx. Whoever is a pacifist, rejects racial theory and is in favour of the democratic majority principle, is still not necessarily a Marxist by a long way. Therefore – and this is of decisive importance for an understanding of his criticism of Marxism – when Hitler spoke of Marxism he did not mean the specifics of the teachings of Karl Marx, for example his economic theory. In the speech already cited at the beginning, he emphasized that he must 'protest most sharply against wanting to number only the Social Democrats and the Communists among the Marxists. They also include all of our present political bourgeoisie, which stands on the ground of parliament, democracy, rejection of battle, internationalism, the rejection of race.'[79]

In *Mein Kampf* Hitler called Marxist theory 'the abbreviated spiritual extract of the commonly valid *Weltanschauung* of today'. For this reason any 'fight by our so-called bourgeois world against it is impossible, even ridiculous, because this bourgeois world is essentially also infused with all of these poisons and pays homage to a *Weltanschauung* which only differentiates itself from that of Marxism by degrees and persons. The bourgeois world is Marxist . . .'[80] Since the middle class had also fallen prey to internationalism, pacifism and the 'majority principle', Hitler concluded: 'On all the great questions of *Weltanschauung*, the world of the middle-class political parties has already put itself on the grounds of Marxism.'[81] This argument shows that Hitler's anti-Marxism had little to do with middle-class anti-Communism. As opposed to the middle-class parties, Hitler admired the Marxist parties and frequently admitted that he had learned much from them.

During the trial after his attempted *putsch* of November 1923, Hitler declared on 26 February 1924 (the opening day of the trial) that Marxism had

...worked with two monstrous instruments. On the one hand with a gigantic mass propaganda, a mass influencing... The second instrument of this movement is a monstrous terror. No movement has shaped the face of the mass with such thorough knowledge as the Marxist movement. It knows that the masses possess respect for strength and determination, and in place of the weakness of the bourgeois and their indecisiveness it has put brutal power and a brutal will, has ruthlessly borne down the individual and confronted the workers with the alternatives, either you decide to become my brother or I will knock you over the head. I came to know this movement in my youth in both of these effects. The middle-class parties do not know it, or do not want to know it.

Hitler then went on to speak about his own, the National Socialist movement:

But this movement has learned from its opponents, it has created two instruments for itself, it has recognized what is necessary. The most enormous enlightenment of the masses and national enlightenment. The spirit of the people is structured in such a way that there is first of all respect for power... For him who is willing to fight with mental weapons, we have the battle with the mind, and for him who wants to fight with the fist, we have the fist. The movement has two instruments, the propaganda machine and, besides it, the SA.[82]

In *Mein Kampf* Hitler primarily derived his principles of propaganda from the observation of Marxist propaganda. He analyzed the 'internal reasons for the successes of Social Democracy' and came to the conclusion that '*If Social Democracy is confronted by a theory of greater veracity, but with the same brutality of execution, the latter will win*, even if only after a most heavy battle.' During his time in Vienna, said Hitler, 'both the teachings as well as the technical instruments of Social Democracy' had become clear to him. 'It is a tactic that has been developed under the exact calculation of all human weaknesses, whose results must almost automatically lead to success, if the opposite side does not also learn to fight poison gas with poison gas.' The example of Social Democracy had also made the 'importance of physical terror against the individual, against the mass' clear to him. 'Here, too, an exact calculation of the psychological effect. The terror at work, in the factory, in the meeting hall and during mass rallies will always be accompanied by success, as long as it is not opposed by just as great a terror.' In the famous sixth chapter of *Mein Kampf* on propaganda Hitler wrote, right at the beginning:

During my attentive pursuit of all the political activities, propaganda activity had always been of extraordinary interest to me. In it I saw an instrument which especially the socialist-Marxist organizations wielded and knew how to employ with masterly cleverness. I learned to understand early on that the correct application of propaganda was really an art which was, and remained, almost completely unknown to the middle-class parties.

VII: Self-Assessment in the Political Spectrum

In the fifth chapter of the second volume of *Mein Kampf* Hitler criticized the popular movement and cited Marxism as an example of the effectiveness of negative, destructive criticism:

> It is a sign of a lack of deeper insight into historic development when the so-called populists today place great value on constantly insisting that they have no intention whatsoever of engaging in *negative criticism* but only in the *work of building up*. A stammering that is as childishly idiotic as it is typically 'populist', and proof of how even contemporary history passed through these brains without leaving a trace. *Marxism* also had an objective, and it too knows the *work of building up* (even if this is only the establishment of the despotism of international world finance Jewry!), but before that it has spent *seventy years* during which it *offered criticism*, and destructive divisive criticism at that, and continued to criticize, so long until by this incessantly corroding acid, the old state had been eroded and brought down. Only then did its so-called 'building up' begin. And this is natural, right, and logical.

The fact that Marxism primarily addressed itself to the working class was also a good example for Hitler's own strategy: 'What our middle class always looked at with a shaking of the head, the fact that only the so-called uneducated masses belonged to Marxism, was in reality the precondition for its success.' His conviction of the superiority of the spoken word, the speech, over the written word, i.e. propaganda in leaflets and scientific treatment in books, he also explained by referring to Marxism:

> What has given Marxism its astonishing power over the masses is not at all the formal written work of Jewish thought but the enormous spoken propaganda wave which over the years has seized upon the masses... What has won the millions of workers to Marxism is not the written work of Marxist apostles but the untiring and truly gigantic work of propaganda by tens of thousands of untiring agitators, starting with great apostles of incitement all the way down to the little union bureaucrat and the trustee and the discussion speaker. It is the hundreds of thousands of meetings in which, standing on the tables of the smoke-filled rooms of inns, these popular speakers hammered away at the masses and were therefore able to gain a fabulous knowledge of this human material, which then enabled them even more to select the most appropriate weapons for the attack upon the citadel of public opinion. And these were again the gigantic mass demonstrations, these hundred-thousand-man parades which burned the conviction into the little miserable human being, that as a little worm he was still a part of a huge dragon under whose blazing breath the hated bourgeois world would one day go up in fire and flames, and the proletarian dictatorship celebrate the final victory.

We have already seen, in Chapter 3.3, that Hitler ridiculed the weak dramaturgy of bourgeois rallies. In contrast, he admired the 'always blind discipline' Marxist rallies displayed, 'so that the thought of breaking up a Marxist rally could not even occur, at least not to the bourgeois side . . . Here we tried to learn from the study of Marxist and bourgeois rallies, and we did learn.'[83]

Ernst Hanfstaengl reports a conversation about the party flag, which Hitler had designed himself, in which he permitted himself a critical remark about the swastika being displayed in black: 'As a sun symbol, I can only imagine the swastika in glowing red or yellow.' Hitler answered:

> But then we cannot use red as the basic colour, and I refuse to depart from that. Some years ago I was once a witness to a Social Democratic mass rally in the Lustgarten in Berlin, and I can assure you that for the staging of mass rallies there is only one colour which affects people, and that is red, the colour of the revolution![84]

This otherwise quite unimportant example shows how strongly Hitler was orientated towards Marxist methods of propaganda.

When Hitler criticized the Austrian Home Defence formations in the *Illustrierte Beobachter* on 31 May 1930 because they refused to understand 'that the dissolution of Marxism automatically also meant the dissolution of the middle-class parties', he reproached them with the statement that only Marxism had assessed the world of the middle-class parties correctly:

> Nobody recognized the impotence of these formations more clearly than Marxism did. It knows how to treat these parties, that means on the one hand it makes them jump in the most brutal fashion, and on the other it gives them a little piece of bread and butter from time to time.[85]

These were exactly the tactics Hitler also applied so successfully.

Let us summarize. Hitler's relationship to Marxism was determined by a strange ambivalence. On the one hand he admired it, regarded the Marxist movement as an example and tried to learn from it. On the other hand he rejected Marxist ideology because it denied the principle of 'eternal battle' as well as the principles of race and personality. His criticism of Marxism – and we should emphasize this once again here – was not directed exclusively against any specific points in the teachings of Karl Marx and was different in many respects from bourgeois anti-Marxism. Nolte has defined Fascism as an 'anti-Marxism which attempts to destroy by the development of a radically opposed but still related ideology and the application of almost identical but still characteristically reshaped methods, but always within the impenetrable framework of national self-assertion and autonomy'.[86] This definition does indeed come very close to the essence of National Socialism. However, National Socialism *should not* be primarily interpreted as anti-Marxism. It was rather an alternative, competing revolutionary movement which did not have the destruction of Marxism as its main objective but which had to destroy it, *not despite*, but *because of* its proximity to it.

There are many examples in history of ideologies or religions combating each other all the more sharply and ruthlessly when they are relatively closely related, or when they have a common origin. G. Schramm's thesis that 'The Christians have caused the Jews so much suffering not *despite* the Jews being so closely related to them but *because* this is so'[87] also applies *mutatis mutandis* to the relationship between Hitlerism and Marxism. Just as the Communists in the Weimar Republic waged their sharpest and most ruthless fight against the Social Democrats ('Social Fascists'), not despite, but because of, their common origin, Hitler had to fight Marxism more determinedly than, for example, conservatism, with which he had very little in common. The typical ambivalence of admiration and fear so characteristic for Hitler's relationship to Marxism perhaps becomes clear in a particular way in the example of his position towards Stalin and the Soviet Union.

d. Hitler's Position towards Stalin

Hitler's assessment of the Soviet Union and Stalin once again demonstrates the contradiction between propaganda and Hitler's actual views and insights. While he never tired in his speeches of attacking the 'Jewish-Bolshevist' conspiracy, no later than from 1940 onwards he was well aware that Stalin was not the representative of Jewish interests but had eliminated the Jews and was now pursuing a nationalistic Russian policy in the tradition of Peter the Great. Hitler first alluded to the *possibility* of such a development in his 'Second Book', written in 1928:

> However, it is conceivable that in Russia itself an inner change within the Bolshevist world could take place insofar as the Jewish element could perhaps be forced aside by a more or less Russian national one. Then it could also not be excluded that the present real Jewish-capitalist-Bolshevist Russia could be driven to national-anti-capitalist tendencies. In this case, which perhaps appears to be announcing itself in certain things, it would then become conceivable, however, that Western European capitalism would seriously take a position against Russia.

What Hitler later stated as a fact, namely Russia's change from a 'Jewish dictatorship' into a national Russian anti-capitalist state, he described in 1928 as being a possibility and a tendency.[88]

For the time being, however, Hitler remained sceptical towards this possible development, or at least warned against an over-estimation of this tendency in his public statements. In an article which appeared in the *Illustrierte Beobachter* on 9 February 1929, for example, he wrote:

> Since I am on the subject of Russia, I would also like to forearm myself with caution here against the constantly recurring reports of 'growing anti-Semitism' in Russia. For twelve years the 'advance of anti-Semitism' is constantly being announced in Russia. Even popular authors frequently write this. In reality, however, the Jew is more firmly in the saddle there than ever before.

Hitler also spoke of the 'apparently anti-Semitic *Herr* Stalin'.[89]

In another article in the *Illustrierte Beobachter* on 30 March 1929 he again discussed this topic in detail: 'I have always regarded it as being bad that in almost our total national and even popular press, reports on the "progress" of anti-Semitism in Russia are circulated with a certain frightening regularity.' In reality the Jew

> ... was more firmly in the saddle in Russia today than ever before. But that small anti-Semitic twitches are turned into great actions also has something to do with certain emigrant circles who are still dreaming of the reinstatement of the House of Romanov and even in part make their living out of this. How improbable such hopes are could be learned from studying history. When revolutions are broken again, the new masters are still not the old ones. In the battle against the revolution a new generation of fighters and leaders grows up. It is just as childish as it is indecent to think that after the victory won by their battle, leaders with iron wills and men with the most courageous hearts will place the leadership back into the hands of those weak people who once before proved unable to hold the rudder and then fled abroad to escape the storm.

Hitler initially also regarded the conflict between Stalin and Trotsky as a mock battle, as his articles in the *Illustrierte Beobachter* show. Here, he said on 30 March 1929, only a 'gigantic comedy [was being] staged'.[90]

He was no longer quite so sure in an article published in mid-January 1930, in which he wrote:

> Stalin is a Bolshevist, and as such perhaps a counterpart of Trotsky, but maybe not even that. After a repeated thorough consideration of Trotsky's latest published work, I myself even today still have reasonable doubts whether the whole apparent conflict is not just a brilliantly staged comedy ... But even if this opinion of mine were to be mistaken, the conflict between Trotsky and Stalin would still only be a battle between two rivals. The view that the Jew Trotsky is standing against the anti-Semite Stalin is not based on anything, is even ridiculous ... Stalin himself does not even have to be circumcised, his associates, in any case, consist of at least nine-tenths genuine Hebrews. His action is the continuation of the complete uprooting of the Russian nation for its total subjugation under the dictatorship of the Jew.[91]

It is difficult to determine when Hitler finally revised his assessment of the conflict between Stalin and Trotsky and came to the view he later constantly advocated, that Stalin had emancipated himself from the Jews and was pursuing a national and anti-Jewish policy. Goebbels reported in his diary on 25 January 1937 that Hitler had not yet completely made up his mind about the events in Russia and his assessment of Stalin:

> In Moscow another show trial. This time solely against Jews again. Radek etc. *Führer* still doubtful whether not with hidden anti-Semitic tendency after all. Perhaps Stalin wants to drive the Jews out after all. The military is also supposed to be strongly anti-Semitic. Therefore keep eyes open. For the time being remain in wait and see position.[92]

On 10 July 1937 Goebbels noted: 'In the case of Russia he [Hitler] no longer sees his way. Stalin must be sick in the head. Otherwise you cannot explain his regiment of blood.'[93]

From early 1940 onwards, however, there were an increasing number of statements made by Hitler in which his admiration for Stalin and the Bolshevist regime become clear. These, no doubt, also served the purpose of defending the pact he had concluded with Stalin in 1939. For example, he wrote a letter to Mussolini on 8 March 1940: 'Since Stalin's final victory, Russia is doubtless experiencing a change of the Bolshevist principle in the direction of a national Russian form of life.'[94] But even after the attack on the USSR, when Hitler no longer had an alliance to justify, he clung to his positive assessment of Stalin and increasingly took the view of Bolshevism already long held within the circles of the 'conservative revolution'.[95] On 23 September 1941, for example, Koeppen noted the following statement by Hitler:

> Stalin was one of the greatest of living men because he succeeded in forging a state out of this Slavic family of rabbits, albeit only with the harshest of compulsion. For this he naturally had to avail himself of the Jews, because the thin Europeanized class which had formerly carried the state had been exterminated, and these forces would never again grow up out of the actual Russianhood.[96]

Of course, this assessment did not prevent Hitler from continuing to spread the thesis of Jewish Bolshevism in his speeches for propaganda purposes. In his address to the soldiers on the Eastern Front on the occasion of the great offensive against Moscow, Hitler declared on 1 October 1941:

> Now, my comrades, you have personally become acquainted with the 'paradise of the workers and farmers', yourselves with your own eyes. In a country which, because of its space and fertility, could feed the whole world, a poverty reigns such as is inconceivable for us Germans. This is the result of a Jewish rule lasting almost 25 years now, which as Bolshevism, is in its profoundest depths only the vilest form of capitalism. The supporters of this system in both cases are the same: Jews and only Jews![97]

In a speech on 8 November 1941 Hitler also rejected the view – quite in contrast to his internal statements – that the 'national tendency' had won out in Russia. In the final analysis, Stalin was nothing but 'an instrument in the hands of this all-powerful Jewry'.[98] At a session of the *Reichstag* on 26 April 1942 Hitler repeated that in the Soviet Union 'Jewry was exercising its exclusive dictatorship'.[99]

In contrast to these public propaganda statements, Hitler said in a table talk in early January 1942 that 'Stalin is seen as the man who had intended to help the Bolshevist idea to victory. In reality he is only Russia, the continuation of Tsarist pan-Slavism! For him Bolshevism is only a means to an end. It serves as a camouflage *vis-à-vis* the Germanic and Romanic nations.'[100] One had to admire Stalin, said Hitler in another talk, because 'he did not let "the Jew" into art'.[101] On 24 July 1942 he claimed during a table talk that, 'in front of Ribbentrop Stalin had made no bones at all about the fact that he was only waiting for the moment of maturity of their own intelligentsia in the USSR in order to make an end of the Jewry he still needed today as a leadership'.[102]

Picker reports on numerous further talks in which Hitler expressed his admiration for Stalin or defended him against critical remarks. Hitler had always, for example, become angry when someone called Stalin a former 'bank robber'. Hitler would then immediately defend Stalin with the declaration that Stalin had not carried out his bank robberies as a private person nor for the benefit of his own pocket, 'but as a revolutionary and in order to finance the Communist movement'.[103] For Stalin, said Hitler on 22 July 1942, 'one had to have respect in any case. In his way he is quite a brilliant chap!'[104]

Heinrich Heim also noted many positive statements by Hitler about Stalin. On 26 August 1942 Hitler said:

> If Stalin had continued to work for another ten to fifteen years Soviet Russia would have become the most powerful nation on earth, 150, 200, 300 years may go by, that is such a unique phenomenon! That the general standard of living rose, there can be no doubt. The people did not suffer from hunger. Taking everything together we have to say: They built factories here where two years ago there was nothing but forgotten villages, factories which are as big as the Hermann Göring Works. They have railways that are not even marked on the maps. Here with us we argue about the tariffs before the railway is even built. I have a book about Stalin; one has to say: That is an enormous personality, a real ascetic, who has brought that huge empire together with an iron fist. Only when someone says that is a social state, then that is a gigantic swindle! It is a national capital state: 200 million people, iron, manganese, nickel, oil, petroleum and what you like – unlimited. At the head a man who said: Do you think the loss of 13 million people is too much for a great idea?[105]

The things Hitler admired in Stalin become particularly clear in this statement: the consistency, even brutality ('iron fist'), with which Stalin – even with the sacrifice of millions of people – implemented the 'great idea' and created a powerful industrial state impressed Hitler. In Stalin he saw his own reflection, namely the executor of the dictatorship of modernization who did not shrink from the employment of even the most brutal methods.

On the other hand he called Bolshevism's social claim 'a gigantic swindle'. Karl Thöt, Reichs stenographer at *Führer* headquarters from September 1942 until the end of the war, noted on 4 February 1943:

> The *Führer* then compared the socialism of the Russians with our own German socialism. When the Russian had, for instance, built a factory somewhere, he then simply collected everybody in the region who was at all still able to work, but he only created living quarters fit for human beings for the commissars and the technical staff. The workers, on the other hand, had to look for their own shelters in the most primitive holes. When we in Germany built a new factory, then the construction of the factory only ate up a fraction of what was spent in addition for a homestead for the workers fit for human beings. The high level of culture of the German worker simply demanded a suitable recompense in addition to his work. He had built the great works in Salzgitter, for example, and for this he had had to create a whole new city, which now already numbered over 100,000 people and would soon grow to a quarter of a million. For this streets had to be built, squares, electricity, sewage, but also theatres, motion picture theatres and all sorts of other cultural facilities. The Russian did not give any thought at all to any of this. He left his people in their primitiveness and this now enabled him to conduct a far more total sort of war.[106]

Hitler cited these arguments, since this was the only way he could still explain the difference between National Socialism and Bolshevism and its comparative superiority, because otherwise he had 'inwardly fallen prey to the Russian example', as Scheidt writes in his notes. He had, said Scheidt, 'lost the conflict of the *Weltanschauung* he had preached for so long or the crusade on the intellectual level right from the start. From then on his evaluation of man and life was no longer different in any way from that of Communism.' Hitler learned 'to admire the rigour of the system there ... He began to suspect that he had been mistaken in Stalin and his remarks expressed admiration, even showed that his example appeared to him as an ideal which would not let him rest':

> Hitler began secretly to admire Stalin. From then on his hatred was determined by envy ... He clung to the hope that he could defeat Bolshevism with its own weapons if he copied it in Germany and the occupied regions ... He increasingly held the Russian methods up to his associates as being exemplary. We cannot fight this battle for existence without their hardness and ruthlessness, he was wont to say. He rejected any objections as being bourgeois.[107]

After 20 July 1944, for example, Hitler bemoaned the fact that he had not purged the *Wehrmacht* like Stalin had and converted it into a National Socialist revolutionary army. Speer reports on a meeting of ministers on 21 July 1944:

> Today he [Hitler] realized that in his case against Tuchatshevsky Stalin had taken the decisive step for a successful waging of the war. By having liquidated the General Staff he had made room for fresh forces, who no longer stemmed from the age of the Tsars. He had formerly always held the accusations at the Moscow trials of 1937 to be trumped up. Now, after the experience of 20 July he was wondering whether there had not been something to them after all. While he did not have any evidence for it, Hitler continued, he could still no longer exclude a treasonable co-operation between the two general staffs.[108]

Two months before the assassination attempt, in a presentation to generals and officers, Hitler had said:

> This problem has been completely solved in Bolshevist Russia. Completely unequivocal situations, clear unequivocal statements by the officer to these points of view, which concern the state, to the whole of expert opinion and with this, naturally, an unequivocal relationship to allegiance, a completely clear relationship. In Germany this whole process was unfortunately interrupted much too quickly by the war, because you can be sure that these courses which take place today would perhaps never have become necessary if the war had not come about. Instead the total planned education of the German officer corps, just as of all German soldiers before entry into the *Wehrmacht*, would have been uniformly carried out step by step. That would have gone step by step according to the procedure that I found to be right, namely without breaking any china, in other words without destroying what is good, to inevitably reach the objective set slowly but surely. Therefore there is nothing left in this struggle except to try to make up for whatever can be made up.[109]

Goebbels wrote in his diary on 16 March 1945:

> I refer the *Führer* to my review of the book by the Soviet General Staff on the Soviet marshals and generals and add that I had the impression we could not in any way compete with this selection of leaders. The *Führer* agrees with me completely. Our generals are too old and used up and National Socialist thinking and posture are completely foreign to them. A large number of our generals do not even want victory by National Socialism. The Soviet generals, in contrast, are not only fanatically convinced of Bolshevism, they also fight just as fanatically for its victory, which naturally gives the Soviet generals a gigantic superiority. The *Führer* is determined to reform the *Wehrmacht* to such an extent during the war that it will come out of the war with a fundamentally National Socialist posture.[110]

What Hitler therefore primarily admired in Stalin was his revolutionary consistency in the elimination of the former élites. He himself had not had this consistency, and, as we have seen, traced his failure in part to this. Hitler's admiration for Stalin was not only an expression of the respect he felt for him personally; his relationship with Stalin also reflected his ambivalent position on Marxism/Communism, which was always characterized by simultaneous fear and admiration. Hitler admired Stalin's revolutionary consistency above all, but exactly this consistency, which went far further than his own, also made him afraid, and made Bolshevism appear as the only serious opponent.

We must note another important result of this chapter. Hitler was – and this is incontestable – most certainly a fanatical Jew-hater, but he also used anti-Semitism for purely tactical or propaganda reasons. Hitler himself no longer believed in the thesis of 'Jewish Bolshevism' that German propaganda kept repeating as a stereotype, but this did not prevent him from continuing to use this abstruse claim for reasons of propaganda. A basic question to raise would be how far, and until when, Hitler believed in the thesis of Marxism as the instrument of Jewry, and how far he only used it because it fitted in with the principles of propaganda he developed in *Mein Kampf*:

> Moreover, the art of all truly great leaders of the people through all the ages primarily consisted in not only being able to fragment the attention of a nation, but always to be able to concentrate it against only one opponent. The more unified the deployment of this will of a nation to fight is, the greater the magnetic attraction of a movement will become, and the more powerful the force of the blow. It is a part of the genius of a great leader to always make opponents that are even far apart [i.e., in this case, capitalism and Marxism—R.Z.] appear to belong to only one category [i.e. as an instrument of Jewry in the battle for world domination—R.Z.], because the appearance of various enemies can easily lead, in the case of weak and insecure characters, to the beginning of doubts in the justice of their own position.[111]

In his programmatic speech on 27 February 1925 Hitler also declared that it was 'psychologically wrong to set several battle objectives' and it was correct 'to only choose one enemy so that everybody can see, this is the sole guilty'. And this enemy, said Hitler, was the Jews.[112]

It is therefore only consistent that Hitler continued to speak about 'Jewish Bolshevism' even though he himself no longer shared this view. While Hitler himself was readily able to see matters with discrimination, he did not trust the mass to. Hitler developed his most important principle of propaganda in *Mein Kampf*: 'In this there is not much differentiation, but only a positive or a negative, love or hate, right or wrong, truth or lie, never half this, half that, or partially and so forth.'[113] It is therefore understandable why in his public statements Hitler rarely expressed his real opinion of the Social Democrats and the Communists. With regard to Hitler's revolutionary self-assessment and

Hitler: The Policies of Seduction

his self-evaluation within the political spectrum, this aspect is of the greatest importance, just as, on the other hand, he judged Italian Fascism and the reactionary Franco regime in Spain far more negatively than one might be led to believe by his public avowals of friendship.

e. Hitler's Criticism of Italian Fascism and the Reactionary Franco Regime in Spain

It is difficult to identify the exact point in time when Hitler began critically to address himself to Fascism. Before the conclusion of the alliance with Italy – which was purely power-political and in no way ideologically motivated[114] – he did not want to endanger this part of his foreign policy by negative or derogatory statements made in public, and in war it is only natural that one does not voluntarily supply the enemy with additional ammunition for propaganda by drawing his attention to conflicts within one's own camp. Nonetheless we know from intimates of Hitler, and from his table talks, that he was highly critical of Italian Fascism. While Hitler proclaimed repeatedly that National Socialism and Fascism were related in Weltanschauung,[115] or spoke of the 'community of the Fascist and National Socialist revolution',[116] his criticism of the Italian system grew increasingly sharp, particularly after his visit to Italy in 1938.[117]

Highly enlightening is the comparison of a speech Hitler gave on 30 January 1942 with a table talk the day after. In his speech he declared that 'both revolutions', the Fascist and the National Socialist, 'had taken almost the identical course':

> During the past few weeks I have read quite a lot about the Italian Fascist revolution in the few hours of free time I had, and it seemed to me as if I had the history of my own party before me, so similar, so much the same, the same struggle, the same enemies, the same opponents, the same arguments. It is truly a strange marvel.[118]

The following evening Hitler repeated this view in his table talk, but then followed it with statements that were not intended for the public but only for the intimate circle of his audience at the dinner table. Hitler first stated that, while the Italian people were idealists, 'the leadership is reactionary':

> It is a difference like between day and night when you see real Fascists or not. The social class we have to deal with is cosmopolitan just like with us... The *Duce* came along with his revolution perhaps one year too soon: the Reds would have killed the court, he would have become head of state. That throng would have disappeared.[119]

On the one hand Hitler recognized the common aspects between the Fascist and the National Socialist revolution; on the other, however, he criticized time and again the continuing influence in Italy of the church, the king and reactionary generals. One should never forget, Hitler once said to Rosenberg, that Mussolini in Italy did not have the same sort of position he himself had in Germany.[120] And, in fact, in Italy the former forces – king, generals and church – still had a decisive influence, so that Italy could hardly be described as a totalitarian regime. 'The *Duce* has problems', Hitler said, 'because his armed forces think royalist, because the Vatican international has its seat in Rome, and because the state, as opposed to the people, is only half-Fascist.'[121]

Hitler also criticized the social backwardness of Fascist Italy: 'One of the socially most sick bodies in the new Europe is Hungary, then Italy,' he remarked on 5 November 1941: 'Wealth on the one hand and a broad deprived mass on the other.'[122] He accused Mussolini of a lack of revolutionary consistency in the battle against the church. The *Duce* himself was a free thinker, said Hitler on 13 December 1941, 'but he started making concessions, whereas in his place I would have turned more to the revolutionary side. I would march into the Vatican and get the whole crowd out. I would say: sorry, I made a mistake! But they would be gone!'[123]

Hitler criticized not only the influence of the church on the Fascist state, but in principle the power which the upper classes still had:

> A positive selection will not take place until this Mafia of the upper world has been removed. It is just as vile as a Mafia of the underworld: a conspiracy of interests which, as stupid as they may be in themselves, have still retained the animal instinct of recognizing talent! They are the most impertinent opponents of talent! Things will not improve in Italy until they get a clear *Führer* state![124]

After Mussolini's downfall in July 1943 Hitler saw one of the reasons for this development in the fact that the Fascists had involved themselves with the 'capitalist elements'. On 12 May 1944 he said to the Slovakian President Tiso:

> But Fascism also bears a part of the blame, it had become too superficial. Of the leadership class, which had changed far too often, only the *Duce* had remained the same. The other leading personalities had let themselves become involved with capitalist elements such as Volpi [Italian banker and Chairman of the Fascist Association of Industry 1934–43—R.Z.] and had then become contaminated by wealth. As opposed to Italy, the *Führer* today was still surrounded by the same people who had already been with him twenty years ago. But the *Führer* had not tolerated any black marketeers near him. On the contrary, he had prevented leading personalities from developing business interests. Nobody in the *Reichstag* was permitted to hold a seat on a supervisory board. Ciano, for example, had been a poor man.[125]

We have already seen, in Chapter IV.4, how much importance Hitler attached to the question of politicians holding seats on supervisory boards or owning shares. He accused Fascism of, instead of breaking the rule of capital, allying itself with it and thereby having been corrupted.

When in February 1945 Hitler analyzed the reasons for his failure, he admitted that the alliance with Italy had been one of his greatest mistakes. It had prevented Germany from joining up with the Islamic liberation movements:

> The Italian ally, stated plainly, was in our way everywhere. Because of him we were unable to initiate a completely new policy in North Africa. Under the given circumstances it was self-evident that Italy would claim this region for herself, and the *Duce* always raised this claim. But if we had only had the possibility of liberating the Islamic nations ruled by France. Such an uprising would have had unforeseeable effects in Egypt and the Middle East subjugated by Britain. By linking our fate to that of the Italians, such a policy became unthinkable. And all the while the Islamic world was living in expectation of our victory. The peoples in Egypt, Iraq and the whole Middle East were prepared to revolt. We should have done everything to help them, to strengthen their courage, as our advantage and our duty demanded. That we were allied to the Italians paralyzed us, and in addition created an unease among our Muslim friends, because in their eyes we had become, deliberately or not, accomplices of their oppressors ... Only the Italians prevented us from playing one of our best cards in this theatre of the war. This consisted of declaring all of the peoples under a French protectorate to be independent and bringing about a general uprising in the regions oppressed by the British.[126]

Let us summarize: Hitler frequently emphasized the communality between Fascism and National Socialism during the 'time of struggle', i.e. during the movement phase.[127] In the system phase, however, he saw substantial differences. The church, the king, reactionary generals and capitalists still held important positions of power in Italy. Mussolini had made concessions instead of proceeding against them revolutionarily. Domestically, the Fascists had allied themselves with reactionary, monarchist and capitalist forces. Abroad they pursued an outdated colonial policy which prevented Germany from developing alliances with revolutionary movements of liberation. What Hitler admired in Stalin, namely his revolutionary consistency in the removal of élites, he found lacking in Fascism.

Hitler criticized the reactionary Franco regime in Spain far more harshly than Fascism, however. While Hitler supported Franco and the Falange during the civil war in 1936–39, he became, no later than from 1940 on, one of the sharpest critics of the regime and regretted not having supported the other side, 'the Reds', during the civil war. Franco, who in Germany he would not even have made into a district leader,[128] this 'born subaltern', was incapable in political matters and had, 'in recognition of his unproductivity ... completely given himself into the hands of the Catholic Church'.[129]

VII: Self-Assessment in the Political Spectrum

If it had not been for the danger that Bolshevism would reach over into Europe, said Hitler in a table talk on 19/20 February 1942, 'I would not have stopped the revolution in Spain: the clerics would have been exterminated! If the clerics were to come to power here with us, Europe would fall back into the dark Middle Ages!'[130] Hitler repeatedly criticized Franco's policy of friendship with the church.[131] Of all people 'the clerics and the monarchists, who were also the deadly enemies of the German national uprising' had, said Hitler on 7 June 1942, joined together in Spain to seize the leadership of the nation. Therefore, 'one need not wonder if a new civil war came along in which the Falangists would have to join the Reds in order to master the clerical and monarchist vermin'.[132] This remark shows that Hitler was politically far closer to the 'Reds' than to monarchist or clerical forces. Moreover, as Fritz Todt had confirmed to him, the red Spaniards did not feel themselves

> ... to be 'Reds' in our sense of the term. They call themselves revolutionaries, and in their diligence and work achievement they display quite a valuable posture. Therefore we can do nothing wiser than to keep as many of them in reserve – starting with the forty thousand in our camps – for an eventual new civil war breaking out in Spain. Together with the Falangists of the old sort they were still the most dependable.

The Franco people were lucky, said Hitler, that they had gained the support of Italy and Germany during the first civil war, 'because as the red Spaniards kept asserting, they had been forced to seek the support of Soviet Russia, not for ideological reasons but for lack of any other support, and had thereby been forced into an otherwise undesirable political minefield'.[133] Hitler said to his architect Hermann Giesler that he believed that, had he known Franco's political objectives and the man personally in 1936, his sympathies would have been 'more on the side of those who were against the feudal system and the clerics'. He had no objections to a Spanish socialism, but he feared that Spain could become a satellite of the Soviets.[134]

Hitler repeatedly prophesied that in Spain there would 'soon be a revolution again'.[135] The end of the fatal political development in Spain would 'be an explosion ... Here too an elementary law again. The parasites do not recognize that, by their greed, they are also destroying the ground on which they stand.'[136] In February 1945 Hitler remarked self-critically that it had been a mistake to ally himself with a regime 'that holds my sympathy less than ever before, a regime of plutocratic exploiters in the leading reins of the clerics!' It was an unforgivable mistake by Franco that he had not been capable of reconciling the Spanish nation after the end of the civil war,

> ... that he had put the Falangists on ice, whom Spain had to thank for the help we supplied, and that he treated former opponents who were not all real Reds as

bandits. It is not a good solution to outlaw half the country while a minority of exploiters gets rich at the expense of all – with the blessing of the clerics. I am sure that there were very few Communists among the so-called Reds in Spain. We were deceived because, had I known the true facts, I would never have permitted our aircraft to be used to destroy the starving and to reinstate the Spanish nobility and black frocks into their medieval prerogatives.[137]

What conclusions can we draw from Hitler's position on Social Democracy and Communism on the one hand and Fascism and the reactionary Franco regime on the other? The most important point is that it would be mistaken to place Hitler's political position on the right edge of the spectrum. Hitler felt himself to be far closer to the 'Reds', as the example of Spain shows, than to the reactionary forces. That Hitler was a revolutionary is also shown by the analysis of his position towards Stalinism on the one hand and Fascism on the other: while he admired the revolutionary consistency with which Stalin removed the former élites, he criticized Fascism for having come to an arrangement with the reactionary and capitalist forces and having left them in possession of important positions of power.

VIII
Final Considerations

'Was Hitler a Revolutionary?' was the title of an article by a Marxist historian published in 1978, in which he answered the question with a clear 'No'. Describing National Socialism as a revolutionary movement was linked to the intention to thereby discredit true revolutionary movements.[1] This, however, is certainly not the intention of our study, even though we have come to the conclusion that we cannot understand National Socialism unless we take seriously Hitler's self-understanding that he was a revolutionary.

Hitler's road as a revolutionary began with the experience of a revolution whose character as a 'real revolution' he denied. In his early speeches Hitler described the November revolution as a 'so-called revolution', because, in social and political conditions, it had not brought any really fundamental changes based on a *Weltanschauung*. He nevertheless still recognized the achievements of the November revolution. He did not in any way lament the breakdown of the monarchy. In his early speeches he variously declared that he was basically not opposed to a republic as a form of constitution, but only an opponent of the republic of Weimar. He sharply rejected those reactionary forces whose objective was the reinstatement of an outdated social order. Later he frequently admitted his recognition and admiration of the Social Democrats, whose achievement in having abolished the monarchy he valued highly. Hitler's position towards the November revolution therefore differed substantially from that of his conservative and reactionary contemporaries. In the November revolution Hitler saw something like a forerunner to his own National Socialist revolution.

As opposed to many of his conservative contemporaries, Hitler fundamentally affirmed the right to revolution; he even expressly proclaimed 'an obligation to rebellion'. As his reason for the right to revolt, he developed a revolutionary constitutional theory. The state was not, as the conservative admirers of the authoritarian state believed, an 'end in itself', something holy, which found its justification in itself, in its mere existence, but was only 'a means to an end' – and this end was 'the preservation of the nation'. When the state no longer fulfilled this end, the people had the right to remove the state by means of a revolution. For Hitler the characteristic of a revolution was that it meant the victory of a *Weltanschauung,* according to whose maxims all political, economic, social and cultural conditions were radically restructured, as had happened, for example, during the Russian October Revolution. Since Hitler fundamentally affirmed a right to revolution, his view of historic revolutions such as the French Revolution of 1789 or the German revolution of 1848 was not negative, even when he regarded their slogans as being illusory.

Initially Hitler still envisaged a revolution as an act of violence during which the old holders of power were removed. He rejected taking part in parliamentary elections because he feared the party would thereby lose its revolutionary character and finally degenerate into a system party. After his attempt on 9 November 1923 to overthrow the existing system by force failed, however, he developed the tactic of the 'legal revolution'. In this his main concern was to continue consistently to advocate the revolutionary claim of the movement despite the 'principle of legality' he was pursuing. That he was able to continue to advocate his revolutionary claim convincingly even though he confessed to 'legality' was also due – as Hitler himself emphasized – to the fact that he had already proved in November 1923 that he really was a revolutionary. But even though Hitler clung to the 'course of legality' he had proclaimed for eight years, not only many of his adherents but he himself too had doubts from time to time whether it would not be better after all to seize power by means of a violent revolt. On the other hand, Hitler was aware that the concept of the 'legal revolution' was a new form of revolution well suited to the German mentality, one which equated best to the contradictory needs of the masses for a revolutionary change of society on the one side and the preservation of the traditional values of authority, obedience and discipline on the other. After the seizure of power he therefore specifically emphasized time and again that one of the greatest upheavals in history had taken place in an extraordinarily moderate and disciplined form, as compared to the 'bloody' and 'chaotic' revolutions in history. Despite its 'moderate' form, for Hitler and his adherents the NS revolution was an event in world history. He believed that with his revolution he had inaugurated a 'turning point in world history', whose true importance perhaps only posterity would be able to understand in full measure.

As an objection to calling Hitler a revolutionary, the claim is sometimes raised that on 30 June 1934 he liquidated Röhm's SA and the NSBO, the truly revolutionary wing of the NS movement. In interpreting the events of the so-called 'Röhm *putsch',* however, it is of primary importance to consider the following facts. For a long time Hitler was unable to reach a decision in the conflict between Röhm's SA and the *Reichswehr*. This inability to decide was – as on 8/9 November 1923 – the expression of an actualization of his ambivalent personality structure, which Wilhelm Reich has aptly described with the words: 'Rebellion against authority accompanied by simultaneous acceptance and subordination.' In the 'Röhm affair', Röhm and the SA's 'revolutionary' claim corresponded to Hitler's 'rebellious' revolutionary tendency, while for him the *Reichswehr* doubtless continued to play the role of a respected and feared authority. Hitler's being torn back and forth is reflected in many contradictory statements in which he first proclaimed the end of the revolution, only then to decisively demand its continuation and completion. Because Hitler was unable to decide between Röhm and the *Reichswehr*, Röhm's opponents finally presented themselves as such massive frauds that Hitler actually began to believe in his intention to conduct a *putsch*, so that his only remaining possibility was to take the bull by the horns. Several statements by Hitler indicate that he subsequently came to regret his action against Röhm. It was not in any way Hitler's objective actually to end the revolution, even though he declared publicly that the revolution was now ended; in reality he wanted to continue it in a different form.

What, then, was the content of this Hitlerian revolution? What social, economic and political objectives was he pursuing? Against previously accepted opinion, Hitler attached great importance to the social question. He wanted to solve the social question by improving the chances of advancement for the worker, by increasing social mobility. He was, as we have demonstrated by our analysis of numerous public and private statements made between 1920 and 1944, a vehement proponent of 'equal opportunity', which, like all of his social and economic objectives however, was only to be realized within the 'German national community'. The issue for him was not the best possible development of the individual, but the optimization of the benefit for the 'German national community'. For Hitler the individual as such was unimportant. What was important was his function and benefit for the national community, and this was best served, in Hitler's view, if traditional class barriers were overcome and all 'national comrades' given the opportunity to take part in the socio-Darwinistically defined battle for social advancement. In this way he hoped to be able to form a new élite which could replace the bourgeoisie.

Hitler primarily accused the middle class of an unsocial position, profit greed and undisguised materialism. By rejecting justified social demands, the bourgeoisie had driven the workers into the arms of the Marxist parties. Proletarian class consciousness was only an understandable reaction to bourgeois class conceit. Furthermore, the middle class had falsified and discredited the national idea by impermissibly identifying its own egoistic class interests with the national interest. A central constantly repeated accusation Hitler made against the middle class was weakness, lack of energy and cowardice. Hitler saw the reason for this 'cowardice' in the material living conditions of this class, i.e. in that the middle class – as opposed to the working class – was a propertied class and therefore lived in constant fear of the loss of this property. The accusation of 'cowardice' can only be understood within the context of Hitler's socio-Darwinistic *Weltanschauung*. One of Hitler's fundamental precepts was that in the eternal battle of the stronger against the weaker, the weaker will finally be destroyed. In his view this applied to individuals as well as to social groupings and even whole nations. The middle class, he concluded, was at the end of its mission because of its cowardice, weakness and lack of energy. This class was incapable of political leadership and had to be replaced by a qualified élite. Hitler hoped to gain this élite primarily from among the working class. For him the workers were, as he stated it, the 'source of strength and energy'. As opposed to the middle class, they were courageous and ready to fight. He therefore concentrated his efforts primarily on gaining the support of the working class. One of the key objectives of his revolution was the ideological upgrading of manual labour and the increase of the social prestige of the worker. The increase of social prestige of the worker was not only to serve the objective of the better integration of this class; at least as important was Hitler's intention to create the conditions for greater social mobility by relativizing traditional social status. The upgrading of manual labour was, as Hitler explained in *Mein Kampf*, the necessary condition for increasing the readiness of children from middle-class families to enter occupations of manual labour, and thereby simultaneously create the conditions for the social advancement of the children of workers.

While the working class and bourgeoisie were – against commonly held beliefs – the key groups which determined Hitler's programmes, the lower middle class and the farmers played only a subordinate role in his thinking. Hitler's objective was the creation of a 'national community' in which class barriers were to be abolished. Existing traditions, 'class conceit' and 'class consciousness' were to be broken down by a process of continuous re-education. The process of ideological levelling was to be accompanied by an actual equalization in many sectors of life.

Even more important for Hitler than the revolutionizing of the social structure of society was the revolutionary restructuring of the economy. Our study has shown that the long-promulgated opinion that Hitler held business in low esteem and understood nothing about economic matters can no longer be upheld. It is also impermissible, as Henry Turner does, to deduce Hitler's

VIII: Final Considerations

contempt for the economy from his statement about the 'secondary role of the economy'. This statement was only intended to convey that, in the final analysis, it was the framework of conditions set by politics which was decisive for positive economic development. If this functional link was no longer recognized, a danger which existed in particular in times of an economic upturn, this led, said Hitler, to political collapse and thereby ultimately also to economic collapse. Business was completely unsuited to becoming the common platform for the various classes and therefore the base for the development of a state, because in business there were always necessarily diverging interests. An ideology which declared business interests to be primary interests ultimately led to the dissolution of the social order. This decay could not be stopped by continuing to pursue its cause, namely to disregard the primacy of politics, but only by abolishing the functional contexts now recognized as being harmful, according to which the economy determines politics, and turning it around. But, according to Hitler, this implied a process against the interest links between politics and business with consistency. He therefore vehemently criticized the influence of business associations on politics, and the 'bribing' of leading politicians by means of positions on supervisory boards and shares. These far-reaching implications of Hitler's demand for the creation of the primacy of politics, which leads in the end to a revolutionizing of the relationship between politics and economy and which is irreconcilable with the capitalist economic system, has previously been largely overlooked by research, which, among other things, probably has to do with the fact that the realities in the Third Reich contradicted this demand for a strict separation of business and politics – thus, for example, Hitler's criticism of Speer's system of 'self-administration of industry' and his toleration of the corruption of Gauleiters and other party big-wigs.

Hitler wanted to establish a mixed economic order in place of the capitalist system, in which elements of a free and planned economy would be united into a new synthesis. Hitler valued the economic principle of competition, which he defined as a special case of the socio-Darwinistic principle of selection and as the motor for continuous dynamic industrial progress. On the other hand, he also criticized the market economy ideology according to which the common good 'automatically' resulted from the pursuit of their egoistic profit interests in the market place by private entrepreneurs.

That Hitler recognized the legal form of private ownership does not mean much in view of the fact that he rejected the free entrepreneurial power of disposition over the means of production. This exemplified Hitler's method, both in economics and in politics, of maintaining the outer form, like the legal form of private ownership, but eroding the content to such a degree that he was ultimately able to destroy it more effectively and with less opposition than would have been possible by any other method. In Hitler's view the entrepreneur was nothing more than a representative of the state and had to fulfil the objectives it set unconditionally. Our study has shown that one of the most important means of reaching this objective was Hitler's constant – open or veiled – threat of nationalization. If the free economy was incapable of achieving the objectives it had been set, he threatened time and again, then the state would take this task into its own hands. His actions in the case of the foundation of the Hermann-Göring-Werke and the Volkswagen Werke demonstrated that this was no empty threat.

The conflicts with business on the one hand and the successes achieved with the application of the system of business planning on the other led to an increasing radicalization of Hitler's criticism of the system of free trade. In this his admiration for the Soviet economic system played a large role – a fact which has previously been overlooked by research. From his memorandum on the Four-Year Plan, but also later from his table talks and his remarks to his associates, it becomes clear that Hitler's conviction of the superiority of the Soviet over the capitalist economic system was an important motive for his enforced destruction of the system of free enterprise in Germany.

In the end Hitler even considered the nationalization of important parts of the German economy, such as the large public share companies, the power industry and all other sectors which produced 'raw materials necessary for survival'. The implementation of a system of planning was not only conditioned upon the necessities of rearmament and war. In contrast to the opinion advanced by Ludolf Herbst, after the war Hitler did not intend to reduce intervention by the state, but rather to extend the system of planned economy. As far as the planned direction of the economy was concerned, Hitler said, this was still only the beginning.

While he rejected the capitalist system of the western industrialized nations, Hitler still admired the technical-industrial standard of development reached in the United States. In this respect America was an example for him which he tried to emulate. In a directive for the press, Hitler expressly forbade using the technical-industrial level of the US as a propaganda argument against that country.

The view that Hitler advocated an anti-modernistic agrarian ideology and planned to opt out of industrial society is based upon a misunderstanding and can no longer be upheld. The settlement of farmers in the *Lebensraum* to be conquered in the East, as planned by Hitler, was not intended to initiate the 'reagrarianization' of German society but only to heal the disturbed relationship between agriculture and industry and to create the conditions for a

VIII: Final Considerations

relatively autarkic greater European economic order. In this, the settlement of farmers was only *one* function of the *Lebensraum* in the East. Besides this, it was of outstanding importance as a source of raw materials and a market, something that has previously been overlooked. For Hitler the conquest of 'ground' did not only mean gaining new agricultural areas, but just as much securing new sources of raw materials and energy. The conquest of the Russian raw material sources would, according to Hitler's vision, facilitate an enormous upturn of industrial production and ultimately even permit Germany to catch up with and surpass the highly industrialized USA.

Hitler was not an opponent of technical progress and industrialization. Quite the opposite. He believed in a quasi-natural law according to which there was a trend towards a constant increase of human demands, a trend which, in the age of mass communications and with the US as the example, would even increase. Nor was Hitler's belief in progress fundamentally affected by his scepticism towards certain negative consequences of modern industrial society, such as the destruction of the environment (which he frequently criticized).

The social revolution triggered by National Socialism, whose content was modernism, was not in any way in contrast to Hitler's intentions. Hitler not only welcomed the process of industrialization and the increase in social mobility but deliberately supported this development, for example by dissolving traditional regional ties through the abolition of the independent states. Hitler believed in a historic trend towards centralization caused by the development of mass communications and transportation technology, which would create the conditions for the advancement of industrial development. Hitler did not reject any of these trends – industrialization, the reduction of class barriers, the dissolution of regional ties – but saw himself as the deliberate executor of this process of modernization. The alleged contradiction between intention and effect, objectives and means, of the revolution set off by National Socialism does not exist, at least as far as Hitler is concerned.

While Hitler was a vehement proponent of modern industrial society and also approved its social consequences, i.e. the increase in social mobility, he was simultaneously just as dedicated an opponent of the democratic pluralistic model of society. He criticized democracy as a system in which the majority allegedly ruled but, being too dumb to exercise political power, in actual fact only permitted itself to be manipulated by the press. This was in the hands of big capital which, by means of controlling 'public opinion' and bribing leading politicians with seats on supervisory boards etc., exercised the actual political power in a democracy. It was therefore not the common good, i.e. the interests of the nation, which determined policy in a democracy, but rather the individual and special interests of powerful groups. In a democracy the bourgeoisie, originally only an economic élite, had also become the political élite, very much to the misfortune of the nation.

Hitler intended to replace democracy and its 'majority principle' by the rule of a new revolutionary élite which he called 'the historic minority'. Hitler developed a theory on the recruitment of an élite which can be summarized as follows. The propaganda of the revolutionary party had to be as radical and uncompromising as possible, so that the 'cowardly' middle-class opportunists were frightened off from the start. Only those elements should be attracted who did not shrink from the ostracism attached to the affirmation of a radical ideology. The physical dangers the SA men were exposed to, for instance, were for Hitler a touchstone for whether these party comrades were really 'brave' and 'courageous' fighters or 'cowardly' opportunists. It is astonishing that racial arguments play hardly any role in Hitler's theory on the recruitment of an élite. Within the framework of his socio-Darwinistic *Weltanschauung* it was not important what a person looked like, but whether he was brave and courageous. These characteristics, which the members of the party proved not only by accepting ostracism, but under certain circumstances also persecution, or at least serious disadvantages, were infallibly attributes of the 'heroic racial elements' of the German people.

This theory of the recruitment of an élite was, of course, no longer valid in the system phase, because now that an endorsement of National Socialism no longer brought social disadvantages but only advantages, the opportunists and 'fair-weather boys' were more likely to join the party. Since Hitler did not succeed in developing convincing principles for the recruitment of an élite in the system phase, he clung all the more to his 'old fighters' who had proved themselves in 'the time of struggle'. But since these did not possess the necessary bureaucratic and administrative knowledge, he was forced to a large extent to lean on the old élites which he had actually set out to replace. While the 'concept of taming' advocated by bourgeois conservative forces such as Papen and Hugenberg failed, Hitler was not the undisputed victor in this alliance. At the end of his life he had to admit that his revolution had failed for lack of a new revolutionary élite. Since such an élite was lacking, he had had to continue to depend on the old élites. He had entered into an alliance with them because he had considered them to be weak, politically incapable and cowardly, and he therefore hoped that he could easily use them or, should this fail, at least be able to get rid of them relatively easily.

His assessment of the Marxist Left, particularly the Communists, was entirely different. Because they too – as opposed to the middle-class parties – 'fanatically' advocated a *Weltanschauung*, because they were brave, courageous and determined, he both admired and feared them at the same time, a position which was also characteristic of Hitler's view of Jewry, which he regarded as the 'puppet master' of historic revolutions, i.e. as the 'historic minority' which was capable of effectively organizing revolutions and carrying them out. But because Hitler was convinced of the superiority and effectiveness of Marxist (and generally 'Jewish') forms and methods of fighting, he feared this opponent far more than the middle-class forces he considered to be cowardly, weak and incapable.

At the end of his life, however, Hitler was to regret that he had not proceeded against the bourgeois right to the same degree as against his Marxist opponents. In the final analysis he was betrayed by his own ideology, which said that only the Marxist enemies had to be dealt with with consistency, because only they were brave and courageous, while the bourgeois opportunists could not become dangerous to him. But the resistance which actually became dangerous for Hitler recruited itself from the ranks of the old nobility and bourgeois power élites. This is an indication that the revolutionary Hitler should not be classified as belonging on the right side of the political spectrum. What also speaks against this is the fact that in his internal statements he expresses an astonishing degree of sympathy for Communists and Social Democrats and an admiration for Stalin and the Soviet system, whereas he became increasingly more critical of Italian Fascism and regretted the support he had given the reactionary Franco regime in Spain with the statement that he should rather have supported the 'red Spaniards'. Hitler, by the way, never regarded himself as being a right-wing politician – nor, of course, as left-wing – but as a revolutionary who, in a situation in which none of the great social classes and political streams was able to assert itself, had created a 'third platform' in National Socialism, a synthesis between nationalism and socialism.

In this study we have reconstructed the key social, economic and political elements of this *Weltanschauung*, which we will call 'Hitlerism' (because there was no such thing as *the* national socialist *Weltanschauung*), from Hitler's original statements. What we have not been able to do systematically is to provide an answer to the question of how far Hitler was able to implement his concepts in reality. This remains a topic for research. We have, however, been able to show in several examples that in certain sectors, particularly in the field of economics, Hitler was able to realize his concepts at least partially. In other areas the picture is contradictory. Hitler's objective of increasing social mobility, an improvement of the possibilities for advancement for members of the socially underprivileged classes, was certainly realized in part:

It has long been overlooked that social advancement in the Third Reich was not only symbolic. Grunberger reported that total upward mobility during the six years of peace of the Third Reich had been twice as large as during the last six years of the Weimar Republic.[2] Governmental bureaucratic organizations and private industry associations had absorbed one million people who came out of the working class.[3]

Dahrendorf and Schoenbaum have already pointed out that the increase in social mobility was one of the important results of the social revolution triggered by National Socialism. It has previously been mainly overlooked, however, that not only was this process deliberately initiated by Hitler, but the objectives he aimed for lay far beyond the results actually achieved. In education policy, for instance, the creation of equal opportunities for all 'members of the national community' was only partially achieved, namely in the National Socialist élite schools.

The fact that, during the twelve years of his rule, not all of Hitler's concepts were completely realized can be explained by a number of objective and subjective factors. During the early years of his rule, Hitler had to make many allowances for his conservative allies. This is particularly true for the period up to Hindenburg's death, but also thereafter. He did not succeed in developing a new revolutionary élite in all sectors of society, which would have secured the realization of his ideas. A further factor must be added. During six of the twelve years of his rule he was at war. While the war favoured the realization of Hitler's concepts in some areas, for example in the economic field, it stood in the way of the implementation of many others, because Hitler certainly did not want to risk a conflict with powerful social groups during a war.

Added to these objective difficulties there was a subjective inability on Hitler's part to convert his ideas effectively into deeds. This inability is linked to a strange trait of Hitler's, which we can also observe in his foreign policy and his waging of the war. Hitler frequently only saw the 'broad principle' and the 'minute detail'. In the waging of war, for example, while he often did have a feeling for strategic considerations, he also worried about such details as the positioning of explosive charges on canal bridges.[4] What he often lacked, however, was an understanding of the intermediary links. In foreign policy he had set his big objectives, and identified his two ideal allies (Britain and Italy), but he had never taken the intermediary steps into his planning, without which the realization of the 'big idea' could not be achieved. He was therefore frequently forced to improvise, which he sometimes carried out masterfully but sometimes lackadaisically. This also applies to the field of social policy. Here too, as we have demonstrated, Hitler developed great objectives and explained them quite logically within the framework of his *Weltanschauung*, but he largely lacked the ability for a really *systematic* implementation of these concepts. What interested Hitler were only the long-term objectives and their explanation in terms of *Weltanschauung* on the one hand and the most minute details on the other. When he found the living conditions of the crew of a passenger liner he had inspected to be unsocial, or he was told about the deficiencies in the quarters of the Reichs autobahn workers,[5] he tried to provide relief. Such problems could still occupy him intensively and years later in his table talks. But this had little to do with the development of systematic concepts for the implementation of his ideas. Hans Mommsen is correct when – in this instance referring to foreign policy – he says that Hitler had been 'a man of improvisation, of experimentation, of the inspiration of the moment'.[6] On the other hand Hitler developed a firmly fixed *Weltanschauung* which was consistent within itself. He was a 'pragmatist' with axiomatically fixed objectives. And, as we have seen in this study, this applies not only to Hitler's foreign and racial policy but also to his concepts of social, economic and domestic policy.

At the beginning of this study we explained why we felt it to be necessary to draw attention to these aspects of Hitler's *Weltanschauung*, which have hardly been examined hitherto. We argued that, while we already know a great deal about Hitler's concepts in foreign and racial policy, his social, economic and domestic objectives have barely been investigated. As important as the analysis of Hitler's foreign policy programme and his racial ideology may be, it can hardly contribute anything, as Eberhard Jäckel repeatedly emphasizes in his study *Hitler's Weltanschauung*, to the clarification of the decisive question of how this man was able to gain the support of a large part, and finally of the overwhelming majority, of the German nation.

In our study we too have admittedly only investigated and discussed a part of Hitler's Weltanschauung, even though, in our view, a very important one. In doing so, we also had to include Hitler's foreign policy concepts in our analysis. What Trevor-Roper conclusively demonstrated for the first time in his 1960 article on Hitler's war aims was confirmed, namely that the conquest of *Lebensraum* in the East was a constant of Hitler's programme. However, research to date has not sufficiently taken the degree to which this objective was determined by Hitler's economic considerations into account. Hitler derived his demand that the German nation had to conquer new *Lebensraum* in Russia from purely economic considerations. The policy of a 'peaceful conquest of the world by economic means' through an economic policy orientated towards export was an illusion, because it too would ultimately have led to war, as the First World War had demonstrated. In addition, the practical possibility of such a policy was declining anyway because of the industrialization of formerly under-developed countries caused by capital export from the old capitalist countries, and leading to a shrinking of the markets. The strategy of economic expansion also led to the development of a imbalance between agriculture and industry. A primarily export-orientated economic strategy could therefore only apparently, i.e. temporarily, 'solve' the contradiction between population and base of subsistence. The actual solution lay in the extension of the *Lebensraum*, which could naturally only be achieved by force. We can see at this point how closely linked Hitler's arguments of economic and foreign policy were.

What is the relationship between Hitler's social, economic and domestic policy concepts we have investigated in this study and his foreign policy? A commonly held interpretation says that social and economic policy was purely functionally directed towards the coming war, and was intended to make Germany internally so strong, productive and firm that the war directed outwardly could be waged. This view is not totally wrong, because Hitler himself did see the close connection between domestic, social, economic and foreign or war policy. Like all of his generation, he had been marked by the experiences of the First World War – for example the blockade – and had come to the conclusion that no successful conduct of a war was possible without a solution to the central problems of economic and social policy.

On the other hand, the common interpretation of the links between domestic and foreign policy is too narrow, because it misinterprets the war as being an overriding objective or axiom of Hitler's policy and one-sidedly assumes the primacy of foreign policy in Hitler's thinking. This somewhat one-sided and abbreviated picture of Hitler has perhaps something to do with the fact that from 1933 to 1939 he concentrated heavily on foreign policy, and that during the war years his attention was increasingly absorbed by the military events so that he turned ever more from a politician into a 'commander'.

This, as well as the understandable concentration of research after the war on the analysis of the policy which finally led to the greatest and most destructive war in the history of the world to date, as well as on the 'final solution of the Jewish question' – i.e. the previously unknown phenomenon of a systematic mass murder organized with 'German thoroughness' – led to a tendency to interpret those sectors which only came into the field of vision later (social and economic policy, for example) exclusively in terms of their functional relationship to the war and the 'final solution'. An example of such a view is that of E. Jäckel, who cites Hitler's frequently repeated statement that the state, the economy etc. were only 'means to an end' as proof of his thesis that all of Hitler's objectives of domestic policy had only been intended to serve his two central objectives of foreign and racial policy. We cannot agree

VIII: Final Considerations

with this interpretation. Hitler wrote in *Mein Kampf*, for example, that 'foreign policy is also only a means to an end', and defined the end as being 'exclusively the fostering of our own nation'.[7] If we were to take the wording 'means to an end' as an indication of Hitler's 'opportunism' or of the secondary importance of certain political sectors for his *Weltanschauung*, we would have to conclude that foreign policy too was only of secondary importance for Hitler, or that in foreign policy he had only thought and acted opportunistically, as Jäckel insinuates for Hitler's economic and social policy (by pointing to Hitler's wording of 'means to an end').[8] The view, however, that with the term 'end' Hitler had always meant the war or the 'removal of the Jews', cannot be demonstrated by the sources.

The concept that Hitler's objectives of social, economic and domestic policy were exclusively directed towards the war and the 'removal of the Jews' implies, when taken to its logical conclusion, that after the 'successful' conclusion of the 'final solution' and the victorious ending of the war, all of Hitler's social, economic and domestic objectives would necessarily have become redundant or without further importance. Hitler's statements on social and economic policy, as well as those in completely different areas not investigated here, such as church policy, show, on the other hand, that he only regarded the conditions for a radical solution of the questions as existing 'after the war'.[9] After the war, Goebbels noted in his diary on 22 January 1940 as the result of a meeting with Hitler, 'the *Führer* wants to stay in office for a few more years, carry out social reforms and his buildings and then retire'.[10] That the post-war period would be marked by the realization of far-reaching social changes was also a condition under which the DAF, above all, was already working on detailed concepts for restructuring in the areas of wage and salary policy, occupational training, health care, pensions and social housing, to name but a few. The realization of these post-war concepts, which Marie-Luise Recker has portrayed in detail,[11] should not be assessed too sceptically. The propagandistic purpose which Recker emphasizes, namely to strengthen the will of the population to continue the war, was not the key issue. Quite the opposite. Goebbels repeatedly advocated generally maintaining 'silence on this embarrassing topic',[12] 'particularly in view of the impossibility today of doing anything at all'.[13] This does not mean that Hitler and Goebbels rejected the social reforms planned by the DAF. On the contrary, Hitler had expressly assigned these tasks to Ley against massive opposition, and Goebbels, too, regarded Ley's plans for a reform of old age security, for example, as being 'very generous' and noted: '[They] grasp the problem by the roots. The intention is to publish the drafts of the appropriate legislation on the occasion of the signing of the armistice'.[14] Only the victorious conclusion of the war and the conquest of *Lebensraum* in the East, went Hitler's premise, could create the necessary material foundation for the execution of far-reaching social reforms. If Hitler sometimes opposed the massive demands by the DAF, then this was because 'power is the only thing that will lead us out of our situation, not theory'[15] and now the 'space [is lacking] to feed our nation'.[16]

In principle, the social restructuring concepts of the DAF largely corresponded to the social and economic principles of Hitler's ideas as we have portrayed them in this study. It would be mistaken, in this context, to try to discover a contradiction between these in many respects quite progressive social restructuring concepts and Hitler's objective of conquering *Lebensraum*. In Hitler's *Weltanschauung* these various elements came together into a closed system and were conditional upon each other.

Within the framework of Hitler's *Weltanschauung* neither the conquest of *Lebensraum* in the East nor the 'removal of the Jews' was overriding, even though both objectives were certainly very important to him. What was overriding was his socio-Darwinistic concept of the 'eternal battle' and the national principle. From these standpoints Hitler derived all his other concepts and objectives of domestic, economic, social, foreign and racial policy. And it is of little help if we attempt to sort the importance of individual objectives into an hierarchical order after the fact. What is important is that all the elements formed a unified whole, a logical system, which can be traced back to two or three fundamental axioms.[17]

Even if we assume – and this cannot be proved – that Hitler's social, economic and domestic objectives that we have analyzed had only been means to the end of waging war, it would still be true that the selection of exactly *these* means (because a given end does not automatically lead to *one* exclusive means but can be pursued by a plethora of alternative means) can only be explained when we consider that Hitler always made his affirmation or rejection of concrete concepts dependent on whether they were in agreement with those basic axioms of his *Weltanschauung*, which for him were the yardsticks for the assessment of all concrete questions.

Notes

I. Introduction

1. *Testament*, p. 73.
2. Windisch, p. 143.
3. On the 'theory of underestimation', see Schreiber, p. 27 *et seq.*
4. For this point of view compare Rauschning, *Nihilism*, pp. 50–6, 294, 305, 308; and also Rauschning, *Conversations*, p. 127 *et seq.*
5. Jäckel, *Weltanschauung*, p. 93.
6. Dimitroff, p. 10.
7. Reich, *Mass Psychology*, p. 103.
8. Sering, p. 785 *et seq.*
9. Pollock, *New Order*, pp. 111, 117, 123 *et seq.*; also Pollock, *State Capitalism*.
10. Rauschning, *Nihilism*, pp. 29, 40, 43, 48, 35, 51 *et seq.*, 57, 347 *et seq.*
11. Bullock, *Hitler*, pp. 239, 259.
12. Görlitz and Quint, p. 368 *et seq.*
13. Mau, p. 126.
14. Faul, p. 563 *et seq.*
15. Bracher, *Seizure of Power*, *passim*.
16. Mosse, *Introduction*, p. 40; Mosse, *Everyday Life*, p. 7.
17. Mosse, *Introduction*, p. 39.
18. Mosse, *Daily Life*, pp. 5, 19.
19. Compare Wippermann, *Theories of Fascism*, p. 89 *et seq.*
20. Dahrendorf, pp. 432 *et seq.*, 436 *et seq.*
21. Schoenbaum, pp. 26, 107, 333.
22. Hennig, pp. 31, 86 *et seq.*; Kühnl, *Review*, p. 35.
23. Mommsen, *Epilogue*, p. 353.
24. Mommsen, *Schoenbaum review*, p. 138.
25. Mommsen, *Epilogue*, pp. 359–63.
26. Fest, *Hitler*, pp. 656 *et seq.*, 1035 *et seq.*
27. *Ibid.*
28. Compare Hillgruber, *Fest Review*, p. 161; Hillgruber, *Research on Hitler*, p. 600; Schöllgen, *Problem*, p. 425 *et seq.*; and Hildebrand, *Hitlerism*, p. 60.
29. Graml, *Problems*, p. 86.
30. See Fest, *op. cit.*, pp. 318, 380, 658, 1031.
31. Bracher, *Controversies*, pp. 70, 93 *et seq.*
32. Weber, *Revolution*, pp. 441, 447, 451.
33. Nolte, *Revolutions*, pp. 395–8, 406 *et seq.*

34. Möller, p. 47.
35. The edition begun by Jäckel is being continued at the Institute for Contemporary History in Munich.
36. See the works by Turner, Barkai, Krüger, Herbst and Teichert; also Chapter IV.1 of the present study.
37. Nolte, *Fascism*, p. 53.
38. Nolte, *Theories*, p. 16.
39. Nolte, *Fascism*, pp. 52–4.
40. See Fest, *op. cit.*, p. 457.
41. On this see Chapter VII.3 of the present study.
42. Domarus, p. 1422.
43. Speech printed in addendum to Picker, here p. 491.
44. *MK*, p. 149.
45. Zmarzlik, p. 246.
46. See the article by Aigner, 'Hitler and World Domination'.
47. See Chapter III.2 of the present study.
48. Speech on 1 October 1933, *VB* No 267 of 3 October 1933.
49. Domarus, p. 1421.
50. Hitler on 23 November 1939, Domarus, p. 1424.
51. Fest, *op. cit.*, p. 21.
52. Jäckel, *Weltanschauung*, p. 22.
53. Turner, *Fascism and Anti-Modernism*, p. 165.
54. The objection was raised against Trevor-Roper, who had been the first to point out the inner consistency of Hitler's thinking (compare Trevor-Roper, *Hitler's War Aims*, p. 32 *et seq.*), 'whether, by not only declaring the fundamental line, but also the whole core of the personality to be uniform and deliberate, we were not coming to an over-stylizing' (Herzfeld in the discussion of Trevor-Roper's theses at the International Congress to Contemporary History in Munich, November 1959, in Freudenfeld, p. 142).
55. See Michalka, *Research on Hitler*, pp. 168–75.
56. Broszat, *Plea*, p. 384 *et seq.*

II. Hitler and the Revolution

1. *MK*, p. 223 *et seq.*
2. *Complete Recordings*, p. 295 (4 January 1921); p. 322 (20 February 1921); p. 607 (12 April 1922); p. 674 (7 August 1922).
3. 'Today they speak of a *revolution*; we did not have one . . .' *Complete Recordings*, p. 583 (23 February 1922).
4. *Ibid.*, p. 644.
5. *Ibid.*, p. 938 (17 June 1923).
6. *Ibid.*, p. 946 (6 July 1923).
7. *VB* edition 283a, special No 17, 6 December 1929 (= *VB* No 284, 7 December 1929), open letter to Schäffer. *VB* No 171 of 20/21 July 1930, speech of 18 July 1930.
8. Speech at the *Reichstag* on 30 January 1934, brochure, p. 7.
9. *VB* No 81 of 22 March 1934, speech of 21 March 1934; *VB* No 188 of 6 July 1936, speech of 5 July 1936.
10. Wagener, p. 471.

Notes

11. *VB* No 80 of 21 March 1934, speech of 19 March 1934.
12. Speech at the *Reichsparteitag* 1937 to the DAF on 11 September 1937, brochure, p. 68.
13. Schoenbaum, p. 84.
14. *Complete Recordings*, p. 127 (27 April 1920); p. 134 (19 May 1920); p. 143 (11 June 1920); p. 208 (25 August 1920); p. 214 (25 August 1920); p. 619 (12 April 1922): p. 733 (20 November 1922); p. 757 (8 December 1922); p. 764 (13 December 1922); p. 1018 (27 September 1923); p. 1027 (2 October 1923); p. 1050 (30 October 1923); p. 1213 (27 March 1924); *MK* p. 380.
15. Speech on 11 September 1926, *VB* special No, BayHStA; speech on 6 March 1927, BA/NS 26/54, f. 132; speech on 23 January 1928, *VB* No 20; speech on 31 August 1928, *VB* No 204; speech on 27 October 1928, BA/NS 26/55, f. 18 *et seq.*; speech on 6 March 1929, BA/NS 26/55, f. 11; speech on 24 February 1931, *VB* No 57.
16. *Complete Recordings*, p. 467 (31 August 1921).
17. *Ibid.*, p. 515 (11 November 1921); p. 671 (28 July 1922); p. 901 (17 April 1923).
18. *Ibid.*, p. 956 (1 August 1923).
19. *Ibid.*, p. 963 (5 August 1923).
20. *Ibid.*, p. 1014 (16 September 1923).
21. *Ibid.*, p. 1022 (30 September 1923).
22. *IB*, No 44 of 2 November 1929, p. 571. Also *VB* No 259 of 8 November 1929, speech on 6 November 1929, as well as 'open letter from Adolf Hitler to Count Soden', *VB* No 259 of 8 November 1929.
23. Wagener, p. 88 *et seq.*, p. 91.
24. Meissner, p. 322 *et seq.*
25. Domarus, p. 229 (government statement to the Enabling Law of 23 March 1933) as well as speech at the *Reichstag* on 30 January 1934, brochure, p. 27.
26. Bouhler I/II, p. 162 *et seq.* (24 February 1940).
27. Meissner, p. 430.
28. Wiedemann, p. 140 *et seq.*
29. Frank, p. 296 *et seq.*
30. Dietrich, p. 246.
31. Speer, p. 124.
32. *Monologues*, p. 64 (also Koeppen, 21 September 1941).
33. *Ibid.*, p. 161.
34. *Ibid.*, p. 248.
35. Picker, p. 418; also p. 186 (4 April 1942).
36. Giesler, p. 382.
37. Speer, p. 67.
38. Wiedemann papers, collection Irving in IfZ, Munich, not numbered.
39. Scheidt, post-war recordings, IfZ Munich, collection Irving, p. 607 *et seq.*
40. Dietrich, p. 244.
41. Frank, p. 296.
42. Conversation with Tiso on 12 May 1944, Hillgruber, *Statesmen*, vol. II, p. 452.
43. Scheidt, *op. cit.*, p. 607.
44. *Complete Recordings*, p. 131 (11 May 1920); p. 608 (12 April 1922); p. 653 *et seq.* (21 July 1922); p. 682 (17 August 1922); p. 754 (4 December 1922); p. 1199 (27 March 1924).
45. *Ibid.*, pp. 357–9 (notes for a speech, 8 April 1921).
46. *Ibid.*, p. 996 *et seq.*, notes for a speech, 5 September 1923; also p. 1003, speech on 5 September 1923.

47. *Ibid.*, p. 1042, speech on 20 October 1923.
48. *MK*, pp. 553–5; also p. 598.
49. *Der National-Sozialist*. Information brochure of the Gau Leadership Württemberg and the District Group Stuttgart of the NSDAP, set 2, No 2, Hitler's speech to a membership meeting of the District Group Stuttgart on 8 July 1925, p. 3 (BayHStA, collection of press clippings 1172).
50. *VB* No 212, speech on 11 September 1926 (special issue, BayHStA, collection of press clippings 1172).
51. *VB* No 81 of 8 April 1927, speech on 6 April 1927.
52. BA/NS 26/55, ff. 10–12, speech on 6 July 1928.
53. *VB* special No of 13 October 1928, BayHStA, collection of press clippings 1172.
54. BA/NL von Epp 24/3, ff. 5/6 (= *VB* 48/49 of 26/27 February 1929), speech on 24 February 1929; also The National Socialist Manifesto to the *Reichsparteitag* 1929, Hitler's opening address on 2 August 1929, *VB* No 178 of 3 August 1929.
55. Wagener, p. 465.
56. Hitler's closing address at the *Reichsparteitag* 1937, brochure, p. 79.
57. Domarus, p. 1837, speech on 12 February 1942. In fact Todt 'did not come into Hitler's circle as a royalist or imperialist reactionary, but because of his social and national convictions. In other words, he came to the NSDAP from the left and not from the right' (Seidler, *Todt*, p. 24).
58. Domarus, p. 2195, speech on 30 January 1945.
59. *Complete Recordings*, p. 347, article of 13 March 1921.
60. *Ibid.*, p. 373, article of 28 April 1921.
61. *Ibid.*, p. 406, notes to a speech on 24 May 1921.
62. *Ibid.*, p. 1007, speech on 12 September 1923.
63. *Ibid.*, p. 1199, before the people's court, 24th day of the trial (27 March 1924); also speech on 9 November 1927, BA/NS 26/54, f. 191 and speech on 9 November 1928, BA/NS 26/55, f. 134 *et seq.*
64. *Complete Recordings*, p. 323, article of 20 February 1921, italics in the original.
65. *Ibid.*, p. 411, speech on 24 May 1921.
66. *Ibid.*, p. 630, speech on 21 April 1922.
67. *Ibid.*, p. 676, speech on 11 August 1922.
68. *Ibid.* p. 900, speech on 17 April 1923; also p. 910, speech on 24 April 1923.
69. *Ibid.*, p. 1007, speech on 12 September 1923.
70. *Ibid.*, p. 1202, before the people's court, 24th day of the trial (27 March 1924).
71. *VB* special issue of 15 July 1925, BayHStA, collection of press clippings 1172; similarly BA/NS 26/54, f. 157, speech on 26 March 1927; BA/NS 26/54, f. 167, speech on 17 June 1927.
72. *VB* No 11 of 14 January 1928, speech on 12 January 1928.
73. *VB* of 23/24 September 1928, speech of 21 September 1928.
74. See, for example, BA/NL Streicher 125, f. 19, speech on 8 December 1928; *IB* of 6 July 1929; Domarus, p. 242, speech of 23 March 1933.
75. *Complete Recordings*, p. 411, speech on 24 May 1921.
76. *Ibid.*, p. 1009, speech on 12 September 1923.
77. Wagener, p. 472.
78. *Complete Recordings*, p. 671, speech on 28 July 1922.
79. *Ibid.*, p. 89 (16 September 1919); p. 266 *et seq.* (24 November 1920); p. 411 *et seq.* (24 May 1921); p. 579 (20 February 1922); p. 615 (12 April 1922); p. 645 (22 June 1922); p. 677 (11 August 1922).

80. *Ibid.*, p. 405 (22 May 1921); p. 466 (31 August 1921); p. 690 (18 September 1922); p. 699 (1 October 1922); p. 779 (3 January 1923); p. 782 (11 January 1923); p. 931 (29 May 1923); p. 954 (1 August 1923).
81. Mohler, p. 48 *et seq.*
82. Schwierskott, p. 79.
83. Moeller, pp. 16, 161.
84. Ullmann, cited in Mohler, p. 50.
85. Jung, p. 620.
86. Moeller, pp. 23, 150, 217.
87. *Ibid.*, p. 219; also p. 227 *et seq.*
88. *Ibid.*, pp. 15, 20.
89. *Complete Recordings*, p. 646, speech on 22 June 1922.
90. In this speech and in *Mein Kampf* Hitler stated that the purpose of the state is the 'preservation of the race'. In his later speeches he rarely used the term 'race' and preferred the term 'national community' or 'nation'. In a speech in 1930, for example, he declared that at the top of the NS *Weltanschauung* was the basic tenet that the people did not exist for the state but the state for the people: 'First, and far ahead on top, stands the term "nation".' (*VB* No 222 of 16 September 1930). Hitler made similar statements on many other occasions – see, among others, 16 September 1935, closing address at the *Reichsparteitag* 1935, brochure, p. 77; 5 November 1937, Domarus, p. 761; 20 February 1938, speech at the *Reichstag*, brochure, p. 6; speech on 26 May 1944, *MGM* 2/76, p. 145. Hitler's thinking in the early years was far more strongly influenced by racial theories than in his later years. A remark by Hitler in the Bormann dictations is also of interest in this context: 'We only speak about the Jewish race out of linguistic laziness, because in the actual sense of the word and from the point of view of genetics there is no Jewish race.' (*Testament*, p. 68).
91. Jäckel takes Hitler's statement that the state is only a means to an end as proof for his thesis that Hitler had 'not been interested in constitutional matters' and had thought and acted opportunistically on matters of domestic policy (Jäckel, *Weltanschauung*, pp. 87, 93). According to Jäckel's interpretation, 'end' always meant the conquest of *Lebensraum* or 'removal of the Jews', which cannot, however, be proved by Hitler's statements. For a criticism of Jäckel's interpretation of Hitler's 'means to an end' wording, see also remarks in Chapter VIII of the present work. Jäckel is correct, however, when he states that this wording originated with the conflict over the constitutional form of the state (*ibid.*, p. 79), but his view that Hitler had not assigned this problem 'any importance' (*ibid.* p. 79) is apparently due to Jäckel's confusing Hitler's keeping this matter open for tactical reasons with actual indifference, and his failure to differentiate between Hitler's propaganda and his *Weltanschauung*.
92. *MK*, pp. 104 *et seq.*, 421, 425–7, 433 *et seq.*
93. *VB* special issue No 87a of 15/16 April 1927, speech on 13 April 1927, BayHstA collection of press clippings 1172.
94. BA/NS 26/54, f. 176 *et seq.*, speech on 9 November 1927.
95. *ZB*, pp. 143, 69.
96. BA/NS 26/55, f. 36, speech on 18 September 1928.
97. BA/NL Streicher No 125, f. 19, speech on 8 December 1928; also Preiss, p. 88 *et seq.*
98. *VB* No 65 of 17/18 March 1929, speech of 15 March 1929.
99. BA/NS 26/56, f. 151, speech on 9 April 1929 (excerpt published in *VB* No 83 of 10 April 1929).
100. *VB* No 259 of 8 November 1929, letter of 8 November 1929.

101. See *Monologues*, pp. 140 *et seq.*, 214 *et seq.*, 243, 271 *et seq.*, 352 *et seq.*, 426. Picker, entry 'jurist' in the register.
102. Obviously an attempt at justification for the bloody suppression of the so-called 'Röhm *putsch*' on 30 June 1934.
103. Frank, p. 153.
104. Speech in the *Reichstag* on 30 January 1937, brochure, p. 16.
105. Goebbels, Diaries, SF vol. 3, p. 55, entry for 23 February 1937.
106. Goebbels, *Speeches*, vol. 1, p. 133 (15 November 1933).
107. *Complete Recordings*, p. 411, speech on 24 May 1921.
108. *Ibid.*
109. *Ibid.*, p. 172, speech on 6 August 1920.
110. *Ibid.*, p. 127, speech on 27 April 1920.
111. *Ibid.*, p. 206, notes for a speech, 25 August 1920, also p. 217, speech on 25 August 1920.
112. Goebbels, *Speeches*, vol. 1, p. 110 (10 May 1933).
113. *Ibid.*, p. 131 (15 November 1933).
114. Speech in the *Reichstag* on 20 February 1938, brochure, p. 9.
115. Domarus, p. 1837 (12 February 1942).
116. *Monologues*, p. 296 (26 February 1942).
117. There is no confirmation to be found in any of the sources for Otto Strasser's claim that Hitler had told him during a disputation in May 1930 that there was no such thing as an economic, political or social revolution but only a racial revolution by the racially inferior lower class against the ruling higher race (Strasser, p. 56). As we have demonstrated, Hitler already admitted at least the possibility of political revolution in his early speeches. Moreover, the tendency we can recognize in the alleged statement, to equate the ruling class with the higher and the lower class with the inferior race, diametrically contradicts Hitler's views (see Chapter III.3.a/b of the present study). The words Strasser puts into Hitler's mouth here are also not credible, because he allegedly recommended Rosenberg's book to Strasser, which was 'the most overpowering of its kind'. Once he had read this book he would recognize that all revolutions in history had been 'nothing but racial battles' (Strasser, p. 56). We know, however, that Hitler made very derogatory remarks about the Rosenberg book after it appeared (in 1930 to Krebs, p. 179) and stayed with this assessment (see Picker, p. 213, 11 April 1942; and Wiedemann, p. 193 *et seq.*). This, as well as other examples, shows that the statements attributed to Hitler by Strasser in the disputation on 21/22 May 1930 should not be cited uncritically as genuine statements by Hitler, which is frequently done in the literature, however (see, among others, Kühnl, *NS Left*, pp. 69, 85, 87, where these statements are cited as proof of Hitler's pro-capitalist position). Bullock's statement that 'what Hitler allegedly said according to this report agrees with his well-known views' (Bullock, p. 137) only applies to a part of the disputation. What we must keep in mind is that with his description of the disputation, which Strasser published as a polemical treatise ('Minister's Armchairs or Revolution') immediately after his break with Hitler, he was attempting to split the NS left away from the party. For this purpose he had, of course, to portray Hitler as a traitor to the revolution, to socialism and to the interests of the workers (see Zitelmann, *Adolf Hitler*, 1989, pp. 56–60). Since quite independently of this there are fundamental doubts about the credibility of Otto Strasser's statements (see, among others, Moreau, p. 137; Stachura, pp. 4, 20, 131 *et seq.*; and Kissenkoetter, p. 29), we should be very sceptical of his report on the disputation of 21/22 May 1930 in those parts that cannot be supported by other sources.

118. On the 'spiritual revolution', or rather 'the revolution of convictions', see *Complete Notes*, p. 239 (24 September 1920); BA/NS 26/56, f. 86 (3 April 1929); *IB*, 6 April 1929; *VB* No 222, 16 September 1930; Wagener, p. 326; 1 September 1933, speech at the *Reichsparteitag*, brochure, p. 24; *VB* No 122, 1 May 1939; and Domarus, p. 1837 (12 February 1942).
119. Speech on 16 December 1925, in *VB* special issue, BayHStA, collection of press clippings 1172.
120. Jochmann, *The Battle for Power*, p. 97 *et seq.*, speech on 28 February 1926.
121. *MK*, pp. 508, 597.
122. *VB* of 5 April 1927, speech on 2 April 1927.
123. *VB* No 270 of 23 November 1927, speech on 21 November 1927.
124. *VB* No 80 of 21 March 1934, speech on 19 March 1934.
125. *VB* No 27 of 27 January 1936, speech on 25 January 1936.
126. Domarus, p. 140, speech on 17 October 1932.
127. *VB* of 12 September 1934, closing address at the *Reichsparteitag*, 10 September 1934; italics in the *VB*.
128. *VB* No 57 of 26 February 1935, speech on 24 February 1935.
129. Speech on 26 May 1944, in *MGM* 2/76, p. 146 *et seq.*
130. Hanfstaengl, p. 45.
131. *MK*, pp. 532, 597.
132. Kotze and Krausnick, p. 274, speech on 10 November 1938.
133. Speech on 26 May 1944, in *MGM* 2/76, p. 159.
134. Goebbels, Diary, 45, p. 115, entry for 5 March 1945.
135. *Complete Recordings*, p. 158, speech on 6 July 1920. It is not clear in this case, however, whether he is referring to the revolution of 1789 or to the proclamation of the republic in September 1870 he so often cited.
136. *Ibid.*, p. 231, speech on 20 September 1920.
137. *Ibid.*, p. 296, 12 January 1921.
138. *Ibid.*, p. 794, 18 January 1923.
139. *Ibid.*, p.1007, 12 September 1923.
140. *MK*, p. 609.
141. *IB*, 4th year set, No 28 of 13 July 1929, p. 321.
142. *ZB*, p. 221; *IB* 4th year set, No 8 of 16 February 1929, p. 88.
143. *IB*, 4th year set, No 8 of 16 February 1929, p. 88.
144. *ZB*, p. 82.
145. *VB* No 250 of 7 September 1934, speech at the cultural conference of the *Reichsparteitag* given on 5 September 1934.
146. Speech at the cultural conference of the *Reichsparteitag* on 9 September 1936, brochure, p. 25.
147. *Ibid.*, p. 27.
148. *Monologues*, p. 123 (2 November 1941).
149. Wagener, p. 116.
150. It is not clear here whether Hitler is threatening a National Socialist revolution or evoking the danger of a Communist revolution. The fact that at the time Hitler was actually toying with the idea of a violent revolt speaks in favour of the first interpretation. Quote from interview with the London *Daily Mail*, 15 September 1932, in Domarus, p. 137.
151. Bracher, *Controversies*, p. 68.
152. Goebbels in his radio address on the boycott of the Jews on 1 April 1933. Cited in

Bracher, *Controversies*, p. 68.
153. *Complete Notes*, p. 322, article on 20 February 1921.
154. *Ibid.*, p. 1007, speech on 12 September 1923.
155. *Ibid.*, p. 1202, 27 March 1924, before the people's court, 24th day of trial.
156. BA/NL Streicher, No 125, f. 2, speech on 8 December 1928. In abbreviated and edited form, this speech is also contained in Preis, p. 88 *et seq*.
157. *IB*, 4th year set, issue 27 of 6 July 1929, p. 305.
158. Domarus, p. 242, speech on 23 March 1933.
159. *IB*, 3rd year set, issue 25 of 10 November 1928, p. 304.
160. *IB*, 4th year set, issue 4 of 26 January 1929, p. 40.
161. Domarus, p. 841, speech on 31 March 1938.
162. *Ibid.*, p. 436, speech on 6 August 1934.
163. *Ibid.*, p. 1078, speech on 14 February 1939.
164. Goebbels, Diaries, SF, vol. 4, p. 34, entry for 6 February 1940.
165. Compare Chapter VI.2.a of the present study.
166. Compare Chapter VII.3.c of the present study.
167. Hillgruber, *Statesmen II*, p. 464. Conversation with Hungarian Minister President Sztójay on 7 June 1944.
168. Thies, *Architect*, p. 41 *et seq*.
169. *Complete Recordings*, p. 247, speech on 18 October 1920.
170. *Ibid.*, p. 282, article of 1 January 1921.
171. *Ibid.*, p. 448, speech on 29 July 1921.
172. *Ibid.*, pp. 460, 462, notes for a speech on 26 August 1921.
173. *Ibid.*, p. 651, reply to a memorandum, 17 July 1921.
174. *Ibid.*, p. 436, to the committee of the NSDAP, 14 July 1921.
175. *Ibid.*, p. 583, speech on 23 February 1922; similarly p. 726, speech on 9 November 1922.
176. *Ibid.*, p. 652, reply to a memorandum, 17 July 1922.
177. *Ibid.*, p. 671, speech on 28 July 1922.
178. *Ibid.*, p. 753, speech on 4 December 1922.
179. *Ibid.*, p. 779, speech on 3 January 1922.
180. *Ibid.*, p. 792, speech on 15 January 1923.
181. *Ibid.*, p. 832, notes for a speech on 20 February 1923.
182. *Ibid.*, p. 975, interview with *The World*, 19 August 1923.
183. *Ibid.*, p. 1028, speech on 7 October 1923.
184. *Ibid.*, p. 1039, speech on 19 October 1923.
185. *Ibid.*, p. 1042, speech on 20 October 1923.
186. *Ibid.*, p. 1052, 8 November 1923.
187. *Ibid.*, Hitler's defence before the people's court, p. 1061 *et seq*., particularly pp. 1084 *et seq*., 1097, 1107, 1117.
188. *Monologues*, p. 262 (3/4 February 1942). Hitler expressed himself in the same vein in his commemorative speech on 8 November 1935, Domarus, p. 553.
189. *Monologues*, p. 262 (3/4 February 1942).
190. *MK*, pp. 104, 127, 111 *et seq*., 114 *et seq*., 379.
191. BA/NS 26/56, f. 28 *et seq*., speech on 6 March 1929 (also published in *VB* No 57 of 8 March 1929).
192. *VB* No 279 of 1/2 December 1929, speech on 29 November 1929.
193. *VB* of 16 September 1930.
194. Domarus, p. 327, speech of 8 November 1933.

195. *Ibid.*, p. 553, speech of 8 November 1935.
196. Letter of 7 August 1930 from Gregor Strasser to the dentist Erckmann, in Kissenkoetter, p. 196.
197. For this see the excellent study by Moreau.
198. Goebbels, Diaries, SF, vol. 2, p. 211.
199. *Ibid.*, pp. 214, 216, 217.
200. Vogelsang, p. 262.
201. Goebbels, Diaries, SF, vol. 2, pp. 218, 221 *et seq.*
202. Heiden I, p. 309.
203. Aretin, p. 139 *et seq.*
204. Vogelsang, p. 262 *et seq.*
205. Goebbels, *Kaiserhof*, p. 145.
206. Goebbels, Diaries, SF, vol. 2, p. 226.
207. Rauschning, *Conversations*, pp. 23 *et seq.*, 32.
208. *Ibid.*, p. 31.
209. Personal statement to the author by Mr Fritz Tobias, Hannover.
210. Wagener, p. 473.
211. Domarus, p. 128, 16 August 1932.
212. Goebbels, *Kaiserhof*, p. 152.
213. Picker, p. 323 *et seq.* (21 May 1942).
214. Wagener, pp. 58, 71.
215. Frank, p. 129, statement by Hitler on 30 January 1933.
216. Domarus, p. 237, speech on 23 March 1933.
217. *Ibid.*, p. 248, proclamation of 28 March 1933.
218. *VB* No 115 of 25 April 1933, speech on 22 April 1933.
219. Opening address at the *Reichsparteitag* on 1 September 1933, brochure, p. 13 *et seq.*
220. Domarus, p. 310, speech on 14 October 1933.
221. *VB* No 299 of 26 October 1933, speech on 24 October 1933.
222. Speech in the *Reichstag* on 30 January 1934, brochure, pp. 3, 27, 37.
223. Domarus, p. 364, interview with Ward Price on 17 February 1934.
224. *VB* No 80 of 21 March 1934, speech on 19 March 1934.
225. *VB* No 81 of 22 March 1934, speech on 21 March 1934.
226. Domarus, p. 424, speech on 13 July 1934.
227. *VB* No 249 of 6 September 1934, speech on 5 September 1934.
228. Domarus, p. 478, speech on 30 January 1935.
229. *VB* No 142 of 22 May 1935, speech on 21 May 1935.
230. *VB* No 123 of 2 May 1936, speech on 1 May 1936.
231. Closing address at the *Reichsparteitag* 1936, brochure, p. 69; Bouhler I/II, p. 344 (speech on 10 December 1940); *ibid.*, p. 392, speech on 30 January 1941.
232. Speech in the *Reichstag* on 30 January 1937, brochure, pp. 4–12.
233. *VB* No 179 of 28 June 1937, speech on 27 June 1937.
234. Opening address at the *Reichsparteitag* 1937, brochure, pp. 13, 16.
235. Speech in the *Reichstag* on 20 February 1938, brochure, p. 9 *et seq.*
236. Domarus, p. 835, speech on 25 March 1938.
237. *Ibid.*, p. 2085, speech on 30 January 1944.
238. Hillgruber, *Statesmen II*, p. 528, conversation on 4 December 1944.
239. Compare Bracher, *Seizure of Power*, Chapter 2.
240. Reich, *Mass Psychology*, p. 54; final sentence in italics.
241. Domarus, p. 411, speech on 13 July 1934.

242. BA/NS 26/54, f. 195, speech on 9 November 1927 (in abbreviated form also in *VB* of 11 November 1927).
243. *MK*, p. 225.
244. *Monologues*, p. 353 (recording of 20 August 1942).
245. BA/NL von Epp 24/3, f. 20 *et seq.*, speech on 24 February 1929 (also published in *VB* No 48/49 of 26/27 February 1929).
246. On this see Maser, *Führer Legend*, where the thesis of Hitler's inability to take decisions is developed and documented in detail on the basis of the sources. However, the thesis of a *Führer* lacking in decisiveness is not as new as Maser attempts to portray. See, for example, Olden pp. 191, 196, 301, 351, 355, 374, 377 *et seq.*, 402 *et seq.*; Trevor-Roper, *Final Days*, pp. 126, 169; Bullock, *Hitler*, pp. 176, 782; Heiber, pp. 34, 58; Gisevius, pp. 290, 314, 348, 373; Fest, pp. 751, 834; Stern, pp. 155, 168; and Carr, pp. 27, 30, 32, 39, 42, 50, 62, 65, 139, 147.
247. Maser, *Führer Legend*, p. 289.
248. Domarus, p. 654, speech on 8 November 1936; our italics.
249. *Complete Recordings*, p. 1062, before the people's court, first day of the trial, 26 February 1924.
250. Fromm, p. 248 *et seq.*
251. Broszat, *Social Motivation*, pp. 94, 97.
252. Sontheimer, pp. 368, 362.
253. Mohler, pp. 207, 295.
254. Kemmernich, *The Causal Law of World History*, cited here in Mohler, p. 30 *et seq.*
255. *VB* No 205 of 4 September 1928, speech on 2 September 1928.
256. Compare Thies, Chapters II.2 and II.3.
257. BA/NS 26/56, f. 154, speech on 9 April 1929 (published in abbreviated form in *VB* No 83 of 10 April 1929).
258. Wagener, p. 135.
259. *VB* No 234 of 22 August 1933, speech on 19 August 1933; similarly also *VB* No 267 of 3 October 1933, speech of 1 October 1933.
260. Domarus, p. 477, speech on 25 January 1935.
261. *Ibid.*, p. 481, speech on 11 February 1935.
262. *VB* No 122 of 2 May 1935, speech on 1 May 1935.
263. Opening address at the *Reichsparteitag* 1935, brochure, p. 12.
264. Domarus, p. 554, speech on 8 November 1935.
265. *Ibid.*, p. 563, speech on 15 January 1936.
266. Speech in Breslau on 22 March 1936, brochure, 'The Führer's Battle for World Peace', p. 53; italics in the original.
267. *Ibid.*, speech on 24 March 1936, p. 56.
268. Domarus, p. 627, speech on 3 July 1936.
269. Speech in the *Reichstag* on 30 January 1937, brochure, p. 3.
270. Speech at the *Reichsparteitag* on 12 September 1937, brochure, p. 74; italics in the original.
271. *Ibid.*, p. 84, closing address on 13 September 1937; italics in the original.
272. Domarus, p. 778, speech on 22 January 1938.
273. Speech in the *Reichstag* on 20 February 1938, brochure, p. 4.
274. Speech at the *Reichsparteitag* on 19 September 1938, brochure, p. 51.
275. Speech to the Winter Help Campaign on 5 October 1938, in 'Führer Speeches to the Winter Help Campaigns 1937 and 1938', p. 15; italics in the original.
276. Domarus, p. 983, speech on 10 December 1938.

277. *Ibid.*, p. 984.
278. Speech in the *Reichstag* on 30 January 1939, brochure, p. 5.
279. Domarus, p. 1181, speech on 1 May 1939.
280. Bouhler I/II, p. 301, speech on 8 November 1940.
281. *Ibid.*, p. 379, speech on 30 January 1941.
282. *Ibid.*, p. 392.
283. *Monologues*, p. 155, 17/18 December 1941.
284. *Ibid.*, p. 297, 26 December 1942.
285. Domarus, p. 1865, speech on 25 April 1942.
286. *Ibid.*, p. 1978, speech on 30 January 1943.
287. On the Röhm controversy and 30 June 1934 compare the works of Mau, Bennecke, Sauer (*Mobilization*), Bloch and Jamin.
288. Mau, p. 126 *et seq.*; also Fest, pp. 648 *et seq.*, 656 *et seq.*
289. See Kershaw, pp. 72–81.
290. Communiqué by the Reichs Cabinet on 3 July 1934, Domarus, p. 406.
291. Domarus, p. 405.
292. Files of the RK, Minister's meeting on 3 July 1934, p. 1358.
293. Goebbels, *Speeches*, vol. 1, p. 157; radio address on 10 July 1934.
294. Domarus, p. 420, speech in the *Reichstag* on 13 July 1934.
295. *Ibid.*, p. 415.
296. In a conversation with *Obergruppenführer* (General) Lutze, cited in Sauer, *Mobilization*, p. 337.
297. Cited in Sauer, *Mobilization*, p. 483, n. 257.
298. Gisevius, p. 180.
299. Maser, *Führer Legend*, p. 314. Other authors, too, have drawn attention to Hitler's lack of decisiveness in the Röhm affair: Olden, pp. 355, 364 *et seq.*, 378 *et seq.*; Heiden I, pp. 421, 426, 431; and Mau, p. 128.
300. Reich, *Mass Psychology*, p. 54.
301. Bennecke, p. 7.
302. In his book *Hitler's War*, pp. 400 *et seq.*, 420 *et seq.*, Irving has cited several cases in which Hitler had intended to impose his deviating opinion on various generals or to criticize them, but in the decisive situation had then not dared to do so.
303. Domarus, p. 219, appeal of 10 March 1933.
304. Files of the RK, pp. 205–7, letter to Papen of 11 March 1933.
305. Domarus, p. 221, address on 12 March 1933.
306. *VB* No 115 of 25 April 1933, speech on 22 April 1933; italics in *VB*.
307. *VB* No 167 of 16 June 1933, speech on 14 June 1933.
308. *VB* No 169/70 of 18/19 June 1933, speech on 16 June 1933.
309. *VB* No 185 of 4 July 1933, speech on 2 July 1933; italics in *VB*.
310. *VB* No 189 of 8 July 1933, speech on 6 July 1933. In the recordings of Reichs Deputy von Epp, Hitler's statements are reported as follows: 'The big task is now to firm up the revolution. History has shown that there are more revolutions which succeeded in the first wave than there are which could be maintained afterwards. Revolution should not be a permanent condition, as if the first revolution had to be followed by a second, and the second by a third. We have conquered so much that we will need quite some time to digest it.. The slogan of the second revolution was justified as long as there were still positions in Germany which could have served as points of crystallization for a counter-revolution. This is no longer the case. We leave no doubt that we are prepared, if necessary, to drown such an attempt in blood. A second

revolution could therefore only be directed against the first.' (Files of the RK, address Hitler's of 6 July 1933, p. 630 *et seq.*) Hitler also rejected the view that a revolution consisted of 'replacing a businessman with another *Weltanschauung* by a businessman with our *Weltanschauung*'. In business, *Weltanschauung* was not the essential issue (*ibid.*, p. 631). The National Socialists certainly had the power 'to take any managing director out', and there were 'probably many who deserved being taken out'. But, within the party, 'trained people for economic policy were spread just as thinly as in the areas of foreign policy and normal bureaucracy' (*ibid.*, p. 632). Here Hitler was opposing the attempts by unqualified people from the party and the SA to remove businessmen and take over their positions. He was well aware that this had nothing in common with a change in the actual economic structure and could only lead to serious disturbances within the economy. Hitler's address to the conference of Reichs deputies on 28 September 1933 had a similar thrust to that of the statements cited above. Compare Files of the RK, p. 864 *et seq.*, particularly p. 868.

311. Speech at the cultural meeting of the *Reichsparteitag* on 1 September 1933, brochure, p. 22.
312. Speech in the *Reichstag* on 30 January 1934, brochure, p. 40.
313. *VB* No 80 of 21 March 1934, speech on 19 March 1934.
314. *Monologues*, p. 296, entry for 26 February 1942; our italics.
315. Domarus, p. 424, speech on 13 July 1934.
316. Goebbels, Diary, 45, entry on 28 March 1945, p. 409.
317. Speer, p. 405.
318. Cited in Fest, p. 976 *et seq.*; similarly Speer, p. 399.
319. Compare p. 418 *et seq.* of the present study.
320. Domarus, p. 424, speech to the district leaders on 29 April 1937 in Vogelsang.
321. Mau, p. 126.
322. Domarus, p. 411 *et seq.*, speech on 13 July 1934.
323. *Ibid.*, p. 445, appeal to the German nation and the NSDAP on 20 August 1934.
324. *Ibid.*, p. 447 *et seq.*, proclamation at the *Reichsparteitag* on 5 September 1934.
325. *Ibid.*, p. 459, speech on 9 November 1934.
326. Compare Diehl-Thiele, p. 19. On p. 17 *et seq.* Diehl-Thiele cites fourteen statements by Hitler between 1933 and 1935 which 'demonstrate the interplay between driving forward and holding back of the revolutionary impetus . . . of the movement'.
327. *VB* No 142 of 22 May 1935, speech in the *Reichstag* on 21 May 1935.
328. Speech at the *Reichsparteitag* on 13 September 1935, brochure, p. 49.
329. *Ibid.*, p. 81, closing address on 16 September 1935.
330. Hillgruber, *Statesmen I*, p. 373, conversation with Italian Minister of Justice Grandi on 25 November 1940.
331. *Monologues*, p. 229, recording on 25 January 1942.
332. *Ibid.*, p. 102, recording of 24 October 1941.
333. Perhaps this was one reason why Hitler addressed himself relatively frequently to the possibility of a revolution directed against him, even though in reality there were no indications whatsoever of the possibility or probability of such a revolution. The condition for such a revolution, said Hitler in a speech on the fifteenth anniversary of the founding of the NSDAP, was that the forces 'decide to go the same way I did. That means a nameless one would have to come along and begin the same struggle I began, but with one difference: I defeated democracy through its own insanity. But no democrat can do away with us. We have destroyed the conditions for beginning such a game again for the next few centuries.' (*VB* No 57 of 26 February 1935, speech on

24 February 1935). Hitler continued to believe that he could reduce the chances of a revolution directed against him by increasing social mobility and the creation of 'equal opportunity' (see Chapter III.2 of the present study): 'This will provide the greatest security for the state and the national community against revolutionary intentions and the destructive trend of time. Because the danger always threatens from the overlooked, but in their depths most creative talents, never from the only negative critics and carpers . . . The true revolutionaries of world stature have always been the leadership talents who were overlooked or not accepted by a conceited, ossified, closed society. It is therefore in the interest of the state to continually test by means of a best selection what talents there are within a nation and how they can be usefully employed.' (speech in the *Reichstag* on 30 January 1939, brochure, p. 17). In the event of a revolution or domestic unrest, Hitler had, as he remarked on 14 September 1941, given the *Reichsleiter SS* the directive to 'remove everything held in the concentration camps from this world; with this the mass has had its leaders taken from it' (*Monologues*, p. 59, recording of 14/15 September 1941). Picker records a similar statement on 7 July 1942: 'If one wished to prevent revolutions, one had . . . as soon as the situation became critical – knock off the asocial breed. But one could only do this if one had already got a hold of the asocial elements in time and collected them in concentration camps.' (Pickert, p. 430). On 7 May 1943 Hitler declared in a speech that there was no danger of a revolt: 'The people would never consider something like that. A Jewish leadership for it does not exist. In a heavy crisis the criminals would not be let loose on the people, but stood up against the wall.' (Domarus, p. 2012). Even though Hitler declared repeatedly that a revolution in Germany was impossible (see, for example, Domarus, p. 1777, 8 November 1941, and a statement to Mussolini on 29 April 1942, Hillgruber, *Statesmen II*, p. 71), he still occupied himself with the possibility of a revolt. To Speer he is alleged to have said: 'It is not completely impossible that I might be forced one day to take unpopular measures. Perhaps there will be a revolt then. Provisions must be made for such a case: All of the windows on this square [i.e. the Adolf-Hitler-Platz in Berlin] will be given heavy steel bullet-proof shutters, the doors must also be out of steel, and the only entry into the square will be closed off by a heavy iron gate. The centre of the Reich must be capable of being defended like a fortress.' (Speer, p. 173 with a similar statement by Hitler).
334. Speech on 26 May 1944 in *MGM* 2/76, p. 159.
335. Jung, p. 283.
336. Jung's definition of revolution is portrayed by Jenschke, pp. 58–74.
337. Jenschke, p. 60 *et seq.*
338. Moeller, pp. 149, 283.
339. Goebbels, Diaries, SF, vol. 4, p. 543, entry for 18 March 1941.
340. Moeller, p. 214; see also p. 237.
341. Sauer, *Mobilization*, p. 285.
342. Cited in Sauer, *Mobilization*, p. 285 *et seq.*

III. Hitler's Social Objectives and His Assessment of the Major Classes of Modern Society

1. *Monologues*, p. 122, entry for 2 November 1941.
2. *Complete Recordings*, p. 199 *et seq.*, speech on 13 August 1920.
3. *Ibid.*, p. 619, speech on 12 April 1922.

4. *MK*, pp. 34, 110, 369–74.
5. *VB* special issue, speech on 15 July 1925 ('Speech by a man who is forbidden to speak'), BayHStA, collection of press clippings 1172.
6. *VB* special issue, speech on 16 December 1925, BayHStA, collection of press clippings 1172.
7. See, for example, BA/NS 26/54, p. 148, speech on 26 March 1927.
8. *Ibid.*, p. 160.
9. BA/NS 26/52, f. 31, speech on 6 August 1927.
10. STA Erlangen III.220.H.1., f. 29, speech on 3 July 1931.
11. Proclamation at the *Reichsparteitag* on 7 September 1937, brochure, p. 17.
12. *Monologues*, p. 322, entry for 1 August 1942.
13. Domarus, p. 2084, speech on 30 January 1944.
14. Meissner, p. 332.
15. *MK*, p. 22 *et seq.*
16. In older biographies Hitler is often portrayed as an asocial beggar who led a life on the fringe of society in the dubious company of down-and-outs and petty criminals. This picture, however, is based on unreliable sources and is certainly not in accordance with reality. But it is also doubtful whether the opposite is true. Based on calculations he made about Hitler's financial situation, Werner Maser attempted to show that he was quite well off (Maser, *Hitler: Legend, Myth, Reality*, p. 73 *et seq.*, but also Toland, p. 52 *et seq.*). These appraisals, which in part are based on assumptions and are also uncertain because we do not know how quickly Hitler spent his money, do not provide any definite parameters for his financial situation.
17. *MK*, pp. 23–33.
18. *Monologues*, p. 72, entry for 27/28 September 1941. Hitler also made similar statements in several speeches. See Domarus, p. 267, speech on 10 May 1933; *ibid.*, p. 302, speech on 23 September 1933; and *MGM*, 2/76, p. 145, speech on 26 May 1944.
19. *MK*, pp. 23, 30.
20. *Complete Recordings*, p. 657, speech on 28 July 1922.
21. *Ibid.*, p. 675, speech on 11 August 1922.
22. *MK*, p. 347 *et seq.*
23. Compare pp. 162–8 of the present study.
24. BA/NS 26/54, f. 147 *et seq.*, speech on 26 March 1927, also published in Preiss, pp. 42–64, but in abbreviated form.
25. *Ibid.*, p. 127, speech on 6 March 1927.
26. Speech to the DAF on 10 May 1933, in Young, *Germany Wants Work and Peace*, p. 42.
27. *Monologues*, p. 290, entry for 22 February 1942.
28. *Ibid.*, p. 296, entry for 26 February 1942.
29. Compare p. 93 of the present study, statement of 2 November 1941.
30. But Goebbels declared on 9 July 1943, 'What was formerly a cheap slogan for [the] gallery now became a fact. The way was open for the competent! We Germans did not become equal in our rights and duties, but *equal* in the opportunities.' Goebbels, *Speeches*, vol. 2, p. 245.
31. Jochmann, W., *Monologues*, Introduction, p. 26.
32. Compare *VB* special issue, speech on 15 July 1925, BayHStA, collection of press clippings 1172; BA/NS 26/54, f. 163, speech on 26 March 1927; *ibid.*, f. 169, speech on 17 June 1927; BA/NSD 71/56, f. 20, speech on 26 June 1927; BA/NS 26/55, f. 40 *et seq.*, speech on 18 September 1928; BA/NL Streicher No 124, f. 24, speech on 30 November

1928 (published in Preiss, p. 139 *et seq.* as speech on 30 November 1929); BA/NS 26/57, f. 15, speech on 31 August 1930; BA/NS 26/52, f. 97 *et seq.*, speech on 8 November 1930; and STA Erlangen, III.220.H.1., f. 9, speech on 26 June 1931.
33. *Complete Recordings*, p. 172, speech on 6 August 1920; *ibid.*, p. 231, speech on 20 September 1920; *MK*, pp. 421, 492 *et seq.*; BA/NS 26/55, f. 42, speech on 18 September 1928; *ibid.*, f. 14, speech on 27 October 1928; Preiss, p. 112, speech on 4 August 1929; *VB* No 280 of 3 December 1929, speech on 29 November 1929; BA/NS 26/52, f. 99 *et seq.*, speech on 8 November 1930; Domarus, p. 71, speech on 27 January 1932; closing address at the *Reichsparteitag* on 3 September 1933, brochure, pp. 33, 36; Domarus, p. 373, speech on 25 March 1934; and Kotze and Krausnick, p. 338, speech on 26 June 1944 (mistakenly dated to early July 1944).
34. So too Mosse, *Daily Life*, p. 16.
35. Wagener, p. 286; italics in the original.
36. *Ibid.*, p. 288; similarly p. 292.
37. Closing address at the *Reichsparteitag* on 14 September 1936, brochure, p. 66.
38. Picker, p. 314, recording of 20 May 1942. For similar statements on the purely national claim of National Socialism see speech at the *Reichsparteitag* on 1 September 1933, brochure, p. 23: speech at the *Reichsparteitag* on 13 September 1937, brochure, p. 93; Kotze and Krausnick, p. 249, speech on 8 November 1938; speech in the *Reichstag* on 30 January 1939, brochure, p. 24; Domarus, p. 1126, speech on 1 April 1939; *Testament*, p. 99, dictation of 21 February 1945; and Goebbels, *Speeches*, vol. 1, pp. 279, 305, 379.
39. Hofer, *National Socialism*, p. 30.
40. *Complete Recordings*, p. 178, speech on 7 August 1920.
41. *Ibid.*, p. 296, speech on 12 January 1921.
42. *Ibid.*, p. 495, notes for a speech on 30 September 1921.
43. *Ibid.*, p. 837, speech on 26 February 1923.
44. *Ibid.*, p. 965, speech on 5 August 1923.
45. *Ibid.*, p. 368, article of 24 April 1921.
46. *MK*, pp. 477–82.
47. *MK*, p. 481 *et seq.*
48. Compare the study by Tallgren on the importance of heroism in Hitler's *Weltanschauung*.
49. *MK*, p. 482.
50. Compare pp. 162–8 of the present study.
51. Jochmann, *In Battle*, p. 95, speech on 28 February 1926.
52. BA/NS 26/54, f. 144, speech on 26 March 1927.
53. *VB* No 81 of 8 April 1927, speech on 6 April 1927.
54. *VB* No 84 of 12 April 1927, speech on 9 April 1927.
55. BA/NS 26/54, f. 169, speech on 17 June 1927; similarly BA/NS 26/54, f. 4, speech on 6 August 1927.
56. BA/NL Streicher No 125, f. 25 *et seq.*, speech on 30 November 1928.
57. *IB*, 3rd year set, issue 32 of 29 December 1928, p. 396; similarly BA/NS 26/56, f. 137, speech on 9 April 1929.
58. *IB*, 5th year set, issue 9 of 1 March 1930, p. 133.
59. Wagener, pp. 350, 426–31, 439 *et seq.*
60. *VB* No 169/70 of 18/19 June 1933, speech on 16 June 1933.
61. Closing address at the *Reichsparteitag* on 3 September 1933, brochure, p. 40 *et seq.*; italics in the original.

62. Domarus, p. 373, interview on 25 March 1934.
63. *VB* of 12 September 1934, speech on 10 September 1934 (closing address).
64. Schoenbaum, Chapter 8, 'Possibilities for Advancement in the Third Reich'.
65. Closing address at the *Reichsparteitag* on 14 September 1936, brochure, pp. 68, 77 *et seq*.
66. Speech in the *Reichstag* on 30 January 1937, brochure, p. 13.
67. Kotze and Krausnick, p. 140, speech on 29 April 1937.
68. *VB* No 123 of 3 May 1937, speech on 1 May 1937.
69. Proclamation at the *Reichsparteitag* on 7 September 1937, brochure, p. 16 *et seq*.; compare p. 91.
70. Closing address at the *Reichsparteitag* on 12 September 1938, brochure, p. 64. Compare the opening proclamation at the *Reichsparteitag* on 6 September 1938, *ibid.*, p. 20.
71. Speech in the *Reichstag* on 30 January 1939, brochure, pp. 17, 46.
72. Bouhler I/II, p. 323, speech on 14 November 1940.
73. *Ibid.*, p. 350, speech on 10 December 1940.
74. Scholtz, pp. 45, 133, 170, 257, 272 *et seq.*, 268, 274, 291.
75. Lingelbach, p. 211 *et seq*.
76. Sonnenberger, p. 325.
77. Bouhler I/II, p. 350 *et seq.*, speech on 10 December 1940.
78. *Monologues*, p. 49, entry for 27/28 July 1941.
79. Koeppen Notes, report No 32 on 18 September 1941, lunch.
80. *Monologues*, p. 72, entry for 27/28 September 1941.
81. *Ibid.*, p. 114 *et seq.*, entry for 29 October 1941.
82. *Ibid.*, p. 120, entry for 1/2 November 1941.
83. *Ibid.*, p. 123, entry for 2 November 1941.
84. *Ibid.*, p. 215, entry for 20 January 1942.
85. *Ibid.*, p. 237 *et seq.*, entry for 27 January 1942.
86. Bouhler III, p. 175, speech on 30 January 1942.
87. Picker, p. 219, entry for 12 April 1942.
88. *Ibid.*, p. 330 *et seq.*, entry for 21 May 1942.
89. Schoenbaum, p. 304 *et seq*. Unfortunately, the modernizing effect of the NS revolution on the Army and its relationship to the state cannot be described in more detail here. For this see the excellent study by K. J. Müller, *Army and Third Reich*, particularly pp. 40 *et seq.*, 55.
90. Domarus, p. 1922 *et seq.*, speech on 30 September 1942.
91. *Ibid.*, p. 1941, speech on 8 November 1942.
92. Schoenbaum, p. 305.
93. Domarus, p. 1941, speech on 8 November 1942.
94. BA/NS 6/161, f. 6, conversation with Mussert on 10 December 1942.
95. Hillgruber, *Statesmen*, vol. II, p. 256 *et seq.*, conversation with Horthy on 17 April 1943.
96. Domarus, p. 2085, speech on 30 January 1944.
97. *MGM* 2/76, p. 152, speech on 26 May 1944.
98. *Ibid.*, p. 153; compare pp. 150, 156.
99. Hillgruber, *Statesmen II*, p. 463, conversation with Sztójay.
100. Kotze and Krausnick, p. 352 *et seq.*, speech on 26 June 1944 (erroneously dated early July 1944).
101. Bouhler I/II, p. 175, speech on 24 February 1940; *ibid.*, p. 399 *et seq.*, speech on 30

January 1941; *Monologues*, p. 377, entry on 29 August 1942; Hillgruber, *Statesmen II*, p. 527 (4 December 1944); Domarus, p. 2206, speech on 24 February 1945; and Goebbels, Diary, 45, p. 203. But also compare Domarus, p. 702, for the statements by Hitler on 23 June 1937 not cited here.
102. Dietrich, pp. 36, 126.
103. *Complete Recordings*, p. 262 *et seq.*, speech on 19 November 1920.
104. *Ibid.*, p. 269, speech on 30 November 1920.
105. *Ibid.*, p. 315, article on 8 February 1921.
106. *Ibid.*, p. 551, article on 23 January 1922.
107. *Ibid.*, p. 707, memorandum on 22 October 1922.
108. *Ibid.*, p. 736, speech on 21 November 1922.
109. *Ibid.*, p. 739.
110. *Ibid.*, p. 840, speech on 26 February 1923.
111. *Ibid.*, p. 912, speech on 24 April 1923.
112. *MK*, pp. 47 *et seq.*, 352 *et seq.*
113. *VB* special issue, speech on 15 July 1925, BayHStA, collection of press clippings 1172.
114. *VB* special issue, speech on 16 December 1925, BayHStA, collection of press clippings 1172.
115. BA/NS 26/54, f. 148, speech on 26 March 1927.
116. *Ibid.*, f. 160.
117. *VB* No 69 of 23 March 1928, speech on 21 March 1928.
118. BA/NS 26/56, f. 33, speech on 6 March 1929 (compare *VB* No 57 of 8 March 1929).
119. *VB* No 47 of 26 February 1930, speech on 24 February 1930.
120. *IB*, 5th year set, issue 44 of 1 November 1930, p. 765.
121. Speech at the *Reichsparteitag* on 11 September 1937 to the DAF, brochure, p. 72.
122. Kotze and Krausnick, p. 237, speech on 8 November 1938.
123. *IB*, 5th year set, issue 10 of 8 March 1930, p. 149. Compare BA/NS 26/55, f. 28, speech on 18 September 1928.
124. *Monologues*, p. 51, entry for 2 August 1941.
125. Compare Chapter IV.3 of the present study.
126. *VB* of 8 March 1927, speech on 6 March 1927.
127. BA/NS 26/54, f. 161, speech on 26 March 1927.
128. *ZB*, p. 122.
129. Wagener, pp. 188, 388.
130. STA Erlangen III.220.H.1., f. 21, speech on 3 July 1931.
131. *Monologues*, p. 220, entry for 24 January 1942.
132. Picker, p. 176, entry for 1 April 1942.
133. BA/NS 26/54, f. 126–33, speech on 6 March 1927.
134. Preiss, p. 41, speech on 23 March 1927.
135. BA/NS 26/54, f. 159, speech on 26 March 1927.
136. *VB* No 81 of 8 April 1927, speech on 6 April 1927.
137. BA/NSD, 71/56, speech on 26 June 1927, printed in a brochure published by the NSDAP Group Marktredwitz, here p. 23 *et seq.*
138. BA/NS 26/52, f. 30, speech on 6 August 1927.
139. BA/NS 26/55, f. 50, speech on 18 September 1928.
140. *Ibid.*, f. 90, speech on 18 October 1928.
141. BA/NS 26/56, f. 18, speech on 6 March 1929.
142. *VB* No 178 of 3 August 1929, opening address at the *Reichsparteitag* on 2 August 1929.
143. BA/NS 26/57, f. 37, speech on 5 November 1930.

144. *Complete Recordings*, p. 1031, speech on 14 October 1923. Compare *ibid.*, p. 1046, notes for a speech on 30 October 1923; and *ibid.*, p. 1049, speech on 30 October 1923.
145. *Ibid.*, p. 1219, article in April 1924.
146. *Ibid.*, p. 1226.
147. Compare *MK*, pp. 186 *et seq.*, 414, 422, 598.
148. *MK*, p. 552.
149. *Complete Recordings*, p. 956, speech on 1 August 1923.
150. *VB* special issue 'The Social Mission of National Socialism', speech on 16 December 1925, BayHStA, collection of press clippings 1172.
151. *VB* No 212, special issue, speech on 11 September 1926, BayHStA, collection of press clippings 1172.
152. BA/NS 26/54, f. 155 *et seq.*, speech on 26 March 1927. Compare *VB* of 5 April 1927, speech on 2 April 1927.
153. *ZB*, p. 82.
154. BA/NL Streicher No 125, f. 23, speech on 8 December 1928 (published in edited form in Preiss, p. 88 *et seq.*).
155. BA/NL von Epp 24/3, f. 3-5, (compare *VB* 48/49 of 26/27 February 1929).
156. *IB* 4th year set, issue 41 of 12 October 1929, p. 521.
157. *VB* No 269, article of 20 November 1929.
158. *IB* 4th year set, issue 47 of 23 November 1929, p. 617.
159. *IB* 5th year set, issue 1 of 4 January 1930, p. 5.
160. *VB* No 47 of 26 February 1930, speech on 24 February 1930.
161. In a meeting with the Bulgarian Regency Council (Cyrill, Filoff, Michoff) Hitler said on 17 March 1944: 'The only real enemy which Germany faced in her heavy struggle was Bolshevism, which roused its adherents to fanaticism by combining idealistic objectives with the gratification of criminal instincts.' Hillgruber, *Statesmen II*, p. 387.
162. See, for example, BA/NS 26/54, f. 114, speech on 6 March 1927; BA/NSD 71/56, f. 8, speech on 26 June 1927; BA/NS 26/55, f. 2, speech on 27 October 1928; BA/NL Streicher, No 125, f. 8 *et seq.*, speech on 30 November 1928; *VB* No 101 of 2 May 1929; Preiss p. 127, speech on 30 November 1929; BA/NS 26/57, f. 3, speech on 31 August 1930; Preiss p. 153, speech on 7 September 1930; and Domarus, p. 227, speech on 21 March 1933.
163. See Borowsky, p. 79, or Toland, p. 488; and in contrast Fest, p. 457.
164. Compare *Complete Recordings*, p. 867 (6 April 1923); *MK*, p. 522; *VB* special issue, speech on 15 July 1925, BayHStA, collection of press clippings 1172; Preiss, p. 34, speech on 23 March 1927; *VB* No 69, speech on 21 March 1938; BA/NS 26/55, f. 60–1, speech on 18 October 1928; BA/NL Streicher, f. 2–3, speech on 30 November 1928; *VB* No 279, speech on 29 November 1929; BA/NS 26/57, f. 3–5, speech on 31 August 1930; Preiss, p. 154, speech on 7 September 1930; and Domarus p. 204, speech on 10 February 1933.
165. Compare *Complete Recordings*, pp. 551 (23 January 1922), 912 (24 April 1923); *MK*, p. 237 ('Mental Senility'); *ZB*, pp. 44, 64, 78, 90, 113, 116, 134, 189, 212; and *IB* of 22 December 1928.
166. *Complete Recordings*, p. 541, information leaflet of 7 January 1922.
167. *Ibid.*, p. 433, article of 5 June 1921.
168. *IB* of 28 June 1930.
169. Speech at the *Reichsparteitag* on 6 September 1938, brochure, p. 32.
170. Koeppen Notes of 5 September 1941.
171. *Monologues*, p. 122, entry on 2 November 1941.

172. BA/NS 26/54, f. 169, speech on 17 June 1927.
173. *IB* 4th year set, issue 40 of 5 October 1929, p. 505.
174. Kotze and Krausnick, p. 220, speech on 20 May 1937.
175. Speech on 23 November 1937, pub. in appendix in Picker, p. 481 *et seq.*, here p. 489 *et seq.*
176. Speech at the *Reichsparteitag* on 6 September 1928, brochure, p. 18.
177. Picker, p. 186 *et seq.*, entry on 4 April 1942. Compare speech on 25 May 1944, in *MGM* 2/76, p. 158.
178. *Complete Recordings*, p. 281, article of 1 January 1921.
179. *Ibid.*, p. 433, article on 5 June 1921.
180. *Ibid.*, p. 509, letter of 27 October 1921.
181. *Ibid.*, p. 550 *et seq.*, article of 23 January 1922.
182. *Ibid.*, p. 710, speech on 25 October 1922.
183. *Ibid.*, p. 778, speech on 3 January 1923.
184. *Ibid.*, p. 911, speech on 24 April 1923.
185. *MK*, pp. 367, 548, 590.
186. *VB* No 23 of 28 January 1928, speech on 26 January 1928.
187. *ZB*, pp. 212, 215, 222.
188. *IB* 4th year set, issue 39 of 28 September 1929, p. 493.
189. *Ibid.*, issue 42 of 19 October 1929, p. 537.
190. Compare Chapter III.3.b of the present work.
191. Koeppen Notes of 5 September 1941, lunch.
192. *Monologues*, p. 122 *et seq.*, entry for 2 November 1941.
193. *Ibid.*, p. 238, entry for 27 January 1942.
194. *Ibid.*, p. 250, entry for 1 February 1942.
195. Picker, p. 184, entry for 4 April 1942.
196. *Monologues*, p. 328, entry for 5 August 1942.
197. Domarus, p. 2205, speech on 24 February 1945.
198. Further statements by Hitler in which he speaks about 'the cowardly bourgeoisie' can be found in BA/NS 26/55, f. 7, speech on 6 July 1928; *IB* of 17 November 1928; BA/NL Streicher 125, f. 22, 30 November 1928; BA/NL von Epp, No 24/3, f. 4: *VB* No 178, speech on 2 August 1929; *VB* No 259, letter by Hitler of 8 November 1929; *VB* No 269, speech on 20 November 1929; *IB* of 2 August 1930; STA Erlangen III.220.H.1., f. 26, speech on 26 June 1931; Domarus, p. 391, speech on 28 March 1933; *Monologues*, p. 156, entry for 23/24 December 1941; Picker, p. 176, entry for 1 April 1942; and *ibid.*, p. 204, entry for 8 April 1942.
199. *Complete Recordings*, p. 619, speech on 12 April 1922.
200. *Ibid.*, p. 703, memorandum of 22 October 1922.
201. *Ibid.*, p. 908, speech on 20 April 1923.
202. Compare the following sources: Jochmann, *In Battle*, pp. 96, 111, speech on 28 February 1926; BA/NS 26/54, f. 155, speech on 26 March 1927; *VB* No 81, speech on 6 April 1927; *ZB*, p. 195; BA/NS 26/55, f. 20, speech on 27 October 1928; *VB* No 178, speech on 2 August 1929; *VB* No 47, speech on 24 February 1930; speech at the *Reichsparteitag* on 14 September 1936, brochure, p. 79; and *Monologues*, p. 324, entry for 3 August 1942.
203. *MK*, p. 108.
204. Jochmann, *In Battle*, p. 95, speech on 28 February 1926.
205. *VB* No 69 of 23 March 1928, speech on 21 March 1928.
206. Conversation with Romanian Head of State Antonescu on 2 September 1943, in

Hillgruber, *Statesmen II*, p. 306. Hitler made a similar statement on 18 October 1943 in a meeting with the Bulgarian Regency Council (Hillgruber, *Statesmen II*, p. 322 *et seq.*) and in his new year address on 1 January 1944 (Domarus, p. 2073).
207. Compare Chapter VI.2 of the present study.
208. STA Erlangen, III.220.H.1., f. 26, speech on 26 June 1931; also *ibid.*, p. 28.
209. Speech at the congress of the DAF on 10 May 1933, in 'Young Germany Wants Work and Peace . . .', p. 48 *et seq.*
210. *VB* No 169/70 of 18/19 June 1933, speech on 16 June 1933.
211. Closing address at the *Reichsparteitag* on 3 September 1933, brochure, p. 38 *et seq.*
212. Compare speech on 10 September 1934, in *VB*; Kotze and Krausnick, p. 238, speech on 8 November 1938; and *MGM* 2/76, p. 149 *et seq.*, speech on 26 May 1944.
213. *MK*, pp. 451, 772, 774.
214. *VB* No 118 of 26 May 1926, speech on 22 May 1926.
215. *VB* No 212, special issue, speech on 11 September 1926, BayHStA, collection of press clippings 1172.
216. BA/NS 26/54, f. 150, speech on 26 March 1927.
217. *VB* No 48 of 26/27 February 1928, speech on 24 February 1928.
218. *ZB*, p. 82.
219. *VB* special issue of 13 October 1928, speech on 10 October 1928, BayHStA, collection of press clippings 1172.
220. BA/NS 26/55, f. 111 (p. 20), speech on 27 October 1928; similarly BA/NS 26/56, f. 34, speech on 6 March 1929.
221. *IB* 4th year set, issue 10 of 9 March 1929, p. 113.
222. *Ibid.*, issue 13 of 30 March 1929, p. 151.
223. *Ibid.*, issue 41 of 12 October 1929, p. 521.
224. *VB* No 286 of 10 December 1929, speech on 7 December 1929.
225. *IB* 5th year set, issue 1 of 4 January 1930, p. 7.
226. *Ibid.*, issue 26 of 28 June 1930, p. 405.
227. *Ibid.*, issue 39 of 27 September 1930, p. 665.
228. Wagener, p. 71; similarly *ibid.*, p. 468.
229. *VB* No 299 of 26 October 1933, speech on 24 October 1933. See also Hitler's letter of 11 November 1933 to Papen, in which he writes, 'I very much have the feeling that our bourgeoisie was unfortunately saved too soon. It would have been better, perhaps, to give it six weeks of Bolshevism so that it would have become acquainted with the difference between the red revolution and our uprising.' (Files of the RK, p. 207).
230. Closing address at the *Reichsparteitag* on 14 September 1936, brochure, p. 68.
231. Speech in the *Reichstag* on 30 January 1939, brochure, p. 18 *et seq.*
232. Bouhler I/II, p. 162, speech on 24 February 1940.
233. *Ibid.*, p. 164.
234. Conversation with Szálasi on 4 December 1944, Hillgruber, *Statesmen II*, p. 527.
235. Domarus, p. 2183, speech on 1 January 1945.
236. *Ibid.*; also *ibid.*, p. 2195, speech on 30 January 1945.
237. *Ibid.*, p. 2196.
238. BA/NS 26/54, f. 200 *et seq.*, speech on 9 November 1927.
239. Wagener, p. 374, February 1931.
240. Preiss, p. 189, speech on 4 September 1932.
241. Speech at the *Reichsparteitag* on 12 September 1938, brochure, p. 60 *et seq.*
242. *Complete Recordings*, p. 175, speech on 7 August 1920.
243. Domarus, p. 350 *et seq.*, conversation with Johst, pub. on 27 January 1934.

244. Closing address at the *Reichsparteitag* on 12 September 1938, brochure, p. 58 *et seq.*
245. Falter in Michalka, 'Seizure of Power', p. 55. Compare Falter, Lindenberger and Schumann, 'Elections'; Falter, 'Elections and Voter Behaviour', in Bracher, Funke and Jacobsen, 'The Weimar Republic 1918-1933'; Hänisch, 'Determinants of Social Structure'; Falter and Hänisch, 'The Susceptibility of Workers'; and Falter, 'The Workers Provided the Majority of Hitler's Voters'. On membership in the NSDAP see Kater, *The Nazi Party*. An overview of newer empirical analyses of the membership and voters of the NSDAP is contained in Manstein's study 'The Members and Voters of the NSDAP 1919–1933'. On the relationship between the working class and National Socialism compare the excellent study by Mai. Mai rightly points out that until now the relationship between the working class and National Socialism has been 'primarily perceived and treated under the aspect of resistance, social protest and refusal' by research (p. 573), whereby the obvious success of National Socialism among the working class has been largely blended out. Mai even goes as far – and probably quite rightly – as to speak of a 'social and historic taboo being put on this topic' (p. 573). Mai demonstrates that by the end of 1932 the *Nationalsozialistische Betriebszellenorganisation* [National Socialist Company Organization—H.B.], in which only a part of the NSDAP's members from the working class were organized, had even overtaken the RGO [Reich Union Organization—H.B.] and the Hirsch-Dunker'sche Gewerksvereine [left-wing/liberal union which rejected class war—H.B.] as far as the number of members was concerned (p. 611), whereby the NSBO 'did not primarily organize "atypical" groups of workers or the declassed, but blue- and white-collar workers of all levels of qualification, branches, company sizes and confessions in all regions' (p. 612). Also compare the study by Kele, *Nazis and Workers*.
246. BA/NS 26/55, f. 103; italics in the shorthand notes.
247. BA/NL Streicher, No 125, f. 2 *et seq.*, speech on 30 November 1928.
248. *VB* No 101 of 2 May 1929. Compare closing address at the *Reichsparteitag* on 10 September 1934, *VB* of 12 September 1934. Bouhler I/II, p. 409, speech on 24 February 1941.
249. *Complete Recordings*, p. 155 *et seq.*, letter of 3 July 1920 to Constantin Hierl.
250. *Ibid.*, p. 199, speech on 13 August 1920; p. 298 *et seq.*, article of 27 January 1921.
251. *Ibid.*, p. 175, speech on 7 August 1920.
252. *Ibid.*, p. 366, speech on 21 April 1921.
253. *Ibid.*, p. 590, speech on 1 March 1922.
254. *Ibid.*, p. 702, memorandum of 22 October 1922.
255. *Ibid.*, p. 912, speech on 24 April 1923.
256. *Ibid.*, p. 1042, speech on 20 October 1923; also *ibid.*, p. 1230, conversation with Hans Lutz on 25 April 1924.
257. *MK*, pp. 108, 111, 349, 509, 511.
258. *Complete Recordings*, p. 782, speech on 11 January 1923; similarly, *ibid.*, p. 799, article of 25 January 1923.
259. Compare pp. 422–7 of the present study.
260. *MK*, pp. 196–203.
261. BA/NS 26/54, f. 200, speech on 9 November 1927.
262. BA/NS 26/52, f. 34, speech on 6 August 1927.
263. *VB* No 270 of 23 November 1927, speech on 21 November 1927.
264. *VB* No 69 of 23 March 1928, speech on 31 March 1928.
265. Stachura, 'The Critical Turning-Point', pp. 90–9, here particularly pp. 90, 94; similarly Stachura, 'Gregor Strasser' p. 67 *et seq.*; critically Manstein p. 38 *et seq.*

266. Goebbels, Diaries, SF, vol. 1, p. 226.
267. Cited in Kissenkoetter, p. 36.
268. *VB* of 2/3 September 1928, speech on 31 August 1928.
269. BA/NL Streicher, No 125, f. 22, speech on 30 November 1928 (dated 30 November 1929 in Preiss).
270. Wagener, p. 321. While this statement by Hitler is most probably authentic based on the discussion up to this point, there is no confirmation in the sources for Strasser's claim that Hitler had told him, 'we will never be able to count on being able to gain the workers to any greater degree' (Strasser, p. 56). On the criticism of Strasser as a source, also see note 117 on p. 458.
271. Opening proclamation at the *Reichsparteitag* on 1 September 1933, brochure, p. 11.
272. Speech at the 2nd Working Congress of the DAF on 16 May 1934, in *VB* No 138 of 18 May 1934.
273. *Monologues*, p. 280, entry for 17 February 1942.
274. Picker, p. 187, entry for 4 April 1942. Compare Hitler on 27 February 1925: 'Reason may deceive a person treacherously, but you never lose your instinct . . . instinct is stable, it does not totter nor waver.' (Hitler's speech at the first big mass rally after refounding of the NSDAP, brochure, p. 11). In his 'Second Book' Hitler writes: 'The man of the people has a better counsellor here [instinct]. In place of the pondering wisdom of our intellectuals he sets the surety of his instinct [feeling] and the belief of his heart.' (*ZB*, p. 76). Compare also speech on 12 April 1931 in *VB* No 105 and speech on 8 September 1938 in *VB* No 253.
275. Speech at the *Reichsparteitag* on 6 September 1938, brochure, p. 32, *ibid.*, pp. 16, 58.
276. Kotze and Krausnick, p. 241 *et seq.* Further statements by Hitler on the intellectuals are in *Complete Recordings*, p. 539, speech on 5 January 1922; *MK*, p. 727; Wagener, pp. 57, 260, 321; speech on 10 May 1933, brochure, p. 55 *et seq.*; Domarus, p. 291, speech on 30 July 1933; speech in the *Reichstag* on 30 January 1934, brochure, p. 33; Kotze and Krausnick, p. 139, speech on 29 April 1937; *ibid.*, pp. 273, 277, 281 *et seq.*, speech on 10 November 1938; and *Monologues*, p. 373, entry for 29 August 1942.
277. Bouhler I/II, p. 329.
278. Goebbels, Diaries, SF, vol. 4, p. 252, entry for 25 July 1940.
279. Koeppen Notes, report No 27 of 5 September 1941, lunch.
280. *Monologues*, p. 65, entry for 21 September 1941.
281. Koeppen Notes, report No 40 of 4 October 1941, lunch.
282. *Monologues*, p. 123, entry for 2 November 1941.
283. *Ibid.*, p. 209, entry for 16/17 January 1941.
284. *Ibid.*, p. 310, entry for 1 March 1942.
285. Picker, p. 204 *et seq.*, entry for 8 April 1942.
286. *Ibid.*, p. 281, entry for 11 May 1942.
287. *Monologues*, p. 237, entry for 27 January 1942.
288. Picker, p. 183, entry for 3 April 1942.
289. *Ibid.*, p. 314 *et seq.*, entry for 20 May 1942.
290. *Monologues*, p. 364, entry for 25 August 1942.
291. Further sources in which Hitler emphasizes either the priority of gaining the working class or generally lauds the 'masses' as a source of 'strength' and 'energy' (as opposed to the bourgeoisie) are *ZB*, p. 76; Preiss, p. 116, 4 August 1929; *IB* of 1 March 1930; Domarus, p. 139, 15 October 1932; *ibid.*, p. 175, 4 January 1933; speech in the *Reichstag* on 30 January 1939, brochure, p. 16; Bouhler I/II, p. 316, 8 November 1940; and Bouhler III, p. 180 *et seq.*, 30 January 1942.

292. *MK*, pp. 385 *et seq.*, 482 *et seq.*, 486.
293. Recker, p. 87 *et seq.*
294. BA/NS 26/55, f. 30, speech on 18 September 1928.
295. Domarus, p. 260, speech on 1 May 1933.
296. Compare Schoenbaum, p. 114.
297. Files of the RK, p. 288 *et seq.*, meeting of 4 April 1933. Köhler is correct in his study of the labour service: 'After his taking over [of] the government, the primary value of the labour service for Hitler unquestionably lay in the fact that it offered the possibility of realizing the concept of the National Socialist national community.' (Köhler, p. 256). Also see the study by Hussmann who sets up the equation 'labour service = German socialism' (Hussmann, p. 11).
298. Domarus, p. 212, interview on 20 February 1933.
299. *Ibid.*, p. 262, speech on 1 May 1933.
300. *Ibid.*, p. 302 *et seq.*, speech on 23 September 1933.
301. *VB* No 127 of 3 May 1934, speech on 1 May 1934; italics in *VB*.
302. Compare the speeches on 6 September 1934 in *VB* No 250; at the *Reichsparteitag* on 12 September 1935, brochure, p. 43; at the *Reichsparteitag* on 10 September 1936, brochure, p. 40 *et seq.*; on 1 May 1937 in *VB* No 121/22 of 1/2 May 1937; and on 1 May 1939 in *VB* No 122.
303. Kotze and Krausnick, p. 157, speech on 29 April 1937.
304. Goebbels, Diaries, SF, vol. 3, p. 26, entry for 28 January 1937.
305. *Ibid.*, p. 104, entry for 8 April 1937.
306. *Monologues*, p. 49, entry for 27/28 July 1941.
307. *Ibid.*, p. 238, entry for 27 January 1942.
308. Similar statements can be found in the following sources: *Complete Recordings*, p. 89 (16 September 1919); *ibid.*, p. 98 (10 December 1919); *ibid.*, p. 149 (19 June 1920); *VB* special issue, speech on 16 December 1925, BayHStA, collection of press clippings 1172; *ZB*, p. 64; BA/NS 26/55, f. 29, speech on 18 September 1928; *ibid.*, f. 73, speech on 18 October 1928; BA/NL Streicher, No 125, f. 24, speech on 8 December 1928; BA/NS 26/57, f. 39, speech on 5 November 1930; BA/NL Streicher, No 126, f. 20 *et seq.*, speech on 13 November 1930; STA Erlangen, III.220.H.1., f. 26 *et seq.*, speech on 3 July 1931; Domarus, p. 260, speech on 1 May 1933; speech at the *Reichsparteitag* on 13 September 1935, brochure, pp. 47, 50; speech at the *Reichsparteitag* on 12 September 1936, brochure, p. 50 *et seq.*; speech on 6 October 1936, brochure, p. 28; Kotze and Krausnick, p. 216, speech on 20 May 1937; *Monologues*, p. 238, entry for 27 January 1942; and Kotze and Krausnick, p. 353, speech on 26 June 1944.
309. *Complete Recordings*, p. 97, speech on 10 December 1919.
310. *Ibid.*, p. 213. Similarly *ibid.*, p. 135 (26 May 1920); and *ibid.*, p. 890 *et seq.* (13 April 1923).
311. *Ibid.*, p. 262, speech on 19 November 1920; similarly *ibid.*, p. 269.
312. BA/NS 26/54, f. 160, speech on 26 March 1927; *ibid.* f. 31, speech on 6 August 1927.
313. BA/NS 26/55, f. 116, speech on 9 November 1928.
314. BA/NS 26/58, f. 2, speech on 5 March 1932.
315. Domarus, p. 1079, speech on 14 February 1939.
316. *Monologues*, p. 52, entry for 2 August 1941.
317. Bouhler I/II, p. 295 *et seq.*, speech on 8 November 1940.
318. *Ibid.*, p. 321 *et seq.*, speech on 14 November 1940.
319. Compare Lampert, p. 192 *et seq.*
320. Compare Härter, p. 61. During the NS period vacation rose from an average of 3 to

an average of 6–12 days.
321. *Germany Reports*, 3rd year set 1936, p. 1487 *et seq.*: 'As far as can be determined, as compared to before, vacation regulations have been generally improved.'
322. *Germany Reports*, cited here in Schäfer, p. 116. Nolte, 'Marxism and National Socialism', p. 395 *et seq.* cites similar statements from the camp of Social Democrat emigrants. One of the most enlightening pointers, says Nolte, is the statement by Viktor Schiff, a former *Vorwärts* editor, that, despite its overwhelmingly proletarian population, the electoral district of Chemnitz-Zwickau was one of the first in which the National Socialists gained an absolute majority of the votes (Nolte, *ibid.*, p. 396, n. 20).
323. *Complete Recordings*, p. 156, letter of 3 July 1920.
324. *Ibid.*, p. 697, speech on 28 September 1922.
325. *MK*, p. 22.
326. *MK*, p. 108 *et seq.*; also compare p. 130.
327. *IB* 3rd year set, issue 32 of 29 December 1928, p. 396.
328. *VB* No 281 of 4 December 1929, speech on 29 November 1929. Further sources in which Hitler criticizes the ruination of the lower middle class by the big department stores are: speech on 22 February 1929, in *VB*; BA/NS 26/56, ff. 57–9, 67, speech on 3 April 1929; *ibid.*, ff. 132 *et seq.*, 137, speech on 9 April 1929; speech on 6 December 1929, in *VB*; and *IB* of 25 January 1930.
329. Compare Turner, *Fascism and Anti-Modernism*.
330. Compare Chapter V of the present study.
331. *Complete Recordings* 1905–1924, compiled and published by E. Jäckel and A. Kuhn.
332. Compare Chapter V.1.b of the present study.
333. *MK*, p. 151 *et seq.*
334. BA/NS 26/55, f. 91, speech on 18 October 1928.
335. BA/NL Streicher, No 125, f. 25 *et seq.*, speech on 30 November 1928; similarly *ibid.*, ff. 12, 19, speech on 8 December 1928.
336. Heberle, p. 154.
337. Compare Schreiber, p. 181 *et seq.*, with appropriate bibliography. Compare the sociological study of elections by Heberle: 'Rural Population and National Socialism'.
338. BA/NS 26/56, f. 60, speech on 3 April 1929 (also pub. in *VB* No 78 of 5 April 1929).
339. Domarus, p. 174, speech on 3 January 1933.
340. *Ibid.*, p. 206, speech on 10 February 1933.
341. Speech to German agriculture on 5 April 1933, in 'Young Germany Wants Work and Peace', p. 28 *et seq.*
342. *VB* No 267 of 3 October 1933, speech on 1 October 1933.
343. Wiedemann, *The Man . . .*, p. 69 *et seq.*
344. Compare Chapter V.1.b of the present study.
345. *Monologues*, p. 332, speech on 6 August 1942.
346. *Complete Recordings*, p. 586, notes for a speech on 1 March 1922.
347. *MK*, p. 372 *et seq.*
348. *MK*, pp. 671–4.
349. *Complete Recordings*, p. 774, letter to E. Scharrer, end of December 1922.
350. *MK*, p. 676 *et seq.*
351. G. Mai states: 'In Hitler's early statements on the unions, we can quite clearly recognize a certain admiring respect for the organizational achievement and the power of the [free] unions, which is linked to a very clear recognition of how such an apparatus can be instrumentalized. On the other hand, as subsidiary organs of

Notes

"Marxism", as instruments of class war, the unions had to be bitterly opposed.' (Mai, p. 576). This ambivalent relationship (admiration/fear/need to fight ruthlessly) was, as we will show, characteristic of Hitler's total relationship to Marxism. See Chapter VII.3.a–c of the present study.

352. Mason, *Social Policy*, pp. 193, 194, 198, 249, 250, 252.
353. Bürckel himself was the son of a craftsman. From 1926 to 1944 he was Gau leader of Gau Rhineland-Palatinate, extended in 1935 to Gau 'Saarpfalz' and in 1942 to Gau 'Westmark'. See biographical data in Hüttenberger, p. 213.
354. Mason, *Social Policy*, p. 254; compare also Recker, pp. 128–54. There is now available important documentation by T. Harlander and G. Fehl (ed.) on housing policy. See my review in *Süddeutsche Zeitung* No 97 of 28 April 1987.
355. BA/NS 26/54, f. 203, speech on 9 November 1927 (also pub. in *VB* of 11 November 1927).
356. BA/NL Streicher, No 125, f. 3 *et seq.*, speech on 30 November 1928.
357. *VB* No 105 of 15 April 1931, speech on 12 April 1931.
358. Speech to the DAF on 10 May 1933, in 'Young Germany Wants Work and Peace', p. 55.
359. Compare Chapter VI.1.b of the present study.
360. Speech on the opening of the third Winter Help Campaign 1935/36, in 'Führer Speeches to the Winter Help Campaign 1933–1936', p. 12 *et seq.*
361. Compare Chapter IV.4 of the present study.
362. Speech on 16 December 1925, *VB* special issue, BayHStA, collection of press clippings 1172; similarly BA/NS 26/54, f. 168, speech on 17 June 1927.
363. BA/NL Streicher, No 126, f. 28, speech on 13 November 1930; similarly speech at the *Reichsparteitag* on 11 September 1937, brochure, p. 70.
364. Domarus, p. 694 *et seq.*, interview with Abel Bonnard on 20 May 1937.
365. Compare the statements on p. 450 *et seq.* in 'Final Considerations' of the present study.
366. *Monologues*, p. 65, entry for 22/23 September 1941.
367. *Ibid.*, p. 72 *et seq.*, entry for 27/28 September 1941.
368. Picker, p. 289, entry for 12 May 1942.
369. *Ibid.*, p. 297, entry for 14 May 1942.
370. Schoenbaum, p. 151.
371. Picker, p. 477, entry for 28 July 1942.
372. Domarus, p. 1874, speech on 26 April 1942.
373. Herbst, p. 190.
374. *Ibid.*, pp. 193, 205, 207.
375. Compare Schoenbaum, p. 226 *et seq.*
376. Rupp, p. 26.
377. Goebbels, cited in Winkler, *Female Labour*, p. 48.
378. *Ibid.*
379. Prinz, p. 334. In his work Prinz comes to very similar conclusions as does this study. In contrast to previously accepted interpretations, he stresses that 'in the end the complete relinquishing of status considerations, as well as the relative liquidation of the "collar line" caused by the increased advancement of workers into salaried positions, was not only the result of "natural" requirements of war. What becomes clear is that the party and the labour front in particular made use of the more stringent requirements of war as a vehicle for the social demand of the levelling of the differences between hourly and salaried employees.' (*ibid.*, p. 279 *et seq.*) Labour policy of the regime was therefore 'only explainable to a minor part by the exigencies

Hitler: The Policies of Seduction

of rearmament' (*ibid.*, p. 322). Based on these results, Prinz also came to a rejection of the thesis of the contradiction between allegedly 'archaic objectives' and 'modern means' in the policy of National Socialism (*ibid.*, pp. 325, 336).
380. Domarus, p. 300, speech on 13 September 1933.
381. *Ibid.*, p. 376, speech on 17 April 1934.
382. Speech on the opening of the Winter Help Campaign 1934/35 on 9 October 1934, in 'Führer Speeches to the Winter Help Campaign 1933–1936', p. 6 *et seq.*
383. Speech on the opening of the third Winter Help Campaign 1935/36, *ibid.*, p. 14 *et seq.*
384. *IB* 5th year set, issue 6 of 8 February 1930, p. 85.
385. Domarus, p. 162, letter of 2 December 1932 to Reichenau.
386. Domarus, p. 261, speech on 1 May 1933.
387. Speech in the *Reichstag* on 30 January 1939, brochure, p. 15.
388. Wagener, p. 135 (statement by Hitler *circa* September 1930).
389. Compare p. 88 of the present study.
390. *VB* No 185 of 4 July 1933, speech on 2 July 1933; italics in *VB*.
391. Domarus, p. 288, speech on 9 July 1933. Similarly proclamation at the opening of the *Reichsparteitag* on 1 September 1933, brochure, p. 15; and *VB* No 135 of 11 November 1933, speech on 10 November 1933.
392. *VB* No 127 of 3 May 1934, address on the occasion of a visit to the Reichs Chancellory on 1 May 1933 by workers' representatives.
393. *VB* No 249 of 6 September 1934, speech on 5 September 1934.
394. Proclamation at the opening of the *Reichsparteitag* on 11 September 1935, brochure, p. 25 *et seq.*
395. *Ibid.*, p. 80 *et seq.*, closing address on 16 September 1935; italics in original.
396. Speech at the 4th annual convention of the DAF, *Reichsparteitag* on 12 September 1936, brochure, p. 54; italics in original.
397. *Ibid.*, p. 78, closing address on 14 September 1936; italics in original.
398. Speech on 6 October 1936 to the fourth Winter Help Campaign, in 'Führer Speeches to the Winter Help Campaign 1933–1936', p. 28.
399. Speech in the *Reichstag* on 30 January 1937, brochure, p. 25.
400. Kotze and Krausnick, p. 85, speech on 24 February 1937.
401. *VB* No 123 of 3 May 1937, speech on 1 May 1937.
402. Speech to the DAF at the *Reichsparteitag* on 11 September 1937, brochure, p. 68 *et seq.*
403. Speech on 5 October 1937 to the opening of the Winter Help Campaign 1937/38, in 'Führer Speeches to the Winter Help Campaign 1937 and 1938', p. 4 *et seq.*; italics in the original.
404. Domarus, p. 855, speech on 1 May 1938.
405. Speech at the *Reichsparteitag* on 9 September 1938, brochure, p. 52.
406. Domarus, p. 1581, speech on 4 September 1940; our italics.
407. Bouhler I/II, p. 338, speech on 10 December 1940.
408. Picker, p. 378, entry for 23 June 1942.
409. Mason, *Social Policy*, p. 24.
410. *Ibid.*, p. 25.
411. Notes by Quartermaster-General of the Army, General of Artillery Eduard Wagner, cited in Mason, *Social Policy*, p. 25.
412. *MGM* 2/76, p. 160, speech on 26 May 1944.
413. *Complete Recordings*, p. 168, speech on 1 August 1920.
414. Preiss, p. 83, speech on 21 August 1927.

415. Domarus, p. 1367, speech on 10 October 1939. On 4 September 1940 Goebbels called the war the 'great equalizer'. On 17 November 1942 he declared, 'This war is the continuation of our revolution. This war has a social character. *It* will primarily give us the opportunity to complete what we mean by *socialism*'. The revolution had, said Goebbels on 9 July 1943, 'removed the differences between the classes and levels of education of our nation in a great melting process. The longer the war lasts, the more it makes us all equal.' Goebbels, *Speeches*, vol. 2, pp. 48, 156, 251. Italics in the speech.
416. Domarus, p. 1922, speech on 30 September 1942.
417. *Ibid.*, p. 1941, speech on 8 November 1942.

IV. Hitler's Central Objective: The Revolutionizing of Politics and Economics and the Restructuring of the Economic System

1. Bullock, *Hitler*, p. 384. Lochner writes in his study published in 1955 that 'Hitler never seriously occupied himself with economic matters' (Lochner, p. 31). Similarly Kroll, p. 424; Fischer, p. 31 *et seq.*; and Ludwig, p. 75. Blaich (1971) also still writes that 'the leading man of the party, Adolf Hitler, had scant interest in problems of business and economic policy' (Blaich, p. 7). Milward (1975) believes that 'the *Führer* himself, together with the leading men of his regime, had precious little understanding and respect for economic policy, and in fact tended not to accept its conditions and to doubt the applicability of the solutions it offered' (Milward, p. 456). It was therefore a 'paradox', says Milward, 'that Hitler, who knew virtually nothing about economics, decided in favour of a strategy [the *Blitzkrieg* strategy—R.Z.] which was economically so successful' (Milward, p. 462). Turner believes that Hitler had 'never achieved even a basic understanding of political economy' and that his relationship to economic questions had been marked by 'a lack of knowledge' (Turner, *Big Business*, p. 92).
2. For this economic programme compare Kroll, p. 426 *et seq.*; and Barkai, *Economic System*, p. 37 *et seq.*
3. Letter from Schacht to Hitler on 29 August 1932, cited in Barkai, *Economic System*, p. 41.
4. Meeting of ministers on 8 February 1933, Files of the RK, p. 55.
5. Compare p. 222 *et seq.* of the present study.
6. Guillebaud, Claude William, *The Economic Recovery of Germany from 1933 to the Incorporation of Austria in March 1938* (London, 1939), p. 101, cited here in Grotkopp, p. 314.
7. This argument is, for example, used by Erbe, p. 23 *et seq.*
8. Grotkopp, p. 287.
9. See also the deviating opinion by Erbe, p. 167.
10. Barkai, *Economic System*, p. 9. Similarly also Schoenbaum, p. 150; and Haffner, pp. 30–4.
11. By J. D. Heyl.
12. Compare Turner, *Hitler's View*; Barkai, *Economic View*; Barkai, *Social Darwinism*; Krüger; Herbst (particularly pp. 84–92); and Teichert, pp. 206, 218.
13. Krüger, p. 263.
14. *Ibid.*, p. 282. Compare Turner, *Hitler's View*, p. 89 *et seq.*; Barkai, *Social Darwinism*, p. 416; Herbst, p. 25 *et seq.*; and Teichert, p. 206 *et seq.*
15. Important points of departure can be found in the contributions by Barkai, Krüger, Herbst and Teichert.

16. Wagener, p. 112 *et seq.*
17. Speech in the *Reichstag* on 30 January 1937, brochure, p. 20.
18. Kotze and Krausnick, p. 185 *et seq.*, speech on 20 May 1937.
19. Speech in the *Reichstag* on 30 January 1939, brochure, p. 34 *et seq.*
20. Conversation with Cudahy on 23 May 1941, Hillgruber, *Statesmen I*, p. 556.
21. *Monologues*, p. 88 *et seq.*, entry for 15 October 1941. The final remark refers to the dissertation of former Reichs Foreign Minister Gustav Stresemann, who had obtained his PhD in 1900 with a thesis on 'The Development of the Bottled Beer Market in Berlin'.
22. Schacht, cited here in Bullock, *Hitler*, p. 363. In their Hitler biography, Görlitz and Quint attribute to Hitler 'a sometimes admirable, sometimes fatal tendency in this day and age of specialization and fragmentation of the sciences . . . to reduce all problems to a simple denominator' (p. 482).
23. Domarus, p. 580, interview on 21 February 1936. In his speech on 20 May 1937 in Berchtesgaden to construction workers about National Socialist economic policy, Hitler said: 'And for me it is a stroke of great luck when I am again given the opportunity to return to where I came from, namely to the people. And it is also wonderful for me to speak to the broad masses, to the unsophisticated people, because that forces one to express problems that are in themselves complicated in very simple terms, and because one is then forced to think in simple terms oneself, and because this simple way of thinking is a base for all true insights.' (Kotze and Krausnick, p. 184).
24. *Monologues*, p. 139, entry for 12 November 1941.
25. *Ibid.*, p. 256, entry for 2 February 1942.
26. Speech on 30 May 1942, printed in appendix to Picker, p. 499.
27. Otto von Zwiedineck-Südenhorst, 1871–1957, from 1921 professor of economics at the University of Munich.
28. *Monologues*, p. 411 *et seq.*, entry for 19 May 1944.
29. On this point compare the studies by Kroll and Grotkopp.
30. Barkai draws attention to the fact that Feder's theory or suggestions are 'not at all "warped" as is normally assumed'. He shares the view expressed previously by Gustav Stolper that 'Schacht hardly did anything else besides adopting Feder's ideas to the orthodoxies of the existing monetary system' (Stolper, cited in Barkai, *Economic Concept*, p. 6; also Barkai, *Economic System*, p. 28 *et seq.*).
31. Compare *MK*, p. 228 *et seq.*; and p. 268 *et seq.* of the present study.
32. Pollock, *State Capitalism*, p. 88; Pollock, *New Order*, p. 124.
33. Compare Mason, *Primacy*.
34. Compare Barkai, *Social Darwinism*, p. 407 *et seq.*; and Herbst, p. 78 *et seq.*
35. Turner, *Hitler's View*, p. 90. Barkai has quite rightly rejected this interpretation and critically remarked that 'contempt . . . was a somewhat misleading term' because Hitler had been 'well aware of the importance of business' and had not underestimated it at all (Barkai, *Social Darwinism*, p. 407).
36. *Complete Recordings*, p. 836, speech on 26 February 1923.
37. *Ibid.*, p. 913, speech on 24 April 1923.
38. *Ibid.*, p. 992, appeal of 2 September 1923.
39. *Ibid.*, p. 1020, speech on 30 September 1923.
40. *Ibid.*, p. 1218, article of April 1924.
41. *MK*, pp. 164 *et seq.*, 166 *et seq.*, 255 *et seq.*, 362, 427.
42. Speech on 16 December 1925, *VB* special issue 'The Social Mission of National Socialism', BayHStA, collection of press clippings 1172.

43. Jochmann, *In Battle*, p. 87 *et seq.*, speech on 28 February 1926.
44. BA/NS 26/54, f. 150, speech on 26 March 1927 (also compare *ibid.*, f. 160).
45. *VB* special issue 87a of 15/16 April 1927, speech on 13 April 1927, BayHStA, collection of press clippings 1172. Compare Hitler's secret brochure for industrialists (August 1927) in Turner, *Fascism and Capitalism*, here p. 56.
46. *VB* No 91 of 19 April 1928, speech on 17 April 1928.
47. *ZB*, p.61; similarly *ibid.*, p. 124.
48. That is, in the *Bürgerbräukeller* in Munich on 8/9 November 1923 when Hitler carried out his attempted *putsch*.
49. BA/NS 26/55, f. 138, speech on 9 November 1928.
50. BA/NL Streicher, No 125. f. 16, speech on 30 November 1928.
51. BA/NS 26/55, f. 162 *et seq.*, speech on 7 December 1928.
52. BA/NL Streicher, No 125, f. 8, speech on 8 December 1928.
53. BA/NS 26/56, f. 18, 25 *et seq.*, speech on 6 March 1929.
54. *VB* No 281, speech on 29 November 1929.
55. *IB* 5th year set, issue 17 of 26 April 1930, p. 261.
56. Domarus, p. 227, speech on 21 March 1933.
57. *Ibid.*, p. 233, speech on 23 March 1933.
58. Speech in the *Reichstag* on 30 January 1934, brochure, pp. 22, 30.
59. *VB* No 127 of 3 May 1934, speech on 1 May 1934.
60. Speech at the *Reichsparteitag* on 11 September 1935, brochure, p. 40 *et seq.*
61. Memorandum, August 1936, *VjHfZg* (1955), p. 208.
62. Compare Chapter IV.5 of the present study.
63. Speech at the *Reichsparteitag* on 9 September 1936, brochure, pp. 16, 26, 37.
64. Kotze and Krausnick, p. 136 *et seq.*, speech on 29 April 1937.
65. *VB* No 90 of 31 March 1938, speech on 30 March 1938.
66. Koeppen Notes, report No 46 of 18 October 1941.
67. *Monologues*, p. 118, entry for 1 November 1941.
68. Goebbels, Diaries, SF, vol. 4, p. 98, entry for 5 April 1940.
69. Bouhler I/II, p. 324, speech on 14 November 1940.
70. Cited in Kissenkoetter, p. 61.
71. Bouhler I/II, p. 345, speech on 10 December 1940.
72. *Monologues*, p. 118 *et seq.*, entry for 1 November 1941. Stanley Baldwin, 1867–1947, came from British heavy industry and was Prime Minister from 1935 to 1937. Neville Chamberlain, 1869–1940, was an industrialist and Prime Minister from 1937 to 1940. The claim that these men were interested in a war with Germany for business reasons, or that for Britain the war had purely capitalist interest, was constantly repeated by Hitler and also played an important role in propaganda. See Domarus, p. 1359 (19 September 1939); *ibid.*, p. 1441 (1 January 1940); *ibid.*, p. 1525 (15 June 1940); *ibid.*, p. 1541 *et seq.* (19 July 1940); *ibid.*, pp. 1577, 1580 (4 September 1940); *ibid.*, p. 1772 (8 November 1941); *ibid.*, p. 1906 (1 September 1942); *ibid.*, p. 1943 (8 November 1942); *ibid.*, p. 2056 (8 November 1943); *ibid.*, p. 2237 (29 April 1945); Bouhler I/II, p. 314 (8 November 1940); *ibid.*, pp. 346–52 (10 December 1940); *ibid.*, pp. 368–76 (1 January 1941); *ibid.*, pp. 398, 401 (30 January 1941); Bouhler III, pp. 22, 24 (4 May 1941); *ibid.*, pp. 159, 161 (31 December 1941); *Monologues*, p. 93 (15 October 1941); *ibid.*, p. 119 (1 November 1941); *ibid.*, p. 379 (31 August 1942); Picker, p. 401 (1 July 1942); Hillgruber, *Statesmen II*, p. 277 (29 April 1943); and *ibid.* p. 422 (22 April 1944).
73. Picker, p. 139, entry for 24 March 1942.
74. *Ibid.*, p. 171, entry for 31 March 1942.

75. *Ibid.*, p. 212, entry for 10 April 1942.
76. *Ibid.*, p. 467, entry for 26 July 1942.
77. Mommsen, *National Socialism*, p. 702.
78. Irving, *Hitler's War*, p. xi: 'My conclusion on completing the research startled even me: while Adolf Hitler was a powerful and relentless military commander, the war years saw him as a lax and indecisive political leader who allowed affairs of state to rot. In fact he was probably the weakest *leader* Germany has known in this century.'; p. xv: 'My central conclusion, however, is that Hitler was a less than omnipotent *Führer* and that his grip on his immediate subordinates weakened as the war progressed.'
79. Attention should be drawn here to what in our view are justified objections, particularly as formulated by K. Hildebrand. See his contributions *NS without Hitler?*; *Monocracy or Polycracy?*; and *Hitlerism*.
80. Picker, pp. 467–70, entry for 26 July 1942.
81. Decrees by the Party Office, vol. 1, p. 20 *et seq.*, circular letter 124/42. Compare also circular letter of 30 September 1942, R/152/42, *ibid.* p. 21 *et seq.*, in which the 'acceptance of favours' is forbidden by 'the *Führer* of the movement' and in this context, for example, a warning is issued against accepting invitations to go hunting etc.
82. Decrees by the Party Office, vol. 4, p. 14 *et seq.*, here p. 16.
83. Cited in Herbst, p. 270.
84. *Ibid.*, Ohlendorf to Himmler on 16 October 1942, cited in Herbst, p. 270.
85. Hüttenberger, p. 200.
86. Turner, *Hitler's View*, p. 95.
87. Barkai, *Social Darwinism*, pp. 408–12.
88. Wagener, p. 321 (September 1931).
89. *Ibid.*, p. 479 (spring 1932).
90. *Ibid.*, p. 116 (early summer 1930). Compare elsewhere, where Wagener reports similar statements by Hitler: p. 183 (autumn 1930); p. 206 (autumn 1930?); p. 298 *et seq.* (1931); p. 335 (1931); and p. 415 (January 1932).
91. *Ibid.*, p. 208 *et seq.* (autumn 1930).
92. *Ibid.*, p. 443 (not dated).
93. *Ibid.*, p. 215 (September 1930).
94. *Ibid.*, p. 204 (autumn 1930).
95. *Ibid.*, p. 292 *et seq.*, (1931).
96. *Ibid.*, p. 268 (early 1931).
97. *Ibid.*, p. 291 (1931).
98. *Ibid.*, p. 353 (June 1930).
99. *Ibid.*, p. 106 (early summer 1930).
100. BA/NL Streicher, No 126, f. 16, speech on 13 November 1930.
101. *VB* No 138 of 18 May 1934, speech on 16 May 1934.
102. Speech in the *Reichstag* on 21 May 1935, in *VB* No 142 of 22 May 1935.
103. *VB* of 7 October 1935, speech on 6 October 1935.
104. Memorandum to the Four-Year Plan, in *VjHfZg* (1955), p. 209.
105. Speech at the *Reichsparteitag* on 9 September 1936, brochure, p. 37.
106. Opening proclamation at the *Reichsparteitag* on 9 September 1936, brochure, pp. 17, 20 *et seq.*
107. Speech in the *Reichstag* on 30 January 1937, brochure, p. 21 *et seq.*
108. *VB* No 52 of 21 February 1937, speech on 20 February 1937.
109. Ludwig, p. 163.

110. Opening proclamation at the *Reichsparteitag* on 7 September 1937, brochure, p. 20 et seq.
111. Frank, p. 367 (May 1938).
112. *VB* No 122 of 2 May 1938, speech on 1 May 1938.
113. The index of wholesale prices rose between 1933 and 1938 as follows: in Germany 16 per cent, in Great Britain 30 per cent and in the United States 34 per cent. See Hardach, p. 77, n. 18.
114. *Ibid.*, p. 77.
115. Hardach is objecting to Fischer's thesis, who wrote in his study 'German Economic Policy 1918–1945' published in 1968: 'It is one of the paradoxes of the National Socialist era that the leadership of the state had no concept for the ordering of this economy which it so strongly abused, but that for twelve years it experimented without system and senselessly tried this and that, so that those concerned never found any peace.' (Fischer, p. 77). Based on the results of our study, this view can no longer be upheld in this form.
116. Hardach, p. 80 *et seq.*
117. Conversation on 25 November 1940 with the Italian Minister of Justice Grandi, Hillgruber, *Statesmen I*, p. 373.
118. *Monologues*, p. 50, entry for 27/28 July 1941.
119. *Ibid.*, p. 56, entry for 8–11 August 1941; our italics.
120. Picker, p. 419, entry for 5 July 1942; our italics.
121. Goebbels, Diaries, SF, vol. 3, p. 641, entry for 14 November 1939.
122. Picker, p. 452, entry for 22 July 1942.
123. Scheidt, *Post-war Recordings*, IfZ Munich, pp. 24, 310 *et seq.*, 666 *et seq.*
124. Conversation with Mussolini on 22 April 1944, Hillgruber, *Statesmen II*, p. 422 *et seq.*
125. Dietrich, p. 188.
126. Speer, p. 369. The fear industry had about the extension of a system of planned economy that Speer reports on was also reinforced by several statements of the party. Herbst, for example, writes that the *Völkische Beobachter*, the central organ of the NSDAP, 'occasionally appeared to be not far removed from the idea a planned economy' (Herbst, p. 329). Herbst also cites from an article in the *VB* of 19 August 1944: 'What is the sense today, when we are aspiring to new forms of the economy, of sitting like Iphigenia on Taurian shores and pining for the memories of the past. Economic forms are nothing more than a function of the amount of production, and since we are aspiring to a new dimension of production we must accept new economic forms.' (Herbst, p. 330). Herbst formulates the misgivings many industrialists had in view of the increasing state direction during the war: '. . . were not many industrialists being set aside by the means of power of the state, which could lead to the beginning of an expropriation? And was private property still secure, simply because a nationalization was not taking place? Was not a form of state economy announcing itself in this economic system under state control, which could renounce nationalization because it no longer needed it?' (Herbst, p. 328). The enforced closing down of companies within the framework of 'total war' also nourished such fears among small businessmen. While on the one hand assurances were given that these factories could re-open after the war, on the other the suspicion that in fact 'the war was being used as a motor for social changes' kept receiving new nourishment (Herbst, p. 224). On 14 February 1943, for example, an article appeared in the periodical *Das Reich* with the provocative title: 'Shops under the Magnifying Glass'. It said, among other things, that 'not all the owners of the companies closed down could expect that their factories

would open again after the war' (cited in Herbst, p. 224).
127. The dating to early June 1944 found in Kotze and Krausnick (p. 335 *et seq.*) and Domarus (p. 2112) is incorrect. Compare Herbst, p. 333, n. 324.
128. Speer, p. 369.
129. Kotze and Krausnick, p. 337 *et seq.*, speech on 26 June 1944.
130. *Ibid.*, pp. 341–3.
131. Speer, p. 369 *et seq.*; our italics.
132. Kotze and Krausnick, p. 336, speech on 26 June 1944.
133. *Ibid.*, p. 348.
134. Speer, p. 371. Herbst misinterprets Hitler's speech on 26 June 1944 to industrialists in the armaments industry. In Hitler's statements he sees a 'clear rejection of a planned economy' and states that he, like Ohlendorf (Ministry of Economics) and Speer, believed that 'the German economic order in the post-war era should be based on private ownership and private initiative' (Herbst, p. 337). In contrast to this, Speer quite rightly pointed out that Hitler's avowal of a free economy had been 'unclear', and that the speech had not fulfilled its purpose, namely to soothe the fears of the industrialists about the extension of the system of planned economy after the end of the war. Herbst objects to this and states: 'Hitler clearly avowed his commitment to private property as the base for the future economic order and announced in the case of a German victory that "the private initiative of the German economy will experience its greatest era" (Herbst, p. 335). Since Herbst does not take into account that the only purpose of this speech was to dispel the fears of the industrialists, he finds it 'strange' that Hitler refused, against Speer's request, to have the speech published: 'It must remain unclear whether it was the linguistic condition of the speech or its content which made it disappear in the safe.' (Herbst, p. 335). In our view, however, this is neither 'unclear' nor 'strange', any more than the fact that Hitler frequently committed slips of the tongue and did not concentrate. In contrast to his usual custom, he had not completely prepared the speech himself but had primarily kept to Speer's notes. Herbst also contradicts himself fundamentally when he claims on the one hand that Hitler favoured a reduction of state intervention after the war (Herbst, p. 128 *et seq.*) and was serious in his support of a free economy after the war, but writes, on the other hand, that a National Socialist government 'could hardly have taken the road into a free economy, even if it had wished to attempt this – something which cannot be assumed with any certainty' (Herbst, p. 433; also compare p. 459). While there were intentions within the Ministry of Economics to reduce state direction after the war, the criticism by Ohlendorf – who had held an important position in the ministry from December 1943 on – shows that his middle class ideology had nothing in common with Hitler's concept of National Socialism. Ohlendorf laments, for instance, that in all aspects of life the individual was being 'equated' to the soldier, he criticizes the uniformity of life, the orientation of production to requirements, 'norming' and mass production, as well as, fundamentally, that in the system of planned economy the individual 'was being subordinated to the economy' (see Herbst, p. 286 *et seq.*).
135. Domarus, p. 2196, speech on 30 January 1945.
136. *Testament*, p. 106, dictation of 24 February 1945.
137. Barkai, *Economic System*, p. 10 *et seq.*
138. *Ibid.*, p. 56.
139. *Ibid.*, p. 139; also Kroll, pp. 477–96.
140. *Ibid.*, p. 155 *et seq.*
141. Petzina, pp. 159–63.

142. The forms of control of the economy are described in detail in Kroll, pp. 539–61; Petzina, pp. 153–77; and Blaich, pp. 10–18.
143. Compare Petzina, p. 10; and Barkai, *Economic System*, p. 171 *et seq.*
144. Barkai, *Economic System*, p. 177.
145. *Ibid.*, pp. 59–86.
146. Compare Sombart, *Future*, p. 18 *et seq.*
147. Compare table in Barkai, *Economic System*, p. 179.
148. Broszat, *State*, p. 378.
149. Compare Turner, *Hitler's View*, pp. 95 *et seq.*, 103 *et seq.*
150. Here Pollock is discussing the views expressed by Franz L. Neumann and A. R. L. Gurland. See their contributions in Horkheimer and Pollock, *Economy, Law and the State under National Socialism*.
151. Pollock, *New Order*, p. 113.
152. Compare Turner, *Hitler's View*, p. 103 *et seq.*
153. *Complete Recordings*, p. 177, speech on 7 August 1920.
154. *Ibid.*, p. 206 *et seq.*, speech on 25 August 1920.
155. *Ibid.*, p. 213; also p. 217.
156. *Ibid.*, p. 252, speech on 26 October 1920.
157. *Ibid.*, p. 520, circular of 19 November 1921.
158. *Ibid.*, p. 521 *et seq.*, information leaflet of 19 November 1921.
159. *Ibid.*, p. 941, speech on 1 July 1923.
160. *Ibid.*, p. 945, speech on 6 July 1923.
161. *Ibid.*, p. 915, speech on 27 April 1923.
162. *Ibid.*, p. 660, speech on 28 July 1922; similarly *ibid.*, p. 719, speech on 2 November 1922; *ibid.*, p. 799, article of 25 January 1923; and *ibid.*, p. 1219, article of April 1924.
163. *Ibid.*, p. 992, appeal on 2 September 1923.
164. Goebbels, Diary, 25/26, p. 72, entry for 13 April 1926. Turner believes that it was quite possible that Hitler had deliberately exaggerated his position in order to tie Goebbels, whose left-wing convictions he was familiar with, to him. It is also conceivable that Goebbels, being influenced by his own wishful thinking, attributed more far-reaching concepts to Hitler than he actually had. While this can certainly not be excluded, Turner does admit that 'There remains the remarkable discrepancy between Hitler's noticeable efforts not to address himself to concrete socio-economic questions in public and his obvious willingness to at least discuss radical changes within his private circle.' (Turner, *Hitler's View*, p. 112 *et seq.*).
165. Goebbels, Diary, 25/26, p. 92, entry for 23 July 1926.
166. Compare BA/NS 26/55, f. 26, speech on 18 September 1928; *VB* special issue, speech on 10 October 1928, BayHStA, collection of press clippings 1172; BA/NS 26/55, f. 68, speech on 18 October 1928; and *IB* of 22 December 1928.
167. Wagener, p. 107 (early summer 1930).
168. Strasser, pp. 65, 67, conversation on 22 May 1930.
169. Schumann interprets the respective clause of the law as follows: 'The entrepreneur was given far-reaching powers within his own company so that the various companies could be more easily employed via their management for the realization of National Socialist economic objectives.' (Schumann, p. 122).
170. Blaich, p. 18, n. 133 with mention of sources.
171. Turner, *Big Business*, p. 86 *et seq.*
172. *Ibid.*, pp. 87 *et seq.*, 157 *et seq.*, 164 *et seq.*
173. *Ibid.*, p. 87.

174. *Ibid.*, p. 122.
175. *Ibid.*, p. 142 *et seq.*
176. On the effect of the speech see the critical analysis by Turner, *Fascism and Capitalism*, p. 96 *et seq.*; and Turner, *Big Business*, p. 264 *et seq.*
177. Domarus, p. 72 *et seq.*, speech on 26 January 1932. Nolte, who in his 'European Civil War', underlines the importance of anti-Communism in Hitler's *Weltanschauung* very one-sidedly, cites this statement as clear proof that 'Hitler's ideology was primarily negatively determined by his opposition to the Soviet Union and Communism.' (Nolte, *Civil War*, p. 217). Just like Marxist authors who have always interpreted this speech as proof of Hitler's pro-capitalist views, Nolte takes Hitler's speech out of its context and overlooks the fact that it was not Hitler's intention to disclose his *Weltanschauung* to the industrialists but to reduce the reservations they had as a result of the anti-capitalist propaganda of the NSDAP.
178. Domarus, pp. 231–7, speech on 23 March 1933.
179. Closing address at the *Reichsparteitag* on 3 September 1933, brochure, p. 35: 'Because it is illogical to declare private property to be morally justified because the ability to achieve is not equal in human beings due to their different talents, and therefore the results of these individual achievements are so different that in their administration one has to consider the ability to achieve, but then on the other hand to claim an equal ability for all in the total administration of life, in the field of politics.'
180. Speech on 9 October 1934 at the opening of the Winter Help Campaign 1934/35, in '*Führer* Speeches to the Winter Help Campaigns 1933–1936', p. 7 *et seq.*
181. Bouhler I/II, p. 324, speech on 14 November 1940. For the underlying facts see Barkai, *Economic System*, p. 157 *et seq.*
182. Bouhler I/II, p. 345, speech on 10 December 1940.
183. *Monologues*, p. 385, entry for 3 September 1942.
184. Kotze and Krausnick, p. 339, speech on 26 June 1944; our italics.
185. *VB* No 343 of 9 December 1935, speech on 26 June 1935; our italics.
186. Memorandum on the Four-Year Plan, August 1936, *VjHfZg* (1955), p. 209.
187. Lochner, p. 211 *et seq.*
188. Goebbels, Diaries, SF, vol. 3, p. 80.
189. *Ibid.*, p. 81.
190. *Ibid.*, p. 257.
191. Kotze and Krausnick, p. 199 *et seq.*, speech on 20 May 1937.
192. Petzina, p. 102 *et seq.*
193. Cited in *ibid.*, p. 104.
194. *Ibid.*, p. 104 *et seq.*
195. Kotze and Krausnick, p. 201, speech on 20 May 1937.
196. *Ibid.*, p. 201 *et seq.*; Speer, p. 218.
197. Cited in Kluke, p. 348.
198. *Ibid.*, p. 352. Compare the biography by Herbert A. Quint (pseudonym von Frankenberg): *Porsche: The Way of an Era* (Stuttgart, 1951), p. 190 *et seq.*
199. *VB* No 49 of 18 February 1939, speech on 17 February 1939.
200. Quint, *Porsche*, p. 191.
201. Goebbels, Diary, 42/43 (Lochner), p. 86, entry for 14 February 1942.
202. Picker, p. 136, entry for 24 March 1942; our italics.
203. Bucharin, *Theory of Subjective Values*, p. 23 *et seq.*; italics in the original.
204. Picker, p. 138 *et seq.*, entry for 24 March 1942.
205. *Ibid.*, p. 141, entry for 25 March 1942, countersigned by Bormann.

206. *Ibid.*, p. 461 *et seq.*, entry for 26 July 1942.
207. Compare Ludwig, p. 181.
208. Ludwig, p. 182, also points out the contradiction between the two statements.
209. Note of 21 October 1942 by Himmler, cited in Georg, p. 146.
210. Report by Staff W about the organization and assignment of Office Group W, July 1944, cited in Georg, p. 145.
211. Georg, p. 146.
212. *Complete Recordings*, p. 193, speech on 13 August 1920.
213. *Ibid.*
214. The confusion of terms with Hitler becomes clear in a speech on 19 November 1920, for example, in which he equates 'employer' with 'brain worker' and 'employee' with 'manual worker'. *Complete Recordings*, p. 259; similarly, *ibid.*, p. 912, speech on 24 April 1923.
215. *Complete Recordings*, p. 220, speech on 31 August 1920.
216. *Ibid.*, p. 689, speech on 10 September 1922. Similarly *ibid.*, p. 328, speech on 28 February 1921; and *ibid.*, p. 405, article of 22 May 1921.
217. *Ibid.*, p. 741, notes for a speech on 22 November 1922.
218. Picker, p. 136, entry on 24 March 1942.
219. *MK*, pp. 228–34.
220. So also the interpretation of this statement from *Mein Kampf* in Fischer, p. 53 *et seq.*
221. *Complete Recordings*, p. 526, letter of 29 November 1921 to an unknown.
222. Hitler claims this in *Mein Kampf*, p. 234. He repeats his claim to having read Marx's central work in a speech on 26 May 1944, and even states that he had gone through it several times, although 'its whole weakness' had become clear to him (compare speech in *MGM* 2/76, p. 146). Without wishing to underestimate Hitler's intellectual abilities, we must doubt this.
223. Wagener, p. 257.
224. Ziegler, p. 15.

V. Hitler: An Opponent of Modern Industrial Society? Modernistic and Anti-Modernistic Elements in Hitler's *Weltanschauung*

1. Turner, *Fascism and Anti-Modernism*, p. 164.
2. Turner, *Hitler's View*, p. 93. This interpretation has been widely accepted in research and even forms the basis of various comparisons between National Socialism and other 'Fascisms'. Bernd Martin, for example, writes in an essay in which he compares the Italian, German and Japanese systems that Hitler's 'objective of a reagrarianization of the whole society on the base of conquered *Lebensraum*' had been a specific aim of National Socialism (Martin, p. 61; compare p. 62). Time and again a 'basic contradiction' is assumed, which allegedly consisted of 'wanting to carry out a pre-modern utopia of racial-agrarian world domination, but with the means of modern big technology and the organizational form of big industry' (Dülffer, p. 193). In his study, L. Herbst was the first to cast doubts upon this thesis (see Herbst, p. 86, n. 252, p. 88). Herbst is not able, however, to prove his thesis that the conquest of *Lebensraum* had not served reagrarianization from the sources, but states that – based on Hitler's objective of restructuring society and industry in such a way that they would be capable of waging war at any time – it was simply 'improbable' that he had pursued the objective of the reagrarianization of the Reich. The argument that the objective of

reagrarianization stipulated by Turner was 'improbable based on Hitler's thought premises' (Herbst, p. 88) is, of course, not sufficient to refute this thesis, since it is possible that certain of Hitler's objectives and premises contradicted each other and he did not follow his own logic.

3. Turner, *Fascism and Anti-Modernism*, p. 166.
4. Turner, *Hitler's View*, p. 94. See also Turner, *Big Business*, p. 96: 'His [Hitler's] concept of economic autarky remained restricted and archaic in its fixation on agriculture. The infinite and enormously valuable industrial resources which the exccecution of his grandiose plan of conquest would have provided for Germany were at best of secondary importance to him. During the years in which Hitler aspired to the rule of one of the most highly developed industrial countries in the world, agriculture held the top position in his considerations for the future.'
5. Compare, for example, *MK*, p. 726 *et seq.*; *VB* special issue, speech on 16 December 1925, BayHStA, collection of press clippings 1172; Hitler's secret brochure for industrialists (1927) in Turner, *Fascism and Capitalism*, here p. 51 *et seq.*; *ZB*, p. 53 *et seq.*; BA/NS 26/55, f. 44, speech on 18 September 1928; *VB* special issue, speech on 10 October 1928, BayHStA, collection of press clippings 1172; BA/NS 26/55, f. 65 *et seq.*, speech on 18 October 1928; Preiss, p. 129 *et seq.* (30 November 1929); BA/NS 26/57, f. 9 *et seq.*, speech on 31 August 1930; STA Erlangen III.220.H.1., f. 5 *et seq.*, speech on 3 July 1931; Kotze and Krausnick, p. 189 *et seq.*, speech on 20 May 1937; and Picker, p. 495 *et seq.* (appendix, speech on 30 May 1942). See also the discussion of this theory of Hitler's in Jäckel, *Weltanschauung*, p. 104 *et seq.*
6. Characteristic of this way of looking at things is an article by Hitler on 29 December 1928 in which he analyzes the reasons for the current border conflict between Bolivia and Paraguay: 'As is almost always the case, here too the superficial reasons assume a relatively minor character. This is a conflict about borders which, however, are only to be regarded as the ultimate trigger for a conflict that goes far deeper. Bolivia is cut off from the sea by Paraguay. This is the reason for a devaluation of the extraordinarily great amount of natural resources available in Bolivia. These consist not only of minerals, but also of oil reserves, and in such enormous dimensions that it becomes understandable why it is primarily American capital which appears here as the interested party.' (*IB* 3rd year set, issue 32 of 29 December 1928, p. 392). To Wagener Hitler said that 'in modern times . . . wars are again the result of economic conflicts of interest' (Wagener, p. 203). Characteristic of Hitler's belief in the economic causality of war was also his fear, as expressed to Wagener, that, in the case of a failure of Roosevelt's economic policy, America would be forced into a 'policy of economic imperialism'. 'Prosperity' could then 'only be enforced by a war, a war which removed the economic competition from Europe, and if possible also Japan, for good, and which secured the big world markets of the future for America: South America and China, possibly also Russia.' (*Ibid.*, p. 296). On another occasion Hitler told Wagener that 'this export obsession is an "addiction" which forms one of the main reasons for war' (*ibid.*, p. 329). Hitler also traced America's entry into the First World War back solely to her economic interests: see, for example, his speech in the *Reichstag* on 30 January 1939, brochure, p. 44; Domarus, p. 1170, speech on 28 April 1939; and *ibid.*, p. 1801, speech on 11 December 1941.
7. *Monologues*, p. 76, entry for 10 October 1941.
8. *Complete Recordings*, p. 123, speech on 17 April 1920.
9. *Ibid.*, p. 135, speech on 26 May 1920.
10. *Ibid.*, p. 148, speech on 17 June 1920.

11. *MK*, p. 157, also p. 693.
12. Compare *Complete Recordings*, p. 123 (17 April 1920); *ibid.*, p. 135 (26 May 1920); *ibid.*, p. 148 (17 June 1920); *ibid.*, p. 230 (20 September 1920); *ibid.*, p. 334 *et seq.*, (6 March 1921); *ibid.*, p. 676 (11 August 1922); *ibid.*, p. 874 (10 April 1923); *ibid.*, p. 889 *et seq.* (13 April 1923); *MK*, pp. 156, 693; BA/NS 26/54, f. 120, speech on 6 March 1927; *ibid.*, f. 149, speech on 26 March 1927; *ibid.*, f. 15, speech on 6 August 1927; *ibid.*, f. 184, speech on 9 November 1927; BA/NSD 71/56, f. 14, speech on 26 June 1927; *VB* No 270, speech on 23 January 1928; *VB* No 91, speech on 17 April 1928; *VB* special issue, speech on 10 October 1928, BayHStA, collection of press clippings 1172; BA/NS 26/55, f. 79, speech on 18 October 1928; *ibid.*, f. 108, speech on 27 October 1928; *ibid.*, f. 120 *et seq.*, speech on 9 November 1928; *VB* No 272, speech on 21 November 1928; BA/NL Streicher No 125, f. 17, speech on 30 November 1928; BA/NS 26/56, f. 32, speech on 6 March 1929; Preiss, p. 135, speech on 30 November 1929; BA/NS 26/57 ff. 9–11, speech on 31 August 1930; Wagener, p. 208 (autumn 1930); Bouhler I/II, p. 380, speech on 30 January 1941; and *Monologues*, p. 45, entry on 22/23 July 1941.
13. *Monologues*, loc. cit.
14. Haller, p. 42.
15. Compare Böhme, *Appeals and Speeches by German Professors During the First World War*, where the thesis that the trade competition between Britain and Germany was the cause of the war is expounded by, among others, Prof. Ulrich von Wilamowitz-Moellendorff (p. 60), Erich Marcks (p. 86 *et seq.*), Hermann Oncken (p. 109) and Reinhard Seeberg (p. 131).
16. Hanfstaengl, p. 52.
17. Stegemann, pp. 6–10.
18. BA/NS 26/52, f. 14 *et seq.*, speech on 6 August 1927.
19. Preiss, p. 77 *et seq.*, speech on 21 August 1927.
20. In his widely read book *The German Economy in the 19th Century*, first published in 1930, Sombart argues that it would be wrong to assume 'that international trade relations are gaining a relatively increasing importance for modern economy. The opposite is true. For the German economy at least, developments during the past decades at least have led to the result of *a reduction of the share of foreign trade movements in the total achievement of economic activity.*' (p. 428). The absolute increase of export, went Sombart's thesis, equated to a relative reduction of its importance.
21. Sombart, *The Future of Capitalism*. On p. 37 he writes: 'Linked to this development is the ending of the third condition of the former world economy, the strange exchange of goods between Western Europe and the other countries in the world. This will not be able to be maintained, in so far as the industrialization of the agricultural nations already mentioned continues. The ability of these nations to absorb industrial products will be reduced, industrial export by Western Europe shrink together.'
22. Sombart, *The Changes of Capitalism*, p. 246 *et seq.* Compare also the contribution by Prof. E. Salin, Basle, pub. in 1932: 'The economy of the early nineteenth century, seized by crisis, was able to get rid of its domestic over-production in the non-capitalist countries, and by involving the pre- and non-capitalist countries in the web of high capitalism, continued to increase their production, their sales, and their returns ... Today there are not only former agricultural countries which have themselves become industrialized as a result of the Great War, capitalism today is also running into anti-capitalist ideas and movements all over the world.' (Salin, p. 4). The widely accepted

thesis of the shrinking of markets and the resultant collapse of world economy was not uncontested. For a criticism see the article by M. Victor, 'The So-called Law of the Declining Importance of Foreign Trade', published in 1932 in the *Weltwirtschaftliche Archiv* (World Economic Archives).

23. Strasser's statements after an interview with A. Barkai; see Barkai, *Economic System*, p. 57n.

24. Fried, *Autarky*, p. 12. Compare the same author's *The End of Capitalism*, p. 168 *et seq.* The two books by Fried are compilations of the author's articles published from 1929 onwards in the periodical *Die Tat*.

25. Compare Hitler's statements in his speech on 21 August 1929 (cited on p. 275), in which he explained the inevitability of war in view of increased competition for the shrinking markets, with the following passage from Bucharin's study 'Imperialism and World Economy': 'Therefore the chase after markets inevitably leads to conflicts between the "national" groups of capital. *The enormous growth of productivity and the reduction of free markets to a minimum which is taking place in recent times, the customs duty policy of the powers, which is a consequence of the rule of capital, and the increase in the difficulties of realizing the values of goods, are producing a condition in which war technology has the final word.*' (Bucharin, *Imperialismus und Weltwirtschaft* [Vienna-Berlin, 1929], p. 94; italics in the original). 'So here too the internationalization of economic life is inevitably leading to a decision of the controversial questions by fire and sword.' (*ibid.*, p. 112; italics in the original). Peter Krüger, who in his essay about Hitler's 'National Socialist Economic Findings' was the first to draw attention to the latter's thesis of the shrinking of markets, cites the following passage from Rosa Luxemburg as a parallel to the appropriate passage in Hitler's 'Second Book' (cited here on p. 277): 'Hand in hand with those methods, since the beginning of the nineteenth century goes the export of the accumulated capital from Europe to the non-capitalist countries of the other continents, where on new fields, on the ruins of domestic foms of production, it finds a new circle of customers for its goods, and therefore a further possibility of accumulation. And so, thanks to the interplay with non-capitalistic social circles and countries, capitalism spreads ever wider by accumulating at their expense, while at the same time eroding and pushing them aside step by step in order to take their place. But the more capitalist countries take part in this chase after areas of accumulation, and the fewer the non-capitalist regions become which are still available for world expansion of capital, the more bitter the competition of capital for those areas of accumulation will become, the more will its excursions on the world stage turn into a chain of economic and political catastrophes: world crises, wars, revolutions.' (Luxemburg, *Complete Works*, vol. 5 [Berlin (East), 1975], p. 430, cited here in Krüger, p. 271). Krüger comments: 'Leaving aside the important differences in the points of departure, in the moral position, the diction and the conclusions, this reasoning by Rosa Luxemburg is, in essence, reflected in the passage cited from Hitler's "Second Book".' (Krüger, p. 271).

26. Teichert, pp. 9, 15.

27. *ZB*, p. 60 *et seq.*; compare *ibid.*, p. 122.

28. BA/NS 26/55, f. 78, speech on 18 October 1928.

29. *Ibid.*, f. 80.

30. BA/NL Streicher, No 125, f. 17 (also compare f. 19), speech on 30 November 1928.

31. See, for example, BA/NL Streicher, No 125, f. 13 *et seq.*, speech on 8 December 1928; Preiss, p. 135, speech on 30 November 1929; STA Erlangen III.220.H.1., speech on 26 June 1931; *ibid.*, ff. 9, 12, speech on 3 July 1931; and Files of the RK, p. 389 (26 May 1933).

32. Domarus, p. 75 *et seq.*, speech on 26 January 1932; compare *ibid.*, p. 173, speech on 3 January 1933.
33. Notes by Lieutenant-General Liebmann on Hitler's statements before the commanders of the Army and the Navy on the occasion of a visit to General of Infantry *Freiherr* von Hammerstein-Equord in his apartment on 3 February 1933, cited in K. J. Müller, *The Army and the Third Reich*, p. 263. On the interpretation of the passage cited see Zitelmann, *Adolf Hitler: A Political Biography*, p. 93 *et seq.*
34. *VB* No 142 of 22 May 1935, speech on 21 May 1935.
35. Domarus, p. 750, speech on 5 November 1937.
36. *MK*, p. 255.
37. BA/NS 26/55, f. 77 *et seq.*, speech on 18 October 1928.
38. *Ibid.*, f. 91.
39. BA/NS 26/55, f. 108, speech on 27 October 1928.
40. BA/NL Streicher, No 125, f. 18 *et seq.*, speech on 30 November 1928 (in Preiss under 30 November 1929, p. 135 *et seq.*).
41. *Ibid.*, f. 14 *et seq.*, speech on 8 December 1928.
42. Chapter III.3.d of the present study.
43. It is therefore not a coincidence that Turner, who cites Hitler's criticism of the big city as proof of his anti-modernism, is able to quote only a single passage from Hitler's 'Second Book', which Hitler wrote in 1928 (see Turner, *Fascism and Anti-Modernism*, p. 166, n. 14).
44. *VB* special issue No 87a of 15/16 April 1927, speech on 13 April 1927, BayHStA, collection of press clippings 1172.
45. *VB* No 20 of 25 January 1928, speech on 23 January 1928.
46. *ZB*, pp. 61 *et seq.*, 201.
47. BA/NS 26/55, f. 44, speech on 18 September 1928.
48. On Hitler's demand for the 'removal of the Jews' see Jäckel, *Weltanschauung*, pp. 55–78.
49. BA/NL Streicher, No 125, f. 9, speech on 30 November 1928.
50. *Ibid.*, f. 19, speech on 8 December 1928.
51. *VB* No 280 of 3 December 1929, speech on 29 November 1929.
52. STA Erlangen III.220.H.1., f. 10 *et seq.*, speech on 3 July 1931.
53. Wagener, pp. 388, 423.
54. Compare *Monologues*, p. 332 *et seq.*, entry for 6 August 1942.
55. Koeppen Notes on 4 October 1941 (dinner).
56. *Monologues*, p. 299, entry for 26 February 1942.
57. Picker, p. 261, entry for 3 May 1942.
58. Compare pp. 282–6 of the present study. The investigation by Erhard Forndran on 'The Founding of the City and Industry of Wolfsburg and Salzgitter' comes to a similar conclusion in its analysis of national Socialist urban development policy. The hostility towards big cities to be found with Feder and other National Socialists, says Forndran, 'should not be exaggerated', because, firstly, there were certainly other views of the big city within National Socialism, and secondly even Feder emphasized that 'The big city cannot be rejected in general; it is only insufficient in its contemporary form and no longer equates to the modern requirements which are addressed to a community of people in which each is an equal individual link capable of life within the great national community.' (Feder, cited in Forndran, p. 62). Hitler and the other leading personalities of the NSDAP were aware, says Forndran, that their objectives could not be achieved by a Germany which had been developed back into an agricultural

country: 'They rejected the big city which they found' but not the big city itself (*ibid.*, p. 62). 'The frequently cited hostility of National Socialism towards the big city gradually lost its importance for urban development and housing policy.' (*ibid.*, p. 64). Forndran is basically correct, but he too starts off from an original 'ideology of reagrarianization' (*ibid.*, p. 63), from which the National Socialists only turned away later – for military and economic considerations. What applies to many valuable individual studies is also true for Forndran's investigation: from their detailed investigations the authors come to conclusions which cannot be reconciled with the positions still dominating research (e.g. 'reagrarianization', 'hostility towards big cities') and therefore attempt to bring their conclusions into line – at least, approximately – with these positions without calling them into fundamental doubt. Forndran therefore states that Hitler's issue had been 'the amalgamation of agrarian and industrial value concepts', that he had been sceptical of the big city, having recognized it as the fount and condition for modernity (*ibid.*, p. 62), that the National Socialists had only turned away from their original ideology of reagrarianization later on (*ibid.*, p. 63 *et seq.*), and so forth.

59. On the developments of 'Hitler's Position Towards Britain' see the excellent contribution under this title by A. V. N. Woerden. Woerden shows that from 1928 onwards Hitler advocated the theory of Britain's 'imperial isolationism' (Woerden, p. 223), which he did not give up even later on (*ibid.*, p. 237 *et seq.*). Even after the beginning of the war 'he continued to hope that it would be possible to "push Britain out of the war, even to possibly gain her as an ally"' (*ibid.*, p. 240). The latter thesis is confirmed by the Goebbels diaries. See SF, vol. III, p. 606; and vol IV, pp. 218, 225, 232, 234. See also Zitelmann, *Adolf Hitler* (1989), pp. 134 *et seq.*, 143–6.

60. *MK*, p. 154; also *ibid.*, p. 691 *et seq.*

61. Hitler's two differing autarky concepts were also recognized by Fischer, p. 75, Petzina, p. 20, and Herbst, p. 66, without, however, their taking the relevance of 'temporary autarky' for alliance policy into consideration.

62. *MK*, p. 152.

63. *ZB*, p. 102.

64. Compare, for example, Domarus, p. 1237 (22 August 1939); *Monologues*, p. 58, entry for 19/20 August 1941; and *ibid.*, p. 366, entry for 26 August 1942. But Hitler only accepted war for the purpose of the extension of *Lebensraum* as being necessary: 'Nations on an impossible terrain will basically always have the desire to extend their terrain, therefore their *Lebensraum*, at least as long as they are healthily led. This process, originally only founded in the worry about subsistence, appeared to be so beneficial in its happy solution that it gradually achieved the fame of success itself. That means the extension of terrain, which had its original reasons in mere expediency, became a heroic deed in the course of human development, which then also occurred when the original conditions or reasons were lacking. The attempt to adjust *Lebensraum* to the increased population then became unmotivated wars of conquest, which in their non-motivation already carried the seed of their subsequent set-back. The answer to this is pacifism. There has been pacifism in the world ever since there has been war whose sense no longer lay in the conquest of territory for the nourishment of a nation. Since then it has become the constant companion of war. It will disappear again as soon as war has stopped being an instrument of greedy or power-hungry individuals or nations, and as soon as it has again become the final weapon with which a nation fights for its daily bread.' (*ZB*, p. 80; see also the basic statements on 'War and Peace', *ibid.*, p. 48 *et seq.*).

65. *VB* special issue of 13 October 1928, speech on 10 October 1928, BayHStA, collection of press clippings 1172.
66. BA/NS 26/55, f. 77, speech on 18 October 1928.
67. 'We live in a time when all of the wisely led nations and states are attempting to make themselves economically as independent as possible from abroad.' STA Erlangen III.220.H.1., f. 7, speech on 26 June 1931.
68. Strasser, p. 65 (22 May 1930).
69. *Ibid.*, p. 64.
70. Domarus, p. 234, speech on 23 March 1933.
71. *VB* No 142 of 22 May 1935, speech on 21 May 1935.
72. Memorandum to the Four-Year Plan, August 1936, *VjHfZg* (1955), pp. 206, 210.
73. Domarus, p. 749 *et seq.*, speech on 5 November 1937.
74. Compare speech at the *Reichsparteitag* on 11 September 1935, brochure, p. 23; *VB* No 52, speech on 20 February 1937; Kotze and Krausnick, p. 212, speech on 20 May 1937; *VB* No 179, speech on 27 June 1937; speech at the *Reichsparteitag* on 6 September 1938, brochure, p. 25; and *VB* No 49, speech on 17 February 1939.
75. Speech in the *Reichstag* on 30 January 1939, brochure, p. 33 *et seq.*
76. *Monologues*, p. 62, entry on 17/18 September 1941.
77. Compare Hillgruber, *The Factor America*.
78. *Monologues*, p. 69 *et seq.*, entry for 25 September 1941.
79. *Ibid.*, p. 78, entry for 13 October 1941.
80. In 1913 Heidelberg professor Friedrich Bergius had succeeded in adding hydrogen to carbon under high pressure, by which he was able to construct a molecule similar to that of petroleum. In 1941 he received a patent for this 'process of coal liquefaction'.
81. *Monologues*, p. 94, entry for 18 October 1941.
82. Koeppen Notes, report No 46 of 18 October 1941, lunch.
83. *Monologues*, p. 109, entry for 26/27 October 1941.
84. Conversation on 27 November 1941 with Finnish Foreign Minister Witting, Hillgruber, *Statesmen I*, p. 640 *et seq.* Similar statement on the same day by Hitler to Hungarian Foreign Minister Bardossy, *ibid*. p. 649.
85. Picker, p. 473, entry for 27 July 1942.
86. *Monologues*, p. 336, entry on 9 August 1942.
87. Kotze and Krausnick, p. 351, speech on 26 June 1944.
88. *Testament*, p. 104, (24 February 1945).
89. Teichert, p. 7 *et seq.*
90. *Ibid.*, p. 1.
91. Fried, *Autarky*, p. 41. Also compare the publications for and against autarky listed in the appendix of Fried's book.
92. Goerdeler, cited in Grotkopp, p. 218; also *ibid.*, pp. 217–30.
93. Fried, *op. cit.*, pp. 9, 23, 44, 52.
94. Sombart, *Future*, pp. 41, 44.
95. *ZB*, p. 102.
96. *Monologues*, p. 48, entry for 27 July 1941.
97. *Ibid.*, p. 54 *et seq.*, entry for 8–11 August 1941.
98. *Ibid.*, p. 58, entry for 19/20 August 1941.
99. *Ibid.*, p. 63, entry for 17/18 September 1941.
100. *Ibid.*, p. 70, entry for 25 September 1941.
101. Koeppen Notes, report No 40 of 4 October 1941, dinner.
102. *Monologues*, p. 139, entry for 12 November 1941.

103. Picker, p. 202, entry for 7 April 1942.
104. *Monologues*, p. 332, entry for 6 August 1942.
105. *Ibid.*, p. 335 *et seq.*, entry for 9 August 1942.
106. Turner, *Hitler's View*, p. 94.
107. *ZB*, pp. 99, 123, 173.
108. *VB* special issue of 13 October 1928, speech on 10 October 1928, BayHStA, collection of press clippings 1172.
109. *VB* No 272 of 22 November 1928, speech on 21 November 1928.
110. BA/NS 26/57, f. 9, speech on 31 August 1930.
111. STA Erlangen III.220.H.1., f. 3 *et seq.*, speech on 26 June 1931.
112. *Ibid.*, f. 8, speech on 3 July 1931.
113. Wagener, p. 296 *et seq.* (1931).
114. Hanfstaengl, p. 252.
115. Domarus, p. 271, speech on 17 May 1933.
116. *Ibid.*, p. 1177, speech on 24 April 1939.
117. *Monologues*, p. 59, entry on 19/20 August 1941.
118. Koeppen Notes, report No 31 of 17 September 1941, lunch.
119. *Monologues*, p. 70, entry for 25 September 1941.
120. Compare Chapter V.1.e of the present study.
121. *Monologues*, p. 78, entry for 13 October 1941.
122. Koeppen Notes, report No 46 of 18 October 1941, dinner.
123. *Monologues*, p. 110, entry for 26/27 October 1941.
124. Koeppen Notes, report No 52 of 26 October 1941, dinner.
125. *Monologues*, p. 264, entry for 4 February 1942.
126. Picker, attachment to p. 495, speech on 30 May 1942.
127. *Monologues*, p. 336, entry for 9 August 1942.
128. *Ibid.*, p. 371, entry for 28 August 1942.
129. Conversation with Mussert on 10 December 1942, BA/NS 6/161, p. 4.
130. Goebbels, *Speeches*, vol. 2, p. 136; italics in the original. At the beginning of the campaign against Russia Goebbels still wanted to hide these economic motives of the war for *Lebensraum*. Three days after the attack in the Soviet Union he wrote in his diary: 'I also do not permit the economic advantages of a victory over Moscow to be treated yet. Our polemics are totally on the political level.' (Goebbels, Diaries, SF, vol. 4 p. 715, entry for 25 June 1941).
131. *Monologues*, p. 63, entry for 17/18 September 1941.
132. Koeppen Notes, report No 32 of 19 September 1941, lunch.
133. *Monologues*, p. 70, entry for 25 September 1941.
134. *Ibid.*, p. 78, entry for 13 October 1941.
135. Conversation on 14 February 1942 with the Croatian ambassador Budak, Hillgruber, *Statesmen II*, p. 63 *et seq.*
136. *Monologues*, p. 331, entry for 6 August 1942.
137. Compare Tallgren, pp. 88–95.
138. *Monologues*, p. 334, entry for 8 August 1942.
139. Koeppen Notes, report No 32 of 18 September 1941, lunch.
140. *Monologues*, p. 70, entry for 25 September 1941.
141. Speer, p. 322.
142. Koeppen Notes, report No 46 of 18 October 1941, dinner.
143. *Monologues*, p. 90, entry for 17 October 1941.
144. *Ibid.*, p. 299, entry for 26 February 1942.

145. *Ibid.*, p. 90 *et seq.*, entry for 17 October 1941.
146. Compare Herbst, p. 88.
147. *ZB*, p. 60.
148. STA Erlangen III.220.H.1., f. 6, speech on 26 June 1931.
149. Files of the RK, p. 105 (24 April 1933).
150. *Ibid.* A note by *Ministerialrat* Willuhn on a reception of Hitler's for representatives from eastern Germany on 26 April 1933 contains the following remark by Hitler: 'Germany's world markets were constantly shrinking. The world economic conference would have to deal with the question of the regulation of the sale of machines to the raw material countries.' (Files of the RK, p. 389).
151. *Monologues*, p. 70, entry for 25 September 1941.
152. *Ibid.*, p. 244, entry for 31 January 1942.
153. See *MK*, pp. 150, 728 *et seq.* Jacobsen points out quite correctly that this military-geographic aspect of the demand for *Lebensraum* has previously received far too little attention (Jacobsen, *Karl Haushofer*, vol. 1, p. 253, here in the context of a very interesting comparison of the definition of *Lebensraum* with Ratzel, Haushofer and Hitler). The importance of the military-geographical motive of the demand for *Lebensraum* – which was, however, secondary to the economic considerations we have discussed here – demonstrates how little a monocausal derivation of the *Lebensraum* function from agrarian considerations (the settlement of farmers) does justice to Hitler's concept.
154. BA/NS 26/54, f. 117, speech on 6 March 1927.
155. *Ibid.*, f. 140 *et seq.*, speech on 26 March 1927.
156. See *MK*, p. 146.
157. *ZB*, p. 120 *et seq.*
158. STA Erlangen III.220.H.1., f. 3, speech on 26 June 1931.
159. *VB* No 265 of 22 September 1933, speech on 20 September 1933. The text of Hitler's speech at the second meeting of the General Council of Economics is reproduced in Files of the RK, pp. 805–21, with special attention to p. 811 *et seq.*
160. Domarus, p. 576 *et seq.*, speech on 15 February 1936. Compare Hitler's remark in a conversation with leading industrialists on 29 May 1933: 'I believe the industry connected with the motor car to be the most powerful and successful in the future', in Files of the RK, p. 513.
161. *Monologues*, p. 73, entry on 27/28 September 1941.
162. *Ibid.*, p. 256, entry on 2 February 1942.
163. Picker, p. 418 *et seq.*, entry on 5 July 1942.
164. Kotze and Krausnick, p. 346, speech at the end of June 1944.
165. Teichert, p. 217. Compare the article by Heyl.
166. Schäfer. p. 117. Compare p. 117 *et seq.*, where Schäfer lists many examples of this orientation towards consumption.
167. Schäfer, p. 150.
168. Cited in Burchardt, *War Economy*, p. 92. As Burchardt emphasizes, the fear played a role here that a situation could recur such as that towards the end of the First World War which finally led to the outbreak of the November revolution. Hitler's reluctance to coutenance a mobilization such as 'total war' would have required, however, is linked to his fundamental conviction of the central importance of man's material needs, which stood in contrast to his repeated demand for 'idealistic convictions'. Hitler's position, which – seen superficially – contradicted the requirements of the waging of the war, is therefore evidence that he attributed extraordinary importance

to questions of the economy and was in this sense more of a 'materialist' than an 'idealist'.
169. Compare Turner, *Fascism and Anti-Modernism*, p. 171 *et seq.*
170. *Ibid.*, p. 162.
171. *ZB*, pp. 123–7.
172. *MK*, p. 479.
173. Article by Engel, p. 35 *et seq.*, 5 September 1938.
174. *Monologues*, p. 255, entry for 2 February 1942.
175. Fried, *End*, pp. 91–3.
176. This, as well as the subsequent sentences of the quotation, were naturally intended as propaganda. We have seen that, in reality, Hitler believed in the actual technical-industrial superiority of the United States, which was, however, to be overcome.
177. Picker, p. 155, entry for 28 March 1942 (Hitler directive of 27 March 1942 to correspondents).
178. BA/NS 26/54, f. 126 *et seq.*, speech on 6 March 1927.
179. BA/NSD 71/56, brochure pub. by the NSDAP district group Marktredwitz, p. 16, speech on 26 June 1927.
180. Strasser, p. 62 (22 May 1930).
181. Kühnl, *NS Left*, p. 159.
182. Compare Wagener, pp. 290, 387, 432; and Domarus, p. 502, speech on 1 May 1935.
183. Knox is correct when he writes on p. 11: 'Hitler was a good old nineteenth-century positivist.'
184. Wagener, p. 207.
185. Domarus, p. 373, interview on 25 March 1934.
186. Compare the speeches at the annual automobile and motorcycle shows already cited.
187. *Monologues*, p. 95, entry for 19 October 1941.
188. *Ibid.*, p. 242, entry for 28/29 January 1942.
189. *Ibid.*, p. 275, entry for 9 February 1942.
190. *Ibid.*, p. 306 *et seq.*, entry for 28 February 1942.
191. Picker, p. 282, entry for 11 May 1942.
192. *Ibid.*, p. 351, entry for 3 June 1942.
193. *Ibid.*, p. 474, entry for 28 July 1942.
194. Compare Carr, p. 110 *et seq.*
195. Haffner, p. 34.
196. Compare Ludwig, p. 210 *et seq.*
197. *Ibid.*, p. 248 *et seq.*
198. *Ibid.*, p. 200.
199. Compare Ludwig, p. 319 *et seq.*; also Seidler, p. 139 *et seq.*
200. Picker, p. 443, entry for 18 July 1942.
201. Ludwig, p. 328.
202. Picker, p. 407, entry for 3 July 1942.
203. *Monologues*, p. 399, entry for 13 June 1943.
204. Compare Ludwig, p. 58 *et seq.*
205. Sieferle, p. 210; compare Fried, *End*, pp. 4, 15, 21, 141, 165.
206. Sombart, W., *German Socialism* (Berlin, 1934), p. 43. Cited in Sieferle, p. 215.
207. So, too, the conclusions by Herf, pp. 189–216. Fritz Todt's positive position on technology is now very well documented; see Seidler, *Fritz Todt*, pp. 39–93.
208. F. Nonnenbruch, review of 'German Socialism', *VB* No 278 of 5 October 1934, cited in Sieferle, p. 285, n. 90.

209. Nonnenbruch, F., *Politics, Technology and Spirit* (Munich, 1939), p. 56, cited in Sieferle, p. 223.
210. Mohler, p. 207. In his stimulating study *Reactionary Modernism*, Herf comes to a different conclusion. According to Herf, while leading members of the 'conservative revolution' vehemently rejected the tradition of the Enlightenment, at the same time they did affirm modern industry and technology. Herf's results may well lead to a correction of the previous view of the 'conservative revolution' in this respect, but also need to be relevated themselves because, particularly in comparison with National Socialism, anti-modernistic tendencies were more strongly developed among leading members of this school than Herf's study would make this appear.
211. Compare Mohler, pp. 67, 210.
212. Compare Chapter III.3.a/b of the present study.
213. Bouhler I/II, p. 320, speech on 14 November 1940.
214. *Monologues*, p. 39, entry for 5 July 1941.
215. The allusion is to the Fischer-Tropsch process developed in 1926 at the Kaiser Wilhelm Insitute for Coal Research.
216. *Monologues*, p. 53 *et seq.*, entry on 2 August 1941.
217. Compare Giesler, p. 218 *et seq.*
218. *Ibid.*, p. 231 *et seq.*
219. *Monologues*, p. 74, entry for 28 September 1941.
220. Picker, p. 426, entry for 7 July 1942.
221. *Ibid.*, p. 475 *et seq.*, entry for 28 July 1942.
222. *Ibid.*, p. 282, note 247.
223. Compare, for example, Engel Notes, p. 35 *et seq.* (5 September 1938).
224. Giesler, p. 286 *et seq.*
225. *Ibid.*, pp. 288–90.
226. *Ibid.*, p. 197.
227. Sieferle, p. 217.
228. *Naturschutz 15*, 1934, p. 208. Cited in Sieferle, p. 217.
229. Reichs Ministerial Bulletin for Forest Administration. Also Official Bulletin for the Highest Office for Conservation 2, 8 (1938), p. 43 *et seq.* Cited in Gröning, p. 11, n. 40.
230. Gröning, p. 1.
231. Minister for Science, Art and Public Education 1933, cited in Gröning, p. 6.
232. Compare Sieferle, p. 217.
233. Cited in Gröning, p. 12.
234. *Ibid.*, p. 13.
235. Ludwig, p. 337. Also compare Seidler, *Fritz Todt*, pp. 112–20.
236. Letter by Todt on 16 March 1935 to the 'Reichsautobahn' company for transmission to all the Higher Construction Offices. Cited in Ludwig, p. 337.
237. Cited in Seidler, *op.cit.*, p. 113.
238. Ludwig, p. 338.
239. Sieferle, p. 220.
240. In his book *Under the Ban of the Myth*, F. W. Doucet has attempted to demonstrate the importance of symbols, archetypes etc. for the mass appeal of National Socialism, and many authors have quite rightly pointed to the pseudo-religious component in Hitler's rhetoric and to his image as a 'Messiah' as one of the reasons for his success. See, for example, Olden, pp. 88, 170, 275 *et seq.*, 410 et seq; Windisch, p. 134 *et seq.*; Görlitz and Quint, pp. 287, 303, 630; Heiber, p. 53; Domarus, pp. 569, 641, 1008; Fest,

p. 458 *et seq.*; Waite, pp. 27 *et seq.*, 191, 343; Stern, pp. 91, 93 *et seq.*, 184–6; Carr, pp. 17 *et seq.*, 179; Toland, pp. 194, 294, 302, 425 *et seq.*, 428, 484 *et seq.*, 486, 539, 593; and Kershaw, pp. 13, 26, 31, 33, 51, 66, 91, 139, 140, 142, 191.
241. Speech at the cultural conference of the *Reichsparteitag* on 6 September 1938, brochure, p. 38 *et seq.*
242. Domarus comments correctly: 'While Hitler did not mention the names of Rosenberg and Himmler, everyone knew whom he meant by the cult adherents he had admonished.' (p. 893).
243. Turner, *Fascism and Anti-Modernism*, p. 163 *et seq.*
244. *Monologues*, p. 67, entry for 23 September 1941.
245. *Ibid.*, p. 84 *et seq.*, entry for 14 October 1941.
246. *Ibid.*, p. 103, entry for 24 October 1941.
247. *Ibid.*, pp. 285–7, entry for 20/21 February 1942.
248. Picker, p. 356, entry for 5 June 1942.
249. *Ibid.*, p. 213, entry for 11 April 1942.
250. Speer, pp. 108, 136.
251. Goebbels, Diaries, SF, vol. 2, p. 505, entry for 21 August 1935.
252. *MGM* 2/76, p. 146, speech on 26 May 1944.
253. *Complete Notes*, p. 88, letter of 16 September 1919.
254. Heiden I, p. 346; also *ibid.*, p. 111.

VI. Hitler's Concepts and Objectives in His Domestic Policies

1. *Complete Notes*, p. 658, speech on 28 July 1922.
2. *Ibid.*, p. 799, article of 25 January 1923; italics in the original. Similarly *ibid.*, p. 822, speech on 29 January 1923; and *ibid.*, p. 838, speech on 26 February 1923.
3. *Ibid.*, p. 1048, speech on 30 October 1923.
4. Unfortunately Tallgren's work on the role of heroism in Hitler's *Weltanschauung* has been noticed far too little by research. See our review: Zitelmann, *Hitler's Successes*, p. 55 *et seq.*
5. *Complete Recordings*, p. 1066, before the people's court, 1st day of the trial, 26 February 1924.
6. *MK*, p. 82.
7. *MK*, pp. 39, 54–9.
8. *MK*, pp. 83–97.
9. BA/NS 26/54, f. 169, speech on 17 June 1927.
10. BA/NSD 71/56, f. 20, speech on 26 June 1927.
11. BA/NS 26/54, f. 7, speech on 6 August 1927.
12. These accusations can be found in the following sources: Preiss, p. 82 (20/21 August 1927); BA/NS 26/54, f. 197, speech on 9 November 1927; *VB* No 270, speech on 21 November 1927; *VB* No 11, speech on 12 January 1928; *ZB*, p. 68; BA/NS 26/55, f. 43, 51, speech on 18 September 1928; *ibid.*, f. 87 *et seq.*, speech on 18 October 1928; *ibid.*, f. 16, speech on 27 October 1928; BA/NL von Epp 24/3, f. 8, speech on 24 February 1929; BA/NS, f. 19, speech on 6 March 1929; BA/NS 26/52, f. 100, speech on 8 November 1930; and Domarus, p. 72, speech on 27 January 1932.
13. BA/NS, 26/52, f. 31, speech on 6 August 1927; similarly *VB* No 270, speech on 21 November 1927; BA/NS 26/52, f. 100, speech on 8 November 1930.
14. BA/NL Streicher, No 125, f. 26, speech on 30 November 1928; similarly BA/NS 26/

55, f. 89, speech on 18 October 1928.
15. Opening proclamation at the *Reichsparteitag* on 1 September 1933, brochure, p. 18.
16. See Hitler's explanations about the function of the plebiscite: *VB* No 315, speech on 10 November 1933; Domarus, p. 333, speech on 19 November 1933; *ibid.*, p. 442 *et seq.*, speech on 17 August 1934; brochure, 'The Führer's Battle for World Peace', p. 41 (14 March 1936), pp. 47, 49 *et seq.* (20 March 1936), p. 55 (22 March 1936), p. 61 (26 March 1936) and pp. 68, 70 (27 March 1936); Domarus, p. 840 (29 March 1938); and *Monologues*, p. 237, entry for 27 January 1942.
17. Kotze and Krausnick, p. 132, speech on 29 April 1937.
18. *Ibid.*, p. 134 *et seq.* While Hitler could be sure of a large measure of acceptance among the population after successes in foreign policy such as the *Anschluss* of Austria, for example, the result of a plebiscite during the final years of the war would have been doubtful. Hitler therefore repeatedly emphasized that in such a situation the *Führer* alone bore the responsibility and it was impossible to let the people take part in the fundamental decision on the ending of the war. Compare Hitler's remarks during a meeting with the Bulgarian Regency Council on 16 March 1944, Hillgruber, *Statesmen II*, p. 376, or his speech to generals and officers on 26 May 1944, *MGM* 2/76, p. 160.
19. See Böhret *et al.*, pp. 60 *et seq.*, 195–205.
20. *Complete Recordings*, p. 271, notes for a speech on 8 December 1920.
21. BA/NS 26/55, ff. 60, 64, speech on 18 October 1928.
22. *ZB*, p. 85.
23. It should be noted that in those days – at least in Germany there was no *explicit* pluralistic political understanding in the sense of a theory with such a designation. Hitler's criticism is therefore not directed against such a theory, but against manifestations within society, or a political understanding which we today would call 'pluralistic'.
24. See Böhret *et al.*, p. 286 *et seq.*
25. Compare p. 212 of the present study.
26. Note missing in the original book.
27. *VB* No 171 of 20/21 July 1930, speech on 18 July 1930.
28. BA/NL Streicher No 125, f. 4, speech on 24 July 1930.
29. Wagener, p. 209; italics in the original.
30. *Ibid.*, p. 71.
31. BA/NS 26/57, f. 35 *et seq.*, speech on 5 November 1930.
32. BA/NS 26/52, f. 94, speech on 8 November 1930. The speech is also published in *Die Ortenau* No 57 (1977), pp. 296–312, with comments by J. Thies. See also BA/NL Streicher, No 126, f. 17, speech on 13 November 1930; and *VB* No 105, speech on 12 April 1931.
33. Speech on 10 May 1933, in 'Young Germany Wants Work and Peace', p. 50.
34. Speech in the *Reichstag* on 30 January 1934, brochure, p. 22. Compare *VB* No 127, speech on 1 May 1934; and *VB* No 138, speech on 16 May 1934.
35. *VB* of 12 September 1934, speech on 10 September 1934 (closing address at the *Reichsparteitag*). See also 'Führer Speeches to the Winter Help Campaign 1933–1936', p. 11 *et seq.*, speech on 8 October 1935.
36. Brochure: 'The Führer's Battle for World Peace', p. 34, speech on 12 March 1936.
37. Proclamation at the *Reichsparteitag* on 9 September 1936, brochure, p. 21.
38. *VB* No 279 of 5 October 1936, speech on 4 October 1936.
39. Kotze and Krausnick, p. 124 *et seq.*, speech on 29 April 1937; see also p. 174.

40. *Ibid.*, p. 127 *et seq.*, speech on 29 April 1937.
41. Domarus, p. 1365, speech on 19 September 1939.
42. Bouhler I/II, p. 390, speech on 30 January 1941.
43. Preiss, p. 69, speech on 9 June 1927.
44. BA/NS 26/55, f. 24, speech on 18 September 1928.
45. *ZB*, p. 87.
46. Speech on 10 May 1933, in 'Young Germany Wants Work and Peace', p. 48.
47. Closing address at the *Reichsparteitag* on 12 September 1938, brochure, p. 67.
48. Bouhler I/II, p. 321 *et seq.*, speech on 14 November 1940.
49. *Ibid.*, p. 341 *et seq.*, speech on 10 December 1940.
50. *Ibid.*, p. 343.
51. Compare Chapter IV.4 of the present study.
52. Bouhler I/II, p. 383, speech on 30 January 1941.
53. Kettenacker, p. 106.
54. *MK*, p. 379; also p. 84.
55. BA/NL Streicher, No 15, f. 28, speech on 30 November 1928.
56. *IB* 4th year set, issue 9 of 2 March 1929, p. 101.
57. STA Erlangen III.220.H.1., f. 10, speech on 26 June 1931.
58. Domarus, p. 71, speech on 27 January 1932.
59. Speech at the cultural conference of the *Reichsparteitag* on 9 September 1936, brochure, p. 28.
60. *VB* No 171 of 20/21 July 1930, speech on 18 July 1930.
61. Domarus, p. 564, speech on 15 January 1936.
62. Bouhler I/II, p. 391, speech on 31 January 1941.
63. *VB* No 57 of 26 February 1935, speech on 24 February 1935; similarly Goebbels, *Speeches*, vol. 1, p. 272.
64. Kotze and Krausnick, p. 128 *et seq.*, speech on 29 April 1937.
65. Domarus, p. 739, speech on 3 October 1937.
66. *VB* No 122 of 2 May 1939, speech on 1 May 1939.
67. Picker, p. 166 *et seq.*, entry for 31 March 1942.
68. *Ibid.*, p. 213 *et seq.*, entry for 11 April 1942.
69. *Ibid.*, p. 477, entry for 28 July 1942.
70. *MGM* 2/76, p. 146 *et seq.*, speech on 26 May 1944.
71. *Complete Recordings*, p. 557 *et seq.*, speech on 30 January 1922. Similarly *ibid.*, p. 279, article of 1 January 1921; *ibid.*, p. 443, notes for a speech on 20 July 1921; *ibid.*, p. 622, speech on 12 April 1922; *ibid.*, p. 700, speech on 14 October 1922; *ibid.*, p. 726, speech on 9 November 1922; *ibid.*, p. 738, speech on 21 November 1922; *ibid.*, p. 745, speech on 30 November 1922; and *ibid.*, p. 798, article of 25 January 1923.
72. *Ibid.*, p. 708, speech on 25 October 1922.
73. *Ibid.*, p. 671, speech on 28 July 1922.
74. *MK*, p. 114 *et seq.*
75. Compare p. 62 of the present study.
76. *MK*, pp. 441, 651–8; italics in the original.
77. BA/NS 26/54, f. 8, speech on 12 June 1925.
78. 'The National Socialist', information leaflet of the Württemberg Gau leadership and Stuttgart district group of the NSDAP, No 2, July 1925, speech by Hitler on 8 July 1925, p. 3, BayHStA, collection of press clippings 1172.
79. Preiss, p. 32 *et seq.*, speech on 26 September 1925.
80. Compare p. 139 *et seq.* of the present study.

Notes

81. Jochmann, *In Battle*, p. 73 *et seq.*, speech on 28 February 1926. For Hitler's positive view of pre-war Social Democracy, particularly his idealization of the USPD, see Chapter VII.3.a of the present study.
82. That Hitler also mentioned these bourgeois circles, who according to his inner convictions only disposed 'heroic' attributes in the most rare of cases, was a concession to his bourgeois audience.
83. Jochmann, *op. cit.*, p. 78 *et seq.*, speech on 28 February 1926.
84. See BA/NS 26/54, f. 137 (26 March 1927); *ibid.*, f. 170 (17 June 1927); BA/NL Streicher, No 125, f. 32 (30 November 1928); *ibid.*, f. 24, 26 (8 December 1928); BA/NS 26/55, f. 19 (6 March 1929); Preiss, pp. 118–21 (4 August 1929); *IB* of 1 March 1930; BA/NS 26/57, f. 40 *et seq.* (5 November 1930); BA/NS 26/52, f. 96 (8 November 1930); BA/NL Streicher No 126, f. 23 *et seq.* (13 November 1930); STA Erlangen III.220.H.1., f. 25 *et seq.* (26 June 1931); and *ibid.*, f. 23 (3 July 1931).
85. *VB* No 205 of 4 September 1928, speech on 2 September 1928.
86. BA/NL von Epp 24/3. f. 10, speech on 24 February 1929.
87. Wagener, p. 189 *et seq.*, end of 1930/beginning of 1931.
88. Compare *VB* No 250 'Culture' speech on 5 September 1934; speech at the *Reichsparteitag* on 12 September 1936, brochure, p. 50; Kotze and Krausnick, pp. 84, 107, speech on 24 February 1937; speech at the *Reichsparteitag* on 13 September 1937, brochure, p. 81; speech in the *Reichstag* on 20 February 1938, brochure, p. 8; speech at the *Reichsparteitag* on 6 September 1938, brochure, p. 19; Kotze and Krausnick, p. 238 *et seq.*, speech on 8 November 1938; Domarus, p. 1421, speech on 23 November 1939; *ibid.*, p. 2050, speech on 8 November 1943; *ibid.* p. 2164, speech on 12 November 1944; Bouhler I/II, p. 174, speech on 24 February 1940; *ibid.*, p. 315, speech on 8 November 1940; *ibid.*, p. 414, speech on 24 February 1941; Bouhler III, p. 181 *et seq.*, speech on 30 January 1942; *Monologues*, p. 173, entry for 3/4 January 1942; *ibid.*, p. 209, entry for 16/17 January 1942; and *ibid.*, p. 265, entry for 4 February 1942.
89. 'The National Socialist', information leaflet of the Württemberg Gau leadership and Stuttgart district group of the NSDAP, No 2, speech on 8 July 1925, p. 3; italics in the original.
90. *MK*, p. 656.
91. *MK*, p. 656 *et seq.*; italics in the original.
92. BA/NS 26/55, f. 34, speech on 18 September 1928; *ibid.*, f. 62, speech on 18 October 1928.
93. Fest, p. 403 *et seq.* These and other statements about the number of members of the NSDAP are based on the official party statistics, but the true number has not yet been ascertained. On the one hand the numbers in the statistics may be too low, because all those members who ended their membership before 1 January 1935 (deadline for the statistics) through resignation, expulsion or death but who had nonetheless filled the ranks of the party at one time or another were not taken into account. On the other hand the numbers may be too high because losses were not taken into account. On this problem see Manstein, pp. 143–64.
94. Numbers according to Kater, *Social Change*, p. 43.
95. Speech in the *Reichstag*, brochure, p. 34 *et seq.*
96. *VB* of 12 September 1934, closing address at the *Reichsparteitag* on 10 September 1934.
97. Schirach, p. 87. Schirach, however, does not understand the true meaning of this remark by Hitler.
98. Kater, *Methodological Considerations*, p. 179 *et seq.*

99. Kotze and Krausnick, pp. 141–5, speech on 29 April 1937.
100. Speech on 23 November 1937, pub. in the appendix to Picker, p. 489 *et seq.*
101. Compare Chapters III.2 and III.3.a/b of the present study.
102. The fact of the 'chaos of power' so characteristic of the Third Reich was pointed out very early in research on Hitler. See Heiden I, pp. 417, 421 *et seq.*; Trevor-Roper, *Final Days*, pp. 40 *et seq.*, 219 *et seq.*; Bullock, *Hitler*, pp. 293, 393, 663; Görlitz and Quint, pp. 357 *et seq.*, 387, 399, 543; Görlitz, pp. 94, 97, 116; Bracher, *German Dictatorship*, pp. 233, 376; Bracher, *Controversies*, p. 64; Sauer, *Mobilization of Force*, p. 291 *et seq.*; Mommsen, *Rise*, pp. 17, 26, 28 *et seq.*; Mommsen, *Hitler's Position*; Stern, pp. 14, 111, 168; Carr, pp. 62 *et seq.*, 66; Burchardt, *Historic Greatness*, pp. 27, 33; Irving, *Hitler's War*, p. 566; Fest, pp. 616, 923; and Haffner, p. 47. Also compare Michalka, *The Research on Hitler*, p. 133 *et seq.*
103. Compare the controversy between Hildebrand and Mommsen in Hirschfeld and Kettenacker, *The Führer State*.
104. See Carr, p. 64 *et seq.*
105. See Maser, *Führer Legend*, p. 65.
106. Carr, p. 66 *et seq.*
107. Speer, p. 225.
108. *Monologues*, p. 143, entry for 19 November 1941.
109. Compare the conversation on 19 April 1938 between Hitler and Sepp Dietrich (*SS Obergruppenführer* and General of the *Waffen-SS*), Engel Notes, p. 19. Hitler said that he intended to develop the SS troop as an élite, which would be kept small, however, 'otherwise it is no longer an élite'.
110. *Monologues*, p. 168, entry of 3/4 January 1942.
111. Picker, p. 471, entry on 27 July 1942, note by *Reichsleiter* Bormann; our italics.
112. *Ibid.*, p. 480, entry 31 July 1942.
113. *Ibid.*, p. 382, entry for 24 June 1942.
114. Compare *ibid.*, p. 383; also pp. 398–403 of the present study.
115. Wiedemann, p. 94.
116. Kater speaks about 'Hitler's always continuing protection motivated by sentimentality' of the Gauleiterss (Kater, *Social Change*, p. 39). Hitler's loyalty to these men, most of whom were 'old fighters', is also noted in Hüttenberger, p. 198 *et seq.*
117. *MK*, p. 657.
118. Bouhler I/II, p. 414, speech on 24 February 1941.
119. *Monologues*, p. 173, entry for 3/4 January 1942.
120. *Ibid.*, p. 205, entry for 16/17 January 1942. Compare Goebbels, *Speeches*, vol. 1, pp. 117, 125, 130, 250.
121. Mommsen, *Leadership Groups*, p. 157.
122. Compare *ibid.*, p. 174 *et seq.* Characteristic of the mood among the National Socialists after the aborted assassination attempt on 20 July 1944 is an address on 31 October 1944 by Ohlendorf to members of the Security Service: 'We did not go into this battle on a firm foundation . . . Neither the *Wehrmacht* nor industry, for example, could be newly structured according to National Socialism.' In both sectors one had been forced, said Ohlendorf, 'to develop evolutionarily' and had had neither 'the possibility' nor 'the time to proceed like Stalin'. In Ohlendorf's view, the 20th of July had disclosed that the 'forces' left in their positions of leadership in 1933 did 'not wish for victory . . . in this war', because this would be tantamount to 'the victory of the revolution'. Now, after 20 July one had begun 'to revolutionize this *Wehrmacht*' and 'in the area of the economy' the same development was going on. Herbst comments

quite rightly: 'The threatening defeat reinforced the demand for the National Socialist revolution because one was being made to feel the superiority of a revolutionary regime, the Soviet one, on one's own body, and simultaneously believed that in the assassins and the bourgeois circles they represented, one had found a guilty party for the military defeat. Mobilization and revolutionization as tendencies now become confused, and are nourished by the hope that a revolutionary storm will be unleashed which will not only sweep away the foundations of the old outdated and encapsulated social and economic order but also defeat the foreign enemy' (Herbst, p. 344 *et seq.*). Herbst also points out that business circles followed the information on the American economic system with growing attention: 'It may safely be assumed that, for many businessmen, such information reinforced the already existing disposition not to regard a victory by the Western Allies as the greatest possible evil.' (*ibid.*, p. 332). Many industrial leaders 'were looking towards the collapse of the political system with disinterest . . . In this context one was primarily trusting in the capitalistic sense of reality of Wall Street' after a German defeat (*ibid.*, p. 381). Business knew that after a defeat it would be virtually impossible 'without help from outside' to overcome the economy of deprivation with all of its accompanying dirigistic elements and the danger of sliding down into a centrally administered economy' (*ibid.*, p. 459).

123. *Testament*, pp. 72 *et seq.* (14 February 1945).
124. *Ibid.*, p. 110 (25 February 1945).
125. Hitler developed this and the subsequent line of argument in greatest detail in his speech at the *Reichsparteitag* on 3 September 1933, brochure, p. 33 *et seq.*
126. Speech at the culture conference of the *Reichsparteitag* on 1 September 1933, brochure p. 23.
127. Closing address at the *Reichsparteitag* on 3 September 1933, brochure, pp. 37, 41.
128. Wagener, p. 349 *et seq.*, June 1930.
129. *Monologues*, p. 237, entry for 27 January 1942.
130. *MGM* 2/76, p. 149, speech on 26 May 1944.
131. Cited in Ackermann, p. 114.
132. *Ibid.*, p. 115 *et seq.*
133. Goebbels, Diaries, SF, vol. 2, p. 633, entry on 26 June 1936.
134. *Ibid.*, p. 632, entry on 24 June 1936.
135. *Ibid.*, vol. 3, p. 257, entry on 7 September 1937.
136. *Ibid.*, p. 316, entry on 28 October 1937.
137. Jäckel, *Weltanschauung*, p. 87. That Hitler had not made any legal provisions for the succession is incorrect. Jäckel corrects his statement in *Hitler's Rule*, p. 161, n. 42. Also compare p. 383 of the present study.
138. *MK*, p. 673.
139. Krebs has not dated these statements by Hitler, but they were certainly made before 1932, because that was the year in which Krebs was ejected from the NSDAP by Hitler personally.
140. Krebs, p. 128. In later years Hitler also referred to the British example: 'The English still do not have a constitution today. Their constitution is the unwritten law which is alive within them without need of it being written down. And to take part in this unwritten law, that is what gives the individual that position of pride in anything having to do with the nation.' *Monologues*, p. 121, entry for 1/2 November 1941.
141. Compare Domarus, p. 232, speech on 23 March 1933; *ibid.*, p. 321, speech on 18 October 1933; and speech in the *Reichstag* on 30 January 1937, brochure, p. 46.
142. Meissner, p. 311.

143. Wagener, p. 412, December 1931.
144. Domarus, p. 292, speech on 6 August 1933.
145. Files of the RK, p. 1385, n. 4.; also Kube, p. 72.
146. Domarus, p. 1316, speech on 1 September 1939.
147. Goebbels, Diaries, SF, vol. 3, p. 630, entry for 3 November 1939.
148. *Ibid.*, vol 4, p. 492, entry for 5 February 1941.
149. Picker, pp. 164–71, entry for 31 March 1942.
150. *Ibid.*, p. 172 *et seq.*
151. *Ibid.*, p. 383 *et seq.*, entry for 24 June 1942.
152. Domarus, p. 1424, speech on 23 November 1939.
153. Conversation with Mussolini on 19 July 1943, Hillgruber, *Statesmen II*, p. 289.
154. *Testament*, p. 110, dictation on 25 February 1945.
155. 'Hitler gave serious consideration to the question of succession and began to study the problem. He discussed it with the head of the Reichs Chancellory Lammers, whom he had also given the rank of a Reichs Minister. The regulation of the succession by adoption as in the Roman Empire was discussed as an example. In addition Lammers had Professor Percy Ernst Schramm prepare a study on the regulation of the succession in the elective empire of the old Holy Roman Empire of the German Nation – a form, however, which was hardly taken into consideration.' (Scheidt, *Postwar Recordings*, IfZ, Irving collection, p. 432).
156. Compare von Lang, *Schirach*, p. 312,
157. Scheidt, *op. cit.*, pp. 432–4. On Göring's loss of power during the Second World War see Kube, pp. 324–46.
158. Kershaw, *Hitler Myth*.
159. *Complete Recordings*, p. 916, speech on 27 April 1923.
160. *Ibid.*, p. 932, speech on 29 May 1923.; also *ibid.*, p. 933, speech on 1 June 1923.
161. Tyrell, p. 167.
162. *MK*, pp. 72 *et seq.*, 99, 378 *et seq.*, 501; italics in the original.
163. BA/NS 26/54, f. 6, 11 *et seq.*, speech on 12 June 1925.
164. Krebs, p. 138; Schirach, pp. 89, 92.
165. Domarus, p. 182, speech on 22 January 1933.
166. Closing address at the *Reichsparteitag* on 16 September 1935, brochure, p. 83 *et seq.*
167. *Complete Recordings*, p. 1033, speech on 14 October 1923.
168. Jochmann, *In Battle*, p. 80 *et seq.*, speech on 28 February 1926.
169. *MK*, p. 593 *et seq.*
170. Jochmann, *op. cit.*, p. 81, n. II. Compare Kurt Detlev Möller, *The Final Chapter: History of the Capitulation of Hamburg* (Hamburg, 1947), p. 98 *et seq.*
171. 'You should not imagine that National Socialism expresses itself in wishing or demanding that the old flags fly again, that the old authoritarian state is erected again . . .' (*Complete Recordings*, p. 1014. speech on 16 September 1923). In *Mein Kampf* Hitler wrote about the monarchy: 'This form demands therefore: never talk back, but accept anything and everything His Majesty deigns to graciously want. But exactly here is where the dignity of the free man was most required, otherwise the monarchic institutions would one day have to fall because of this grovelling, because it was grovelling and nothing else!' (*MK*, p. 258 *et seq.*). 'Just as the authorities in the old police state, today our administrations still only regard the citizen as an underling, who, being politically under age, requires constant spoon-feeding.' (*Monologues*, p. 120, entry for 1/2 November 1941).
172. *Monologues*, p. 50, entry for 1/2 August 1941.

173. Compare Chapter II.2 of the present study.
174. *Complete Recordings*, p. 127, speech on 27 April 1920.
175. *Ibid.*, p. 443, notes for a speech on 29 July 1921.
176. *Ibid.*, p. 924, speech on 4 May 1923.
177. *Ibid.*, p. 1004, speech on 5 September 1923.
178. Compare *ibid.*, p. 733, conversation with Truman Smith on 20 November 1922; *ibid.*, p. 925, speech on 6 May 1923; *ibid.*, p. 988, speech on 21 August 1923; *ibid.*, p. 1028, speech on 7 October 1923; and *ibid.*, p. 1039, speech on 10 October 1923.
179. Domarus, p. 127, interview on 16 August 1932.
180. *Ibid.*, p. 694, speech on 20 May 1937; *ibid.*, p. 833, speech on 25 March 1938; *ibid.*, p. 842, speech on 1 April 1938.
181. Wiedemann, p. 74.
182. Goebbels, Diaries, SF, vol. 2, p. 475.
183. *Ibid.*, p. 594.
184. Preiss, p. 68, speech on 9 June 1927.
185. BA/NS 26/55, f. 51, speech on 18 September 1928.
186. BA/NS 26/56, f. 19 *et seq.*, speech on 6 March 1929.
187. Wagener, p. 124 (summer 1930); similarly *ibid.*, pp. 188, 246 *et seq.*, 292.
188. Opening proclamation at the *Reichsparteitag* on 1 September 1933, brochure, p. 17 *et seq.*
189. Speech in the *Reichstag* on 30 January 1934, brochure, pp. 15, 52. There are numerous similar statements by Hitler on record: 'We wild Germans are better democrats than other nations.' (Domarus, p. 433, interview on 5 August 1934). 'If democracy is only supposed to be the executor of the will of the people, then we are better democrats than all of our opponents in most of the so-called democracies in the world.' (*VB* No 249 of 6 September 1934, opening proclamation at the *Reichsparteitag* on 5 September 1934). 'Germany too has a "democratic" constitution. Today's German government of the National Socialist state has also been called by the people and feels itself just as responsible to the people.' (*VB* No 142 of 22 May 1935, speech in the *Reichstag* on 21 May 1935). 'I have not removed democracy, but only simplified it by not holding myself accountable to the 47 parties, but to the German nation itself.' (speech on 16 March 1936, brochure 'The *Führer*'s Battle for World Peace'; see also *ibid.*, p. 56, speech on 24 March 1936, p. 65, speech on 27 March 1936, and p. 71, speech on 28 March 1936). 'They speak about democracies and dictatorships and have not yet even understood that an upheaval has taken place in this country whose result – if democracy is to make any sense at all – must be called democratic in the highest sense of the word. With unerring certainty we are steering towards an order which – just as in all the rest of life – will secure a natural and sensible process of selection in the sector of political leadership, through which the really able brains of our nation will be identified for the leadership of the nation without regard for birth, origin, name or fortune . . . Is there a more splendid and beautiful socialism or a more truthful democracy than that National Socialism which makes it possible, thanks to its organization, that among millions of German boys, any one whom Providence may wish to make use of, can find the way up to the top of the nation.' (speech in the *Reichstag* on 30 January 1937, brochure, p. 12). Similarly also Kotze and Krausnick, p. 140, speech on 29 April 1937; *ibid.*, p. 256, speech on 8 November 1938; Picker, appendix, p. 488, speech on 23 November 1937; and speech in the *Reichstag* on 30 January 1939, brochure, p. 24.
190. Compare Lenin, *Theses*, p. 468; Stalin, *Works*, vol. 6, p. 103; and Mao, *Works*, vol.

Hitler: The Policies of Seduction

4, p. 445.
191. Compare the quotation from Hitler's speech in the *Reichstag* on 30 January 1937 cited in note 189. Hitler argues similarly in his speech on 29 April 1937; Kotze and Krausnick, p. 140.
192. *MK*, pp. 624, 636–44.
193. *IB* 3rd year set, issue 25 of 10 November 1928, p. 304. Similarly BA/NS 26/55, f. 177–9, speech on 7 December 1928; and *IB* of 16 February 1929.
194. Compare Bracher, *Seizure of Power*, pp. 192–202.
195. Opening proclamation at the *Reichsparteitag* on 1 September 1933, brochure, p. 19 *et seq.*; italics in the original.
196. Speech in the *Reichstag* on 20 February 1938, brochure, p. 34 *et seq.*; our italics.
197. Dahrendorf, p. 435.
198. *Monologues*, p. 119 *et seq.*, entry for 1/2 November 1941.
199. *Ibid.*, p. 139 *et seq.*, entry for 16 November 1941.
200. Picker, p. 260, entry for 3 May 1942.
201. *Ibid.*, p. 382 *et seq.*, entry for 24 June 1942.
202. *Ibid.*, p. 455, entry for 22 July 1942.
203. *Ibid.*, p. 462, entry for 26 July 1942.
204. Wagener, p. 301.
205. On Hitler's 'inability to take decisions' see Olden, pp. 191, 196, 301, 351, 355, 374, 377 *et seq.*, 402 *et seq.*; Heiden I, pp. 242, 315 *et seq.*, 344, 356 *et seq.*, 419, 426; Bullock, *Hitler*, pp. 282 *et seq.*, 782; Görlitz and Quint, pp. 283, 306, 465; Gisevius, pp. 290, 314, 348, 373; Heiber, pp. 34, 58; Fest, pp. 751, 834: Stern, pp. 155, 168; Waite, pp. 206, 210; Maser, *Early History*, p. 375 *et seq.*; Maser, *Führer Legend*, pp. 9 *et seq.*, 18, 24 *et seq.*, 33 *et seq.*, 51, 52, 56 *et seq.*, 69, 72, 96, 103, 106, 139, 142, 155, 179, 184, 190, 192 *et seq.*, 269, 289, 293, 339, 346, 401; Carr, pp. 27, 30, 32, 39, 42, 50, 62, 65, 139, 147; and Irving, *Hitler's War*, pp. xi, 67, 445, 690.
206. Maser, *Führer Legend*, p. 58 *et seq.*

VII. Hitler's Self-Assessment in the Political Spectrum

1. Haffner, p. 60. Möller writes: 'The NSDAP cannot be sorted into a simple left-right schema.' (Möller, *The End*, p. 28). Hildebrand also believes that the Third Reich 'basically could not be assigned to the political Left nor to the political Right, its orientation was neither clearly revolutionary nor clearly reactionary, but was a phenomenon *sui generis* which possessed its own historic power' (Hildebrand, *The Third Reich*, p. 109). Plack, on the other hand, believes that 'We can leave it at that, that Nazism was a typically right-wing movement.' (Plack, p. 256).
2. Dahrendorf, pp. 442–4.
3. Cited in Mommsen, *View of Society*, p. 90.
4. *Ibid.*, p. 92
5. Cited in *ibid.*, p. 91.
6. *Complete Recordings*, p. 204, speech on 13 August 1920; italics in the original.
7. *Ibid.*, p. 576, speech on 17 February 1922; also *ibid.*, pp. 571, 574, notes for this speech.
8. Domarus, p. 129, interview on 16 August 1932.
9. *Monologues*, p. 51, entry for 2 August 1941.
10. Strauss interview on 29 September 1979 in the *Bayerische Rundfunk*, cited in Plack, p. 252.

11. *Complete Recordings*, p. 250, speech on 26 October 1920.
12. *Ibid.*, p. 259, speech on 19 November 1920.
13. *Ibid.*, p. 440, notes for a speech on 20 July 1921.
14. *Ibid.*, p. 470, letter to G. Seifert on 6 September 1921; italics in the original.
15. *Ibid.*, p. 698, speech on 28 September 1922.
16. *Ibid.*, p. 837, speech on 26 February 1923.
17. *Ibid.*, p. 837; also *ibid.*, p. 840, italics in the original.
18. *Ibid.*, p. 912, speech on 12 April 1923.
19. *MK*, pp. 364, 726.
20. BA/NS 26/52, f. 25, speech on 6 August 1927.
21. Compare speech on 16 December 1925, *VB* special issue, BayHStA, collection of press clippings 1172; and BA/NSD 71/56, f. 9, 24, speech on 26 June 1927.
22. *VB* No 101 of 2 May 1929.
23. *VB* No 47 of 26 February 1930, speech on 24 February 1930.
24. Wagener, p. 368 *et seq.*, February 1931.
25. Bouhler I/II, p. 409, speech on 24 February 1941.
26. *Monologues*, p. 146, entry for 30 November 1941.
27. Bouhler III, p. 183, speech on 30 January 1942.
28. *MGM* 2/76, p. 155, speech on 26 May 1944.
29. Compare pp. 133–41 of the present study.
30. On the concepts and objectives of domestic policy of these forces, see Hoffmann, pp. 226–54; and Mommsen, *View of Society*.
31. Below, p. 403.
32. Martin Lipset is correct when he objects to the unconsidered use of the terms 'right' and 'left' and argues that the schematic use of these terms suggests that extremist movements or dictatorships could only occur on the left or the right, whereas the centre of the political continuum would always defend democracy (Lipset, 'Fascism: The Left, the Right, and the Centre'). But when Lipset then simply interprets National Socialism as being an extreme of the centre, and the middle classes at that, then the objection must be raised 'that in the established Fascist regimes – Germany and Italy – the influence of the middle classes on the guidelines of policy became ever more unimportant. Before, during, and after the appearance of Fascist parties there were organizations which were similarly composed sociologically. The functions and objectives of Fascism cannot be explained in terms of its social base.' (Wippermann, *Theories of Fascism*, p. 93 *et seq.*).
33. Marx, *Communist Manifesto*, p. 43.
34. Nolte, for example, writes that National Socialism '*was not* based on the melding of nationalism and socialism. Within it, every synthesis must permit us to recognize the essence and tradition of *both* elements.' (Nolte, *Fascism*, p. 388). If we were to follow Nolte's phenomenological method, however, it would be unavoidable to reconstruct this key point of National Socialist self-understanding in particular. In his study on *Varieties of Fascism: Doctrines of Revolution in the Twentieth Century*, published in 1964, Eugen Weber on the other hand emphasizes the revolutionary character of 'Fascism' and defines National Socialism as the amalgamation of a 'collectivistic nationalism' (p. 21 *et seq.*) and a 'utilitarian socialism' (p. 30 *et seq.*).
35. *Complete Recordings*, p. 665, speech on 28 July 1922. Also *ibid.*, p. 200, speech on 13 August 1920; *ibid.*, p. 659, speech on 28 July 1922; and *ibid.*, p. 621, speech on 12 April 1922.
36. *Ibid.*, p. 822, speech on 29 January 1923.

37. Compare *ibid.*, p. 200, speech on 13 August 1920.
38. BA/NS 26/54, ff. 131–4, speech on 6 March 1927.
39. *VB* No 84 of 12 April 1927, speech on 9 April 1927.
40. Compare Thalheimer, *On Fascism*.
41. Jäckel, who explicitly bases himself on the Marxist theory of Bonapartism, presents a rather 'un-Marxist' version in his study *Hitler's Rule* because he mixes the socio-economic term 'class' with terminology which serves to classify political-ideological positions or to characterize certain constitutional concepts. Compare our criticism in *Süddeutsche Zeitung* No 75 of 31 March 1987.
42. Jäckel, *Weltanschauung*, p. 152 *et seq.*
43. Thalheimer, p. 28.
44. BA/NS 26/52. ff. 92–4, speech on 8 November 1930.
45. BA/NL Streicher No 126, ff. 9 *et seq.*, 15–19, speech on 13 November 1930.
46. When Hitler's opponents within the party – i.e. the adherents of the left wing around Otto Strasser who were expelled from the party in 1930 or resigned from it – claim that Hitler had described socialism as a 'Jewish invention' (Krebs, p. 46) and said that 'if the people have something to eat and their fun, then they have their socialism' (*ibid.*, p. 143; similarly Strasser, p. 56), this is not credible, firstly because there is no proof to be found in any of the other sources and secondly because the attempt to 'unmask' Hitler as a traitor to the socialist ideal of National Socialism is too obvious. In his 'Second Book' Hitler explicitly declares: 'I am a socialist' (*ZB*, p. 78), as he does in numerous conversations with Otto Wagener. After the seizure of power Hitler also confessed to being a socialist; he even stressed that the socialist character of the Reich had to be emphasized with the greatest consistency (speech at the *Reichsparteitag* on 14 September 1936, brochure, p. 78).
47. Bouhler I/II, p. 411 *et seq.*, speech on 24 February 1941.
48. Compare Domarus, p. 1766, speech on 3 October 1941; and *ibid.*, p. 1869, speech on 26 April 1942.
49. Compare Hildebrand, *The Third Reich*, p. 110.
50. *Complete Recordings*, p. 914, speech on 27 April 1923.
51. Compare Maser, *Early History*, p. 132.
52. *MK*, pp. 39, 44–54, 589 *et seq.*; italics in the original.
53. Compare p. 360 *et seq.* of the present study.
54. BA/NS 26/54, f. 1, speech on 12 June 1925.
55. Wagener, pp. 346–8, 459.
56. Compare p. 37 of the present study.
57. Koeppen Notes, report No 32 of 18 September 1941, dinner. Fritz Tobias considers 'such a servility on the part of Severing to be completely impossible', and was kind enough to put documents at our disposal which support this judgement (letter of 13 August 1988 by Fritz Tobias to the author). In Tobias' view, the reports that Severing had repeatedly volunteered to 'issue' appeals to the social democratic workers are based on rumours which were being spread by the Communists at the time. Severing did, however, declare in an interview with the *Kölnische Zeitung* on 30 December 1934: 'I wish as emphatically as before that the day of the vote may bring an impressive majority for the return of the Saar district to Germany. My position on the Saar was never an expression of my party-political belief, but a natural expression of my national feelings and objectives which have not been affected by a change of the regime.'
58. *Monologues*, p.161, entry for 28/29 December 1941.

59. *Ibid.*, p. 248 *et seq.*, entry for 1 February 1942.
60. *Ibid.*, p. 240, entry for 27 January 1942.
61. *Ibid.*, p. 363, entry for 24 August 1942. The background is as follows. On 12 May 1919 the faction of the SPD decided against five votes to have its speaker declare in the National Convention that the peace conditions in their present form were unacceptable for Germany. Scheidemann declared for the government: '. . . who can, as an honest man – I do not even want to say as a German – only as an honest man who is true to his word, enter into such conditions? Which hand would not wither away that had laid us into such chains? This treaty is unacceptable for the Reichs government.'
62. Nolte, *Civil War*, p. 470.
63. In the introduction to his book *The European Civil War*, Nolte writes: 'This book is based on the assumption that the central motivation of Hitler's feelings and ideology actually was his hate- and fear-filled relationship to Communism, that with this he was only articulating in a particularly intensive way what numerous German and non-German contemporaries also felt, and that all of these feelings and fears were not only understandable but to a large extent also comprehensible and even justified up to a certain point.' (p. 16). The 'actual experience of Hitler, and the most moving one', had been 'with a high degree of probability the experience of Bolshevism, or Communism' (p. 120). Here Nolte is exaggerating the importance of anti-Communism in Hitler's ideology.
64. BA/NS 26/54, f. 8, speech on 12 June 1925.
65. Speech on 28 February 1926, Jochmann, *In Battle*, p. 97 *et seq.*
66. Wagener, p. 349, June 1930.
67. *Ibid.*, p. 431.
68. Speech at the opening of the third Winter Help Campaign 1935–36 on 8 October 1935, in 'Führer Speeches to the Winter Help Campaign 1933–1936', here p. 17.
69. Ley, p. 212.
70. *Monologues*, p. 51, entry for 2 August 1941.
71. Ernst Torgler, chairman of the faction of the KPD from 1929 to 1933, was one of the principal defendants in the *Reichstag* Arson Trial. He was acquitted and in 1935 released from the protective custody to which he had subsequently been condemned, after he had given the National Socialists material for their anti-Communist propaganda. He was expelled from the KPD in 1935.
72. *Monologues*, p. 52, entry for 2 August 1941.
73. *IB* 3rd year set, issue 22 of 20 October 1928, p. 267; *IB* 4th sear set, issue 39 of 28 September 1929, p. 493; *IB* 5th year set, issue 1 of 4 January 1930, p. 5.
74. *Monologues*, p. 122, entry for 2 November 1941.
75. *Ibid.*, p. 161, entry for 28/29 December 1941.
76. Conversation with the Bulgarian Regency Council on 17 March 1944, Hillgruber, *Statesmen II*, p. 387.
77. The analysis of the National Socialist understanding of Marxism is an important aim of research. There are some initial points of departure in Nolte, 'Marxism and National Socialism', who, however, places his emphasis on the portrayal of the relationship of Marxism to National Socialism but still manages to produce interesting results. On Hitler's position towards Marxism Nolte writes, with referral to Chapter 11 (vol. 1) of *Mein Kampf*: 'In this, the historic process Hitler describes is obviously, even if on a far lower intellectual level, the same one Marx and Engels had in mind, and the negative basic feelings are not without similarities: economic liberalism converts everything into mere goods, makes human relationships imper-

sonal, founds a purely formal democracy as well as a press which is directed by interest groups, and estranges people from their world to the point where the share, and therefore anonymity, becomes the key element or hallmark of business life. And in Hitler an experience with Marxism repeats itself, which is frequently attested to by unsophisticated people in particular: the scales suddenly fall from his eyes.' (Nolte, 'Marxism and National Socialism', p. 392 *et seq.*). As opposed to Marxism, however, Hitler did not see the causes of this event in a manner of production based on the accumulation of added value, but as a machination by the Jews (*ibid.*, p. 393). This is an interpretation by Nolte which is not completely wrong, but which in our view does not do justice to Hitler's view of the phenomena in question.

78. *VB* of 5 April 1927, speech on 2 April 1927.
79. *Ibid.*
80. *MK*, p. 420; similarly p. 361.
81. *VB* No 178 of 3 August 1929, speech on 2 August 1929; similarly *VB* of 4 January 1930.
82. *Complete Recordings*, p. 1064 *et seq.*, before the people's court, 1st day of the trial, 26 February 1924.
83. *MK*, pp. 44 *et seq.*, 193, 505, 509, 528 *et seq.*, 547; italics in the original.
84. Hanfstaengl, p. 196. When Hitler turned to the time of struggle in the table talks on 8 April 1942 he declared that at the time his primary objective had been to gain the working class: in the selection of red for the posters, for example, he had aligned himself with the Marxist parties (Picker, p. 205).
85. *IB* No 22 of 31 May 1930, p. 341.
86. Nolte, *Fascism*, p. 51; italics in the original.
87. Schramm, p. 320.
88. *ZB*, p. 153 *et seq.*
89. *IB* 4th year set, issue 6 of 9 February 1929, p. 64.
90. *Ibid.*, issue 13 of 30 March 1929, p. 149.
91. *IB* 5th year set, issue 2 of 11 January 1930, p. 21. Hitler repeated his assessment of Stalin as an agent of Jewry on 8 February 1930; see *IB*, issue 6, p. 85.
92. Goebbels, Diaries, SF, vol. 3, p. 21, entry for 25 January 1937.
93. *Ibid.*, p. 198, entry for 10 July 1937.
94. ADAP D VIII, p. 685 *et seq.* Cited here in Hillgruber, *Statesmen I*, p. 78, n. 3. Hitler made a similar statement to Sven Hedin on 4 March 1940 (see Hillgruber, *op.cit.*), as well as in a conversation with Mussolini on 18 March 1940 (*ibid.*, p.96). Also compare Hitler's statements on 20 January 1941 at a conference of German and Italian military experts, Domarus, p. 1655.
95. Compare the study by Louis Dupeux 'The Revolutionary-Conservative Image of Bolshevism', esp. p. 216 *et seq.*
96. Koeppen Notes, report No 37 on 23 September 1941, dinner.
97. Domarus, p. 1756, speech on 1 October 1941.
98. *Ibid.*, p. 1773, speech on 8 November 1941.
99. *Ibid.*, p. 1867, speech on 26 April 1942.
100. *Monologues*, p. 180, entry for 5/6 January 1942.
101. Picker, p. 133, entry for 23 March 1942.
102. *Ibid.*, p. 457, entry for 24 July 1942.
103. *Ibid.*, p. 447.
104. *Ibid.*, p. 452, entry for 22 July 1942.
105. *Monologues*, p. 366, entry for 26 August 1942.
106. Thöt Notes, Irving collection, IfZ, p. 14 *et seq.*, entry for 4 February 1943.

107. Scheidt Notes, Irving collection, IfZ, pp. 311 *et seq.*, 667.
108. Speer, p. 399.
109. *MGM* 2/76, p. 143, speech on 26 May 1944.
110. Goebbels, Diary, 45, p. 263 *et seq.*, entry for 16 March 1945.
111. *MK*, p. 129.
112. Hitler's speech on 27 February 1925 at the first big mass meeting after the refounding of the NSDAP, brochure p. 9 *et seq.*
113. *MK*, p. 201.
114. Compare Jäckel, *Weltanschauung*, p. 32.
115. Domarus, p. 375 (25 March 1934); *ibid.*, p. 735 (27 September 1937).
116. *Ibid.*, p. 737, speech on 28 September 1937. Compare *ibid.*, p. 1215, speech on 25 June 1939; *ibid.*, p. 1523 (10 June 1940); *ibid.*, p. 1553 (19 July 1940); Bouhler I/II, p. 414 *et seq.*, speech on 24 February 1941; and *Monologues*, p. 328, entry for 5 August 1942.
117. Compare Wiedemann, p. 140 *et seq.*; Engel Notes, p. 23; Dietrich, p. 246; Frank p. 296 *et seq.*; Speer, p. 124; Giesler, p. 382; and Meissner, p. 430.
118. Bouhler III, p. 198 *et seq.*, speech on 30 January 1942.
119. *Monologues*, p. 245 *et seq.*, entry for 31 January 1942.
120. *Rosenberg Diary*, p. 103, entry for 3 March 1940.
121. *Monologues*, p. 75, entry for 25/26 September to 11 October 1941. Similarly *ibid.*, p. 328, entry for 5 August 1942; and Picker, p. 459, entry for 24 July 1942.
122. *Monologues*, p. 129, entry for 5 November 1941.
123. *Ibid.*, p. 151 *et seq.*, entry for 13 December 1941.
124. *Ibid.*, p. 278, entry for 17 February 1942.
125. Conversation with Tiso on 12 May 1944, Hillgruber, *Statesmen II*, p. 452.
126. See *Testament*, pp. 84–7, dictation of 17 February 1945.
127. Compare *Monologues*, p. 43, entry for 22 July 1941; Picker, p. 237, entry for 23 April 1942; and Domarus, p. 1868, speech on 26 April 1942.
128. Thus Hitler in October 1940 to Hans Frank; see Frank, p. 227.
129. Conversation with Mussolini on 19 January 1941, Hillgruber, *Statesmen I*, p. 438 *et seq.*
130. *Monologues*, p. 284, entry for 19/20 February 1942.
131. Compare Picker, p. 357, entry for 5 June 1942; and *ibid.*, p. 361 *et seq.*, entry for 7 June 1942.
132. *Ibid.*, p. 362, entry for 7 June 1942.
133. *Ibid.*, p. 428 *et seq.*, entry for 7 July 1942.
134. Giesler, p. 421.
135. Conversation with the Bulgarian ambassador Draganoff on 14 August 1942, Hillgruber, *Statesmen II*, p. 102.
136. *Monologues*, p. 323, entry for 1 August 1942.
137. *Testament*, p. 60 *et seq.*, dictation on 10 February 1945.

VIII. Final Considerations

1. Petzold, p. 186.
2. Compare Grunberger, p. 56. The period of comparison selected, however, does not appear to be very sensible, although this does not change the correctness of the contention that social mobility in the Third Reich increased markedly.
3. Schäfer, p. 117.

4. An example of this is in Irving, *Hitler's War*, pp. 86, 111.
5. On the latter compare Ley, p. 213.
6. Mommsen, review by H.-A. Jacobsen in *MGM* 7/1970, p. 183.
7. *MK*, p. 686 *et seq.*
8. 'Hitler only had two real objectives, one in foreign policy and the other in racial policy. Under his leadership Germany had to conquer new *Lebensraum* in the East, and it had to remove the Jews. The state and its constitution, domestic, economic and social policy, the party, its programme and its ideology – everything was only the means to this dual end. Hitler was therefore indeed an opportunist to a large extent...' (Jäckel, *Weltanschauung*, p. 93).
9. With reference to the church he said on 25 October 1941: 'I am forced to pile up an enormous lot within me, but this does not mean that what I take notice of without being able to react to it immediately is extinguished within me. It is entered into an account; one day the book will be pulled forth. I also had to hold back with the Jews for a long time. There is no point in artificially creating additional difficulties for yourself. The more cleverly you proceed the better.' (*Monologues*, p. 108). As he specifically underlined, Hitler saw his task after the war (*Monologues*, p.150, entry for 13 December 1941) as consisting of solving 'the church question': 'I cannot give them [the clerics—R.Z.] the answer now, but it all goes into my big notebook. The time will come when I call them to account and make short shrift of it.' (*ibid.*, p. 272, entry for 8 February 1942). With regard to Hitler's long-term plans for the church, see *Rosenberg Diary*, p. 32 (28 June 1934); *ibid.*, p. 57 (24 February 1935); *ibid.*, p. 103 (3 March 1940); Engel Recordings, p. 30 (6 August 1938); *ibid.*, p. 71 *et seq.*, (20 January 1940); *ibid.*, p. 106 (20 May 1941); speech in the *Reichstag* on 30 January 1939, brochure, p. 49; Hillgruber, *Statesmen I*, p. 228; *Monologues*, p. 40 *et seq.* (11/12 July 1941); *ibid.*, p. 82 *et seq.* (14 October 1941); *ibid.*, p. 135 (11 November 1941); *ibid.*, p. 136 (12 November 1941); *ibid.*, p. 234 (25/26 January 1942); *ibid.*, p. 302 *et seq.* (26 February 1942); *ibid.*, p. 337 (11 August 1942); Picker, p. 201 *et seq.* (7 April 1942); *ibid.*, pp. 414–17 (4 July 1942); Domarus, p. 2019 (mid-June 1943); Dietrich, p. 170; Wiedemann, p. 88; and Below, p. 256 *et seq.*
10. Goebbels, Diaries, SF, vol. 4, p. 20, entry for 22 January 1940.
11. Compare our discussion in *NPL* 1/1986, p. 138 *et seq.*
12. Goebbels, Diaries, SF, vol. 4, p. 394, entry for 16 June 1941.
13. *Ibid.*, p. 698, entry for 17 June 1941.
14. Goebbels, Diaries, BA/NL 118/15, p. 5, entry for 9 July 1941.
15. This is how Goebbels reports the view that Hitler stated in a conversation on 3 June 1937. Goebbels, Diaries, SF, vol. 4, p. 164.
16. Hitler in a conversation with Goebbels on 8 May 1937, *ibid.*, p. 138.
17. Compare p. 26 *et seq.* of the present study.

Bibliography

Note: Only literature that has been cited in the study is listed here.

A. Unpublished sources

I. Bayerisches Hauptstaatsarchiv (Central Bavarian State Archives), BaHStA
VB special issues, information leaflets of the NSDAP etc.: collection of press clippings 1172 (formerly Rehse Collection).

II. Bundesarchiv (Federal Archives) Coblenz
NS 6/161: recording by Bormann about a meeting Hitler/Mussert.
NS 26/52-62: Hitler speeches.
NS 26/389: Hitler speeches.
NSD 71/56: Hitler speeches.
NL Epp 24/3: Hitler speeches.
NL Streicher 125/26: Hitler speeches. *Note: We have not taken into account the hand-written corrections made by Dr Preiss to the shorthand text of Hitler's speeches.*
NL Goebbels 118: diary of Dr Goebbels.
R/6/34a, F. 1-82: Notes by Rosenberg's personal assistant Dr W. Koeppen to Hitler's table talks.

III. Institut für Zeitgeschichte (Institute for Contemporary History) Munich, IfZ
Stenographic diary kept by Reichs stenographer Karl Thöt (FHQu.), 11 September 1942 to 23 May 1945 (Irving collection).
Rittmeister (ret.) *Dr* Wilhelm Scheidt, post-war notes and articles (Irving collection).
Captain Fritz Wiedemann, private papers 1936 to 1941, not numbered.
General of Infantry (ret.) Liebmann, private papers ED 1.
Völkischer Beobachter (National Observer), Bavarian edition, sets 1925 to 1932.
Illustrierter Beobachter (Illustrated Observer), sets 1928 to 1930.

IV. Stadt und Universitätsbibliothek (City and University Library) Frankfurt
Völkischer Beobachter (National Observer), North German edition, sets 1933 to 1945.

V. Stadtarchiv (City Archives) Erlangen, STA Erlangen
Hitler speeches III.220.H.1.

B. Published sources

Files of the Reichs Chancellory. Hitler Government 1933–1938. Pub. for the Historic Commission of the Bavarian Academy of Sciences by Konrad Repgen, for the Federal

Archives by Hans Booms. Vol. 1: 30 January to 31 August 1933, documents 1–206, ed. by Karl-Heinz Minuth; vol. 2: 12 September 1933 to 27 August 1934, documents 207–384, ed. by Karl-Heinz Minuth, Boppard/Rhine 1983. Cited as Files of the RK.

Bouhler, P., (pub.), *Der grossdeutsche Freiheitskampf. Reden Adolf Hitlers.* (The Battle for Freedom of Greater Germany. Adolf Hitler's Speeches). Vols. I/II: 1 September 1939 to 16 March 1941; vol. III: 16 March 1941 to 15 March 1942 (Munich, 1940–43).

Deutschland-Berichte der Sozialdemokratischen Partei Deutschlands (Sopade) (Germany Reports of the German Social Democratic Party), 1st year set 1934 to 7th year set 1940 (Frankfurt/M., 1982).

Domarus, M., *Hitler: Reden und Proklamationen 1932–1945. Kommentiert von einem deutschen Zeitgenossen* (Hitler: Speeches and Proclamations 1932–1945. Commented on by a German contemporary) (Wiesbaden, 1973).

Die Tagebücher von Joseph Goebbels: Sämtliche Fragmente (The Diaries of Joseph Goebbels: The Complete Fragments), pub. by Elke Fröhlich on behalf of the Institute for Contemporary History and in Connection with the Federal Archives. Part I: Notes 1924–1941, 4 vols. (Munich/New York/London/Paris, 1987). Cited as Goebbels, Diaries, SF.

Das Tagebuch von Joseph Goebbels 1925/26 (The Diary of Joseph Goebbels 1925/26), pub. by H. Heiber with further documents (Stuttgart, 1961). Cited as Geobbels, Diary, 25/26.

Goebbels, J., *Vom Kaiserhof zur Reichskanzlei: Eine historische Darstellung in Tagebuchblättern* (From the *Kaiserhof* to the *Reichskanzlei*: A Historic Portrayal in Pages from a Diary) (Munich, 1934). Cited as Goebbels, *Kaiserhof.*

Goebbels Tagebücher aus den Jahren 1942–43 (Goebbels Diaries of the Years 1942–43), pub. by Louis P. Lochner with further documents (Zürich, 1948). Cited as Goebbels, Diary, 42/43.

Goebbels, J., *Tagebücher 1945* (Diary 1945), with an introduction by Rolf Hochhuth (Bergisch Gladbach, 1980). Cited as Goebbels, Diary, 45.

Goebbels-Reden 1932–1939 (Goebbels Speeches 1932–1939), vol. 1, pub. by Helmut Heiber (Munich, 1971).

Goebbels-Reden 1939–1945 (Goebbels Speeches 1939–1945), vol. 2, pub. by Helmut Heiber (Munich, 1972).

Harlander, T. and Fehl, G., (pub.), *Hitlers Sozialer Wohnungsbau 1940–1945: Wohnungspolitik, Baugestaltung und Siedlungsplanung* (Hitler's Social Housing 1940–1945: Housing Policy, Building and Urban Planning) (Hamburg, 1986). Articles and legal foundations on housing policy, building and urban planning from the periodical *Der Soziale Wohnungsbau in Deutschland.*

Heeresadjutant bei Hitler 1938-1943 (Army Adjutant to Hitler 1938–1943) (Stuttgart, 1974). Notes by Major Engel, pub. and commented on by H. von Kotze. Cited as Engel Notes.

Hillgruber, A., (pub.), *Staatsmänner und Diplomaten bei Hitler* (Statesmen and Diplomats with Hitler) (Frankfurt/M., 1967 and 1970). Confidential notes on conversations with representatives of foreign countries 1939–44, 2 vols.

Hitler, A., *Sämtliche Aufzeichnungen 1905–1924* (Complete Notes 1905–1924), pub. by E Jäckel and A. Kuhn (Stuttgart, 1980). The forged documents were not taken into account: compare Jäckel and Kuhn, *Neue Erkenntnisse zur Fälschung von Hitler-Dokumenten* (New Insights into the Forging of Hitler Documents), *VjHfZg* 1984, pp. 163–9. Cited as *Complete Notes.*

Hitler, A., *Mein Kampf.* Two volumes in one book: vol. 1: An Accounting; vol. 2: The National Socialist Movement (Munich, 1939), 419–423rd edns. Cited as *MK.*

Die Rede Adolf Hitlers in der ersten grossen Massenversammlung (Münchener Bürgerbräu-

Bibliography

Keller am 27.2.1925) bei der Wiederaufrichtung der NSDAP(Adolf Hitler's Speech at the First Big Mass Rally [on 27 February 1925 at the Munich Bürgerbräukeller] at the Resurrection of the NSDAP) (Munich, 1925).
'Der Weg zum Wiederaufstieg: Hitler's geheime Broschüre für Industrielle 1927' ('The Road to Recovery: Hitler's Secret Brochure for Industrialists 1927'), in Turner, *Faschismus und Kapitalismus* (Fascism and Capitalism), pp. 41–59.
Hitlers Zweites Buch (Hitler's Second Book: A Document from 1928) (Stuttgart, 1961). Introduced and commented on by G. L. Weinberg, with a preface by H. Rothfels. Cited as ZB.
Hitlers Auseiandersetzung mit Brüning (Hitler's Dispute with Brüning) (Munich, 1932).
Das Junge Deutschland will Arbeit und Frieden (Young Germany Wants Work and Peace) (Berlin, 1933). Speeches by the Reichs Chancellor of the New Germany Adolf Hitler, with an introduction by *Dr* Josef Goebbels.
Das Recht der Deutschen Arbeit: Adolf Hitler und Staatsrat Dr Ley zum Recht der Arbeit (The Law of German Work: Adolf Hitler and State Counsellor Dr Ley on the Law of Work) (Munich, 1933). Compiled by *Dr* Karl Sell.
Die Reden Hitlers am Reichsparteitag 1933 (Hitler's Speeches at the *Reichsparteitag* 1933) (Munich, 1934).
Die Rede des Führers Adolf Hitler am 30. Jan. 1934 im Deutschen Reichstag (The Speech by the Führer Adolf Hitler on 30 January 1934 in the German *Reichstag*) (Leipzig, 1934). With the Law on the Reconstruction of the German Reich and the Reasons by Reichs Minister *Dr* Frick.
Führer-Reden zum Winterhilfswerk 1933–1936 (*Führer* Speeches on the Winter Help Campaign 1933–1936) (Munich/Berlin, 1937).
Die Reden Hitlers am Parteitag der Freiheit 1935 (Hitler's Speeches at the Party Convention of Freedom 1935) (Munich, n.d.).
Der Parteitag der Freiheit vom 10.–16. September 1935 (The Party Convention of Freedom from 10–16 September 1935) (Munich, 1935). Official Report on the course of the *Reichsparteitag*, with all the Convention speeches.
Freiheit für Deutschland. Friede für Europa (Freedom for Germany. Peace for Europe) (n.d.). Speech by the *Führer* in the Historic Session of the *Reichstag* on 7 March 1936. Special issue No 33 of the *SS-Standarte*.
Des Führers Kampf um den Weltfrieden (The Führer's Battle for World Peace) (Munich, 1936). Speeches 12 March 1936 to 28 March 1936.
Hitlers Denkschrift zum Vierjahresplan 1936 (Hitler's Memorandum on the Four-Year Plan 1936). Documentation, with an introduction by Wilhelm Treue, *VjHfZg*, 3rd year set 1955, 2nd issue, pp. 184–210.
Reden des Führers am Parteitag der Ehre 1936 (Speeches by the *Führer* at the Party Convention of Honour 1936) (Munich, 1936).
Rede des Führers und Reichskanzlers Adolf Hitler vor dem Reichstag am 30. Januar 1937 (Speech by the *Führer* and Reichs Chancellor Adolf Hitler before the *Reichstag* on 30 January 1937) (Berlin, 1937).
Reden des Führers am Parteitag der Arbeit 1937 (Speeches by the *Führer* at the Party Convention for Work 1937) (Berlin, 1939).
Führer-Reden zum Winterhilfswerk 1937 und 1938 (*Führer* Speeches on the Winter Help Campaign 1937 and 1938) (Berlin, 1939).
Führerbotschaft an Volk und Welt (*Führer* Message to the Nation and the World) (Munich, 1938). Speech in the *Reichstag* on 20 February 1938.
Reden des Führers am Parteitag Grossdeutschland 1938 (Speeches by the *Führer* at the Party

Convention Greater Germany 1938) (Munich, 1939).

Ausgewählte Reden des Führers 1938 (Selected Speeches by the *Führer* 1938) (Berlin, 1938). Speech by Field Marshal Hermann Göring at the Party Convention Greater Germany; special issue for the *Wehrmacht*.

Rede des Führers vor dem 1. Grossdeutschen Reichstag am 30. Januar 1939 (Speech by the *Führer* to the 1st Greater German *Reichstag* on 30 January 1939) (Munich, 1939).

Führer-Reden zum Kriegswinterhilfswerk 1939 und 1940 (*Führer* Speeches to the War Winter Help Campaign 1939 and 1940) (Berlin, 1940).

Kampf bis zum Sieg! Rede des Führers vor der Alten Garde am 8. November 1940 (Fight Until Victory! Speech by the *Führer* to the Old Guard on 8 November 1940) (Munich, n.d.).

Führer-Rede zum Kriegswinterhilfswerk 1941/42 (*Führer* Speech to the War Winter Help Campaign 1941/42) (Berlin, 1941). Together with the speech by Reichs Minister *Dr* Goebbels and the Report on the War Winter Help Campaign 1940/41.

Hitlers Ansprache vor Generalen und Offizieren am 26. Mai 1944 (Hitler's Speech to Generals and Officers on 26 May 1944). Documentation by H.-H. Wilhelm, *MGM* 2/76, pp. 123–70.

Hitlers Wollen. Nach Kernsätzen aus seinen Schriften und Reden (What Hitler Wanted. According to Key Statements from his Writings and Speeches), pub. by W. Siebarth (Munich, 1940).

Adolf Hitler spricht. Ein Lexikon des Nationalsozialismus (Adolf Hitler Speaks. A Dictionary of National Socialism) (Leipzig, 1934).

Sozialismus wie ihn der Führer sieht (Socialism as the *Führer* Sees It) (Munich, 1935). Words by the *Führer* on Social Questions. Compiled by F. Menstre.

Hitler, A., *Monologe im Führerhauptquartier 1941–1944* (Monologues at *Führer* Headquarters 1941–1944) (Hamburg, 1980). The recordings by Heinrich Heims, pub. by Werner Jochmann. Cited as *Monologues*.

Hitlers Tischgespräche im Führerhauptquartier 1941–42 (Hitler's Table Talks at *Führer* Headquarters 1941–42) (Wiesbaden, 1983). Notes by Henry Picker. Cited as Picker.

Hitlers politisches Testament. Die Bormann-Diktate vom Februar und April 1945 (Hitler's Political Testament. The Bormann Dictations of February and April 1945) (Hamburg, 1981). With an essay by Hugh R. Trevor-Roper and an epilogue by André François-Poncet. Cited as *Testament*.

Hofer, W., *Der Nationalsozialismus. Dokumente 1933–1945* (National Socialism. Documents 1933–1945) (Frankfurt/M., 1957).

Jochmann, W., *Im Kampf um die Macht* (In the Battle for Power) (Frankfurt, 1960). Hitler's Speech to the Hamburg National Club of 1919.

Kotze, H. and Krausnick, H., *"Es spricht der Führer"* ('The Führer Speaks') (Gütersloh, 1966). Seven selected speeches by Hitler.

Ley, R., *Wir alle helfen dem Führer. Deutschland braucht jeden Deutschen* (We All Help the *Führer*. Germany Needs Every German) (Munich, 1937).

Preiss, H., *Adolf Hitler in Franken. Reden aus der Kampfzeit* (Adolf Hitler in Frankonia. Speeches from the Time of Struggle) (Nuremberg, 1939).

Rauschning, H., *Gespräche mit Hitler* (Talks with Hitler) (Zürich, 1940).

Das politische Tagebuch Alfred Rosenbergs aus den Jahren 1934/35 und 1939/40 (The Political Diary of Alfred Rosenberg from 1934/35 and 1939/40) (Göttingen-Berlin-Frankfurt/M., 1956). Pub. and commented on by *Dr* Hans-Günther Seraphim.

Verfügungen/Anordnungen/Bekanntgaben Decrees/Orders/Announcements), vols. I–VI (Munich, 1943/44). Issued by the Party Office. Cited as Decrees by the Party Office.

C. Contemporary works

Dimitroff, G., *Arbeiterklasse gegen Faschismus* (Working Class Against Fascism) (Munich, n.d.). Report presented on 2 August 1935 to Item 2 of the Agenda of the Seventh World Congress of the Communist International: 'The Offensive by Fascism and the Tasks of the Communist International in the Battle for the Unity of the Working Class'.

Heiden, K., *Adolf Hitler. Eine Biographie. Bd. 1: Das Zeitalter der Verantwortungslosigkeit, Bd. 2: Ein Mann gegen Europa* (Adolf Hitler. A Biography. Vol. 1: The Age of Irresponsibility; vol. 2: One Man Against Europe) (Munich, 1980). Unaltered reprint, Zürich, Europa-Verlag, 1936/37–1980.

Horkheimer/Pollock/Neumann et al., *Wirtschaft, Recht und Staat im Nationalsozialismus* (Economy, Law, and the State under National Socialism) (Frankfurt/M., 1981). Analyses by the Institute for Social Research 1939–1942, pub. by H. Dubiel and A. Söllner.

Jung, E. J., *Die Herrschaft der Minderwertigen. Ihr Zerfall und ihre Ablösung durch ein Neues Reich* (The Rule of the Inferior. Their Downfall and Their Replacement by a New Reich) (Berlin, 1930).

Moeller van den Bruck, A., *Das Dritte Reich* (The Third Reich) (Hamburg, 1931).

Neumann, F., *Behemoth. Structure and Practice of National Socialism* (New York, 1942).

Olden, R. *Hitler the Pawn* (London, 1936).

Pollock. F., 'Staatskapitalismus' ('State Capitalism'), in Horkheimer et al., *Wirtschaft, Recht und Staat im Nationalsozialismus*, pp. 81–109.

———, 'Ist der Nationalsozialismus eine neue Ordnung?' ('Is National Socialism a New Order?'), in *Wirtschaft, Recht und Staat im Nationalsozialismus*, pp. 111–28

Rauschning, H., *Die Revolution des Nihilismus* (The Revolution of Nihilism) (Zürich, 1964). Newly pub. by Golo Mann.

Reich, W., *Die Massenpsychologie des Faschismus* (The Mass Psychology of Fascism) (Frankfurt, 1977). First pub. in 1933; new enlarged edn 1942.

Sering, P. (pseud. for Richard Löwenthal), 'Der Faschismus' ('Fascism'), in *ZfS* No 24/25 (September/October 1935), pp. 765–87.

Spengler, O., *Der Mensch und die Technik* (Man and Technology) (Munich, 1931). Contribution to a philosophy of life.

Thalheimer, A., 'Über den Faschismus' ('On Fascism'), in Abendroth, W., (pub.) *Faschismus und Kapitalismus* (Fascism and Capitalism) (Frankfurt/M., 1979), pp. 19–39. Theories about the social causes and the function of Fascism.

D. Memoirs and subjective portrayals post-1945

Aretin, E. v., *Krone und Ketten. Erinnerungen eines bayerischen Edelmanns* (Crown and Chains. Memoirs of a Bavarian Noble), pub. by Karl Buchheim and K. O. von Aretin (Munich, 1955).

Below, N. von, *Als Hitlers Adjutant 1937-45* (As Hitler's Adjutant 1937–45) (Mainz 1980).

Dietrich, O., *Zwölf Jahre mit Hitler* (Twelve Years with Hitler) (Cologne, 1955).

Frank, H., *Im Angesicht des Galgen* (In View of the Gallows) (Munich-Gräfelfing, 1953). Interpretation of Hitler and his age based on personal experiences and insights. Written in the Nuremberg Court Prison.

Ein anderer Hitler. Bericht seines Architekten Hermann Giesler. Erlebnisse–Gespräche–Reflexionen (A Different Hitler. Report by his Architect Hermann Giesler. Experiences–Conversations–Reflections) (Leoni a. Starnberger See, 1982). Cited as Giesler.

Hanfstaengl, E., *Zwischen Weissem und Braunen Haus* (Between the White House and the Brown House) (Munich, 1970). Memoirs of a political outsider.

Krebs, A., *Tendenzen und Gestalten der NSDAP* (Tendencies and Figures of the NSDAP) (Stuttgart, 1959). Recollections from the early days of the Party.

Meissner, O., *Staatssekretär unter Ebert–Hindenburg–Hitler* (State Secretary under Ebert–Hindenburg–Hitler) (Hamburg, 1950). The road of Fate of the German nation 1918–1945 as I experienced it.

Schirach, B. von, *Ich glaubte an Hitler* (I Believed in Hitler) (Hamburg, 1967).

Speer, A., *Erinnerungen* (Memoirs) (Frankfurt/M.–Berlin, 1969).

Strasser, O., *Mein Kampf. Eine politische Autobiographie* (My Struggle. A Political Autobiography) (Frankfurt/M., 1969).

Wagener, O., *Hitler aus nächster Nähe* (Hitler from Close Up) (Frankfurt/M.–Berlin–Vienna, 1978). Notes by a confidant, 1929–1932. Pub. by H. A. Turner.

Wiedemann, F., *Der Mann der Feldherr werden wollte* (The Man Who Wanted to Become a Commander) (Velbert-Kettwig, 1964). Events and experiences of Hitler's superior in the First World War and his subsequent personal adjutant.

Ziegler, H. S., *Adolf Hitler aus dem Erleben dargestellt* (Adolf Hitler Portrayed from Experience) (Göttingen, 1964).

E. Portrayals

(a) Literature on NS Economic and Social Policy as well as on the ideological background of Hitler's Weltanschauung

Barkai, A., 'Die Wirtschaftsauffassung der NSDAP' ('The Economic Concept of the NSDAP'), in *Aus Politik und Zeitgeschichte*, supplementary to the weekly *Das Parlament*, B 9/75, pp. 3–16. Cited as Barkai, *Economic Concept*.

———, *Das Wirtschaftssystem des Nationalsozialismus* (The Economic System of National Socialism) (Cologne 1977). The historic background 1933–36. Cited as Barkai, *Economic System*.

———, 'Sozialdarwinismus und Antiliberalismus in Hitlers Wirtschaftskonzept' ('Social Darwinism and Anti-Liberalism in Hitler's Economic Concept'), in Henry A. Turner Jr., 'Hitlers Einstellung zu Wirtschaft und Gesellschaft vor 1933' ('Hitler's Position on the Economy and Society before 1933'), in *GuG*, 3rd year set, pp. 406–17. Cited as Barkai, *Social Darwinism*.

———, *Vom Boykott zur "Entjudung". Der wirtschaftliche Existenzkampf der Juden im Dritten Reich 1933–1945* (From the Boycott to 'De-Jewing'. The Economic Fight for Existence of the Jews in the Third Reich 1933–1945) (Frankfurt/M., 1988).

Blaich, F., 'Wirtschaftspolitik und Wirtschaftsverfassung im Dritten Reich' ('Economic Policy and Organization in the Third Reich'), in *Aus Politik und Zeitgeschichte*, supplement to the weekly *Das Parlament*, B 8/71, pp. 3–18.

Burchardt, L., *Die Auswirkungen der Kriegswirtschaft auf die deutsche Zivilbevölkerung im Ersten und im Zweiten Weltkrieg* (The Effects of the War Economy on the German Population in the First and Second World Wars), *MGM* 1/1974, pp. 65–97.

Erbe, R., *Die nationalsozialistische Wirtschaftspolitik 1933-1939 im Lichte der modernen Theorie* (National Socialist Economic Policy 1933–1939 in the Light of Modern Theory) (Zürich, 1958).

Fischer, W., *Deutsche Wirtschaftspolitik 1918-1945* (German Economic Policy 1918–

1945), 3rd edn (Opladen, 1968).
Fried, F., *Das Ende des Kapitalismus* (The End of Capitalism) (Jena, 1931).
———, *Autarkie* (Autarky) (Jena, 1932).
Garraty, J., 'The New Deal. National Socialism and the Great Depression', in *AHR*, vol. 78, No 4, October 1973, pp. 907-44.
Georg, E., *Die wirtschaftlichen Unternehmungen der SS* (The Business Enterprises of the SS) (Stuttgart, 1963).
Grotkopp, W., *Die grosse Krise. Lehren aus der Überwindung der Wirtschaftskrise 1929/32* (The Great Crisis. Conclusions from the Overcoming of the Economic Crisis 1929/32) (Düsseldorf, 1954).
Grunberger, R., *Das Zwölfjährige Reich. Der deutsche Alltag unter Hitler* (The Twelve Year Reich. German Daily Life Under Hitler) (Vienna–Munich–Zürich, 1972).
Hardach, K., *Wirtschaftsgeschichte Deutschlands im 20. Jahrhundert* (German Economic History in the 20th Century) (Göttingen, 1976).
Härter, K., *Der Konflikt zwischen dem Reichsarbeitsministerium und der Deutschen Arbeitsfront als wesentliches Strukturmerkmal der Sozialpolitik des Dritten Reiches* (The Conflict Between the Reichs Labour Ministry and the German Labour Front as an Essential Structural Element of Social Policy in the Third Reich), unpublished MS (TH Darmstadt, 1984).
Hayek, F. A., *Der Weg zur Knechtschaft* (The Road to Bondage) (Munich, 1994). New edn of the economic classic, with an introduction by Otto *Graf* Lambsdorff.
Hennig, E., *Thesen zur deutschen Sozial- und Wirtschaftsgeschichte 1933 bis 1938* (Theses on German Social and Economic History 1933 to 1939) (Frankfurt/M., 1973).
Herbst, L., *Der Totale Krieg und die Ordnung der Wirtschaft* (Total War and the Structuring of the Economy) (Stuttgart, 1982). The war economy amidst politics, ideology and propaganda 1939-45.
Heyl, J. D., 'Hitler's Economic Thought: A Reappraisal', in *Central European History*, 6, 1973/74, pp. 83–96.
Hussmann, P., *Der deutsche Arbeitsdienst* (The German Labour Service) (Berlin, 1935). A constitutional investigation of the idea and structure of the German Labour Service and its position within the overall structure of the State.
Kluke, P., 'Hitler und das Volkswagenprojekt' ('Hitler and the Volkswagen Project'), in *VjHfZg*, October 1960, pp. 341-83.
Köhler, H., *Arbeitsdienst in Deutschland* (Labour Service in Germany) (Berlin, 1967). Plans and forms of realization until the introduction of obligatory Labour Service in 1935.
Kroll, G., *Von der Weltwirtschaftskrise zur Staatskonjunktur* (From the World Economic Crisis to State Control) (Berlin, 1958).
Krüger, P., 'Zu Hitlers "nationalsozialistischen Wirtschaftserkenntnissen"' ('On Hitler's "National Socialist Economic Insights"'), in *GuG* 6th year set, 1980, pp. 263–82.
Lampert, H., 'Staatliche Sozialpolitik im Dritten Reich' ('State Social Policy in the Third Reich'), in Bracher *et al.*, *National Socialist Dictatorship 1933-1945* (q.v.), pp. 177–205.
Lochner, L. P., *Die Mächtigen und der Tyrann* (The Powerful and the Tyrant) (Darmstadt, 1955). German industry from Hitler to Adenauer.
Ludwig, K. H., *Technik und Ingenieure im Dritten Reich* (Technology and Engineers in the Third Reich) (Düsseldorf, 1974).
Mason, T. W., *Arbeiterklasse und Volksgemeinschaft* (Working Class and National Community) (Opladen, 1975). Documents and material on German labour policy 1936–39, Cited as Mason, *Working Class*.
———, *Sozialpolitik im Dritten Reich* (Social Policy in the Third Reich) (Opladen, 1978).

Cited as Mason, *Social Policy*.

———, 'Der Primat der Politik – Politik und Wirtschaft im Nationalsozialismus' ('The Primacy of Politics – Politics and Economy under National Socialism'), in Michalka, *Nationalsozialistische Aussenpolitik* (q.v.), pp 117–47. Cited as Mason, *Primacy*.

Milward, A. S., 'Der Einfluss ökonomischer und nicht-ökonomischer Faktoren auf die Strategie des Blitzkrieges' ('The Influence of Economic and Non-Economic Factors on the Strategy of the *Blitzkrieg*') in Michalka, *Nationalsozialistische Aussenpolitik* (q.v.), pp. 455–70.

Petzina, D., *Autarkiepolitik im Dritten Reich* (Autarky Policy in the Third Reich) (Stuttgart, 1968). The National Socialist Four-Year Plan.

Pool, J. and S., *Hitlers Wegbereiter zur Macht* (Hitler's Helpers to Power) (Berne–Munich, 1979). How Hitler's rise became possible through secret German and international financial sources.

Prinz, M., *Vom neuen Mittelstand zum Volksgenossen* (From the New Middle Class to National Comrade) (Munich 1986). Development of the social status of salaried employees from the Weimar Republic to the end of the NS era.

Quint, H. A., (pseud. for von Frankenberg), *Porsche. Der Weg eines Zeitalters* (Porsche. The Way of an Age) (Stuttgart, 1951).

Recker, M. L., *Nationalsozialistische Sozialpolitik im Zweiten Weltkrieg* (National Socialist Social Policy in the Second World War) (Munich, 1985).

Rupp, L. J., *Mobilizing Women For War: German and American Propaganda 1939–1945* (Princeton, 1978).

Salin, E., 'Von den Wandlungen der Weltwirtschaft in der Nachkriegszeit' ('Developments in World Economics in the Post-War Period'), in *Weltwirtschaftliches Archiv*, 35th vol. (1932 I), pp. 1–33.

Schoenbaum, D., *Die braune Revolution* (The Brown Revolution) (Munich, 1980). A social history of the Third Reich.

Schumann, H.-G., *Nationalsozialismus und Gewerkschaftsbewegung* (National Socialism and the Union Movement) (Hannover–Frankfurt/M. 1958). The destruction of the German unions and the build-up of the 'German Labour Front'.

Smelser, R. M., 'Die nationalsozialistische Machtergreifung als sozial-integrierender Prozess: Überlegungen zur NS Sozialpolitik' ('The National Socialist Seizure of Power as a Process of Social Integration: Considerations on NS Social Policy'), in Michalka, *National Socialist Seizure of Power* (q.v.), pp. 220–30.

Sombart, W., *Die deutsche Volkswirtschaft im Neunzehnten Jahrhundert* (German Political Economy in the Nineteenth Century) (Berlin, 1903).

———, 'Die Wandlungen des Kapitalismus' ('Developments of Capitalism'), in *Weltwirtschaftliches Archiv*, 28th vol. (1928 II), pp. 243–56.

———, *Die Zukunft des Kapitalismus* (The Future of Capitalism) (Berlin, 1932).

Teichert, E., *Autarkie und Grossraumwirtschaft in Deutschland 1930–1939* (Autarky and Large-Area Economics in Germany 1930–1939) (Munich, 1984). Export policy concepts between the economic crisis and the Second World War.

Turner, H. A., 'Verhalfen die deutschen "Monopolkapitalisten" Hitler zur Macht?' ('Did the German "Monopoly Capitalists" Help Hitler Gain Power?'), in Turner, *Faschismus und Kapitalismus in Deutschland* (q.v.), pp. 9–32.

———, 'Hitlers Einstellung zu Wirtschaft und Gesellschaft vor 1933' ('Hitler's Position on the Economy and Society before 1933'), in *GuG*, 1976, issue 1, pp. 87–117.

———, *Die Grossunternehmer und der Aufstieg Hitlers* (Big Business and Hitler's Rise) (Berlin, 1985). Cited as Turner, *Big Business*.

Victor, M., 'Das sogenannte Gesetz der abnehmenden Aussenhandelsbedeutung' ('The So-Called Law of Diminishing Importance of Foreign Trade'), in: *Weltwirtschaftliches Archiv,* 36th vol. (1932 II), pp. 59–85.

Winkler, D., *Frauenarbeit im "Dritten Reich"* (Female Labour in the 'Third Reich') (Hamburg, 1977).

(b) General

Ackermann, J., *Heinrich Himmler als Ideologe* (Heinrich Himmler as an Ideologist) (Göttingen–Zürich–Frankfurt/M., 1970).

Aigner, D., 'Hitler und die Weltherrschaft' ('Hitler and World Rule'), in Michalka, *Nationalsozialistische Aussenpolitik* (q.v.), pp. 49–69.

Allardyce, G., 'What Fascism Is Not: Thoughts on the Deflation of a Concept', in *AHR,* vol. 84 (1979), pp. 367–88.

Backes, U.; Janssen, K.-H.; Jesse, E.; Köhler, H.; Mommsen, H.; and Tobias, F., *Reichstagsbrand. Aufklärung einer historischen Legende* (Fire in the *Reichstag.* Clearing Up a Historic Legend), 2nd enlarged edn (Munich, 1987).

Bennecke, H., *Die Reichswehr und der "Röhm Putsch"* (The Reichswehr and the 'Röhm Putsch') (Munich–Vienna, 1964).

Benz, W., 'Die Abwehr der Vergangenheit. Ein Problem nur für Historiker und Moralisten?' ('Defending Against the Past. Only a Problem for Historians and Moralists?'), in Diner, D., (pub.), *Ist der Nationalsozialismus Geschichte?* (q.v.), pp. 17–33.

Bloch, C., *Die SA und die Krise des NS-Regimes 1934* (The SA and the Crisis of the NS Regime 1934) (Frankfurt/M., 1970).

Böhme, K., (pub.), *Aufrufe und Reden deutscher Professoren im Ersten Weltkrieg* (Proclamations and Speeches by German Professors during the First World War) (Stuttgart, 1975).

Böhnke, W., *Die NSDAP im Ruhrgebiet 1920–1933* (The NSDAP in the Ruhr District 1920–1933) (Bonn–Bad Godesberg, 1974).

Böhret, C., Jann, W. et al., *Innenpolitik und politische Theorie. Ein Studienbuch* (Domestic Policy and Political Theory. A Reader) (Opladen, 1982).

Borowsky, P., *Adolf Hitler* (Hamburg, 1978).

Bracher, K. D., *Die deutsche Diktatur. Entstehung, Struktur, Folgen des Nationalsozialismus* (The German Dictatorship. Origin, Structure, Consequences of National Socialism) (Frankfurt/M.–Berlin–Vienna, 1979). New enlarged edn with introduction to the 6th edn and extended bibliography. Cited as Bracher, *German Dictatorship.*

———, *Zeitgeschichtliche Kontroversen um Faschismus, Totalitarismus, Demokratie* (Controversies in Contemporary History on Fascism, Totalitarianism, Democracy) (Munich, 1980). Cited as Bracher, *Controversies.*

Bracher, K. D.; Funke, M.; and Jacobsen, H. A.(pub.), *Nationalsozialistische Diktatur 1933–1945. Eine Bilanz* (National Socialist Dictatorship 1933–1945. A Balance Sheet) (Bonn, 1983).

———, *Die Weimarer Republik 1918–1933* (The Weimar Republic 1918–1933) (Düsseldorf, 1987). Politics, economy and society.

Bracher, K. D.; Schulz, G.; and Sauer, W., *Die nationalsozialistische Machtergreifung* (The National Socialist Seizure of Power) (Frankfurt/M.–Berlin–Vienna, 1979). Studies on the building of a totalitarian system of rule in Germany 1933–34. Cited as Bracher, *Seizure of Power.*

Broszat, M., *Der Nationalsozialismus* (National Socialism) (Hannover, 1960). *Weltanschauung* – programme and reality. Cited as Broszat, *Weltanschauung*.

———, 'Betrachtungen zu "Hitlers Zweitem Buch"' ('Reflections on "Hitler's Second Book"'), in *VjHfZg* 4/1961, pp. 417–29. Cited as Broszat, *Second Book*.

———, *Der Staat Hitlers* (Hitler's State) (Munich, 1983). Foundation and development of its internal structure. Cited as Broszat, *State*.

———, 'Soziale Motivation and Führer-Bindung des Nationalsozialismus' ('Social Motivation and Führer Attachment of National Socialism'), in Michalka, *Nationalsozialistische Aussenpolitik* (q.v.), pp. 92–116. Cited as Broszat, *Social Motivation*.

———, 'Hitler und die Genesis der "Endlösung"' ('Hitler and the Genesis of the "Final Solution"'), in *VjHfZg* 25 (1977), pp. 739–75. On the theses by David Irving.

———, 'Enthüllung? Die Rauschning-Kontroverse' ('Disclosure? The Rauschning Controversy'), in Graml, H., and Henke, K.-D., (pub.), *Nach Hitler. Der schwierige Umgang mit unserer Geschichte* (q.v.), pp. 249–51.

———, 'Plädoyer für eine Historisierung des Nationalsozialismus' ('Plea for a Historicization of National Socialism'), in *Merkur* (1985), pp. 373–85.

Broszat, M.; Fröhlich, E.; and Grossmann, A., (pub.), *Bayern in der NS-Zeit III*. (Bavaria during the NS Third Period) (Munich–Vienna, 1981). Rulership and society in conflict, Part B. Cited as Broszat, *Bavaria III*.

Broszat, M.; Fröhlich, E.; and Wiesemann, F., (pub.), *Bayern in der NS-Zeit* (Bavaria during the NS Period), vol. 1 (Munich–Vienna, 1977). Social situation and political behaviour of the population as reflected in confidential reports. Cited as Broszat, *Bavaria I*.

Broszat, M., and Möller, H., (pub.), *Das Dritte Reich. Herrschaftsstruktur und Geschichte* (The Third Reich. Rulership Structure and History) (Munich, 1983).

Bucharin, N., *Die Politische Ökonomie des Rentners* (The Political Economy of the Pensioner) (Vienna, 1926; reprint Frankfurt/M., 1966). The value and profit theory of the Austrian School.

Bullock, A., 'Hitler und die Ursprünge des Zweiten Weltkrieges' ('Hitler and the Origins of the Second World War'), in Niedhart, G., *Kriegsbeginn 1939* (q.v.), pp. 124–62.

———, *Hitler. A Study in Tyranny* (Kronberg/Ts., 1977). German version of the 'completely revised edition, 1964'.

Burchardt, L., *Hitler und die historische Grösse* (Hitler and Historical Greatness) (Konstanz, 1979).

Carr, W., *Adolf Hitler. Persönlichkeit und politisches Handeln* (Adolf Hitler. Personality and Political Activity). Stuttgart–Berlin–Cologne–Mainz, 1980.

Carsten, F. L., 'Interpretations of Fascism', in Laqueur, W., *Fascism. A Reader's Guide* (q.v.), pp. 415–33.

Dahrendorf, R., *Gesellschaft und Demokratie in Deutschland* (Society and Democracy in Germany) (Munich, 1965).

Davidson, E., *Wie war Hitler möglich?* (How Was Hitler Possible?) (Düsseldorf–Vienna, 1980).

Deuerlein, E., *Hitler, Eine politische Biographie* (Hitler. A Political Biography) (Munich, 1969).

Dickmann, F., 'Machtwille und Ideologie in Hitlers aussenpolitischen Zielsetzungen vor 1933' ('The Will to Power and Ideology in Hitler's Foreign Policy Objectives before 1933'), in *Spiegel der Zeit* (Münster Westphalia, 1964). Festive edn pub. by K. Repgenon on 10 April 1964 for Max Braubach and S. Skalweit, pp. 915–41.

Diehl-Thiel, P., *Partei und Staat im Dritten Reich* (Party and State in the Third Reich) (Munich, 1971). Investigation of the relationship between the NSDAP and the general administration of the State; student issue.

Diner, D., (pub.), *Ist der Nationalsozialismus Geschichte?* (Is National Socialism History?) (Frankfurt, 1987). On the historization and the historians' dispute.

Doucet, F. W., *Im Banne des Mythos* (Under the Ban of the Myth) (Esslingen am Neckar, 1979). The psychology of the Third Reich.

Dülffer, J., 'Die Machtergreifung und die Rolle der alten Eliten im Dritten Reich' ('The Seizure of Power and the Role of the Old Elites in the Third Reich'), in Michalka, *National Socialist Seizure of Power* (q.v.), pp. 182–94.

Dupeux, L., *"Nationalbolschewismus" in Deutschland 1919–1933* ('National Bolshevism' in Germany 1919–1933) (Munich, 1985). Communist strategy and conservative dynamics.

Falter, J. W., 'Die Arbeiter machten den Grossteil der Wählerschaft Hitlers aus' ('The Workers Comprised the Greater Part of Hitler's Voters'), in *Frankfurter Rundschau*, 21 December 1982, p. 12.

——, 'Die Wähler der NSDAP 1928–1933: Sozialstruktur und parteipolitische Herkunft' ('The Voters of the NSDAP 1928–1933: Social Structure and Party-Political Origin'), in Michalka, *National Socialist Seizure of Power* (q.v.), pp. 47–59.

——, 'Wahlen und Wählerverhalten unter besonderer Berücksichtigung des Aufstiegs der NSDAP nach 1928' ('Elections and Voter Behaviour under Special Consideration for the Rise of the NSDAP after 1928'), in Bracher *et al.*, (pub.), *Die Weimarer Republik 1918–1933* (q.v.), pp. 484–504.

Falter, J. W., and Hänisch, D., 'Die Anfälligkeit von Arbeitern gegenüber der NSDAP bei den Reichstagswahlen 1928–1933' ('The Susceptibility of Workers for the NSDAP in the ReichstagElections 1928–1933'), in *Archiv für Sozialgeschichte*, XXVI, 1986, pp. 179–216.

Falter, J. W.; Lindenberg, T.; and Schumann, S., *Wahlen und Abstimmungen in der Weimarer Republik* (Elections and Plebiscites in the Weimar Republic) (Munich 1986). Material on voter behaviour 1919–33.

Faul, E., 'Hitlers Über-Machiavellismus' ('Hitler's Over-Machiavellism'), in *VjHfZg*, 4/1954, pp. 344–72.

Fest., J. C., *Hitler. Eine Biographie* (Hitler. A Biography) (Frankfurt/M.–Berlin–Vienna, 1973).

Forndran, E., *Die Stadt- und Industriegründungen Wolfsburg und Salzgitter* (The Founding of the City and Industry of Wolfsburg and Salzgitter) (Frankfurt/M.–New York, 1984). Decision processes in the National Socialist system of rule.

Frei, N., *Nationalsozialistische Eroberung der Provinzpresse* (National Socialist Conquest of the Provincial Press) (Stuttgart, 1980). Bringing in line, self-adjustment and resistance in Bavaria.

——, *Der Führerstaat* (The *Führer* State) (Munich, 1987). National Socialist rule, 1933–45.

Freudenfeld, B., (pub.), *Stationen der deutschen Geschichte 1919–1945* (Stages of German History 1919–1945) (Stuttgart, 1962). International Congress on Contemporary History, Munich.

Fromm, E., *Arbeiter und Angestellte am Vorabend des Dritten Reiches* (Hourly and Salaried Employees on the Eve of the Third Reich) (Stuttgart, 1980). A socio-psychological study edited and published by Wolfgang Bonss.

Funke, M., (pub.), *Hitler, Deutschland und die Mächte* (Hitler, Germany and the Powers) (Kronberg/Ts., 1978). Material on the foreign policy of the Third Reich.

Geiss, I., *Die Habermas-Kontroverse. Ein deutscher Streit* (The Habermas Controversy. A German Conflict) (Berlin, 1988).

Gisevius, H. B., *Adolf Hitler. Eine Biographie – Versuch einer Deutung* (Adolf Hitler. A

Biography – Attempt at an Interpretation) (Munich–Zürich, 1967).
Gordon Jr., H. J., *Hitlerputsch 1923. Machtkampf in Bayern 1923–1924* (Hitler *Putsch* 1923. Battle for Power in Bavaria 1923–1924) (Munich, 1978).
Görlitz, W., *Adolf Hitler* (Göttingen–Berlin–Frankfurt/M., 1960).
Görlitz, W., and Quint., H. A., *Adolf Hitler, Eine Biographie* (Adolf Hitler. A Biography) (Stuttgart, 1952).
Graml, H., 'Probleme einer Hitler-Biographie' ('The Problems of a Hitler Biography'), in *VjHfZg* 22 (1974), pp. 76–92. Critical remarks to Joachim C. Fest.
Graml, H. and Henke, K.-D., (pub.), *Nach Hitler. Der schwierige Umgang mit unserer Geschichte* (After Hitler. The Difficult Treatment of Our History) (Munich, 1986). Contributions by Martin Broszat.
Gröning, G. and Wolschke, J., 'Naturschutz und Ökologie im Nationalsozialismus' ('Conservation and Ecology Under National Socialism'), in *Die alte Stadt*, 10 (1983), pp. 1–17.
Haffner, S., *Anmerkungen zu Hitler* (Comments on Hitler) (Hamburg, 1981).
Haller, J., *Die Aera Bülow* (The Bülow Era) (Stuttgart–Berlin, 1922). A historical-political study.
Hamilton, R., *Who Voted for Hitler?* (Princeton, 1982).
Hänel, W., *Hermann Rauschnings "Gespräche mit Hitler" – eine Geschichtsfälschung* (Hermann Rauschning's 'Conversations with Hitler' – a Falsification of History) (Ingolstadt, 1984). Reworked version of the unabridged presentation at the Conference of the Research Society for Contemporary History, Ingolstadt, on 14 May 1983.
Hänisch, D., *Sozialstrukturelle Bestimmungsgründe des Wahlverhaltens in der Weimarer Republik* (Socio-Structural Reasons for Voter Behaviour in the Weimar Republic) (Duisburg, 1983). An aggregate data analysis of the results of the *Reichstag* elections from 1924 to 1933.
Hass, G., 'Faschismus in Deutschland und Zweiter Weltkrieg' ('Fascism in Germany and the Second World War'), in Lozek, G., et al., *Kritik der bürgerlichen Geschichtsschreibung* (Criticism of Middle Class History Writing) (Cologne, 1973). Handbook, pp. 199–215.
Heberle, R., *Landbevölkerung und Nationalsozialismus* (Rural Population and National Socialism) (Stuttgart, 1963). A sociological study of political decision making in Schleswig-Holstein from 1918 to 1932.
Hehl, U. von, 'Die Kontroverse um den Reichstagsbrand' ('The Controversy on the Fire in the Reichstag'), in *VjHfZg* 36 (1988), pp. 259–80.
Heiber, H., *Adolf Hitler. Eine Biographie* (Adolf Hitler. A Biography) (Berlin, 1960).
Heisig, K. *Die politischen Grundlagen in Hitlers Schriften, Reden und Gesprächen im Hinblick auf seine Auffassung von Staat und Recht* (The Political Foundations in Hitler's Writings, Speeches and Conversations with regard to his View of the State and the Law) (Cologne 1965). Diss. lex.
Herf, J., *Reactionary Modernism. Technology, Culture and Politics in Weimar and the Third Reich* (Cambridge–London–New York–New Rochelle–Melbourne–Sydney, 1986).
Hilderbrand, K., 'Der "Fall Hitler". Bilanz und Wege der Hitler-Forschung' ('"Case Hitler". Outcome and Ways of Research on Hitler'), in *NPL* XIV set (1969), pp. 375–86.
———, *Deutsche Aussenpolitik 1933–1945 – Kalkül oder Dogma?* (German Foreign Policy 1933–1945 – Calculation or Dogma?), 4th edn (Stuttgart–Berlin–Cologne–Mainz, 1980). With an epilogue 'The History of German Foreign Policy (1933–1945) in the Judgement of Recent Research: Results, Controversies, Perspectives'.
———, 'Hitlers "Programm" und seine Realisierung 1939–1942' ('Hitler's "Programme" and its Realization, 1939–1942'), in Niedhart, G., *Kriegsbeginn 1939* (q.v.), pp. 178–224.
———, 'Innenpolitische Antriebskräfte der nationalsozialistischen Aussenpolitik' ('The

Domestic Policy Forces Motivating National Socialist Foreign Policy'), in Funke, M., *Hitler, Deutschland und die Mächte* (q.v.), pp. 223–38.

——, 'Hitlers Ort in der Geschichte des preussisch-deutschen Nationalstaates' ('Hitler's Place in the History of the German-Prussian National State'), in *HZ* 217 (1974), pp. 584–632.

——, 'Nationalsozialismus oder Hitlerismus?' ('National Socialism or Hitlerism?'), in Bosch, M. (pub.), *Persönlichkeit und Struktur in der Geschicht*, Düsseldorf, 1977, pp. 55–61.

——, 'Monokratie oder Polykratie? Hitlers Herrschaft und das Dritte Reich' ('Monocracy or Polycracy? Hitler's Rule and the Third Reich'), in Hirschfeld, G., and Kettenacker, L., (pub.), *Der "Führerstaat". Mythos und Realität* (q.v.), pp. 73–97.

——, *Das Dritte Reich* (The Third Reich) (Munich–Vienna, 1980).

——, 'Nationalsozialismus ohne Hitler?' ('The Third Reich Without Hitler?'), in *GWU* 1980/5, pp. 289–304. The Third Reich as an object of research for the science of history.

Hillgruber, A., 'Der Faktor Amerika in Hitlers Strategie 1938–1941' ('The America Factor in Hitler's Strategy 1938–1941'), in Michalka, *Nationalsozialistische Aussenpolitik* (q.v.), pp. 493–525.

——, 'Zum Kriegsbeginn im September 1939' ('To the Beginning of the War in September 1939'), in Niedhart, *Kriegsbeginn 1939* (q.v.), pp. 163–77.

——, 'Kontinuität und Diskontinuität in der deutschen Aussenpolitik von Bismarck bis Hitler' ('Continuity and Discontinuity in German Foreign Policy From Bismarck to Hitler'), in Ziebura, G., (pub.), *Grundfragen der deutschen Aussenpolitik seit 1871* (q.v.), pp. 15–47.

——, 'Die "Endlösung" und das deutsche Ostimperium als Kernstück des rassenideologischen Programms des Nationalsozialismus' (1972) ('The "Final Solution" and the German Empire in the East as Key Element of the Racial-Ideological Programme of National Socialism'), in Funke, *Hitler, Deutschland und die Mächte* (q.v.), pp. 94–114.

——, 'Rezension von Joachim C. Fest, "Hitler. Eine Biographie"' ('Review of Joachim C. Fest, "Hitler. A Biography"'), in *HZ*, vol. 219, pp. 161–5.

——, 'Tendenzen, Ergebnisse und Perspektiven der gegenwärtigen Hitler-Forschung' ('Tendencies, Results and Perspectives of Contemporary Research on Hitler'), in *HZ*, vol. 226 (1978), pp. 600–21.

Hirschfeld, G., and Kettenacker, L., (pub.), *Der "Führerstaat". Mythos und Realität* (The '*Führer* State'. Myth and Reality) (Stuttgart, 1981). Studies on the structure and policies of the Third Reich.

"Historikerstreit" ('The Historian's Debate') (Munich–Zürich, 1987). The documentation of the controversy on the singularity of the National Socialist destruction of the Jews.

Hoffmann, P., *Widerstand, Staatsstreich, Attentat* (Resistance, *Coup d'Etat*, Assassination) (Frankfurt/M.–Berlin–Vienna, 1974). The battle of the opposition to Hitler.

Hüttenberger, P., *Die Gauleiter* (The Gau Leaders) (Stuttgart, 1969). A study on the development of the power structure in the NSDAP.

Irving, D., *Hitler's War* (London–Sydney–Auckland–Toronto, 1979).

——, *Hitlers Weg zum Krieg 1933–1939* (Hitler's Road to War 1933–1939) (Munich, 1981).

Jäckel, E., *Hitlers Weltanschauung* (Stuttgart, 1981). Outline of a regime; extended and revised edn.

——, *Hitlers Herrschaft* (Hitler's Rule) (Stuttgart, 1981). Implementation of a *Weltanschauung*.

Jäckel, E., and Rohwer, J., (pub.), *Der Mord an den Juden im Zweiten Weltkrieg* (The

Murder of the Jews in the Second World War) (Stuttgart, 1985). Process of decision and realization.

Jacobsen, H. A., *Nationalsozialistische Aussenpolitik 1933–1938* (National Socialist Foreign Policy 1933–1938) (Frankfurt/M.–Berlin, 1968).

———, *Karl Haushofer. Leben und Werk* (Karl Haushofer. Life and Work) ((Boppard am Rhein, 1979). Vol. I: Life 1869–1946 and selected texts on geopolitics.

Jamin, M., 'Zur Rolle der SA im nationalsozialistischen Herrschaftssystem' ('The Role of the SA in the National Socialist System of Rule'), in Hirschfeld, G., and Kettenacker, L., (pub.), *Der "Führerstaat". Mythos und Realität* (q.v.), pp. 329–60.

Jenschke, B., *Zur Kritik der konservativ-revolutionären Ideologie in der Weimarer Republik* (Criticism of Conservative-Revolutionary Ideology in the Weimar Republic) (Munich, 1971). *Weltanschauung* and Politics of Edgar Julius Jung.

Jesse, E., '"Vergangenheitsbewältigung" in der Bundesrepublik Deutschland' ('"Coming to Terms with the Past" in the Federal Republic of Germany'), in *Der Staat*, vol. 26, 1987, issue 4, pp. 539–65.

———, 'Der Reichstagsbrand und seine "Aufklärer"'. ('The Fire in the Reichstag and its "Investigators"'), in K. Corino, (pub.), *Gefälscht! Betrug in Literatur, Kunst, Musik, Wissenschaft und Politik* (Falsified! Fraud in Literature, Art, Music, Science and Politics) (Nördlingen, 1988), pp. 106–27. A falsification scandal comes to an end.

———, 'Ist der "Historikerstreit" ein "historischer Streit"' ('Is the "Historian's Debate" a "Historic Conflict?"'), in *Zeitschrift für Politik*, 2/1988, pp. 163–97. A discussion of the literature.

Joachimsthaler, A., *Korrektur einer Biographie. Adolf Hitler 1908–1920* (Correction of a Biography. Adolf Hitler 1908–1920) (Munich, 1989).

Jones, J. S., *Hitlers Weg begann in Wien 1907–1913* (Hitler's Road Began in Vienna 1907–1913) (Wiesbaden–Munich, 1980).

Kater, M. H., 'Sozialer Wandel in der NSDAP im Zuge der nationalsozialistischen Machtergreifung' ('Social Change in the NSDAP in Connection with the National Socialist Seizure of Power'), in Schieder, W., *Faschismus als soziale Bewegung* (Fascism as a Social Movement) (Hamburg, 1976), pp. 25–67.

———, 'Methodologische Überlegungen über Möglichkeiten und Grenzen einer Analyse der sozialen Zusammensetzung der NSDAP von 1925 bis 1945' ('Methodological Considerations about the Possibilities and Limitations of an Analysis of the Social Composition of the NSDAP from 1925 to 1945'), in Mann, R., (pub.), *Die Nationalsozialisten* (q.v.), pp. 155–85.

———, *The Nazi Party. A Social Profile of Members and Leaders 1919–1945* (Cambridge, Mass., 1983).

Kele, M. H., *Nazis and Workers. National Socialist Appeals to German Labor 1919–1933* (Chapel Hill, 1972).

Kershaw, I., *Der Hitler-Mythos* (The Hitler Myth) (Stuttgart, 1980). Public opinion and propaganda in the Third Reich. With an introduction by M. Broszat.

Kettenacker, L., 'Sozialpsychologische Aspekte der Führer-Herrschaft' ('Socio-Psychological Aspects of the *Führer* Rule'), in Hirschfeld, G., and Kettenacker, L., (pub.), *Der "Führerstaat". Mythos und Realität* (q.v.), pp. 98–132.

Kissenkoetter, U., *Gregor Strasser und die NSDAP* (Gregor Strasser and the NSDAP) (Stuttgart, 1978).

Knox, MacG., 'Conquest, Foreign and Domestic, in Fascist Italy and Nazi Germany', in *JMH* 56 (1984), pp. 1–57.

Krausnick, H., 'Stationen des nationalsozialistischen Herrschaftssystems (30. Juni 1934–

Fritschkrise 1938–20. July 1944)' ('Stages of the National Socialist System of Rule [30 June 1934–Fritsch Crisis 1938–20 July 1944]), in Freudenfeld, B., (pub.), *Stationen der deutschen Geschichte 1919–1945* (q.v.), pp. 114–40.

Kube, A., *Pour le mérite und Hakenkreuz. Hermann Göring im Dritten Reich* (*Pour le mérite* and Swastika. Hermann Göring in the Third Reich) (Munich, 1986).

Kühnl, R., *Die nationalsozialistische Linke 1925–1930* (The National Socialist Left 1925–1930) (Meisenheim am Glan, 1966). Cited as Kühnl, *NS Left*.

———, *Faschismustheorien* (Theories of Fascism) (Reinbeck bei Hamburg, 1979). Texts on the discussion of Fascism. 2: A Guideline.

———, 'Der deutsche Faschismus' ('German Fascism'), in *NPL* XV set (1970). National Socialism and the Third Reich in individual investigations and overall portrayals. Cited as Kühnl, *Review*.

Lang, J. v., *Der Sekretär. Martin Bormann: Der Mann, der Hitler beherrschte* (The Secretary. Martin Bormann: The Man Who Controlled Hitler) (Munich–Berlin, 1987). 3rd completely revised edn.

———, *Der Hitler-Junge. Baldur von Schirach. Der Mann, der Deutschlands Jugend erzog* (The Hitler Youth. Baldur von Schirach. The Man Who Brought Up Germany's Youth) (Hamburg, 1988).

Laqueur, W., *Fascism. A Reader's Guide. Analyses, Interpretations, Bibliography* (Berkeley–Los Angeles, Ca., 1978).

Lenin, V. I., 'Thesen über bürgerliche Demokratie und Diktatur des Proletariats' ('Theses on Bourgeois Democracy and the Dictatorship of the Proletariat') in Lenin, *Gegen den Revisionismus* (Against Revisionism) (Berlin, DDR, 1959), pp. 461–72. First Congress of the Communist International, 4 March 1919.

Lingelbach, K. C., *Erziehung und Erziehungstheorien im nationalsozialistischen Deutschland* (Education and Educational Theories in National Socialist Germany) (Weinheim–Berlin–Basle 1970). Origin and development of the dominant theoretical educational streams in Germany in 1933–45, their political functions and their relationship to the extra-scholastic educational practice of the Third Reich.

Lipset, S. M., 'Der "Faschismus", die Linke, die Rechte und die Mitte' ('"Fascism", the Left, the Right, and the Centre'), in Nolte, E., *Theorien über den Faschismus* (q.v.), pp. 449–91.

Lukacs, J., *Hitler. Geschichte und Geschichtsschreibung* (Hitler. History and Historical Writing) (Munich, 1997).

Mai, G., 'Die Nationalsozialistische Betriebszellenorganization' ('The National Socialist Company Cell Organization'), in *VjHfZg* 31 (1983), pp. 573–613. The relationship between the working class and National Socialism.

Mann, R., (pub.), *Die Nationalsozialisten* (The National Socialists) (Stuttgart, 1980). Analyses of Fascist movements.

Manstein, P., *Die Mitglieder und Wähler der NSDAP 1919–1933* (The Members and Voters of the NSDAP 1919–1933) (Frankfurt/M.–Berne–New York–Paris, 1988). Investigation of their class composition.

Mao Tse-tung, *Ausgewählte Werke* (Selected Works), vols. I–IV (Peking, 1968–69).

Martin, B., 'Zur Tauglichkeit eines übergreifenden Faschismus-Begriffs' ('On the Usefulness of an Overriding Definition of Fascism'), in *VjHfZg* 29 (1981), pp. 48–73. A comparison of Japan, Italy and Germany.

Marx, K., and Engels, F. 'Manifest der Kommunistischen Partei' ('Manifesto of the Communist Party'), in Marx and Engels, *Selected Writings in Two Volumes* (Berlin, 1971), vol. 1, pp. 17–57.

Marx, K., *Das Kapital* (Capital). Volume One, Book I: 'The Production Process of Capital';

Volume Three, Book III: 'The Total Process of Capitalist Production'. MEW, vols. 23 and 25 (Berlin, 1972 and 1979). A criticism of political economy.

Maser, W., *Adolf Hitler. Legende–Mythos–Wirklichkeit* (Adolf Hitler. Legend–Myth–Reality) (Cologne, 1971).

———, *Der Sturm auf die Republik. Frühgeschichte der NSDAP* (The Storm Against the Republic. The Early History of the NSDAP) (Frankfurt/M.–Berlin–Vienna, 1981).

———, *Adolf Hitler. Mein Kampf* (Esslingen, 1981). History, excerpts, comments; 6th completely revised and extended edn.

———, *Adolf Hitler. Das Ende der Führer-Legende* (Adolf Hitler, The End of the *Führer* Legend) (Düsseldorf–Vienna, 1980).

Mau, H., 'Die "Zweite Revolution" – Der 30. Juni 1934' ('The "Second Revolution" – 30 June 1934'), in *VjHfZg* 1st year set (1953), pp. 119–37.

Michalka, W., (pub.), *Nationalsozialistische Aussenpolitik* (National Socialist Foreign Policy) (Darmstadt, 1978).

———, 'Wege der Hitler-Forschung: Problemkreise, Methoden und Ergebnisse. Eine Zwischenbilanz' ('The Ways of Research on Hitler: Problems, Methods and Results. A Provisional Summary'), in *Quaderni di storia* No 8 (1978), pp. 157–90, and No 10 (1979), pp. 123–51.

———, 'Hitler im Spiegel der Psycho-History' ('Hitler in the Reflection of Psycho-History') in *Francia*, vol. 8 (1980), pp. 595–611. On new interdisciplinary attempts at interpretation in the research on Hitler.

——— (pub.), *Die nationalsozialistische Machtergreifung* (The National Socialist Seizure of Power) (Paderborn–Munich–Vienna–Zürich, 1984).

Mohler, A., *Die Konservative Revolution in Deutschland 1918–1932* (The Conservative Revolution in Germany 1918–1932) (Stuttgart, 1950). An outline of its *Weltanschauung*.

Möller, H., 'Die nationalsozialistische Machtergreifung – Konterrevolution oder Revolution?' ('The National Socialist Seizure of Power – Counter Revolution or Revolution?'), in *VjHfZg* No 1 (1983), pp. 25–51.

———, 'Das Ende der Weimarer Demokratie und die nationalsozialistische Revolution von 1933' ('The End of the Weimar Democracy and the National Socialist Revolution of 1933'), in Broszat, M., and Möller, H., (pub.), *Das Dritte Reich. Herrschaftsstruktur und Geschichte* (q.v.), pp. 9–37.

Mommsen, H., 'Gesellschaftsbild und Verfassungspläne des deutschen Widerstandes' ('View of Society and Constitutional Plans of the German Resistance'), in *Der deutsche Widerstand gegen Hitler* (German Resistance Against Hitler) (Cologne–Berlin, 1966), pp. 73–168. Four historic critical studies, pub. by Walter Schmitthenner and Hans Buchheim. Cited as Mommsen, *View of Society*.

———, *Nachweis der Schizophrenie* (Proof of Schizophrenia), in *Der Spiegel*, 22nd year set, No 36, 2 September 1968, pp. 138–40. Review of D. Schoenbaum, 'The Brown Revolution'. Cited as Mommsen, *Schoenbaum review*.

———, 'Rezension von H.-A. Jacobsen, Nationalsozialistische Aussenpolitik 1933–1938' ('Review of H.-A. Jacobsen, National Socialist Foreign Policy 1933–1938'), in *MGM* 7, 1970.

———, 'Nationalsozialismus' ('National Socialism'), in *Sowjetsystem und demokratische Gesellschaft* (Soviet System and Democratic Society), vol. IV (Freiburg–Basle–Vienna, 1971), pp. 695–713. A comparative encyclopedia. Cited as Mommsen, *National Socialism*.

———, 'Zur Verschränkung traditioneller und faschistischer Führungsgruppen in Deutschland beim Übergang von der Bewegungs- zur Systemphase' ('On the Interlinking of Traditional and Fascist Leadership Groups in Germany at the Transition from the

Movement to the Systems Phase'), in Schieder, T., (pub.), *Faschismus als soziale Bewegung* (q.v.), pp 157–81. Cited as Mommsen, *Leadership Groups*.

———, 'Der Nationalsozialismus' ('National Socialism'), in *Meyers Enzyklopädisches Lexikon*, vol. 16 (Mannheim–Vienna–Zürich, 1976), pp. 785–90. Cumulative radicalization and self-destruction of the regime. Cited as Mommsen, *Cumulative Radicalization*.

———, 'Nationalsozialismus oder Hitlerismus?' ('National Socialism or Hitlerism?'), in Bosch, *Persönlichkeit und Struktur in der Geschichte* (Personality and Structure in History) (Düsseldorf, 1977), pp. 62–71. Historic stocktaking and didactic implications. Cited as Mommsen, *Hitlerism*.

———, 'Ausnahmezustand als Herrschaftstechnik des NS-Regimes' ('The Emergency Situation as a Technique of Rule in the NS Regime'), in Funke, M., (pub.), *Hitler, Deutschland und die Mächte* (q.v.), pp. 40–5. Cited as Mommsen, *Emergency Situation*.

———, 'Aufstieg der NSDAP und nationalsozialistisches Herrschaftssystem' ('The Rise of the NSDAP and the National Socialist System of Rule'), in Mannzmann, A., (pub.), *Hitlerwelle und historische Fakten* (The Hitler Wave and Historic Facts) (Königstein/Ts., 1979), pp. 14–59. With an overview of the literature and a collection of material on Neo-nazism. Cited as Mommsen, *Rise*.

———, 'Hitlers Stellung im nationalsozialistischen Herrschaftssystem' ('Hitler's Position within the National Socialist System of Rule'), in Hirschfeld, G., and Kettenacker, L., (pub.), *Der "Führerstaat". Mythos und Realität* (q.v.), pp. 43–72. Cited as Mommsen, *Hitler's Position*.

———, *Nachwort zu: Schoenbaum. Die braune Revolution* (Epilogue to: Schoenbaum. The Brown Revolution) (q.v.), pp. 352–68. Cited as Mommsen, *Epilogue*.

———, 'Die Realisierung des Utopischen' ('The Realization of the Utopian'), in *GuG* 9 (1983), pp. 381–420. The 'Final Solution' of the Jewish Question in the Third Reich.

Moreau, P., *Nationalsozialismus von links* (National Socialism from the Left) (Stuttgart, 1985). The 'Fighting Community Revolutionary National Socialism' and Otto Strasser's 'Black Front' 1930–35.

Mosse, G. L., *Ein Volk, ein Reich, ein Führer* (One People, One Reich, One Führer) (Königstein/Ts., 1979). The popular rrigin of National Socialism (German version of *The Crisis of the German Ideology*, 1964). Cited as Mosse, *One People*.

———, 'Einführung. Die Entstehung des Faschismus' ('Introduction. The Development of Fascism'), in *Internationaler Faschismus 1920–1945* (German book version of *The Journal of Contemporary History*) (Munich, 1966), pp. 29–45. Cited as Mosse, *Introduction*.

———, *Der nationalsozialistische Alltag* (National Socialist Daily Life) (German version of *Nazi Culture*, 1966) (Königstein/Ts., 1978). Life under Hitler. Cited as Mosse, *Daily Life*.

Müller, K.-J., (pub.), *Der deutsche Widerstand 1933–1945* (German Resistance 1933–1945) (Paderborn–Munich–Vienna–Zürich, 1986).

———, *Armee und Drittes Reich 1933–1939* (The Army and the Third Reich 1933–1939) (Paderborn, 1987). Portrayal and documentation in cooperation with E. W. Hansen.

Niedhart, G., (pub.), *Kriegsbeginn 1939* (Beginning of the War 1939) (Darmstadt, 1976). Unleashing or start of the Second World War?

Nipperdey, T., 'Kann Geschichte objektiv sein?' ('Can History Be Objective?'), in *GWU* 1979/6, pp. 329–42.

Nolte, E., *Die faschistischen Bewegungen* (The Fascist Movements) (Munich, 1982). The crisis of the Liberal system and the development of Fascism.

———, *Der Faschismus in seiner Epoche* (Fascism in Its Age) (Munich–Zürich, 1979). Action Française, Italian Fascism and National Socialism. Cited as Nolte, *Fascism*.

———, *Theorien über den Faschismus* (Theories on Fascism) (Cologne, 1976). Cited as

Nolte, *Theories.*

———, 'Konservatismus und Nationalsozialismus' ('Conservatism and National Socialism'), in Nolte, E., *Marxismus, Faschismus, Kalter Krieg* (Marxism, Fascism, Cold War) (Stuttgart, 1977), pp. 117–35. Presentations and articles 1964–76.

———, 'Marxismus und Nationalsozialismus' ('Marxism and National Socialism'), in *VjHfZg* 31 (1983), pp. 389–417.

———, 'Europäische Revolutionen des 20. Jahrhunderts' ('European Revolutions of the 20th Century'), in Michalka, *National Socialist Seizure of Power* (q.v.), pp. 395–410. The National Socialist seizure of power in its historical context.

———, *Der europäische Bürgerkrieg 1917–1945* (The European Civil War 1917–1945), 5th revised and extended edition (Munich, 1997). National Socialism and Bolshevism.

———, *Das Vergehen der Vergangenheit* (The Crime of the Past) (Berlin-Frankfurt/M., 1987). Answer to critics in the so-called 'historians' dispute'.

Petzold, J., 'War Hitler ein Revolutionär?' ('Was Hitler a Revolutionary?'), in *BdiP* 1978, pp. 186–204. On the topic of modernism and anti-modernism in the discussion about Fascism.

Plack, A., *Wie oft wird Hitler noch besiegt?* (How Often Will Hitler Be Defeated Again?) (Düsseldorf, 1982).

Rohlfes, J., 'Objektivität und Parteilichkeit im Geschichtsunterricht' ('Objectivity and Taking Sides in the Teaching of History'), in Süssmuth, H., (pub.), *Geschichtsdidaktische Positionen. Bestandsaufnahme und Neuorientierung* (Didactic Positions in History. Stocktaking and Reorientation) (Paderborn–Munich–Zürich, 1980), p. 337–81.

Sauer, W., 'Die Mobilmachung der Gewalt' ('The Mobilization of Violence'), in Bracher, K. D., et al., *Die nationalsozialistische Machtergreifung*, part III (Cologne–Opladen, 1974).

———, 'National Socialism: Totalitarianism or Fascism?', in *AHR*, December 1967 (LXXIII), pp. 404–24.

Schäfer, H. D., *Das gespaltene Bewusstsein* (The Split Consciousness) (Munich–Vienna 1982). German culture and real life. 1933–45.

Schieder, T., *Hermann Rauschnings "Gespräche mit Hitler" als Geschichtsquelle* (Hermann Rauschning's 'Conversations with Hitler' as a Historical Source) (Opladen, 1972).

———, 'Stichwort "Revolution"' ('Cue "Revolution"'), in *The Soviet System and Democratic Society. A Comparative Encyclopedia*, vol. V (Freiburg–Basle–Vienna, 1972).

Schieder, T., (pub.), *Faschismus als soziale Bewegung* (Fascism as a Social Movement) (Hamburg 1976). Germany and Italy compared.

Schöllgen, G., 'Das Problem einer Hitler-Biographie' ('The Problem of a Hitler Biography') in *NPL*, set XXIII/4 (1978), pp. 421–34. Considerations based on more recent portrayals of the Hitler case.

Scholtz, H., *NS-Ausleseschulen* (NS Elite Schools) (Göttingen, 1973). Boarding schools as a means of rule in the *Führer* State.

Schramm, G., 'Die Juden als Minderheit in der Geschichte – Versuch eines Resümees' ('The Jews as a Minority in History – Attempt at a Résumé'), in Martin B. and Schulin, E., (pub.), *The Jews as a Minority in History* (Munich, 1981), pp. 316–34.

Schreiber, G., *Hitler Interpretationen 1923–1983* (Interpretations of Hitler 1923-1983) (Darmstadt, 1988).

Schwierskott, H.-J., *Arthur Moeller van den Bruck und der revolutionäre Nationalismus in der Weimarer Republik* (Arthur Moeller van den Bruck and Revolutionary Nationalism in the Weimar Republic) (Göttingen–Berlin–Frankfurt/M., 1962).

Seidler, F. W., *Fritz Todt. Baumeister des Dritten Reiches* (Fritz Todt. Master Builder of the Third Reich) (Munich–Berlin, 1986).

Sieferle, R. P., *Fortschrittsfeinde? Opposition gegen Technik und Industrie von der*

Romantik bis zur Gegenwart (Enemies of Progress? Opposition Against Technology and Industry from the Romantic Period until the Present) (Munich, 1984).

Smelser, R., *Robert Ley, Hitler's Labour Front Leader* (Oxford–New York–Hamburg, 1988).

Smelser, R., and Zitelmann, R., (pub.), *Die braune Elite. 22 biographische Skizzen* (The Brown Elite. 22 Biographical Sketches) (Darmstadt, 1989).

Sonnenberger, F., 'Der neue "Kulturkampf". Die Gemeinschaftsschule und ihre historischen Voraussetzungen' ('The New "*Kulturkampf*". The Comprehensive School and its Historic Preconditions'), in Broszat, M., *et al.*, *Bayern in der NS-Zeit III.* (q.v.), pp. 235–327.

Sontheimer, K., *Antidemokratisches Denken in der Weimarer Republik* (Anti-Democratic Thinking in the Weimar Republik) (Munich, 1962). The political ideas of German Nationalism, 1918–33.

Stachura, P. D., 'Der kritische Wendepunkt?' ('The Critical Turning-Point?'), in *VjHfZg* 26, 1978, pp. 66–99. The NSDAP and the *Reichstag* elections of 20 May 1928.

——, *Gregor Strasser and The Rise of Nazism* (London–Boston–Sydney, 1983).

Stalin, J. W., *Werke* (Works), vols. 1–13 (Berlin, DDR, 1950).

Stegemann, H., *Geschichte des Krieges* (The History of the War), vol. 1 (Stuttgart–Berlin, 1917).

Stein, P., *Die NS-Gaupresse 1925-1933* (The NS Gau Press 1925–1933). Research report.

——, Criticism of Sources – New Stocktaking (Munich–New York–London–Oxford–Paris, 1987).

Stern, J. P., *Hitler – Der Führer und das Volk* (Hitler – The *Führer* and the People) (Munich, 1981).

Tallgren, V., *Hitler und die Helden* (Hitler and the Heroes). Annales Academiae Scientiarum Fennicae. Dissertationes Humanarum Litterarum 29. (Suomalainen Tiedeakatemia, Helsinki, 1981). Heroism and *Weltanschauung*.

Thamer, H.-U., Verführung und Gewalt. Deutschland 1933–1945 (Seduction and Force. Germany 1933–1945) (Berlin, 1986).

Thies, J., *Architekt der Weltherrschaft* (Architect of World Rule) (Königstein/Ts., 1980). Hitler's 'final objectives'.

Tobias, F., 'Auch Fälschungen haben lange Beine' ('Forgeries Have Long Legs Too'), in K. Corino, (pub.), *Gefälscht! Betrug in Literatur, Kunst, Musik, Wissenschaft und Politik* (Falsified! Fraud in Literature, Art, Music, Science and Politics) (Nördlingen, 1988), pp. 91–105. President of the Senate Rauschning's 'conversations with Hitler'.

Toland, J., *Adolf Hitler* (Bergisch Gladbach, 1981).

Trevor-Roper, H. R., *Hitlers letzte Tage* (Hitler's Final Days) (Frankfurt/M.–Berlin–Vienna, 1973). Cited as Trevor-Roper, *Final Days*.

——, 'Einleitung' ('Introduction'), in *Hitlers politisches Testament. Die Bormann-Diktate vom Februar und April 1945* (q.v.), pp. 17–40. Cited as Trevor-Roper, *Introduction*.

——, 'Hitlers Kriegsziele' ('Hitler's War Aims'), in Michalka, W., *Nationalsozialistische Aussenpolitik* (q.v.), pp. 31–48.

Turner, H. A., *Faschismus und Kapitalismus in Deutschland* (Fascism and Capitalism in Germany) (Göttingen, 1980). A study in the relationship between National Socialism and business.

Tyrell, A., *Vom "Trommler" zum "Führer"* (From 'Drummer' to '*Führer*') (Munich, 1975). The changes in Hitler's self-understanding between 1919 and 1924 and the development of the NSDAP.

Vogelsang, T., *Reichswehr, Staat und NSDAP* (Reichswehr, State and NSDAP) (Stuttgart, 1962). Contributions to German History 1930–32.

Weber, E., *Varieties of Fascism. Doctrines of Revolution in the Twentieth Century* (New York–Cincinnati–Toronto–Melbourne–London, 1964).

———, 'Revolution? Counterrevolution? What Revolution?', in Laqueur, W., *Fascism. A Reader's Guide. Analyses, Interpretations, Bibliography* (q.v.), pp. 435–67.

Wehler, H.-U., *Entsorgung der deutschen Vergangenheit?* (Disposal of Germany's Past?) (Munich, 1988). A polemic essay in the 'historians' dispute'.

Weissmann, K., *Der Weg in den Abgrund* (The Way Into the Abyss) (Munich 1997). Germany under Hitler, 1933–45; 2nd revised and extended edn.

Wendt, B.-J., *Grossdeutschland. Aussenpolitik und Kriegsvorbereitung des Hitler-Regimes* (Greater Germany. Foreign Policy and Preparation for War by the Hitler Regime) (Munich, 1987).

Windisch, H., *Führer und Verführte* (Leader and Misled) (Seebruck am Chiemsee, 1946). Death dance and rebirth: an analysis of German Fate.

Winkler, H. A., 'Mittelstandsbewegung oder Volkspartei?' ('Movement of the Middle Class or Popular Party?'), in Schieder, W., *Faschismus als soziale Bewegung* (q.v.), pp. 97–118. On the social base of the NSDAP.

Wippermann, W., *Faschismustheorien* (Theories of Fascism) (Darmstadt, 1980). On the current state of the discussion.

Woerden, A. V. N. van, 'Hitlers Verhältnis zu England: Theorie, Vorstellung und Politik' ('Hitler's Relationship to England: Theory, Concept and Politics'), in Michalka, *Nationalsozialistische Aussenpolitik* (q.v.), pp. 220–43.

Ziebura, G., (pub.), *Grundfragen der deutschen Aussenpolitik seit 1871* (Basic Questions of German Foreign Policy since 1871) (Darmstadt, 1975).

Zitelmann, R., 'Hitlers Erfolge – Erklärungsversuche in der Hitler-Forschung' ('Hitler's Successes – Attempts at Explanation in Hitler Research), in *NPL* set XXVII/1,(1982), pp. 47–69.

———, 'Soziale Zielsetzungen und revolutionäre Motive in Hitlers Weltanschauung als Forschungsdesiderat' ('Social Objectives and Revolutionary Motives in Hitler's *Weltanschauung* as a Desideratum of Research') (TH Darmstadt, 1983). Unpub. MS.

———, 'Der Nationalsozialismus' ('National Socialism'), in Fetscher, I., and Münkler, H., (pub.), *Pipers Handbuch der politischen Ideen* (Piper's Handbook of Political Ideas), vol. 5: Present: From the Age of Imperialism to the New Social Movements (Munich, 1987), pp. 327–32.

———, *Adolf Hitler. Eine politische Biographie* (Adolf Hitler. A Political Biography) (Göttingen–Zürich, 1989).

Zmarzlik, H.-G., 'Der Sozialdarwinismus in Deutschland als geschichtliches Problem' ('Social Darwinism in Germany as a Historical Problem'), in *VjHfZg* 11 (1963), pp. 246–73.

Abbreviations

AHR	*American Historical Review*
AuZB	*Aus Politik und Zeitgeschichte.* Beilage zur Wochenzeitung *Das Parlament* (Politics and Contemporary History. Supplement to the periodical *Das Parlament*)
BA	Bundesarchiv Koblenz (Federal Archives, Coblenz)
BayHStA	Bayerisches Hauptstaatsarchiv, München (Central Bavarian State Archives, Munich)
BdiP	Blätter für deutsche und internationale Politik (Leaflets for German and International Politics)
CEH	Central European History
GuG	*Geschichte und Gesellschaft* (History and Society)
GWU	*Geschichte in Wissenschaft und Unterricht* (History in Science and Education)
HZ	*Historische Zeitschrift* (Historical Magazine)
IB	*Illustrierter Beobachter* (Illustrated Observer)
JMH	*Journal of Modern History*
MK	*Mein Kampf* (Hitler)
MGM	*Militärgeschichtliche Mitteilungen* (Information on Military History)
NPL	*Neue Politische Literatur* (New Political Literature)
QdS	*Quaderni di Storia* (Historical Quarterly)
SF	*Sämtliche Fragmente* (Complete Fragments) of Goebbels' diaries.
STA Erlangen	Stadtarchiv Erlangen (Erlangen City Archives)
VB	*Völkischer Beobachter* (National Observer).
VVjHfZg	*Vierteljahreshefte für Zeitgeschichte* (Quarterly for Contemporary History)
WA	*Weltwirtschaftliches Archiv* (World Economic Archives)
ZB	*Zweites Buch* (Second Book) (Hitler)
ZfS	*Zeitschrift für Sozialismus* (Magazine for Socialism)

Index of Names

A
Adenauer, Konrad, 314
Antonescu, Ion, 140, 530
Aretin, Erwein Freiherr von, 67
Aretin, Karl Otmar Freiherr von, 9 *et seq.*
Aristotle, 335
Auer, Erhard, 417
August Wilhelm, Prince, 366

B
Baldwin, Stanley Earl of Bewdley, 218, 481
Balfour, Arthur James, 276
Bárdossy, László von, 493
Barkai, Avraham, 222, 237 *et seq.*, 480
Barth, Emil, 42
Beck, Ludwig, 404
Below, Nicolaus von, 409
Benjamin, Walter, 29
Bergius, Friedrich, 292, 493
Bismarck, Otto Prince von, 131, 136, 169, 344, 388, 396 *et seq.*, 400
Blaich, Fritz, 479
Blomberg, Werner von, 86
Bonnard, Abel, 182
Bormann, Martin, 183, 218 *et seq.*, 236, 294, 374, 384, 386, 457
Bose, Herbert von, 84, 409
Bracher, Karl Dietrich, 18, 21
Braun, Otto, 417
Broszat, Martin, 9, 32, 79
Brüning, Heinrich, 200, 417
Bucharin, Nicolai Ivanovich, 258, 276, 490
Budak, Mile, 305
Bullock, Alan, 18, 21, 198
Burchardt, Lothar, 495
Bürckel, Josef, 179

C
Canaris, Wilhelm, 409
Carr, William, 370
Chamberlain, Arthur Neville, 218, 481
Charlemagne, 355
Chiang Kai-shek, 147
Ciano, Galeazzo, Count di Cortellazo, 435
Confucius, 115
Copernicus, Nikolaus, 335
Cudahy, John, 204
Cyrill (Bulgarian Prince), 470

D
Dahrendorf, Ralf, 18–20, 23, 28, 109, 114, 270, 398, 404, 448
Danton, Georges Jacques, 56
Darré, Richard Walther, 176, 270, 332, 334
Dietrich, Otto, 36 *et seq.*, 120 *et seq.*, 234
Dietrich, Sepp, 502
Dimitroff, Georgi, 15
Domarus, Max, 25
Doucet, Friedrich W., 497

E
Ebert, Friedrich, 37, 42, 56, 102, 381, 417
Eisner, Kurt, 242, 397
Engel, Gerhard, 26, 316, 502
Engels, Friedrich, 509
Epp, Franz Xaver Ritter von, 463
Erzberger, Matthias, 56, 418

F
Falter, Jürgen W., 151
Faul, Erwin, 18

535

Favre, Jules, 59
Feder, Gottfried, 205, 243, 263, 267 et seq., 326, 480, 491
Fest, Joachim C., 9, 21, 25, 29, 366
Filoff, Bogdan D., 470
Fischer, Franz, 235
Fischer, Wolfram, 483
Flick, Friedrich, 351
Forndran, Erhard, 491 et seq.
Forster, Albert, 68
Franco, Francisco, 26, 415, 434, 436 et seq., 447
Frank, Hans, 26, 36 et seq., 49, 70, 91, 230
Frick, Wilhelm, 220, 383
Fried, Ferdinand, (pseudonym of Friedrich Zimmermann), 276, 294 et seq., 317, 490
Friedrich II, King of Prussia, 54, 58, 149, 333
Fromm, Erich, 78
Funk, Walther E., 221

G

Gambetta, Léon, 59
Genghis Khan, 232
Georg, Enno, 262
Gerke, Adolf, 326
Giesler, Hermann, 37, 326–8, 437
Gisevius, Hans Bernd, 86
Goebbels, Joseph, 26, 49, 51 et seq., 55, 58, 61, 66–9, 86, 89, 92, 156, 159, 167, 185 et seq., 216, 232, 244, 253, 257, 303, 324, 334, 379, 382 et seq., 392 et seq., 406, 429, 432, 451, 466, 479, 485, 492, 512
Goerdeler, Carl-Friedrich, 295, 404, 409
Goethe, Johann Wolfgang von, 320
Göring, Hermann, 84, 86, 185, 254 et seq., 383, 386
Görlitz, Walter, 18
Graml, Hermann, 21
Grandi di Mordano, Dino Count, 91, 232
Gross, Walter, 379
Grotkopp, Wilhelm, 200
Grunberger, Richard, 448
Guillebaud, Claude William, 199
Gurland, A. R. L., 485

H

Haffner, Sebastian, 322, 404

Halder, Franz, 404
Haller, Johannes, 274
Hammerstein-Equord, Kurt Freiherr von, 491
Hanfstaengl, Ernst, 26, 54, 274, 301, 426
Hardach, Karl, 231, 483
Hassell, Ulrich von, 404, 409
Hedin, Sven, 510
Heiden, Konrad, 335
Heim, Heinrich, 430
Held, Heinrich, 67
Helldorf, Wolf (Heinrich) Count von, 67
Herbst, Ludolf, 185, 444, 483 et seq., 487, 503
Herf, Jeffrey, 497
Hess, Rudolf, 92, 382 et seq., 387
Heydrich, Reinhard, 397
Hierl, Konstantin, 152, 171
Hildebrand, Klaus, 414, 482, 506
Hildebrandt, Friedrich, 115, 117
Hilferding, Rudolf, 418
Himmler, Heinrich, 84, 86, 221, 261 et seq., 270, 331 et seq., 334, 375, 378, 382
Hindenburg, Paul von Beneckendorff und von, 15, 31, 36, 60, 67 et seq., 84 et seq., 117, 381 et seq., 392, 448
Horkheimer, Max, 16
Horthy von Nagybánya, Nikolaus, 118
Hossbach, Friedrich, 279, 290
Hugenberg, Alfred, 147, 165, 446
Hüttenberger, Peter, 502

I

Irving, David, 219, 463, 482
Ivan IV, The Terrible, 63

J

Jäckel, Eberhard, 9, 14, 23, 30 et seq., 143, 335, 379, 382, 403, 412, 449 et seq., 457, 503, 508
Jacobsen, Hans-Adolf, 495
Jochmann, Werner, 99
Johst, Hanns, 149
Josef II, 58
Jouvenal, Bertrand de, (French journalist), 204
Jung, Edgar Julius, 44, 84, 91, 409

K

Kahr, Gustav Ritter von, 63
Kautsky, Karl, 418
Keppler, Wilhelm, 326
Kershaw, Ian, 287
Kettenacker, Lothar, 351
Keynes, John Maynard, 200, 205, 231, 277
Koch, Erich, 306
Koeppen, Werner, 115, 159, 216, 285, 298, 301, 306, 417, 429
Krebs, Albert, 381, 389, 458
Krüger, Peter, 200, 490

L

Lafferentz, Dr, 256
Lammers, Hans Heinrich, 218 et seq., 220, 504
Landfried, Friedrich W., 220
Lawaczeck, Franz, 261
Lenin, (pseudonym of Uljanov, Vladimir Ilyitsh), 15, 274, 395
Ley, Robert, 179, 256, 321, 324, 420, 451
Liebmann, Kurt, 278, 491
Liedig, Franz Maria, 405
Linge, Heinz, 402
Lingelbach, Karl Christoph, 114
Lipset, Seymour Martin, 507
List, Friedrich, 239
Litt, Theodor, 114
Löbe, Paul, 417
Lochner, Louis P., 108, 166, 253, 320
Louis XIV, 55
Ludendorff, Erich, 296
Ludwig, Karl-Heinz, 322, 339 et seq.
Lueger, Karl, 173
Luther, Martin, 83
Luxemburg, Rosa, 276, 490

M

Mac-Mahon, Marie Edmé Comte de, 59
Mai, Gunther, 473, 476 et seq.
Mao Tse-tung, 147, 395
Marat, Jean-Paul, 56
Marcks, Erich, 489
Marcuse, Herbert, 16
Martin, Bernd, 487

Marx, Karl, 23, 266, 268, 410, 423, 426, 487, 509 et seq.
Maser, Werner, 77, 86, 402, 462, 466
Mason, Timothy W., 179 et seq., 194
Mau, Hermann, 18, 85
May, Karl, 305
Meissner, Otto, 36, 95, 381 et seq.
Metternich, Klemens Wenzel Prince von, 147
Michoff, Nikola, 470
Milward, Alan S., 479
Moeller van den Bruck, Arthur, 44 et seq., 91 et seq., 320
Mohler, Armin, 43, 324
Möller, Horst, 23 506
Mommsen, Hans, 9, 20, 219, 373, 404, 449
Mosse, George L., 18
Müller, Adam Heinrich, 239
Mussert, Anton Adriaan, 118, 303
Mussolini, Benito, 37, 67, 230, 234, 386, 435 et seq., 465, 510

N

Napoleon I, 55, 80, 320
Napoleon III, 59
Naumann, Friedrich, 410
Neumann, Franz L., 485
Nolte, Ernst, 22–4, 143, 145, 419, 426, 476, 486, 507, 590 et seq.
Nonnenbruch, Fritz, 324
Noske, Gustav, 37

O

Ohlendorf, Otto, 202 et seq., 484
Oncken, Hermann, 489
Oster, Hans, 404, 409

P

Papen, Franz von, 17, 39, 84, 147 et seq., 165, 199, 382, 409, 446, 472
Peter I, the Great, 427
Petzina, Dieter, 238, 254
Picker, Henry, 37, 69, 218, 327, 384, 430, 465
Plack, Arno, 506
Pollock, Friedrich, 16, 241, 250, 485
Popitz, Johannes, 404, 409

Porsche, Ferdinand, 255 et seq.
Prinz, Michael, 186, 477
Ptolemy, 335

Q
Quint, Herbert, (pseudonym of Frankenberg, Richard von), 18, 256

R
Radek, Karl, 429
Rauschning, Hermann, 17 et seq., 68
Recker, Marie-Luise, 451
Reemtsma, Philipp, 259
Reich, Wilhelm, 15, 76, 441
Reichenau, Walter von, 189
Reusch, Paul, 246
Ribbentrop, Joachim von, 430
Robespierre, Maximilien de, 56
Röhm, Ernst, 69, 72, 74, 76, 78, 84–9, 92, 440 et seq.
Romanov dynasty, 428
Roosevelt, Franklin Delano, 301, 318, 488
Rosenberg, Alfred, 26, 270, 331–4, 378, 458
Rousseau, Jean-Jacques, 395
Rupp, Leila J., 186
Rupprecht von Wittelsbach, Crown Prince of Bavaria, 35
Rust, Bernhard, 113

S
Schacht, Hjalmar, 179, 198, 204, 366
Schäfer, Hans-Dieter, 314
Schall, Adolf von, 256
Scheidemann, Philipp, 37, 42, 56, 417 et seq., 509
Scheidt, Wilhelm, 26, 37 et seq., 233 et seq., 387, 431
Scherff, Walther, 37
Schiff, Viktor, 476
Schirach, Baldur von, 26, 368, 387, 389
Schleicher, Kurt von, 67, 189
Schoenbaum, David, 18–20, 23, 34, 109, 117, 184, 270, 448
Schoenichen, Walther, 329
Scholtz, Harald, 112 et seq.
Schönerer, Georg Ritter von, 64, 93, 140

Schramm, Gottfried, 427
Schramm, Percy Ernst, 504
Schumann, Hans-Gerd, 485
Schuschnigg, Kurt Ritter von, 421
Seeberg, Reinhard, 489
Seifert, Alwin, 330
Seldte, Franz, 165, 179
Sering, Paul, (pseudonym of Löwenthal, Richard), 16
Severing, Carl, 37, 417, 508
Seyss-Inquart, Arthur, 329
Sieferle, Rolf Peter, 330
Soden-Fraunhofer, Count August Maria, 35, 49
Sombart, Werner, 239, 276 et seq., 295, 323
Speer, Albert, 26, 36 et seq., 89, 220 et seq., 234 et seq., 240, 250, 260, 306, 314, 322, 324, 334, 432, 443, 465, 483 et seq.
Spengler, Oswald, 320
Spiecker, Carl, 417
Stachanov, Alexy, 232
Stachura, Peter D., 155 et seq.
Stalin, Josef Wissarionovich, 61, 89, 232, 355, 395, 422, 427–33, 438, 447, 502, 512
Starhemberg, Ernst Rüdiger Prince von, 421
Stegemann, Hermann, 274
Stinnes, Hugo, 209, 243
Stolper, Gustav, 480
Strasser, Gregor, 65 et seq., 156, 244, 364, 394
Strasser, Otto, 66, 244 et seq., 276, 288, 319 et seq., 458, 474, 508
Strauss, Franz Josef, 405
Stresemann, Gustav, 480
Sulla, Lucius Cornelius, 63
Szálasi, Ferenc, 75, 146
Sztójay, Döme von, 61, 119

T
Tallgren, Vappu, 339
Teichert, Eckart, 276, 294
Thalheimer, August, 412
Thälmann, Ernst, 420 et seq.
Thies, Jochen, 61, 82
Thöt, Karl, 26, 436
Thyssen, Fritz, 351
Tiso, Josef, 37, 435
Tobias, Fritz, 68, 508

Index of Names

Todt, Fritz, 40, 322, 324, 326, 329 *et seq.*, 437, 456
Torgler, Ernst, 421, 509
Treviranus, Gottfried Reinhold, 418
Trevor-Roper, Hugh R., 454
Troost, Paul Ludwig, 382
Trott zu Solz, Adam von, 404
Trotsky, (pseudonym of Bronstein, Leo), 144, 428
Tuchatshevsky, Michail Nikolaievich, 432
Turner, Henry Ashby, 19, 23, 30, 206, 222, 246, 271, 299, 315, 332, 442, 485, 487, 491
Tyrell, Albrecht, 388

V

Valentin, Veit, 14, 147
Volpi, Giuseppe Count, 435
Voltaire, (pseudonym of François Marie Arouet), 333

W

Wagener, Otto, 34, 36, 39, 43, 58, 60 *et seq.*, 80, 100, 106 *et seq.*, 127, 145, 148, 157, 189, 201, 222 *et seq.*, 245, 268, 284, 301, 320, 345, 363, 377, 382, 394, 401, 408, 416, 420, 488, 508
Weber, Eugen, 22, 507
Weinstock, Heinrich, 114
Wels, Otto, 59
Wiedemann, Fritz, 26, 36, 176, 372, 392
Wilamowitz-Moellendorff, Ulrich von, 489
Wilhelm II, 405
Wilson, Thomas Woodrow, 45
Winkler, Dörte, 186
Wirth, Joseph, 418
Witting, Rolf, 292, 493
Witzleben, Erwin von, 404
Woerden, A. V. N., 492

Y

Yorck von Wartenburg, Count Peter, 404
Young, Owen D., 35, 366

Z

Ziegler, Hans Severus, 268
Zwiedineck-Südenhorst, Otto von, 205